# Microsoft® Office 365®
# PowerPoint® 2021

## Comprehensive

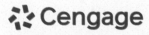

Australia • Brazil • Canada • Mexico • Singapore • United Kingdom • United States

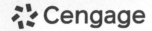

**New Perspectives Series®, Microsoft®
Office 365® & PowerPoint®
2021 Comprehensive**
Jennifer Campbell

SVP, Product: Erin Joyner

VP, Product: Thais Alencar

Product Director: Mark Santee

Senior Product Manager: Amy Savino

Product Assistant: Ciara Horne

Learning Designer: Zenya Molnar

Content Manager: Christina Nyren

Digital Delivery Quality Partner: Jim Vaughey

Developmental Editors: Michael Sanford

VP, Product Marketing: Jason Sakos

Director, Product Marketing: Danaë April

Executive Product Marketing Manager: Jill Staut

IP Analyst: Ann Hoffman

IP Project Manager: Anjali Kambli

Production Service: Lumina Datamatics, Inc.

Designer: Erin Griffin

Cover Image Source: Hiroshi Watanabe
/Getty Images

Mac Users: If you're working through this product using a Mac, some of
the steps may vary. Additional information for Mac users is included with
the Data files for this product.

Disclaimer: This text is intended for instructional purposes only; data is fictional and does not belong to any real persons or companies.

Disclaimer: The material in this text was written using Microsoft
Windows 10 and Office 365 Professional Plus and was Quality Assurance
tested before the publication date. As Microsoft continually updates the
Windows 10 operating system and Office 365, your software experience
may vary slightly from what is presented in the printed text.

Windows, Access, Excel, and PowerPoint are registered trademarks of
Microsoft Corporation. Microsoft and the Office logo are either registered trademarks or trademarks of Microsoft Corporation in the United
States and/or other countries. This product is an independent publication and is neither affiliated with, nor authorized, sponsored, or
approved by, Microsoft Corporation.

Some of the product names and company names used in this book have
been used for identification purposes only and may be trademarks or
registered trademarks of Microsoft Corporation in the United States and/
or other countries.

For product information and technology assistance, contact us at
**Cengage Customer & Sales Support, 1-800-354-9706  or
support.cengage.com.**

For permission to use material from this text or product, submit all
requests online at **www.copyright.com.**

Library of Congress Control Number: 2022935105

Student Edition ISBN: 978-0-357-67225-9
Looseleaf ISBN: 978-0-357-67226-6*
*Looseleaf available as part of a digital bundle

**Cengage**
200 Pier 4 Boulevard
Boston, MA 02210
USA

Cengage is a leading provider of customized learning solutions with
employees residing in nearly 40 different countries and sales in more
than 125 countries around the world. Find your local representative at
**www.cengage.com.**

To learn more about Cengage platforms and services, register or access
your online learning solution, or purchase materials for your course, visit
**www.cengage.com.**

**Notice to the Reader**

Printed in Mexico
Print Number: 2     Print Year: 2023

# BRIEF CONTENTS

# TABLE OF CONTENTS

## POWERPOINT MODULES

### Planning, Developing, and Giving a Presentation
*Preparing a Presentation for a Resort* . . . . . . . . . . **PRES 1**

## Module 3 Applying Advanced Formatting to Objects

## Module 4 Advanced Animations and Distributing Presentations

## Module 5 Integrating PowerPoint with Other Programs

*Creating a Presentation for a Rowing*

## Module 6 Customizing Presentations and the PowerPoint Environment

*Creating a Presentation for a City-Wide Green*

# Getting to Know Microsoft Office Versions

Cengage is proud to bring you the next edition of Microsoft Office. This edition was designed to provide a robust learning experience that is not dependent upon a specific version of Office.

Microsoft supports several versions of Office:

- **Office 365:** A cloud-based subscription service that delivers Microsoft's most up-to-date, feature-rich, modern productivity tools direct to your device. There are variations of Office 365 for business, educational, and personal use. Office 365 offers extra online storage and cloud-connected features, as well as updates with the latest features, fixes, and security updates.

- **Office 2021:** Microsoft's "on-premises" version of the Office apps, available for both PCs and Macs, offered as a static, one-time purchase and outside of the subscription model.

- **Office Online:** A free, simplified version of Office web applications (Word, Excel, PowerPoint, and OneNote) that facilitates creating and editing files collaboratively.

Office 365 (the subscription model) and Office 2021 (the one-time purchase model) had only slight differences between them at the time this content was developed. Over time, Office 365's cloud interface will continuously update, offering new application features and functions, while Office 2021 will remain static. Therefore, your onscreen experience may differ from what you see in this product. For example, the more advanced features and functionalities covered in this product may not be available in Office Online or may have updated from what you see in Office 2021.

For more information on the differences between Office 365, Office 2021, and Office Online, please visit the Microsoft Support site.

Cengage is committed to providing high-quality learning solutions for you to gain the knowledge and skills that will empower you throughout your educational and professional careers.

Thank you for using our product, and we look forward to exploring the future of Microsoft Office with you!

# Using SAM Projects and Textbook Projects

SAM Projects allow you to actively apply the skills you learned live in Microsoft Word, Excel, PowerPoint, or Access. Become a more productive student and use these skills throughout your career.

## To complete SAM Textbook Projects, please follow these steps:

SAM Textbook Projects allow you to complete a project as you follow along with the steps in the textbook. As you read the module, look for icons that indicate when you should download **sam¹⬇** your SAM Start file(s) and when to upload **sam¹⬆** the final project file to SAM for grading.

Everything you need to complete this project is provided within SAM. You can launch the eBook directly from SAM, which will allow you to take notes, highlight, and create a custom study guide, or you can use a print textbook or your mobile app. Download IOS or Download Android.

To get started, launch your SAM Project assignment from SAM, MindTap, or a link within your LMS.

## Step 1: Download Files

- Click the "Download All" button or the individual links to download your **Start File** and **Support File(s)** (when available). You <u>must</u> use the SAM Start file.

- Click the Instructions link to launch the eBook (or use the print textbook or mobile app).

- Disregard any steps in the textbook that ask you to create a new file or to use a file from a location outside of SAM.

- Look for the SAM Download icon **sam¹⬇** to begin working with your start file.

- Follow the module's step-by-step instructions until you reach the SAM Upload icon **sam¹⬆**.

- Save and close the file.

## Step 2: Save Work to SAM

- Ensure you rename your project file to match the Expected File Name.

- Upload your in-progress or completed file to SAM. You can download the file to continue working or submit it for grading in the next step.

## Step 3: Submit for Grading

- Upload the completed file to SAM for immediate feedback and to view the available Reports.

  - The **Graded Summary Report** provides a detailed list of project steps, your score, and feedback to aid you in revising and re-submitting the project.

  - The **Study Guide Report** provides your score for each project step and links to the associated training and textbook pages.

- If additional attempts are allowed, use your reports to assist with revising and resubmitting your project.

- To re-submit the project, download the file saved in step 2.

- Edit, save, and close the file, then re-upload and submit it again.

## For all other SAM Projects, please follow these steps:

To get started, launch your SAM Project assignment from SAM, MindTap, or a link within your LMS.

## Step 1: Download Files

- Click the "Download All" button or the individual links to download your **Instruction File**, **Start File**, and **Support File(s)** (when available). You <u>must</u> use the SAM Start file.

- Open the Instruction file and follow the step-by-step instructions. Ensure you rename your project file to match the Expected File Name (change _1 to _2 at the end of the file name).

## Step 2: Save Work to SAM

- Upload your in-progress or completed file to SAM. You can download the file to continue working or submit it for grading in the next step.

## Step 3: Submit for Grading

- Upload the completed file to SAM for immediate feedback and to view available Reports.

    - The **Graded Summary Report** provides a detailed list of project steps, your score, and feedback to aid you in revising and resubmitting the project.

    - The **Study Guide Report** provides your score for each project step and links to the associated training and textbook pages.

- If additional attempts are allowed, use your reports to assist with revising and resubmitting your project.

- To re-submit the project, download the file saved in step 2.

- Edit, save, and close the file, then re-upload and submit it again.

For additional tips to successfully complete your SAM Projects, please view our Common Student Errors Infographic.

# Planning, Developing, and Giving a Presentation

## Preparing a Presentation for a Resort

## Case | Outer Island Hotel and Resort

Outer Island Hotel and Resort is a hotel on Sanibel Island in Florida. The hotel was recently bought by the national hotel chain, Castle Hotels. Castle Hotels spent the last year renovating Outer Island Hotel and Resort. They hired Theary Him to create a marketing campaign to attract new corporate business to the hotel. As part of the campaign, Theary plans to visit large companies all over the United States to describe the services and amenities of the hotel and to convince them to schedule their next convention, sales meeting, or corporate retreat at the hotel. She needs to create a presentation to help her do this.

In this module, you'll learn how to plan presentations by determining their purposes and outcomes and by analyzing the needs and expectations of your audience. You'll also understand the importance of identifying a clear focus for the presentations and outlining your key points, and how to apply this information as you develop an introduction, organized body, and conclusion for presentations. You'll learn about the types of visuals and handouts you can use to support the content of a presentation and about the criteria for assessing the situation and facilities for giving the presentation. Finally, you will learn the value of rehearsing your delivery and preparing your appearance, and how to evaluate your performance.

### Objectives

#### Session 1
- Understand presentations and presentation media
- Learn about common forms of presentations
- Understand how to identify a presentation's purposes and desired outcomes
- Identify an audience's demographics and the audience's relationship to the presenter
- Learn how to recognize the needs and expectations of an audience

#### Session 2
- Understand the importance of determining the focus for a presentation
- Learn how to identify the key points of a presentation
- Understand how to develop an effective introduction, body, and conclusion
- Explore types of visuals and handouts

#### Session 3
- Identify the ways to deliver a presentation
- Learn how to prepare for audience questions and participation
- Understand what to focus on when rehearsing a presentation
- Consider aspects of your appearance
- Consider the steps for setting up for a presentation
- Learn how to evaluate your performance

### Starting Data Files

There are no starting Data Files needed for this module.

# Session 1 Visual Overview:

Knowing whether the presentation will be delivered by a person either in front of a live audience or over the Internet, or if it will be self-running, affects how you will use presentation media.

Presentations can be informative, persuasive, or demonstrative.

Understanding what you want your listeners to know, think, feel, or do after listening to your message helps keep you focused on your audience's needs.

Determine the form of the presentation

Determine the purpose of the presentation

Identify the desired outcome

## Form, Purpose, and Outcome

| What form is the presentation? | ☐ Real-time | ☐ Self-running |
|---|---|---|

What is the primary purpose of your presentation? Check one and add specific details.

☐ Inform:

☐ Persuade:

☐ Demonstrate or train:

What is the primary desired outcome of your presentation? Specifically, what should the audience know, think, feel, or do after listening to your message?

Does your presentation have a secondary purpose? Check one and add specific details.

☐ Inform:

☐ Persuade:

☐ Demonstrate or train:

☐ None

If there is a secondary purpose, what is the secondary desired outcome?

# Planning a Presentation

Identifying your audience's relationship to you can help you determine the appropriate style for your presentation.

Learning the characteristics of your audience will help you deliver an effective presentation.

Determine
the
audience's
relationship
to you

Determine
the
demographics
of the
audience

**Audience Analysis, continued**

How will your listeners use this information? Check and explain all that apply.

- [ ] Make decisions:

## Audience Analysis

Who is your audience? Check all that apply and add details about each.

- [ ] Peers:

- [ ] Managers:

- [ ] Employees:

- [ ] Strangers:

What characteristics do you know about your audience? Check all that apply and add details about each selected characteristic.

- [ ] Age:

- [ ] Education:

- [ ] Cultural background:

- [ ] Other:

What level of expertise does your audience have with regards to your topic? Add details to describe the selected level of expertise.

- [ ] Expert:

- [ ] Intermediate:

- [ ] Beginner/Some knowledge:

- [ ] Complete novice:

# Understanding Presentations and Presentation Media

A **presentation** is a talk in which the person speaking—the **presenter**—is communicating with an audience in an effort to explain new concepts or ideas, sell a product or service, entertain, train the audience in a new skill or technique, or achieve a wide variety of other goals. The ability to give an interesting and informative presentation is an important skill for students and professionals in all types of businesses.

Some talented presenters are able to simply stand in front of an audience and speak. They don't need any **presentation media**—the visual and audio aids that you display to support your points—because they are able to captivate the audience and clearly explain their topics simply by speaking. Most of us, however, want to use presentation media to help hold the audience's interest and enhance their understanding. Presentation media is also a valuable reinforcement tool for those who process learning visually.

Presentation media can include photos, lists, music, video, and objects that the presenter shows or shares with the audience. You can also use the following tools to display presentation media:

- Presentation software, such as Microsoft PowerPoint
- Whiteboard
- Flip chart
- Posters
- Overhead transparencies
- Handouts
- Chalkboard

Presentation software like PowerPoint makes it very easy for presenters to create bulleted lists of information points. This sometimes results in all of the presenter's content listed on a screen behind them, which they then proceed to read to their audience. Since most people can read faster than someone can speak, the audience finishes reading the words before the presenter finishes speaking, and then sits, bored, waiting for the presenter to move on to new information. Even if the presenter has additional information to communicate, the audience, anticipating that they will be able to read the information on the screen, has probably stopped listening. Sometimes visuals contain so many words that to make them all fit, the presenter must use a small font, making it difficult or impossible for the audience to read, leading to frustration as well as boredom (see Figure 1).

| Figure 1 | A bored audience member |
| --- | --- |

Yuri Acurs/Shutterstock.com

Although brief bulleted lists can be very helpful when the presenter is explaining facts, people attend presentations to hear the speaker and perhaps to see diagrams or other illustrations that will help them understand and retain the information. When you give a presentation, you should take advantage of this opportunity to thoroughly engage your audience. For example, if you display a graphic that supports your statements, your presentation will be more interesting, and the audience will pay attention to you and what you are saying, rather than tuning you out while trying to read words on the screen (see Figure 2).

| Figure 2 | An interested, engaged audience |
| --- | --- |

Rawpixel.com/Shutterstock.com

In order to deliver a successful presentation, you need to spend time developing it. There are three stages to developing a presentation: planning, creating, and preparing your delivery. In this session, you will focus on the planning stage.

# Planning a Presentation

When you plan a presentation, you need to consider some of the same factors you consider when planning a written document—your purpose, your audience, and the information you want to convey. Planning a presentation in advance will improve the quality of your presentation, make it more effective and enjoyable for your audience, make you better prepared to deliver it, and, in the long run, save you time and effort.

As you plan your presentation, you should ask yourself the following questions:

• Will I deliver the presentation real-time in front of a live audience or in a webinar, or will it be a self-running presentation? If it is real-time, will it be recorded for later viewing?
• What are the purposes and desired outcomes of this presentation?
• Who is the audience for my presentation, and what do they need and expect?

The following sections will help you answer these questions so that you can create a more effective presentation, and enable you to feel confident in presenting your ideas.

# Determining the Form of the Presentation

Usually when someone refers to a presentation, they mean an oral presentation given by a presenter to a live audience. When giving an oral presentation, a person might present to a small audience in a room the size of a classroom, to an audience in a hall large enough to require using a microphone, or over the Internet in webinar format. A **webinar** is a presentation in which the audience signs in to a shared view of the presenter's computer screen and either can hear the speaker through the screen, or calls in to a conference call to hear the presenter over the telephone line. If the presenter is using video technology, such as a webcam, the webinar audience will be able to see the presenter as well. Depending on the webinar software, the audience might also be able to participate by asking questions verbally or posting them to an area of the screen.

With PowerPoint and other presentation software, you can also create a presentation that is self-running or that is controlled by the person viewing it. Sometimes, this type of presentation includes recorded audio, but often it includes only the presentation content. This type of presentation can be challenging to create because the person who prepares the content needs to avoid making it simply a substitute for a written document.

If you are presenting in front of a live audience, you can use facial expressions and body language to help convey your points. If presenting in person, or with some webinar formats, you can also see your audience's facial expressions and body language, which can help to indicate how they are feeling about your presentation. For example, if you see confused expressions, you might decide to pause for questions. If you are presenting via a webinar, you need to make sure all the visuals that you use to help explain your points are very clear, and you need to figure out how to interact with your audience in a way that won't disrupt the flow of your presentation. If the presentation will be self-running or pre-recorded, the content will need to be compelling enough on its own to make the audience want to watch the entire presentation. For this reason, the content of a self-running or pre-recorded presentation must be even more visually interesting because the presenter will not have the opportunity to directly engage the audience.

# Determining the Presentation's Purposes and Desired Outcomes

When you are planning a presentation, you need to know what the purpose of the presentation is. Most presentations have one of three purposes: to inform, to persuade, or to demonstrate.

## Determining the Purposes

**Informative presentations** are designed to inform or educate. This type of presentation provides the audience with background information, knowledge, and specific details about a topic that will enable them to gain understanding, make informed decisions, or increase their expertise on a topic. Examples of informative presentations include:

- Summary of research findings at an academic conference
- Briefings on the status of projects
- Overview, reviews, or evaluations of products and services
- Reports at company meetings

**Persuasive presentations** are designed to persuade or sell. They have the specific purpose of influencing how an audience feels or acts regarding a particular position or plan, or trying to convince the audience to buy something. Persuasive presentations are usually designed as balanced arguments involving logical as well as emotional reasons for supporting an action or viewpoint. Examples of persuasive presentations include:

- Recommendations of specific steps to take to achieve goals
- Sales presentations to sell a product or service
- Motivational presentations

**Demonstrative** (or **training**) **presentations** show an audience how something works, educate them on how to perform a task, or help them to understand a process or procedure. Sometimes you will provide listeners with hands-on experience, practice, and feedback so they can correct their mistakes and improve their performances. Examples of demonstrative presentations include:

- Software demonstrations
- Process explanations
- Employee training
- Seminars and workshops
- Educational classes and courses

You should always identify the primary purpose of your presentation. However, presenters often have more than one goal, which means your presentation might have additional, secondary purposes. For example, the primary purpose of a presentation might be to inform an audience about a wildlife preserve and describe it to them. But the secondary purpose might be to raise funds for that preserve. Identifying the primary purpose of a presentation helps you focus the content; however, by acknowledging secondary purposes, you can be prepared to answer or deflect questions until after the presentation so that the primary purpose remains the focus of the presentation.

Figure 3 summarizes the three categories of presentation purposes and their goals.

**Figure 3**     **Purposes for giving presentations**

| Purpose | Goal | Examples |
|---|---|---|
| Informative | Present facts and details | Summary of research findings, status reports, briefings, discussions of products and services |
| Persuasive | Influence feelings or actions | Recommendation reports, sales presentations, motivational presentations |
| Demonstrative (Training) | Show how something works and provide practice and feedback | Software demos, process explanations, employee training, seminars and workshops, educational courses |

When Theary gives her presentation about the hotel, her primary purpose will be to persuade the people in her audience to book the Outer Island Hotel and Resort for company events. Her secondary purpose will be to convince her audience members to consider visiting the hotel on their next vacation.

## Identifying Desired Outcomes

In addition to determining the purpose of a presentation, you should also consider what you hope to achieve in giving your presentation. That means you need to determine the desired outcomes of your presentation—what you want your listeners to know, think, feel, or do after listening to the message. Focusing on the desired outcomes of your presentation forces you to make it more audience-oriented. Just as when you determined the purpose of your presentation, you might find that although you have a primary desired outcome, secondary outcomes might be acceptable as well.

You should be able to concisely express the purpose and desired outcomes of your presentation. Writing down the purpose and desired outcomes helps you decide what to include in the presentation, enabling you to create a more effective presentation. A good statement of your purpose and desired outcomes will also help when you write the introduction and conclusion for your presentation. Consider the following examples of specific purpose statements with specific outcomes:

- **Purpose:** To demonstrate a newly purchased projector that staff members can use for giving presentations to small groups.
  **Outcome:** Staff members will understand how to use the new equipment.

- **Purpose:** To inform department heads at a college about the benefits of a new website where students can receive tutoring.
  **Outcome:** Audience will understand the benefits of the program.
  **Secondary Purpose:** To persuade department heads to recruit tutors for the program.
  **Secondary Outcome:** Department heads will ask their faculty to identify potential tutors.

The desired outcome of Theary's presentation is that the event planners at the companies she visits will book their companies' events at the Outer Island Hotel and Resort.

Figure 4 shows a basic worksheet for helping determine the form, purpose, and outcome of a presentation. This worksheet is filled out with Theary's information.

| Figure 4 | Form, Purpose, and Outcome worksheet for hotel presentation |

## Form, Purpose, and Outcome

| What form is the presentation? | ☒ Real-time | ☐ Self-running |

What is the primary purpose of your presentation? Check one and add specific details.

☐ Inform:

☒ Persuade: Persuade companies to book their conventions and corporate retreats at Outer Island Hotel.

☐ Demonstrate or train:

What is the primary desired outcome of your presentation? Specifically, what should the audience know, think, feel, or do after listening to your message?

The audience will know about all the services and amenities available at Outer Island Hotel and Resort. As a result, they will want to book their company's next convention or corporate retreat at the hotel.

Does your presentation have a secondary purpose? Check one and add specific details.

☐ Inform:

☒ Persuade: Persuade audience members to book their next vacation or family reunion at Outer Island Hotel and Resort.

☐ Demonstrate or train:

☐ None

If there is a secondary purpose, what is the secondary desired outcome?
Audience members will want to book their next vacation or family reunion at the hotel.

# Analyzing Your Audience's Needs and Expectations

The more you know about your audience, the more you'll be able to adapt your presentation to their needs. By putting yourself in your audience's shoes, you'll be able to visualize them as more than just a group of passive listeners, and you can anticipate what they need and expect from your presentation. Anticipating the needs of your audience also increases the chances that your audience will react favorably to your presentation.

The first step in analyzing your audience is to determine their relationship to you. If you are speaking to your peers, you could adopt a less formal style than if you are speaking to your managers or people who report to you. Also, if you are speaking to people who know you and your credentials, you might be able to present in a more informal, familiar manner than if you are speaking to people who have never met you.

The second step in analyzing your audience is to find out about their demographics. **Demographics** are characteristics that describe your audience. Some of the demographics that affect your presentations are:

- **Age**—People of different age groups vary in terms of attention span and the way they absorb information. For example, children have shorter attention spans and generally can't sit still as long as adults, so presentations to children should be divided into short sessions interspersed with physical activity.
- **Cultural background**—Each culture has its own expectations for how to write, speak, and communicate, including nonverbal conventions such as gestures and body movement. It is important to remember that cultural differences can occur even in the same country.
- **Expertise**—Audiences with specialized training expect examples that use terms and concepts from their field. Audiences who are unfamiliar with a topic will require more definitions and explanation to understand the presentation.

# Insight

## Understanding the Needs of an International Audience

If you're presenting to an international audience, whether over the Internet or in person, it is important to understand the different cultural expectations that international audiences may have for your presentation, including expectations for nonverbal communication. These cultural expectations are subtle but powerful, and you can immediately create a negative impression if you don't understand them. For example, audiences from cultures outside the United States may expect you to speak and dress more formally than you are used to in the United States. In addition, some cultures may take offense at certain topics or jokes.

There are no universal guidelines that would enable you to characterize the needs of all international audiences; however, there are some commonsense recommendations. You should analyze the hand gestures and symbols you use routinely to see if they have different meaning for other cultures. Be cautious about using humor because it is easy to misinterpret. Most importantly, take special care to avoid using cultural stereotypes, even if you think they are positive or well-meaning.

Also avoid using idioms or phrases that might not be widely used outside of your area or country, such as "the cat's out of the bag" or "jump on the bandwagon."

Understanding who your audience is and their needs and expectations helps you adapt the content of your presentation to a particular audience. Figure 5 shows a worksheet that Theary used to analyze the needs and expectations of her audience.

**Figure 5**    **Audience Analysis worksheet for the hotel presentation**

## Audience Analysis

**Who is your audience? Check all that apply and add details about each.**

☐ Peers:

☐ Managers:

☐ Employees:

☒ Strangers: Decision makers at large companies in the United States who decide where the company will hold off-site meetings.

**What characteristics do you know about your audience? Check all that apply and add details about each selected characteristic.**

☒ Age: Adults probably between ages 25 and 65

☒ Education: Most will be college educated, some will have advanced degrees

☒ Cultural background: Varied

☐ Other:

**What level of expertise does your audience have with regards to your topic? Add details to describe the selected level of expertise.**

☒ Expert: Audience members most likely will have experience booking and attending corporate conventions, seminars, sales meetings, and corporate retreats, and they know what services and amenities they want.

☐ Intermediate:

☐ Beginner/Some knowledge:

☐ Complete novice:

### Audience Analysis, continued

**How will your listeners use this information? Check and explain all that apply.**

☒ Make decisions: Decide whether to book a corporate event at the hotel

☐ Perform a task:

☒ Form an opinion: Form an opinion about Outer Island Hotel and Resort

☒ Increase understanding: Learn about the upgraded services and amenities of the hotel

☐ Follow a process:

☐ Other:

**Proskills**

## Teamwork: Planning Collaborative Presentations

Because much of the work in business and industry is collaborative, it's only natural that some presentations are created and presented by a team of people. These types of presentations are referred to as collaborative presentations and they provide many benefits, including:

- Sharing a greater range of expertise and ideas
- Provoking more discussion due to different presentation styles and a wider range of information being shared
- Providing more people with exposure and the rewards of a task accomplished
- Allowing more people to gain valuable experience in communicating ideas

In addition to creating compelling content, a successful collaborative presentation depends on your group's ability to plan thoroughly and practice together. To ensure a successful group presentation, consider the following as you plan your presentation:

- Involve the whole team in the planning.
- Show respect for the ideas of all team members, and be sensitive to personality and cultural differences among the team members.
- Convey clear time constraints to each speaker and ensure that all speakers are prepared to limit themselves to the time allotted.
- Plan for the transitions between speakers.

In this session you learned how to plan a presentation and to consider the needs and expectations of your audience. In the next session, you will learn about the steps for creating the content of a presentation.

# Review

### Session 1 Quick Check

1. Describe the difference between a presentation and presentation media.
2. What are the three stages of developing a presentation?
3. List the three categories of presentation purposes.
4. Give an example of each category of presentation purpose.
5. Why is it important to focus on the desired outcomes of a presentation?
6. List three examples of audience demographics.

# Session 2 Visual Overview:

A presentation's focus can be based on the chronology of events, a geography or region, categories or classifications, a particular component or segment, or a point of view.

An effective introduction should engage the audience and state the purpose for your presentation.

Information gathered from a variety of sources can help support your statements, as long as the information is accurate and up-to-date and the source is reputable.

**Establish a focus and identify key points**

**Write an introduction**

**Gather and evaluate information**

## Focus and Organization

| How will you focus your presentation? Select one and describe the selected strategy. | |
|---|---|
| ☐ Time or chronology | ☐ Geography or region |
| ☐ Category or classification | ☐ Component or element |
| ☐ Segment or portion | ☐ Point of view |

Explanation:

What are your key points of your presentation?

How will you gain your audience's attention? Select one and describe the selected strategy.

| | |
|---|---|
| ☐ Anecdote | ☐ Statistic or relevant data |
| ☐ Quotation, familiar phrase, or definition | ☐ Question(s) |
| ☐ Current problem or issue | ☐ Comment about audience or occasion |
| ☐ State purpose | |

Explanation:

| Will you provide an overview of your presentation? | ☐ Yes | ☐ No |
|---|---|---|

If so, how?

# Creating a Presentation

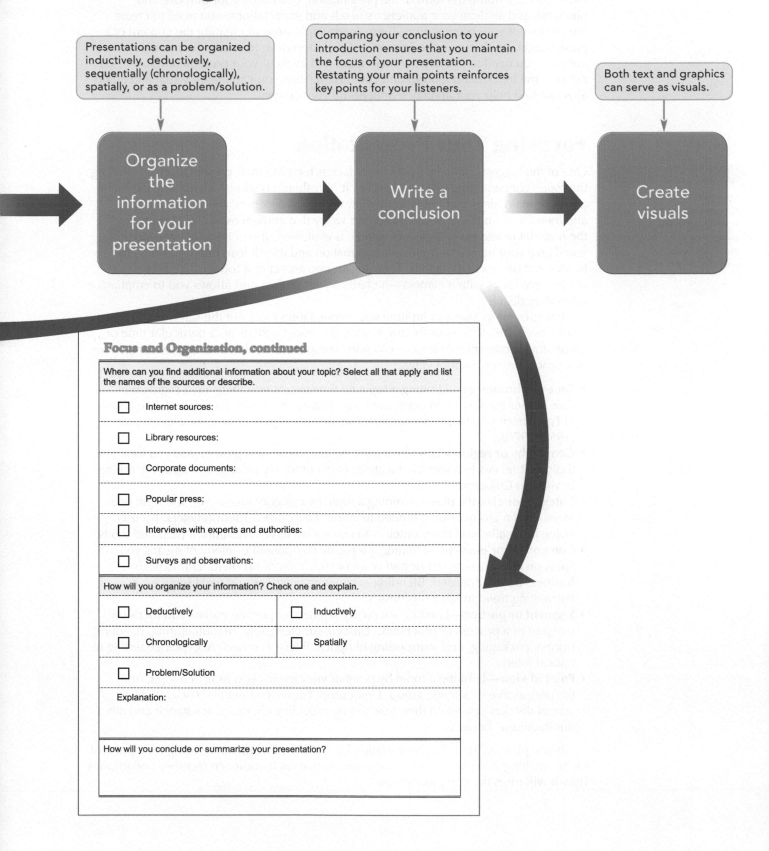

Presentations can be organized inductively, deductively, sequentially (chronologically), spatially, or as a problem/solution.

Comparing your conclusion to your introduction ensures that you maintain the focus of your presentation. Restating your main points reinforces key points for your listeners.

Both text and graphics can serve as visuals.

**Organize the information for your presentation**

**Write a conclusion**

**Create visuals**

### Focus and Organization, continued

Where can you find additional information about your topic? Select all that apply and list the names of the sources or describe.

☐ Internet sources:

☐ Library resources:

☐ Corporate documents:

☐ Popular press:

☐ Interviews with experts and authorities:

☐ Surveys and observations:

How will you organize your information? Check one and explain.

☐ Deductively             ☐ Inductively

☐ Chronologically         ☐ Spatially

☐ Problem/Solution

Explanation:

How will you conclude or summarize your presentation?

# Creating the Presentation

Once you determine the form of the presentation, determine your purpose and outcome, and analyze your audience's needs and expectations, you need to create the content of your presentation. There are multiple steps to creating the content of a presentation. As shown in the Session 2 Visual Overview, to create the presentation's content, you need to identify the main ideas and focus of your presentation, and then develop the introduction, body, and conclusion. Then you can create visual and audio aids that will help your audience understand your content.

# Focusing Your Presentation

**Tip**

If your audience's experience level is unknown to you, you can prepare background slides that you can access during your presentation as needed.

One of the biggest challenges presenters face is focusing their presentations by limiting the topic, concentrating on one aspect of it. You should begin by identifying the major points or main ideas that are directly relevant to your listeners' needs and interests, and then focus on those. Some presenters worry that audiences will not understand the material unless every aspect of a topic is explained. If you try to cover everything, you'll give your audience irrelevant information and they'll lose interest as they try to filter out unnecessary details. Focusing on one aspect of a topic is like bringing a picture into focus with a camera—it clarifies your subject and allows you to emphasize interesting details.

Strategies for focusing or limiting your presentation topic are the same as those you would use to create a focus for any written document—focus on a particular time or chronology, geography or region, category, component or element, segment or portion of a procedure, or point of view.

- **Time or chronology**—Limiting a topic by time means you focus on a segment of time, rather than trying to cover the entire history of a topic. *Unfocused:* The history of Egypt from 640 to 2000. *Focused:* The history of Egypt during the Nasser years (1952–1970).
- **Geography or region**—Limiting a topic by geography or region means you look at a topic as it relates to a specific location. *Unfocused:* Fly fishing. *Focused:* Fly fishing in western Colorado.
- **Category or classification**—Limiting a topic by category means you focus on one member of a group or on a limited function. *Unfocused:* Thermometers. *Focused:* Using bimetallic-coil thermometers to control bacteria in restaurant-prepared foods.
- **Component or element**—Limiting a topic by component or element means you focus on one small aspect or part of an organization or problem. *Unfocused:* Business trends. *Focused:* Blending accounting practices and legal services, a converging trend in large businesses.
- **Segment or portion**—Limiting a topic by segment or portion means you focus on one part of a process or procedure. *Unfocused:* Designing, manufacturing, handling, storing, packaging, and transporting of optical filters. *Focused:* Acceptance testing of optical filters.
- **Point of view**—Limiting a topic by point of view means you look at a topic from the perspective of a single group. *Unfocused:* Employee benefits. *Focused:* How school districts can retain their teachers by providing childcare assistance and other nontraditional benefits.

Theary plans to focus her presentation by limiting the topic to focusing on a point of view—making sure she describes the resort so that each audience member understands how it will meet the company's needs.

# Identifying Your Key Points

Once you have determined your focus, you need to identify the key points of your presentation. To help you continue to design your presentation with the listener in mind, phrase the key points as the conclusions you want your audience to draw from the presentation.

As you identify the key points, order them in a numbered list with the most important idea listed first and the least important point listed last. This will help you maintain the focus and ensure that the most important points receive the most attention. For example, the key points of Theary's presentation about the Outer Island Hotel and Resort are:

1. The hotel was recently completely renovated.
2. The resort has many amenities and services that will appeal to large groups.
3. The hotel will work with the company to create the perfect event.

Once you've established a focus and identified your key points, you need to create the introduction, body, and conclusion of your presentation. Good presentations start with an effective introduction, continue with a well-organized body, and end with a strong conclusion.

# Developing an Introduction

The introduction, or opening statement, of a presentation enables you to gain your listeners' attention, establish a relationship with your audience, and preview your key points. The introduction sets the tone for the entire presentation. An inadequate introduction can ruin the rest of your presentation no matter how well you've prepared. Consider these guidelines to avoid common mistakes:

- Don't begin by apologizing about any aspect of your presentation, such as how nervous you are or your lack of preparation. Apologies can cause the audience to lose faith in your credibility as a presenter or expert on your topic.
- Don't use gimmicks to begin your presentation, such as asking the audience to repeat a phrase, singing a song, or ringing a bell. Members of your audience may not know how to respond or will feel uncomfortable.
- Avoid trite, flattering, or phony statements, such as, "Ladies and gentlemen, it is an unfathomable honor to be in your presence." Gaining respect requires treating your audience as your equal.
- Be cautious when using humor. It's difficult to predict how audiences will respond to jokes and other forms of humor. Also, what one person or group finds humorous might offend another person or group.

## Gaining Your Audience's Attention

The purpose of the introduction is to provide the listeners with an organizational overview of your presentation; however, it is also important to remember that the introduction provides the audience with their first impression of you and your presentation. Even if your audience is interested in your topic, they can be easily distracted, so it's important to create an effective introduction that will immediately grab their attention. A truly effective introduction captures the attention of your audience and establishes a rapport with them. Some effective ways to gain your audience's attention are:

- Share anecdotes.
- Discuss statistics and quantitative data.
- Mention a quotation, familiar phrase, or definition.
- Ask questions.
- Raise a current problem or issue.
- Comment about the audience or occasion.
- State the purpose of the presentation.

### Share Anecdotes

Sharing anecdotes (short stories or personal experiences that demonstrate a specific point) is a very effective method of gaining your audience's attention. Anecdotes allow your audience to relate to you as a person and make your topic more relevant. For example, Theary could begin her presentation by describing a recent successful event held at the hotel:

"Last month, Worldwide Phone Systems held their annual sales meeting at Outer Island Hotel and Resort. They needed a room large enough to serve 800 people dinner and with a stage for presenting awards. We were able to remove a moveable wall between our two largest ballrooms and accommodate them. They also wanted to ensure that attendees seated farthest from the stage would be able to clearly see the people on the stage. We provided two 10 foot by 10 foot screens located on either side of the stage so that even someone at the back table could clearly see the stage. Finally, they asked us to arrange outings during the day. We arranged several activities for their attendees including tee times at the resort, kayaking and canoeing tours, a guided tour of the J.N. Ding Darling National Wildlife Refuge, and a tour of Sanibel Historical Museum and Village. The events director at Worldwide told me that it was the most successful sales meeting they had for the last 10 years."

### Discuss Statistics and Quantitative Data

Another way to engage your audience is to discuss interesting statistics and quantitative data relating to the needs of your audience. To be effective, make sure that the statistics and data you use are current, accurate, and easily understood.

In Theary's presentation, she could share statistics and data about the number of sunny days on Sanibel Island.

### Mention a Quotation, Familiar Phrase, or Definition

Short quotes, familiar phrases, or definitions are another way to gain your audience's attention. This strategy works because your audience wants to know how the quote, phrase, or definition relates to your topic, and this leads naturally into the rest of your talk. Castle Hotels has been running a national marketing campaign to raise brand awareness, and their slogan has been repeated for months in online, television, radio, and print ads. The slogan is, "You are our number one VIP." Theary could begin by quoting that slogan and emphasizing that it is not just a slogan, it is the way she and the hotel employees will treat each and every guest.

### Ask Questions

Asking questions to introduce your topic can be effective if the questions are thought-provoking and the issues are important. This can be especially effective in small group settings or situations where you're attempting to find new ways to approach ideas. Asking audience members to give tentative answers to an informal quiz or questionnaire allows you to adjust your presentation to accommodate their responses.

**Tip**

If an audience member calls out humorous or otherwise unwanted answers to your questions, be polite, but redirect your audience to the focus of your presentation.

Rhetorical questions (questions you don't expect the audience to answer) are especially effective. Rhetorical questions engage the audience right away because the audience members instinctively reply to the question internally.

In her presentation, Theary could emphasize the hotel's dedication to making sure every guest is satisfied by asking the rhetorical question "Have you ever had a disappointing customer service experience?" and then following that statement with examples of how customer service issues have been handled successfully in the past.

## Raise a Current Problem or Issue

Another way to grab the attention of your audience is to raise a current problem or unresolved issue. This provides you with an opportunity to suggest a change or a solution to the problem. By defining a problem for your audience, you develop a common ground upon which you can provide insight, examine alternatives, and make recommendations.

In Theary's presentation, she could address the current issue of climate change by describing the hotel's commitment to the environment. For example, new solar panels provide 70% of the hotel's electricity, the hotel has agreements with a local agency to compost food waste, and new, automatic shut-off systems for air conditioners and lights in guest rooms, conference rooms, and common area rest rooms were installed.

## Comment About the Audience or Occasion

To show your enthusiasm about the group you're addressing, as well as about your topic, you can make comments about the audience or occasion. If you do this, your comments should be brief and sincere. Referring to the occasion can be as simple as Theary saying, "Thank you so much for allowing me to describe our newly renovated hotel and resort and how we can meet your needs for your next sales meeting, corporate retreat, or convention."

## State the Purpose of the Presentation

Simply announcing your purpose works well as an introduction if your audience is already interested in your topic or if your time is limited. Most audiences, however, will appreciate a more creative approach than simply stating, "I'm going to try to convince you that Outer Island Hotel and Resort is the best place to schedule your next event." For example, in Theary's presentation, she might say something like, "I am here to describe our beautiful hotel and location."

Figure 6 summarizes the ways to gain your audience's attention.

| Figure 6 | Ways to gain your audience's attention |
| --- | --- |

| Method | Result |
| --- | --- |
| Share anecdotes | Helps audience relate to you as a real person |
| Discuss statistics and quantitative data | Increases audience interest in topic |
| Mention a quotation, familiar phrase, or definition | Leads in well to remainder of presentation |
| Ask questions | Gets audience thinking about topic |
| Raise a current problem or issue | Prepares audience to consider solutions or recommendations for change |
| Comment about the audience or occasion | Enables you to show your enthusiasm |
| State the purpose of the presentation | Works well if audience is already interested |

## Providing an Overview of Your Presentation

After you have gained the attention of your audience, you might choose to provide them with an overview of your presentation. Overviews, sometimes called advance organizers or previews, prepare your audience for the points that will follow. They can be very effective for longer presentations or for presentations that cover complex or technical information. Overviews help your audience remember your presentation by providing a road map of how it is organized. Overviews should be brief and simple, stating what you plan to do and in what order. After you've given your audience an overview of your presentation, it's important that you follow that same order.

Once you've created your introduction, you're ready to develop the body of your presentation.

# Developing the Body of Your Presentation

The body of your presentation is where you present pertinent information, supporting evidence, and important details. To develop the body, you need to gather information on your key points, determine the organizational approach, add supporting details and other pertinent information, and provide transitions from one point to the next.

## Gathering Information

Most of the time, you'll give presentations on topics about which you're knowledgeable and comfortable. Other times, you might have to give presentations on topics that are new to you. In either case, you'll need to explain the reasoning behind your statements, provide support for claims, present sensible recommendations, and anticipate objections to your statements or conclusions. This means you need to go beyond your personal experience and do in-depth research to provide relevant and up-to-date information, verifiable facts, truthful statistics, and expert testimony (see Figure 7). Always remember to cite your sources for facts, quotes, and other information.

You can find additional information on your topic by consulting the following:

- Internet sources, including blogs, Twitter feeds, recorded webinars, and podcasts— Be sure to verify that the source is credible.
- Library resources—You can access library resources, such as books, encyclopedias, academic journals, government publications, and other reference materials, using the library's computerized catalog, indexes, and professional database services.
- Corporate documents and office correspondence—Since using these materials might violate your company's nondisclosure policy, you might need to obtain your company's permission or get legal clearance to use the information.
- Popular press items from newspapers, radio, TV, the web, and magazines—This information, geared for general audiences, provides large-scale details and personal opinions that may need to be supplemented by additional research.
- Interviews with experts and authorities in the field or other members of your organization—Talking to other people who are knowledgeable about your topic will give you additional insight.
- Surveys and observations—If you do your own interviews, surveys, and observations, be prepared with a list of specific questions, and always be respectful of other people's time.

| Figure 7 | Gathering information from a variety of sources |

Duplass/Shutterstock.com

## Evaluating Information

**Tip**

Some sources have the look and feel of authoritative, research-based information, but are skewed by politics, profits, or personal opinions.

Not all of the information you gather will be of equal value. You must evaluate the information you gather by asking whether it is accurate, up-to-date, and reputable. When evaluating Internet sources in particular, it's important that you ascertain whether the websites you use as sources contain a bias or viewpoint that influences the information, such as a sales pitch.

You should also evaluate whether the information is pertinent to your particular topic. The scope of some topics is so broad, you will need to whittle down the information to only that which serves to clarify or enhance the specific key points of your presentation. Consider whether the information supports your purpose and focus.

For her presentation, Theary collected the following additional information: a list of all the upgrades that were done, a complete list of the activities offered by the resort, the number of rooms and meeting areas available, statistics from the National Oceanic and Atmospheric Administration about the average temperature and number of sunny days on the island, menus from the hotel and area restaurants, and a schedule of the free shuttles to and from the airport.

## Organizing Your Information

After you have fully researched your topic and evaluated the information you've gathered, you're ready to organize the information in an understandable and logical manner so that your listeners can easily follow your ideas. You should choose an organizational approach for your information based upon the purpose, audience, and situation of each presentation. Sometimes your company or supervisor might ask you to follow a specific organizational pattern or format in giving your presentations. Other times you might be able to choose your own organizational approach. Some common organizational options include deductive, inductive, chronological, spatial, and problem-solution.

**Deductive organization** means that you present your conclusions or solutions first, and then explain the information that led you to your conclusions. See Figure 8. Deductive organization is the most common pattern used in business because it presents the most important or bottom-line information first.

**Figure 8** **Deductive organization**

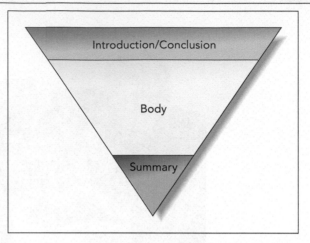

When you begin with the individual facts and save your conclusions until the end of your presentation, you are using **inductive organization**. See Figure 9. Inductive organization is useful when your purpose is to persuade your audience to follow an unusual plan of action, or you feel your audience might resist your conclusions. However, inductively organized presentations can be more difficult to follow because the most important information may come at the end of the presentation.

**Figure 9** **Inductive organization**

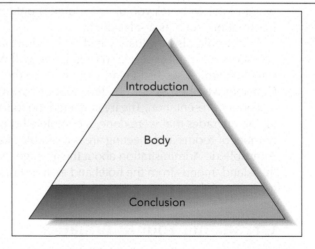

Organizing Theary's presentation in a deductive manner would mean that Theary would begin by stating that the hotel is the best place in the country to hold an event, and then describe all the amenities and facts about the hotel and the area. If Theary organized her presentation inductively, she would do the opposite. She would start by describing the amenities and facts about the hotel and conclude by stating the hotel is the obvious choice for the next company event.

When you use **sequential** or **chronological organization**, you organize information in a step-by-step fashion or according to a time sequence. See Figure 10. Sequential organization works best when you must demonstrate a procedure, train someone to use a piece of equipment, or explain the evolution of a concept. Failing to present sequential information in the proper order can leave your listeners confused and might result in wasting time and resources.

| Figure 10 | Sequential (chronological) organization |
| --- | --- |

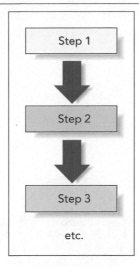

If Theary decided to organize her presentation sequentially, she could describe a typical guest's experience at the hotel from the time they check in through the time they check out.

**Spatial organization** is used to provide a logical and effective order for describing the physical layout of an item or system. See Figure 11.

| Figure 11 | Spatial organization |
| --- | --- |

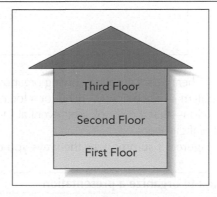

To organize her presentation spatially, Theary would describe the hotel's various areas, such as the guest rooms, the conference rooms, the indoor and outdoor eating areas, the golf course, and so on.

**Problem-solution organization** consists of presenting a problem, outlining various solutions to the problem, and then explaining the solution you recommend. See Figure 12. Problem-solution presentations work best for recommending a specific action or solution.

| Figure 12 | Problem-solving organization |
|---|---|

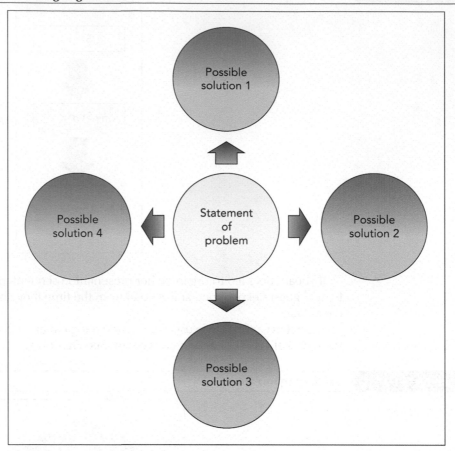

If Theary uses problem-solving organization in her presentation, she would present the problem—the company's need for a location for their event—and then recommend her solution—that they book their event at Outer Island Hotel and Resort because it will meet all of their needs.

Figure 13 summarizes the ways you can organize a presentation.

| Figure 13 | Ways to organize a presentation |
|---|---|

| Organizational Pattern | Explanation of Pattern |
|---|---|
| Deductive | Present conclusions or solutions first |
| Inductive | Present conclusions or solutions last |
| Sequential (Chronological) | Order by sequence or time |
| Spatial | Order by space or position |
| Problem/Solution | Present problem and various solutions, then recommend solution |

## Developing Your Conclusion

Conclusions are valuable because they allow you to restate your key points, thus helping your listeners remember important information from your presentation. You can also suggest appropriate actions and recommend further resources. The conclusion is the last thing your audience hears and sees, and will likely stay with them longer than individual points you made—if it's effective. Therefore, you should give the same amount of attention and effort to developing the conclusion as you did to your introduction.

The following suggestions will help you create an effective conclusion:

- Use a clear transition to move into your conclusion. This will signal your audience that you're moving from the body of your presentation to the closing statements. Avoid ending with a trite statement like "I see my time is up, so I'll stop here," which sends a general message to your audience that you did not develop a conclusion or prepare adequately to present all the relevant information in the amount of time available.
- Keep your conclusion short and simple. Audiences appreciate speakers who keep their presentations within the allotted time limit.
- Make sure the conclusion reiterates only the central points or essential message of your presentation. Don't introduce new ideas; simply remind your audience why they should care about your topic. Audiences won't appreciate a rehash of your entire presentation.
- Relate your conclusion to your introduction. Consider writing your conclusion at the same time you write your introduction to make sure that they both provide the same focus. Whenever you write your conclusion, compare it to your introduction to make sure they are complementary.
- If your purpose was to persuade your audience to take a specific action, use your conclusion to suggest what the audience should do now.
- If possible, suggest where your audience can find additional resources by providing website addresses, email addresses, phone numbers, or physical addresses.

Theary could conclude her presentation by stating, "You have many options when choosing the location of your next corporate event. I hope I have convinced you that the beautiful Outer Island Hotel and Resort on Sanibel Island is the place you should choose."

Figure 14 shows a worksheet Theary used to determine the focus and organization for her presentation.

Figure 14    Focus and Organization worksheet for hotel presentation

## Focus and Organization

**How will you focus your presentation? Select one and describe the selected strategy.**

- [ ] Time or chronology
- [ ] Geography or region
- [ ] Category or classification
- [ ] Component or element
- [ ] Segment or portion
- [x] Point of view

Explanation:
Although the hotel has many services and amenities for all travelers, the emphasis will be on the advantages and usefulness to a corporate audience.

**What are your key points of your presentation?**
The new renovation and upgrades, excellent customer service, and the business services available

**How will you gain your audience's attention? Select one and describe the selected strategy.**

- [ ] Anecdote
- [ ] Statistic or relevant data
- [ ] Quotation, familiar phrase, or definition
- [ ] Question(s)
- [ ] Current problem or issue
- [x] Comment about audience or occasion
- [ ] State purpose

Explanation: Be enthusiastic while introducing self and introducing the hotel so that the audience immediately understands that the hotel is a good solution for where to book their next event.

**Will you provide an overview of your presentation?**    [ ] Yes    [x] No

If so, how?

## Focus and Organization, continued

**Where can you find additional information about your topic? Select all that apply and list the names of the sources or describe.**

- [x] Internet sources: collect good reviews about the hotel and the area
- [ ] Library resources:
- [x] Corporate documents: specific information about the renovations
- [x] Popular press: locate good reviews of the purchase of the hotel by Castle Hotels and the renovations
- [ ] Interviews with experts and authorities:
- [x] Surveys and observations: responses from survey cards filled out by recent guests at the hotel

**How will you organize your information? Check one and explain.**

- [ ] Deductively
- [ ] Inductively
- [ ] Chronologically
- [x] Spatially
- [ ] Problem/Solution

Explanation:
Describe the physical hotel space—the guest rooms, the conference spaces, the restaurants and catering services, including the beachside bistro, the business center, the amenities including the private beach, pools, golf course, tennis courts, salon, spa, and fitness center.

**How will you conclude or summarize your presentation?**
Reiterate how nice the renovated hotel is, how satisfied guests have been, and make sure all contact information is posted and available in handouts.

# Creating Visuals

Once you have written the content of your presentation, you can create your visuals. As you create your visuals, remember that they are intended to clarify your points, not contain the full content of your presentation. The exception to this is when you are creating a self-running or pre-recorded presentation that users can view on their own. Even then, you need to remember that you are creating a presentation, not a document, so the information should be communicated in a creative manner, not just via long bulleted lists.

Using visuals to supplement your presentation does the following:

- Increases the listeners' understanding—Visuals are especially helpful in explaining a difficult concept, displaying data, and illustrating the steps in a process.
- Helps listeners remember information—Audiences will remember information longer when visuals highlight or exemplify the main points, review conclusions, and explain recommendations.
- Adds credibility to the presentation—Speakers who use visuals in their presentation are judged by their audiences as more professional and better prepared.
- Stimulates and maintains the listeners' attention—It's much more interesting to see how something functions, rather than just hear about it.

The primary thing to remember is that the visuals are supposed to enhance the audience's understanding and help keep their attention. Visuals shouldn't draw attention to themselves in such a way as to distract from your main points.

## Using Text as Visuals

When you use text as visuals, you allow your audience to absorb the information you are conveying by reading as well as listening. This can help audience members retain the information presented. Text can be formatted as bulleted lists or treated like a graphic.

A common pitfall for presenters is to use too much text. You don't want your presentation to turn into a bedtime story with you reading all the words on your visual as the audience falls asleep. Therefore, if you use bulleted lists, keep the bullet points short. Bullet points should be brief descriptions of your main points, giving your audience a broad overview of what you will be discussing and serving as reminders to help you remember what you want to say.

Instead of creating a bulleted list, one alternative is to display key words in a decorative, large font. You could also use relevant images as the bullets, or use a photo of a person accompanied by dialog balloons, like those in a drawn comic, that contain the text you want to display. Compare the four visuals shown in Figure 15. The text in the first visual is clear enough, but the second is visually more interesting. The third visual uses graphical bullets that relate to the text in each bullet point, and the fourth eliminates text completely and just uses images.

| Figure 15 | A simple bulleted list and alternatives |
| --- | --- |

### Hybrid Automobiles

- Better gas mileage
- Reduced emissions
- Possible tax breaks

### Hybrid Automobiles

Better gas mileage

Reduced emissions

Possible tax breaks

### Hybrid Automobiles

  Better gas mileage

  Reduced emissions

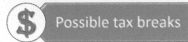  Possible tax breaks

Hybrid Automobiles

microstock3D/Shutterstock.com; romvo/Shutterstock.com

When you use text as a visual, keep in mind the following:

- If you are creating a visual that you will display to an audience while you are speaking in front of them, follow the 7x7 Rule, which says that when you display bulleted lists, use no more than seven bullet points per visual, with no more than seven words per bullet. Some presenters restrict themselves to 4x4—no more than four bullet points per visual or page with no more than four words per bullet.
- Keep phrases parallel. For example, if one bulleted item starts with a verb (such as "Summarize"), the other bulleted items should also start with a verb (such as "Include," "List," or "Review").
- Use basic, plain fonts in a size large enough to be read from the back of the room. Only use decorative fonts for a single word or a few related words for maximum impact.
- Use dark-colored text on a light or white background to make it easy for the audience to quickly read the content. Do not layer text on top of a busy background graphic because the text will be difficult to read and the graphic will compete with the text for the audience's attention.
- Proofread your presentations. One sure way to reduce your credibility as a presenter is to have typographical errors in your presentation. It is especially important to double-check the spelling of proper names.

In her presentation, Theary could list facts about the hotel, such as the number of guest rooms, the square footage of meeting space available, the number of restaurants on site, and so on, in a bulleted list.

## Using Graphics as Visuals

You can help your listeners comprehend and retain the ideas from your presentation by supplementing it with effective graphics. A **graphic** is a picture, shape, design, graph or chart, diagram, or video. The old adage "A picture is worth a thousand words" especially applies to presentations because listeners understand ideas more quickly when they can see and hear what you're talking about.

You can choose from many types of visuals for your presentations: tables (text and numerical), graphs and charts (such as bar, line, pie, organizational, and flow), illustrations (such as drawings, diagrams, maps, and photographs), and video. Selecting appropriate visuals for your purpose is a matter of knowing the strengths and weaknesses of the types of visuals. For example, if you want your audience to know facts and figures, a table might be sufficient; however, if you want your audience to make a particular judgment about the data, then a bar graph, line graph, or pie chart might be better. If you want to show processes and procedures, diagrams are better than photographs.

In Theary's presentation, she might want to present data describing the the average monthly temperatures on the island and the number of rainy days they have each month. She could read a summary of the numbers, as shown in Figure 16.

**Figure 16**     **Temperature and rainy day data as a presenter would read it**

"The average high temperature on Sanibel Island in the winter is 79 and the average low temperature is 59. In the summer, the average high temperature is 90 and the average low temperature is 72. Most months, we have only three to five days with rain. In the summer, we do have more days with rain—about 15 per month. But it usually rains for about an hour in the late afternoon."

Source: National Oceanic and Atmospheric Administration

However, this is not the most interesting way of communicating the data. By using visuals, Theary can present the same data in a format that's easier to understand, and more interesting. For example, she could present the data in tabular format, as shown in Figure 17.

**Figure 17**     **Temperature and rainy day data in tabular format**

| High | Low | Rainy | Days |
|------|-----|-------|------|
| January | 75 | 54 | 3 |
| February | 77 | 55 | 3 |
| March | 80 | 59 | 4 |
| April | 85 | 63 | 3 |
| May | 89 | 69 | 5 |
| June | 91 | 73 | 13 |
| July | 91 | 75 | 15 |
| August | 92 | 75 | 15 |
| September | 90 | 74 | 12 |
| October | 86 | 69 | 5 |
| November | 81 | 62 | 3 |
| December | 77 | 57 | 3 |

Source: National Oceanic and Atmospheric Administration

Although presenting the data in this manner does allow the audience members to read and absorb the numbers as Theary is speaking, some people can't visualize what this means. Tables are good for showing exact numbers, but they are not as good for showing trends or for illustrating how one number compares to another. To do this, Theary could create a column chart to show the temperature data, as shown in Figure 18.

**Figure 18**    Temperature data in a column chart

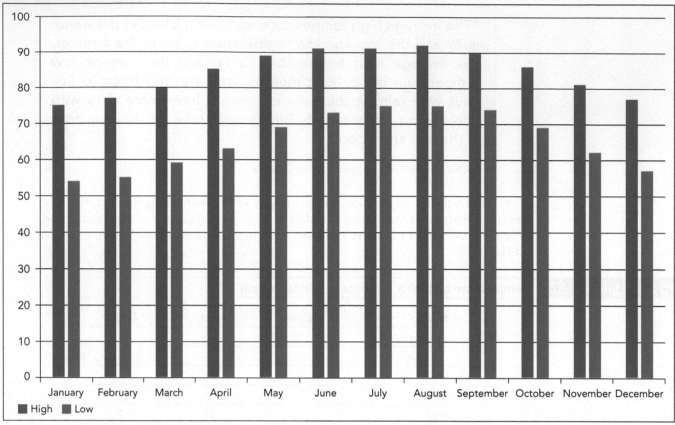

Source: National Oceanic and Atmospheric Administration

Column and bar graphs (graphs that use horizontal or vertical bars to represent specific values) are useful for comparing the value of one item to another over a period of time or a range of dates or values. A column chart could be a good choice to show the number of days with rain each month. But using a column chart for the average temperature data puts more emphasis on comparing the average high and low temperature each month.

Theary doesn't think the column chart is the best way to communicate the temperature data. Instead, she will use a line chart with two lines—one to show the average high temperatures and one to show the average low temperatures. For the number of days with rain, she will use an area chart. See Figure 19.

**Figure 19**    **Temperature data in a line chart and rainy day data in an area chart**

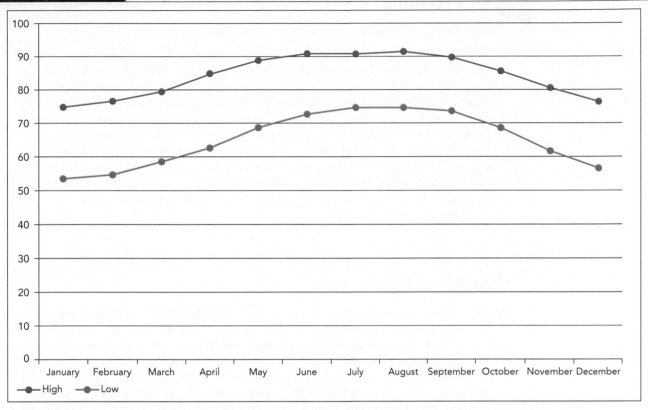

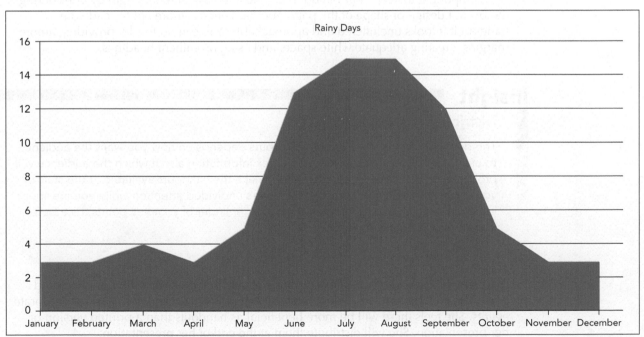

Source: National Oceanic and Atmospheric Administration

The line chart gives a clear picture of the temperatures. The area chart coveys a sense of volume. Theary plans to use both charts as visuals during her presentation. She also plans to include photos showing the hotel's private beach on a beautiful sunny day, the golf course, the wildlife preserve on the island, and people paddleboarding and kayaking. She is considering showing a video of very short clips of happy people engaged in various activities at the resort.

**Proskills**

### Decision Making: Accessible Presentations

Graphics-based visuals may not be accessible to viewers of your presentation who require assistive technologies that read the contents. With any non-text visuals, ensure that they have alternative text. Alternative text, also called alt text, is descriptive text added to an object. The assistive reading device will read the alt text to the audience member, so it should describe the graphic in enough detail that the audience member will be able to understand without seeing it. For example, if you are including a chart, describe the chart type, the labels, and the key details of the chart. Presentation software, including PowerPoint, have features that can be used to check accessibility. It will alert you to any graphics that do not contain alt text, as well as enable you to check the reading order of slide content to ensure that the assistive reader will present the information in the correct order.

## Creating Handouts

**Handouts** are documents you give to your audience before, during, or after your presentation and can be printed to distribute to a live audience, or made available digitally to participants in a webinar. Handouts can be a version of your presentation, but they can also be brochures, an instruction manual, booklets, or anything you think will help the audience remember your key points. The information in handouts should complement, rather than compete with, the information contained in your presentation.

It's important to keep your handouts simple and easy to read. Begin by considering the overall design or shape of the page. Your audience is more apt to read your handout if it looks uncluttered and approachable. You can do this by providing ample margins, creating adequate white space, and using prominent headings.

## Insight

### Distributing Handouts

The decision of when to distribute handouts depends on how you want the audience to use them. If you are presenting complex information about which the audience will probably need to take notes, you should make the handouts available at the start of your presentation. If you want the audience's undivided attention while you are speaking and your handouts will serve simply as a reminder of your key points, distribute them after your presentation.

Theary has new brochures for corporate clients that describe all the services and amenities the hotel and resort can offer the event organizer and the guests at corporate events. She feels these will be more beneficial as handouts than a printed version of her presentation. She will distribute them at the end of her presentation.

After developing the content of a presentation and creating supporting visuals, you can begin to prepare to deliver your presentation. You will learn how to prepare for delivering a presentation in the next session.

# Review

## Session 2 Quick Check

1. List at least three methods for focusing your topic.
2. Why is it a good idea to order your key points in a numbered list with the most important idea listed first and the least important point listed last?
3. List at least three ways to gain your audience's attention.
4. What is the difference between organizing your presentation deductively and inductively?
5. Why are conclusions important?
6. If you use bulleted lists as visuals, what is a good rule of thumb for how much text should be shown at one time?
7. What is a graphic?
8. What is a handout?

# Session 3 Visual Overview:

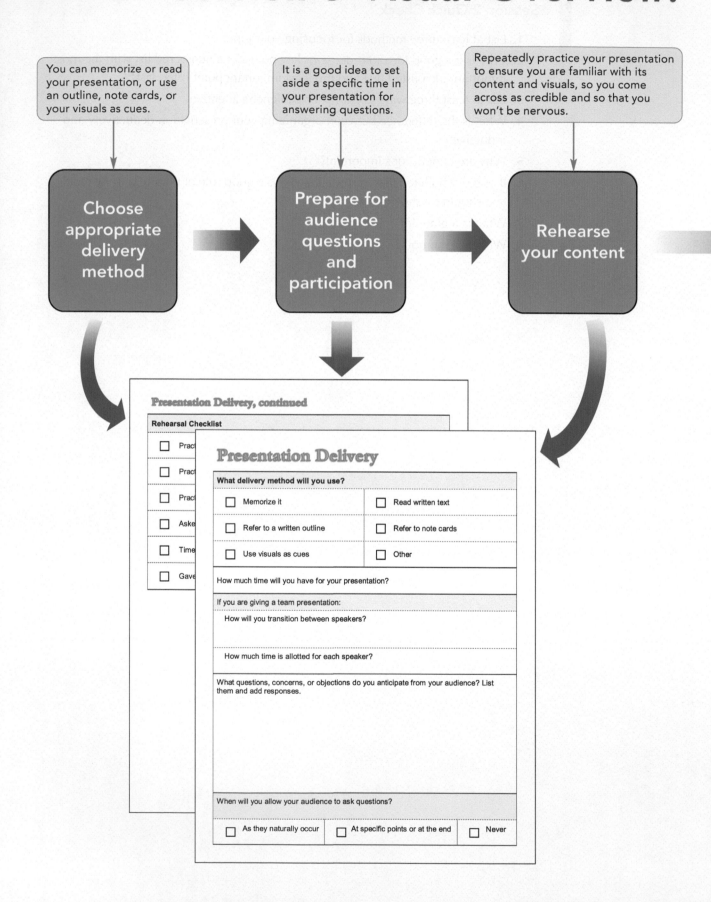

You can memorize or read your presentation, or use an outline, note cards, or your visuals as cues.

It is a good idea to set aside a specific time in your presentation for answering questions.

Repeatedly practice your presentation to ensure you are familiar with its content and visuals, so you come across as credible and so that you won't be nervous.

**Choose appropriate delivery method**

**Prepare for audience questions and participation**

**Rehearse your content**

**Presentation Delivery, continued**

**Rehearsal Checklist**

- [ ] Prac
- [ ] Prac
- [ ] Prac
- [ ] Aske
- [ ] Time
- [ ] Gave

**Presentation Delivery**

**What delivery method will you use?**

- [ ] Memorize it
- [ ] Read written text
- [ ] Refer to a written outline
- [ ] Refer to note cards
- [ ] Use visuals as cues
- [ ] Other

How much time will you have for your presentation?

If you are giving a team presentation:

How will you transition between speakers?

How much time is allotted for each speaker?

What questions, concerns, or objections do you anticipate from your audience? List them and add responses.

When will you allow your audience to ask questions?

- [ ] As they naturally occur
- [ ] At specific points or at the end
- [ ] Never

# Delivering a Presentation

It is important to dress appropriately for your presentation.

Check that all your equipment is working properly, make sure the room is arranged so that all audience members can clearly see you, or that your background is clean and professional for a webinar.

Obtaining feedback on your presentation and its delivery will help improve your future presentations.

**Evaluate your appearance**

**Set up the location for your presentation**

**Evaluate your performance**

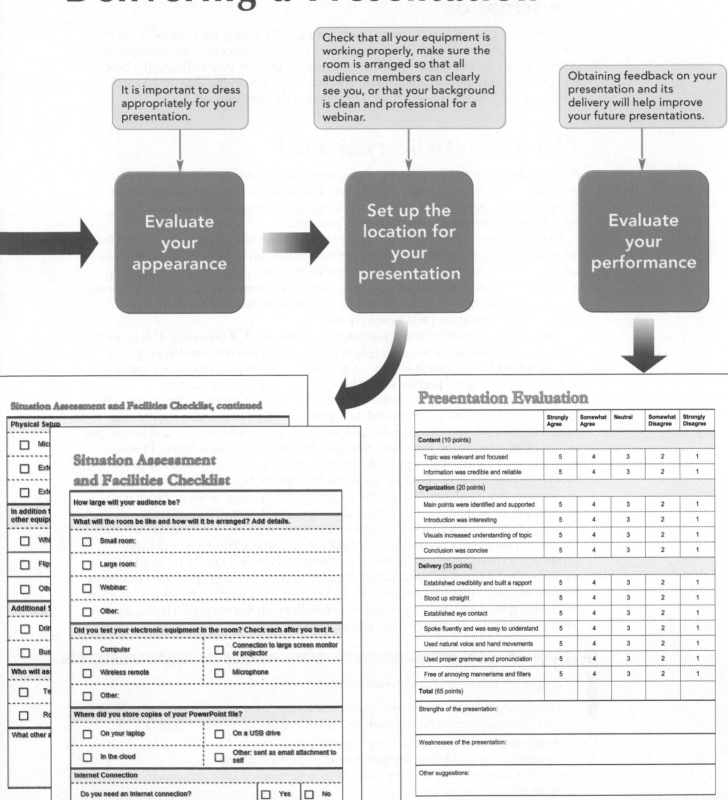

## Situation Assessment and Facilities Checklist, continued

**Physical Setup**

- [ ] Mic
- [ ] Exte
- [ ] Exte

In addition other equip

- [ ] Whi
- [ ] Flip
- [ ] Oth

Additional

- [ ] Drin
- [ ] Bus

Who will ass

- [ ] Te
- [ ] R

What other a

## Situation Assessment and Facilities Checklist

**How large will your audience be?**

**What will the room be like and how will it be arranged? Add details.**

- [ ] Small room:
- [ ] Large room:
- [ ] Webinar:
- [ ] Other:

**Did you test your electronic equipment in the room? Check each after you test it.**

- [ ] Computer
- [ ] Connection to large screen monitor or projector
- [ ] Wireless remote
- [ ] Microphone
- [ ] Other:

**Where did you store copies of your PowerPoint file?**

- [ ] On your laptop
- [ ] On a USB drive
- [ ] In the cloud
- [ ] Other: sent as email attachment to self

**Internet Connection**

| | | |
|---|---|---|
| Do you need an Internet connection? | [ ] Yes | [ ] No |
| If yes, did you check it in the room with your laptop, tablet, or smartphone to make sure you know how to connect and that it is reliable? | [ ] Yes | [ ] No |

## Presentation Evaluation

| | Strongly Agree | Somewhat Agree | Neutral | Somewhat Disagree | Strongly Disagree |
|---|---|---|---|---|---|
| **Content** (10 points) | | | | | |
| Topic was relevant and focused | 5 | 4 | 3 | 2 | 1 |
| Information was credible and reliable | 5 | 4 | 3 | 2 | 1 |
| **Organization** (20 points) | | | | | |
| Main points were identified and supported | 5 | 4 | 3 | 2 | 1 |
| Introduction was interesting | 5 | 4 | 3 | 2 | 1 |
| Visuals increased understanding of topic | 5 | 4 | 3 | 2 | 1 |
| Conclusion was concise | 5 | 4 | 3 | 2 | 1 |
| **Delivery** (35 points) | | | | | |
| Established credibility and built a rapport | 5 | 4 | 3 | 2 | 1 |
| Stood up straight | 5 | 4 | 3 | 2 | 1 |
| Established eye contact | 5 | 4 | 3 | 2 | 1 |
| Spoke fluently and was easy to understand | 5 | 4 | 3 | 2 | 1 |
| Used natural voice and hand movements | 5 | 4 | 3 | 2 | 1 |
| Used proper grammar and pronunciation | 5 | 4 | 3 | 2 | 1 |
| Free of annoying mannerisms and fillers | 5 | 4 | 3 | 2 | 1 |
| **Total** (65 points) | | | | | |
| Strengths of the presentation: | | | | | |
| Weaknesses of the presentation: | | | | | |
| Other suggestions: | | | | | |

# Preparing for the Delivery of an Oral Presentation

If you need to give an oral presentation, planning and creating the content of your presentation and creating your visuals are only part of the necessary preparation. In order to give a successful presentation, you need to prepare your delivery. The best oral presentations are prepared well in advance. As shown in the Session 3 Visual Overview, the first step in preparing is to choose a delivery method.

# Choosing a Delivery Method

After you have created the content of your presentation, you need to decide if you want to memorize it exactly, read it word for word, or review it thoroughly so that glancing at keywords or your visuals is enough of a trigger to indicate which information to present at a given point in your talk.

Some presenters like to write their entire presentation out, word for word, and then memorize it so they can recite the presentation to the audience from memory. If you've never given a presentation before, this might be the best approach. If you are using presentation media, you can also use your visuals as reminders of the points you want to make. This works well for speakers who are comfortable speaking in front of an audience and who know their topic very well.

You could read your written presentation word for word, if necessary. This is not the most engaging method of presenting, however, because you may tend to keep your head down and your voice low. It is better if you can maintain eye contact with your audience and use good posture so that your voice is loud and clear.

Written or memorized presentations don't leave a lot to chance, so they work well in formal settings when you must stick to a topic and stay on schedule. They're also helpful if you think you'll forget what you prepared, or become nervous and tongue-tied as a result of your inexperience with the topic or with giving presentations. However, once you've memorized your presentation, it's not easy to alter it in response to changes in time limits or audience questions. Perhaps the biggest drawback to written or memorized presentations is that it's difficult to sound natural while reading your presentation or reciting it from memory, causing your listeners to lose interest.

Another delivery approach is to create an outline on paper or notecards that you can use to deliver your presentation without memorization. This type of delivery allows you to have a more natural-sounding presentation and the ability to adapt it for audience questions or participation. You still need to thoroughly review your notes to avoid leaving out crucial information, lacking precision when explaining your ideas, or stumbling because you are nervous or unfamiliar with the material. Having a paper backup is crucial if the presentation equipment fails.

## Insight

### Giving an Impromptu Presentation

Impromptu presentations involve speaking without notes, an outline, or memorized text. Impromptu presentations work best when you're in the following situations:

- Extremely familiar with your topic and audience
- Speaking to a small, intimate group, or in your office setting
- More interested in getting the views of your audience than in persuading them or giving them specific information

Generally, you should be wary of impromptu presentations because they leave too much to chance. Speaking without notes may result in taking too much time, saying something that offends your audience, or appearing unorganized. If you think you might be asked to give an impromptu presentation, jot down some notes beforehand so you'll be prepared.

Theary will prepare her oral delivery and memorize it. She knows her material well, so she plans to use her visuals as cues rather than written notes.

# Preparing for Audience Interaction

Allowing your audience to ask questions or actively participate in your presentation by offering their own ideas makes the presentation more personal for your audience. This also helps to keep them interested.

## Anticipating Audience Questions

You need to decide whether you want your audience to have an opportunity to ask questions or actively participate in your presentation. You should welcome the idea of questions from the audience, rather than trying to avoid them (see Figure 20). The absence of questions may indicate that your audience had no interest in what you said or that you spoke for too long. Adopting the attitude that interested listeners will have questions enables you to anticipate and prepare for the questions your audience will ask.

| Figure 20 | Interested listeners have questions |

iStock.com/Nicola Katie

If you plan to invite your audience to ask questions, you need to decide when you want this to happen. The size of your audience and the formality of the presentation might affect this decision. For example, four or five co-workers in a small conference room or webinar would probably expect to be able to interrupt your presentation and ask questions or express their own views, whereas a large audience would not. Webinar software often enables your audience members to raise their hands virtually to indicate that they have a question. This function can be disabled if you do not plan on taking questions.

Allowing people to ask questions freely during your presentation means that the questions will be relevant and the answers will make sense to all members of the audience. If you allow this, keep an eye on the time and be prepared to halt questions if you need to. To allow you a little more control, you can build time for questions into your presentation as you transition from one section to another. Some speakers rely on a colleague to monitor questioners and keep timing so that they can stay focused.

If you allow questions during the presentation, the audience may bring up topics that will be covered later in your presentation. To keep your presentation focused, explain that the question will be addressed later, and then make a note to yourself to restate the question at the appropriate point during the presentation.

You can also ask your audience to hold all questions until the end of your presentation. If you do this, you will have more control over the time. However, people might forget their questions by the end of the presentation, and other audience members might not pay any attention at all to a question about something you discussed 30 minutes earlier. If delivering a webinar, the chat feature can be used by the audience to pose questions that you can answer when it's appropriate.

If you decide to open the presentation to questions, you should prepare a few that you can pose in case no one responds when you invite questions. You can start with "I've often been asked…" or "A question that comes up frequently is…" This can be especially helpful if you build in time at the end of your presentation for answering questions, but no one has any.

When preparing for questions, keep in mind the following:

- Announce your plan for handling questions at the beginning of your presentation. If you don't plan to allow questions during your presentation, perhaps let people know they can approach you later.
- Repeat questions to make sure everyone in the audience hears them.
- If you don't understand a question, ask the questioner to rephrase it.
- Be prepared to answer questions about information in your presentation that is new, controversial, or unexpected.
- If you can't answer a question, admit it, indicate you will find out the answer and report back to the group, and then move on.
- If one person is completely confused and asks too many questions, especially questions that most of the audience already know the answer to, ask this person to talk to you after the presentation so that the focus of your presentation doesn't get derailed.
- Don't be defensive about hostile questions. Treat every person's question as important, and respond courteously.
- Keep your answers brief. If you need additional time to respond to a question, arrange for it after your presentation.
- Be prepared to end a question-and-answer session; for example, state, "We have time for one more question."
- Consider offering to answer questions after the session, or provide your contact information and invite people to send you questions.
- Consider practicing your presentation in front of someone whose experience level with your topic matches your audience's. Listening to their questions may help you anticipate questions your audience could raise, and help you shape and clarify your content.

Theary anticipates that during her presentation audience members might have questions such as, "What is the discounted rate for guest rooms if we book our event at the hotel?" and "If we arrange an outdoor activity for our attendees and it rains, what can we offer our group instead?"

## Preparing for Audience Participation

**Tip**

Don't coerce people into participating. Always ask for volunteers. Putting reluctant members of your audience on the spot embarrasses everyone.

If you involve your audience in your presentation, they will pay closer attention to what you have to say. For example, an easy way to get the audience to participate is to start with a question and invite responses, or to stop partway through to discuss a particularly important point. You can also allow audience members to answer others' questions, contribute their own ideas, or ask for volunteers to help with a demonstration. Alternatively, you could ask audience members to give answers to an informal quiz or questionnaire, and then adjust your presentation to accommodate their responses. Allowing the audience to actively participate in your presentation can be especially effective in small group settings or situations where you're attempting to find new ways to approach ideas.

If you decide to allow your audience to participate in your presentation, you need to take extra precautions to avoid losing control of your presentation. Here are some tips to help you handle audience participation:

- Be prepared with tactful ways to interrupt a participant who monopolizes the time. If necessary, you can simply state, "You have some interesting points, but I want to give others a chance to comment before we move on."
- State a limit on the length of each response (such as 30 seconds) or the number of responses.
- Be prepared to halt comments that are taking too much time by saying something such as "These are great comments, but I'm afraid I need to move on as we have a limited amount of time."
- If you are inexperienced with handling audience participation, consider allowing it only at the end of your presentation.

During her presentation, Theary will ask members of the audience to relate their good and bad experiences when staying at hotels.

Now that you've determined how you want to deliver your presentation and you're prepared to interact with your audience, it's time to practice delivering the presentation.

# Rehearsing the Presentation

Once the presentation content has been created, enhanced, and perfected, and you have determined your delivery method, it is time to prepare you, the presenter. Even the most knowledgeable speakers rehearse to ensure they know how the topics flow, what the main points are, how much time to spend on each point, and where to place emphasis. Presenters who try to stand up and "wing it" in front of a crowd usually reveal this amateur approach the moment they start speaking—by looking down at their notes, rambling off topic, losing track of what they are saying, or turning their backs on the audience frequently to read information displayed on-screen. To avoid this, you need to rehearse your presentation (see Figure 21).

| Figure 21 | Confidence comes with practice |

silentalex88/Shutterstock.com

**Tip**

Consider rehearsing for job interviews using the same techniques as you use for rehearsing for a presentation.

Begin by simply going over the key points of the presentation in your mind. Then rehearse your presentation in private until you are comfortable with the content. Next, practice in front of a few close friends so that they can offer critiques and you can get a feel for what it will be like speaking to an audience. Pay special attention to what your friends say about key aspects of your presentation, such as your introduction, main points, and conclusion. Then, rehearse your presentation again.

During your rehearsals, practice using your visuals to support your points. Know when to pause for a moment to let your audience absorb a visual, and know when to switch to the next visual. Also, time your presentation to make sure it is the correct length. Pay attention to the timing as you are speaking so that you know approximately how much time you have left by where you are in the presentation.

Finally, if you have a video camera, you can record yourself and then review the video. Watching video evidence of your performance often reveals weaknesses that you don't want your audience to see or that your friends or family may be unwilling or unable to identify.

As you rehearse, you should remember to focus on the following areas:

- Connecting to your audience
- Being aware of your body language
- Establishing eye contact
- Speaking in a pleasant, natural, confident voice
- Using proper grammar and pronunciation
- Avoiding fillers

# Insight

## Overcoming Nervousness

Just thinking about speaking in front of other people may cause your heart to beat faster and your palms to sweat. You aren't alone. Feeling nervous about giving a presentation is a natural reaction. But you don't need to let nervousness interfere with your giving a successful presentation. Being nervous is not all bad. It means your adrenaline is flowing, and you'll have more energy and vitality for your presentation. In most instances, your nervousness will pass once you begin speaking. Sometimes, however, nervousness arises from feelings of inadequacy or from worrying about problems that could occur during a presentation. The most effective way to overcome your nervousness and deliver a smooth presentation is to carefully plan and prepare your presentation, and then to practice, practice, practice.

Experienced public speakers have learned several means of overcoming nervousness:

- Think positively about your presentation. Be optimistic and enthusiastic about your opportunity to gain experience. Visualize yourself as calm and confident.
- Work with your nervousness. Realize that some nervousness is normal and will help make your presentation better. Remember, your audience isn't nearly as concerned about your nervousness as you are.
- Give yourself plenty of time before your presentation. Devote a few minutes before-hand to relax and review your presentation notes.
- Start by looking at your audience and smiling. Then take a few slow breaths to calm yourself before you begin to speak.
- Don't expect everything to be perfect. Have backup plans in case something goes wrong, and be prepared to handle problems with grace and a sense of humor.
- Think about why your audience is there—to learn something from you. When you focus your mind on meeting the needs of your audience, you begin to forget about yourself and how the audience might respond to you.
- Observe other presenters. Make a list of the things they do that you like, and try to implement them in your own presentations. Likewise, note any annoying mannerisms or speech patterns so that you don't duplicate them in your presentation.

## Connecting to Your Audience

How an audience perceives a speaker can sometimes be more important than what the speaker says; therefore, it is important to establish a connection with your audience. Begin by introducing yourself and describing your credentials for speaking on your topic. Being aware of your demeanor—your body language, how often you make eye contact, and how you speak—will help you build a rapport with the audience. You often know if you have made a connection with your audience by their behavior and expressions. If your message is getting across, they will instinctively affirm what you're saying by returning your gaze, nodding their heads, or smiling. In Figure 22, the audience is smiling, nodding, and appears engaged with the presenter. If your message is not getting across and you see confused, puzzled, or frustrated expressions, you can make adjustments accordingly. This can be difficult to gauge in a webinar, but you should deliver your online presentations as if you can see the audience, and make eye contact with the camera.

| Figure 22 | Establish a connection with your audience |

iStock.com/kupicoo

## Being Aware of Your Body Language

Nonverbal communication is the way you convey a message without saying a word. Most nonverbal communication deals with how you use your body when interacting with people—how you look, stand, and move—in other words, your body language. In your everyday life, your body language is unconscious. However, by becoming aware of your body language, you can use it consciously to help you communicate more effectively.

Start by becoming aware of your posture. Refrain from slouching, as your audience may interpret this to mean that you don't care or you're insecure.

Be aware of your hand movements as you speak. The best position for your hands is to place them comfortably by your side, in a relaxed position. As you talk, it's fine to use hand gestures to help make a point, but be careful not to overdo it. Informal presentations lend themselves to more gestures and movement than do formal presentations where you're standing in front of a microphone on a podium. But giving a formal presentation doesn't mean you should hide behind the lectern or behave like a robot. Even formal presentations allow for gestures that are purposeful, spontaneous, and natural.

It is important to recognize your unique mannerisms (recurring or unnatural movements of your voice or body) that can be annoying, such as raising your voice and eyebrows as if you are talking to children; playing with your car keys, a pen, or equipment; or fidgeting, rocking, and pacing. All of these mannerisms can communicate nervousness. If they are pervasive, they will detract from your presentation because your audience will start paying attention to your mannerisms instead of to your topic. Consider asking a friend whether your gestures are distracting, and then practice speaking without them.

Resist the temptation to glance at your watch or cell phone; you don't want to send a signal that you'd rather be someplace else or that you are anxious to have the presentation completed.

## Establishing Eye Contact

One of the most common mistakes presenters make is failing to establish eye contact with their audience. Speakers who keep their eyes on their notes, stare at their visuals, or look out over the heads of their audience create an emotional distance between themselves and their listeners. A better method is to look directly at your listeners or at the camera, even if you have to pause to look up. Smiling and making eye contact sends the message that you want to connect and that you can be trusted (see Figure 23).

**Figure 23**  ▶  **Establish eye contact**

iStock.com/kupicoo

To establish eye contact in an in-person presentation, look at individuals; do not just scan the audience. Focus on a particular member of the audience for just a second or two, then move on to someone else until you eventually get to most of the people in the audience or, if the audience is large, to most parts of the presentation room. Do not focus exclusively on one or two members of the audience because that will likely make those people feel uncomfortable.

## Speaking in a Pleasant, Natural, Confident Voice

The best presentations are those in which the presenter appears confident and speaks naturally in a conversational manner. No one enjoys a presentation when the speaker drones on endlessly in a monotone voice. When delivering your presentation, speak with enthusiasm, with authority, and with a smile. When you project your voice with energy, passion, and confidence, your audience will automatically pay more attention to you. However, be careful not to overdo it. Speaking too loudly or using an overly confident or arrogant tone will quickly turn off an audience and make them stop listening altogether.

Also, try to avoid raising the tone of your voice at the end of statements as if you were asking a question. This is sometimes referred to as uptalking or upspeaking. If you make statements that sound as if you are asking a question, you will sound less confident and knowledgeable.

## Using Proper Grammar and Pronunciation

One of the best ways to be seen as a credible speaker is to use proper grammar and pronunciation. To assure you're pronouncing a word correctly, check its pronunciation in a dictionary. Make sure you are using the correct pronouns. For example, many people misuse "me," I,", and "myself." Consider whether you would say "this is a picture of I" or "this is a picture of me." You then know that you would say "this is a picture of Pat and me," not "this is a picture of Pat and I." Also, avoid using "myself" when you mean "me." Myself is reflexive, meaning that it refers to something you do to yourself. Many people say "You can ask myself," but that is impossible—only you can ask yourself. The correct grammar is "You can ask me."

## Avoiding Fillers

Fillers consist of sounds, words, and phrases such as *um*, *ah*, *like*, and other breaks in speech that dilute a speaker's message. Fillers don't add any value, yet add length to sentences. At best, they can make you sound unprofessional. At worst, they can distract your audience and make your message incomprehensible.

Theary used the worksheet shown in Figure 24 to help her when practicing the delivery of her presentation. Note that she still needs to practice in front of others to get their feedback.

| Figure 24 | Presentation Delivery worksheet for the hotel presentation |
| --- | --- |

**Proskills**

### Verbal Communication: Avoiding Business Jargon

Business jargon has crept into our everyday language more and more over the past several years, to the point that many expressions are cliché. As you prepare your delivery, avoid using business jargon. For example, avoid saying things like "in my wheel-house," "leverage our content," "using all our available bandwidth," "drill down to the solution," and "we need a hard stop here." Think about what you're trying to say and break it down into its simplest, most direct terms. If your audience is used to hearing business jargon, they'll tune out your message because they've heard it all before. If your audience is not used to hearing business jargon, they'll spend most of their time trying to figure out what exactly you're trying to tell them. And if your audience is spending time figuring out what you just said, they are no longer listening to what you are currently saying. After you prepare your oral delivery, go back through and replace any jargon with simple direct language that anyone could understand.

## Referring to Visuals During Your Presentation

As you rehearse your presentation, you'll need to plan how to manage and present your visuals so they effectively support your content. Follow these simple guidelines for effectively using visuals when giving your presentation:

- Introduce and interpret the visual. Explain to your audience what they should be looking at in the visual and point to what is important.
- If the visual is text, don't read it word for word; use it as a cue for what you want to say next.
- In a real-time presentation, stand to the side, not in front, of the visuals and avoid turning your back on your audience as you refer to a visual. Practice how you will introduce visuals in a webinar, and consider whether they will be handheld or embedded into your presentation.
- Display the visual as you discuss it and remove the visual after you're through discussing it. Don't let your visuals get ahead of or behind your verbal presentation.

## Evaluating Your Appearance

Before a single word is spoken in a presentation, the audience sizes up the way the presenter looks. Your appearance creates your audience's first impression of you, so make sure your dress and grooming contribute to the total impression you want to convey to your audience. You want to make sure you look professional and competent. Dress appropriately for the situation, and in a manner that doesn't detract from your presentation. For example, for a formal presentation, you should wear business attire. Consider your audience and situation, but always make sure your appearance is neat, clean, and well-coordinated, and that you choose appropriate clothing. For example, the presenters shown in Figure 25 are appropriately dressed to speak in a professional setting. Even if you are delivering a webinar, dress in a complete outfit (including shoes) in case you have to stand or move at any point.

**Figure 25**    **Dress appropriately**

DW labs Incorporated/Shutterstock.com

# Setting Up for Your Presentation

It's important to include the setup, or physical arrangements, for your presentation as a critical element of preparation. Even the best-planned and practiced presentation can fail if your audience can't see or hear your presentation, or if they're uncomfortable. You've probably attended a presentation where the speaker stepped up to the microphone only to find that it wasn't turned on. Or, the speaker tried to start a PowerPoint presentation but nothing appeared on the screen or it was displayed incorrectly.

Much of the embarrassment and lost time can be prevented if you plan ahead. Make sure the equipment works and make sure you know how to use it, especially if it works differently from equipment with which you are familiar. Of course, there are some things over which you have no control. For example, if you're giving your presentation as part of a professional conference, you can't control whether the room you're assigned is the right size for your audience. You often can't control what projection systems are available, the thermostat setting in the room, or the quality of the sound system. But you can control many of the factors that could interfere with or enhance the success of your presentation, if you consider them in advance.

## Preparing Copies of Your Content

Electronic storage can be damaged or files erased, and physical handouts and posters can be accidentally destroyed, for example, by getting wet. Therefore, it's always a good idea to have backups or copies of your visuals. You should do this even if you have sent a copy of your visuals to the person hosting or coordinating the conference or will be presenting using your own laptop or device.

If you prepared a presentation file, you should make backups of the file on a portable storage device, such as a USB drive. If you are traveling on a plane, consider carrying a copy of your presentation in your carry-on bag and another copy in your checked bags. In addition, send a copy of the presentation via email to yourself and a colleague on an email service that you can access via the web, or store a copy of the presentation file in the cloud, such as on Microsoft OneDrive, where you can easily retrieve it if necessary.

If you have handouts or posters, consider making extra copies of them and storing them separately from the original versions. This might not be possible in the case of posters, but you could take photos of the posters and bring your camera or storage card with you so that you could recreate the posters if something happens to the originals.

## Assessing the Technology and Staff Available

You need to think about the technology you will be using. Check with your host or the presentation organizer ahead of time to make sure you know the type of equipment that will be available in the presentation room or what app you will be using for a webinar. If you are planning to use presentation software such as PowerPoint, you need to make sure the presentation is sent to whomever will be delivering the presentation. If you need to access the Internet during your presentation, obtain the password, if needed, and make sure you test the connection. If you have posters that need to be displayed, make sure an easel or place to mount the posters is available as well as thumbtacks or adhesive. If you want to take notes that people can see, make sure there are markers and a whiteboard available.

Whether you are presenting in person or in a webinar, verify that the presentation tools you need are available and that your presentation software is loaded and has access to your presentation. If using your own computer or device, make sure it is charged ahead of time (see Figure 26). Then open the presentation file and start the presentation to make sure that it will be displayed correctly. Make sure that each visual is displayed as you expect it to be. Do this well in advance of the time you are scheduled to give your presentation.

**Figure 26    Setting up for an in-person presentation**

pook_jun/Shutterstock.com

If you will be provided with a computer or projection device, rather than you using your own, take the time to familiarize yourself with that equipment and make sure you know exactly which folder your presentation is stored in. Consider bringing your own laptop or device as a backup just in case the one provided to you doesn't display the presentation file correctly.

Even with the most carefully laid plans, unexpected problems can come up. If you are giving a presentation at a large facility, such as in a conference room at a hotel, make sure you know how to contact the appropriate staff in case you have technical or other problems.

## Becoming Familiar with the Setup

For an in-person presentation, it's helpful to know the size and shape of the room where your presentation will occur and the seating arrangement. The setting for a presentation can affect audience expectations and, therefore, will dictate the appropriate level of formality. A small conference room with a round table and moveable chairs would call for a much more informal presentation than a large lecture hall with fixed seating. If you wish to make changes to the room setup, such as adjusting the lighting or temperature, or moving chairs, be sure to ask the staff at the venue.

For a webinar, find out ahead of time what format the presentation will be in. Will the audience be able to see you the entire time as well as your presentation? Will you be able to see audience members? Will the chat or "raise hand" features be enabled? If so, will someone be monitoring them?

## Identifying Other Needed Supplies

In addition to your presentation visuals, you should make sure that you have any other supplies that you need. For example, make sure you have chargers for devices with rechargeable batteries and power cords and extension cords. If you need them, make sure a whiteboard or flip chart is available. You should also have pen and paper in case you need to take notes.

If you are going to have handouts, make sure you have enough copies for all your audience members. Even if you don't plan to pass out business cards to everyone in the room, make sure you have some with you in case someone asks for one.

Finally, it's also a good idea to have a glass of water or water bottle available in case your throat or lips get dry.

Figure 27 shows a worksheet Theary used to assess the situation and facilities for this and other presentations.

Figure 27    Situation Assessment and Facilities Checklist worksheet for the hotel presentation

## Situation Assessment and Facilities Checklist

| How large will your audience be? 2-15 people |
|---|

**What will the room be like and how will it be arranged? Add details.**

☒ Small room: conference rooms on site at companies

☐ Large room:

☐ Webinar:

☐ Other:

**Did you test your electronic equipment in the room? Check each after you test it.**

| ☒ Computer | ☒ Connection to large screen monitor or projector |
|---|---|
| ☒ Wireless remote | ☐ Microphone |
| ☐ Other: | |

**Where did you store copies of your PowerPoint file?**

| ☒ On your laptop | ☒ On a USB drive |
|---|---|
| ☒ In the cloud | ☒ Other: sent as email attachment to self |

**Internet Connection**

| Do you need an Internet connection? | ☒ Yes | ☐ No |
|---|---|---|
| If yes, did you check it in the room with your laptop, tablet, or smartphone to make sure you know how to connect and that it is reliable? | ☐ Yes | ☒ No |

## Situation Assessment and Facilities Checklist, continued

**Physical Setup**

☐ Microphone height OK, if applicable

☒ Extension cords available if you need them

☒ Extension cords and other wires out of the way

**In addition to your PowerPoint file, laptop, and projection equipment, do you have other equipment available to use?**

| ☐ Whiteboard | ☐ White board markers and eraser |
|---|---|
| ☐ Flip chart | ☐ Permanent marker |
| ☐ Other: | |

**Additional Supplies**

| ☒ Drinking water | ☐ Paper and pen |
|---|---|
| ☒ Business cards | ☒ Other: brochures |

**Who will assist you with the equipment and other situational aspects?**

| ☐ Technical support staff | ☐ Friend or colleague |
|---|---|
| ☐ Room monitor | ☒ Other: designated person at each company |

What other aspects must you consider for your presentation?
None

For her presentation, Theary will most likely have technical support from each company's IT staff. Remember, she will be traveling from one company to another. This means she will not be able to change the arrangement of chairs in the various conference rooms she will be presenting in. She will not be able to adjust the room temperature. And she will not be able to access the room in which she will be speaking ahead of time to become familiar with its setup. She will arrive at each company 30 minutes before the time for her meeting so that she can connect her laptop to a large screen monitor or to her projector and check to make sure that her presentation file will be displayed correctly. She will not be using a whiteboard, posters, or a flip chart.

Theary feels confident that she has done everything possible to prepare for her presentation.

# Evaluating Your Performance

**Tip**

If you ask someone to critique your presentation, be prepared to take criticism. Even if you think the criticism is unjustified, ask yourself, "How can I use this criticism to improve my presentation?"

An important step in any presentation (and the step that is most often left out) is to review your performance after it is over to determine how you can improve your next presentation. Evaluating your performance and setting goals for improvement ensures that your next presentation will be even better than your last one. After you give your oral presentation, you can also ask your audience to evaluate your presentation. Having written feedback or a numerical score for each aspect of your presentation can be especially helpful in highlighting where you have room for improvement.

You can evaluate your own performance or ask friends or audience members to evaluate your presentation. Theary plans to ask her staff, other managers at the hotel, and her supervisor to evaluate her presentation using the Presentation Evaluation sheet shown in Figure 28.

| Figure 28 | Presentation Evaluation worksheet |

## Presentation Evaluation

|  | Strongly Agree | Somewhat Agree | Neutral | Somewhat Disagree | Strongly Disagree |
|---|---|---|---|---|---|
| **Content** (10 points) | | | | | |
| Topic was relevant and focused | 5 | 4 | 3 | 2 | 1 |
| Information was credible and reliable | 5 | 4 | 3 | 2 | 1 |
| **Organization** (20 points) | | | | | |
| Main points were identified and supported | 5 | 4 | 3 | 2 | 1 |
| Introduction was interesting | 5 | 4 | 3 | 2 | 1 |
| Visuals increased understanding of topic | 5 | 4 | 3 | 2 | 1 |
| Conclusion was concise | 5 | 4 | 3 | 2 | 1 |
| **Delivery** (35 points) | | | | | |
| Established credibility and built a rapport | 5 | 4 | 3 | 2 | 1 |
| Stood up straight | 5 | 4 | 3 | 2 | 1 |
| Established eye contact | 5 | 4 | 3 | 2 | 1 |
| Spoke fluently and was easy to understand | 5 | 4 | 3 | 2 | 1 |
| Used natural voice and hand movements | 5 | 4 | 3 | 2 | 1 |
| Used proper grammar and pronunciation | 5 | 4 | 3 | 2 | 1 |
| Free of annoying mannerisms and fillers | 5 | 4 | 3 | 2 | 1 |
| **Total** (65 points) | | | | | |
| Strengths of the presentation: | | | | | |
| Weaknesses of the presentation: | | | | | |
| Other suggestions: | | | | | |

# Review

## Session 3 Quick Check

1. What is a good approach for delivering a presentation if you are not used to giving them?
2. What is one benefit of allowing audience members to ask questions during a presentation at the point when questions occur to them?
3. Name three reasons why you should rehearse your presentation.
4. Why is being aware of your body language helpful when giving presentations?
5. What are fillers and why should you avoid them?
6. Why should you create backups or copies of your visuals?
7. If you will be using a computer and projector or large screen monitor to display a presentation file, what should you do when you arrive at the facility where you will be giving your presentation?
8. Why is it useful to evaluate your performance?

# Practice

## Review Assignments

A team of 50 people from Castle Hotels will be attending a meeting at the Outer Island Hotel and Resort. Theary's supervisor wants Theary to describe her marketing campaign to them and to give a shortened version of the presentation she gave to event directors at companies. The supervisor also wants Theary to add details about the hotel renovations to her presentation because most of the Castle Hotels team do not know exactly what was done. The presentation will be given in a conference room at the hotel, and Theary will have 30 minutes.

Complete the following steps (note that your instructor may provide you with files containing the different worksheets you need to complete):

1. Complete a Purposes and Outcomes worksheet for Theary's presentation.
2. Complete an Audience Analysis worksheet for Theary's presentation.
3. Complete a Focus and Organization worksheet for Theary's presentation, using the following information:
   a. Keep in mind that the audience is composed of hotel professionals who already know what Castle Hotels offer people. This audience is accustomed to professional presentations that are focused on a single topic.
   b. Prepare an introduction for the presentation using rhetorical questions that ask the audience to remember times when they attended corporate events.
   c. Prepare a conclusion for the presentation that includes a fictional quote from a very positive review of the hotel that someone posted on a social media site after the renovations were finished.
4. Complete a Presentation Delivery worksheet for Theary's presentation (skip the Rehearsal Checklist). Include at least three questions (and fictional responses) that you think the audience will have.
5. Describe what Theary should wear for her presentation. (Remember, her audience consists of corporate professionals.)
6. Complete a Situation and Media Assessment Worksheet for Theary's presentation. Assume the following:
   a. Theary will have access to a large screen monitor to which she can connect her laptop.
   b. A microphone will be available.
   c. Theary has a wireless remote to switch from one visual to another.
   d. Theary does not need a connection to the Internet.
   e. A tech support employee of the hotel will be available to assist.
7. Divide into groups of two and deliver a one-minute presentation to your partner. Present a topic that Theary would cover or any topic of your choice. Have your partner fill out a Presentation Evaluation worksheet for you. Then have your partner present, and you fill out a Presentation Evaluation worksheet for your partner.

## Module 1

### Objectives

**Session 1.1**
- Plan and create a new presentation
- Create a title slide and slides with lists
- Edit and format text
- Move and copy text
- Duplicate, rearrange, and delete slides
- Change the theme and theme variant
- Close a presentation

**Session 1.2**
- Open an existing presentation
- Insert and crop photos
- Resize and move objects
- Modify photo compression options
- Convert a list to a SmartArt diagram
- Create speaker notes
- Check the spelling
- Run a slide show
- Print slides, handouts, speaker notes, and the outline

# Creating a Presentation

## Presenting Information About an Insurance Company

## Case | Southwest Insurance Company

Southwest Insurance Company is an insurance company with offices all over the American Southwest, including one in Houston, Texas. Anthony Scorsone, a sales manager in the Houston office, recently hired you as his assistant. Anthony frequently visits companies to try to convince them to offer insurance plans from Southwest Insurance Company to their employees. Many businesses have opened offices in the Houston area over the past several years. Anthony wants to use a PowerPoint presentation when he visits these businesses. He asks you to prepare a presentation to which he will later add data and cost information.

**Microsoft PowerPoint** (or simply **PowerPoint**) is a complete presentation app that lets you produce professional-looking presentation files and then deliver them to an audience. In this module, you'll use PowerPoint to create a file that includes text, graphics, and speaker notes. Anthony can use the presentation as a starting point for his more comprehensive sales pitch. Before you give the presentation to Anthony, you'll check the spelling, run the slide show to evaluate it, and print the file.

### Starting Data Files

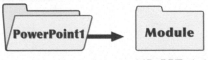

**Module**

NP_PPT_1-1.pptx
Support_PPT_1_Doctor.jpg
Support_PPT_1_Family.jpg
Support_PPT_1_Hands.jpg

**Review**

NP_PPT_1-2.pptx
Support_PPT_1_Anthony.jpg
Support_PPT_1_Meeting.jpg
Support_PPT_1_Standing.jpg
Support_PPT_1_Woman.jpg

**Case1**

NP_PPT_1-3.pptx
Support_PPT_1_Application.jpg
Support_PPT_1_Building.jpg
Support_PPT_1_Key.jpg
Support_PPT_1_Sophia.jpg

**Case2**

Support_PPT_1_Beach.jpg
Support_PPT_1_Black.jpg
Support_PPT_1_Blue.jpg
Support_PPT_1_Ensemble.jpg
Support_PPT_1_Pink.jpg

# Session 1.1 Visual Overview:

The **Quick Access Toolbar** contains buttons for frequently used commands. You can click the Customize Quick Access Toolbar button (the small arrow on the right) to add and remove commands.

The ribbon is organized into tabs. Each **tab** contains buttons for performing related activities or tasks.

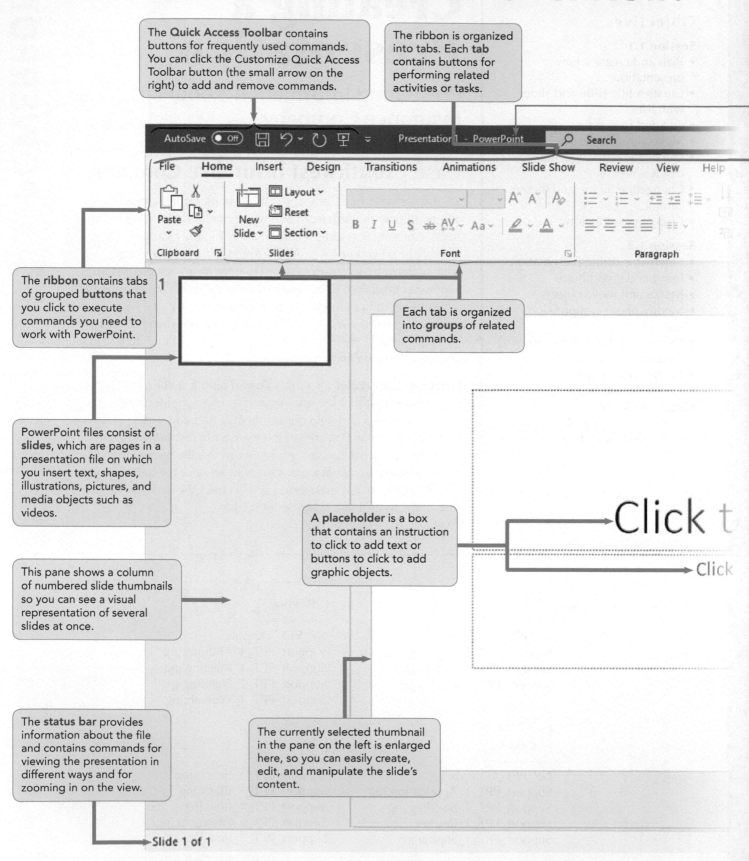

The **ribbon** contains tabs of grouped **buttons** that you click to execute commands you need to work with PowerPoint.

Each tab is organized into **groups** of related commands.

PowerPoint files consist of **slides**, which are pages in a presentation file on which you insert text, shapes, illustrations, pictures, and media objects such as videos.

A **placeholder** is a box that contains an instruction to click to add text or buttons to click to add graphic objects.

This pane shows a column of numbered slide thumbnails so you can see a visual representation of several slides at once.

The **status bar** provides information about the file and contains commands for viewing the presentation in different ways and for zooming in on the view.

The currently selected thumbnail in the pane on the left is enlarged here, so you can easily create, edit, and manipulate the slide's content.

# The PowerPoint Window

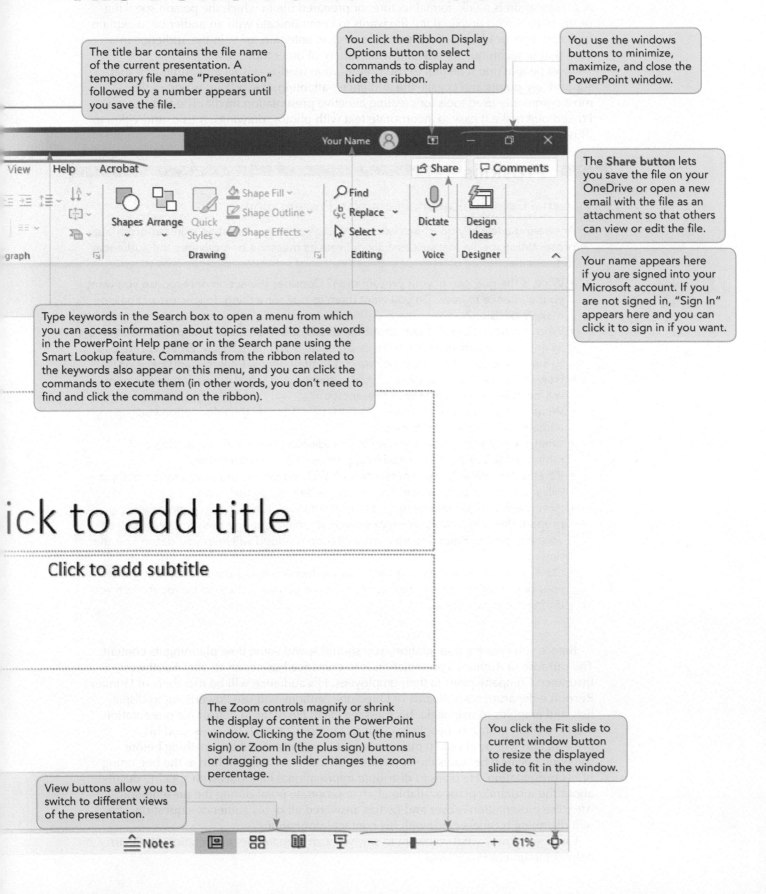

The title bar contains the file name of the current presentation. A temporary file name "Presentation" followed by a number appears until you save the file.

You click the Ribbon Display Options button to select commands to display and hide the ribbon.

You use the windows buttons to minimize, maximize, and close the PowerPoint window.

The **Share button** lets you save the file on your OneDrive or open a new email with the file as an attachment so that others can view or edit the file.

Your name appears here if you are signed into your Microsoft account. If you are not signed in, "Sign In" appears here and you can click it to sign in if you want.

Type keywords in the Search box to open a menu from which you can access information about topics related to those words in the PowerPoint Help pane or in the Search pane using the Smart Lookup feature. Commands from the ribbon related to the keywords also appear on this menu, and you can click the commands to execute them (in other words, you don't need to find and click the command on the ribbon).

The Zoom controls magnify or shrink the display of content in the PowerPoint window. Clicking the Zoom Out (the minus sign) or Zoom In (the plus sign) buttons or dragging the slider changes the zoom percentage.

You click the Fit slide to current window button to resize the displayed slide to fit in the window.

View buttons allow you to switch to different views of the presentation.

# Planning a Presentation

A **presentation** is a talk, formal lecture, or prepared file in which the person speaking or the person who prepared the file wants to communicate with an audience to explain new concepts or ideas, sell a product or service, entertain, or train the audience in a new skill or technique, or any of a wide variety of other topics.

Most people find it helpful to use **presentation media**—visual and audio aids that support key points and engage the audience's attention. PowerPoint is one of the most commonly used tools for creating effective presentation media. The features of PowerPoint make it easy to incorporate text with photos, drawings, music, and video to illustrate key points of a presentation.

 **Proskills**

### Verbal Communication: Planning a Presentation

Answering a few key questions will help you create a presentation using appropriate presentation media that successfully delivers its message or motivates the audience to take an action.

- What is the purpose of your presentation? Consider the action or response you want your audience to have. Do you want them to buy something, follow instructions, or make a decision?
- Who is your audience? Think about the needs and interests of your audience as well as any decisions they will make because of what you have to say. What you choose to say to your audience must be relevant to their needs, interests, and decisions.
- How will you ensure members of your audience with visual or hearing impairments will be able to experience your presentation?
- What are the main points of your presentation? Identify the information your audience will find most relevant.
- What presentation media will help your audience absorb the information and remember it later? Do you need lists, photos, charts, and/or tables?
- What is the format for your presentation? Will you deliver the presentation orally or will you create a presentation file for people to view on their own?
- How much time do you have for the presentation? Keep that in mind as you prepare the presentation content so that you have enough time to present all of your key points. Practicing your presentation out loud will help you determine the timing.
- Consider whether distributing handouts will help your audience follow along with your presentation or steal their attention when you want them to be focused on you during the presentation.

Before you create a presentation, you should spend some time planning its content. The purpose of Anthony's presentation is to convince businesses to offer Southwest Insurance Company plans to their employees. His audience will be members of Human Resource departments or Boards of Directors. Anthony will use PowerPoint to display lists and graphics to help make his message clear. He plans to deliver his presentation orally to small groups of people in conference rooms at each business, and his presentation will be about 10 minutes long. He will not distribute anything before speaking because he wants the audience's full attention to be on him at the beginning of his presentation. He plans to distribute informational handouts with specific details about the insurance plans available at an appropriate point during the presentation. After the presentation is over and he has answered all of his audience's questions, he will distribute business cards with his contact information.

Once you know what you want to say, you can prepare the presentation media to help communicate your ideas.

# Starting PowerPoint and Creating a New Presentation

PowerPoint is a tool you can use to create and display visual and audio aids on slides to help clarify the points you want to make in your presentation. You also can use PowerPoint to create a presentation that people view on their own without you.

When PowerPoint starts, Backstage view appears, showing the Home screen. **Backstage view** is the view that contains commands that allow you to manage the file and program settings. When you first start PowerPoint, the actions available to you in Backstage view are to create a new PowerPoint file, open an existing PowerPoint file, view your Account settings, submit feedback to Microsoft, and open the PowerPoint Options dialog box to change app settings.

You'll start PowerPoint now.

**To start PowerPoint:**

▶ 1. **sam** ⬇ On the Windows taskbar, click the **Start** button ⊞. The Start menu opens.

▶ 2. On the Start menu, scroll the list of apps on the left, and then click **PowerPoint**. PowerPoint starts and displays the Home screen in Backstage view. Options for creating new presentations appear in a row at the top of the screen, and if you have recently viewed PowerPoint files, they appear below this row. See Figure 1–1.

| Figure 1–1 | Home screen in Backstage view |
|---|---|

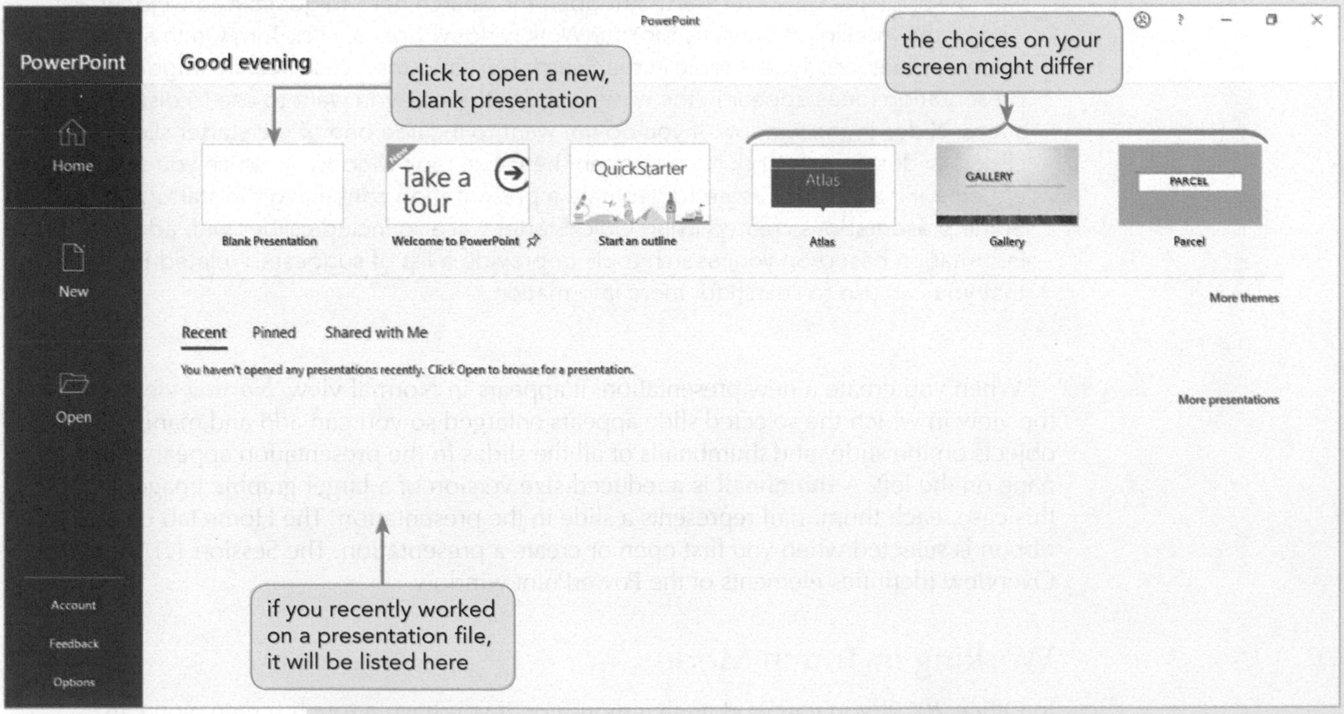

**Tip**

To create a new blank presentation when PowerPoint is already running, click the File tab on the ribbon, click New in the navigation pane, and then click Blank Presentation.

3. Click **Blank Presentation**. Backstage view closes and a new presentation window appears. The temporary filename "Presentation1" appears in the title bar. There is only one slide in the new presentation—Slide 1.

   **Trouble?** If you do not see the area on the ribbon that contains buttons and you see only the ribbon tab names, click the Home tab to expand the ribbon and display the commands, and then in the bottom-right corner of the ribbon, click the Pin the ribbon button ⊞.

   **Trouble?** If the window does not appear maximized, click the Maximize button ▣ in the upper-right corner.

Because you just started PowerPoint, you clicked Blank presentation on the Home screen. If PowerPoint was already running and you wanted to create a new, blank presentation, you would click the File tab, click New in the navigation pane, and then click Blank Presentation on the New screen in Backstage view.

## Insight

### Using QuickStarter

QuickStarter is a feature in PowerPoint that creates slide titles based on a topic you enter. To use QuickStarter when you first start PowerPoint, click QuickStarter on the Home screen. If you already are using PowerPoint, click the File tab, click New, and then click QuickStarter on the New screen. The Search here to get started window opens. (The first time you use this feature, the Welcome to PowerPoint QuickStarter window appears. Click Get started to open the Search here to get started window. Also, if the Intelligent Services for Your Work window opens, click Turn On to start using the feature.) Type a topic in the Search box, and then click Search. Suggested presentation ideas appear in the window. Click the one you want to use to display starter slides in the window. If you do not want to include one of the starter slides, click it to deselect it. Click Next to open the Pick a look window, in which you select a theme. Finally, click Create to generate a presentation containing the starter slides. Some presentations created using QuickStarter will also include slides with additional information based on your search topic or provide a list of suggested related topics that you can use to search for more information.

When you create a new presentation, it appears in Normal view. **Normal view** is the view in which the selected slide appears enlarged so you can add and manipulate objects on the slide, and thumbnails of all the slides in the presentation appear in the pane on the left. A **thumbnail** is a reduced-size version of a larger graphic image. In this case, each thumbnail represents a slide in the presentation. The Home tab on the ribbon is selected when you first open or create a presentation. The Session 1.1 Visual Overview identifies elements of the PowerPoint window.

### Working in Touch Mode

In Office 2019, you can work with a mouse or, if you have a touch screen, you can work in Touch Mode. In **Touch Mode**, the ribbon increases in height, the buttons are larger, and more space appears around buttons so you can more easily use your finger or stylus to tap screen elements. Also, in the placeholders on the slide, "Double tap" replaces the instruction telling you to "Click." Note that the figures in this text show the screen with Mouse Mode on. You'll switch to Touch Mode and then back to Mouse Mode now.

**Note:** The following steps assume that you are using a mouse. If instead you are using a touch device, please read these steps, but don't complete them, to continue working in Touch Mode.

## To switch between Touch Mode and Mouse Mode:

▶ **1.** On the Quick Access Toolbar, click the **Customize Quick Access Toolbar** button . A menu opens. The Touch/Mouse Mode command near the bottom of the menu does not have a checkmark next to it.

**Trouble?** If the Touch/Mouse Mode command has a checkmark next to it, press the Esc key to close the menu, and then skip Step 2.

▶ **2.** On the menu, click **Touch/Mouse Mode**. The menu closes, and the Touch/ Mouse Mode button appears on the Quick Access Toolbar.

▶ **3.** On the Quick Access Toolbar, click the **Touch/Mouse Mode** button . A menu opens listing Mouse and Touch. The icon next to Mouse is shaded to indicate it is selected.

**Trouble?** If the icon next to Touch is shaded, press ESC to close the menu and skip Step 4.

▶ **4.** On the menu, click **Touch**. The menu closes, and the ribbon increases in height so that there is more space around each button on the ribbon. Notice that the instructions in the placeholders on the slide changed by replacing the instruction to "Click" with the instruction to "Double tap." See Figure 1–2. Now you'll change back to Mouse Mode.

| Figure 1–2 | PowerPoint window with Touch Mode active |

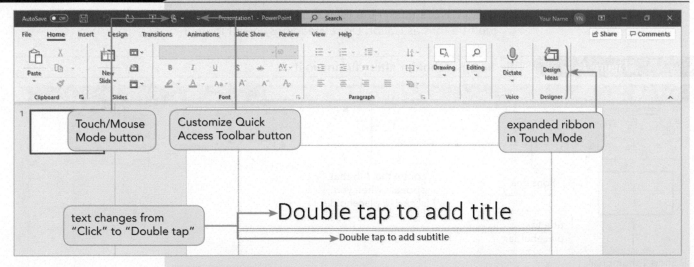

**Trouble?** If you are working with a touch screen and want to use Touch Mode, skip Steps 5 and 6.

▶ **5.** Click the **Touch/Mouse Mode** button , and then click **Mouse**. The ribbon and the instructions change back to Mouse Mode defaults, as shown in the Session 1.1 Visual Overview.

▶ **6.** Click the **Customize Quick Access Toolbar** button , and then click **Touch/ Mouse Mode** to deselect this option and remove the checkmark. The Touch/ Mouse Mode button disappears from the Quick Access Toolbar.

# Creating a Title Slide

The **title slide** is the first slide in a presentation. It usually contains the presentation title and other identifying information, such as a company name or logo, a company's slogan, or the presenter's name. The **font**—a set of letters, numbers, and symbols that all have the same style and appearance—used in the title and subtitle may be the same or may be different fonts that complement each other.

The title slide contains two objects called text placeholders. A **text placeholder** is a placeholder designed to contain text and that contains a prompt that instructs you to click to add text and might describe the purpose of the placeholder. The large placeholder on the title slide is for the presentation title. The small placeholder is for a subtitle. Once you enter text into a text placeholder, the instructional text disappears and it becomes an object called a text box. A **text box** is an object that contains text.

When you click in the placeholder, the insertion point appears. The **insertion point** is a blinking vertical line that indicates where new text will be inserted. Also, a new tab, the Shape Format tab, appears on the ribbon. This tab is a contextual tab. A **contextual tab** appears only in context—that is, when a particular type of object is selected or is active—and contains commands for modifying that object.

You'll add a title and subtitle for Anthony's presentation now. Anthony wants the title slide to contain the company name and slogan.

### To add the company name and slogan to the title slide:

1. On **Slide 1**, move the pointer to position it in the title text placeholder (where it says "Click to add title") so that the pointer changes to the I-beam pointer Ⅰ, and then click. The insertion point replaces the placeholder text, and the Shape Format contextual tab appears as the rightmost tab on the ribbon. Note that in the Font group on the Home tab, the Font box identifies the title font as Calibri Light (Headings). See Figure 1–3.

| Figure 1–3 | Title text placeholder after clicking in it |
| --- | --- |

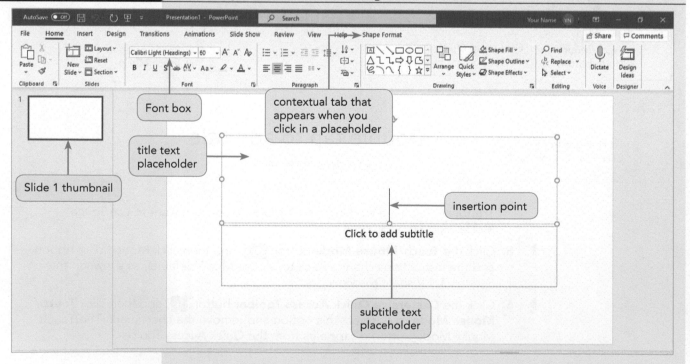

2. Type **Southwest Insurance Corp** in the placeholder. The placeholder is now a text box.

3. Click a blank area of the slide. The border of the text box disappears, and the Shape Format tab no longer appears on the ribbon.

4. Click in the subtitle text placeholder (where it says "Click to add subtitle"), and then type **Best in Health Care Since 1990** in the placeholder. Notice in the Font group that the subtitle font is Calibri (Body), a font that works well with the Calibri Light font used in the title text.

5. Click a blank area of the slide.

## Saving and Editing a Presentation

Once you have created a presentation, you should name and save the presentation file. You can save the file on a hard drive or a network drive, on an external drive such as a USB drive, or to your account on OneDrive, Microsoft's free online storage area.

### To save the presentation for the first time:

1. On the Quick Access Toolbar, point to the **Save** button 🔲. A box called a ScreenTip appears. A **ScreenTip** is a label that appears when you point to a button or object, which may include the name, purpose, or keyboard shortcut for the object, and may include a link to associated help topics.

2. Click the **Save** button 🔲. The Save this file dialog box opens, which you use to save a file on OneDrive. To save a new presentation on your hard drive or an external drive, you use the Save As screen.

3. Click the More options link. The Save As screen in Backstage view appears. See Figure 1–4. The navigation pane is the pane on the left that contains commands for working with the file and program options. Recently used folders on the selected drive appear in a list on the right.

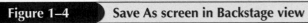

**Figure 1–4**    Save As screen in Backstage view

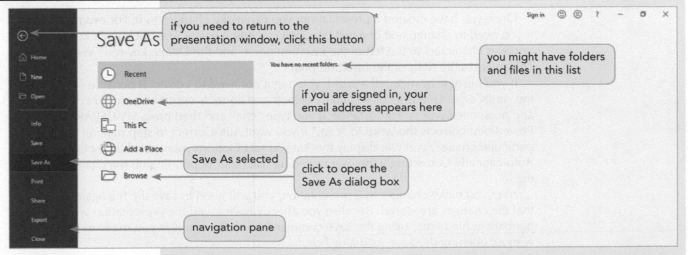

▶ **4.** Click **Browse**. The Save As dialog box opens, similar to the one shown in Figure 1–5.

**Figure 1–5**   Save As dialog box

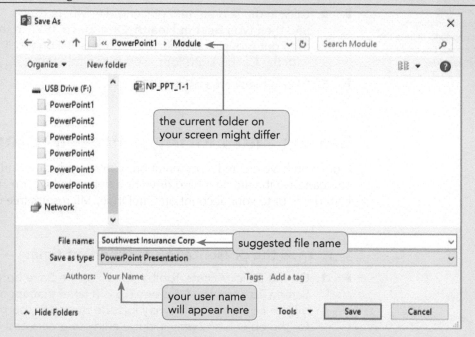

▶ **5.** Navigate to the drive and folder where you are storing your Data Files, and then click in the **File name** box. The suggested file name, Southwest Insurance Corp, is selected.

▶ **6.** Type **NP_PPT_1_NewBusiness** to replace the selected text in the File name box.

▶ **7.** Click **Save**. The file is saved, the dialog box and Backstage view close, and the presentation window appears again with the new file name in the title bar.

Once you have created a presentation, you can make changes to it. For example, if you need to change text in a text box, you can edit it easily. The Backspace key removes characters to the left of the insertion point, and the Delete key removes characters to the right of the insertion point.

If you mistype or misspell a word, you might not need to correct it because the **AutoCorrect** feature automatically detects and corrects commonly mistyped and misspelled words. For instance, if you type "cna" and then press SPACEBAR, PowerPoint corrects the word to "can." If you want AutoCorrect to stop making a particular change, you can display the AutoCorrect Options menu, and then click Stop Automatically Correcting. (The exact wording will differ depending on the change made.)

After you make changes to a presentation, you will need to save the file again so that the changes are stored. Because you already have saved the presentation with a permanent file name, using the Save command saves the changes you made to the file without opening the Save As dialog box.

**To edit the text on Slide 1 and save your changes:**

1. On Slide 1, click the title, and then press **LEFT ARROW** or **RIGHT ARROW** as needed to position the insertion point to the right of the word "Corp."

2. Press **BACKSPACE** four times. The four characters "Corp" to the left of the insertion point are deleted.

3. Type **Company**. (Do not type the period.) "Southwest Insurance Company" now appears as the title.

4. In the subtitle text box, click to the left of the word "Best" to position the insertion point in front of that word, type **Teh**, and then press **SPACEBAR**. "Teh" is corrected to "The" after you press SPACEBAR. "The Best in Health Care Since 1990" now appears as the subtitle.

5. Move the pointer over the word "**The**." A small, faint rectangle appears below the first letter of the word. This rectangle indicates that an autocorrection was made.

   **Trouble?** If you can't see the rectangle, point to the letter "T," and then slowly move the pointer down until it is on top of the rectangle.

6. Move the pointer on top of the rectangle so that it changes to the AutoCorrect Options button ▣▾, and then click the **AutoCorrect Options** button ▣▾. A menu opens, as shown in Figure 1–6. You can change the word back to what you originally typed, instruct PowerPoint to stop making this type of correction in this file, or open the AutoCorrect dialog box.

| Figure 1–6 | AutoCorrect Options button menu |
| --- | --- |

7. Click **Control AutoCorrect Options**. The AutoCorrect dialog box opens with the AutoCorrect tab selected. See Figure 1–7.

**Figure 1–7**   **AutoCorrect tab in the AutoCorrect dialog box**

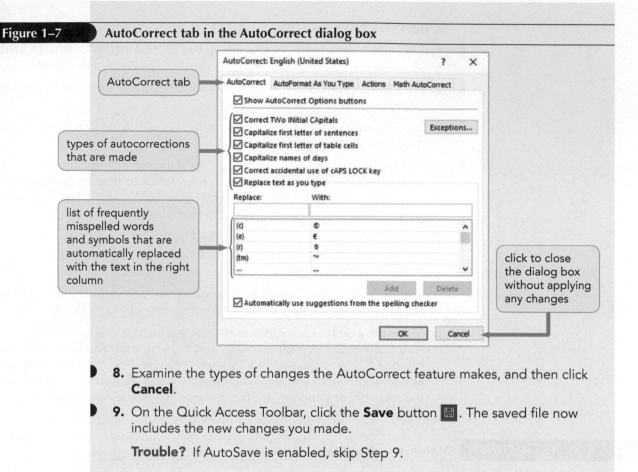

8. Examine the types of changes the AutoCorrect feature makes, and then click **Cancel**.

9. On the Quick Access Toolbar, click the **Save** button 🖫 . The saved file now includes the new changes you made.

**Trouble?** If AutoSave is enabled, skip Step 9.

# Adding New Slides

Now that you've created the title slide, you need to add more slides. Every slide has a **layout**, which is the arrangement of placeholders on the slide. The title slide uses the Title Slide layout. A commonly used layout is the Title and Content layout, which contains a title text placeholder for the slide title and a content placeholder. A **content placeholder** is a placeholder designed to contain text or graphic objects.

To add a new slide, you use the New Slide button in the Slides group on the Home tab. When you click the top part of the New Slide button, a new slide is inserted with the same layout as the current slide, unless the current slide is the title slide. In that case, the new slide has the Title and Content layout. If you want to create a new slide with a different layout, click the arrow on the bottom part of the New Slide button to open a gallery of layouts, and then click the layout you want to use.

You can change the layout of a slide at any time. To do this, click the Layout button in the Slides group to display the same gallery of layouts that appears in the New Slide gallery, and then click the slide layout you want to apply to the selected slide.

As you add slides, you can switch from one slide to another by clicking the slide thumbnails in the Slides pane. You need to add several new slides to the file.

### To add new slides and apply different layouts:

1. Make sure the Home tab is displayed on the ribbon.

2. In the Slides group, click the top part of the **New Slide** button. A new slide appears, and its thumbnail appears in the pane on the left below the Slide 1 thumbnail. The new slide has the Title and Content layout applied. This layout contains a title text placeholder and a content placeholder. An orange

border appears around the new Slide 2 thumbnail, indicating that it is the current slide.

3. In the Slides group, click the **New Slide** button again. A new Slide 3 is added. Because Slide 2 had the Title and Content layout applied, Slide 3 also has that layout applied.

4. In the Slides group, click the **New Slide arrow** (the bottom part of the New Slide button). A gallery of the available layouts appears. See Figure 1–8.

**Figure 1–8**    **Gallery of layouts on the New Slide menu**

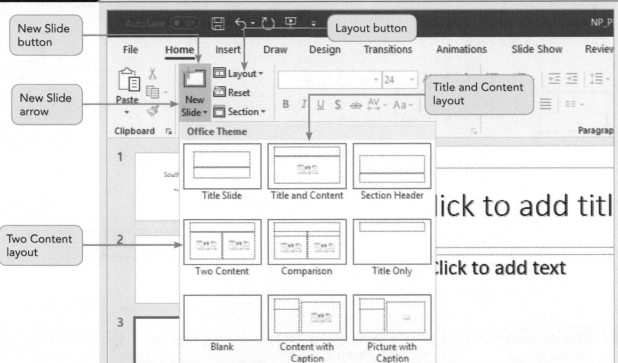

New Slide button

New Slide arrow

Two Content layout

Layout button

Title and Content layout

5. In the gallery, click the **Two Content** layout. The gallery closes, and a new Slide 4 is inserted with the Two Content layout applied. This layout includes three objects: a title text placeholder and two content placeholders.

6. In the Slides group, click the **New Slide** button twice. New Slides 5 and 6 are added to the presentation. Because Slide 4 had the Two Content layout applied, that layout is also applied to the new slides. You need to change the layout of Slide 6.

7. In the Slides group, click the **Layout** button. The same gallery of layouts that appeared when you clicked the New Slide arrow appears. The shading behind the Two Content layout indicates that it is applied to the current slide.

8. Click the **Title and Content** layout. The layout of Slide 6 changes to Title and Content.

   **Trouble?** If the Design Ideas pane opens, click its Close button ☒.

9. In the Slides group, click the **New Slide** button to add Slide 7 with the Title and Content layout.

10. Add one more new slide with the Two Content layout. There are now eight slides in the presentation. In the pane that contains the slide thumbnails, some thumbnails have scrolled out of view, and vertical scroll bars appear along the right side of both panes in the program window.

**11.** In the pane that contains the slide thumbnails, drag the scroll box to the top of the vertical scroll bar, and then click the **Slide 2** thumbnail. Slide 2 appears in the program window and is selected in the pane that contains the slide thumbnails. See Figure 1–9.

**Figure 1–9** **Slide 2 with the Title and Content layout**

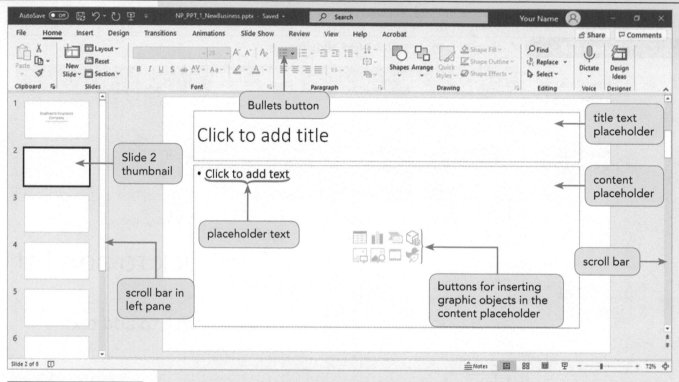

**12.** On the Quick Access Toolbar, click the **Save** button. The changes you made are saved in the file.

**Tip**

If you accidentally close a presentation without saving changes and need to recover it, click the File tab, click Open in the navigation bar, and then click the Recover Unsaved Presentations button.

# Creating Lists

You can use a list to help explain a topic or concept. If you are preparing an oral presentation (one that you give in front of an audience), lists on your slides should enhance the oral presentation, not replace it. If you are preparing a self-running presentation (one that others will view on their own), list items might need to be longer and more descriptive.

Each item in a list is a paragraph. Items in a list can appear at different levels. A first-level item is a main item in a list. A second-level item is an item beneath and indented from a first-level item. A third-level item is an item beneath and indented from a second-level item, and so on. All items below the first level are subitems. A **subitem** is any item in a list that is beneath and indented from a higher-level item.

Usually, the size of the text in subitems on a slide is smaller than the size of the text in the level above. Text is measured in points. A **point** is the unit of measurement used for text size. One point is equal to 1/72 of an inch. Text in a book typically is printed in 10- or 12-point type. Text on a slide in a presentation that will be shown to an audience needs to be much larger so that the audience can easily read it.

## Creating a Bulleted List

A **bulleted list** is a series of paragraphs, each beginning with a bullet character, such as a dot or checkmark. Subitems in a list often begin with a different or smaller bullet symbol. Use bulleted lists when the order of the items is not important.

You need to create a bulleted list that describes the types of insurance plans that Southwest Insurance Company offers and one that highlights why it would be the best insurance company for businesses to create a relationship with.

### To create a bulleted list on Slides 2 and 3:

1. On Slide 2, click in the title text placeholder (with the placeholder text "Click to add title"), and then type **Types of Plans**. (Do not type the period.)

2. In the content placeholder, click any area where the pointer is the I-beam pointer ‖ (anywhere except on one of the buttons in the center of the placeholder). The placeholder text "Click to add text" disappears, the insertion point appears, and a light gray bullet symbol appears.

3. Type **Life** in the placeholder. As soon as you type the first character, the icons in the center of the content placeholder disappear, the bullet symbol darkens, and the content placeholder changes to a text box. On the Home tab, in the Paragraph group, the Bullets button ⊞ is shaded to indicate that it is selected.

4. Press **ENTER**. The insertion point moves to a new line, and a light gray bullet appears on the new line.

5. Type **Health**, and then press **ENTER**. The bulleted list now consists of two first-level items, and the insertion point is next to a light gray bullet on the third line in the text box. On the Home tab, in the Font group, the point size in the Font Size box is 28 points.

6. Press **TAB**. The bullet symbol and the insertion point indent one-half inch to the right, the bullet symbol changes to a smaller size, and the number in the Font Size box changes to 24. See Figure 1–10.

**Figure 1–10**    Subitem created on Slide 2

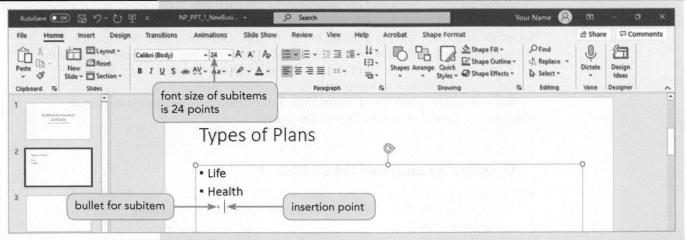

**7.** Type **HMO** and then press **ENTER**.

**8.** Type **PPO**, press **ENTER**, type **POS**, and then press **ENTER**. A fourth subitem is created. You will change it to a first-level item using a key combination. In this book, when you need to press two keys at the same time, the keys will be separated by a plus sign.

**9.** Press **SHIFT+TAB**. The bullet symbol and the insertion point shift back to the left margin of the text box, the bullet symbol changes back to the larger size, and 28 again appears in the Font Size box because this line is now a first-level bulleted item.

**10.** Type **Disability**, and then press **ENTER**. A fourth first-level item is created. You need to enter subitems for the "Disability" first-level item.

**11.** On the Home tab, in the Paragraph group, click the **Increase List Level** button ⬚. Clicking the Increase List Level button is an alternative to pressing TAB to create a subitem.

**12.** Type **Long-term**, press **ENTER**, type **Short-term**, and then press **ENTER**. A third second-level item is created. You need to create a fourth first-level item.

**13.** In the Paragraph group, click the **Decrease List Level** button ⬚. Clicking the Decrease List Level button is an alternative to pressing SHIFT+TAB to change a lower-level item to a higher-level item.

**14.** Type **Stable**. The list now contains four first-level items.

If you add more text than will fit in the content placeholder, **AutoFit** adjusts the font size and line spacing to make the text fit. When AutoFit is active, the AutoFit Options button ⬚ appears below the text box. You can click this button and then select from among several options, including turning off AutoFit for this text box and splitting the text between two slides. Although AutoFit can be helpful, be aware that it also enables you to crowd text on a slide, making the slide more difficult to read.

## Creating a Numbered List

A **numbered list** is a group of paragraphs in which each one is preceded by a number, with the paragraphs numbered consecutively. The numbers can be followed by a separator character, such as a period or parenthesis. Generally, you use a numbered list when the order of the items is important. For example, you would use a numbered list if you are presenting a list of step-by-step instructions that need to be followed in sequence to complete a task successfully.

You will create a numbered list on Slide 5 to explain why Southwest Insurance Company is a good choice for businesses to use.

**To create a numbered list on Slide 5:**

**1.** In the pane containing the thumbnails, click the **Slide 5** thumbnail to display Slide 5, and then type **Choose Southwest Insurance** in the title text placeholder.

**2.** In the left content placeholder, click the placeholder text.

**3.** On the Home tab, in the Paragraph group, click the **Numbering** button ⬚. The Numbering button is selected, the Bullets button is deselected, and in the content placeholder, the number 1 followed by a period replaces the bullet symbol.

**Trouble?** If a menu containing a gallery of numbering styles appears, you clicked the Numbering arrow on the right side of the button. Click the Numbering arrow again to close the menu, and then click the left part of the Numbering button.

4. Type **Reliable**, and then press **ENTER**. As soon as you start typing, the number 1 darkens to black. After you press ENTER, the insertion point moves to the next line, next to the light gray number 2.

5. Type **Customer-focused**, and then press **ENTER**. The number 3 appears on the next line.

6. In the Paragraph group, click the **Increase List Level** button. The third line is an indented subitem under the second item, and the number 3 changes to a number 1 in a smaller font size than the first-level items.

7. Type **Dedicated customer service team**, press **ENTER**, type **24/7 support**, and then press **ENTER**.

8. In the Paragraph group, click the **Decrease List Level** button. The fifth line becomes a first-level item, and the number 3 appears next to it.

9. Type **Dependable**. The list now consists of three first-level numbered items and two subitems under number 2.

10. In the second item, click before the word "Customer," and then press **ENTER**. A blank line is inserted above the second item.

11. Press **UP ARROW**. A light-gray number 2 appears in the blank line. The item on the third line in the list is still numbered 2.

12. Type **Trustworthy**. As soon as you start typing, the new number 2 darkens in the second line, and the number of the third item in the list changes to 3. Compare your screen to Figure 1–11.

**Figure 1–11**     **Numbered list on Slide 5**

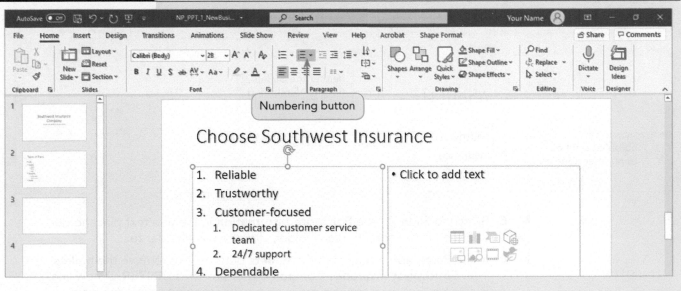

## Creating an Unnumbered List

An **unnumbered list** is a list that does not have bullets or numbers preceding each item. Unnumbered lists are useful when you want to present information on multiple lines, but you do not want to start each item with a bullet or number.

Each item in lists is a paragraph. When you press ENTER to create a new item, you create a new paragraph with a little bit of extra space between the new item and the previous item. Sometimes, you don't want to create a new item, or you do not want extra space between lines. In that case, you can create a new line without creating a new paragraph by pressing SHIFT+ENTER. When you do this, the insertion point moves to the next line, but there is no extra space above it. If you do this in a bulleted or numbered list, the new line will not have a bullet or number next to it because it is not a new item.

You need to create a slide that highlights the company's name. Also, Anthony asks you to create a slide containing contact information.

### To create unnumbered lists on Slides 4 and 7:

1. In the pane containing the thumbnails, click the **Slide 4** thumbnail to display Slide 4. Slide 4 has the Two Content layout applied.

2. Type **About Us** in the title text placeholder, and then in the left content placeholder, click the placeholder text.

3. On the Home tab, in the Paragraph group, click the **Bullets** button ⊟. The Bullets button is no longer selected, and the bullet symbol disappears from the content placeholder.

4. Type **Southwest**, press **ENTER**, type **Insurance**, press **ENTER**, and then type **Company**. (Do not type the period.) Compare your screen to Figure 1–12.

**Figure 1–12**    **Unnumbered list on Slide 4**

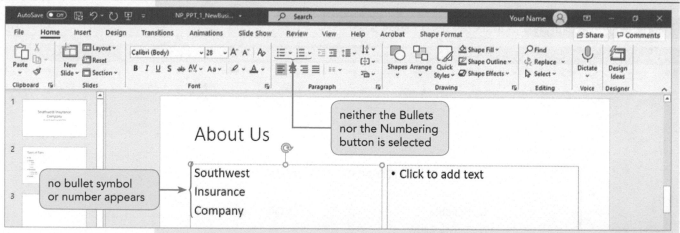

5. Switch to Slide 7, type **For More Information** in the title text placeholder, and then in the content placeholder, click the placeholder text.

6. In the Paragraph group, click the **Bullets** button ⊟ to remove the bullets, type **Southwest Insurance Company**, and then press **ENTER**. A new line is created, but there is extra space above the insertion point. You want the address information to appear on multiple lines, but without the extra spacing between each line.

7. Press **BACKSPACE** to delete the new line and move the insertion point back to the end of the first line, and then press **SHIFT+ENTER**. The insertion

point moves to the next line. There is no extra space above the line, and the insertion point is aligned below the first character in the first line.

8.  Type **9720 Birch Blvd.**, press **SHIFT+ENTER**, and then type **Houston, TX 77002**. (Do not type the period.) You need to insert the phone number on the next line, Anthony's email address on the line after that, and the website address on the last line. The extra space above these lines will set this information apart from the address and make it easier to read.

9.  Press **ENTER** to create a new line with extra space above it, type **(281) 555-0187**, press **ENTER**, type **a.scorsone@sic.example.com**. (Do not type the period.)

    **Trouble?** If the first character in the email address changed to an uppercase letter "A," move the pointer on top of the "A" so that the AutoCorrect rectangle appears, move the pointer on top of the AutoCorrect rectangle so that the AutoCorrect Options button appears, click the AutoCorrect Options button, and then click Undo Automatic Capitalization.

10. Press **ENTER**. The insertion point moves to a new line with extra space above it, and the email address you typed changes color to blue and is underlined.

    When you type text that PowerPoint recognizes as an email or website address and then press SPACEBAR or ENTER, the text is automatically formatted as a link that can be clicked during a slide show. Formatted links generally appear in a different color and are underlined.

11. Type **www.sic.example.com**, and then press **SPACEBAR**. The text is formatted as a link. Anthony plans to click this link during his presentation to show the audience the website, so he wants it to stay formatted as a link. However, there is no need to have the email address formatted as a link.

12. Right-click **a.scorsone@sic.example.com**. A shortcut menu opens.

13. On the shortcut menu, click **Remove Link**. The email address is no longer formatted as a link. Compare your screen to Figure 1–13.

| Figure 1–13 | List on Slide 7 |
| --- | --- |

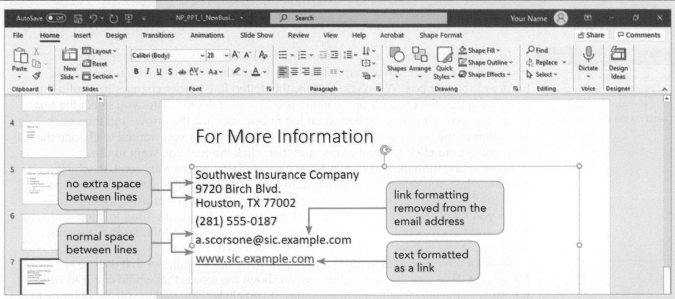

14. On the Quick Access Toolbar, click the **Save** button to save the changes.

# Formatting Text

Slides in a presentation should have a consistent look and feel. For example, the slide titles and the text in content placeholders should be in complementary fonts. There are times, however, when you need to change the format of text. For instance, you might want to make specific words bold to make them stand out more.

The commands in the Font group on the Home tab are used to apply formatting to selected text. Figure 1–14 describes the buttons in this group.

**Figure 1–14**    **Formatting commands in the Font group on the Home tab**

| Button | Name | Description |
|---|---|---|
| Calibri (Body) ▾ | Font | Change the font. |
| 11 ▾ | Font Size | Change the font size; click a size on the menu or type any value between 1 and 3600 in increments of 0.1 (for example, 42.4). |
| A˄ | Increase Font Size | Increase the font size to the next size up listed on the Font Size menu. |
| A˅ | Decrease Font Size | Decrease the font size to the next size down listed on the Font Size menu. |
| A◇ | Clear All Formatting | Remove formatting of selected text. |
| B | Bold | Format text as bold. |
| I | Italic | Italicize text. |
| U | Underline | Underline text. |
| S | Text Shadow | Apply a shadow to text. |
| ab | Strikethrough | Add a line through text. |
| AV ▾ | Character Spacing | Change the spacing between characters. |
| Aa ▾ | Change Case | Change the case of selected text (for example, change to all uppercase). |
| ✎ ▾ | Text Highlight Color | Add a highlight color to selected text. |
| A ▾ | Font Color | Change the color of text. |

**Tip**

To remove all formatting from selected text, click the Clear All Formatting button in the Font group.

To apply formatting to text, you must first select either the text or the text box. If you want to apply the same formatting to all the text in a text box, you can click the border of the text box. When you do this, the dotted line border changes to a solid line to indicate that the contents of the entire text box are selected. After you select the text or the text box, you click the button on the ribbon, or click the arrow, and then click an option in the menu or gallery that opens. For example, if you wanted to change the font, you would click the Font arrow, and then click the font you want to use.

Some of the formatting commands are also available on the Mini toolbar, which appears when you select text with the mouse or when you right-click on a slide. The **Mini toolbar** is a small toolbar that appears next to text you select using the mouse or when you right-click a slide and that contains the most frequently-used text formatting commands, such as bold, italic, font color, and font size. If the Mini toolbar appears, you can use the buttons on it instead of those in the Font group.

Some of the commands in the Font group have menus or galleries that use the Microsoft Office **Live Preview** feature, which shows the results that would occur in your file, such as the effects of formatting options, if you clicked the option you are pointing to.

Anthony wants the contact information on Slide 7 ("For More Information") to be larger. He also wants the first letter of each item in the unnumbered list on Slide 4 ("About Us") formatted so it is more prominent.

## To format the text on Slides 7 and 4:

1. On Slide 7 ("For More Information"), position the pointer on the border of the text box containing the contact information so that it changes to the move pointer ⛶, and then click the border of the text box. The border changes to a solid line to indicate that the entire text box is selected.

2. On the Home tab, in the Font group, click the **Increase Font Size** button A̅ twice. All the text in the text box increases in size with each click and is now 36 points.

3. In the pane containing the thumbnails, click the **Slide 4** thumbnail to display that slide.

4. In the unnumbered list, click to the left of "Southwest," press and hold **SHIFT**, press **RIGHT ARROW**, and then release **SHIFT**. The letter "S" is selected. See Figure 1–15.

**Figure 1–15** | **Text selected to be formatted**

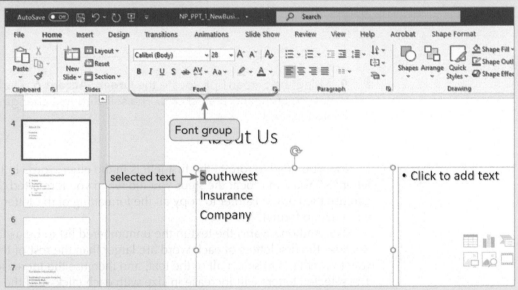

5. In the Font group, click the **Bold** button B. The Bold button becomes selected, and the selected text is formatted as bold.

6. In the Font group, click the **Font Size arrow** to open the Font Size menu, and then click **48**. The selected text is now 48 points.

7. In the Font group, click the **Font Color arrow** A̲ ⌄. A menu containing color options opens.

8. Under Theme Colors, move the pointer over each color, noting the ScreenTips that appear and watching as Live Preview changes the color of the selected text as you point to each color. Figure 1–16 shows the pointer pointing to the Green, Accent 6, Darker 25% color.

**Figure 1–16**   **Font Color menu**

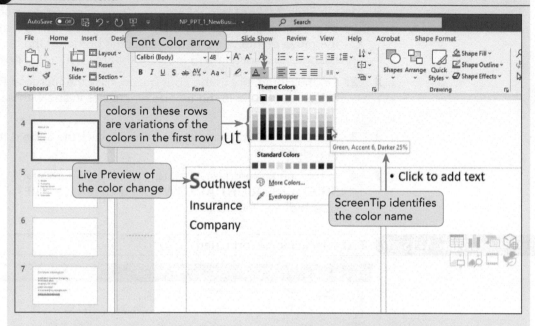

9. Using the ScreenTips, locate the **Green, Accent 6, Darker 25%** color in the last column, and then click it. The selected text changes to the green color you clicked.

Now you need to format the first letters in the other words in the list to match the letter "S." You can repeat the steps you did when you formatted the letter "S," or you can use the Format Painter to copy all the formatting of the letter "S" to the other letters you need to format.

Also, Anthony wants the text in the unnumbered list to be as large as possible. Because the first letters of each word are larger than the rest of the letters, the easiest way to do this is to select all of the text, and then use the Increase Font Size button. The selected letters will increase in size with each click, and the first letters will still be larger.

**To use the Format Painter to copy and apply formatting on Slide 4:**

1. Make sure the letter "S" is still selected.

2. On the Home tab, in the Clipboard group, click the **Format Painter** button , and then move the pointer on top of the slide. The button is selected, and the pointer changes to the Format Painter pointer for text .

3. Position the pointer before the letter "I" in "Insurance," press and hold the mouse button, drag over the letter **I**, and then release the mouse button. The formatting you applied to the letter "S" is copied to the letter "I," and the Mini toolbar appears. See Figure 1–17. The Mini toolbar appears whenever you drag over text to select it.

**Figure 1–17** | **Mini toolbar**

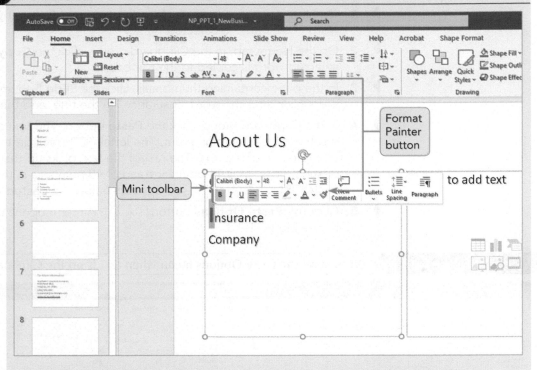

4. On the Mini toolbar, click the **Format Painter** button 🖌, and then drag across the letter "C" in "Company."

5. Click the border of the text box to select the entire text box, and then in the Font group, click the **Increase Font Size** button A˄ five times. In the Font group, the Font Size button indicates that the text is 48+ points. This means that in the selected text box, the text that is the smallest is 48 points and there is some text that is larger.

6. On the Quick Access Toolbar, click the **Save** button 🖫 to save the changes.

# Moving and Copying

You can move and copy text and objects in a presentation using the Clipboard that is part of Windows. The **Clipboard** is a temporary Windows storage area that holds the selections you copy or cut so you can use them later. When you **cut** something, you remove the text or object from a file and place it on the Clipboard. You can also **copy** text or an object, which means you select it and place a duplicate of it on the Clipboard, leaving the text or object in its original location. You can then paste the text or object stored on the Clipboard anywhere in the presentation or in any file in any Windows program. To **paste** something means to place text or an object stored on the Clipboard in a location in a file.

The Clipboard holds only the most recently cut or copied item. As soon as you cut or copy another item, it replaces the previously cut or copied item on the Clipboard. You can paste an item on the Clipboard as many times and in as many locations as you like.

Note that cutting text or an object differs from deleting it. When you press DELETE or BACKSPACE to delete text or objects, they are not placed on the Clipboard and cannot be pasted.

Anthony wants a few changes made to Slides 5 and 2. You'll use the Clipboard as you make these edits.

## To cut, copy, and paste text using the Clipboard:

1. On Slide 4 ("About Us"), double-click the word **Company** in the list. The word "Company" is selected.

2. On the Home tab, in the Clipboard group, click the **Copy** button 🗐. The selected word is copied to the Clipboard.

3. In the pane containing thumbnails, click the **Slide 5** thumbnail to display that slide, click after the word "Insurance" in the title, and then press **SPACEBAR**.

4. In the Clipboard group, click the **Paste** button. The text appears at the location of the insertion point. The letter "C" is still green and is larger than the rest of the text. The rest of the text picks up the formatting of its destination, so it is 44 points instead of 48 points as in the list on Slide 4. The Paste Options button 🗐 (Ctrl)▾ appears below the pasted text.

5. Click the **Paste Options** button 🗐 (Ctrl)▾. A menu opens with four buttons on it. See Figure 1–18.

**Figure 1–18** | Buttons on the Paste Options menu when text is on the Clipboard

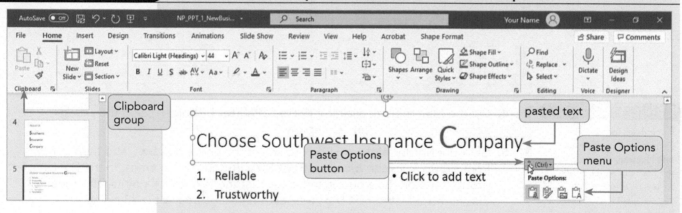

6. Point to each button on the menu, reading the ScreenTips and watching to see how the pasted text changes in appearance. The first button is the Use Destination Theme button 🗐, which is the default choice when you paste text.

7. On the Paste Options menu, click the **Keep Text Only** button 🗐. The pasted text changes so that its formatting matches the rest of the title text.

8. Display Slide 2 ("Types of Plans"). The last bulleted item ("Stable") belongs on Slide 5.

9. In the last bulleted item, position the pointer on top of the bullet symbol so that the pointer changes to the four-headed arrow pointer ✥, and then click. The entire bulleted item is selected.

10. In the Clipboard group, click the **Cut** button 🗴. The last bulleted item is removed from the slide and is placed on the Clipboard.

11. Display Slide 5 ("Choose Southwest Insurance Company"), click after the last item ("Dependable"), and then press **ENTER** to create a fifth first-level item.

12. In the Clipboard group, click the **Paste** button. The bulleted item you cut becomes the fifth first-level item on Slide 5 using the default paste option of Use Destination Theme. The insertion point appears next to a sixth first-level item.

13. Press **BACKSPACE** twice to delete the extra line, and then on the Quick Access Toolbar, click the **Save** button 🖫 to save the changes.

**Tip**

To cut text or an object, you can press CTRL+X. To copy text or an object, press CTRL+C. To paste the contents of the Clipboard, press CTRL+V.

## Insight

### Using the Office Clipboard

The **Office Clipboard** is a temporary storage area in the computer's memory that lets you collect text and objects from any Office document and then paste them into other Office documents. Once you activate the Office Clipboard, you can store up to 24 items on it and then select the item or items you want to paste. To activate the Office Clipboard, click the Home tab. In the Clipboard group, click the Dialog Box Launcher (the small square in the lower-right corner of the Clipboard group) to open the Clipboard pane to the left of the displayed slide.

# Manipulating Slides

You can manipulate the slides in a presentation to suit your needs. For example, if you need to create a slide that is similar to another slide, you can duplicate the existing slide and then modify the copy. If you no longer want to include a slide in your presentation, you can delete it. You can also reorder slides as necessary.

To duplicate, rearrange, or delete slides, you select the slides in the pane containing the thumbnails in Normal view or switch to Slide Sorter view. In **Slide Sorter view** all the slides in the presentation are displayed as thumbnails in the window.

Anthony wants to display a slide that shows the name of the company at the end of the presentation. To create this slide, you will duplicate Slide 4 ("About Us").

### To duplicate Slide 4:

1. Display Slide 4 ("About Us").

2. On the Home tab, in the Slides group, click the **New Slide arrow**, and then click **Duplicate Selected Slides**. A duplicate of Slide 4 appears as a new Slide 5 and is the current slide. If you had selected more than one slide, they would all be duplicated. The duplicate slide doesn't need the title; Anthony just wants to reinforce the company's name.

3. On Slide 5, click anywhere on the title **About Us**, click the text box border to select the text box, and then press **DELETE**. The title and the title text box are deleted, and the title text placeholder reappears.

You could delete the title text placeholder, but you do not need to. When you display a presentation to an audience as a slide show, any unused placeholders do not appear.

Next you need to rearrange the slides. You need to move the duplicate of the "About Us" slide so it becomes the last slide in the presentation because Anthony wants it to remain displayed after the presentation is over. He hopes this visual will reinforce the company's name for the audience. Anthony also wants Slide 6 ("Choose Southwest Insurance Company") moved before the "Types of Plans" slide (Slide 2), and he wants the original "About Us" slide (Slide 4) to be the second slide in the presentation.

## To rearrange the slides in the presentation:

1. In the pane containing the thumbnails, scroll, if necessary, so that you can see Slides 2 and 6, and then click the **Slide 6** ("Choose Southwest Insurance Company") thumbnail. Slide 6 ("Choose Southwest Insurance Company") is the current slide.

2. Point to the **Slide 6** thumbnail, press and hold the mouse button, drag the Slide 6 thumbnail up above the Slide 2 ("Types of Plans") thumbnail, and then release the mouse button. As you drag, the Slide 6 thumbnail follows the pointer and the other slides move down to make room for the slide you are dragging. The "Choose Southwest Insurance Company" slide becomes Slide 2 and "Types of Plans" becomes Slide 3. You'll move the other two slides in Slide Sorter view.

3. On the status bar, click the **Slide Sorter** button ⊞. The view switches to Slide Sorter view. Slide 2 appears with an orange border, indicating that it is selected.

4. On the status bar, click the **Zoom Out** button ⊟ as many times as necessary until you can see all nine slides in the presentation. See Figure 1–19.

**Figure 1–19**    **Slide Sorter view**

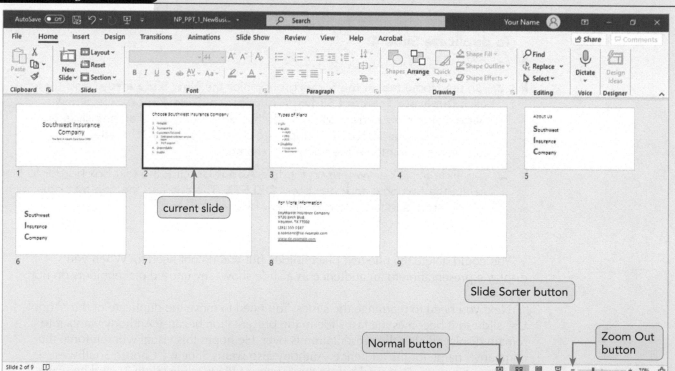

5. Drag the **Slide 5** ("About Us") thumbnail to between Slides 1 and 2. As you drag, the other slides move out of the way. The slides are renumbered so that the "About Us" slide is now Slide 2.

6. Drag the **Slide 6** thumbnail (the slide containing just the name of the company) after the last slide in the presentation (Slide 9).

Now you need to delete the blank slides. To delete a slide, you right-click its thumbnail to display a shortcut menu, and then click Delete Slide on that menu.

You already know that to select a single slide you click its thumbnail. You can also select more than one slide at a time. To select sequential slides, click the first slide, press and hold SHIFT, and then click the last slide you want to select. To select nonsequential slides, click the first slide, press and hold CTRL, and then click any other slides you want to select. When more than one slide is selected, you can delete or duplicate all of the selected slides with one command.

### To delete the blank slides:

▶ 1. Click the **Slide 5** thumbnail (the first blank slide), press and hold **SHIFT**, click the **Slide 8** thumbnail (the last blank slide), and then release **SHIFT**. The two slides you clicked are selected, as well as the slides between them. Holding SHIFT when you click items selects the slides you click as well as the slides between the slides you click. You want to delete only the three blank slides. To select only the slides you click, you need to hold CTRL instead.

▶ 2. Click a blank area of the window to deselect the slides, click the **Slide 5** thumbnail, press and hold **CTRL**, click the **Slide 6** thumbnail, click the **Slide 8** thumbnail, and then release **CTRL**. Only the slides you clicked are selected.

▶ 3. Right-click any of the selected slides. A shortcut menu appears. See Figure 1–20.

| Figure 1–20 | Shortcut menu for selected slides |

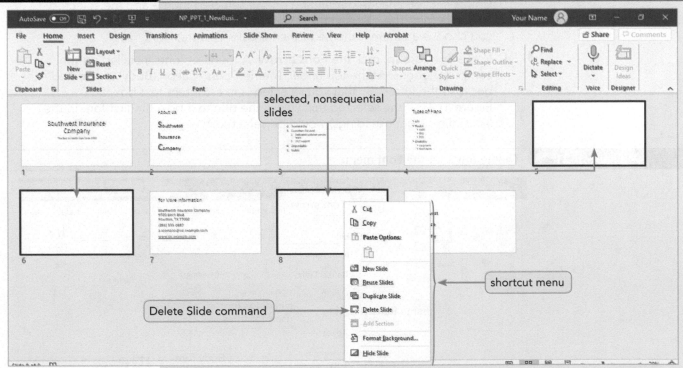

▶ 4. On the shortcut menu, click **Delete Slide**. The shortcut menu closes, and the three selected slides are deleted. The presentation now contains six slides.

▶ 5. On the status bar, click the **Normal** button. The presentation appears in Normal view.

▶ 6. On the Quick Access Toolbar, click the **Save** button to save the changes to the presentation.

### Tip

You can also double-click a slide thumbnail in Slide Sorter view to display that slide in the view the presentation was in prior to being in Slide Sorter view.

# Changing the Theme

A **theme** is a predefined, coordinated set of colors, fonts, graphical effects, and other formats that can be applied to a presentation. In PowerPoint, most themes have variants that have different coordinating colors and sometimes slightly different backgrounds. All presentations have a theme. If you don't choose one, the default Office theme is applied; that is the theme currently applied to the presentation you created.

Every theme has a palette of 12 coordinated colors. You saw the Office theme colors when you changed the color of the text on the "About Us" slide. If you don't like the color palette of the theme you chose, you can change to a different one.

Themes also have a font set. One font, called the Headings font, is used for slide titles. The other font, called the Body font, is used for the rest of the text on a slide. In the Office theme, the Headings font is Calibri Light, and the Body font is Calibri. In some themes, the Headings and Body font are the same font.

Anthony wants you to try changing the theme colors and fonts.

**To examine the current theme and then change the theme color and theme fonts:**

1. Display Slide 5 ("For More Information"). Notice that the link is blue.

2. Display Slide 6, and then, in the unnumbered list, select the green letter **S**.

3. On the Home tab, in the Font group, click the **Font Color arrow** . Look at the colors under Theme Colors. The last column contains shades of green. In that column, the second to last color is selected. The colors in the Theme Colors section change depending on the selected theme and the selected theme colors. The colors in the row of Standard Colors do not change when you choose a different theme or theme color palette.

4. In the Font group, click the **Font arrow**. A menu of fonts installed on the computer opens. At the top under Theme Fonts, Calibri (Body) is selected because the letter "S" that you selected is in a content text box. See Figure 1–21. If the selected text was in the title text box, the first font in the list, Calibri Light (Headings) would be selected.

**Figure 1–21**    Theme fonts on the Font menu

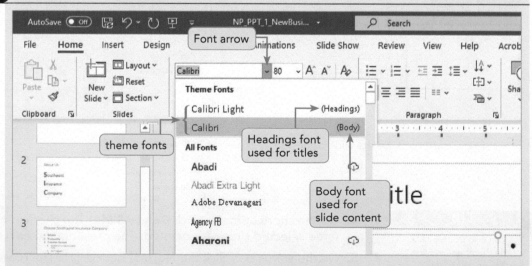

5. On the ribbon, click the **Design** tab. The Design tab is active. See Figure 1–22. In the Themes group, the first theme is the theme applied to the presentation. In this case, it is the Office theme. The second theme is also the Office theme and it is shaded to indicate that it is selected. In the Variants group, the first variant is shaded to indicate that it is selected.

**Figure 1–22**     Themes and variants on the Design tab

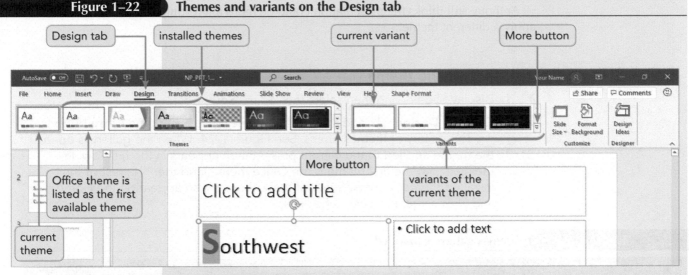

6. In the Variants group, click the **More** button ⬇. A menu opens containing commands for changing the theme colors and the theme fonts. See Figure 1–23.

**Figure 1–23**     More button menu in the Variants group

7. On the menu, point to **Colors** to open a submenu of color palettes, and then click the **Blue Warm** palette. The colored letters on Slide 6 change to a shade of grayish brown.

8. In the Variant group, click the **More** button ⬇, point to **Fonts**, scroll down, and then click **Tw Cen MT-Rockwell**. The font of the list and the title text placeholder on Slide 6 changes.

9. Click the **Home** tab, and then in the Font group, click the **Font Color arrow** 🅰 ⌄. The second to last color in the last column is still selected, but now that column contains shades of grayish brown. The row of Standard Colors is the same as it was when the Office theme colors were applied.

10. In the Font group, click the **Font** arrow. The Headings and Body font have changed to the Tw Cen MT and the Rockwell fonts.

11. Display Slide 5. The link that was blue before you changed the theme colors is now purple.

PowerPoint comes with several installed themes, and many more themes are available online at Office.com. In addition, you can use a custom theme stored on your computer or network.

You can select a different installed theme when you create a new presentation by clicking one of the themes on the New or Home screen in Backstage view. If you want to change the theme of an open presentation, you can choose an installed theme on the Design tab, or you can apply a theme applied to another presentation or a theme stored on your computer or network.

Anthony still thinks the presentation could be more interesting, so he asks you to apply a different theme.

### To change the theme

▶ **1.** Display Slide 6, and then select the "S" in "Southwest."

▶ **2.** Click the **Design** tab, and then in the Themes group, click the **More** button ⯆. The gallery of themes opens. See Figure 1–24. When the gallery is open, the theme applied to the current presentation appears in the first row. In the next row, the first theme is the Office theme, and then the rest of the installed themes appear. Some of these themes also appear on the Home and New screens in Backstage view.

**Figure 1–24**    **Themes gallery expanded**

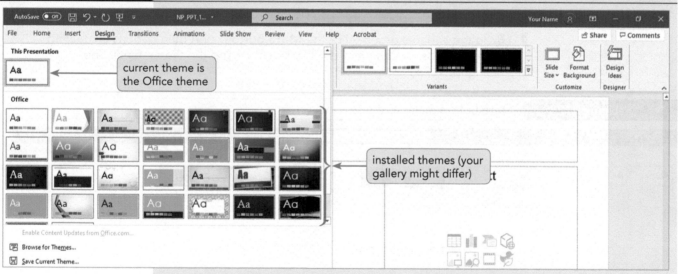

▶ **3.** Point to several of the themes in the gallery to display their ScreenTips and to see a Live Preview of the theme applied to the current slide.

▶ **4.** Click the **Wisp** theme. The gallery closes, and all the slides have the Wisp theme with the default variant (the first variant in the Variants group) applied. The background of the slides changes from white to tan, and the letters that you had colored green on Slide 6 change to a shade of grayish green. In the empty content placeholder on Slide 6, the bullet symbol changed from a circle to an arrow.

▶ **5.** In the Variants group, point to the other three variants to see a Live Preview of each of them, and then click the third variant (the blue one). The letters on Slide 6 change to purple. You prefer the original colors. On the Quick Access Toolbar, click the **Undo** button.

▶ **6.** Click the **Home** tab, and then in the Font group, click the **Font Color arrow** ⯆. The selected color is still the second to last color in the last column, but now the last column contains shades of purple. Again, the row of Standard Colors is the same as it was before you made changes.

**7.** In the Font group, click the **Font arrow**. You can see that the Theme Fonts are now Century Gothic for both Headings and the Body.

**8.** Press **ESC**. The Font menu closes.

After you apply a new theme, you should examine your slides to make sure that they look the way you expect them to. Slide 6 looks fine.

**To examine the slides with the new theme and adjust font sizes:**

**1.** Display Slides 5, 4, 3, and Slide 2. These slides look fine.

**2.** Display Slide 1 (the title slide). The title text is too large with the Wisp theme applied.

**3.** Click anywhere on the title text, and then click the text box border. The entire text box is selected.

**4.** In the Font group, click the **Decrease Font Size** button $\boxed{\text{A}^\vee}$ as many times as necessary until the font size of the title text decreases to 44 points.

**5.** On the Quick Access Toolbar, click **Save** 🔲. The changes to the presentation are saved.

## Insight

### Understanding the Difference Between Themes and Templates

As explained earlier, a theme is a coordinated set of colors, fonts, backgrounds, and effects. A **template** is a file that has a theme applied and contains text, graphics, and placeholders that direct you in creating content for a presentation. You can create and save your own custom templates or find everything from calendars to marketing templates among the thousands of templates available on Office.com. To find a template on Office.com, display the Home or New screen in Backstage view, type keywords in the "Search for online templates and themes" box, and then click the Search button in the box to display templates related to the search terms. To create a new presentation based on the template you find, click the template and then click Create.

If a template is stored on your computer, you can apply the theme used in the template to an existing presentation. If you want to apply the theme used in a template on Office.com to an existing presentation, you need to download the template to your computer first.

# Closing a Presentation

When you are finished working with a presentation, you can close it and leave PowerPoint open. To do this, you click the File tab to open Backstage view, and then click the Close command. If you have only one presentation open, if you click the Close button ☒ in the upper-right corner of the PowerPoint window, you will not only close the presentation, you will exit PowerPoint as well.

You're finished working with the presentation for now, so you will close it. First you will add your name to the title slide.

**To add your name to Slide 1 and close the presentation:**

▶ **1.** On Slide 1 (the title slide), click the subtitle, position the insertion point after "1990," press **ENTER**, and then type your full name.

▶ **2.** Click the **File** tab. Backstage view appears with the Home screen displayed. See Figure 1–25.

**Figure 1–25**    Home screen in Backstage view

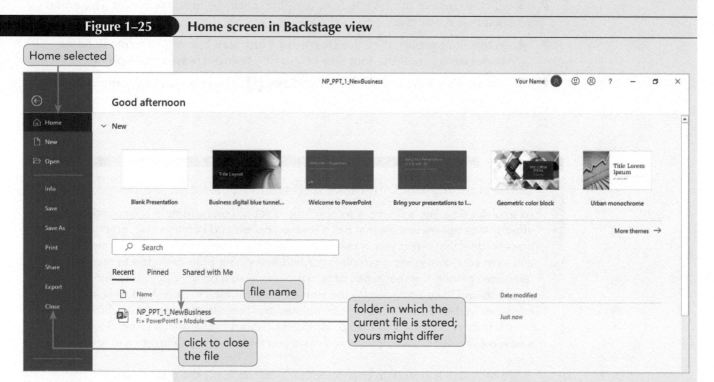

▶ **3.** In the navigation pane, click **Close**. Backstage view closes, and a dialog box opens, asking if you want to save your changes.

▶ **4.** sam ↑ In the dialog box, click **Save**. The dialog box and the presentation close, and the empty presentation window appears.

**Trouble?** If you want to take a break, you can exit PowerPoint by clicking the Close button ☒ in the upper-right corner of the PowerPoint window.

You've created a presentation that includes slides to which you added bulleted, numbered, and unnumbered lists. You also formatted text, manipulated slides, and applied a theme. You are ready to give the presentation draft to Anthony to review.

# Review

## Session 1.1 Quick Check

1. Define "presentation."

2. How do you display Backstage view?

3. What is a slide layout?

4. In addition to a title text placeholder, what other type of placeholder do many layouts contain?

5. What is the term for an object that contains text?

6. What is the difference between the Clipboard and the Office Clipboard?

7. Explain what a theme is and what changes with each variant.

# Session 1.2 Visual Overview:

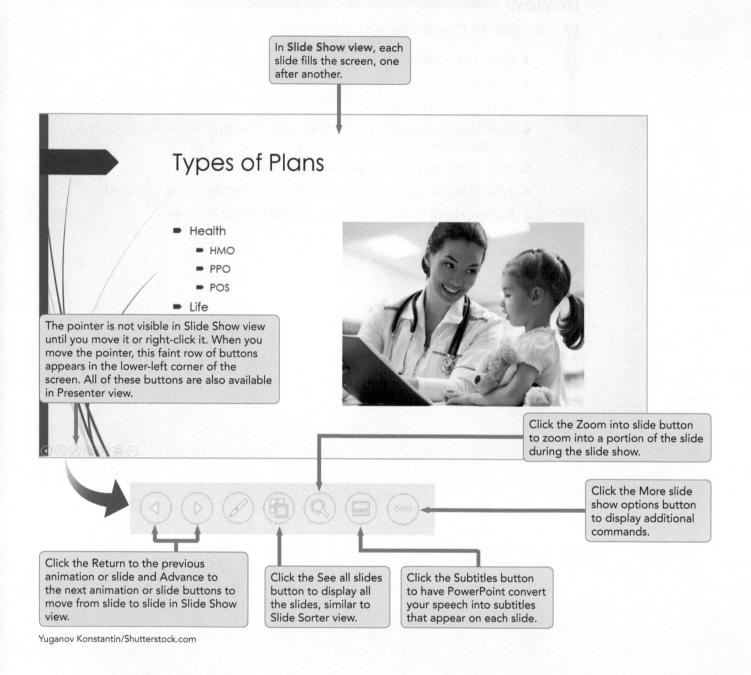

In **Slide Show view**, each slide fills the screen, one after another.

## Types of Plans

- Health
  - HMO
  - PPO
  - POS
- Life

The pointer is not visible in Slide Show view until you move it or right-click it. When you move the pointer, this faint row of buttons appears in the lower-left corner of the screen. All of these buttons are also available in Presenter view.

Click the Zoom into slide button to zoom into a portion of the slide during the slide show.

Click the More slide show options button to display additional commands.

Click the Return to the previous animation or slide and Advance to the next animation or slide buttons to move from slide to slide in Slide Show view.

Click the See all slides button to display all the slides, similar to Slide Sorter view.

Click the Subtitles button to have PowerPoint convert your speech into subtitles that appear on each slide.

Yuganov Konstantin/Shutterstock.com

# Slide Show and Presenter Views

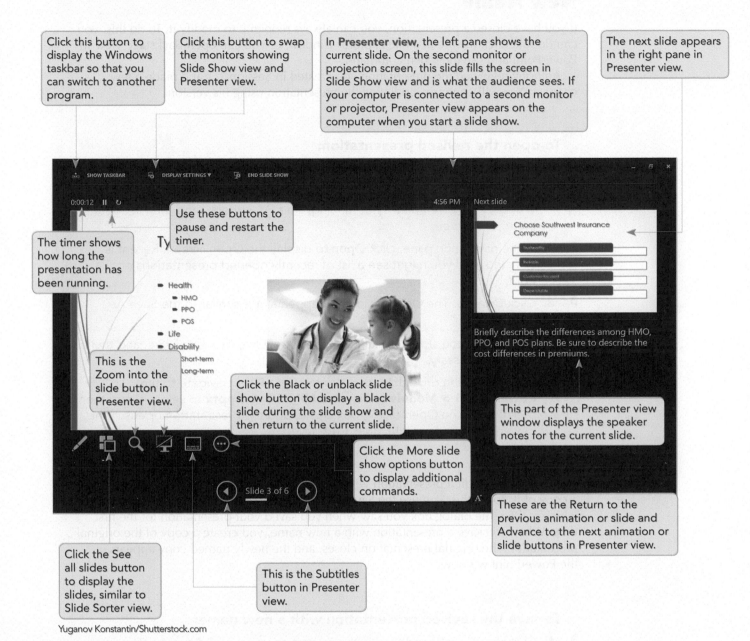

Click this button to display the Windows taskbar so that you can switch to another program.

Click this button to swap the monitors showing Slide Show view and Presenter view.

In **Presenter view**, the left pane shows the current slide. On the second monitor or projection screen, this slide fills the screen in Slide Show view and is what the audience sees. If your computer is connected to a second monitor or projector, Presenter view appears on the computer when you start a slide show.

The next slide appears in the right pane in Presenter view.

Use these buttons to pause and restart the timer.

The timer shows how long the presentation has been running.

This is the Zoom into the slide button in Presenter view.

Click the Black or unblack slide show button to display a black slide during the slide show and then return to the current slide.

Briefly describe the differences among HMO, PPO, and POS plans. Be sure to describe the cost differences in premiums.

This part of the Presenter view window displays the speaker notes for the current slide.

Click the More slide show options button to display additional commands.

These are the Return to the previous animation or slide and Advance to the next animation or slide buttons in Presenter view.

Click the See all slides button to display the slides, similar to Slide Sorter view.

This is the Subtitles button in Presenter view.

Yuganov Konstantin/Shutterstock.com

# Opening a Presentation and Saving It with a New Name

If you have closed a presentation, you can always reopen it to modify it. To do this, you can double-click the file in a File Explorer window, or you can open Backstage view in PowerPoint and use the Open command.

Anthony reviewed the presentation you created in Session 1.1 and made a few changes. You will continue modifying the presentation using his version.

### To open the revised presentation:

1. **sam** ⬇ Click the **File** tab on the ribbon to display the Home screen in Backstage view.

   **Trouble?** If PowerPoint is not running, start PowerPoint, and then in the left pane, click Open.

2. In the navigation pane, click **Open** to display the Open screen. Recent is selected, and you might see a list of recently opened presentations on the right.

3. Click **Browse**. The Open dialog box appears. It is similar to the Save As dialog box.

   **Trouble?** If you store your files on your OneDrive, click OneDrive, and then log in if necessary.

4. Navigate to the drive that contains your Data Files, navigate to the **PowerPoint1 > Module** folder, click **NP_PPT_1-1.pptx** to select it, and then click **Open**. The Open dialog box closes, and the presentation opens in the PowerPoint window, with Slide 1 displayed.

If you want to edit a presentation without changing the original, you need to create a copy of it. To do this, you use the Save As command to open the Save As dialog box, which is the same dialog box you saw when you saved your presentation for the first time. When you save a presentation with a new name, you create a copy of the original presentation, the original presentation closes, and the newly named copy appears in the PowerPoint window.

### To save the revised presentation with a new name:

1. Click the **File** tab, and then in the navigation pane, click **Save As**. The Save As screen in Backstage view appears.

2. Click **Browse** to open the Save As dialog box.

3. If necessary, navigate to the drive and folder where you are storing your Data Files.

4. In the File name box, change the filename to **NP_PPT_1_Revised**, and then click **Save**. The Save As dialog box closes, and a copy of the file is saved with the new name NP_PPT_1_Revised and appears in the PowerPoint window.

# Inserting Pictures and Adding Alt Text

In many cases, graphics are more effective than words for communicating an important point or invoking an emotional reaction. For example, if a sales force has reached its sales goals for the year, including a photo in your presentation of a person reaching the top of a mountain can convey a sense of accomplishment to your audience. To add a graphic to a slide, you can use the buttons in a content placeholder or buttons on the Insert tab.

When you insert a graphic and when specific built-in layouts are applied to the slide, the Design Ideas pane opens containing suggestions for interesting layouts for the slide. You can click one of these layouts to apply it or close the Design Ideas pane without accepting any of the suggestions.

Anthony has a photo that he wants you to insert on Slide 2.

**To insert a photo on Slide 2 and view the Design Ideas:**

1. Display Slide 2 ("About Us"), and then in the content placeholder on the right, click the **Pictures** button. The Insert Picture dialog box opens. This dialog box is similar to the Open dialog box.

2. Navigate to the **PowerPoint1 > Module** folder included with your Data Files, click **Support_PPT_1_Family.jpg**, and then click **Insert**. The dialog box closes, and a picture of a family in front of medical professionals appears in the placeholder and is selected. Text that describes the picture might appear briefly at the bottom of the picture. Also, the Design Ideas pane might open listing suggestions for interesting layouts for this slide. On the ribbon, the contextual Picture Format tab appears and is the active tab. See Figure 1–26.

**Figure 1–26**    Picture inserted on Slide 2

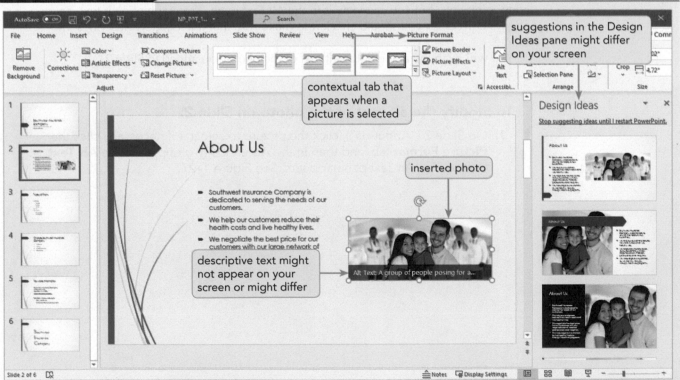

Rob Marmion/Shutterstock.com

**Trouble?** If the Design Ideas pane does not appear, click the Design tab, and then in the Designer group, click the Design Ideas button.

**Trouble?** If the descriptive text does not appear below the picture, do not be concerned. You will display it later.

3. In the Design Ideas pane, click each of the thumbnails to see the effect on the slide. Although Anthony likes some of the layouts suggested in the Design Ideas pane, he wants you to apply the Two Content layout again. First, you need to undo the change you made.

**Tip**

You can click the Redo button on the Quick Access Toolbar to redo an action.

4. On the Quick Access Toolbar, click the **Undo arrow** 🔄. No matter how many thumbnails you clicked in the Design Ideas pane, only one "Apply Design Idea" action is listed in the Undo menu.

5. On the menu, click **Apply Design Idea**. The slide is reset to its original layout.

6. In the Design Ideas pane, in the top-right corner, click the **Close** button ✖. The pane closes.

The layout suggestions in the Design Ideas pane can help you create interesting slides. If you open the Design Ideas pane and it does not contain any suggestions, make sure you are using one of the themes that is included with PowerPoint, and change the slide layout to Title Slide or Title and Content.

Although graphics can make a slide more interesting, people with limited vision might not be able to see them clearly and people who are blind cannot see them at all. People with vision challenges might use a screen reader to view your presentation. A screen reader identifies objects on the screen and produces an audio of the text. Graphics cause problems for users of screen readers unless the graphics have alternative text. **Alternative text**, usually shortened to **alt text**, is descriptive text added to an object.

When you add a picture to a slide, alt text for the picture is automatically created and displayed at the bottom of the picture. The alt text on the picture disappears after a few moments, but you can view it in the Alt Text pane. The automatic alt text is not always correct, so you should check it to make sure that it accurately describes the image.

You will examine and edit the alt text of the photo you added to Slide 2.

### To modify the alt text of the photo on Slide 2:

1. On Slide 2 ("About Us"), click the picture to select it if necessary, click the **Picture Format** tab, and then in the Accessibility group, click the **Alt Text** button. The Alt Text pane appears. See Figure 1–27.

**Figure 1–27**    Alt Text pane open showing automatically generated alt text

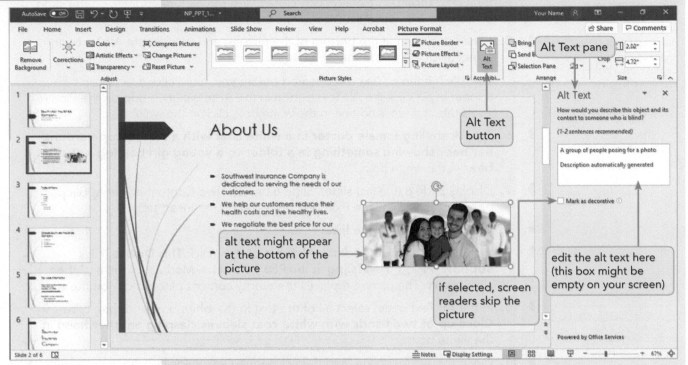

Rob Marmion/Shutterstock.com

**Trouble?** If alt text is not automatically generated, this feature might be turned off on your computer or your computer might not have been able to connect to the Microsoft server. Click in the white box in the Alt Text pane, and then skip Step 2.

2. In the Alt Text pane, in the white box, select all of the text, including the phrase "Description automatically generated."

3. Type **Happy mother, young son, and father standing in front of medical professionals** in the white box. The text you type replaces the selected text. The next time you select the picture, a new command—Generate a description for me—will appear. You could click that command to have the alt text generated again, replacing the text you typed.

4. In the Alt Text pane, in the top-right corner, click the **Close** button ☒.

> **Tip**
>
> Another way to open the Alt Text pane is to click the alt text when it appears on the bottom of the picture when the picture is first inserted.

Anthony has two more photos that he wants you to add to the presentation. He asks you to add the photos to Slides 3 and 6.

**To insert photos on Slides 3 and 6:**

1. Display Slide 3 ("Types of Plans"). This slide has the Title and Content layout applied, so it does not have a second content placeholder. You can change the layout to include a second content placeholder, or you can use a command on the ribbon to insert a photo.

2. Click the **Insert** tab, and then in the Images group, click the **Pictures** button. The Insert Picture From gallery appears.

3. Click **This Device** to select a picture on your computer. The Insert Picture dialog box opens.

**Tip**

To convert pictures to SmartArt, select all the pictures on a slide, click the Picture Format tab, and then click the Picture Layout button in the Picture Styles group.

4. In the PowerPoint1 > Module folder, click **Support_PPT_1_Doctor.jpg**, and then click **Insert**. The dialog box closes, and the picture appears on the slide, covering the bulleted list. You will fix this later.

5. Click the alt text at the bottom of the picture, and then, in the Alt Text pane, select all of the text in the white box.

   **Trouble?** If the alt text disappeared before you could click it or doesn't appear at all, click the Alt Text button in the Accessibility group on the Picture Tools tab. If there is no text in the white box, click in the white box.

6. Type **A smiling female doctor in a white coat with a stethoscope around her neck showing something in a folder to a young girl holding a stuffed bear** in the white box.

7. Display Slide 6 (the last slide). Slide 6 has the Two Content layout applied, but you can still use the Pictures command on the Insert tab.

8. On the ribbon, click the **Insert** tab.

9. In the Images group, click the **Pictures** button, click **This Device**, click **Support_PPT_1_Hands.jpg** in the PowerPoint1 > Module folder, and then click **Insert**. The picture replaces the empty content placeholder on the slide.

10. In the Alt Text pane, select all of the text in the white box, and then type **Close-up of two hands with white coat sleeves clasping another hand** in the white box.

11. Close the Alt Text pane, and then close the Design Ideas pane, if necessary.

 **Proskills**

### Decision Making: Deciding Whether to Allow Alt Text to Be Generated

People are becoming much more aware of privacy concerns when posting information to the cloud or to social media. When you insert a picture on a slide, the picture is sent to Microsoft's servers in order to generate alt text. This means that you are sharing the picture in the cloud. If you are concerned about sharing your private pictures, you can turn this feature off. To do this, click the File tab, and then click Options to open the PowerPoint Options dialog box. On the left, click Ease of Access to display the options for making PowerPoint more accessible. In the Automatic Alt Text section, click the Automatically generate alt text for me check box to deselect it. If you change your mind and you want alt text generated for a specific picture, you can still click the command to generate new alt text in the Alt Text pane.

## Cropping Pictures

Sometimes you want to display only part of a photo. For example, if you insert a photo of a party scene that includes a bouquet of colorful balloons, you might want to show only the balloons. To do this, you can crop the photo. To **crop** means to trim away part of a picture. In PowerPoint, you can crop a picture to any size you want, crop it to a preset ratio, or crop it to a shape.

It can be helpful to display rulers and gridlines in the window to help you crop photos to specific sizes. There are two rulers. One is horizontal and appears above the slide. The other is vertical and appears to the left of the slide. **Gridlines** are evenly spaced horizontal and vertical lines on the slide that help you align objects.

Anthony wants you to crop the photo on Slide 3 ("Types of Plans") to make the dimensions of the final photo smaller without making the images in the photo smaller.

**To crop the photo on Slide 3:**

1. Click the **View** tab, and then in the Show group, click the **Ruler** and the **Gridlines** check boxes. Rulers appear above and to the left of the displayed slide, and the gridlines appear on the slide.

2. Display Slide 3 ("Types of Plans"), click the photo to select it, and then click the **Picture Format** tab, if necessary.

3. In the Size group, click the **Crop** button. The Crop button is selected, and crop handles appear around the edges of the photo just inside the sizing handles. See Figure 1–28.

**Figure 1–28**    Photo with crop handles

Yuganov Konstantin/Shutterstock.com; Rob Marmion/Shutterstock.com

4. Position the pointer directly on top of the middle crop handle on the left side of the picture so that it changes to the left-middle crop pointer ⊣. On the rulers, a red dotted line shows the position of the pointer.

5. Press and hold the mouse button, drag the crop handle to the right until the left cropped edge is on the gridline that aligns with the negative 3-inch mark on the horizontal ruler, and then release the mouse button. The part of the photo that will be cropped off is shaded dark gray. See Figure 1–29.

**Figure 1–29**    **Cropped photo**

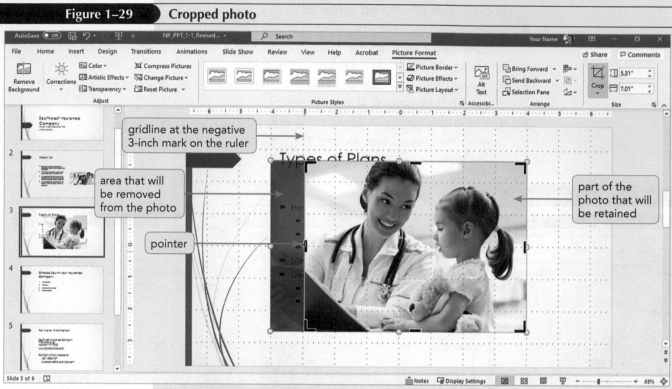

Yuganov Konstantin/Shutterstock.com; Rob Marmion/Shutterstock.com

**6.** Move the pointer on top of the photo so that the pointer changes to the move pointer ✥, press and hold the mouse button, and then drag the photo to the right until the right side of the girl's ponytail is next to the right edge of the visible part of the photo. See Figure 1–30.

**Figure 1–30**    **Photo moved inside cropped area**

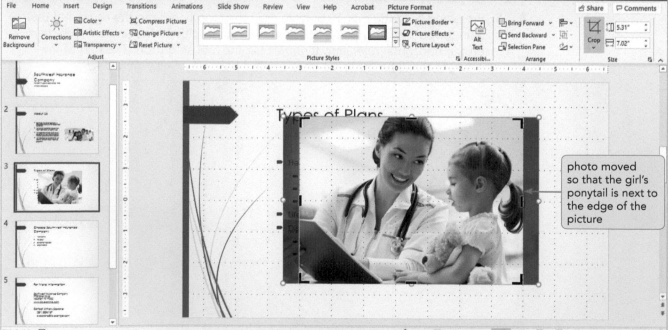

Yuganov Konstantin/Shutterstock.com; Rob Marmion/Shutterstock.com

7. Click the **Crop** button again. The Crop feature turns off, but the photo is still selected, and the Picture Format tab is still the active tab.

When you crop a picture to a shape, the picture fills the shape. Anthony wants you to crop the photo on Slide 6 (the last slide) so that it fills a cross shape.

### To crop the photo on Slide 6 to a shape:

1. Display Slide 6 (the last slide), click the photo to select it, and then click the **Picture Format** tab, if necessary.

2. In the Size group, click the **Crop arrow**. The Crop menu opens. See Figure 1-31.

**Figure 1-31     Crop button menu**

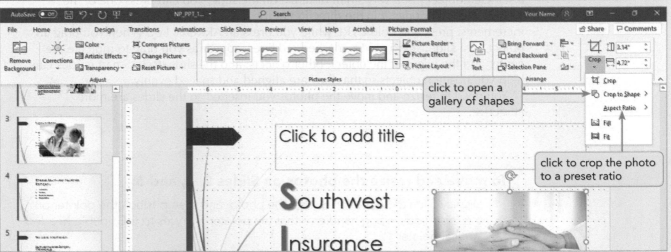

REDPIXEL.PL/Shutterstock.com; Yuganov Konstantin/Shutterstock.com; Rob Marmion/Shutterstock.com

**Tip**

Some SmartArt layouts include shapes with a Pictures button. You can click that button to insert a picture in the shape so that it fills the shape.

3. Point to **Crop to Shape** to open a gallery of shapes, and then in the second row under Basic Shapes, click the **Cross** shape. The photo is cropped to a cross shape. Notice that the rectangular selection border of the original photo is still showing.

4. In the Size group, click the **Crop** button. You can now see the cropped portions of the original, rectangle photo that are shaded gray.

5. Click a blank area of the slide. The picture is no longer selected, and the Home tab is the active tab on the ribbon.

If you want to change how a picture is cropped, you can adjust the crop by selecting the picture and clicking the Crop button again. The cropped portion of the picture will be visible, and you can move the picture inside the crop marks or drag the crop handles to change how the picture is cropped. To change the crop so that the entire picture appears in the shape at its original aspect ratio, click the Fit command on the Crop menu. To change it back so that the picture fills the shape again, click the Fill command on the Crop menu.

# Resizing and Moving Objects

You can resize and move any object to best fit the space available on a slide. One way to resize an object is to drag a sizing handle. **Sizing handles** are small circles at the corners, and often the edges, of a selected object. When you use this method, you can adjust the size of the object so that it best fits the space visually. If you need to size an object to exact dimensions, you can modify the measurements in the Size group on the Format tab that appears when you select the object.

The **aspect ratio** of an object is the proportional relationship between an object's height and width. Pictures and other objects that cause the Picture Format tab to appear when you select them have their aspect ratios locked. This means that if you resize the object by dragging a corner sizing handle or by changing the measurement in either the Height or the Width box in the Size group on the Picture Format tab, both the height and the width of the object will change by the same proportions. However, if you drag one of the sizing handles on the side of the object, you will override the locked aspect ratio setting and resize the object only in the direction you drag. Generally, you do not want to do this with photos because the images will become distorted.

If you want to reposition an object on a slide, you drag it. If you need to move a selected object just a very small distance on the slide, you can press one of the ARROW keys to nudge it in the direction of the arrow. To move it in even smaller increments, press and hold CTRL while you press an ARROW key. When you drag an object on a slide, **smart guides**, dashed red lines, appear as you drag to indicate the center and the edges of the object, other objects, and the slide itself. Smart guides can help you position objects so that they are aligned and spaced evenly.

You need to resize and move the photos you inserted so the slides are more attractive.

### To move and resize the photos on Slides 2, 3, and 6:

1. Display Slide 2 ("About Us"), click the photo, and then position the pointer on the top-middle sizing handle so that the pointer changes to the double-headed vertical pointer ↕.

2. Press and hold the mouse button so that the pointer changes to the thin cross pointer ┼, drag the top-middle sizing handle up approximately two inches, and then release the mouse button. The photo is two inches taller, but the image is distorted. You can undo the change you made.

3. On the Quick Access Toolbar, click the **Undo** button ↺. The photo returns to its original size. You need to resize the photo by dragging a corner sizing handle to maintain the aspect ratio.

4. Click the **Picture Format** tab if necessary, and then note the measurements in the Height and Width boxes in the Size group. The photo is 2.02 inches high and 4.72 inches wide.

5. Position the pointer on the top-left corner sizing handle so that it changes to the double-headed diagonal pointer ⬉, press and hold the mouse button so that the pointer changes to the thin cross pointer ┼, and then drag the top-left sizing handle up. Even though you are dragging in only one direction, because you are dragging a corner sizing handle, both the width and height change proportionately to maintain the aspect ratio of the photo.

6. When the left edge of the photo is aligned with the gridline dots that are below the negative 0.5-inch mark on the horizontal ruler, release the mouse button. In the Height and Width boxes, the measurements changed to reflect the picture's new size.

7. If the measurement in the Shape Height box in the Size group is not 2.5, click in the Shape Height box to select the current measurement, type **2.5**, and then press **ENTER**.

8. Drag the photo so that the right edge of the photo aligns with the right edge of the slide, and the top of the photo is aligned with the top of the bulleted list, as shown in Figure 1–32.

| Figure 1–32 | Repositioning the photo on Slide 2 using smart guides and gridlines |
|---|---|

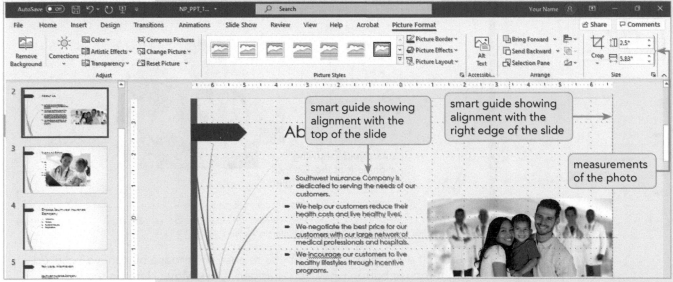

Rob Marmion/Shutterstock.com; Yuganov Konstantin/Shutterstock.com

**Trouble?** If the smart guides do not appear, click the View tab, and then in the Show group, click the Dialog Box Launcher to open the Grid and Guides dialog box. Click the "Display smart guides when shapes are aligned" check box to select it.

9. Release the mouse button. The photo is in its new location.

10. Display Slide 3 ("Types of Plans"), click the photo to select it, and then click the **Picture Format** tab if necessary.

11. In the Size group, click in the **Shape Height** box to select the current measurement, type **4**, and then press **ENTER**. The measurement in the Shape Width box in the Size group changes proportionately to maintain the aspect ratio, and the new measurements are applied to the photo.

12. Drag the photo down and to the right until a horizontal smart guide appears indicating that the top of the photo is about one-eighth of an inch above the top of the bulleted list and aligned with the gridline dots at the $1\frac{3}{8}$-inch mark on the vertical ruler, and a vertical smart guide appears showing that the left edge of the photo aligns with the center of the slide and with the gridline at the 0-inch mark on the horizontal ruler, as shown in Figure 1–33.

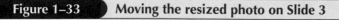

**Figure 1–33** **Moving the resized photo on Slide 3**

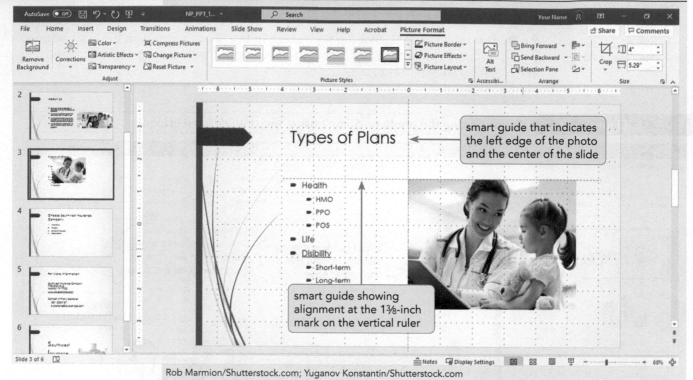

Rob Marmion/Shutterstock.com; Yuganov Konstantin/Shutterstock.com

**Trouble?** If a menu appears after you release the mouse button, you clicked the right mouse button when you dragged. Click Move Here on the menu, and then check to make sure the photo is positioned as described in Step 12.

**13.** When the photo is aligned as shown in Figure 1–33, release the mouse button.

**14.** Display Slide 6 (the last slide), and then position the photo so that the top of the photo aligns with the smart guide that indicates the middle of the title text box and the right edge aligns with the smart guide that indicates the right edge of the title text box.

Text boxes, like other objects that cause the Shape Format tab to appear when selected, do not have their aspect ratios locked. This means that when you resize a text box by dragging a corner sizing handle or changing one measurement in the Shape Height box or the Shape Width box in the Size group, the other dimension does not change.

Like any other object on a slide, you can reposition text boxes. To do this, you must position the pointer on the text box border, anywhere except on a sizing handle, to drag it to its new location.

To improve the appearance of Slide 6, you will resize the text box containing the unnumbered list so that it vertically fills the slide.

## To resize the text box on Slide 6:

1. On Slide 6 (the last slide), click the unnumbered list to display the text box border.

2. Position the pointer on the top-middle sizing handle so that it changes to the double-headed vertical pointer ↕, and then drag the sizing handle up until the top edge of the text box aligns with the top edge of the title text placeholder.

3. Drag the right-middle sizing handle to the left so that the right border of the text box is aligned with the negative 1.5-inch mark on the ruler. Next, you will shift the text box a little to the right.

4. Position the pointer on top of the border of the text box so that it changes to the move pointer ⬩, and then drag the text box to the right so that the right border of the text box aligns with the smart guide that indicates the center of the slide. Even though the title text placeholder will not appear during a slide show, you will delete it to see how the final slide will look.

5. Click the border of the title text placeholder, and then press **DELETE**. See Figure 1–34.

| Figure 1–34 | Slide 6 with resized text box |

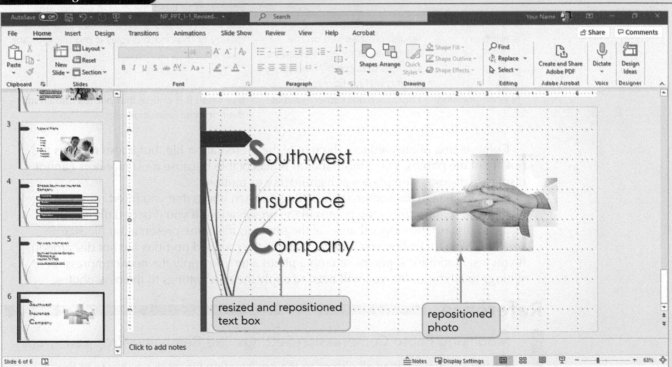

REDPIXEL.PL/Shutterstock.com; Yuganov Konstantin/Shutterstock.com; Rob Marmion/Shutterstock.com

6. Click the **View** tab, and then click the **Ruler** and **Gridlines** check boxes to deselect them. The ruler and the gridlines disappear.

7. Save the changes to the presentation.

# Compressing Pictures

When you save a presentation that contains pictures, you can choose to compress the pictures to make the size of the PowerPoint file smaller. See Figure 1–35 for a description of the compression options available.

**Figure 1–35**    **Photo compression settings**

| Compression Setting | Compression Value | When to Use |
|---|---|---|
| High fidelity | Photos are compressed very minimally, and only if they are larger than the slide. | Use when a presentation will be viewed on a high-definition (HD) display, when photograph quality is of the highest concern, and file size is not an issue. This is the default setting. |
| HD (330 ppi) | Photos are compressed to 330 pixels per inch. | Use when slides need to maintain the quality of the photograph when displayed on HD displays, but file size is of some concern. |
| Print (220 ppi) | Photos are compressed to 220 pixels per inch. | Use when slides need to maintain the quality of the photograph when printed. |
| Web (150 ppi) | Photos are compressed to 150 pixels per inch. | Use when the presentation will be viewed on a low-definition display. |
| E-mail (96 ppi) | Photos are compressed to 96 pixels per inch. | Use for presentations that need to be emailed or uploaded to a webpage or when it is important to keep the overall file size small. |
| Use default resolution | Photos are compressed to the resolution specified on the Advanced tab in the PowerPoint Options dialog box. (The default setting is High fidelity.) | Use when file size is not an issue, or when quality of the photo display is more important than file size. |
| No compression | Photos are not compressed at all. | Use when it is critical that photos remain at their original resolution. |

Compressing photos reduces the size of the presentation file, but it also reduces the quality of the photos. Often this trade-off is acceptable because most monitors cannot display high-resolution photos at high-fidelity resolution.

You can change the compression setting for each photo that you insert, or you can change the settings for all the photos in the presentation. If you cropped photos, you also can discard the cropped areas of the photo to make the presentation file size smaller. (Note that when you crop to a shape, the cropped portions are not discarded.) If you insert additional photos or crop a photo after you apply the new compression settings to all the slides, you will need to apply the new settings to the new photos.

## Reference

### Modifying Photo Compression Settings and Removing Cropped Areas

- After you have added all photos to the presentation file, click any photo in the presentation to select it.
- Click the Picture Format tab. In the Adjust group, click the Compress Pictures button.
- In the Compress Pictures dialog box, click the option button next to the resolution you want to use.
- To apply the new compression settings to all the photos in the presentation, click the Apply only to this picture check box to deselect it.
- To keep cropped areas of photos, click the Delete cropped areas of pictures check box to deselect it.
- Click OK.

You will adjust the compression settings to make the file size of the presentation as small as possible so that Anthony can easily send it or post it for others without worrying about file size limitations on the receiving server.

**To modify photo compression settings and remove cropped areas from photos:**

▶ **1.** On Slide 6 (the last slide), click the photo, and then click the **Picture Format** tab, if necessary.

▶ **2.** In the Adjust group, click the **Compress Pictures** button. The Compress Pictures dialog box opens. See Figure 1–36. Under Resolution, the Use default resolution option button is selected. (If an option in this dialog box is gray and is not available for you to select, the photo is a lower resolution than that option.)

| Figure 1–36 | Compress Pictures dialog box |

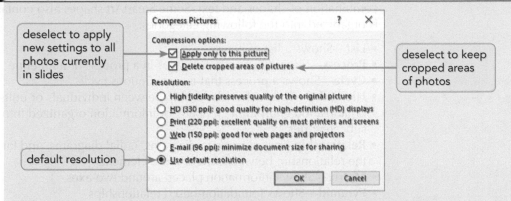

deselect to apply new settings to all photos currently in slides

deselect to keep cropped areas of photos

default resolution

▶ **3.** Click the **E-mail (96 ppi)** option button. This setting compresses the photos to the smallest size available. At the top of the dialog box under Compression options, the Apply only to this picture check box is selected. You want the settings applied to all the photos in the file.

▶ **4.** Click the **Apply only to this picture** check box to deselect it. The Delete cropped areas of pictures check box is also selected. You want the presentation file size to be as small as possible, so you'll leave this option selected.

   **Trouble?** If the Delete cropped areas of pictures check box is not selected, click it.

▶ **5.** Click **OK**.

   The dialog box closes and the compression settings are applied to all the photos in the presentation. You can confirm that the cropped areas of photos were removed by examining the photo on Slide 3. (The photo on Slide 6 was cropped to a shape, so the cropped areas on it were not removed, in case you later change to a different shape cropping.)

▶ **6.** Display Slide 3 ("Types of Plans"), click the photo, and then click the **Picture Format** tab, if necessary.

▶ **7.** In the Size group, click the **Crop** button. The Crop handles appear around the photo, but the portions of the photo that you cropped out no longer appear.

▶ **8.** Click the **Crop** button again to deselect it, and then save the changes to the presentation.

Be sure you deselect the Apply only to this picture check box and be sure you are satisfied with the way you cropped the photo on Slide 3 before you click OK to close the dialog box.

## Insight

### Changing the Default Compression Settings for Pictures

In PowerPoint, the default compression setting for pictures is High fidelity. This means that High fidelity compression is automatically applied to pictures when the file is saved. You can change this setting if you want. To change the settings, click the File tab to open Backstage view, click Options in the navigation pane to open the PowerPoint Options dialog box, click Advanced in the navigation pane, and then locate the Image Size and Quality section. To choose a different compression setting, click the Default resolution arrow, and then select a setting in the list. To prevent pictures from being compressed at all, click the Do not compress images in file check box. Note that these changes affect only the current presentation.

# Converting a List to a SmartArt Graphic

A **SmartArt graphic** is a diagram that shows information or ideas visually using a combination of shapes and text. Some SmartArt shapes also contain pictures. SmartArt is organized into the following categories:

- **List**—Shows a list of items
- **Process**—Shows a sequence of steps in a process or a timeline
- **Cycle**—Shows a process that is a continuous cycle
- **Hierarchy**—Shows the relationship between individuals or units, such as an organization chart for a company or information organized into categories and subcategories
- **Relationship** (including Venn diagrams, radial diagrams, and target diagrams)—Shows the relationship between two or more elements
- **Matrix**—Shows information placed around two axes
- **Pyramid**—Shows foundation-based relationships
- **Picture**—Provides a location for a picture or pictures that you insert

When you create a SmartArt graphic, you need to choose a SmartArt layout. In SmartArt, a **layout** is the shapes and arrangement of the shapes in the SmartArt graphic. Once you create a SmartArt graphic, you can easily change the layout to another one if you want.

A quick way to create a SmartArt graphic is to convert an existing list. There are two ways to do this. First, you can try displaying the Design Ideas pane. When the Design Ideas pane shows options for a slide that contains a list, some of the layouts include the list transformed into a SmartArt graphic. The other way you can create a SmartArt graphic from a list is to click the Convert to SmartArt Graphic button in the Paragraph group on the Home tab.

When you change a list to SmartArt, each first-level item in the list is converted to a shape in the SmartArt. If the list contains subitems, you might need to experiment with different layouts to find one that best suits the information in your list.

## Reference

### Converting a List into SmartArt

- Display the slide containing the list you want to convert to SmartArt.
- If the Design Ideas pane does not open, click the Design tab on the ribbon, and then in the Designer group, click the Design Ideas button.
- In the Design Ideas pane, select the SmartArt and slide layout that you want to use.

*or*

- Click anywhere in the list that you want to convert.
- In the Paragraph group on the Home tab, click the Convert to SmartArt button, and then click More SmartArt Graphics.
- In the Choose a SmartArt Graphic dialog box, select the desired SmartArt category in the list on the left.
- In the center pane, click the SmartArt you want to use.
- Click OK.

Anthony wants you to change the numbered list on Slide 4 into a SmartArt diagram.

### To convert the list on Slide 4 into SmartArt:

1. Display Slide 4 ("Choose Southwest Insurance Company").

2. If the Design Ideas pane does not open, click the **Design** tab on the ribbon, and then, in the Designer group, click the **Design Ideas** button. The Design Ideas pane opens on the right. Your screen will look similar to the one shown in Figure 1–37.

**Figure 1–37**     Design Ideas pane with suggestions for the list on Slide 4

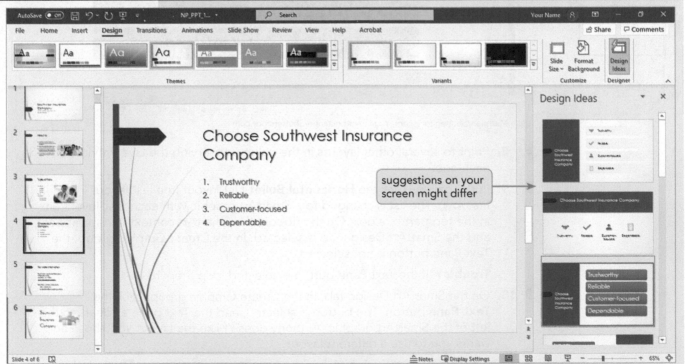

Rob Marmion/Shutterstock.com; Yuganov Konstantin/Shutterstock.com; REDPIXEL.PL/Shutterstock.com

3. In the Design Ideas pane, click several of the thumbnails to see the effect on the slide.

4.  After you are finished exploring the layouts in the Design Ideas pane, click the **Undo** button 🔄 on the Quick Access Toolbar. The slide resets to its original layout.

5.  Close the Design Ideas pane, and then on the slide, click anywhere in the list.

6.  On the ribbon, click the **Home** tab, and then in the Paragraph group, click the **Convert to SmartArt Graphic** button. A gallery opens listing SmartArt layouts.

7.  Point to the first layout. The ScreenTip identifies this layout as the Vertical Bullet List layout, and Live Preview shows you what the list will look like with that layout applied. See Figure 1–38.

**Figure 1–38      Live Preview of the Vertical Bullet List SmartArt layout**

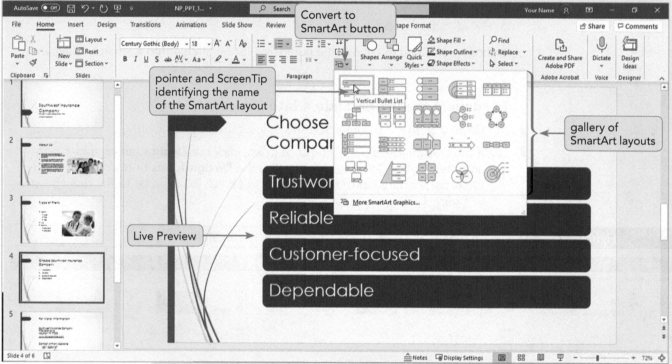

Rob Marmion/Shutterstock.com; Yuganov Konstantin/Shutterstock.com

8.  Point to several other layouts in the gallery, observing the Live Preview of each one.

9.  In the gallery, click the **Horizontal Bullet List** layout (the last layout in the first row). The list is changed to a SmartArt graphic with each first-level item in the top part of a box. On the ribbon, the SmartArt contextual tabs appear, and the SmartArt Design tab is selected. In the Create Graphic group, the Text Pane button is not selected.

    **Trouble?** If the Text Pane button is selected, skip Step 10.

10. On the SmartArt Design tab, in the Create Graphic group, click the **Text Pane** button. The button is selected, and the Text pane appears to the left of the SmartArt graphic. Anthony doesn't like the layout you chose and wants you to use a different layout.

11. On the SmartArt Design tab, in the Layouts group, click the **More** button ⤓. A gallery of SmartArt layouts appears.

12. At the bottom of the gallery, click **More Layouts**. The Choose a SmartArt Graphic dialog box opens. See Figure 1–39. You can click a category in the left pane to filter the middle pane to show only the layouts in that category.

**Figure 1–39**    **Choose a SmartArt Graphic dialog box**

click a category to filter the list on the right to display only that type of layout

scroll to see all the SmartArt layouts

preview, name, and description of selected layout

selected layout

**Horizontal Bullet List**

Use to show non-sequential or grouped lists of information. Works well with large amounts of text. All text has the same level of emphasis, and direction is not implied.

**13.** In the left pane, click **List**, and then in the middle pane, click the **Vertical Box List** layout, using the ScreenTips to identify it. The right pane changes to show a description of that layout.

**14.** Click **OK**. The dialog box closes, and each of the first-level items in the list appears in the colored shapes in the diagram. The items also appear as a bulleted list in the Text pane. See Figure 1–40.

**Figure 1–40**    **SmartArt graphic with the Vertical Box List layout**

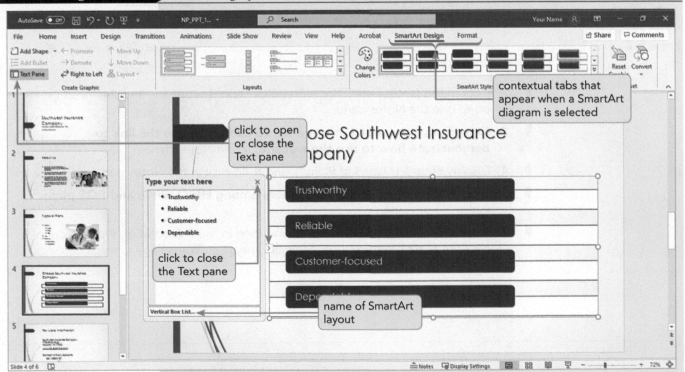

Rob Marmion/Shutterstock.com; Yuganov Konstantin/Shutterstock.com

**15.** To the right of the text pane, click the **Collapse text pane** button. The text pane closes.

# Adding Speaker Notes

**Speaker notes**, or simply **notes**, are information you add about slide content to help you remember to bring up specific points during the presentation. Speaker notes should not contain all the information you plan to say during your presentation, but they can be a useful tool for reminding you about facts and details related to the content on specific slides.

You add notes in the **Notes pane**, which is an area at the bottom of the window that you can use to type speaker notes. The notes are not visible when you present a slide show.

You also can switch to **Notes Page view**, in which a reduced image of the slide appears in the top half of the window and the notes for that slide appear in the bottom half. Notes are not visible to the audience during a slide show.

### To add notes to Slides 3 and 5:

▶ 1. Display Slide 5 ("For More Information"), and then, on the status bar, click the **Notes** button. The Notes pane appears below Slide 5 with "Click to add notes" as placeholder text. See Figure 1–41.

| **Figure 1–41** | Notes pane below Slide 5 |
| --- | --- |

REDPIXEL.PL/Shutterstock.com

▶ 2. Click in the Notes pane. The placeholder text disappears, and the insertion point is in the Notes pane.

▶ 3. Type **Hand out contact information to audience. Use the link to demonstrate how to use the website.** in the Notes pane.

▶ 4. Display Slide 3 ("Types of Plans"), and then click in the Notes pane.

▶ 5. Type **Briefly describe the differences among HMO, PPO, and POS plans.** in the Notes pane.

▶ 6. Click the **View** tab on the ribbon, and then in the Presentation Views group, click the **Notes Page** button. Slide 3 appears in Notes Page view. See Figure 1–42.

**Figure 1-42** Slide 3 in Notes Page view

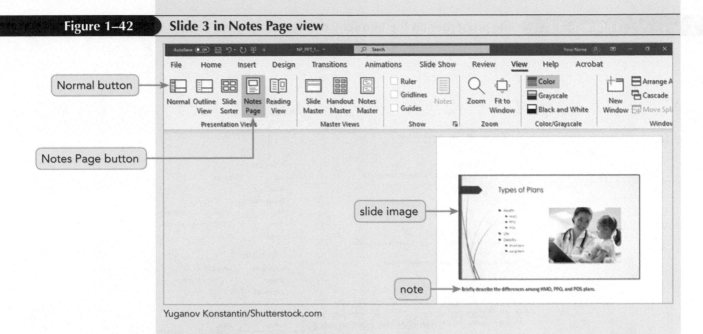

Yuganov Konstantin/Shutterstock.com

**Tip**

Use the Zoom in button on the status bar to magnify the text to make it easier to edit the note.

7. In the note, click after the period at the end of the sentence, press **SPACEBAR**, and then type **Be sure to describe the cost differences in premiums.** (including the period).

8. On the View tab, in the Presentation Views group, click the **Normal** button to return to Normal view. The Notes pane stays open until you close it again.

9. On the status bar, click the **Notes** button to close the Notes pane, and then save the changes to the presentation.

# Editing Common File Properties

File **properties** are identifying information—characteristics—about a file that is saved along with the file that help others understand, identify, and locate the file. Common properties are the title, the author's name, and the date the file was created. You can use file properties to organize presentations or to search for files that have specific properties. To view or modify properties, you need to display the Info screen in Backstage view.

Anthony wants you to modify the Author property by adding yourself as an author and he wants you to add the Company property.

### To add common file properties:

1. On the ribbon, click the **File** tab, and then click **Info** in the navigation pane. The Info screen in Backstage view appears. The document properties appear on the right side of the screen. See Figure 1-43. Because Anthony created the original document, his name is listed as the Author property. Because you saved the file after making changes, your name (or the user name on your computer) appears in the Last Modified By box. You'll add yourself as an author.

**Figure 1–43**    File properties on the Info screen in Backstage view

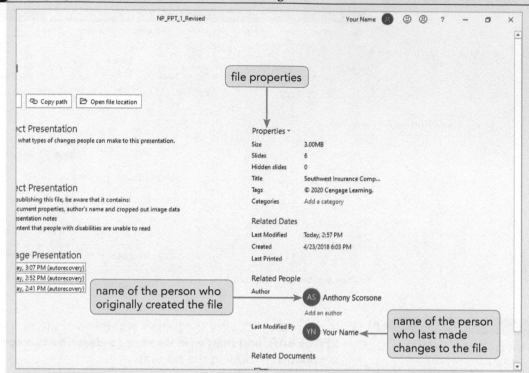

2. In the Related People section, click **Add an author**, type your name in the box that appears, and then click a blank area of the window. You and Anthony are now both listed as the Author property. Next, you need to add the Company property. The Company property does not appear in the list.

3. Scroll down, and then at the bottom of the Properties list, click **Show All Properties**. The Properties list expands to include all of the common document properties, including the Company property.

4. Next to Company, click **Specify the company**, type **Southwest Insurance Company**, and then click a blank area of the screen. You are finished adding properties to the file.

5. Scroll up if necessary, and at the top of the navigation pane, click the **Back** button ⊙ to return to Slide 3 in Normal view.

# Checking Spelling

You should always check the spelling and grammar in your presentation before you finalize it. To make this task easier, you can use PowerPoint's spelling checker. You can quickly tell if there are words on slides that are not in the built-in dictionary by looking at the Spelling button at the left end of the status bar. If there are no words flagged as possibly misspelled, the button is 🗐; if words are flagged, the button changes to 🗐. To indicate that a word might be misspelled, a wavy red line appears under it.

To correct misspelled words, you can right-click a flagged word to see a list of suggested spellings on the shortcut menu, or you can check the entire presentation to locate possible misspellings. To check the spelling of all the words in the presentation, you click the Spelling button in the Proofing group on the Review tab. This opens the Spelling pane to the right of the displayed slide and starts the spell check from the current slide. When a possible misspelled word is found, suggestions for the correct spelling appear. If you want to accept one of the suggested spellings, you can change only the selected instance of the word or all of the instances of the word in the presentation. If the word is spelled correctly, you can ignore this instance of that word or all the instances of that word in the presentation. The pane also lists synonyms for the selected correct spelling.

### To check the spelling in the presentation:

1. Display Slide 2 ("About Us"), and then right-click the misspelled word **incourage** in the fourth bulleted item. A shortcut menu opens listing spelling options. See Figure 1–44.

**Figure 1–44**    **Shortcut menu for a misspelled word**

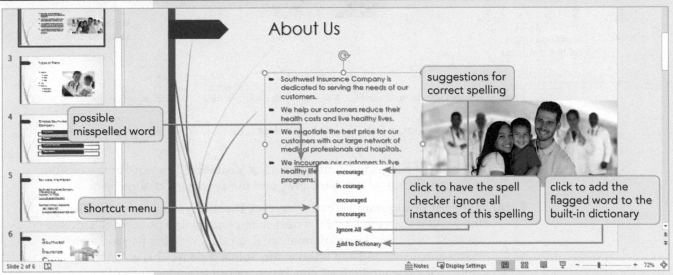

Rob Marmion/Shutterstock.com; Yuganov Konstantin/Shutterstock.com

**Trouble?** If the word "incourage" does not have a wavy red line under it, click the Review tab, and then in the Proofing group, click the Spelling button. The wavy red line should now appear. Right-click "incourage," continue with Step 2, and then do not do Step 3.

2. On the shortcut menu, click **encourage**. The menu closes, and the spelling is corrected.

3. Click the **Review** tab, and then in the Proofing group, click the **Spelling** button. The Spelling pane opens to the right of the displayed slide, and the next possible misspelled word, "Disibility" on Slide 3 ("Types of Plans"), is selected on the slide and in the Spelling pane. See Figure 1–45. In the Spelling pane, the first suggested correct spelling is selected. The selected correct spelling also appears at the bottom of the pane, with synonyms for the word listed below it and a speaker icon next to it.

**Tip**

If words are flagged with blue underlines, right-click the underlined words to see suggestions for fixing the possible grammatical error.

**Figure 1–45** Spelling pane displaying a misspelled word

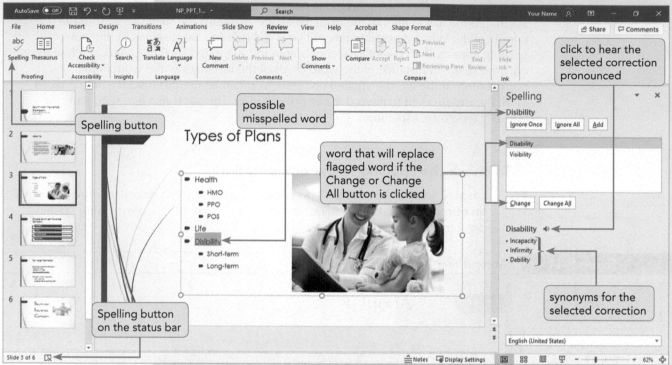

Yuganov Konstantin/Shutterstock.com; Rob Marmion/Shutterstock.com; REDPIXEL.PL/Shutterstock.com

4. In the Spelling pane, click the **speaker** icon ◀)). A voice says the word "Disability."

5. In the list of suggested corrections, click **Visibility**. The word at the bottom of the pane changes to "Visibility," and the synonyms change also.

6. In the list of suggested corrections, click **Disability**, and then click **Change**. The word is corrected, and the next slide containing a possible misspelled word, Slide 5 ("For More Information"), appears with the flagged word, "Scorsone," selected and listed in the Spelling pane. This is Anthony's last name, so you want the spell checker to ignore every instance of this word, not just this instance.

7. In the pane, click **Ignore All**. Because that was the last flagged word in the presentation, the Spelling pane closes, and a dialog box opens telling you that the spell check is complete.

   **Trouble?** If the spell checker finds any other misspelled words, correct them.

8. Click **OK**. The dialog box closes.

9. Display Slide 1 (the title slide). Anthony's last name no longer has a wavy red line under it because you clicked Ignore All when it was flagged as a possible misspelled word on Slide 5.

10. Save the changes to the presentation.

# Running a Slide Show

After you have created and proofed your presentation, you should view it as a slide show to see how it will appear to your audience. You can do this in Slide Show view or in Presenter view.

You can use Slide Show view if your computer has only one monitor and you don't have access to a screen projector. If you have connected your computer to a second monitor or a screen projector, Slide Show view is the way an audience will see your slides. Refer to the Session 1.2 Visual Overview for more information about Slide Show and Presenter views.

In Slide Show and Presenter views, you can move from one slide to another in several ways. Figure 1–46 describes the methods you can use to move from one slide to another during a slide show.

| Figure 1–46 | Methods of moving from one slide to another during a slide show |

| Desired Result | Method |
| --- | --- |
| To display the next slide | • Press SPACEBAR.<br>• Press ENTER.<br>• Press RIGHT ARROW.<br>• Press DOWN ARROW.<br>• Press PGDN.<br>• Press N.<br>• Click the slide.<br>• In Slide Show view, move the pointer to display the buttons in the lower-left corner of the slide, and then click the Advance to the next animation or slide button ⊙.<br>• In Presenter view, click the Advance to the next animation or slide button ⊙.<br>• Right-click the slide, and then on the shortcut menu, click Next. |
| To display the previous slide | • Press BACKSPACE.<br>• Press LEFT ARROW.<br>• Press UP ARROW.<br>• Press PGUP.<br>• Press P.<br>• In Slide Show view, move the pointer to display the buttons in the lower-left corner of the slide, and then click the Return to the previous animation or slide button ◁.<br>• In Presenter view, click the Return to the previous animation or slide button ◁.<br>• Right-click the slide, and then on the shortcut menu, click Previous. |
| To display a specific slide | • In Slide Show view, move the pointer to display the buttons in the lower-left corner of the slide, click the See all slides button ⊞, and then click the thumbnail of the slide you want to display.<br>• In Presenter view, click the See all slides button ▦, and then click the thumbnail of the slide you want to display.<br>• Type the number of the slide you want to display, and then press ENTER.<br>• Right-click the slide, and then on the shortcut menu, click See all slides. |
| To display the first slide | Press HOME. |
| To display the last slide | Press END. |
| To end the slide show | Press ESC.<br>Right-click the slide, and then on the shortcut menu, click End Show. |

Anthony asks you to review the slide show in Slide Show view to make sure the slides look professional.

**Tip**

To start the slide show from the current slide, click the Slide Show button on the status bar.

**To use Slide Show view to view the final presentation:**

1. On the Quick Access Toolbar, click the **Start From Beginning** button ⊞. Slide 1 appears on the screen in Slide Show view. Now you need to advance the slide show.

2. Press **SPACEBAR**. Slide 2 ("About Us") appears on the screen.

3. Click the mouse button. The next slide, Slide 3 ("Types of Plans"), appears on the screen.

4. Press **BACKSPACE**. The previous slide, Slide 2, appears again.

5. Move the mouse to display the buttons in the lower-left corner of the slide, and then click the **See all slides** button ⊙. All of the slides in the file are displayed as thumbnails on the screen, similar to Slide Sorter view.

6. Click the **Slide 5** thumbnail. Slide 5 ("For More Information") appears on the screen.

7. Move the mouse to display the pointer, and then position the pointer on the website address **www.sic.example.com**. The pointer changes to the pointing finger pointer 👆 to indicate that this is a link, and the ScreenTip that appears shows the full website address including "http://". If this were a real website, you could click the link to open your web browser and display the website to your audience. Because you moved the pointer, the faint row of buttons appears in the lower-left corner. See Figure 1–47.

| **Figure 1–47** | **Link and row of buttons in Slide Show view** |
| --- | --- |

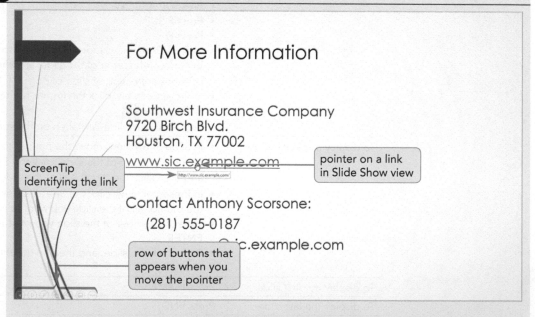

For More Information

Southwest Insurance Company
9720 Birch Blvd.
Houston, TX 77002

www.sic.example.com

ScreenTip identifying the link → http://www.sic.example.com/

pointer on a link in Slide Show view

Contact Anthony Scorsone:
(281) 555-0187
          @sic.example.com

row of buttons that appears when you move the pointer

8. Move the pointer again, if necessary, to display the buttons that appear in the lower-left corner of the screen, and then click the **Return to the previous animation or slide** button ◁ twice to redisplay Slide 3 ("Types of Plans").

   **Trouble?** If you can't see the buttons at the bottom of the screen, move the pointer to the lower-left corner so it is on top of the first button to darken that button, and then move the pointer to the right to see the rest of the buttons.

**9.** Display the buttons at the bottom of the screen again, and then click the **Zoom into the slide** button 🔍. The pointer changes to the zoom in pointer ⊕, and three-quarters of the slide is darkened. See Figure 1–48.

**Figure 1–48**    **Zoom feature activated in Slide Show view**

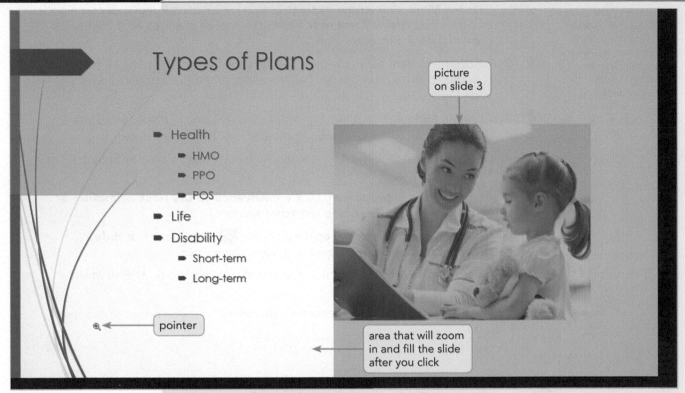

Yuganov Konstantin/Shutterstock.com

**10.** Move the pointer on top of the picture so that the top part of the picture does not appear darkened, and then click the picture. The slide zooms in so that the part of the slide inside the bright rectangle fills the screen, and the pointer changes to the hand pointer 🖐.

**11.** Press and hold the mouse button to change the pointer to the closed fist pointer ✊, and then drag to the right to pull another part of the zoomed in slide into view.

**12.** Press **ESC** to zoom back out to see the whole slide.

Presenter view provides additional tools for running a slide show. In addition to seeing the current slide, you can also see the next slide, speaker notes, and a timer showing you how long the slide show has been running. Refer to the Session 1.2 Visual Overview for more information about Presenter view. Because of the additional tools available in Presenter view, you should consider using it if your computer is connected to a second monitor or projector.

If your computer is connected to a projector or second monitor, and you start a slide show in Slide Show view, Presenter view starts on the computer and Slide Show view appears on the second monitor or projection screen. If, for some reason, you don't want to use Presenter view in that circumstance, you can switch to Slide Show view. If you want to practice using Presenter view when your computer is not connected to a second monitor or projector, you can switch to Presenter view from Slide Show view.

Anthony wants you to switch to Presenter view and familiarize yourself with the tools available there.

## To use Presenter view to review the slide show:

**Tip**

To display the slide show in Reading view, click the Reading view button on the status bar. To advance through the slide show in Reading view, use the same commands as in Slide Show or Presenter view or click the Next and Previous buttons on the status bar.

1. Move the pointer to display the buttons in the lower-left corner of the screen, click the **More slide show options** button to open a menu of commands, and then click **Show Presenter View**. The screen changes to show the presentation in Presenter view.

2. Below the current slide, click the **See all slides** button. The screen changes to show thumbnails of all the slides in the presentation, similar to Slide Sorter view.

3. Click the **Slide 4** thumbnail. Presenter view reappears, displaying Slide 4 ("Choose Southwest Insurance Company") as the current slide.

4. Click anywhere on Slide 4. The slide show advances to display Slide 5 ("For More Information").

5. At the bottom of the screen, click the **Advance to the next animation or slide** button. Slide 6 (the last slide) appears.

6. Click the **More slide show options** button, and then click **Hide Presenter View**. Slide 6 appears in Slide Show view.

7. Press **SPACEBAR**. A black slide appears displaying the text "End of slide show, click to exit."

8. Press **SPACEBAR** again. Presenter view closes, and you return to Normal view.

## Proskills

### Decision Making: Displaying a Blank Slide During a Presentation

Sometimes during a presentation, the audience has questions about the material and you want to pause the slide show to respond. Or you might want the audience to focus its attention on you instead of on the visuals on the screen. In these cases, you can display a black or white blank slide. Some presenters plan to use blank slides and insert them at specific points during their slide shows. Planning to use a blank slide can help you keep your presentation focused. It can also remind you that the purpose of the PowerPoint slides is to provide visual aids to enhance your presentation; the slides themselves are not the presentation.

If you did not create blank slides in your presentation file, but during your presentation you feel you need to display a blank slide, you can easily do this in Slide Show or Presenter view. To display a blank black slide, press B. To display a blank white slide, press W. You can also click the More slide show options button in Slide Show view, click Screen, and then Black Screen or White Screen. In Presenter view, you can click the More slide show options button, point to Screen, and then click Black Screen or White Screen. Or you can right-click the screen, point to Screen on the menu, and then click Black Screen or White Screen. To remove the black or white slide and redisplay the slide that had been on the screen before you displayed the blank slide, press any key on the keyboard or click anywhere on the screen. In Presenter view, you can also click the Black or unblack slide show button to toggle a blank slide on or off.

# Printing a Presentation

Before you deliver your presentation, you might want to print it. PowerPoint provides several printing options. For example, you can print the slides in color, grayscale (white and shades of gray), or pure black and white, and you can print one, some, or all of the slides in several formats.

You use the Print screen in Backstage view to set print options such as specifying a printer and color options. First, you will add your name to the title slide.

### To add your name to the title slide and choose a printer and color options:

1. Display Slide 1, click after "Scorsone" in the subtitle, press **ENTER**, and then type your name.

2. Click the **File** tab to display Backstage view, and then click **Print** in the navigation pane. Backstage view changes to display the Print screen. The Print screen contains options for printing your presentation, and a preview of the first slide as it will print with the current options. See Figure 1–49.

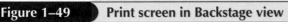

**Figure 1–49**    **Print screen in Backstage view**

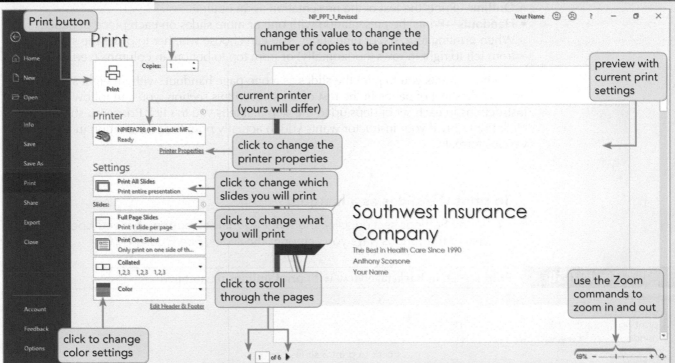

**Trouble?** If your screen does not match Figure 1–49, click the first button below Settings, click Print All Slides, click the second button below Settings, and then click Full Page Slides.

3. If you are connected to a network or to more than one printer, make sure the printer listed in the Printer box is the one you want to use; if it is not, click the **Printer** button, and then click the correct printer in the list.

4. Click the **Printer Properties** link to open the Properties dialog box for your printer. Usually, the default options are correct, but you can change any printer settings, such as print quality or the paper source, in this dialog box.

5. Click **Cancel** to close the Properties dialog box. Now you can choose whether to print the presentation in color, black and white, or grayscale. If you plan to print in black and white or grayscale, you should change this setting so that you can see what your slides will look like without color and to make sure they are legible.

6. Click the **Color** button, and then click **Grayscale**. The preview changes to grayscale.

7. At the bottom of the preview pane, click the **Next Page** button ▶ twice to display Slide 3 ("Types of Plans"). The slides are legible in grayscale.

8. If you will be printing in color, click the **Grayscale** button, and then click **Color**.

In the Settings section on the Print screen, you can click the Full Page Slides button to choose from among several choices for printing the presentation, as described below:

- **Full Page Slides**—Prints each slide full size on a separate piece of paper.
- **Notes Pages**—Prints each slide as a notes page.
- **Outline**—Prints the text of the presentation as an outline.
- **Handouts**—Prints the presentation with one or more slides on each piece of paper. When printing four, six, or nine slides, you can choose whether to order the slides from left to right in rows (horizontally) or from top to bottom in columns (vertically).

Anthony wants you to print the slides as a one-page handout, with all eight slides on a single sheet of paper. In the rest of the steps in this section, you can follow the instructions in each set of steps up to the step that tells you to click Print. You should click Print only if your instructor wants you to actually print the presentation in the various formats.

### To print the slides as a handout:

1. In the Settings section, click the **Full Page Slides** button. A menu opens listing the various ways you can print the slides. See Figure 1–50.

**Figure 1–50**     **Print screen in Backstage view with print options menu open**

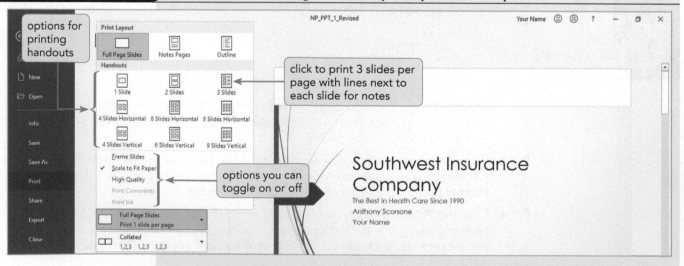

2. In the Handouts section, click **6 Slides Horizontal**. The preview changes to show all six slides in the preview pane, arranged in order horizontally in three rows from left to right. The current date appears in the top-right corner, and a page number appears in the bottom-right corner.

3. At the top of the Print section, click **Print**. Backstage view closes and the handout prints.

Next, Anthony wants you to print the title slide as a full-page slide so that he can use it as a cover page for his handouts.

### To print the title slide as a full-page slide:

1. Click the **File** tab, and then click **Print** in the navigation pane. The Print screen appears in Backstage view. The preview still shows all six slides on one page. "6 Slides Horizontal" appears on the second button in the Settings section because that was the last printing option you chose.

2. In the Settings section, click **6 Slides Horizontal**, and then click **Full Page Slides**. Slide 1 (the title slide) appears as the preview. Below the preview of Slide 1, it indicates that you are viewing Slide 1 of six slides to print.

3. In the Settings section, click the **Print All Slides** button. Note on the menu that opens that you can print all the slides, selected slides, the current slide, or a custom range. You want to print just the title slide as a full-page slide.

4. Click **Print Current Slide**. Slide 1 appears in the preview pane, and at the bottom, it now indicates that you will print only one slide.

5. Click the **Print** button. Backstage view closes and Slide 1 prints.

Recall that you created speaker notes on Slides 3 and 5. Anthony would like you to print these slides as notes pages.

### To print the nonsequential slides containing speaker notes:

1. Open the Print screen in Backstage view again, and then click the **Full Page Slides** button. The menu opens.

2. In the Print Layout section of the menu, click **Notes Pages**. The menu closes, and the preview displays Slide 1 as a Notes Page.

3. In the Settings section, click in the **Slides** box, type **3,5** and then click a blank area of the Print screen.

4. Scroll through the preview to confirm that Slides 3 ("Types of Plans") and 5 ("For More Information") will print, and then click **Print**. Backstage view closes, and Slides 3 and 5 print as notes pages.

Finally, Anthony would like you to print the outline of the presentation. Remember, Slide 6 is designed to be a visual that Anthony can leave displayed at the end of the presentation, so you don't need to include it in the outline.

### To print Slides 1 through 5 as an outline:

▶ **1.** Open the Print screen in Backstage view, click the **Notes Pages** button, and then in the Print Layout section, click **Outline**. The text on Slides 3 and 6 appears as an outline in the preview pane.

▶ **2.** Click in the **Slides** box, type **1-5**, and then click a blank area of the Print screen. See Figure 1–51.

**Figure 1–51**    Print screen in Backstage view with Slides 1–5 previewed as an outline

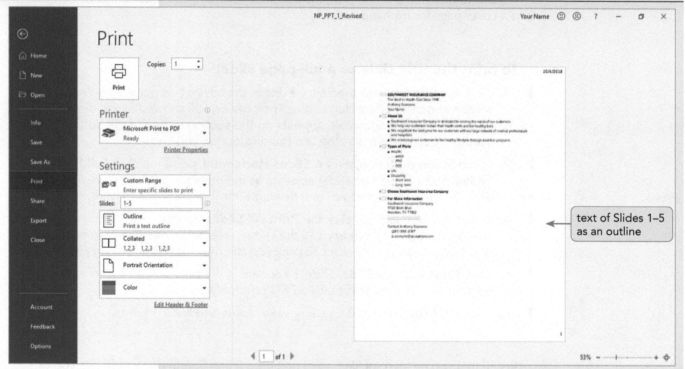

▶ **3.** At the top of the Print section, click the **Print** button. Backstage view closes, and the text of Slides 1–5 prints.

# Closing PowerPoint

When you are finished working with your presentation, you can close PowerPoint. If you only have one presentation open, you click the Close button ☒ in the upper-right corner of the program window. If you have more than one presentation open, clicking this button will close only the current presentation; to close PowerPoint, you need to click the Close button in each of the open presentation's windows.

**To close PowerPoint:**

▶ **1.** In the upper-right corner of the program window, click the **Close** button ☒. A dialog box opens, asking if you want to save your changes. This is because you did not save the file after you added your name to the title slide.

▶ **2.** sam⬆ In the dialog box, click **Save**. The dialog box closes, the changes are saved, and PowerPoint closes.

**Trouble?** If any other PowerPoint presentations are still open, click the Close button ☒ on each open presentation's program window until no more presentations are open to exit PowerPoint.

In this session, you opened an existing presentation and saved it with a new name, changed the theme, added and cropped photos and adjusted the photo compression, and resized and moved objects. You have also added speaker notes and checked the spelling. Finally, you printed the presentation in several forms and exited PowerPoint. Your work will help Anthony give an effective presentation to potential customers of Southwest Insurance Company.

# Review

### Session 1.2 Quick Check

1. What is alt text?
2. Explain what happens when you crop photos.
3. Describe sizing handles.
4. How do you use smart guides?
5. Why is it important to maintain the aspect ratio of photos?
6. How do you convert a list to a SmartArt diagram without using the Design Ideas pane?
7. What is the difference between Slide Show view and Presenter view?
8. List the four formats for printing a presentation.

# Practice

## Review Assignments

Data Files needed for the Review Assignments: NP_PPT_1-2.pptx, Support_PPT_1_Anthony.jpg, Support_PPT_1_Meeting.jpg, Support_PPT_1_Standing.jpg, Support_PPT_1_Woman.jpg

Anthony Scorsone, a sales manager in the Houston office of Southwest Insurance Company, is preparing a presentation for the upcoming summer sales meeting. Because his team has sold so many new policies, he has been asked to give a presentation to the branch managers. He will focus on how they can create new business from their current customers by actively selling the new policy types the company sells. He asks you to begin creating the presentation. Complete the following steps:

1. Start PowerPoint and create a new, blank presentation. On the title slide, type **New Sales Leads** as the title, and then type your name as the subtitle. Save the presentation as **NP_PPT_1_Leads** to the drive and folder where you are storing your files.

2. Edit the slide title by typing **Developing** before "New" so that the title is now "Developing New Sales Leads."

3. Add a new Slide 2 with the Title and Content layout, type **Contact Your Existing Clients** as the slide title, and then in the content placeholder type the following:

   - **Offer new plans**
     - **Auto**
     - **Boat**
     - **Worker's Comp**
   - **Offer competitive package pricing**
   - **Emphasize your personal connection and service**
   - **Contact Anthony Scorsone**

4. Create a new Slide 3 with the Two Content layout, then create a new Slide 4 with the Two Content layout. On Slide 4, add **Recipe for Success** as the slide title, and then type the following as a numbered list in the left content placeholder:

   1. **Offer new products to existing clients**
   2. **Present to local organizations**
      1. **Chamber of Commerce**
      2. **Service organizations**
      3. **Professional organizations**
   3. **Reach out to self-insured with customized packages**

5. Create a new Slide 5 using the Title and Content layout, and then create a new Slide 6 with the Title and Content layout. On Slide 6, add **For More Information** as the slide title.

6. Use the Cut and Paste commands to move the last bulleted item on Slide 2 ("Contact Anthony Scorsone") to Slide 6 as the first bulleted item in the content placeholder.

7. On Slide 6, remove the bullet symbol from the text you pasted, and then add the following as the next two items in the unnumbered list:

   **Email: a.scorsone@sic.example.com**
   **Cell: (281) 555-0187**

8. Click after "Scorsone" in the first item in the list, and then create a new line below it without creating a new item in the list so that there is no extra space above the new line. Type **Sales Manager, Houston Office** on the new line.

9. Remove the link formatting from the email address.

10. Duplicate Slide 2 ("Contact Your Existing Clients"). On the new Slide 3, do the following:

    - Edit the title so it is **Introduce New Products**
    - Edit the first bulleted item so it is **New Products**
    - Delete the second and third first-level bulleted items

11. Delete the blank Slides 4 and 6.

12. Move Slide 3 ("Introduce New Products") so it becomes Slide 2.

13. Change the theme to Banded and choose the second variant.

14. Save your changes, and then close the presentation.

15. Open the file **NP_PPT_1-2.pptx**, located in the PowerPoint1 > Review folder included with your Data Files, add your name as the subtitle on the title slide, and then save it as **NP_PPT_1_ Updated** to the drive and folder where you are storing your files.

16. Change the theme colors to Orange Red. Change the theme fonts to Cambria.

17. Change the layout of Slide 3 ("Contact Your Existing Clients") to Two Content.

18. On Slide 3, insert the picture **Support_PPT_1_Woman.jpg**, located in the PowerPoint1 > Review folder. Add **Woman on the phone at a desk in an office.** as the alt text for this picture.

19. Open the Design Ideas pane if necessary, and then click several of the suggested layouts. When you are finished, close the pane, and then on the Quick Access Toolbar, click the Undo button to reset the slide, and then close the Design Ideas pane.

20. Resize the picture on Slide 3 while maintaining the aspect ratio so that the picture height is 4 inches. Reposition the picture so that its right edge aligns with the right edge of the slide and its top edge aligns with the top edge of the text box containing the list.

21. Change the layout of Slide 4 ("Create Custom Packages for Self-Employed") to Title and Content.

22. On Slide 4, insert the photo **Support_PPT_1_Standing.jpg**, located in the PowerPoint1 > Review folder. Add **Business people standing and chatting in a group, holding glasses of water, in an office setting.** as the alt text for this picture.

23. Resize the picture on Slide 4 while maintaining the aspect ratio so that the picture height is 4 inches. Reposition the picture so that its right edge aligns with the right edge of the slide and its bottom edge aligns with the bottom of the slide.

24. On Slide 5, insert the photo **Support_PPT_1_Meeting.jpg**, located in the PowerPoint1 > Review folder. Add **People in business casual attire at a conference table in an office setting listening to a man speak.** as the alt text for this picture.

25. Resize the picture on Slide 5 while maintaining the aspect ratio so that the picture height is 5 inches.

26. Display the rulers and the gridlines, and then crop 1 inch off the bottom of the picture on Slide 5. Resize the cropped part of the picture so that the head of the man standing is about one-eighth of an inch from the top of the picture. Then crop one-half inch off the right side of the picture.

27. Reposition the picture on Slide 5 so that its right edge aligns with the right edge of the slide, its top edge aligns with the gridline at the 1-inch mark on the vertical ruler, and its bottom edge aligns with the gridline at the negative 3-inch mark on the vertical ruler.

28. On Slide 5, change the width of the text box containing the bulleted list by dragging the sizing handle in the middle of the right border of the text box so that the right border aligns with the gridline at the negative 1-inch mark on the horizontal ruler. Then change the height of the text box by dragging the sizing handle in the middle of the top border down so that the top of the text box aligns with the top of the picture.

29. On Slide 6 ("Recipe for Success"), open the Design Ideas pane and click several of the suggested layouts. Then, on the Quick Access Toolbar, click the Undo button and close the Design Ideas pane.

30. On Slide 6, convert the numbered list to SmartArt using the Vertical Block List layout on the Convert to SmartArt menu.

31. On Slide 6, change the SmartArt layout to the Segmented Process layout.

32. On Slide 6, display the Notes pane, and then type **Some local organizations to consider are the Chamber of Commerce, service organizations, and professional organizations.** as a speaker note. When you are finished, close the Notes pane.

33. On Slide 7 ("For More Information"), increase the size of the text in the unnumbered list to 24 points. Then, in the first bulleted item, select the text "Anthony Scorsone." and format it as bold and 28 points.

34. On Slide 7, insert the picture **Support_PPT_1_Anthony.jpg**, and then **Portrait of Anthony Scorsone** as the alt text for this picture.

35. Crop the photo to the Oval shape. Click the Crop button, and then drag the bottom-middle crop handle up one inch. Reposition the picture so that the top of the picture aligns with the horizontal gridline at the 1-inch mark on the vertical ruler if necessary.

36. Hide the rulers and gridlines.

37. Compress all the photos in the slides to E-mail (96 ppi) and delete cropped areas of pictures.

38. Add your name as an author property, and add **Southwest Insurance Company** as the Company property.

39. Check the spelling in the presentation. Correct the spelling error on Slide 2 by selecting "Liability" as the correct spelling, and the error on Slide 3 by selecting "Emphasize" as the correct spelling. Ignore all instances of Anthony's last name. If you made any additional spelling errors, correct them as well. If your name on Slide 1 is flagged as misspelled, ignore this error. Save the changes to the presentation.

40. Review the slide show in Slide Show and Presenter views.

41. View the slides in grayscale, and then print the following in color or in grayscale depending on your printer: the title slide as a full-page-sized slide; Slides 2 through 7 as a handout on a single piece of paper with the slides in order horizontally; Slide 6 as a notes page; and Slides 2 through 5 and Slide 7 as an outline. Save and close the presentation and PowerPoint when you are finished.

# Apply

## Case Problem 1

**Data Files needed for this Case Problem: NP_PPT_1-3.pptx, Support_PPT_1_Application.jpg, Support_PPT_1_Building.jpg, Support_PPT_1_Key.jpg, Support_PPT_1_Sophia.jpg**

**Upper Coast Bank**  Upper Coast Bank has branches all over the United States. Sophia Baker, the Vice President of Residential Lending at the Hartford, Connecticut branch, hired you as her executive assistant. Sophia wants to create a simple presentation that will help her explain some of the details about applying for a mortgage to first-time home buyers. She asks you to help complete the slides. Complete the following steps:

1. Open the presentation named **NP_PPT_1-3.pptx**, located in the PowerPoint1 > Case1 folder included with your Data Files, and then save it as **NP_PPT_1_Mortgage** to the drive and folder where you are storing your files.

2. Insert a new slide with the Title Slide layout. Add **Mortgage Essentials** as the presentation title on the title slide. In the subtitle text placeholder, type your name. Move this slide so it is the first slide in the presentation.

3. Apply the Frame theme, and then apply the third theme variant.

4. Change the theme fonts to Garamond-TrebuchetMs.

5. On Slide 1 (the title slide), change the font size of the title text to 36 points. Then resize the title text box so it is 2.25 inches wide. If necessary, reposition the title text box so that the left edge of the text box is aligned with the left edge of the subtitle text box and so that there is the same amount of space between the top of the text box and the top slide edge as there is between the bottom of the subtitle text box and the bottom of the slide. Resize the subtitle text box so it is 3.3 inches wide, and then align its left edge with the left edge of the title text box.

6. On Slide 1, insert the picture **Support_PPT_1_Application.jpg**, located in the PowerPoint1 > Case1 folder. Add **Picture of a mortgage application form with a red "Approved" stamp on it and the wooden stamp next to it.** as the alt text.

7. On Slide 1, resize the photo, maintaining the aspect ratio, so that it is 5.84 inches high. Position the photo so that its middle aligns with the middle of the tan rectangle and its right edge aligns with the right edge of the slide.

8. On Slides 2 through 6, increase the size of the text in the bulleted list so the first-level items are 24 points and any second-level items are 20 points.

9. On Slide 4 ("What Are Closing Costs?"), cut the last bulleted item ("$200,000 loan"), and then paste it in on Slide 3 ("What Are Points?") as the third bulleted item. If a blank line is added below the pasted text, delete it.

10. On Slide 3, add the following as second-level items below "$200,000 loan", adjusting the font size to 20 points if necessary:

**2 points (2%) = $4,000**

**3 points (3%) = $6,000**

11. On Slide 2 ("Steps"), convert the bulleted list to SmartArt using the Step Down Process layout. (*Hint*: You need to click More SmartArt Graphics to open the Choose a SmartArt Graphic dialog box.)

12. On Slide 5 ("Documents Needed"), change the layout to Two Content, then insert the picture **Support_PPT_1_Key.jpg**, located in the PowerPoint1 > Case1 folder. Add **Drawing of a hand passing an approved mortgage towards another person's hand holding a key on a key chain shaped like a house.** as the alt text.

13. On Slide 5, resize the picture, maintaining the aspect ratio, so that it is 4.5 inches square, and then position it so that its middle aligns with the middle of the text box containing the bulleted list and its right edge aligns with the left edge of the gray rectangle on the right side of the slide. (*Hint*: Position the picture as close as possible to the edge of the gray rectangle. Then with the picture selected, press RIGHT ARROW or LEFT ARROW to nudge it into the correct position.)

14. On Slide 5, in the last bulleted item, format "and" with italics. Enter **Make sure applicants understand that they need two forms of ID.** as a speaker note, and then close the Notes pane.

15. On Slide 6 ("Contact Information"), remove the link formatting from both the email address and the Internet address of the Mortgages page for the bank.

16. On Slide 6, click before the word "Contact" in the slide title, and then press ENTER three times. Insert the photo **Support_PPT_1_Sophia.jpg**, located in the PowerPoint1 > Case1 folder. Add **Portrait of smiling Sophia Baker.** as the alt text.

17. On Slide 6, crop 1.5 inches off the bottom of the picture, then crop the photo to the Rectangle: Rounded Corners shape.

18. On Slide 6, resize the photo so it is 2.8 inches high, maintaining the aspect ratio. Reposition the photo in the tan rectangle above the title so that the vertical smart guide that appears shows that the photo aligns with the center of the tan rectangle, and the bottom of the photo aligns with the middle of the slide.

19. Add a new Slide 7 with the Content with Caption layout. In the title text placeholder, type **Upper**, and then create a new line without creating a new paragraph. Type **Coast** on the new line, create another new line, and then type **Bank**. In the text placeholder below the title, type **The Friendly Bank**.

20. On Slide 7, change the size of the title text to 48 points and bold, and change its color to Brown, Accent 1, Darker 50%. Change the size of the text below the title to 24 points and make it italic.

21. On Slide 7, add the picture **Support_PPT_1_Building.jpg**, located in the PowerPoint1 > Case1 folder. Add **Photo of Upper Coast Bank building.** as the alt text.

22. Compress all the photos in the presentation to E-mail (96 ppi) and delete cropped portions of photos.

23. Add your name as an author property and add **Upper Coast Bank** as the Company property.

24. Check the spelling in the presentation and correct all misspelled words.

25. Save the changes to the presentation, view the slide show in Presenter view, and then print Slides 1–6 as a handout using the 6 Slides Horizontal arrangement, and print Slide 5 as a notes page.

26. Close the presentation and PowerPoint.

# Create

## Case Problem 2

**Data Files needed for this Case Problem: Support_PPT_1_Beach.jpg, Support_PPT_1_Black.jpg, Support_PPT_1_Blue.jpg, Support_PPT_1_Ensemble.jpg, Support_PPT_1_Pink.jpg**

**Jumpstart Advertising** Joaquin Castillo is an associate account executive at Jumpstart Advertising, an advertising agency in New York City. A national department store recently hired Jumpstart to promote a new line of women's clothing with a vintage look. A new design house named Retro Again designed the clothing line. Joaquin has started a presentation to introduce the design house to his team so that they can create an effective ad campaign. He asks you to finish the presentation. The completed presentation is shown in Figure 1–52. Refer to Figure 1–52 as you complete the following steps:

**Figure 1–52** **Advertising presentation**

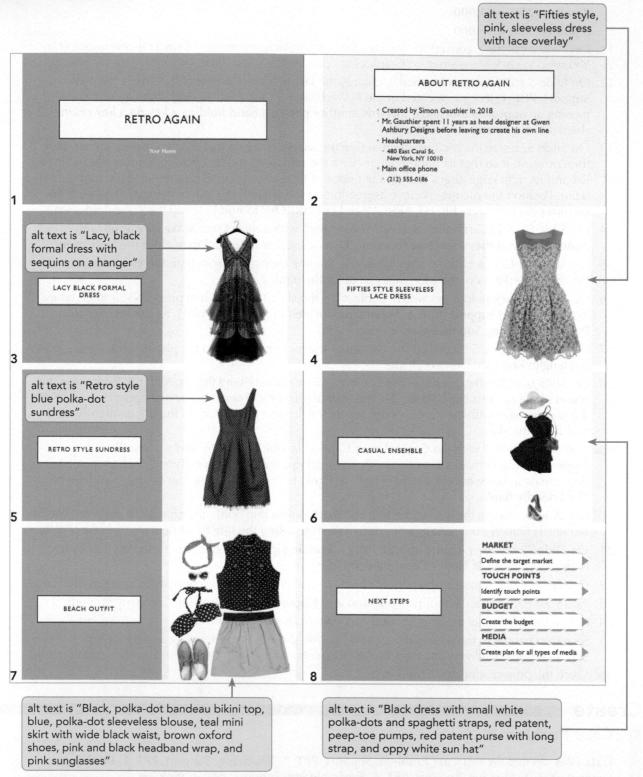

ladyfortune/Shutterstock.com; Maffi/Shutterstock.com; Tarzhanova/Shutterstock.com; urfin/Shutterstock.com; Africa Studio/Shutterstock.com

1. Create a new, blank PowerPoint presentation. Save it as **NP_PPT_1_Retro** to the drive and folder where you are storing your files. Add your name as the subtitle on Slide 1.
2. The theme is the Parcel theme with the first variant.
3. Slide 2 has the Title and Content layout applied. Slides 3 through 8 have the Content with Caption layout applied.
4. On Slides 3 through 8, the text placeholders below the title text are deleted. The title text boxes on Slides 3 through 8 are repositioned so that their middles are aligned with the horizontal grid-lines at the 0-inch mark on the vertical ruler and so their left edges are aligned with the vertical gridline at the negative 6-inch mark on the horizontal ruler.
5. On Slide 2, the text box containing the bulleted list is resized so that the bottom of the text box aligns with the gridlines at the negative 3-inch mark on the vertical ruler and the top aligns with the gridline at the 1-inch mark on the vertical ruler. The first-level items are 26 points, and the second-level items are 22 points.
6. The pictures on Slides 3 through 7 are all located in the PowerPoint1 > Case2 folder included with your Data Files. Each photo is resized so that it is 7.5 inches high. Add the alt text as shown in Figure 1–52.
7. The left edges of the pictures on Slides 3 through 6 are aligned with the gridline at the 1-inch mark on the horizontal ruler. The left edge of the picture on Slide 7 is aligned with the 0.25-inch mark on the horizontal ruler.
8. Compress all the photos in the presentation to E-mail (96 ppi).
9. On Slide 8 ("NEXT STEPS"), type the text in the SmartArt as a bulleted list. Each uppercase word is a first-level item, and each sentence is a second-level item. The SmartArt layout is Vertical Accent List. All the text is 24 points. The first-level items (the words in all uppercase) are bold and Orange, Accent 3, Darker 25%. (*Hint*: Change the color of the text in the first-level items after you convert the list to a SmartArt graphic.)
10. Save the changes to the presentation, and then view the presentation in Slide Show view.
11. Close the presentation and PowerPoint.

**Module** **2**

# Adding Media and Special Effects

## Using Media in a Presentation for a Veterinary Hospital

POWERPOINT

## Objectives

**Session 2.1**
- Apply a theme used in another presentation
- Insert shapes
- Format shapes and pictures
- Duplicate objects
- Rotate and flip objects
- Create a table
- Modify and format a table
- Insert symbols
- Add footers and headers

**Session 2.2**
- Apply and modify transitions
- Animate objects and lists
- Change how an animation starts
- Use the Morph transition
- Add video and modify playback options
- Trim video and set a poster frame
- Understand animation effects applied to videos
- Compress media

## Case | Windsor Veterinary Hospital

Teréza Gonçalves is the client service coordinator at Windsor Veterinary Hospital in Windsor, Ontario. One of her responsibilities is to recruit new clients by promoting hospital services. Because Windsor is on the border of Canada and the United States, Teréza is putting together a presentation to advertise the hospital to potential customers in the United States. Teréza prepared the text of a PowerPoint presentation, and she wants you to add photos and other features to make the presentation more interesting and compelling.

In this module, you will modify a presentation that highlights the state of the art services and competitive costs of the hospital. You will add formatting and special effects to photos and shapes; create a table; insert symbols; add footer and header information to slides, notes, and handouts; add transitions and animations to slides; and add and modify video.

## Starting Data Files

**Module**

NP_PPT_2-1.pptx
Support_PPT_2_Chip.jpg
Support_PPT_2_MRI.jpg
Support_PPT_2_OR.jpg
Support_PPT_2_Running.mov
Support_PPT_2_Teeth.jpg
Support_PPT_2_Theme.pptx
Support_PPT_2_VetDog.jpg

**Review**

NP_PPT_2-2.pptx
Support_PPT_2_Bath.jpg
Support_PPT_2_NewTheme.pptx
Support_PPT_2_Plate.jpg
Support_PPT_2_Sign.jpg
Support_PPT_2_Writing.mov

**Case1**

NP_PPT_2-3.pptx
Support_PPT_2_Calendar.jpg
Support_PPT_2_Cornucopia.jpg
Support_PPT_2_Fourth.jpg
Support_PPT_2_Labor.png
Support_PPT_2_Logo.pptx
Support_PPT_2_Memorial.jpg
Support_PPT_2_NewYear.jpg
Support_PPT_2_Sayings.mp4
Support_PPT_2_Sixty.png

**Case2**

NP_PPT_2-4.pptx
Support_PPT_2_Corporate.jpg
Support_PPT_2_Hospital.jpg
Support_PPT_2_Residential.jpg
Support_PPT_2_School.jpg

# Session 2.1 Visual Overview:

Use the Shape Fill button to change the **fill**, the formatting of the area inside a shape. You can also change the fill of slide backgrounds and text.

To change the color, weight (thickness), or style (solid line, dashed line, and so on) of a shape's border, use the Shape Outline button.

The Shape Format tab appears when a drawing or a text box—including the slide's title and content placeholders—is selected.

The Shape Height box contains the height measurement of the selected shape, and the Shape Width box contains the width measurement.

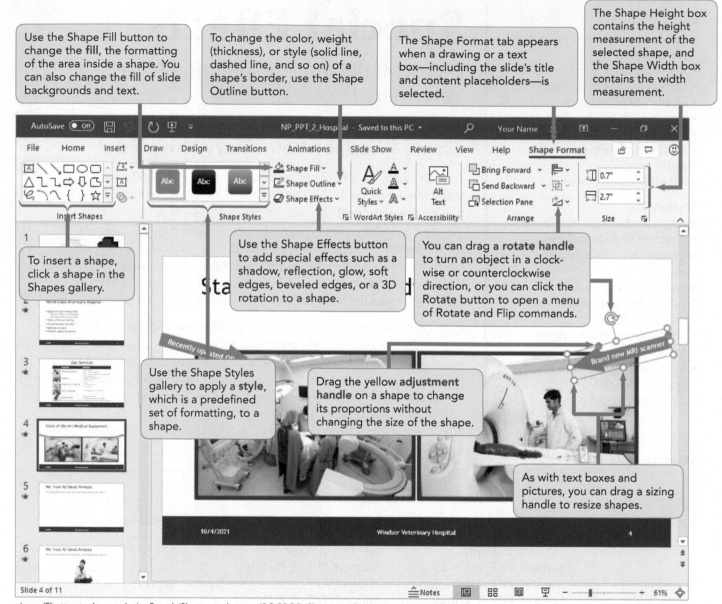

To insert a shape, click a shape in the Shapes gallery.

Use the Shape Effects button to add special effects such as a shadow, reflection, glow, soft edges, beveled edges, or a 3D rotation to a shape.

You can drag a **rotate handle** to turn an object in a clockwise or counterclockwise direction, or you can click the Rotate button to open a menu of Rotate and Flip commands.

Use the Shape Styles gallery to apply a **style**, which is a predefined set of formatting, to a shape.

Drag the yellow **adjustment handle** on a shape to change its proportions without changing the size of the shape.

As with text boxes and pictures, you can drag a sizing handle to resize shapes.

# Formatting Graphics

Use the Reset Picture button to undo formatting and sizing changes you made to a picture.

To change the color, weight (thickness), or style (solid line, dashed line, and so on) of a picture's border, use the Picture Border button.

The Picture Format tab appears when a picture is selected.

Like shapes, the dimensions of the picture appear in the Shape Height and Shape Width boxes.

Use the Picture Styles gallery to apply a style to a picture.

Click the Picture Effects button to add special effects to a picture, such as a shadow, reflection, glow, soft edges, beveled edges, or a 3D rotation.

Like shapes, you can rotate or flip pictures using the Rotate handle or the Rotate button.

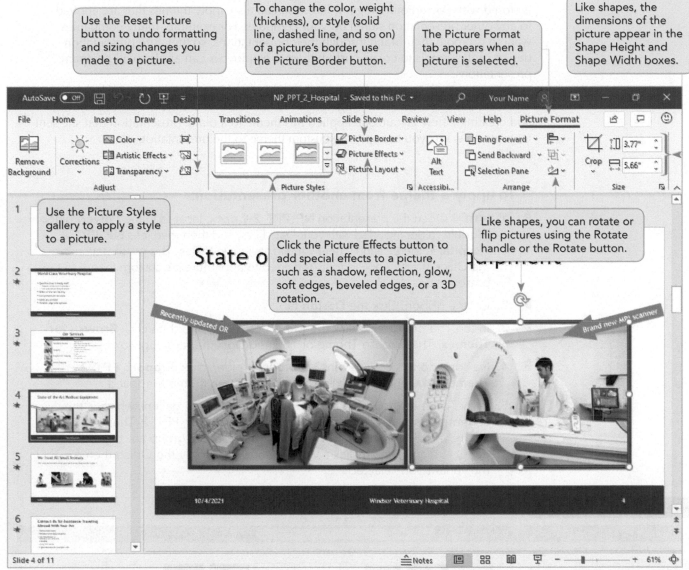

# Applying a Theme Used in Another Presentation

As you learned earlier, you can apply an installed theme by clicking an option in the Themes group on the Design tab. An installed theme is a special type of file that is stored with PowerPoint program files. You can also apply themes that are applied to any other presentation stored on your computer. For example, many companies want to promote their brand through their presentations, so they hire presentation design professionals to create custom themes employees can apply to all company presentations.

Teréza created a presentation describing Windsor Veterinary Hospital. She also created a custom theme by changing the theme fonts and colors, modifying layouts, and creating a new layout. She applied this theme to a blank presentation that she sent to you. She wants you to apply the custom theme to the presentation.

## To apply a theme from another presentation:

1. **sam↓** Open the presentation **NP_PPT_2-1.pptx**, located in the **PowerPoint2 > Module** folder included with your Data Files, and then save it as **NP_PPT_2_ Hospital** in the location where you are saving your files. This presentation has the Office theme applied to it. You need to apply Teréza's custom theme to the presentation.

2. On the ribbon, click the **Design** tab.

3. In the Themes group, click the **More** button ⊽, and then click **Browse for Themes**. The Choose Theme or Themed Document dialog box opens.

4. Navigate to the **PowerPoint2 > Module** folder, click **Support_PPT_2_ Theme.pptx**, and then click **Apply**. The custom theme is applied.

5. In the Themes group, point to the first theme in the gallery, which is the current theme. Its ScreenTip identifies it as Support_PPT_2_Theme. See Figure 2–1. The options that appear in the Variants group are the Office theme variants. If you click a variant, you will reapply the Office theme with the variant you selected.

| Figure 2–1 | Custom theme applied |
| --- | --- |

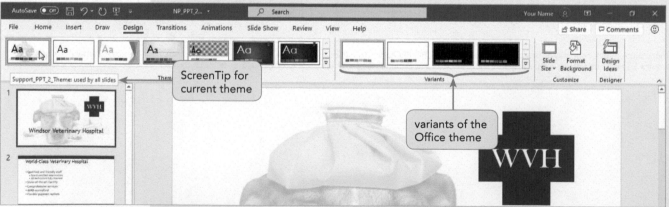

Javier Brosch/Shutterstock.com

After you apply a custom theme, you might need to adjust some of the slides in the presentation. You will check the slides now.

6. Click the **Home** tab, and then on Slide 1 (the title slide), click **Windsor Veterinary Hospital**, the title text.

7. In the Font group, click the **Font arrow**. Notice that Trebuchet MS is the theme font for both the headings and the body text. This is different from the Office theme, which uses Calibri for the body text and Calibri Light for the headings.

8. In the Slides group, click the **Layout button**. The Layout gallery appears. The custom layouts that Teréza created are listed in the gallery, as shown in Figure 2–2.

**Figure 2–2**    Custom layouts in the custom theme

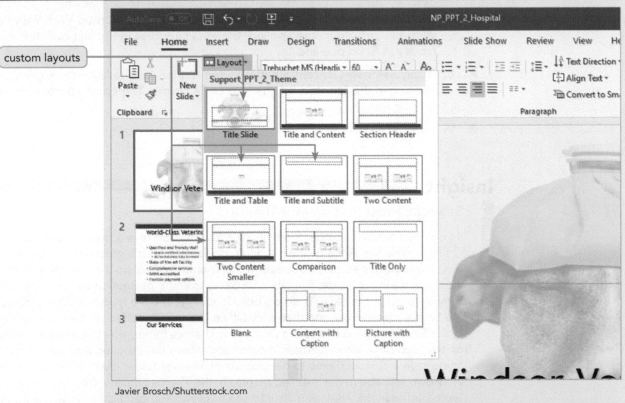

Javier Brosch/Shutterstock.com

9. Press **ESC** to close the Layout gallery.

When you applied the custom theme, the title slide and the slides with the Title and Content and Two Content layouts were changed to use the customized versions of these layouts. Teréza wants you to change the layout of Slide 3 to the custom Title and Table layout, change the layout of Slide 5 to the custom Title and Subtitle layout, and then add the hospital's slogan on Slide 5. You will also examine the other slides to make sure they are formatted correctly with the custom theme applied.

**To examine the slides and apply custom layouts to Slides 3, 5, and 6:**

▶ **1.** Display Slide 2 ("World-Class Veterinary Hospital"). Slide 2 looks fine.

▶ **2.** Display Slide 3 ("Our Services"). You need to apply a custom layout to this slide.

▶ **3.** In the Slides group, click the **Layout** button, and then click the **Title and Table** layout. The custom layout is applied to Slide 3.

▶ **4.** Display Slide 4 ("State of the Art Medical Equipment"). This slide looks fine.

▶ **5.** Display Slide 5 ("We Treat All Small Animals"), and then apply the **Title and Subtitle** layout to it.

▶ **6.** On Slide 5, click in the subtitle text placeholder, and then type **The only person who loves your pets more than we do is you.** (including the period).

▶ **7.** Display Slide 6 ("Contact Us for Assistance Traveling Abroad With Your Pet"). With the custom theme applied, the email address in the last bulleted item does not fit on one line.

▶ **8.** Apply the **Two Content Smaller** layout to Slide 6. The layout is applied and the text in the bulleted list changes to 24 points. The email address now fits on one line.

▶ **9.** Save your changes.

## Insight

### Saving a Presentation as a Theme

If you need to use a custom theme frequently, you can save a presentation file as an Office Theme file. A theme file is a different file type than a presentation file. You can then store this file so that it appears in the Themes gallery on the Design tab. To save a custom theme, click the File tab, click Save As in the navigation bar, and then click Browse to open the Save As dialog box. To change the file type to Office Theme, click the Save as type arrow, and then click Office Theme. This changes the current folder in the Save As dialog box to the Document Themes folder, which is a folder created on the hard drive when Office is installed and where the installed themes are stored. If you save a custom theme to the Document Themes folder, that theme will be listed in its own row above the installed themes in the Themes gallery. (You need to click the More button in the Themes gallery to see this row.) You can also change the folder location and save the custom theme to any location on your computer or network or to a folder on your OneDrive. If you do this, the theme will not appear in the Themes gallery, but you can still access it using the Browse for Themes command on the Themes gallery menu.

## Inserting Shapes

You can add many shapes to a slide, including lines, rectangles, stars, and more. To draw a shape, click the Shapes button in the Illustrations group on the Insert tab, click a shape in the gallery, and then click on the slide to draw a shape at the default size of about one-inch wide, or click and drag to draw the shape the size you want. Like any object, you can resize a shape after you insert it.

You've already had a little experience with one shape—a text box, which is a shape specifically designed to contain text. You can add additional text boxes to slides using the Text Box shape. You can also add text to any shape you place on a slide.

Teréza wants you to add a label describing one of the photos on Slide 4. You will do this with an arrow shape.

**To insert an arrow shape on Slide 4 and add text to it:**

1. Display Slide 4 ("State of the Art Medical Equipment").

2. Click the **Insert** tab, and then in the Illustrations group, click the **Shapes** button. The Shapes gallery opens. See Figure 2–3. In addition to the Recently Used Shapes group at the top, the gallery is organized into nine categories of shapes.

**Figure 2–3**   Shapes gallery

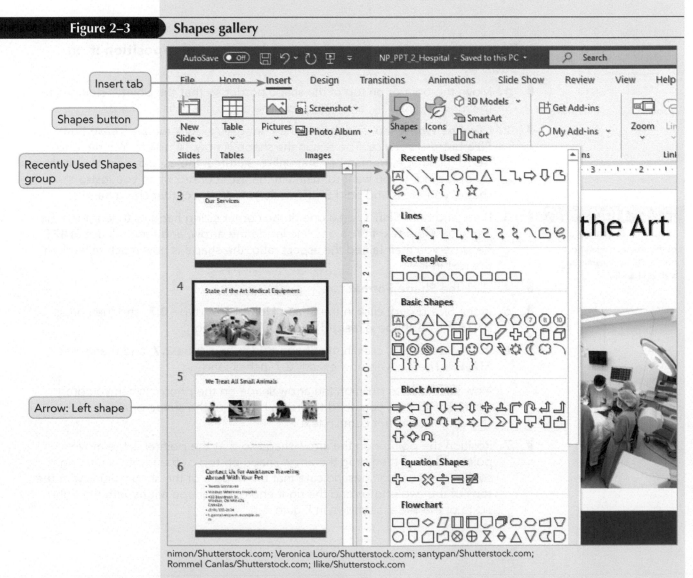

nimon/Shutterstock.com; Veronica Louro/Shutterstock.com; santypan/Shutterstock.com; Rommel Canlas/Shutterstock.com; Ilike/Shutterstock.com

**Tip**

You can also insert a shape using the Shapes gallery in the Drawing group on the Home tab.

3. Under Block Arrows, click the **Arrow: Left** shape ⇦. The gallery closes and the pointer changes to the thin cross pointer ╂.

4. On the slide, click above the photo on the right and below the word "Equipment" in the title. An orange, left-pointing arrow, approximately one-inch long, appears. (Don't worry about the exact placement of the arrow; you will move it later.) The Shape Format tab is the active tab on the ribbon.

5. With the shape selected, type **Brand new MRI scanner** in the arrow. The text you type appears in the arrow, but it does not all fit.

Next you need to resize the shape to fit the text. Then you will move the arrow to a new position on the slide.

### To add text to the arrow shape and resize and reposition it on Slide 4:

1. Move the pointer on top of the shape border so that the pointer changes to the move pointer ⬆, and then click. The entire shape is selected.

2. Click the **Home** tab, and then in the Font group, click the **Decrease Font Size** button A˅ twice. The text in the shape is now 14 points. You need to resize the shape. Remember that unlike pictures, the aspect ratio of a shape is not locked. If you want to maintain the aspect ratio when you resize a shape, you press and hold SHIFT while you drag a corner sizing handle.

**Tip**

To resize from the center of the shape, press and hold CTRL while you drag a sizing handle.

3. Press and hold **SHIFT**, drag one of the corner sizing handles to lengthen the arrow until the text fits on one line inside the arrow, and then release **SHIFT**. Because you maintained the aspect ratio, the shape is now much taller than the text in it.

4. Click the **Shape Format** tab.

5. In the Size group, click in the **Shape Height** box, type **0.7**, and then press **ENTER**. The shape is resized so it is 0.7 inches high.

6. In the Size group, click in the **Shape Width** box, type **2.7**, and then press **ENTER**. The arrow is now exactly 2.7 inches long.

   Now you need to position the arrow shape on the photo. When you drag a shape with text, you need to drag a border of the shape or a part of the shape that does not contain text.

7. Position the pointer on the arrow shape so that the pointer is the move pointer ⬆, and then drag the arrow shape on top of the photo on the right so that the smart guides indicate that the middle of the shape aligns with the tops of the two photos and the right end of the shape aligns with the right edge of the slide, as shown in Figure 2–4.

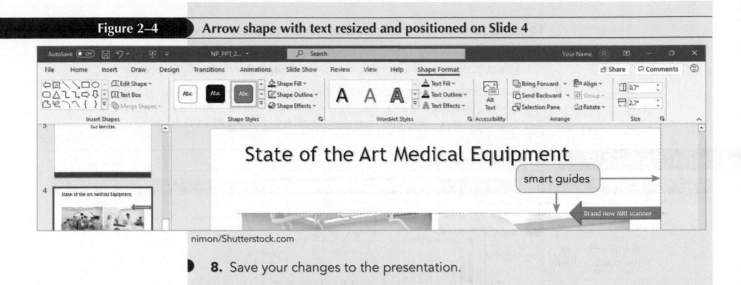

**Figure 2–4**    Arrow shape with text resized and positioned on Slide 4

nimon/Shutterstock.com

**8.** Save your changes to the presentation.

## Insight

### Using the Draw Tab

The Draw tab on the ribbon contains commands that let you draw on a slide. If you have a device with a touchscreen, you can use your finger or a stylus to draw. If you do not have a touchscreen, you can use the mouse. To draw on a slide, click the Draw button, and then choose different colored pens, a pencil, a highlighter, or a pen style called Galaxy, which draws using a glitter effect. You can adjust any of the drawing tools to create a wider or more narrow line. You can click buttons in the convert group to convert your drawings to text, shapes, or mathematical equations. If you want to draw straight lines or align your drawings, you can use the Ruler button on the Draw tab to display a ruler across the slide that you can rotate to whatever position you want. The drawings are also recorded as a video. After you have finished drawing, you can "replay" the drawing action and watch the characters and shapes you drew get redrawn on the slide. The Draw tab appears on the ribbon automatically if you are using a touchscreen device. If the Draw tab does not appear, you can right-click a tab name on the ribbon, click Customize the Ribbon, and then in the Customize the Ribbon list, click the Draw check box to select it.

## Formatting Objects

When you select a shape, including a text box, the Shape Format contextual tab appears. When you select a picture on a slide, the Picture Format contextual tab appears. These tabs contain tools for formatting shapes or pictures. For both shapes and pictures, you can apply borders or outlines and add special effects such as shadows, reflections, a glow effect, soft edges, bevels, and 3-D effects. Some formatting tools are available only for one or the other type of object. For example, the Remove Background tool is available only for pictures, and the Fill command is available only for shapes. Refer to the Session 2.1 Visual Overview for more information about the commands on the Format contextual tabs.

You can apply a style to both shapes and pictures. For example, a picture style can add both a border and a shadow effect to a picture. A shape style could apply a fill color, an outline color, and a shadow effect to a shape.

### Formatting Shapes

You can modify the fill of a shape by filling it with a color, a gradient (shading in which one color blends into another or varies from one shade to another), a textured pattern, or a picture. When you add a shape to a slide, the shape is filled with the Accent 1 color from the set of theme colors, and the outline is a darker shade of that color.

Teréza wants you to change the color of the arrow shape on Slide 4.

### To change the fill, outline, and style of the arrow shapes:

1. On Slide 4 ("State of the Art Medical Equipment"), click the arrow shape to select it, if necessary, and then click the **Shape Format** tab, if necessary.

2. In the Shape Styles group, click the **Shape Fill arrow**. The Shape Fill menu opens. See Figure 2–5. You can fill a shape with a color, a picture, a gradient, or a texture, or you can remove the fill by clicking No Fill.

**Figure 2–5**  Shape Fill menu

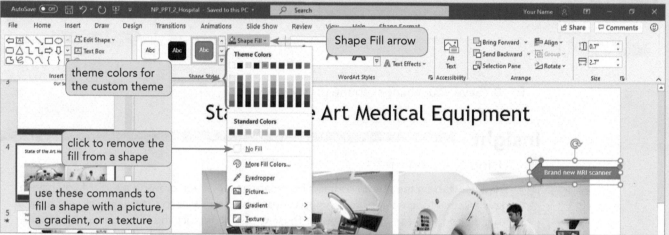

nimon/Shutterstock.com

**Tip**

You can fill a shape with a picture instead of a color. On the Shape Fill menu, click Picture to open the Insert Pictures dialog box, and then click the location of the picture (From a File, Online Pictures, or From Icons).

3. In the Theme Colors section, click the **Tan, Accent 6** square. The fill of the selected arrow changes to tan.

4. Click the **Shape Fill arrow**, point to **Gradient**, and then in the Dark Variations section click the **Linear Right** gradient (in the first column, second row in the Dark Variations section). The shape is filled with a gradient of tan that is darker on the left side of the shape and fades to a lighter shade on the right side of the shape.

5. In the Shape Styles group, click the **Shape Outline arrow**. The Shape Outline menu appears. See Figure 2–6. You can change the color of a shape outline, the width (by clicking Weight), or the style (by clicking Dashes).

**Figure 2–6**  Shape Outline menu

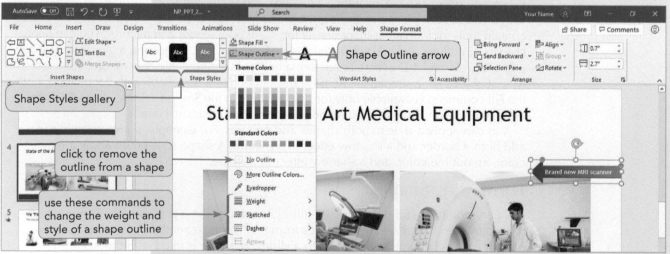

nimon/Shutterstock.com

6. On the menu, point to **Weight**, and then click **6 pt**. The width of the outline increases to six points. Teréza doesn't like this look, so she asks you to apply a style instead.

7. In the Shape Styles group, click the **More** button ⬟. The Shape Styles gallery opens.

8. Scroll down, and then in the Presets section, click the **Colored Fill – Tan, Accent 6, No Outline** style. The style, which fills the shape with tan and removes the outline, is applied to the shape.

**Tip**

To make other adjustments to shapes, in the Insert Shapes group on the Shape Format tab, click the Edit Points button, and then drag the points that appear on the shape. To replace a shape with a different one, click the Edit Shape button, point to Change Shape, and then click the shape you want.

On some shapes, you can drag the yellow adjustment handle to change the shape's proportions. For instance, if you drag one of the adjustment handles on the arrow shape, you would change the size of the arrowhead relative to the size of the arrow.

Teréza wants you to change the shape of the arrow by making the arrowhead larger relative to the size of the arrow shape.

### To adjust the arrow shape:

1. Click the arrow shape, if necessary, to select it. There are two yellow adjustment handles on the arrow shape. One adjustment handle is at the right end of the arrow. The other adjustment handle is at the base of the arrowhead on the top border of the shape.

2. Drag the adjustment handle at the base of the arrowhead to the right so that the bottom edge of the arrowhead is approximately between the letters "a" and "n" in "Brand." Compare your screen to Figure 2–7.

**Figure 2–7**    **Arrow shape after using the adjustment handle**

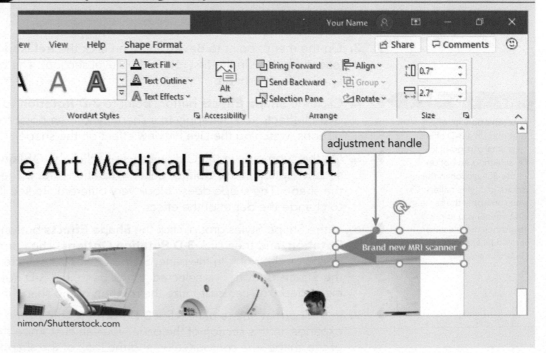

nimon/Shutterstock.com

Another way you can format a shape is to apply effects to it, such as a shadow, reflection, glow, soft edges, bevel, and 3-D rotation effect. Teréza placed a cross shape containing the hospital's initials on Slide 1. She wants you to make the cross shape look three-dimensional.

### To apply 3-D effects to the shape on Slide 1:

1. Display Slide 1 (the title slide), click the cross shape, and then click the **Shape Format** tab.

2. In the Shape Styles group, click the **Shape Effects** button. The Shape Effects menu opens. The menu contains a list of the types of effects you can apply. See Figure 2–8.

**Figure 2–8**    Shape Effects menu

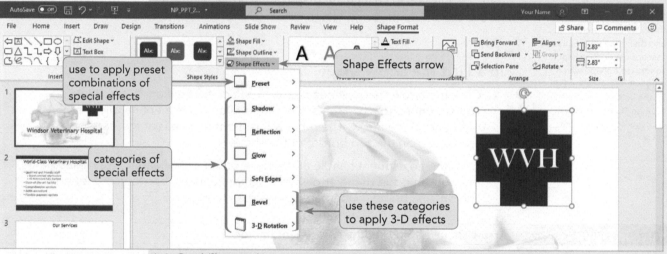

Javier Brosch/Shutterstock.com

3. On the menu, point to **Bevel**, and then click the **Relaxed Inset** button (second button in the first row in the Bevel section). The bevel effect is applied to the shape.

4. Click the **Shape Effects** button, point to **3-D Rotation** to open a submenu of 3-D effects you can apply to a shape, and then point to several of the options, watching the Live Preview effect on the shape.

5. On the submenu, in the Oblique section, click the **Oblique: Top Right** (the second option in the Oblique section) rotation effect. The effect is applied to the shape. The shape doesn't look very different. To see the effect, you need to change the depth of the effect.

6. In the Shape Styles group, click the **Shape Effects** button, point to **3-D Rotation**, and then click **3-D Rotation Options**. The Format Shape pane opens on the right. In the pane, Shape Options is selected at the top, and the Effects button ⬦ is selected. In the pane, the 3-D Rotation section is expanded. You can customize the rotation of the shape in this section.

7. In the Format Shape pane, click **3-D Format**. The 3-D Format section expands. In this section of the pane, you can customize the bevel, the depth of the shape, the contour color, and the look of the shape by changing the material and lighting settings.

   **Trouble?** If the 3-D Format section is not expanded, it was already expanded before you clicked it. Click 3-D Format in the pane again.

8. In the 3-D Format section, in the Depth section, click in the **Size** box, and then edit the number so it is **120 pt**. The shape changes so that the depth is increased to 120 points. The cross now looks three-dimensional.

9. In the Depth section, click the **Color** button , and then click **Dark Blue, Accent 3, Darker 50%**. The color of the depth shading changes to dark blue. Compare your screen to Figure 2–9.

**Figure 2–9**    **Cross shape formatted to look three-dimensional**

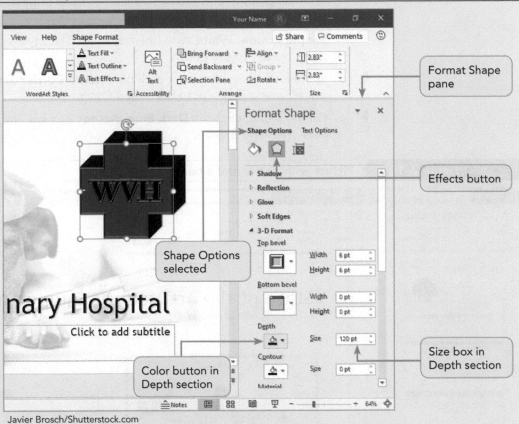

Javier Brosch/Shutterstock.com

10. In the upper-right corner of the Format Shape pane, click the **Close** button .

## Formatting Pictures

You can format pictures as well as shapes. To format pictures, you use the tools on the Picture Format tab.

Teréza wants you to format the pictures on Slide 4 by adding colored borders. To create a border, you could apply a thick outline, or you can apply one of the styles that includes a border and then modify it.

### To format the photos on Slide 4:

1. Display Slide 4 ("State of the Art Medical Equipment"), click the photo on the left, and then click the **Picture Format** tab.

2. In the Picture Styles group, click the **More** button , and then click the **Metal Oval** style (the last style in the last row). The style is applied to the picture. Teréza doesn't like that style.

3. In the Adjust group, click the **Reset Picture** button. The style is removed from the picture, and the picture is reset to its original condition.

4. In the Picture Styles group, click the **More** button , and then click the **Simple Frame, White** style (the first style). This style applies a 7-point white border to the photo.

5. In the Picture Styles group, click the **Picture Border arrow**. The Picture Border menu is similar to the Shape Outline menu.

6. On the menu, click the **Dark Blue, Accent 3** color. The picture border is now blue. See Figure 2–10.

**Figure 2–10** Picture with a style and a border color applied

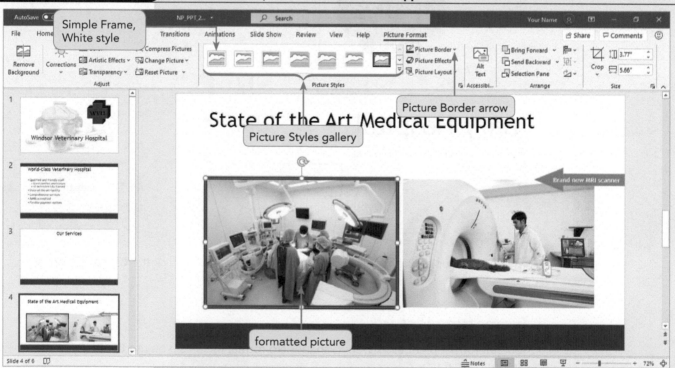

nimon/Shutterstock.com; Javier Brosch/Shutterstock.com

You need to apply the same formatting to the photo on the right on Slide 4. You can repeat the same formatting steps, or you can copy the formatting.

7. With the left photo on Slide 4 still selected, click the **Home** tab.

8. In the Clipboard group, click the **Format Painter** button , and then move the pointer to the slide. The pointer changes to the Format Painter pointer for objects .

9. Click the photo on the right. The style and border color of the photo on the left is copied and applied to the photo on the right.

10. Save your changes.

# Duplicating Objects

Teréza decides she wants you to add an arrow pointing to the picture of the operating room on the left of Slide 4. You could draw another arrow, but instead, you'll duplicate the arrow you just drew so that they have the same style and size. When you duplicate an object, you create a copy of the object, but nothing is placed on the Clipboard. You can only use the Duplicate command to duplicate objects, including text boxes. You cannot use the Duplicate command to duplicate selected text.

**To duplicate the arrow on Slide 4 and edit the text in the shape:**

1. On Slide 4 ("State of the Art Medical Equipment"), click the arrow shape to select it.

2. On the Home tab, in the Clipboard group, click the **Copy arrow** [icon]. A menu opens.

3. On the menu, click **Duplicate**. A duplicate of the arrow appears on the slide.

4. Move the pointer on top of the duplicate shape so that the pointer changes to the I-beam pointer I, and then click before the first word "Brand." The insertion point appears in the shape before "Brand."

   **Trouble?** If the insertion point is not before "Brand," press LEFT ARROW or RIGHT ARROW as needed to move it to the correct position.

5. Press and hold **SHIFT**, click after the last word, "scanner," and then release **SHIFT**. All of the text between the locations where you clicked is selected.

6. Type **Recently updated OR** in the duplicate arrow. The text you type replaces the selected text.

7. Drag the duplicate arrow to the left so that the smart guides indicate that the left edge of the duplicate arrow shape aligns with the left edge of the slide and the duplicate arrow shape aligns with the original arrow shape as shown in Figure 2–11.

> **Tip**
>
> You can also press and hold SHIFT then press an arrow key to select adjacent text.

| Figure 2–11 | Duplicate arrow repositioned on Slide 4 |
| --- | --- |

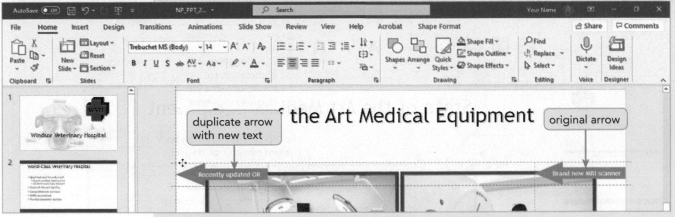

nimon/Shutterstock.com; Javier Brosch/Shutterstock.com

8. Save your changes.

# Rotating and Flipping Objects

You can rotate and flip any object on a slide. To flip an object, you click the Rotate button in the Arrange group on the Shape Format tab or on the Picture Format tab to access the Flip commands on the Rotate menu. To rotate an object, you can use the Rotate commands on the Rotate menu to rotate objects in 90-degree increments. You can also drag the rotate handle that appears above the top-middle sizing handle to rotate a selected object to any position that you want.

Teréza wants you to rotate the arrows on Slide 4 so that they are slanted. Also, the "Recently updated OR" arrow on Slide 4 needs to point to the right. To make that change, you need to flip the arrow.

**To flip the duplicate arrow shape on Slide 4:**

1. On Slide 4 ("State of the Art Medical Equipment"), click the Brand new MRI scanner arrow to select it. The shape border appears with the Rotate handle ⟳ above the shape. The right end of the arrow is touching the right side of the slide.

2. Position the pointer on the **rotate handle** ⟳ so that the pointer changes to the rotate pointer ⟳, and then drag the **rotate handle** ⟳ counter-clockwise to the left until only the bottom corner of the arrow shape is still touching the right side of the slide.

3. Click the **Recently updated OR** arrow, and then drag the rotate handle 180 degrees to the right so that the arrow is pointing to the right. Now the arrow is pointing in the correct direction, but the text in the arrow is now upside down.

4. On the Quick Access Toolbar, click the **Undo** button ↺, and then click the **Shape Format** tab, if necessary.

5. In the Arrange group, click the **Rotate** button. The Rotate menu opens. See Figure 2–12.

**Figure 2–12**    Rotate menu

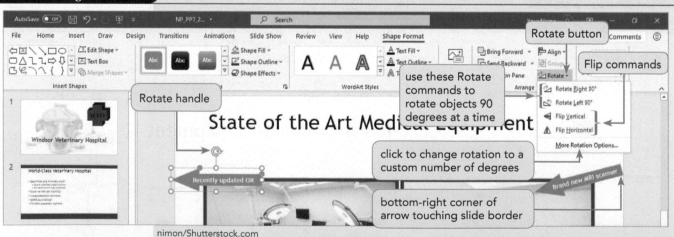

nimon/Shutterstock.com

6. Click **Flip Horizontal**. The arrow flips horizontally and is now pointing right. Unlike when you rotated the arrow, the text is still right-side up.

7. Drag the **rotate handle** clockwise to the right until only the bottom corner of the arrow shape is still touching the left side of the slide. Usually, using the rotate handle is fine, but you can also rotate objects by a precise number of degrees.

8. In the Arrange group, click the **Rotate** button, and then click **More Rotation Options**. The Format Shape pane opens with the Shape Options tab selected and the Size & Properties button 🔲 selected. The Size section is expanded. The value in the Rotation box indicates the number of degrees the object was rotated in a clockwise direction from its original position.

9. If the value in the Rotation box is not 15°, click in the **Rotation** box, edit the value so it is **15°**, and then press **ENTER**.

10. Click the **Brand new MRI scanner** arrow shape. The value in the Rotation box will be a value between 270° and 360°. This is because no matter which way you dragged the rotate handle, the final value in the Rotation box is the number of degrees the object is rotated in a clockwise direction.

11. If the value in the Rotation box is not 345°, click in the **Rotation** box, and then edit the value so it is **345°**, and then press **ENTER**.

12. Close the Format Shape pane, and then save your changes.

# Creating and Formatting a Table

A **table** is a grid of rows and columns that can contain text and graphics. A **cell** is the box where a row and column intersect. Each cell contains one piece of information. **Gridlines** in a table are the nonprinting lines that show cell boundaries. Gridlines create a table's structure.

## Creating a Table and Adding Data to It

Teréza wants you to add a table to Slide 3 that describes some of the services the hospital offers. This table will have three columns—one to list the services, one to give examples of the services, and one to list notes.

## Reference

### Inserting a Table

- On the ribbon, click the Insert tab, and then in the Tables group, click the Table button.
- Click a box in the grid to create a table of that size.

*or*

- In a content placeholder, click the Insert Table button; or, click the Insert tab on the ribbon, click the Table button in the Tables group, and then click Insert Table.
- Specify the numbers of columns and rows, and then click the OK button.

Teréza hasn't decided how many services to include in the table, so she asks you to start by creating a table with four rows.

### To add a table to Slide 3:

1. Display Slide 3 ("Our Services"). You can click the Table button in the content placeholder or you can use the Table command on the Insert tab.

2. Click the **Insert** tab, and then in the Tables group, click the **Table** button. A menu opens with a grid of squares above three commands.

3. Point to the grid, and without clicking the mouse button, move the pointer over the grid. The label above the grid indicates how large the table will be, and a preview of the table appears on the slide. See Figure 2–13.

| Figure 2–13 | Inserting a 3×4 table on Slide 3 |

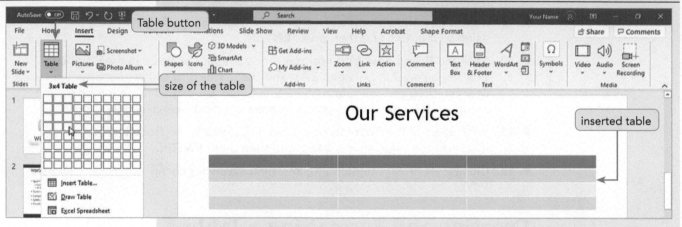

4. When the label above the grid indicates 3×4 Table, click to insert a table with three columns and four rows. A selection border appears around the table, and the insertion point is in the first cell in the first row. On the ribbon, two table contextual tabs appear.

Now you're ready to fill the blank cells with the information about the services. To enter data in a table, you click in the cells in which you want to enter data and then start typing. You can also use the Tab and arrow keys to move from one cell to another.

**To add data to the table:**

1. In the first cell in the first row, type **Service**. The text you typed appears in the first cell.

2. Press **TAB**. The insertion point moves to the second cell in the first row.

3. Type **Details**, press **TAB**, type **Notes**, and then press **TAB**. The insertion point is in the first cell in the second row.

4. In the first cell in the second row, type **Wellness Exams**, press **TAB**, and then type **Vaccinations** in the second cell. You need to add two more lines in the second cell in the second row.

5. Press **ENTER**, type **Nutritional counseling**, press **ENTER**, and then type **Flea, tick, and heartworm prevention**. The height of the second row increased to fit the extra lines of text in this cell.

6. Click in the first cell in the third row, type **Surgery**, and then press **TAB**.

7. In the second cell in the third row, type **Spay and neuter**, press **ENTER**, type **Foreign body removal**, press **ENTER**, and then type **Trauma repair**.

8. Click in the first cell in the last row, type **Diagnostic Imaging**, and then press **TAB**.

9. In the second cell in the last row, type **X-rays**, press **ENTER**, type **CT and MRI scans**, press **ENTER**, and then type **Ultrasounds**.

## Inserting and Deleting Rows and Columns

You can modify the table by adding or deleting rows and columns. You need to add more rows to the table for additional services.

### To insert rows and a column in the table:

▶ 1. Make sure the insertion point is in the last row in the table.

▶ 2. Click the **Layout** tab, and then in the Rows & Columns group, click the **Insert Below** button. A new row is inserted below the current row. See Figure 2–14.

**Figure 2–14**    Table with row inserted

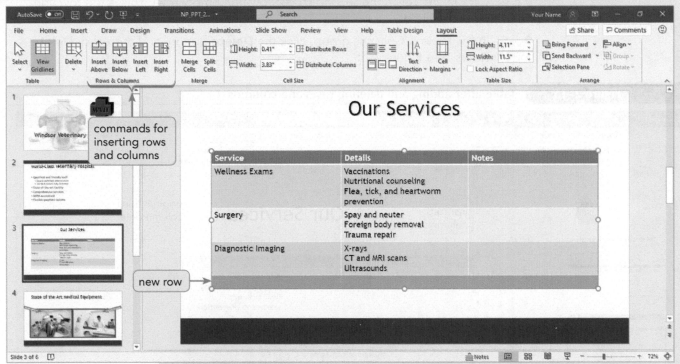

Javier Brosch/Shutterstock.com; nimon/Shutterstock.com

▶ 3. Click in the first cell in the new last row, type **Microchipping**, and then press **TAB**.

▶ 4. Type **Chip frequency is 134.2 kHz**, and then press **TAB**. The insertion point is in the last cell in the last row.

▶ 5. Press **TAB**. A new row is created, and the insertion point is in the first cell in the new row.

▶ 6. Type **Dental Care**, press **TAB**, type **Preventative care**, press **ENTER**, and then type **Treatment of all oral problems**. You need to insert a row above the last row.

▶ 7. In the Rows & Columns group, click the **Insert Above** button. A new row is inserted above the current row, and all of the cells in the new row are selected. You also need to insert a column to the left of the first column.

▶ 8. Click any cell in the first column, and then in the Rows & Columns group, click the **Insert Left** button. A new first column is inserted.

Teréza decided she doesn't want to add notes to the table, so you'll delete the last column. She also decided that she doesn't need the new row you added as the second to last row in the table, so you'll delete that row.

### To delete a column and a row in the table:

1. Click in any cell in the last column in the table. This is the column you will delete.

2. On the Layout tab, in the Rows & Columns group, click the **Delete** button. The Delete button menu opens.

3. Click **Delete Columns**. The current column is deleted, and the entire table is selected.

4. Click in any cell in the second to last row (the empty row). This is the row you want to delete.

5. In the Rows & Columns group, click the **Delete** button, and then click **Delete Rows**. See Figure 2–15.

**Figure 2–15** Table after adding and deleting rows and columns

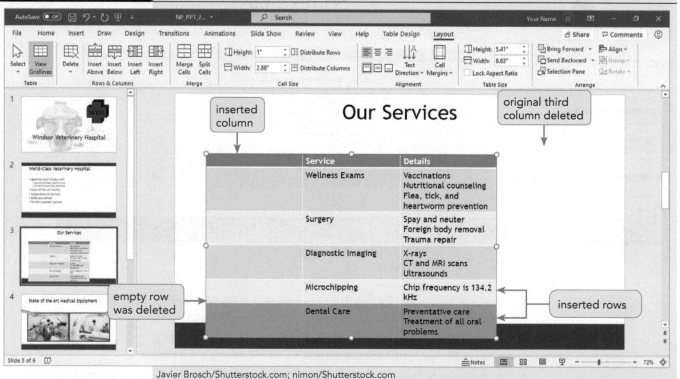

Javier Brosch/Shutterstock.com; nimon/Shutterstock.com

## Formatting a Table

After you insert data into a table, you need to think about how the table looks and whether the table will be readable for the audience. As with any text, you can change the font, size, or color, and as with shapes and pictures, you can apply a style to a table. You can also change how the text fits in the table cells by changing the height of rows and the width of columns. You can also customize the formatting of the table by changing the border and fill of table cells.

You need to change the font size of the text in the table.

**To change the font size of text in the table:**

1. Move the pointer on top of the left edge of the cell containing "Service" so that the pointer changes to the cell selection pointer ➚, and then click. The entire cell is selected, and the Mini toolbar appears. You want to change the size of all the text in the table, so you will select the entire table. Notice that a selection border appears around the table. This border appears any time the insertion point is in a table cell or part of the table is selected.

2. Click the **Layout** tab, if necessary, and then in the Table group, click the **Select** button. The Select menu opens with options to select the entire table, the current column, or the current row.

3. Click **Select Table**. The entire table is selected. Because the selection border appears any time the insertion point is in the table, the only visual cues you have that the entire table is now selected are that no cells in the table are selected, the insertion point is not blinking in any cell in the table, and the Select button is gray and unavailable. See Figure 2–16.

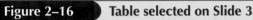

**Figure 2–16**    Table selected on Slide 3

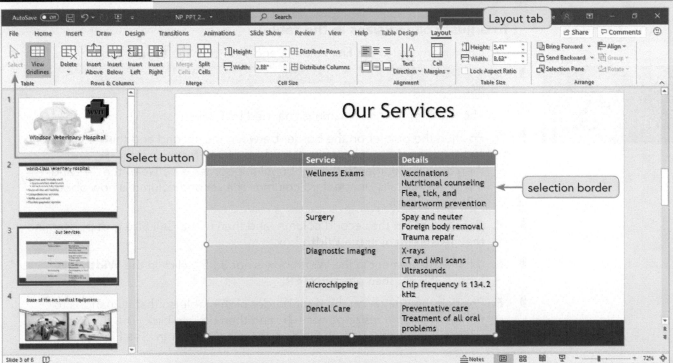

Javier Brosch/Shutterstock.com; nimon/Shutterstock.com

4. On the ribbon, click the **Home** tab.

5. In the Font group, click the **Font Size arrow**, and then click **24**. Because the entire table is selected, the size of all the text in the table changes to 24 points. The height of all the rows in the table increases to fit the larger text size.

6. Move the pointer on top of the top border of the table so that the pointer changes to the move pointer ⊹, and then drag the table up until the top of the table aligns with the top of the slide and so that you can see the last row in the table. The table will be on top of the title.

7. Click any cell in the third column, and then click the **Layout** tab.

8. In the Table group, click the **Select** button, and then click **Select Column**. All of the cells in the third column are selected. You want to change the font size of only the text in the cells below the heading row.

9. Click in the second cell in the third column, press and hold **SHIFT**, and then click in the last cell in the third column. All of the cells in the third column except the first cell are selected.

10. On the ribbon, click the **Home** tab.

11. In the Font group, click the **Font Size arrow**, and then click **18**. The text in the selected cells changes to 18 points and the height of those rows decreases.

Next, you will adjust the column widths to better fit the data. To adjust column widths, you can drag a column border or type a number in the Width box in the Cell Size group on the Layout tab. You can also automatically adjust a column to fit its widest entry by double-clicking its right border.

### To adjust column sizes in the table:

1. Click in any cell in the first column, and then click the **Layout** tab.

2. In the Cell Size group, click the number in the **Width** box, type **1.3**, and then press **ENTER**.

   The width of the first column is changed to 1.3 inches.

> Make sure you change the value in the Width box in the Cell Size group and not the value in the Width box in the Table Size group.

3. Position the pointer on the border between the second and third columns so that the pointer changes to the table column resize pointer +‖+, and then drag the border to the right until the border is between the "e" and the "t" in "Details" in the third column. The second column is now about 3.35 inches wide.

4. Click any cell in the second column, and then in the Cell Size group, examine the measurement in the **Width** box.

5. If the measurement in the Width box is not 3.35", click in the **Width** box, type **3.35**, and then press **ENTER**.

6. Position the pointer on the right border of the table so that it changes to the table column resize pointer +‖+, and then double-click. The third column widens to accommodate the widest entry in the column. See Figure 2–17.

Figure 2-17    Table column widths adjusted

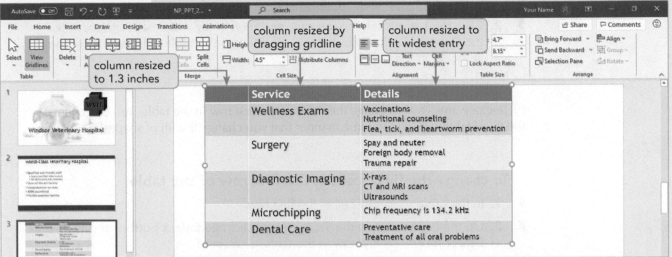

Figure 2-17    Table column widths adjusted

Javier Brosch/Shutterstock.com

**Trouble?** If you have trouble making the pointer change to the table column resize pointer +‖+, move the pointer a little to the left of the right border. If you still can't do it, click the Layout tab, click in the Width box in the Cell Size group, type 4.5, and then press ENTER.

7. Move the pointer on top of the top, bottom, or one of the side borders of the table so that the pointer changes to the move pointer ⛶, and then drag the table down so that the smart guides indicated that the table is centered horizontally and vertically on the slide.

On the Layout tab, in the Alignment group, you can change the alignment of text in cells. Figure 2-18 describes the buttons in the Alignment group that you can use to align text in table cells.

Figure 2-18    Alignment commands on the Layout tab

| Button | Name | Description |
| --- | --- | --- |
| | Align Left | Horizontally align the text along the left edge of the cell. |
| | Center | Horizontally align the text between the left and right edges of the cell. |
| | Align Right | Horizontally align the text along the right edge of the cell. |
| | Align Top | Vertically align the text along the top edge of the cell. |
| | Center Vertically | Vertically align the text between the top and bottom edges of the cell. |
| | Align Bottom | Vertically align the text along the bottom edge of the cell. |

The text in all cells in the table is horizontally left-aligned and vertically aligned at the top of the cells. The table would look better if the text was vertically aligned in the center of the cells.

**To adjust the alignment of text in cells:**

▶  1.  Select the entire table, if necessary.

▶  2.  Click the **Layout** tab if necessary, and then in the Alignment group, click the **Center Vertically** button ▤. The text in the table cells is now centered vertically in the cells.

Teréza wants you to change the color of the first row in the table. You can change the fill of table cells in the same manner that you change the fill of shapes.

**To change the fill of cells in the first row of the table:**

▶  1.  In the table, click any cell in the first row.

▶  2.  On the Layout tab, in the Table group, click the **Select** button, and then click **Select Row**. The first row in the table is selected.

▶  3.  Click the **Table Design** tab.

▶  4.  In the Table Styles group, click the **Shading arrow**. The Shading menu is similar to the Shape Fill menu you worked with earlier. The menu also includes the Table Background command that you can use to fill the table background with a color or a picture.

▶  5.  Click the **Tan, Background 2** color (in the third column), and then click any cell in the table to deselect the row. The menu closes and the cells in the first row are shaded with light tan. The white text is hard to read on the light background.

▶  6.  Move the pointer to the left of the first row so that it changes to the row selection pointer ➡, and then click. The first row is selected.

**Tip**

You can also change the font color of table text using the Font Color button in the Font group on the Home tab.

▶  7.  On the Table Design tab, in the WordArt Styles group, click the **Text Fill arrow** [A ▾], click the **Black, Text 1** color, and then click any cell in the table. The text in the first row changes to black.

Teréza doesn't like the changes you made. She wants you to try formatting the table with a style. When you apply a style to a table, you can specify whether the header and total rows and the first and last columns are formatted differently from the other rows and columns in the table. You can also specify whether to use banded rows or columns, which fills alternating rows or columns with different shading.

**To apply a style to the table:**

▶  1.  Click the **Table Design** tab, if necessary. In the Table Styles group, the second style, Medium Style 2 – Accent 1, is selected. In the Table Style Options group, the Header Row and Banded Rows check boxes are selected, which means that the header row will be formatted differently than the rest of the rows and that every other row will be filled with shading. See Figure 2–19.

**Figure 2–19**    **Current style and options applied to the table**

Javier Brosch/Shutterstock.com

> **2.** In the Table Styles group, click the **More** button ▾. The Table Styles gallery opens.

**Tip**

Select the View Gridlines button on the Layout tab to make the gridlines visible; deselect it to hide the gridlines.

> **3.** Click the **Medium Style 3 – Accent 3** style (in the third row in the Medium section), and then click a blank area of the slide to deselect the table. This style adds borders above and below the top row in the table and below the bottom row. Because the Header Row check box in the Table Style Options group was selected, the first row is formatted differently from the rest of the rows. And because the Banded Rows check box was selected, every other row below the header row is filled with light blue.

Teréza wants you to change the borders between the rows to dark blue instead of white. Borders are different than gridlines. Gridlines are the lines that form the structure of a table. **Borders** are drawn on top of the gridlines. To add borders, you use the buttons in the Draw Borders group on the Table Design tab. Before you change them, the settings are solid-line borders, 1 point wide, and black. See Figure 2–20.

**Figure 2–20**    **Current settings for borders**

Javier Brosch/Shutterstock.com

### To modify the borders of the table:

> **1.** Click the table, and then on the Table Design tab, in the Draw Borders group, click the **Pen Style arrow** ———▾. A menu of line styles appears, including the No Border option. Teréza wants a solid line border, so you will not change the selection.

> **2.** On the menu, click the solid line. The menu closes, the pointer changes to the pencil pointer ✎, and the Draw Table button in the Draw Borders group is selected.

3. In the Draw Borders group, click the **Pen Weight arrow** `1 pt ─────── ▾`, and then click **¼ pt**.

4. In the Draw Borders group, click the **Pen Color arrow**, and then click the **Dark Blue, Accent 3, Darker 50%** color. Now the borders you draw will be one-quarter point, solid, dark blue lines. To add a border, you click the gridline you want to add the border to.

5. Move the pointer on top of the gridline between the first cell in the second row and the first cell in the third row, and then click the mouse button. A one-quarter point, solid, dark blue line appears between the first cells in the second and third rows.

6. Click the gridline between each of the cells in the second and third rows until the border between the second and third rows is a solid line separating the rows.

**Tip**

You can also click the Borders arrow in the Table Styles group and use commands on that menu to apply or remove borders. The borders will be the style, weight, and color specified by the buttons in the Draw Borders group.

7. Create a border line between the third and fourth rows, between the fourth and fifth rows, and between the fifth and sixth rows. You are finished adding borders to the table.

8. In the Draw Borders group, click the **Draw Table** button to deselect it. The pointer changes back to its usual shape. Now that you added the borders, Teréza wants you to remove the shading from every other row.

9. In the Table Style Options group, click the **Banded Rows** check box to deselect it. All of the rows in the table are now filled with white.

## Filling Cells with Pictures

Just as you can fill a shape with a picture, you can do the same with cells. Note that many of the table styles include shaded cells as part of the style definition, so if you want to fill table cells with pictures and apply a table style, you need to apply the table style first. Otherwise, the shading that is part of the table style definition will replace the pictures in the cells.

Teréza wants you to add a picture to each row to make the table more interesting.

**To fill the cells in the first column with pictures:**

1. In the table, click in the first cell in the second row, and then click the **Table Design** tab, if necessary.

2. In the Table Styles group, click the **Shading arrow**, and then click **Picture**. The Insert Pictures window opens. See Figure 2–21.

**Figure 2-21**    Insert Pictures window

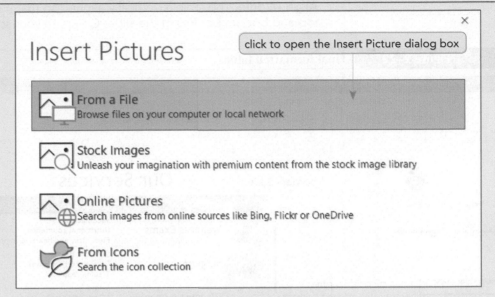

3. Click **From a File**. The Insert Picture dialog box opens.

4. Navigate to the **PowerPoint2 > Module folder**, click **Support_PPT_2_ VetDog.jpg**, and then click **Insert**. The photo fills the cell.

5. Fill the first cells in the next four rows with the following pictures, all located in the **PowerPoint2 > Module** folder: **Support_PPT_2_OR.jpg**, **Support_ PPT_2_MRI.jpg**, **Support_PPT_2_Chip.jpg**, and **Support_PPT_2_Teeth.jpg**.

The photos in the last two rows are too small, and they are distorted because they are stretched horizontally to fill the cells. To fix both of these problems, you'll increase the height of these rows.

### To change row heights in the table:

1. Click in any cell in the second row in the table, and then click the **Layout** tab. In the Height box in the Cell Size group, 1" appears. The second, third, and fourth rows are each one-inch high.

2. Position the pointer to the left of the second to last row in the table so that it changes to the row selection pointer ➡, press and hold the mouse button, drag down until the pointer is to the left of the bottom row in the table, and then release the mouse button. The last two rows in the table are selected.

3. On the Layout tab, in the Cell Size group, click in the **Height** box, type **1**, and then press **ENTER**. The height of the selected rows increases to one inch. Now you will adjust the table's placement on the slide again. This time, you will use the Align commands instead of the smart guides.

4. Click in any cell to deselect the last two rows, and then in the Arrange group, click the **Align** button. A menu with commands for aligning the objects on the slide appears. Because only one object—the table—is selected, selecting a command will align the object to the borders of the slide.

5. Click **Align Center**. The table is horizontally aligned so that it is centered between the left and right borders of the slide.

> **6.** In the Arrange group, click the **Align** button, and then on the menu, click **Align Middle**. The table is vertically aligned so that it is centered between the top and bottom borders of the slide. Compare your screen to Figure 2–22.

**Figure 2–22** **Final formatted table**

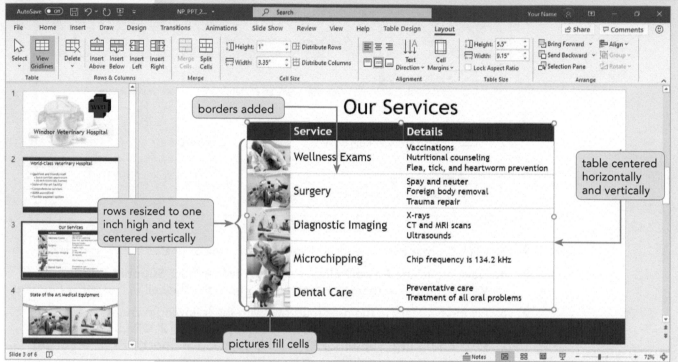

JPC-PROD/Shutterstock.com; nimon/Shutterstock.com; Ivonne Wierink/Shutterstock.com; Africa Studio/Shutterstock.com; Javier Brosch/Shutterstock.com

> **7.** Save the changes to the presentation.

# Inserting Symbols

You can insert some symbols, such as the trademark symbol, the registered trademark symbol, and the copyright symbol, by typing letters between parentheses and letting AutoCorrect change the characters to a symbol. You can insert all symbols, including letters from another alphabet, by using the Symbol button in the Symbols group on the Insert tab.

The hospital's slogan—"The only person who loves your pets more than we do is you."—is trademarked. Teréza wants you to add the trademark symbol ™ after the slogan on Slide 5.

### To insert the trademark symbol:

> **1.** Display Slide 5 ("We Treat All Small Animals"), and then click in the title text box immediately after "Animals."

> **2.** Type **(tm** in the title text box.

> **3.** Type **)** ( close parenthesis). The text "(tm)" changes to the trademark symbol, which is ™. Teréza points out that the trademark symbol should appear after the slogan, not after the slide title.

> **4.** Press **BACKSPACE**. The symbol changes to the characters you typed.

**Tip**

To insert the copyright symbol ©, type (c). To insert the registered trademark symbol ®, type (r).

5. Press **BACKSPACE** four times to delete the four characters, and then click in the text box containing the italicized slogan, immediately after the period after "you."

6. Type **(tm)** after "you." This time, the characters you typed did not change to the trademark symbol. If this happens, you need to use the symbol dialog box to insert the symbol.

7. Press **BACKSPACE** four times to delete the four characters, click the **Insert** tab, and then in the Symbols group, click the **Symbol** button. The Symbol dialog box opens.

8. If "(normal text)" does not appear in the Font box, click the **Font arrow**, and then click **(normal text)**.

9. Click the **Subset arrow**, scroll down, click **Letterlike Symbols**, and then click the trademark symbol (™) as shown in Figure 2–23. (The symbol might be in a different row and column on your screen.) In the bottom-left corner of the Symbol dialog box below "Unicode name," the name of the selected character is "Trade Mark Sign."

**Figure 2–23**   Symbol dialog box with the trademark symbol selected

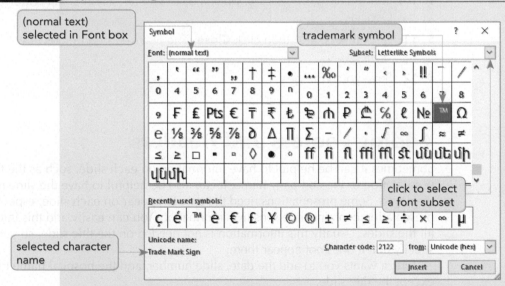

10. Click **Insert**. In the text box containing the slogan, the trademark symbol is inserted.

11. In the dialog box, click **Close**. The dialog box closes.

Teréza's first and last names contain two letters that are not in the English alphabet. You need to correct the spelling of Teréza's first and last names on Slide 6.

**To insert special characters:**

1. Display Slide 6 ("Contact Us for Assistance Traveling Abroad With Your Pet").

2. In the first bulleted item, click after the second "e" in "Tereza," and then press **BACKSPACE**. The second "e" in "Tereza" is deleted.

> **3.** On the Insert tab, in the Symbols group, click the **Symbol** button. The Symbol dialog box opens.

> **4.** At the top of the dialog box, click the **Subset arrow**, scroll the menu up, and then click **Latin-1 Supplement**. The list of symbols in the dialog box scrolls up to display the Latin-1 Supplement section.

> **5.** Click **é**. In the bottom-left corner of the Symbol dialog box, the name of the selected character is "Latin Small Letter E With Acute."
>
>   **Trouble?** If you don't see the letter é, click the down scroll arrow two times and look in the next two rows.

> **6.** Click **Insert**. The letter "é" is inserted on the slide at the insertion point.

> **7.** Click **Close**. The first word in the first bulleted item is now "Teréza."

> **8.** In the first bulleted item, click after the "c" in "Goncalves," and then press **BACKSPACE** to delete the "c."

> **9.** On the Insert tab, in the Symbols group, click the **Symbol** button to open the Symbols dialog box. The first row contains the é that you just inserted. You need to insert ç, which appears two boxes to the left of é.

> **10.** In the dialog box, click **ç**, which has the name "Latin Small Letter C With Cedilla."

> **11.** Click **Insert**, and then click **Close**. The first bulleted item is now "Teréza Gonçalves."

> **12.** Save your changes.

# Adding Footers and Headers

Sometimes it can be helpful to have information on each slide, such as the title of the presentation or the company name. It can also be helpful to have the slide number displayed. Some presentations need the date to appear on each slide, especially if the presentation contains time-sensitive information. You can easily add this information to all the slides. Usually this information is not needed on the title slide, so you can also specify that it does not appear there.

Teréza wants you to add the date, slide number, and the hospital name to each slide except the title slide.

**To add a footer, slide numbers, and the date to slides:**

**Tip**

Click the Insert Slide Number button on the Insert tab to insert the slide number on all of the slides. Click the Date & Time button to open a dialog box listing the current date and time in various formats that you can choose from.

> **1.** On the Insert tab, in the Text group, click the **Header & Footer** button. The Header and Footer dialog box opens with the Slide tab selected.

> **2.** Click the **Footer** check box to select it, and then click in the **Footer** box. In the Preview box on the right, the middle placeholder on the bottom is filled with black to indicate where the footer will appear on slides. See Figure 2–24. Note that the position of the footer, slide number, and date changes in different themes.

**Figure 2–24**     Slide tab in the Header and Footer dialog box

Header and Footer                                           ?     ✕

Slide   Notes and Handouts

Include on slide                                                    Preview

☐ Date and time                                           date
  ◉ Update automatically                                 position
    10/4/2021                          ▼
current date will    Language:              Calendar type:
appear here          English (United States)  ▼   Gregorian        ▼
  ○ Fixed
    10/4/2021                                            footer
type footer text                                          position
here            ☐ Slide number
                ☑ Footer
                                                          slide number
                                                          position
select this check box if
you don't want the    ☐ Don't show on title slide    click to display selected
selected items to                                    items on all slides
appear on the title slide
                                        Apply    Apply to All    Cancel

3. Type **Windsor Veterinary Hospital** in the Footer box.

4. Click the **Slide number** check box to select it. In the Preview box, the box in the bottom-right is filled with black.

5. Click the **Date and time** check box to select it. The options under this check box are no longer dimmed, indicating that you can use them, and in the Preview box, the box in the bottom-left is filled with black. You don't want the date in the presentation to update automatically each time the presentation is opened. You want it to show today's date so people will know that the information is current as of that date.

6. Click the **Fixed** option button, if necessary. Now you want to prevent the footer, slide number, and date from appearing on the title slide.

7. Click the **Don't show on title slide** check box to select it, and then click **Apply to All**. On Slide 6 the footer, date, and slide number are displayed. See Figure 2–25.

**Figure 2–25**     Date, footer, and slide number on Slide 6

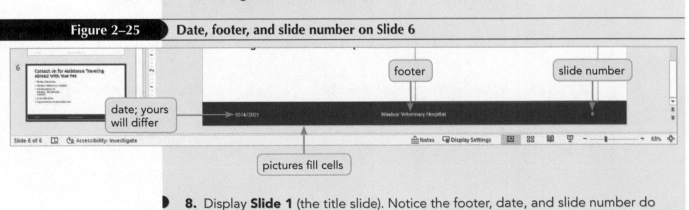

footer          slide number

date; yours
will differ

pictures fill cells

8. Display **Slide 1** (the title slide). Notice the footer, date, and slide number do not appear on the title slide.

Typically, a footer is any text that appears at the bottom of every page in a document. As you saw when you added the footer in the Header and Footer dialog box, in PowerPoint a **footer** is specifically the text that appears in the Footer box on the Slide tab in that dialog box and in the corresponding Footer text box on the slides. This text box can appear anywhere on the slide. In some themes the footer appears at the top of slides. Notes pages and handouts can also have a footer, but you need to add that separately. The text you enter in the Footer box on the Slide tab in the Header and Footer dialog box does not appear on notes pages and handouts.

A header is information displayed at the top of every page in a document. Slides do not have headers, but you can add a header to handouts and notes pages. In PowerPoint a **header** refers only to the text that appears in the Header box on the Notes and Handouts tab in the Header and Footer dialog box. In addition to headers and footers, you can also display a date and the page number on handouts and notes pages.

Teréza plans to distribute handouts when she gives her presentation, so she wants you to add information in the header and footer on handouts and notes pages.

### To modify the header and footer on handouts and notes pages:

1. On the Insert tab, in the Text group, click the **Header & Footer** button. The Header and Footer dialog box opens with the Slide tab selected.

2. Click the **Notes and Handouts** tab. The Page number check box is selected by default, and in the Preview, the lower-right rectangle is bold to indicate that this is where the page number will appear.

3. Click the **Header** check box to select it, click in the **Header** box, and then type **Windsor Veterinary Hospital**.

4. Click the **Footer** check box to select it, click in the **Footer** box, and then type your name.

5. Click the **Apply to All** button. To see the effect of modifying the handouts and notes pages, you need to look at the print preview.

6. Click the **File** tab to open Backstage view, and then in the navigation pane, click **Print**.

7. Under Settings, click the **Full Page Slides** button, and then click **Notes Pages**. The preview shows Slide 1 as a notes page. The header and footer you typed appear, along with the page number. See Figure 2–26.

**Figure 2-26**    Header and footer on the Slide 1 notes page

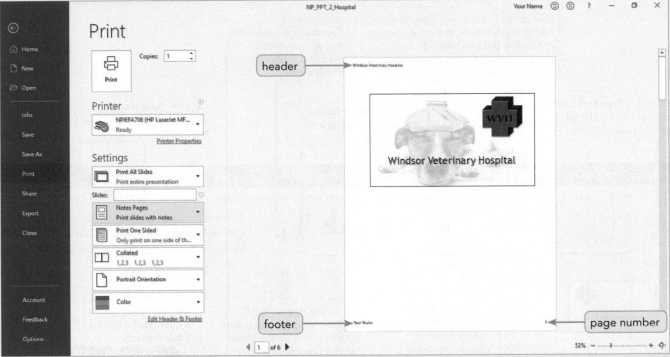

Javier Brosch/Shutterstock.com

**8.** At the top of the navigation bar, click the **Back** button ⬅ to return to Normal view.

**9.** Save your changes.

You have modified a presentation by applying a theme used in another presentation; inserting, formatting, and duplicating pictures and shapes; and inserting a table and characters that are not on your keyboard. You also added footer and header information to slides and handouts. In the next session, you will continue modifying the presentation by applying and modifying transitions and animations, and adding and modifying videos.

# Review

## Session 2.1 Quick Check

1. Which contextual tab appears on the ribbon when you select a shape?

2. What is a style?

3. What is the fill of a shape?

4. In a table, what is the intersection of a row and column called?

5. How do you know if an entire table is selected and not just active?

6. How do you insert characters that are not on your keyboard?

7. In PowerPoint, what is a footer?

# Session 2.2 Visual Overview:

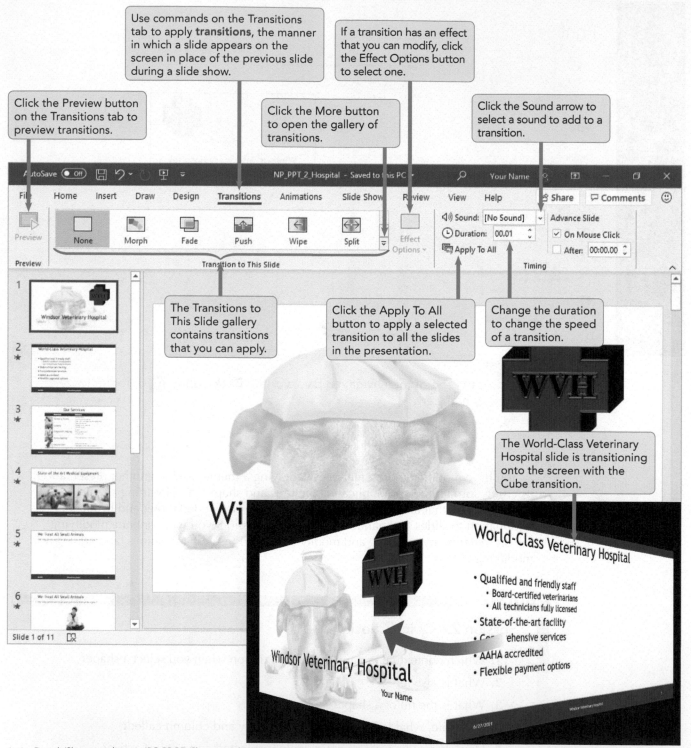

Use commands on the Transitions tab to apply **transitions**, the manner in which a slide appears on the screen in place of the previous slide during a slide show.

If a transition has an effect that you can modify, click the Effect Options button to select one.

Click the Preview button on the Transitions tab to preview transitions.

Click the More button to open the gallery of transitions.

Click the Sound arrow to select a sound to add to a transition.

The Transitions to This Slide gallery contains transitions that you can apply.

Click the Apply To All button to apply a selected transition to all the slides in the presentation.

Change the duration to change the speed of a transition.

The World-Class Veterinary Hospital slide is transitioning onto the screen with the Cube transition.

# Using Animations and Transitions

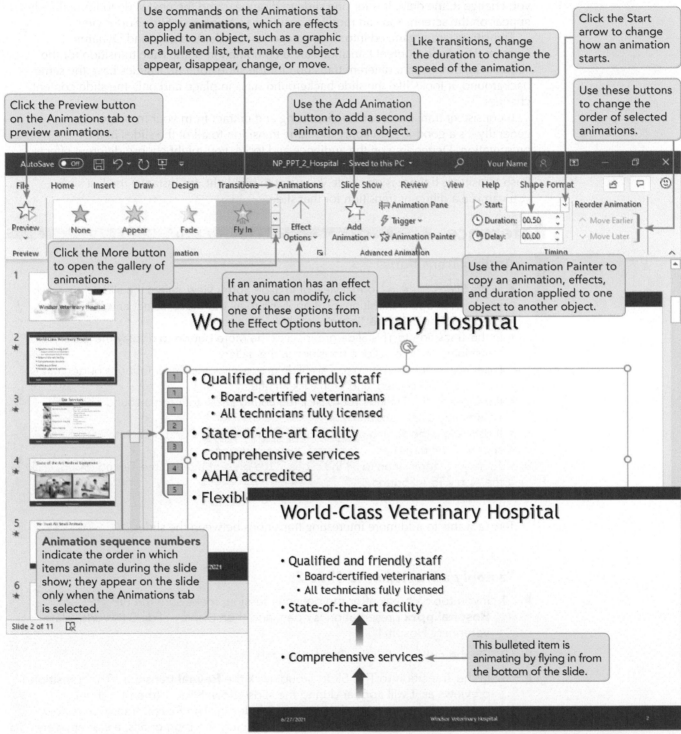

Use commands on the Animations tab to apply **animations**, which are effects applied to an object, such as a graphic or a bulleted list, that make the object appear, disappear, change, or move.

Like transitions, change the duration to change the speed of the animation.

Click the Start arrow to change how an animation starts.

Click the Preview button on the Animations tab to preview animations.

Use the Add Animation button to add a second animation to an object.

Use these buttons to change the order of selected animations.

Click the More button to open the gallery of animations.

If an animation has an effect that you can modify, click one of these options from the Effect Options button.

Use the Animation Painter to copy an animation, effects, and duration applied to one object to another object.

**Animation sequence numbers** indicate the order in which items animate during the slide show; they appear on the slide only when the Animations tab is selected.

This bulleted item is animating by flying in from the bottom of the slide.

# Applying Transitions

The Transitions tab contains commands for changing the transitions between slides. Refer to the Session 2.2 Visual Overview for more information about transitions. Unless you change it, the default is for one slide to disappear and the next slide to immediately appear on the screen. You can modify transitions in Normal or Slide Sorter view.

Transitions are organized into three categories: Subtle, Exciting, and Dynamic Content. Dynamic Content transitions are a combination of the Fade transition for the slide background and a different transition for the slide content. If slides have the same background, it looks like the slide background stays in place and only the slide content changes.

Inconsistent transitions can be distracting and detract from your message, so generally it's a good idea to apply the same transition to all of the slides in the presentation. Depending on the audience and topic, you might choose different effects of the same transition for different slides, such as changing the direction of a Wipe or Push transition. If there is one slide you want to highlight, for instance the last slide, you can use a different transition for that slide.

## Reference

### Adding Transitions

- In the Slides pane in Normal view or in Slide Sorter view, select the slide(s) to which you want to add a transition, or, if applying to all the slides, select any slide.
- On the ribbon, click the Transitions tab.
- In the Transition to This Slide group, click the More button to display the gallery of transitions, and then click a transition in the gallery.
- If desired, in the Transition to This Slide group, click the Effect Options button if it is available to be clicked, and then click an effect.
- If desired, in the Timing group, click the Sound arrow to insert a sound effect to accompany each transition.
- If desired, in the Timing group, modify the time in the Duration box to modify the speed of the transition.
- To apply the transition to all the slides in the presentation, in the Timing group, click the Apply To All button.

Teréza wants to add more interesting transitions between the slides.

### To apply a transition to Slide 2:

1. If you took a break after the previous session, make sure the **NP_PPT_2_ Hospital.pptx** presentation is open, and then display Slide 2 ("World-Class Veterinary Hospital").

2. On the ribbon, click the **Transitions** tab.

3. In the Transition to This Slide group, click the **Reveal** transition. The transition previews as it will appear during the slide show: Slide 1 (the title slide) appears, fades away, and then Slide 2 fades in. The Reveal transition is now selected in the gallery. In the pane containing the thumbnails, a star appears next to the Slide 2 thumbnail. If you missed the preview, you can see it again.

4. In the Preview group, click the **Preview** button. The transition previews again.

5. In the Transition to This Slide group, click the **More** button ⊽. The gallery opens listing all the transitions. See Figure 2–27.

**Figure 2-27**    **Transition to This Slide gallery**

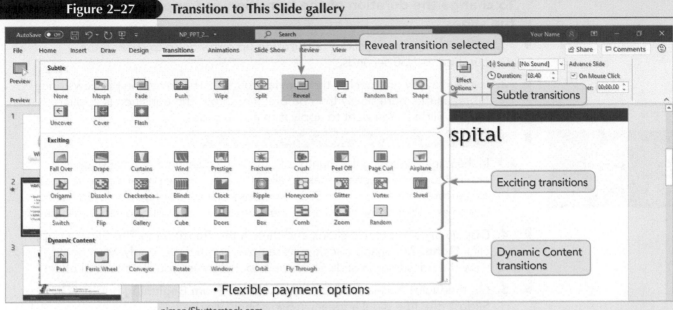

nimon/Shutterstock.com

**6.** Click the **Push** transition. The preview shows Slide 2 slide up from the bottom and push Slide 1 up and out of view.

Most transitions have effects that you can modify. For example, the Peel Off transition can peel from the bottom-left or the bottom-right corner, and the Wipe transition can wipe from any direction. You'll modify the effect of the transition applied to Slide 2.

### To modify the transition effect for Slide 2:

**1.** In the Transition to This Slide group, click the **Effect Options** button. The effects that you can modify for the Push transition are listed on the menu.

**2.** Click **From Right**. The Push transition previews again, but this time Slide 2 slides from the right to push Slide 1 left. The available effects change depending on the transition selected.

**3.** In the Transition to This Slide group, click the **Shape** transition. The transition previews with a brief view of Slide 1, before Slide 2 appears in the center of Slide 1 and enlarges in a circular shape to fill the slide.

**4.** Click the **Effect Options** button. The effects that you can modify for the Shape transition are listed.

**5.** Click **Out**. The preview of the transition with this effect displays Slide 2 in the center of Slide 1 that grows in a rectangular shape to fill the slide.

Finally, you can also change the duration of a transition. The duration is the length of time, or the speed, from the beginning to the end of the transition. To make the transition faster, decrease the duration. To slow the transition down, increase the duration. The duration is measured in seconds.

Teréza likes the Shape transition, but she thinks it is a little fast, so you will increase the duration. Then you can apply the modified transition to all the slides.

**To change the duration of the transition and apply it to all the slides:**

▶ **1.** In the Timing group, click the **Duration** up arrow twice to change the duration to 1.50 seconds.

▶ **2.** In the Preview group, click the **Preview** button. The transition previews once more, a little more slowly than before. Right now, the transition is applied only to Slide 2. You want to apply it to all the slides.

▶ **3.** In the Timing group, click the **Apply To All** button.

In the pane containing the thumbnails, the star indicating that a transition is applied to the slide appears next to all of the slides in the presentation. You want to remove the transition from Slide 1 because that slide will be displayed on the screen as audience members enter the room where you will give your presentation.

▶ **4.** Display Slide 1 (the title slide), and then in the Transition to This Slide group, click **None**. The Shape transition is removed from Slide 1 only. You should view the transitions in Slide Show view to make sure you like the final effect.

▶ **5.** On the Quick Access Toolbar, click the **Start From Beginning** button 🔲. Slide 1 (the title slide) appears in Slide Show view.

▶ **6.** Press **SPACEBAR** or **ENTER** to advance through the slide show. The transitions look fine.

▶ **7.** End the presentation, and then save your changes.

> Make sure you click the Apply To All button or the transition is applied only to the currently selected slide or slides.

# Applying Animations

Animations add interest to a slide show and draw attention to the text or object being animated. For example, you can animate a slide title to fly in from the side or spin around like a pinwheel to draw the audience's attention to that title. Refer to the Session 2.2 Visual Overview for more information about animations.

Animation effects are grouped into four types:

- **Entrance**—Text and objects do not appear on the slide until the animation occurs. This is one of the most commonly used animation types.
- **Emphasis**—Text and objects on the slide change in appearance or move.
- **Exit**—Text and objects leave the screen before the slide show advances to the next slide.
- **Motion Paths**—Text and objects follow a path on the slide.

## Animating Objects

You can animate any object on a slide, including pictures, shapes, and text boxes. To animate an object you click it, and then select an animation in the Animation group on the Animations tab.

# Reference

## Applying Animations

- On the slide displayed in Normal view, select the object you want to animate.
- On the ribbon, click the Animations tab.
- In the Animation group, click the More button to display the gallery of animations, and then click an animation in the gallery.
- If desired, in the Animation group, click the Effect Options button, and then click a direction effect. If the object is a text box, click a sequence effect.
- If desired, in the Timing group, modify the time in the Duration box to modify the speed of the animation.
- If desired, in the Timing group, click the Start arrow, and then click a different setting.

Slide 4 contains two pictures. Teréza wants you to add an animation to the title text on this slide.

### To animate the title on Slide 4:

1. Display Slide 4 ("State of the Art Medical Equipment"), and then click the **Animations** tab on the ribbon. Because nothing is selected on the slide, the animations in the Animation group are gray.

2. Click the **State of the Art Medical Equipment** title text. The animations in the Animation group are green to indicate that they are now available. All of the animations currently visible in the Animation group are entrance animations.

3. In the Animation group, click the **Fly In** animation. The animation previews on the slide, showing the title text fly in from the bottom. In the Timing group, the Start box displays On Click, which indicates that this animation will occur when you advance the slide show by clicking the mouse or pressing SPACEBAR or ENTER. The animation sequence number 1 in the box to the left of the title text box indicates that this is the first animation that will occur on the slide when you advance the slide show. You can preview the animation again if you missed it.

4. In the Preview group, click the **Preview** button. The animation previews again.

5. In the Animation group, click the **More** button. The Animation gallery opens. The animation commands are listed by category, and each category appears in a different color. At the bottom are four commands, each of which opens a dialog box listing all the effects in that category. See Figure 2–28. You will try an emphasis animation.

**Figure 2–28** **Animation gallery**

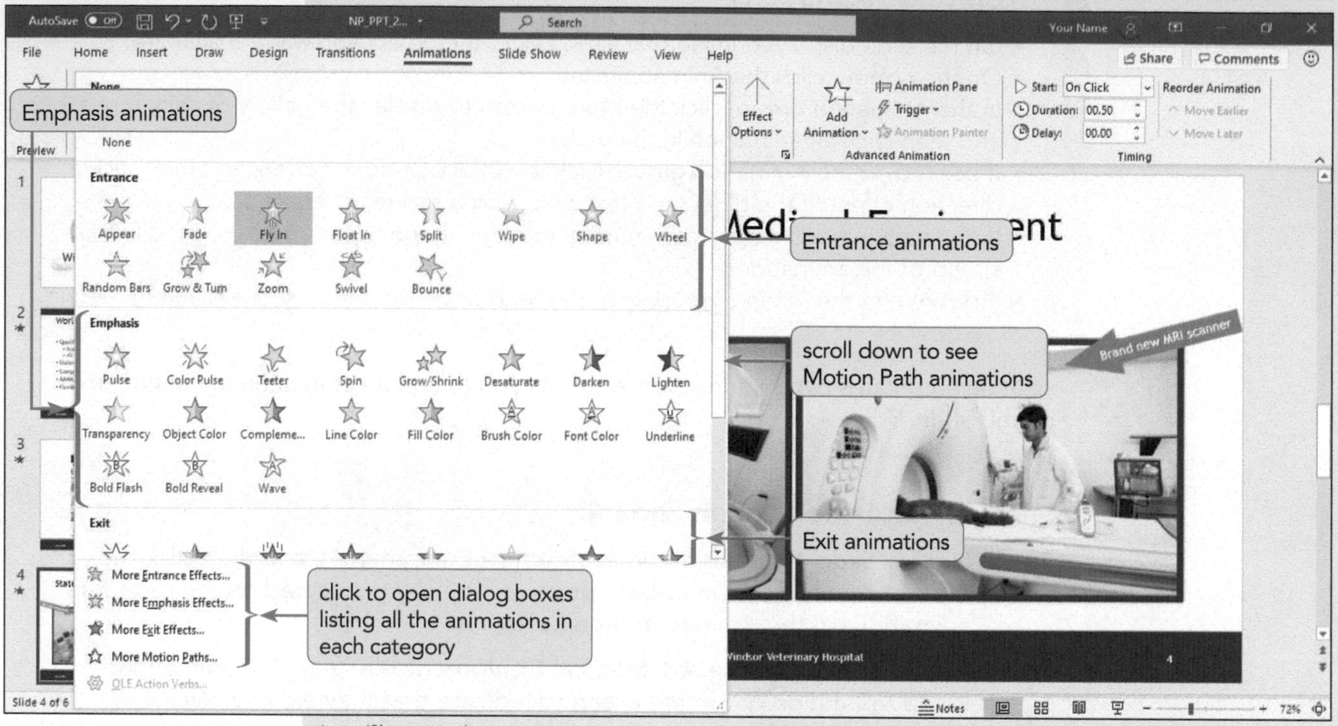

nimon/Shutterstock.com

> **6.** Under Emphasis, click the **Underline** animation. The Underline animation replaces the Fly In animation, and the slide title is underlined in the preview.

The Underline animation you applied to the slide title is an example of an emphasis animation you can apply only to text boxes. You cannot apply this animation to other types of objects, such as pictures or tables.

Slide 4 contains two photos. To focus the audience's attention on one photo at time, you will apply an entrance animation to the photos so that they appear one at a time during the slide show.

### To apply an entrance animation to a photo on Slide 4:

> **1.** On Slide 4 ("State of the Art Medical Equipment"), click the picture on the right.

> **2.** In the Animation group, click the **More** button. Notice that in the Emphasis section, six of the animations, including the Underline animation you just applied to the slide title, are gray, which means they are not available for this object. These six animations are available only for text.

> **3.** In the Entrance section, click the **Split** animation. The picture appears starting from the left and right edges. In the Timing group, On Click appears in the Start box, indicating that this animation will occur when you advance the slide show. The animation sequence number to the left of the selected picture is 2, which indicates that this is the second animation that will occur on the slide when you advance the slide show.

You need to change the direction from which this animation appears, and you want to slow it down.

### To change the effect and duration of an animation:

▶ **1.** In the Animation group, click the **Effect Options** button. This menu contains Direction options.

▶ **2.** Click **Vertical Out**. The preview shows the picture appearing, starting from the center and building out to the left and right edges.

▶ **3.** In the Timing group, click the **Duration** up arrow once. The duration changes from 0.50 seconds to 0.75 seconds.

After you have applied and customized the animation for one object, you can use the Animation Painter to copy that animation to other objects. You will copy the Split entrance animation to the other photo on Slide 4.

### To use the Animation Painter to copy the animation on Slide 4:

▶ **1.** Click the photo on the right.

▶ **2.** In the Advanced Animation group, click the **Animation Painter** button, and then move the pointer onto the slide. The pointer changes to the Animation Painter pointer ⬚.

▶ **3.** Click the photo on the left. The Split animation with the Vertical Out effect and a duration of 0.75 seconds is copied to the photo on the left, and the animation previews.

After you apply animations, you should watch them in Slide Show view to see what they will look like during a slide show. Remember that On Click appeared in the Start box for each animation that you applied, which means that to see the animation during the slide show, you need to advance the slide show.

### To view the animations on Slide 4 in Slide Show view:

▶ **1.** Make sure Slide 4 ("State of the Art Medical Equipment") is displayed.

▶ **2.** On the status bar, click the **Slide Show** button ⬚. When you click this button to start a slide show, the slide show starts from the current slide instead of from the beginning. Slide 4 appears in Slide Show view. Only the title, the arrow shapes, and the footer appear on the slide.

▶ **3.** Press **SPACEBAR** to advance the slide show. The first animation, the emphasis animation that underlines the title, occurs.

▶ **4.** Press **SPACEBAR** again. The photo on the right appears starting at the center of the photo and building out to the left and right edges.

▶ **5.** Click anywhere on the screen. The photo on the left appears with the same animation as the photo on the right.

▶ **6.** Press **ESC**. The slide show ends and Slide 4 appears in Normal view.

Teréza doesn't like the emphasis animation applied to the slide title. It's distracting because the photos are the focus of the slide, not the title. Also, she thinks it would be better if the photo on the left appeared before the photo on the right. Finally, Teréza wants the arrows to animate after each photo appears. To fix these issues, you will remove the animation applied to the title, add entrance animations to the arrows, and change the order of the animations so that the photo on the left animates first, followed by its arrow, then the photo on the right animates followed by its arrow.

### To remove the title animation, animate the arrows, and change the order of the animations:

1. Click the **State of the Art Medical Equipment** title text. In the Animation group, the yellow emphasis animation Underline is selected.

**Tip**

You can also click the animation sequence icon, and then press DELETE to remove an animation.

2. In the Animation group, click the **More** button ⬇, and then at the top of the gallery, click **None**. The animation that was applied to the title is removed, the animation sequence icon no longer appears next to the title text box, and the other two animation sequence icons on the slide are renumbered 1 and 2. Next you will apply animation to the two arrows.

3. Apply the entrance **Wipe** animation to the "Recently updated OR" arrow, and then change its effect option to **From Left**.

4. Apply the entrance **Wipe** animation to the "Brand new MRI scanner" arrow, and then change its effect option to **From Right**. Now you need to select the animation applied to the photo on the left and change it so that it occurs first. You can select the object or the animation sequence icon to modify an animation.

5. Next to the left photo, click the **2** animation sequence icon. In the Animation group, the green Split entrance animation is selected. See Figure 2–29.

**Figure 2–29**   **Animation selected to change its order**

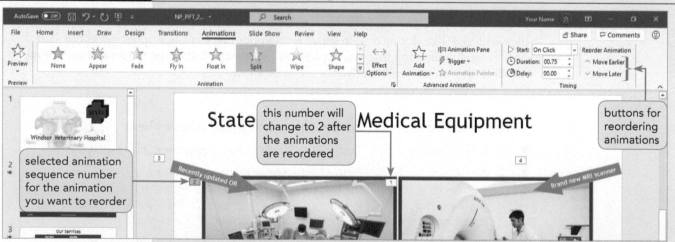

nimon/Shutterstock.com; Javier Brosch/Shutterstock.com

6. In the Timing group, click the **Move Earlier** button. The animation sequence icon next to the photo on the left changes from 2 to 1, and the animation sequence icon next to the photo on the right changes from 1 to 2. Now you need to reorder the animations so that the "Recently updated OR" arrow animates after the picture on the left.

7. Next to the "Recently updated OR" arrow, click the **3** animation sequence icon, and then in the Timing group, click the **Move Earlier** button.

> **8.** In the Preview group, click the **Preview** button. The photo on the left appears, then the "Recently updated OR" arrow, then the photo on the right, and then the "Brand new MRI scanner" arrow.

## Changing How an Animation Starts

Remember that when you apply an animation, the default is for the object to animate On Click, which means when you advance through the slide show. You can change this so that an animation happens automatically, either at the same time as another animation or when the slide transitions, or after another animation or the transition.

Teréza wants the arrows to appear automatically after each photo without the presenter needing to advance the slide show.

### To change how the animation for the arrows start:

> **1.** On Slide 4 ("State of the Art Medical Equipment"), click the **Recently updated OR** arrow. The Wipe entrance animation is selected in the Animation group, and in the Timing group, On Click appears in the Start box.

> **2.** In the Timing group, click the **Start** arrow. The menu lists three choices for starting an animation: On Click, With Previous, and After Previous.

> **3.** Click **After Previous**. Now this arrow will appear automatically after the photo on the left appears. Notice that the animation sequence number next to the arrow changed to 1, the same number as the animation sequence number next to the photo on the left. This is because you will not need to advance the slide show to start this animation.

> **4.** Change the way the animation applied to the "Brand new MRI scanner" arrow starts to **After Previous**.

When you preview an animation, it plays automatically on the slide in Normal view, even if the timing setting for the animation is On Click. To make sure the timing settings are correct, you need to watch the animation in a slide show.

### To view and test the animations:

> **1.** On the status bar, click the **Slide Show** button 🖵. Slide 4 appears in Slide Show view.

> **2.** Press **SPACEBAR**. The photo on the left appears, followed by the "Recently updated OR" arrow.

> **3.** Press **SPACEBAR**. The photo on the right appears, followed by the "Brand new MRI scanner" arrow.

> **4.** Press **ESC** to end the slide show.

When you set an animation to occur automatically during the slide show, it happens immediately after the previous action. You can add a pause before the animation so that there is time between automatic animations. To do this, you increase the time in the Delay box in the Timing group. Like the Duration time, Delay times are measured in seconds.

To give the audience time to look at the first photo before the second photo appears on Slide 4, you will add a delay to the animation that is applied to the photo on the right.

### To add a delay to the animations applied to the arrows:

▶ **1.** On Slide 4 ("State of the Art Medical Equipment"), click the "Brand new MRI scanner" arrow to select it, if necessary. In the Timing group, 00.00 appears in the Delay box.

▶ **2.** In the Timing group, click the **Delay** up arrow four times to change the time to one second. After the photo on the right appears (the previous animation), the "Brand new MRI scanner" arrow will appear after a delay of one second.

▶ **3.** Apply a one-second delay to the animation applied to the "Recently updated OR" arrow.

▶ **4.** On the status bar, click the **Slide Show** button 🖵. Slide 4 appears in Slide Show view.

▶ **5.** Press **SPACEBAR**. The photo on the left appears, and then after a one-second delay, the "Recently updated OR" arrow appears.

▶ **6.** Press **SPACEBAR**. The photo on the right appears, and then after a one-second delay, the "Brand new MRI scanner" arrow appears.

▶ **7.** Press **ESC** to end the slide show, and then save your changes.

## Animating Lists

If you animate a list, the default is for each of the first-level items to animate On Click. This type of animation focuses your audience's attention on each item, without the distraction of items that you haven't discussed yet.

Teréza wants you to add an Entrance animation to the bulleted list on Slide 2. She wants each first-level bulleted item to appear on the slide one at a time so that the audience won't be able to read ahead while she is discussing each point.

### To animate the bulleted list on Slide 2:

▶ **1.** Display Slide 2 ("World-Class Veterinary Hospital"), and then click anywhere in the bulleted list to make the text box active.

▶ **2.** On the Animations tab, in the Animation group, click the **Fly In** animation. The animation previews on the slide as the bulleted items fly in from the bottom. When the "Qualified and friendly staff" item flies in, its subitems fly in with it. After the preview is finished, the numbers 1 through 5 appear next to the bulleted items. Notice that the subitems have the same animation sequence number as their first-level item. This means that the subitems are set to start With Previous or After Previous. See Figure 2–30.

**Figure 2–30**     **Fly In entrance animation applied to a bulleted list with subitems**

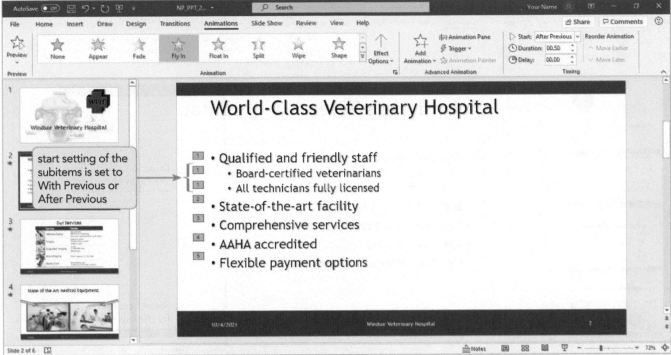

Javier Brosch/Shutterstock.com; JPC-PROD/Shutterstock.com; nimon/Shutterstock.com; Ivonne Wierink/Shutterstock.com; Africa Studio/Shutterstock.com

3. Next to the "Qualified and friendly staff" bulleted item, click the **1** animation sequence icon to select it. In the Timing group, On Click appears in the Start box.

4. Next to the subitem "Board-certified veterinarians," click the **1** animation sequence icon. In the Timing group, With Previous appears in the Start box.

If you wanted to change how the items in the list animate during the slide show, you could change the Start setting of each item, or you could change the sequence effect. Sequence effects appear on the Effect Options menu in addition to the Direction options when you apply an animation to a text box. The default is for the items to appear By Paragraph. This means each first-level item animates one at a time—with its subitems, if there are any—when you advance the slide show. You can change this setting so that the entire list animates at once as one object, or so that each first-level item animates at the same time but as separate objects.

**To examine the Sequence options for the animated list:**

1. Click in the bulleted list, and then in the Animation group, click the **Effect Options** button. The Sequence options appear at the bottom of the menu, below the Direction options, and By Paragraph is selected. See Figure 2–31.

**Figure 2–31** **Animation effect options for a bulleted list**

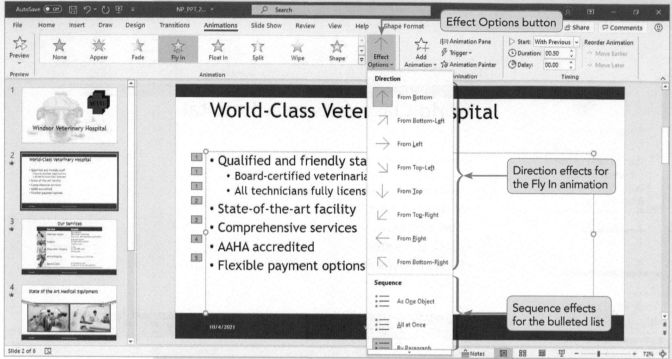

Javier Brosch/Shutterstock.com; JPC-PROD/Shutterstock.com; nimon/Shutterstock.com; Ivonne Wierink/Shutterstock.com; Africa Studio/Shutterstock.com

2. Click **As One Object**. The animation preview shows the entire text box fly in. After the preview, only one animation sequence icon appears next to the text box, indicating that the entire text box will animate as a single object. In the Timing group, On Click appears in the Start box.

3. In the Animation group, click the **Effect Options** button, and then under Sequence, click **All at Once**. The animation previews again, but this time each of the first-level items fly in as separate objects, although they all fly in at the same time. Visually, there is not much of a difference between this option and the As One Object option for the Fly In animation. After the preview, animation sequence icons, all numbered 1, appear next to each bulleted item, indicating that each item will animate separately but you only need to advance the slide show once.

4. Next to the first bulleted item, click the **1** animation sequence icon. In the Timing group, On Click appears in the Start box.

5. Next to the second first-level item ("State-of-the-art facility"), click the **1** animation sequence icon. In the Timing group, With Previous appears in the Start box.

6. In the Animation group, click the **Effect Options** button, and then click **By Paragraph**. The sequence effect changes back to its original setting.

7. Save your changes.

## Proskills

### Decision Making: Just Because You Can Doesn't Mean You Should

PowerPoint provides you with many tools that enable you to create interesting and creative slide shows. Just because a tool is available doesn't mean you should use it. You need to give careful thought before deciding to use a tool to enhance the content of your presentation. One example of a tool to use sparingly is sound effects with transitions. Most of the time you do not need to use sound to highlight the fact that one slide is leaving the screen while another appears. Many people find sound transitions annoying or distracting.

You will also want to avoid using too many or frivolous animations. It is easy to go overboard with animations, and they can quickly become distracting and make your presentation seem less professional. Before you apply an animation, you should know what you want to emphasize and why you want to use an animation. Animations should enhance your message. When you are finished giving your presentation, you want your audience to remember your message, not your animations.

## Using the Morph Transition

The Morph transition is a special transition that essentially combines a transition with an animation. With the Morph transition, you can move an object to a new location on a slide; change the size, shape, and color of an object; and zoom into or out from an object.

To use the Morph transition, you need to follow these steps:

1. Create a slide that contains all of the items you want to appear to change size or position during the slide show.
2. Duplicate that slide or create a second slide with at least one object in common with the first slide.
3. On the duplicate slide, move the object or objects to the new position or make other changes to the objects, such as changing their size or color.
4. Apply the Morph transition to the duplicate slide.

When you use the Morph transition, you might need to place objects in the area outside the actual slide. The area outside of the slide is part of the PowerPoint workspace, but anything positioned in this area will not be visible in Slide Show or Presenter view. To use the workspace, you may need to zoom out.

### To drag objects off Slide 5:

▶ 1. Display Slide 5 ("We Treat All Small Animals"). This slide contains four pictures. During the slide show, each picture needs to appear in the center of the slide and then move out of the way to make space for the next picture. First, you will move all of the pictures off of the slide to the workspace, and then you will zoom out to see more of the workspace.

▶ 2. On the status bar, click the **Zoom Out** button ▬ as many times as needed to change the zoom percentage to 40%.

▶ 3. Drag the first picture (the man sitting with several animals on him) to the left of the slide, using the smart guides to keep it aligned with the other pictures.

▶ 4. Drag the next picture (hands around a yellow bird) off the slide and position it to the left of the first picture.

▶ 5. Drag the next picture (a woman patting a bearded dragon) to the right of the slide, and then drag the last picture (closeup of a dog) to the right of the picture of the woman. See Figure 2–32. This is the starting slide for the Morph transition.

**Figure 2–32**   **Pictures moved off of Slide 5**

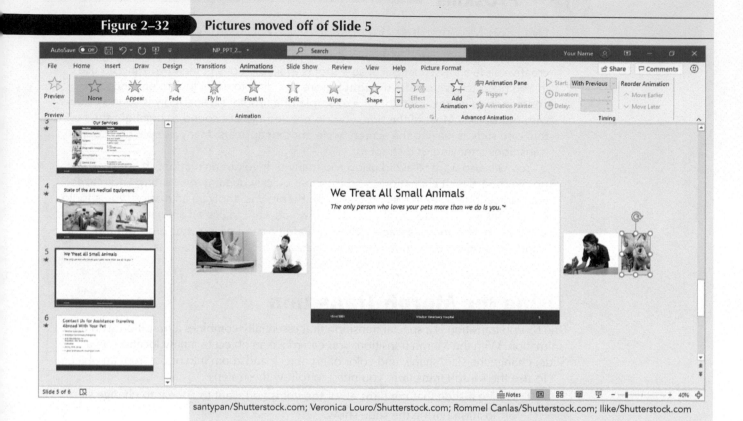

santypan/Shutterstock.com; Veronica Louro/Shutterstock.com; Rommel Canlas/Shutterstock.com; Ilike/Shutterstock.com

The steps in this section instruct you to place the objects at very precise locations. The instructions are specific so that your final file matches the official solution file. If you were creating this for your own use, the placement of the objects off the slide would not need to be so precise. After you place objects in your own files, preview the transition or watch it in Slide Show view, and then decide for yourself if you like the way the objects appear to move or if you want to reposition them for a better effect.

You have created the starting slide for the Morph transition. Next, you need to duplicate the slide and move and change at least one object.

### To duplicate Slide 5 and resize and reposition a photo on Slide 6:

1. In the pane that contains the slide thumbnails, right-click the **Slide 5** thumbnail, and then click **Duplicate Slide**. The new Slide 6 is selected.

2. To the left of Slide 6, click the picture of the man sitting with several animals on him, and then click the **Picture Format** tab.

3. In the Size group, click in the **Shape Height** box, type **4**, and then press **ENTER**.

4. Drag the picture of the man to the center of the slide so that the smart guides show that it is centered both horizontally and vertically.

   **Trouble?** If you have difficulty making the correct smart guides appear, use the Align Center and Align Middle commands in the Arrange group.

5. Click the **Transitions** tab, and then in the Transition to This Slide group, click the **Morph** transition. The Morph transition is applied to Slide 6, and the picture of the man sitting moves onto the slide and resizes as the transition previews.

6. Display Slide 5, and then on the status bar, click the **Slide Show** button 🖵. Slide 5 appears in Slide Show view.

7. Press **SPACEBAR**. Slide 6 appears, and the picture of the seated man slides onto the slide and gets larger.

8. Press **ESC** to end the slide show.

The Morph transition made it look like you had applied both the Fly In animation and the Zoom animation to the picture. Now that you have seen how the Morph transition works, you will repeat the process until the final slide shows all the photos correctly positioned and sized.

### To complete the Morph transition effect for the pictures originally on Slide 5:

1. Duplicate Slide 6. The new Slide 7 is selected. On the Transitions tab, the Morph transition is selected. When you duplicated Slide 6, the transition was copied as well.

2. On Slide 7, change the height of the picture of the seated man to **3.2"**.

3. Drag the picture of the seated man to the lower-right corner of the slide so that the smart guides show that there is the same amount of space below the picture and above the title text box, and so that the right edge of the picture aligns with the right edge of the slide.

4. To the right of the slide, change the height of the picture of the woman patting the bearded dragon to **4"**, and then drag the picture of the woman to the center of the slide.

5. Duplicate Slide 7.

6. On the new Slide 8, change the height of the picture of the woman to **2.3"** and then drag the picture to the left so that the smart guides show that the center of the picture aligns with the top of the picture of the seated man, and so that there is the same amount of space between the right edge of the picture of the woman and the center of the slide as there is between the left edge of the picture of the seated man and the center of the slide.

7. To the left of the slide, change the height of the picture of the yellow bird to **4"**, and then drag the picture of the bird to the center of the slide.

8. Duplicate Slide 8.

9. On the new Slide 9, change the height of the picture of the bird to **2.1"** and then drag it to approximately one-quarter of an inch to the left of the seated man so one smart guide shows that its bottom aligns with the bottom of the picture of the woman and another smart guide appears vertically through the center of the picture of the bird. (This vertical smart guide is indicating that the center of the picture is aligned with the right edge of the text box containing the footer.)

10. To the right of the slide, change the height of the picture of the kitten and puppy to **4"** and then drag it to the center of the slide.

11. Duplicate Slide 9.

12. On the new Slide 10, change the height of the picture of the kitten and puppy to **3.5"** and then position it to the left of the picture of the bird so that the

middle of the picture of the kitten and puppy aligns with the bottom of the picture of the woman and so that there is the same amount of space between the picture of the kitten and puppy and the photos on either side of it.

▶ 13. On the status bar, click the **Fit slide to current window** button ⬦. Compare your screen to Figure 2–33.

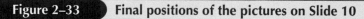

| Figure 2–33 | Final positions of the pictures on Slide 10 |

Rommel Canlas/Shutterstock.com; Ilike/Shutterstock.com; santypan/Shutterstock.com; Veronica Louro/Shutterstock.com

Now that you have created all the necessary slides, you can view the slides in Slide Show view to see the effect of the Morph transition.

### To view Slides 5 through 10 in Slide Show view:

▶ 1. Display Slide 5 (the first "We Treat All Small Animals" slide), and then on the status bar, click the **Slide Show** button 🖵. Slide 5 appears in Slide Show view. The pictures that you positioned to the left and right of the slide are not visible. In the lower-right corner of the screen, the slide number 5 appears.

▶ 2. Press **SPACEBAR**. The picture of the seated man appears from the left, moves to the slide, and grows larger. In the lower-right corner of the screen, the slide number changes to 6.

▶ 3. Press **SPACEBAR**. The picture of the seated person shrinks and moves to the lower right corner of the slide while the picture of the person leaning over a table appears from the right, moves to the center of the slide, and grows in size. Again, the slide number changes.

▶ 4. Press **SPACEBAR** three more times. The other two pictures move onto the slide and are repositioned in their final locations. The changing slide numbers distract from the effect you are trying to create with the Morph transition.

▶ **5.** Press **ESC** to end the slide show, and then click the **Insert** tab.

▶ **6.** In the Text group, click the **Header & Footer** button, click the **Slide number** check box to deselect it, and then click **Apply to All**. Now the changing slide number will not distract the viewer from the Morph transition effect.

You can also use the Morph transition on slides that contain text. You will apply the Morph transition to Slide 2 so that the title on Slide 1 looks like it moves into the footer on Slide 2.

**To apply the Morph transition to Slide 2:**

▶ **1.** Display Slide 1. The title text box contains the text "Windsor Veterinary Hospital."

▶ **2.** Display Slide 2. The footer contains the same text as in the title text box on Slide 1—"Windsor Veterinary Hospital."

▶ **3.** On the ribbon, click the **Transitions** tab, and then click the **Morph** transition. The Morph transition is applied to Slide 2 and previews.

▶ **4.** On the Quick Access Toolbar, click the **Start From Beginning** button ▣. Slide 1 appears in Slide Show view.

▶ **5.** Press **SPACEBAR**. Slide 2 appears in Slide Show view, and as it does, the title text from Slide 1 moves down into the footer on Slide 2.

▶ **6.** Press **SPACEBAR**. The first bulleted item flies onto the screen.

▶ **7.** Press **ESC** to end the slide show, and then save the changes to the presentation.

# Adding and Modifying Video

You can add video to slides to play during your presentation. PowerPoint supports various file formats, including the MPEG-4 format, the Windows Media Audio/Video format, and the QuickTime movie format. After you insert a video, you can modify it by changing playback options, changing the length of time the video plays, and applying formats and styles to the video.

## Adding Video to Slides

To insert a video stored on your computer or network, click the Insert Video button in a content placeholder to open the Insert Video dialog box. You can also click the Video button in the Media group on the Insert tab, and then click This Device to open the same Insert Video dialog box.

# Reference

## Adding Videos Stored on Your Computer or Network

- In a content placeholder, click the Insert Video button to open the Insert Video dialog box, or click the Insert tab on the ribbon, and then in the Media group, click the Video button, and then click This Device to open the Insert Video dialog box.
- Click the video you want to use, and then click the Insert button.
- Choose how the video starts by clicking the Playback tab, and then in the Video Options group:
  - In the Start box, leave the setting as In Click Sequence to have the video start playing when you advance the slide show, when you click anywhere on the video, or when you click the Play button on the video toolbar.
  - Click the Start arrow, and then click Automatically to have the video start automatically when the slide appears in Slide Show view.
  - Click the Start arrow, and then click When Clicked On to have the video start when you click anywhere on the video or when you click the Play button on the video toolbar.
- Click the Play Full Screen check box to select it to have the video fill the screen.
- Click the Rewind after Playing check box to select it to have the poster frame display after the video plays.
- Click the Volume button, and then click a volume level or click Mute.

Teréza gave you a video that she wants you to add to Slide 11. The video shows a happy dog running towards the camera in slow motion.

### To add a video to Slide 11 and play it:

1. Display Slide 11 ("Contact Us for Assistance Traveling Abroad With Your Pet"), and then in the content placeholder, click the **Insert Video** button ▦. The Insert Video dialog box opens.

**Tip**

To link a video to a slide, in the Insert Video dialog box, click the Insert arrow, and then click Link to File.

2. In the **PowerPoint2 > Module** folder, click **Support_PPT_2_Running.mov**, and then click **Insert**. The video is inserted on the slide in place of the content placeholder. The first frame of the video is displayed, and a video toolbar with controls for playing the video appears below it. The video contextual tabs appear on the ribbon. See Figure 2-34.

**Figure 2–34**     Video added to Slide 11

Multifocus/Shutterstock.com; Rommel Canlas/Shutterstock.com; Ilike/Shutterstock.com; santypan/Shutterstock.com; Veronica Louro/Shutterstock.com

4. On the video toolbar, click the **Play** button ▶. The Play button changes to the Pause button ❚❚ and the video plays. Watch the 11-second video (note that this video does not have any sound).

5. Click the **Playback** tab. In the Start box, In Click Sequence appears. This means that the video will start playing during a slide show when you advance the slide show or when you click the video or the Play button on the video toolbar. Next, you'll watch the video in Slide Show view.

6. On the status bar, click the **Slide Show** button 🖥. Slide 11 appears in Slide Show view.

7. Press **SPACEBAR**. The video starts playing because you advanced the slide show.

8. Before the video finishes playing, move the pointer to make it visible, and then click the video. The video pauses. To stop the video from playing, you can click it, or you can move the pointer on top of the video and then click the Pause button on the video toolbar.

   Because you already started playing the video once, if you advance the slide show, the next slide will appear. If you want to start the video playing again, you need to click it or click the Play button on the video toolbar,

9. Move the pointer on top of the video. The video toolbar appears, and the pointer changes to the pointing finger pointer 👆.

10. Click anywhere on the video. The video continues playing from the point it left off.

11. Press **SPACEBAR**. The black slide that indicates the end of the slide show appears.

12. Press **SPACEBAR** again to return to Normal view.

## Insight

### Inserting Pictures and Videos You Find Online

In addition to adding pictures and video stored on your computer or network to slides, you can also add pictures and video stored on websites. To add pictures from a website or OneDrive, you click the Pictures button in the Images group on the Insert tab, and then click Online Pictures. When you do this, the Online Pictures window opens, in which you can use the Bing search engine to search for images stored on the Internet. Your results will be similar to those you would get if you typed keywords in the Search box on the Bing home page in your browser.

To add a video from a website such as YouTube, you click the Video button in the Media group on the Insert tab, and then click Online Video to open a window for inserting a video from a website. In this window, you type or paste the web address of a video stored on a website such as YouTube or Vimeo. A preview of the video appears in the window so you can confirm it. Keep in mind that using online media is subject to each provider's Terms of Use policy.

## Trimming Videos

Keeping your videos short and only showing necessary content helps to keep your audience focused. If a video is too long, or if there are parts at the beginning or end of the video that you don't want to show during the presentation, you can trim it. To do this, click the Trim Video button in the Editing group on the Playback tab, and then, in the Trim Video dialog box, drag the green start slider or the red stop slider to a new position to mark where the video will start and stop.

Teréza wants the video to end right after the dog runs off screen, so she wants you to trim it.

**To trim the video on Slide 11:**

▶  1. On Slide 11 ("Contact Us for Assistance Traveling Abroad With Your Pet"), click the video to select it, and then click the **Playback** tab, if necessary.

▶  2. In the Editing group, click the **Trim Video** button. The Trim Video dialog box opens. See Figure 2–35.

| Figure 2–35 | Trim Video dialog box |

Multifocus/Shutterstock.com

**Trouble?** If the video appears black in the dialog box, click the Play button in the dialog box, and then click the Pause button to stop the playback. The video should appear.

3. Drag the red **Stop** tab to the left until the time in the End Time box is approximately 9.5 seconds.

4. If the number in the End Time box is not 00:09.500, click in the End Time box, click after the last number, edit the time so it is **00:09.500**, and then click **OK**.

5. On the video toolbar, click the **Play** button ▶. The video plays from the beginning but stops playing after 9.5 seconds. The last 1.5 seconds of the video do not play.

6. Save your changes.

## Setting a Poster Frame

The frame that appears on the video object when the video is not playing is called the **poster frame**. The default poster frame for a video is the first frame of the video. You can select any frame from the video or any image stored in a file as the poster frame. If the video is set to rewind, the poster frame will reappear after playing.

Teréza wants you to select a poster frame for the video on Slide 11.

**To set a poster frame for the video on Slide 11:**

1. On Slide 11 ("Contact Us for Assistance Traveling Abroad With Your Pet"), click the video to select it, if necessary, and then click the **Video Format** tab.

**2.** Point to the toolbar below the video. A ScreenTip appears identifying the time of the video at that point. See Figure 2–36.

**Figure 2–36**   **Setting a poster frame**

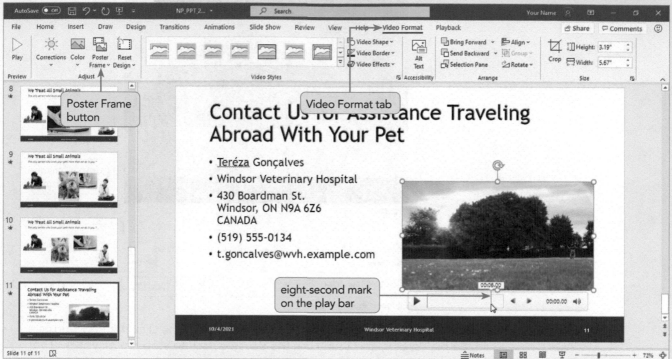

Multifocus/Shutterstock.com; Rommel Canlas/Shutterstock.com; Ilike/Shutterstock.com; santypan/Shutterstock.com; Veronica Louro/Shutterstock.com

**3.** On the video toolbar, click at approximately the 8.00-second mark. The frame at the 8.00-second mark shows the dog in the center of the video object.

> **Trouble?** You might not be able to click at exactly the 8.00-second mark. Click as close to it as you can (for example, 7.99 or 8.05).

**4.** In the Adjust group, click the **Poster Frame** button. The Poster Frame menu opens.

**5.** Click **Current Frame**. The message "Poster Frame Set" appears in the video's play bar, and the frame currently visible in the video object is set as the poster frame.

**6.** On the status bar, click the **Slide Show** button 🖵. Slide 11 appears in Slide Show view. The poster frame shows the dog in the center of the video object.

**7.** Click the video. The video plays. When it is finished, the video object shows the empty field that is at the end of the video.

**8.** Press **ESC** to end the slide show.

---

**Tip**

Like pictures, you can change the brightness and contrast of a video or recolor it using the buttons in the Adjust group. To reset a video, click the Reset Design button in the Adjust group.

---

## Modifying Video Playback Options

You can change several options for how a video plays. The video playback options are listed in Figure 2–37.

**Figure 2–37**    Video playback options

| Video Option | Function |
|---|---|
| Fade Duration | Set the number of seconds to fade the video in at the beginning of the video or out at the end of the video. |
| Volume | Change the volume of the video from high to medium or low or mute it. |
| Start | Change how the video starts:<br>• In Click Sequence means that the presenter can start the video by advancing the slide show, clicking the video object, or clicking the Play button on the video toolbar.<br>• Automatically means that the video will start automatically after the slide appears on the screen during the slide show.<br>• When Clicked On means that the video starts when the presenter clicks the video object or clicks the Play button on the video toolbar. |
| Play Full Screen | The video fills the screen during the slide show. |
| Hide While Not Playing | The video does not appear on the slide when it is not playing; make sure the video is set to play automatically if this option is selected. |
| Loop until Stopped | The video plays until the next slide appears during the slide show. |
| Rewind after Playing | The video rewinds after it plays so that the first frame or the poster frame appears again. |

As you have seen, when you insert a video, its Start setting is set to In Click Sequence. In Click Sequence for a video means the same thing that On Click means for an animation. Anything you do to advance the slide show causes the video to start. If you want to start the video by clicking the video object or the Play button on the video toolbar, set the Start setting to On Click. When On Click is selected, if you click somewhere else on the screen or do anything else to advance the slide show, the video will not play. You can also modify the Start setting so that the video plays automatically when the slide appears during the slide show. The Start setting is on the Playback tab.

In addition to changing the Start setting, you can set a video to fill the screen when it plays during the slide show. If you set the option to play full screen, the video will fill the screen when it plays, covering the slide title and anything else on the slide. You can also set a video to rewind so that it displays the poster frame after it plays.

Teréza wants you to change several playback options of the video on Slide 11. She wants the video to start automatically when Slide 11 appears during a slide show, and she wants it to fill the screen while it plays. When it is finished playing, she wants it to rewind so that the poster frame is on screen again.

### To modify the playback options of the video:

1. On Slide 11 ("Contact Us for Assistance Traveling Abroad With Your Pet"), click the video to select it, if necessary, and then click the **Playback** tab. In the Video Options group, In Click Sequence appears in the Start box. See Figure 2–38.

**Figure 2–38**    **Options on the Playback tab**

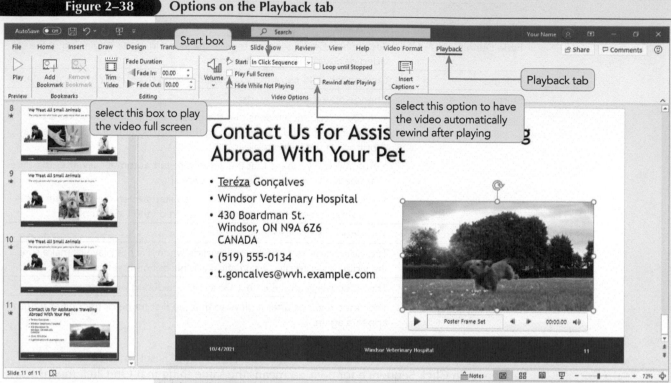

Multifocus/Shutterstock.com; Rommel Canlas/Shutterstock.com; Ilike/Shutterstock.com; santypan/Shutterstock.com; Veronica Louro/Shutterstock.com

**Tip**

You can adjust the volume of a video while it plays, or you can set the default volume by clicking the Volume button in the Video Options group on the Playback tab and then clicking an option on the menu.

2. In the Video Options group, click the **Start** arrow, and then click **Automatically**. Now the video will start automatically when the slide appears during the slide show.

3. In the Video Options group, click the **Play Full Screen** check box to select it. The video will fill the screen while it plays.

4. In the Video Options group, click the **Rewind after Playing** check box to select it. The video will reset to the poster frame after it plays.

5. On the status bar, click the **Slide Show** button 🖵. Slide 11 appears briefly in Slide Show view, and then the video fills the screen and plays. After the video finishes playing, Slide 11 reappears, and the poster frame appears in the video object.

6. Press **ESC** to end the slide show, and then save your changes.

## Understanding Animation Effects Applied to Videos

When you insert a video (or audio) object, two animations are automatically applied to the video or audio object. The first animation is the Play animation. The Play animation is set to On Click. This means that when you advance the slide show, the video will start playing.

The second animation is the Pause animation. This animation has a special setting applied to it called a trigger so that you can click anywhere on the video to play it (or "unpause" it) and click the video again to pause it.

Both the Play and the Pause animations are Media animations. The Media animation category appears in the Animation gallery only when a media object—either video or audio—is selected on a slide.

If you change the Start setting of the video to Automatically, the Start setting of the Play animation is set to After Previous. If there are no other objects on the slide set to animate before the video, the Play animation has an animation sequence number of zero, which means that it will play immediately after the slide transition.

If you change the Start setting of a video on the Playback tab to When Clicked On, the Play animation is removed from the video and only the Pause animation is applied.

To see these animations, click the Animations tab on the ribbon, and then select a video object on a slide. The Pause and Play animations appear in the Animation gallery in the Media category.

You'll examine the video animations now.

**To examine the Media animations applied to the video:**

▶ **1.** On Slide 11 ("Contact Us for Assistance Traveling Abroad With Your Pet"), click the video to select it, if necessary, and then click the **Animations** tab. Because you set this video to start automatically, two animation sequence icons appear next to it, one containing a zero and one containing a lightning bolt. In the Animation group, Multiple is selected because two animations are applied to this video. See Figure 2–39.

**Figure 2–39**    **Two animations applied to a video**

Multifocus/Shutterstock.com; Rommel Canlas/Shutterstock.com; Ilike/Shutterstock.com; santypan/Shutterstock.com; Veronica Louro/Shutterstock.com

▶ **2.** In the Animation group, click the **More** button. The Media category appears at the top of the Animation gallery because a media object is selected.

▶ **3.** Press **ESC**. The gallery closes without you making a selection.

When more than one animation is applied to any object, you need to click each animation sequence icon to see which animation is associated with each icon.

▶ **4.** Click the **0** animation sequence icon. In the Animation group, Play is selected, and in the Timing group, After Previous appears in the Start box. This start setting of the Play animation was changed to After Previous when you selected Automatically in the Start box on the Playback tab.

▶ **5.** Click the **lightning bolt** animation sequence icon. In the Animation group, the Pause animation is selected, and in the Timing group, On Click appears in the Start box. This animation is applied automatically to all videos when you add them to slides. It is because of this animation that you can click anywhere on the video object during a slide show to play or pause it.

> **6.** Click the **Playback** tab.
>
> **7.** In the Video Options group, click the **Start arrow**, click **In Click Sequence**, click the **Animations** tab, and then click the **1** animation sequence icon. In the Animation group, Play is selected, but now On Click appears in the Start box.
>
> **8.** Click the video, and then click the **Playback** tab.
>
> **9.** In the Video Options group, click the **Start arrow**, click **When Clicked On**, and then click the **Animations** tab. There is only one animation applied to the video now. In the Animation group, Pause is selected, and On Click appears in the Start box.
>
> **10.** Change the Start setting of the video back to **Automatically**.

# Compressing Media

As with pictures, you can compress media files. If you need to send a file via email or you need to upload it, you should compress media files to make the final PowerPoint file smaller. When you compress files, you make the final presentation file smaller, but you also lower the quality of the video. You can compress videos using the following settings:

- **Full HD (1080p)**—compresses the videos slightly and maintains the quality of the videos
- **HD (720p)**—compresses the videos to a quality suitable for streaming over the Internet
- **Standard (480p)**—compresses the videos as small as possible

With all of the settings, any parts of videos that you trimmed off will be deleted, similar to deleting the cropped portions of photos.

After you compress media, you should watch the slides containing the videos using the equipment you will be using when giving your presentation to make sure the reduced quality is acceptable. Usually, if the videos are high quality to start with, the compressed quality will be fine. However, if the original video quality was grainy, the compressed quality might be too low, even for evaluation purposes. If you decide that you don't like the compressed quality, you can undo the compression before you close the file.

You will compress the media file you inserted. You need to send the presentation to Teréza via email, so you will compress the media as much as possible.

### To compress the video in the presentation:

> **1.** With Slide 11 ("Contact Us for Assistance Traveling Abroad With Your Pet") displayed, click the **File** tab. Backstage view appears displaying the Info screen.
>
> **2.** Click the **Compress Media** button. A menu opens listing compression choices. See Figure 2–40.

| Figure 2–40 | Compression options on the Info screen in Backstage view |

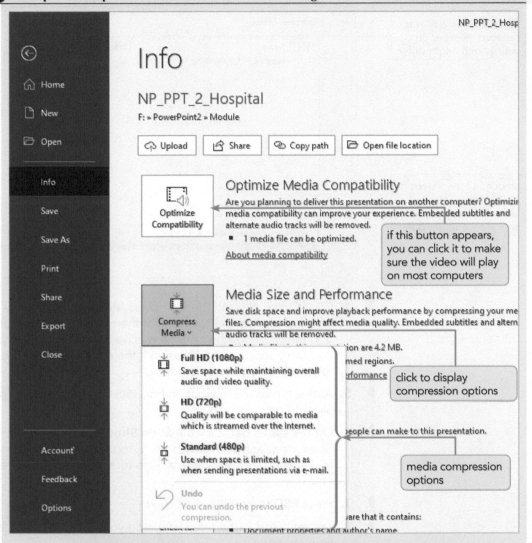

3. Click **Standard (480p)**. The Compress Media dialog box opens listing the video file in the presentation with a progress bar to show you the progress of the compression. After the file is compressed, a message appears in the Status column indicating that compression for the file is complete and stating how much the video file size was reduced. A message also appears at the bottom of the dialog box stating that the compression is complete and indicating how much the file size of the presentation was reduced. Because there is only one video in this presentation, the amount the video was reduced and the amount the presentation was reduced is the same. See Figure 2–41.

Figure 2–41 **Compress Media dialog box**

amount video size was reduced; number on your screen might differ

amount all the videos in the presentation were reduced; number on your screen might differ

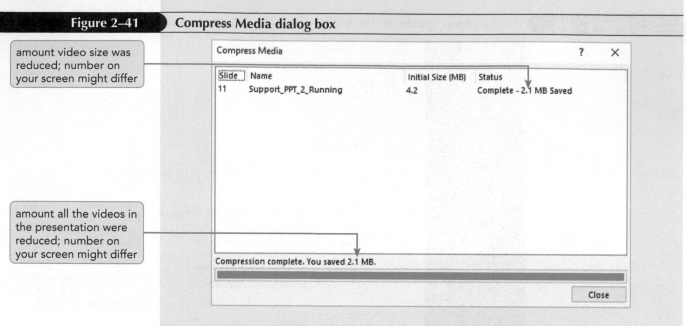

4. Click **Close**. Next to the Compress Media button on the Info screen, the bulleted list lists the total size of the media files in the presentation, states that the presentation's media was compressed to Standard (480p), and that you can undo the compression if the results are unsatisfactory. Now you need to view the compressed videos.

5. At the top of the navigation bar, click the **Back** button ⊙ to display Slide 11.

6. On the status bar, click the **Slide Show** button 🖵 to display the slide in Slide Show view, and then watch the video. The quality is lower, but it is sufficient for Teréza to get the general idea after you send the presentation to her via email.

7. Press **ESC** to end the slide show.

8. Display Slide 1 (the title slide), add your name as the subtitle, and then save your changes.

Now that you have finished working on the presentation, you should view the completed presentation as a slide show.

**To view the completed presentation in Slide Show view:**

1. On the Quick Access Toolbar, click the **Start From Beginning** button 🖵. Slide 1 appears in Slide Show view.

2. Press **SPACEBAR**. Slide 2 ("World-Class Veterinary Hospital") appears in Slide Show view with the Morph transition so the title on Slide 1 moves down to the footer.

3. Press **SPACEBAR** five times to display all the bulleted items, and then press **SPACEBAR** again to display Slide 3 ("Our Services").

4. Press **SPACEBAR** to display Slide 4 ("State of the Art Medical Equipment").

5. Press **SPACEBAR**. The photo on the left appears with the Split animation, and then after a one-second delay, the "Recently updated OR" arrow appears with the Wipe animation.

▶ 6. Press **SPACEBAR**. The photo on the right appears, and then after a one-second delay, the "Brand new MRI scanner" arrow appears.

▶ 7. Press **SPACEBAR**. Slide 5 ("We Treat All Small Animals") appears with only the title, the slogan, and the footer information displayed.

▶ 8. Press **SPACEBAR** five times, watching the pictures move on the screen with the Morph transition.

▶ 9. Press **SPACEBAR**. Slide 11 briefly appears, and then the video fills the screen and plays automatically. When the video is finished, Slide 11 appears again with the poster frame you selected displayed in the video object.

▶ 10. Press **SPACEBAR** to display the black slide that appears at the end of a slide show, and then press **SPACEBAR** once more to return to Normal view.

▶ 11. sam̄ ↟ Close the presentation file.

The final presentation file with transitions, animations, and video is interesting and should enhance Teréza's presentation.

# Review

## Session 2.2 Quick Check

1. What is a transition?

2. What are animations?

3. How do you change the speed of a transition or an animation?

4. When you apply an animation to a bulleted list with subitems, how do the first-level items animate? How do the second-level items animate?

5. What is the Morph transition?

6. What is a poster frame?

7. For a video, what is the difference between the Start setting "On Click" and "In Click Sequence"?

8. What animation is applied to every video that you add to a slide no matter what the Start setting is?

# Practice

## Review Assignments

**Data Files needed for the Review Assignments: NP_PPT_2-2.pptx, Support_PPT_2_Bath.jpg, Support_PPT_2_NewTheme.pptx, Support_PPT_2_Plate.jpg, Support_PPT_2_Sign.jpg, Support_PPT_2_Writing.mov**

The practice manager at Windsor Veterinary Hospital, Brian Sarkar, organizes the hospital's Give Back volunteer program. Through Give Back, hospital employees can participate as volunteers at different events throughout the year. Teréza Gonçalves offered to help Brian run this program. Brian asked Teréza to help him prepare a presentation that he will use to describe the program to new employees. Teréza created the text of the presentation and asked you to find graphics to include. She also wants you to add animations and transitions to make the presentation more interesting. Complete the following steps:

1. Open the presentation **NP_PPT_2-2.pptx**, located in the PowerPoint2 > Review folder included with your Data Files, add your name as the subtitle, and then save it as **NP_PPT_2_Volunteer** to the drive and folder where you are storing your files.

2. Apply the theme from the presentation **Support_PPT_2_NewTheme.pptx**, located in the PowerPoint2 > Review folder.

3. Apply the Uncover transition to any slide. Change the Effect Options to From Bottom, and then change the duration to 0.50 seconds. Apply this transition to all of the slides, and then remove it from Slide 1 (the title slide).

4. On Slide 2 ("What Is Operation Give Back?"), add the trademark sign after "Give Back" and before the question mark.

5. On Slide 2, animate the bulleted list with the Fly In entrance animation, and then change the effect so the items fly in from the left.

6. On Slide 2, animate the slide title with the Float In animation, and then change the effect so that the title floats down from the top. Change the duration of the animation applied to the title to 0.50 seconds, and then change the way it starts so that the animation happens automatically after the previous action.

7. On Slide 2, change the order of the animations so that the title animates first.

8. Change the layout of Slide 3 ("2021 Give Back Days") to the custom Title and Table layout.

9. On Slide 3, insert a 3×3 table. Refer to Figure 2–42 to add the rest of the data to the table. Add a row if needed.

**Figure 2–42     Data for table on Slide 3**

| Description | Date | Requirements |
|---|---|---|
| Groom animals at city animal shelter | Saturday, April 24 | |
| Clean up city dog parks | Saturday, June 19 | |
| Annual fundraiser dinner for city animal shelter | Sunday, September 12 | |

10. In the table, delete the third column (with "Requirements" in the first cell).

11. Apply the Light Style 2 – Accent 6 table style.

12. Add a new first column (to the left of the "Description" column). Fill each cell in the new column (except the first cell) with the following pictures, all located in the PowerPoint2 > Review folder, in order from the second row to the bottom row: **Support_PPT_2_Bath.jpg**, **Support_PPT_2_Sign.jpg**, and **Support_PPT_2_Plate.jpg**.

13. On Slide 3, format the table as follows:

    • Change the font size of all of the text in the table to 24 points. Then change the font size of the text in the top row to 28 points.

    • Change the fill of the first row to Tan, Accent 6, Darker 50%.

- Change the width of the first column to 2". Change the width of the second column to 4.25". And change the width of the third column so it is just wide enough to fit its widest entry (which is 3.6").
- Change the height of rows 2 through 4 to 1.4".
- Align the text in rows 2 through 4 so it is centered vertically.
- Change the border between rows 2 and 3 and the border between rows 3 and 4 to a three-point, solid line border using the Tan, Accent 6, Darker 50% color.

14. Reposition the table so it is centered horizontally on the slide and so the smart guides indicate that there is the same amount of space between the bottom of the table and the bottom of the slide as there is between the top of the title text box and the top of the slide.

15. On Slide 4, move the picture of the man serving the couple above the slide and the picture of the dog and the boy below the slide, using the smart guides to position them so the centers of the pictures align with the center of the slide. Then change the layout to the Section Header layout, and type **Scenes from Last Year** as the title.

16. Duplicate Slide 4. On the new Slide 5, delete the title text, and then change the layout to the Blank layout. Resize the picture of the man serving the couple so it is 7.5 inches high, and then position it on the slide so it is centered both horizontally and vertically on the slide. Apply the Rotated, White style to the picture on the slide, then change the color of the border to Dark Blue, Accent 3, Darker 50%.

17. On Slide 5, insert the Arrow: Right shape. Change the fill to Dark Green, Accent 4, Darker 25%, and change the outline to No Outline.

18. Resize the arrow so it is 1.5 inches high and 5.7 inches wide.

19. With the arrow selected, change the font size to 16 points. Then type **Ben Kim, veterinary technician, waiting tables at last year's fundraiser** in the arrow.

20. Drag the adjustment handle at the base of the arrowhead about one-quarter inch to the left to make the arrowhead larger. (The base of the arrowhead will be between the "e" and the "s" in "tables.")

21. Position the arrow to the left of the man serving the seated couple so the left edge of the arrow aligns with the left edge of the slide and the top of the border around the shape is about one-half inch below the top edge of the slide.

22. Apply the Wipe entrance animation to the arrow, and then change the effect so that it wipes from the left. Change the way the animation starts so that it starts after the previous action. Set a delay of one second.

23. Duplicate Slide 5. On the new Slide 6, reset the picture to remove the style. Then resize the picture so it is 3.75 inches high and center it vertically and horizontally on the slide.

24. On Slide 6, move the picture of the dog and boy onto the slide (it will be on top of the other picture and the arrow will still be visible). Resize the picture of the dog and the boy so it is 7.5 inches high, and then center it horizontally and vertically on the slide.

25. Copy the formatting applied to the picture on Slide 5 to the picture of the dog and boy on Slide 6.

26. Replace the text in the arrow with **Randy, son of Kathy Turner, HR Director, enjoying the dog park after the clean-up last year** on Slide 6.

27. On Slide 6, flip the arrow horizontally, and then position it to the right of the boy so the right edge of the arrow aligns with the right edge of the slide and the bottom of the border around the shape aligns with the horizontal smart guide that appears (the smart guide indicates the top of the picture underneath the picture of the dog and the boy).

28. On Slide 6, change the effect of the animation applied to the arrow so it wipes in from the right.

29. Duplicate Slide 6. On the new Slide 7, reset the picture of the dog and the boy, then resize that picture so it is 3.75 inches high. Delete the arrow. Change the layout to Title Only.

30. On Slide 7, position the photo of the man serving the couple on the left side of the slide, about one inch below the shading under the title text placeholder and so that the left edge of the photo aligns with the left edge of the title text placeholder. Position the photo of the dog and boy to the

right of the other photo so that its right edge aligns with the right edge of the title text placeholder and so its top and bottom align with the photo on the left. Add **Join the Gang!** as the slide title.

31. Apply the Morph transition to Slides 5, 6, and 7.

32. On Slide 8, use the Video button in the Media group on the Insert tab to insert the video **Support_PPT_2_Writing.mov** located in the PowerPoint2 > Review folder. Resize the video so it is 7.5 inches high, and then center it horizontally and vertically on the slide. Trim a bit from the end of the video so the number in the End box is 8.600. Set the poster frame by clicking about one-quarter of an inch from the end of the play bar. It will be approximately the 7.9-second mark. Finally, set the playback options so that the video starts playing automatically and rewinds after playing.

33. On Slide 9 ("Sign Up Today!"), replace the second "e" in "Tereza" with "é" and the "c" in "Goncalves" with "ç."

34. On Slide 9, delete the empty content placeholder. Insert the Arrow: Pentagon shape, and then resize it so that it is two inches high and five inches wide. Type **This way to feel great and help others!** in the shape. Change the font of this text to Bradley Hand ITC, change the font size to 32 points, and then format this text as bold.

35. Fill the shape with the Red, Accent 2 color. Then apply the Linear Down gradient in the Dark Variations section.

36. Format the shape with the Oblique: Bottom Left 3-D effect. Change the Depth of the 3-D format to 40 points. Change the Depth shading color to Red, Accent 2, Darker 50%.

37. Position the shape so that its middle aligns with the horizontal smart guide that indicates the middle of the slide and its left edge aligns with the left edge of the title text box. Then drag the rotate handle on the shape to the left so that the rotate handle is below the "p" in "Up" in the title.

38. Open the Format Shape pane to the Shape Options tab with the Size & Properties button selected and the Size section expanded. If the value in the Rotation box is not 345°, change it to 345°.

39. Add **Give Back Days at WVH** as the footer on all the slides except the title slide, and display the current date (fixed) on all the slides except the title slide. On the notes and handouts, add **Operation Give Back** as the header and your name as the footer, and show page numbers.

40. Compress all the photos in the presentation to E-mail (96 ppi), and then compress the media to Standard (480p).

41. Save your changes, view the slide show, and then close the presentation.

# Apply

## Case Problem 1

**Data Files needed for this Case Problem: NP_PPT_2-3.pptx, Support_PPT_2_Calendar.jpg, Support_PPT_2_Cornucopia.jpg, Support_PPT_2_Fourth.jpg, Support_PPT_2_Labor.png, Support_PPT_2_Logo.pptx, Support_PPT_2_Memorial.jpg, Support_PPT_2_NewYear.jpg, Support_PPT_2_Sayings.mp4, Support_PPT_2_Sixty.png**

**Worldwide Phone Systems** Ibrahim Khan is the director of human resources for Worldwide Phone Systems, a national telecommunications company headquartered in San Jose, California. He recently proposed a new system of paid holidays to the Board of Directors so that all of the employees in the company's diverse workforce will be able to request paid time off to celebrate their own religious or cultural holidays. The Board of Directors approved his plan, and now Ibrahim needs to present the details of the plans to department managers via a webinar. He asks you to help him finish the presentation, which will include photos, a video, and a table to communicate the new policy. Complete the following steps:

1. Open the file named **NP_PPT_2-3.pptx**, located in the PowerPoint2 > Case1 folder included with your Data Files, add your name as the subtitle on Slide 1, and then save it as **NP_PPT_2_Holidays** to the drive and folder where you are storing your files.

2. Apply the theme from the presentation **Support_PPT_2_Logo.pptx**, located in the PowerPoint2 > Case1 folder.

3. Apply the Cut transition to all of the slides in the presentation, then remove the transition from Slide 1 (the title slide).

4. Add **Worldwide Phone Systems** as the footer text. Display the footer text, the slide number, and the current date (using the Fixed option) on all of the slides including the title slide.

5. On Slide 1, draw a rectangle that is 11.7 inches wide and 0.2 inches high. Position the rectangle so it is on top of the date, footer, and slide number at the bottom of the slide. Remove the shape outline, and fill the rectangle with White, Background 1. (Note: You are doing this because you are going to duplicate this slide and apply the Morph transition to the new Slide 2, and this prevents the footer information from appearing on the new Slide 2.)

6. On Slide 1, insert the picture **Support_PPT_2_Calendar.jpg**, located in the PowerPoint2 > Case1 folder. Resize the picture so it is 4.3 inches high. Rotate the picture left by 90 degrees. Position the rotated picture to the left of the slide so that the top of the picture aligns with the top of the slide and so that there is about one-quarter of an inch between the picture and the slide.

7. Duplicate Slide 1. On the new Slide 2, delete your name, and then apply the Title 2 layout.

8. On Slide 2, rotate the picture of the calendar right by 90 degrees so that it is right-side-up. Apply the picture style Thick Matte, Black to the calendar picture, and then change the border color to the Red, Accent 2, Darker 25% color.

9. Position the picture in the upper-left corner of the slide so that the outside of the red border on the top and left side of the picture align with the top and left borders of the white part of the slide.

10. On the picture of the calendar, drag the rotate handle to the left until the top-left corner of the picture border is just touching the outside of the blue border around the slide. Note that when you release the mouse button, the picture will slightly increase in size so that the top-left corner of the picture will overlap the slide border.

11. Confirm that the picture of the calendar is rotated to 345°. If it is not, change the rotation so that it is.

12. Apply the Morph transition to Slide 2. Change the duration of this transition to one second.

13. On Slide 3, animate the bulleted list using the entrance Float In animation with the Float Down effect, and change the duration to 0.50 seconds. Animate the bulleted lists on Slides 5 and 6 using the same animation. On Slide 5, make sure you animate the list on the left first, and then animate the list on the right. Then on Slide 5, change the effect for both lists to All at Once.

14. On Slide 4 ("Five Fixed Holidays"), create a table with three columns and five rows. In the first row, type **Name** in the first cell, **Description** in the second cell, and **Date** in the third cell.

15. In the table, in the "Name" column, starting in the second row, type the following entries: **New Year's Day**, **Memorial Day**, **Labor Day**, and **Thanksgiving Day**. Then in the "Date" column, type the following entries: **January 1**, **Last Monday in May**, **First Monday in September**, and **4th Thursday in November**.

16. In the table, insert a new row between the Memorial Day row and the Labor Day row. In the new row in the "Name" column, type **Independence Day**, and in the "Date" column, type **July 4**.

17. In the table, delete the second column (with the label "Description" in the first row). Then add a new column to the left of the first column.

18. Change the table style to Medium Style 3 – Accent 4. Change the font size of all the text in the table to 24 points, and then align the text so it is centered vertically.

19. In the first column, starting in the second row, fill the cells with the following pictures: **Support_PPT_2_NewYear.jpg**, **Support_PPT_2_Memorial.jpg**, **Support_PPT_2_Fourth.jpg**, **Support_PPT_2_Labor.png**, and **Support_PPT_2_Cornucopia.jpg**.

20. Resize the first column in the table so it is 1.8" wide. Resize the second and third columns to fit their widest entries (2.83" and 4.03", respectively). Resize all the rows except the first row so that they are 0.95" high.

21. Align the table so that its left edge aligns with the left edge of the title text box and its top edge appears below the text in the title text box.

22. Draw one-quarter point black line in the table on the border between the last two cells in the first column. Draw another one-quarter point black line on the border between the first and second cells in the fifth row.

23. On Slide 5 ("Choose Five Floating Holidays"), draw a Rectangle: Rounded Corners shape that is 6.2 inches wide and 0.5 inches high, and then position it so its left edge aligns with the left edge of the title text box and its bottom edge aligns with the smart guide that indicates the top of the footer area. Type **More dates might be added depending on employee needs.** in the shape. Italicize the text in the shape. Change the fill of the shape to Gray, Accent 6, and remove the outline.

24. Change the Start setting of the animation applied to the first bulleted item in each list to With Previous.

25. On Slide 6, insert the picture **Support_PPT_2_Sixty.png** in the empty content placeholder. Add **Image of the number sixty** as alt text. Apply the Grow & Turn entrance animation.

26. Change the order of the animations on Slide 6 so that the picture of "60" animates first. Next, click the animation sequence icon next to "Floating holiday requests," and then move that animation earlier. Finally, change the Start setting of the animation applied to the picture of "60" so that it starts with the previous animation. The end result is that the first bulleted item will animate when you advance the slide show, and its subitems and the picture of "60" will animate with it.

27. Set the duration of the animation applied to the picture of "60" to 0.50 seconds, and then set a delay of 0.50 seconds.

28. On Slide 7, insert the video **Support_PPT_2_Sayings.mp4**, located in the PowerPoint2 > Case1 folder. Set the movie to play automatically and rewind after playing. Set the poster frame to the frame at approximately the 1-second mark.

29. Select the image of the red number sixty on Slide 6, and then compress all the pictures to E-mail (96 ppi). Compress the media to Standard (480p).

30. Save your changes, view the slide show in Slide Show view, and then close the presentation.

# Create

## Case Problem 2

**Data Files needed for this Case Problem: NP_PPT_2-4.pptx, Support_PPT_2_Corporate.jpg, Support_PPT_2_Hospital.jpg, Support_PPT_2_Residential.jpg, Support_PPT_2_School.jpg**

**Abonza Food Services**    Maura Mitchell is the National Food Service Manager for Abonza Food Services, a food service and facilities management company that is contracted to run cafeterias and kitchens for a wide range of industries across the United States and Canada. Because they hire local food service managers frequently, monthly orientation and certification seminars are held in each region to train them. Maura created a presentation to help her with this training. She asks you to finish the presentation. Complete the following steps:

1. Open the presentation **NP_PPT_2-4.pptx**, located in the PowerPoint2 > Case2 folder included with your Data Files, add your name as the subtitle, and then save the presentation as **NP_PPT_2_Manager** to the drive and folder where you are storing your files.

2. Apply the Cube transition to all of the slides in the presentation. Remove the transition from Slide 1.

3. Add as a footer **Updated:** and then type today's date. Show the footer on all the slides except the title slide.

⊕ **Explore** 4. On Slide 1 (the title slide), apply the Appear entrance animation to the title, change the Start setting to After Previous, and then modify the animation so that the letters appear one by one. (*Hint*: Use the Animation group Dialog Box Launcher, and then change the setting in the Animate text box on the Effect tab.) Speed up the effect by changing the delay between letters to 0.1 seconds.

⊕ **Explore** 5. On Slide 1, add the Typewriter sound to the animation applied to the title. (*Hint*: Use the Animate text box again.)

⊕ **Explore** 6. On Slide 1, apply the entrance Flip animation to the reddish-orange shape in the upper-left corner of the slide. (*Hint*: Click More Entrance Effects on the Animations menu.) Change the Start setting of this animation to After Previous.

7. On Slide 1, copy the reddish-orange shape in the upper-left corner of the slide. Paste the copied shape onto Slide 2 ("Industries We Serve"), then remove the animation from the shape on Slide 2. Copy the shape on Slide 2, and then paste it onto the rest of the slides in the presentation.

8. Duplicate Slide 2. On the new Slide 3, change the title to **Schools**.

9. On Slide 3 ("Schools"), move the three photos on the right off the slide to the right, positioned so that they are still aligned with the remaining picture on the slide. (*Hint*: Select all three photos, and then drag them all together as a group.) Keep the photos in the same order as on Slide 2. Resize the picture of the children eating at a cafeteria table so it is five inches high. Position the picture so it is centered horizontally and so the bottom of the photo aligns with the smart guide that indicates the top of the footer text box.

10. Duplicate Slide 3. On the new Slide 4, change the title to **Residential Living**.

11. On Slide 4 ("Residential Living"), drag the picture of the children eating at a cafeteria table off the slide anywhere to the left. Then drag the picture of the group of adults onto the slide, resize it so that it is five inches high. Position the picture so it is centered horizontally and so the bottom of the photo aligns with the smart guide that indicates the top of the footer text box.

12. Duplicate Slide 4. On the new Slide 5, change the title to **Hospitals**.

13. On Slide 5 ("Hospitals"), drag the picture of the adults off the slide anywhere to the left (it doesn't matter if it is on top of the picture of the children). Drag the picture of the person in pink scrubs handing a tray of food to a patient onto the slide, and then resize it so that it is five inches high. Position the picture so it is centered vertically and so the bottom of the photo aligns with the smart guide that indicates the top of the footer text box.

14. Duplicate Slide 5. On the new Slide 6, change the title to **Corporate**.

15. On Slide 6 ("Corporate"), drag the picture of the person in pink scrubs handing a tray of food to a patient off the slide anywhere to the left. Drag the last picture on the right of the slide onto the slide (people standing in line in a cafeteria), and then resize it so that it is five inches high. Position the picture so it is centered horizontally and so the bottom of the photo aligns with the smart guide that indicates the top of the footer text box.

16. Apply the Morph transition to Slides 3 through 6, and then change the transition duration to 1.50 seconds.

⊕ **Explore** 17. Change the effect option on the slides that have the Morph transition applied so that each of the characters in the slide titles morph also.

18. On Slide 7 ("Our Clients"), insert a 2×4 table. Remove the formatting for the Header Row and Banded Rows, and then change the shading for all of the cells to No Fill. Enter the data shown in Figure 2–43 in the table.

**Figure 2–43     Data for the table on Slide 7**

| Schools | Colleges<br>High schools<br>Middle schools<br>Elementary schools |
|---|---|
| Residential Living | Assisted living<br>Retirement homes |
| Hospitals | Patient meals<br>Cafeterias |
| Corporate | Cafeterias<br>Catered events |

19. Insert a new column to the left of the first column. In the new first column, fill the cells with the following pictures, all located in the PowerPoint2 > Case4 folder: **Support_PPT_2_School.jpg**, **Support_PPT_2_Residential.jpg**, **Support_PPT_2_Hospital.jpg**, **Support_PPT_2_Corporate.jpg**.

20. Change the width of the first column to 2". Change the widths of the second and third columns to 2.5" each. Change the height of all of the rows in the table to 1.3". Center-align the table horizontally on the slide and then position it so that the bottom of the table aligns with the top of the footer text box.

21. Format the text in the second column as 24 points and bold. Center the text in the second and third columns vertically in the cells.

22. Select the table, and then remove the table borders. (*Hint*: Use the Borders button in the Table Styles group on the Table Design tab.) You might still see the table gridlines.

23. On Slide 7, insert a rectangle 1.3 inches high and 7 inches wide, and position it on top of the first row in the table so that the text and picture are covered. Use the smart guides to make sure that the top of the rectangle aligns with the top of the table and the sides of the rectangle are aligned with the sides of the table.

24. Apply the Wipe exit animation with the From Left effect to the rectangle. (*Hint*: Make sure you use the Wipe animation in the Exit category, not the Entrance category.)

25. Use the Duplicate command to duplicate the rectangle. Position the duplicated rectangle on top of the second row in the table, using the smart guides to make sure that the top of the duplicate rectangle aligns with the bottom of the first rectangle and the sides of the rectangle are aligned with the sides of the table. Then, duplicate the rectangle covering the second row in the table twice. If needed, position the third and fourth rectangles on top of the last two rows in the table.

⊕ **Explore** 26. Change the fill of each rectangle to the same color as the slide background. (*Hint*: Use the Eyedropper tool on the Shape Fill menu.) Remove the outline from the rectangles.

27. If you still see small lines above or below any rows in the table, click the rectangle covering that row, change its height to 1.35", and then reposition it so all of the row is covered.

28. On Slide 8 ("Health & Safety"), animate the bulleted list with the entrance Split animation. Change the effect to Horizontal In. Apply the same animation to the bulleted list on Slide 9 ("ServSafe Certification").

29. On Slide 9 ("ServSafe Certification"), add the registered trademark symbol ® after "ServSafe" in both the title and in the first bulleted item.

30. Compress all the pictures in the presentation to E-mail (96 ppi).

31. Save your changes, run the slide show, and then close the presentation.

**Module 3**

## Objectives

**Session 3.1**
- Create and modify a SmartArt graphic
- Animate a SmartArt graphic
- Convert a SmartArt graphic to shapes
- Ungroup and group shapes
- Add an audio clip to a slide
- Create and modify a chart
- Insert and format text boxes
- Apply a WordArt style to text

**Session 3.2**
- Remove the background from a photo
- Apply an artistic effect to a photo
- Correct photos using photo editing tools
- Create a custom shape
- Rotate shapes with text
- Fill a shape with a texture and a custom gradient
- Check for accessibility issues and fix them
- Use the Selection pane

# Applying Advanced Formatting to Objects

## Formatting Objects in a Presentation for a Sales and Marketing Company

## Case | MBG Sales and Marketing

Kavita Goyal is a client operations manager for MBG Sales and Marketing, headquartered in Hattiesburg, Mississippi. After a customer service representative speaks to a client who has called to request support or describe a problem, the client receives a follow-up phone call asking them to describe their level of satisfaction with their service experience on a scale of one to five (from extremely satisfied to not at all satisfied). Kavita has noticed a decrease in the percentage of clients who are extremely or very satisfied and an increase in clients who are only somewhat satisfied. Kavita decided she needs to retrain her team so that they will provide greater satisfaction to clients. She asks for your help in enhancing her presentation.

In this module, you will create a SmartArt graphic and a chart and you will insert an audio clip. You will also create a text box, use WordArt styles, and rotate shapes containing text so that the text stays right-side up. You will edit pictures, create a custom shape, and apply advanced formatting to a shape. Finally, you will check the presentation for accessibility.

## Starting Data Files

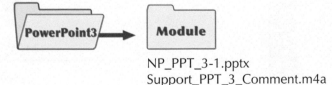

**PowerPoint3** → **Module**

NP_PPT_3-1.pptx
Support_PPT_3_Comment.m4a

**Review**

NP_PPT_3-2.pptx
Support_PPT_3_Compliment.mp3
Support_PPT_3_FollowUp.jpg
Support_PPT_3_Form.jpg
Support_PPT_3_Respect.jpg

**Case1**

NP_PPT_3-3.pptx
Support_PPT_3_Recovery.mp3

**Case2**

NP_PPT_3-4.pptx

# Session 3.1 Visual Overview:

If you need additional tools, click the Edit Data in Microsoft Excel button to open the spreadsheet in an Excel workbook.

When you insert a chart, a spreadsheet appears in which you enter the data to create the chart. A **spreadsheet** (called a worksheet in Microsoft Excel) is a grid of cells that contain numbers and text.

As in a table, the intersection of a row and a column is a **cell**, and you add data and labels in cells. Cells in a datasheet are referenced by their column letter and row number. This cell is cell B1.

Drag this sizing handle to include or exclude columns and rows from the chart.

Colored borders around cells and the shaded cells indicate that they are included in the chart.

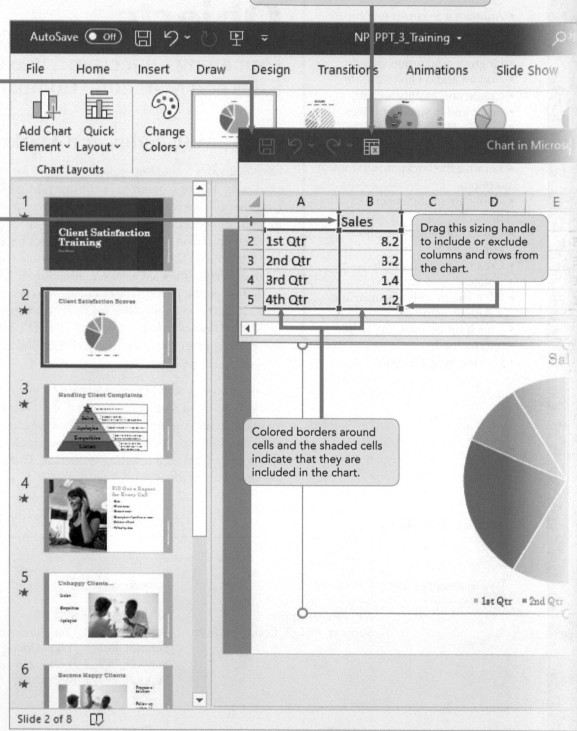

# Creating a Chart on a Slide

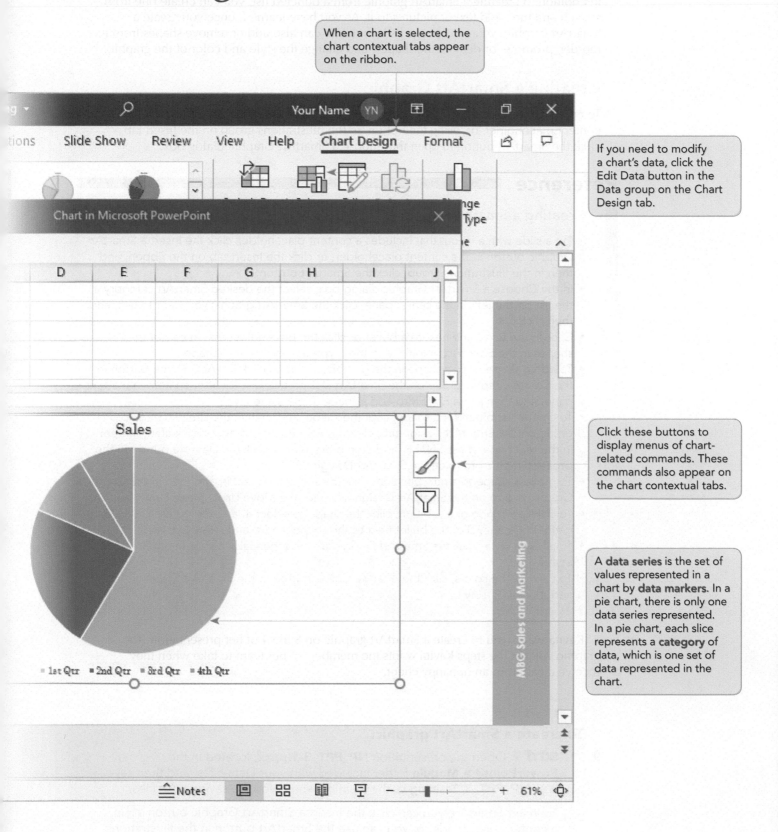

When a chart is selected, the chart contextual tabs appear on the ribbon.

If you need to modify a chart's data, click the Edit Data button in the Data group on the Chart Design tab.

Click these buttons to display menus of chart-related commands. These commands also appear on the chart contextual tabs.

A **data series** is the set of values represented in a chart by **data markers**. In a pie chart, there is only one data series represented. In a pie chart, each slice represents a **category** of data, which is one set of data represented in the chart.

# Working with SmartArt Graphics

In addition to creating a SmartArt graphic from a bulleted list, you can create one from scratch and then add text or pictures to it. As you have learned, once you create a SmartArt graphic, you can change its layout. You can also add or remove shapes from it; reorder, promote, or demote the shapes; and change the style and color of the graphic.

## Creating a SmartArt Graphic

To create a SmartArt graphic, you click the Insert a SmartArt Graphic button in a content placeholder, or, using the ribbon, in the Illustrations group on the Insert tab, click the SmartArt button to open the Choose a SmartArt Graphic dialog box.

## Reference

### Creating a SmartArt Graphic

- On a slide with a layout that includes a content placeholder, click the Insert a SmartArt Graphic button in the content placeholder; or click the Insert tab on the ribbon, and then in the Illustrations group, click the SmartArt button.
- In the Choose a SmartArt Graphic dialog box, select the desired SmartArt category in the list on the left, in the center pane, click the SmartArt graphic you want to use, and then click OK.
- Click in the text pane next to a bullet or click the placeholder text in one of the shapes in the SmartArt graphic, and then type the text for that shape.
- To add a shape, click a shape in the graphic, and then click the Add Shape button in the Create Graphic group on the SmartArt Design tab; or click after an item in the text pane, and then press ENTER to add a shape at the same level.
- To create a subitem for a shape, click the shape, and then in the Create Graphic group on the SmartArt Design tab, click the Add Bullet button; or click after an item in the text pane, press ENTER, and then press TAB or click the Demote button in the Create Graphic group on the SmartArt Design tab.
- To move a shape to a new position, click the shape to select it, and then in the Create Graphic group on the SmartArt Design tab, click the Move Up or Move Down button.
- To delete a shape or a subitem, click the shape to select it, and then press DELETE; or in the text pane, click the bullet next to the shape, and then press DELETE.
- To apply a style, click the SmartArt Design tab, and then click a style in the SmartArt Styles group.
- To change the colors, click the Change Colors button in the SmartArt Styles group, and then click a style.

Kavita wants you to create a SmartArt graphic on Slide 4 of her presentation. The graphic will list the steps Kavita wants the members of her team to take when they receive a call from an unhappy client.

**To create a SmartArt graphic:**

▶ 1. **sam** ⬇ Open the presentation **NP_PPT_3-1.pptx**, located in the **PowerPoint3 > Module** folder included with your Data Files, and then save it as **NP_PPT_3_Training** to the location where you are saving your files.

To insert SmartArt, you can click the Insert a SmartArt Graphic button 🖾 in a content placeholder or you can use the SmartArt button in the Illustrations group on the Insert tab.

2. Display Slide 3 ("Handling Client Complaints"), and then in the content placeholder, click the **Insert a SmartArt Graphic** button . The Choose a SmartArt Graphic dialog box opens.

3. In the list on the left, click **Relationship**, click the **Segmented Pyramid** layout, and then click **OK**. A SmartArt graphic in the shape of a pyramid in sections is inserted on the slide, and the SmartArt Design tab is selected on the ribbon. Kavita wants you to use a pyramid shape that has only one item on each level of the pyramid.

4. On the SmartArt Design tab, in the Layouts group, click the **More** button , and then click **More Layouts** to open the Choose a SmartArt Graphic dialog box.

5. In the list on the left, click **Pyramid**, click the **Basic Pyramid** layout, and then click **OK**. The SmartArt graphic layout is changed to a pyramid with one item of text in each of the three levels in the pyramid. The text is placeholder text.

6. On the SmartArt Design tab, in the Create Graphic group, click the **Text Pane** button to select it, if necessary. The text pane opens next to the graphic. See Figure 3–1. The insertion point is next to the first bullet in the text pane.

**Figure 3–1**     **SmartArt graphic with the text pane open on Slide 3**

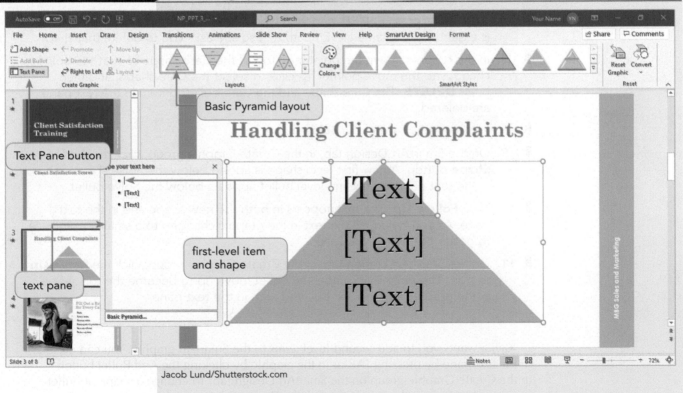

Jacob Lund/Shutterstock.com

Now that you've added the SmartArt graphic to the slide, you can add content to it. You will add first-level items to the graphic, and then reorder the shapes in the graphic by moving them up or down in the graphic and in the bulleted list in the text pane.

## To add text to the SmartArt graphic and move shapes:

1. With the insertion point in the first bulleted item in the text pane, type **Solve**. The text appears in the bulleted list in the text pane and in the top shape in the graphic.

2. In the text pane, next to the second bullet in the list, click **[Text]**. The placeholder text disappears, and the insertion point appears.

3. Type **Apologize**. The text "Apologize" replaces the placeholder text next to the second bullet in the text pane and appears in the middle shape in the graphic.

4. In the graphic, in the bottom shape, click **[Text]**, and then type **Empathize**. The text appears in both the shape and next to the third bullet in the text pane.

5. In the text pane, click after the word "Empathize", and then press **ENTER**. A new bullet is created below the Empathize bullet in the text pane. In the graphic, a new shape is added below the Empathize shape.

   **Trouble?** If a new line is inserted below "Empathize" in the bottom shape in the graphic instead of a new bullet, the insertion point was in the bottom shape of the graphic when you pressed ENTER. Press BACKSPACE to delete the new line, and then repeat Step 5, this time making sure you click in the text pane after the word "Empathize" before you press ENTER.

6. Type **Care**, press **ENTER**, and then type **Listen**. Kavita points out that "Care" is essentially the same as "Empathize", so she asks you to delete that shape.

7. In the graphic, move the pointer on top of the **Care** shape so that the pointer changes to the move pointer ✥, click to select the Care shape, and then press **DELETE**. The Care shape and the Care bulleted item in the text pane are deleted.

8. In the graphic, select the **Solve** shape.

9. On the SmartArt Design tab, in the Create Graphic group, click the **Add Shape** button. A new first-level shape is added below the Solve shape and, in the text pane, a new first-level bullet appears below the Solve bullet.

10. Type **Follow Up**. The text appears in both the new shape and in the text pane. As you typed, all the text in the graphic changed to a smaller point size to better fit the text you typed.

11. On the SmartArt Design tab, in the Create Graphic group, click the **Move Up** button. The Follow Up shape and bullet move up to become the top shape in the graphic and the first bulleted item in the text pane.

Kavita wants you to add second-level items to the SmartArt graphic. You can do this in the text pane by pressing TAB or in the graphic by clicking the Add Bullet button in the Create Graphic group on the SmartArt Design tab. To change a shape or bullet from one level to another, you can click the Demote or Promote buttons in the Create Graphic group on the SmartArt Design tab.

### To add second-level shapes and bullets to the SmartArt graphic:

1. In the graphic, click the **Listen** shape, and then in the Create Graphic group, click the **Add Bullet** button. In the graphic, a shape is added to the right of the Listen shape. In the text pane, a second-level bullet appears below the Listen bullet. See Figure 3–2.

**Figure 3–2** | **Second-level shape added to the Listen shape**

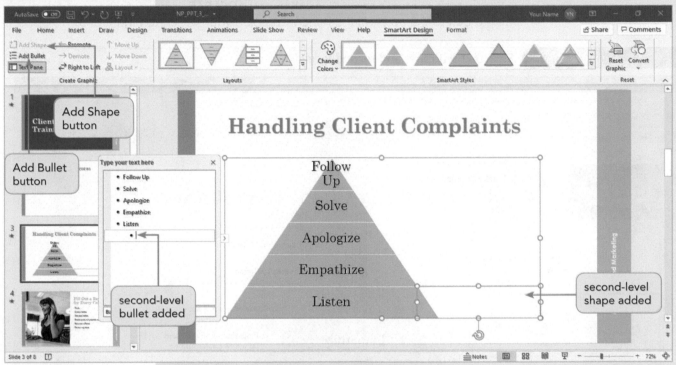

Jacob Lund/Shutterstock.com

**Tip**

To change the shapes in the graphic, select all the shapes, then in the Shapes group on the Format tab, click the Change Shape button to change the shapes to a different shape, or click the Larger or Smaller buttons to change the size of the shapes.

2. Type **Listen to the client.** in the new shape. The text appears in the new shape and next to the second-level bullet in the text pane.

3. Press **ENTER**, and then type **Ask questions if you don't understand.** (including the period). The text is added as another second-level bullet.

4. In the text pane, click after "Empathize", press **ENTER**, and then press **TAB**. A second-level bullet is created below the Empathize bullet in the text pane, and a new shape is added to the right of the Emphasize shape in the graphic.

5. Type **Empathize with the client.**, press **ENTER**, and then type **Do not be condescending.** (including the period).

6. In the graphic, click the **Apologize** shape, in the Create Graphic group, click the **Add Shape** button, and then click the **Demote** button. First, a shape was added below the Apologize shape. After you demoted the shape, the shape moved and appears to the right of the Apologize shape in the graphic. In the text pane, a second-level bullet appears below the Apologize bullet.

7. Type **Apologize even if it is not our fault.** (including the period).

8. Add a shape to contain second-level items next to the Solve shape, and then type the following two items into that new shape:

   **Propose a solution.**

   **Consult with Kavita if you need help.**

**Tip**

To reverse the direction of a SmartArt graphic so the first-level shapes appear in the opposite order, click the Right to Left button in the Create Graphic group on the SmartArt Design tab.

▶ 9. Add a shape to contain second-level items next to the Follow Up shape, and then type the following two items into that new shape:

**Get the contact's name.**

**Follow up within 14 days.**

Kavita asks you to delete the "Get the contact's name." second-level item.

▶ 10. In the text pane or in the shape next to the Follow Up shape, click before "Get the contact's name." and then press **DELETE** as many times as needed to delete the text and the bullet. Compare your screen to Figure 3–3.

**Figure 3–3** ▶ **SmartArt with first and second levels**

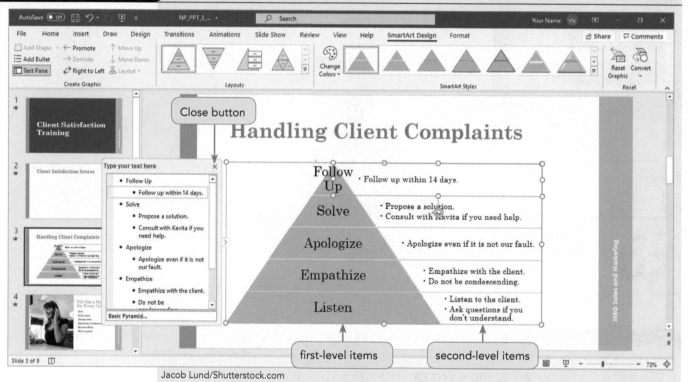

Jacob Lund/Shutterstock.com

▶ 11. In the text pane, click the **Close** button ☒. The text pane closes.

## Changing the Appearance of a SmartArt Graphic

You can change how a SmartArt graphic looks by applying a style and changing its colors. Kavita wants the pyramid to be more colorful.

**To apply a style to the SmartArt graphic and change its colors:**

▶ 1. With Slide 3 ("Handling Client Complaints") displayed, on the SmartArt Design tab, in the SmartArt Styles group, click the **More** button ▼ to open the gallery of styles available for the graphic.

2. In the gallery, in the 3D section, click the **Inset** style. The style of the graphic changes to the Inset style, which gives the shapes a slightly three-dimensional look.

3. In the SmartArt Styles group, click the **Change Colors** button. A gallery of color styles opens.

4. Below Colorful, click the **Colorful – Accent Colors** style. Each shape in the pyramid is a different color.

SmartArt graphics contain multiple objects that are treated as a whole. This means that when you apply a style or other effect to the graphic, the effect is applied to the entire object. You can also apply formatting to individual shapes within the graphic if you want. You just need to select the specific shape first. You can also change the formatting of the text in SmartArt graphics.

You will change the color of the Listen shape, and then you will change the formatting of the text in the first-level shapes.

**To change the color of one shape and format the text in the SmartArt graphic:**

1. In the SmartArt graphic, click the **Listen** shape. A selection box appears around the Listen shape in the graphic.

   **Trouble?** If the Listen shape is not selected, click it again.

2. Click the **Format** tab.

3. In the Shape Styles group, click the **Shape Fill** button, and then click the **Gray, Accent 6, Darker 25%** color (in the last column). The color of the Listen shape changes to the darker gray you selected.

4. In the bottom shape, double-click **Listen**, and then click the **Home** tab. The word "Listen" is selected.

5. In the Font group, click the **Font Size arrow**, and then click **44**. The font size of "Listen" changes to 44 points.

6. Change the font size of **Empathize** to **40** points, change the font size of **Apologize** and **Solve** to **36** points, change the font size of **Follow Up** to **20** points, and then click a blank area of the slide. See Figure 3–4.

**Figure 3–4**    SmartArt with formatted text

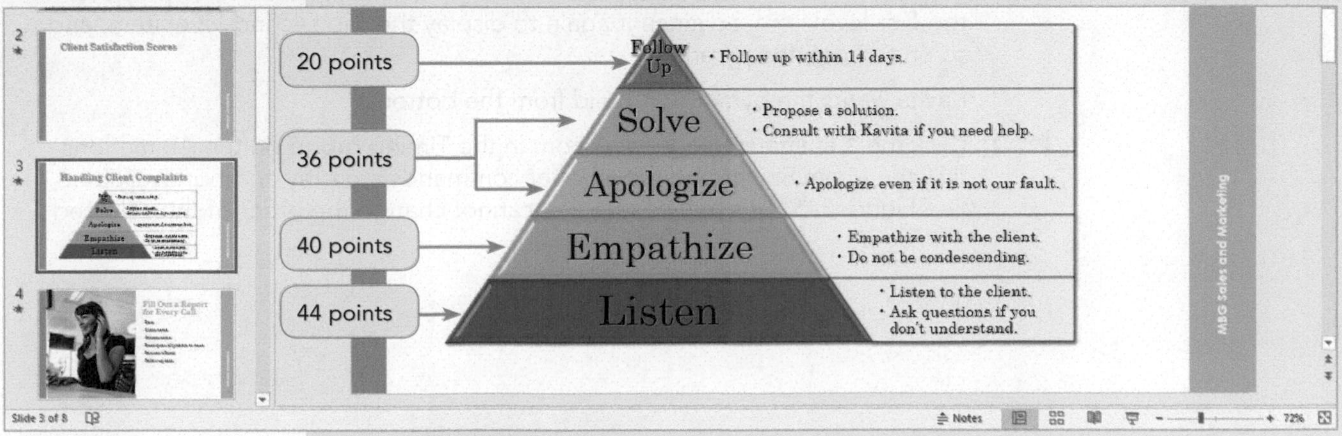

Jacob Lund/Shutterstock.com

## Animating a SmartArt Graphic

You animate a SmartArt graphic in the same way you animate any object. The default is for the entire object to animate as a single object. Similar to a bulleted list, after you apply an animation, you can use the Effect Options button to choose a different sequence effect.

Kavita wants each first-level shape in the SmartArt graphic to appear on the slide one at a time, followed by the associated second-level shape.

**To animate the SmartArt graphic:**

▶ **1.** On Slide 3 ("Handling Client Complaints"), click the SmartArt graphic, and then click the **Animations** tab.

▶ **2.** In the Animation group, click the **Wipe** animation, click the **Effect Options** button, and then click **From Left**. The animation previews, and the SmartArt graphic wipes in from the left. An animation sequence icon appears above and to the left of the graphic.

▶ **3.** Click the **Effect Options** button again. The selected Sequence effect is As One Object.

▶ **4.** Click **Level at Once**, and then watch the preview. The first-level shapes appear all at the same time, followed by the second-level shapes. Two animation sequence icons appear, each overlapping other icons. This indicates that the animation indicated by the sequence icons that are below the top sequence icon on each stack is set to With Previous or After Previous. In this case, each of the first-level shapes would appear, one after the other, when you advance the slide show once. Then, each of the second-level shapes would appear, one after the other, when you advance the slide show once.

▶ **5.** Click the **Effect Options** button, click **Level One by One**, and then watch the preview. Each first-level shape appears one at a time, starting from the top. Then each second-level shape appears, again starting from the top. Ten animation sequence icons appear, indicating that each shape will appear, one at a time, when you advance the slide show. This means you would advance the slide show five times to display each of the first-level items, and then five more times to display each of the second-level items.

▶ **6.** Click the **Effect Options** button, click **One by One**, and then watch the preview. The top shape in the pyramid appears first, then the shape containing its second-level items appears. The rest of the shapes follow in the same fashion. Ten animation sequence icons appear to the left of the graphic. In this case, you would advance the slide show once to display the top first-level item, advance it again to display the top second-level item, and so on through the pyramid.

Kavita wants the pyramid to build from the bottom.

▶ **7.** Click the **1** animation sequence icon. In the Timing group on the Animations tab, the Move Earlier and Move Later commands are gray and not available. See Figure 3–5. This means that you cannot change the order of the selected animation.

**Figure 3–5**    Move commands in the Timing group are unavailable

Jacob Lund/Shutterstock.com; fizkes/Shutterstock.com

Because you cannot change the order in which the shapes in the SmartArt graphic animate, you need to convert the SmartArt graphic bullets and sub-bullets to ordinary shapes. Then you can have the shapes on the bottom of the pyramid appear first, followed by the next shape and so on, building the pyramid from the bottom.

When you convert a SmartArt graphic into shapes, each shape in the graphic becomes an individual object, but all the shapes are grouped together. When objects are **grouped**, they are combined into one object.

You will convert the SmartArt graphic to shapes.

### To convert the SmartArt graphic to shapes:

1. Click the SmartArt graphic to select it, click the **SmartArt Design** tab, and then in the Reset group, click the **Convert** button. See Figure 3–6. The menu that opens contains two options. If you wanted to convert the graphic to a bulleted list, you would click Convert to Text. You want to convert the graphic to its individual shapes.

**Figure 3–6**　**Convert menu on the SmartArt Design tab**

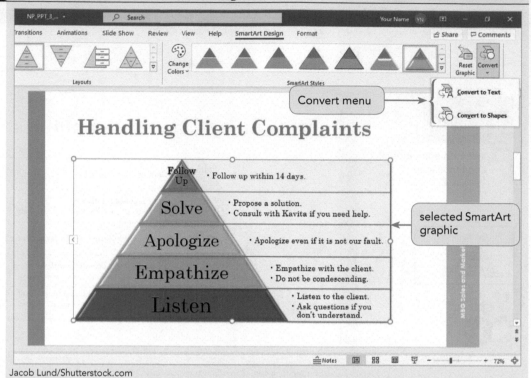

Jacob Lund/Shutterstock.com

2. On the menu, click **Convert to Shapes**. The SmartArt graphic is converted into shapes. On the ribbon, the SmartArt contextual tabs disappear, and the Shape Format contextual tab appears instead. A selection border appears around all of the shapes, indicating that they are grouped into one object. See Figure 3–7. The text in the first-level shapes was changed to white. On the ribbon, the Home tab is selected. First, you are going to change the text in the first-level shapes back to black.

**Figure 3–7**    **SmartArt converted to shapes**

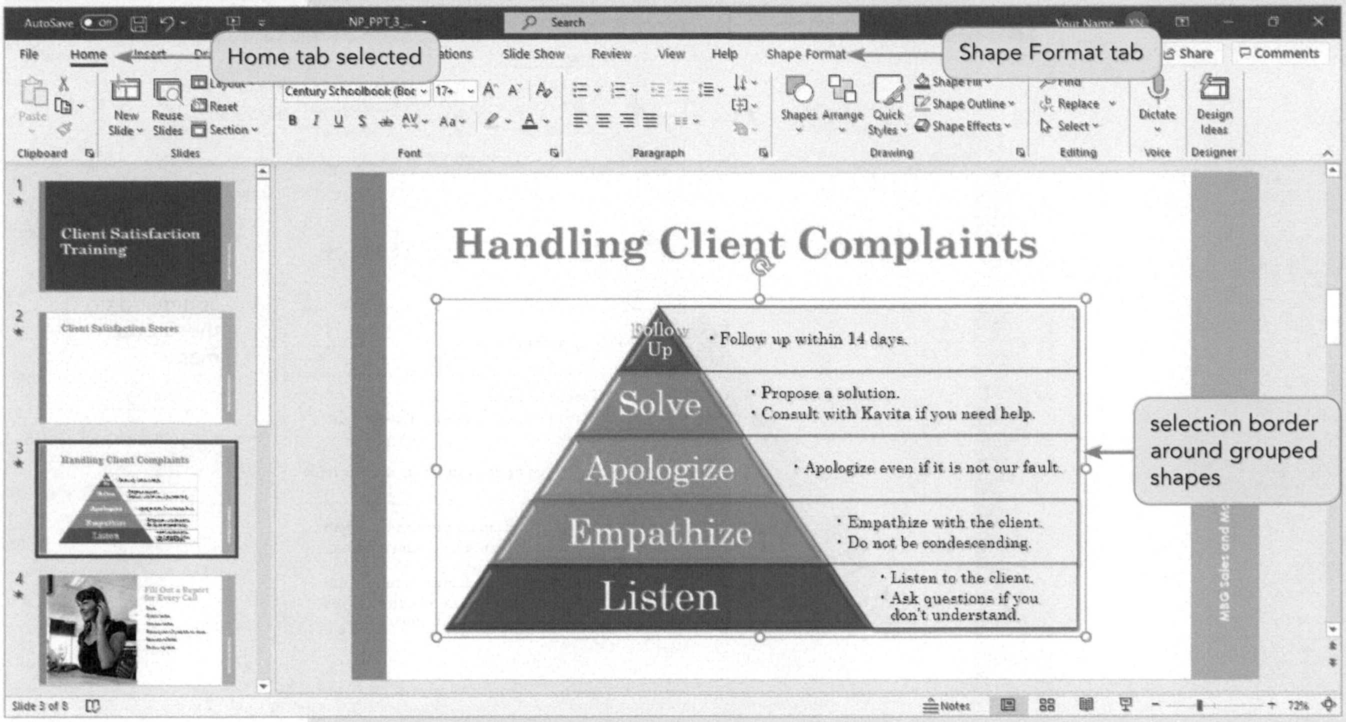

Jacob Lund/Shutterstock.com

> **3.** On the Home tab, in the Font group, click the **Font Color arrow** [A ▾], and then click the **Black, Text 1** color. Because the entire grouped object was selected, all of the text changes to black.

> **4.** On the ribbon, click the **Animations** tab. In the Animation group, None is selected. When you converted the SmartArt graphic, the animation you had applied to the graphic was removed.

Kavita wants the second-level shapes to appear immediately after each first-level shape, as if the shapes were connected. To create this effect, you will first ungroup all the shapes. Next, you will group the shapes at each level, and then animate each group.

### To ungroup and group shapes:

> **1.** Click the **Shape Format** tab, and then in the Arrange group, click the **Group** button. A menu opens. See Figure 3–8. Because the objects are already grouped, the only command available is the Ungroup command.

**Figure 3–8**   **Group menu when a grouped object is selected**

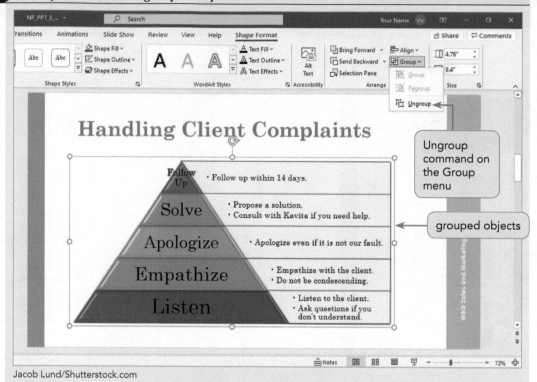

Jacob Lund/Shutterstock.com

> 2. On the menu, click **Ungroup**. The shapes are ungrouped, and each individual shape is selected. Next, you will group the Listen shape and the shape containing its subitems.

> 3. Click a blank area of the slide to deselect the shapes, click the **Listen** shape, press and hold **SHIFT**, click the shape to the right of the Listen shape, and then release **SHIFT**. The two shapes are selected.

> 4. On the Shape Format tab, in the Arrange group, click the **Group** button. The Group menu opens. This time, the Ungroup command is not available because the items are not yet grouped.

> 5. On the menu, click **Group**. The two shapes are grouped as one object and the selection border appears around both of them.

> 6. Working your way up the pyramid, use the **Group** command to group the two shapes in each level of the pyramid.

> 7. Click the grouped **Listen** shape, click the **Animations** tab, and then in the Animation group, click the **Wipe** entrance animation.

> 8. In the Animation group, click the **Effect Options** button, and then click **From Left**. The animation previews and the Listen shape and its subitems wipe on the screen from the left.

> 9. Starting with the Empathize group and working your way up the pyramid, apply the **Wipe** entrance animation with the **From Left** effect to each grouped object. When you are finished, the animation sequence icons should advance from 1 through 5 from the bottom of the pyramid to the top. See Figure 3–9.

| Figure 3–9 | Animations applied to the grouped shapes on Slide 3 |

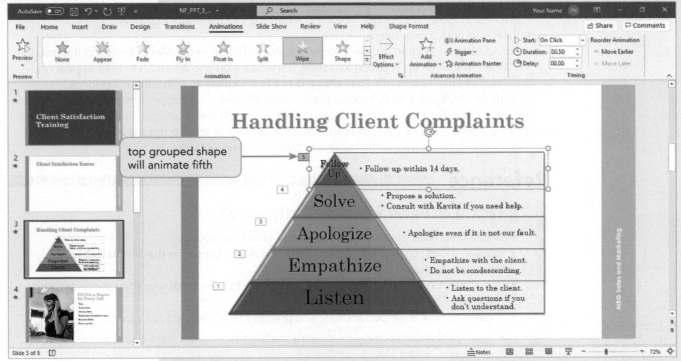

Jacob Lund/Shutterstock.com

**Trouble?** If the animation sequence icons are out of order, click the icon of the animation whose order you want to change, and then in the Timing group on the Animations tab, click the Move Earlier or Move Later button to move the animation earlier or later.

**10.** Save the changes to the presentation.

# Insight

### Inserting Scalable Vector Graphics

In addition to shapes, you can insert icons. The icons are sorted into various categories, such as People, Education, Vehicles, Sports, and so on. To insert icons, click the Insert tab, and then in the Illustrations group, click the Icons button to open the Insert Icons dialog box. Click as many icons as you want to add to the slide, and then click Insert.

When you select an icon on a slide, the Graphic Format tab appears on the ribbon. Similar to the Shape Format tab, you can change the fill color, the outline color, weight, and style of an icon, or apply effects, such as shadows or bevels, to the icon. If you want to change to a different icon, you can click the Change Graphic button in the Change group.

An icon is a scalable vector graphic, which means the icon can be resized, rotated, or recolored without losing any quality. If you want to recolor or manipulate different parts of the icon, you need convert it to a shape or ungroup it. To do this, select the icon, and then in the Change group on the Graphic Format tab, click the Convert to Shape button. Then you can click each shape that makes up the icon and format it any way you want using the tools on the Shape Format tab.

# Adding Audio to Slides

Audio in a presentation can be used for a wide variety of purposes. For example, you might want to add a sound clip of music to a particular portion of the presentation to evoke emotion, or perhaps include a recording of customers expressing their satisfaction with a product or service.

To add a sound clip to a slide, you use the Audio button in the Media group on the Insert tab. When a sound clip is added to a slide, a speaker icon and an audio toolbar appear on the slide, and like videos, the start setting is In Click Sequence. Also similar to videos, the options for changing how the sound plays during the slide show appear on the Playback tab for audio clips. For the most part, they are the same options that appear on the Playback tab for video clips. For example, you can trim an audio clip or set it to rewind after playing. You can also compress audio in the same way that you compress video.

## Reference

### Inserting an Audio Clip into a Presentation

- Display the slide onto which you want to insert the sound.
- On the ribbon, click the Insert tab, click the Audio button in the Media group, and then click Audio on My PC.
- In the Insert Audio dialog box, navigate to the folder containing the sound clip, click the audio file, and then click Insert.
- If desired, click the Playback tab, and then in the Audio Options group:
  - Change the start setting by clicking the Start arrow, and then clicking Automatically or When Clicked On.
  - Click the Hide During Show check box to select it to hide the speaker icon during a slide show.
  - Click the Volume button, and then click a volume level or click Mute.
  - Click the Loop until Stopped check box to select it to play the audio clip continuously until the next action occurs.
  - Click the Rewind after Playing check box to rewind the clip to the beginning after it plays.
- If desired, click the Playback tab, and then in the Editing group:
  - Click the Trim Audio button, and then in the Trim audio dialog box, change the time in the Start Time or End Time boxes to change the point at which the audio clip starts or stops, and then click OK.
  - Increase the time in the Fade In or Fade Out boxes to fade the audio in or out at the beginning or end of the clip.

Kavita wants you to add a sound clip to the last slide in the presentation. The clip is a recording of a client who said that she was extremely satisfied with her customer service experience at MBG.

**Tip**

To record an audio clip, click the Audio button in the Media group on the Insert tab, and then click Record Audio.

**To add a sound clip to Slide 6:**

1. Display Slide 6 (the second "Pathway to Happy Clients" slide), and then click the **Insert** tab on the ribbon.

2. In the Media group, click the **Audio** button, and then click **Audio on My PC**. The Insert Audio dialog box opens.

3. Navigate to the **PowerPoint3 > Module** folder, click **Support_PPT_3_ Comment.m4a**, and then click **Insert**. A speaker icon appears in the middle of the slide with the audio toolbar below it, and the Playback tab is selected on the ribbon. See Figure 3–10. As with videos, the default Start setting is In Click Sequence.

| Figure 3–10 | Speaker icon on Slide 6 |
| --- | --- |

fizkes/Shutterstock.com

4. Drag the speaker icon to the lower-right corner of the slide so it is positioned at the bottom of the blue bar.

5. On the audio toolbar, click the **Play** button ▶. The sound clip, which is a comment from a satisfied client, plays. Kavita wants the clip to play automatically after the slide appears on the screen.

6. On the Playback tab, in the Audio Options group, click the **Start** arrow, and then click **Automatically**. Because the clip will play automatically, there is no need to have the sound icon visible on the screen during a slide show.

7. In the Audio Options group, click the **Hide During Show** check box to select it.

8. Save the changes to the presentation.

## Insight

### Playing Music Across Slides

You can add an audio clip to a slide and have it play throughout the slide show. On the Playback tab, in the Audio Styles group, click the Play in Background button. When you select this option, the Start setting in the Audio Options group is changed to Automatically, and the Play Across Slides, Loop until Stopped, and Hide During Show check boxes become selected. These setting changes ensure the audio clip will start playing when the slide appears on the screen during a slide show and will continue playing, starting over if necessary, until the end of the slide show. To change the settings so that the audio no longer plays throughout the slide show, click the No Style button in the Audio Styles group.

# Adding a Chart to a Slide

**Charts** are graphic elements that illustrate data using bars, columns, dots, lines, or other symbols to make the data easier to understand and to make it easier to see the relationships among the data. Refer to the Session 3.1 Visual Overview for more information about creating charts and using spreadsheets in PowerPoint.

## Creating a Chart

To create a chart, you click the Insert Chart button in a content placeholder or use the Chart button in the Illustrations group on the Insert tab, and then select a chart type. Doing this opens a window containing a spreadsheet with sample data, and a sample chart appears on the slide. When you edit the sample data in the spreadsheet, the chart on the slide changes to reflect the new data.

## Reference

### Creating a Chart

- On a slide with a layout that includes a content placeholder, click the Insert Chart button in the content placeholder; or click the Insert tab, and then, in the Illustrations group, click the Chart button.
- In the Insert Chart dialog box, click the desired chart type in the list on the left.
- In the row of styles, click the desired chart style, and then click OK.
- In the spreadsheet that opens, enter the data that you want to plot.
- If you need to chart fewer rows or columns than are shaded in the spreadsheet, drag the handle in the lower-right corner of the shaded area up to remove rows or to the left to remove columns.
- In the spreadsheet window, click the Close button.

Kavita wants you to create a chart on Slide 2 that illustrates the percentage of clients that are satisfied with their customer service encounters. A pie chart is a good choice when you want to show the relative size of one value compared to the other values and compared to the total set of values.

### To create a chart on Slide 2:

1. Display Slide 2 ("Client Satisfaction Scores"). You can insert a chart by using the Insert Chart button ▥ in a content placeholder or by clicking Chart in the Illustrations group on the Insert tab.

2. In the content placeholder, click the **Insert Chart** button ▥. The Insert Chart dialog box opens. Column is selected in the list of chart types on the left, and the Clustered Column style is selected in the row of styles at the top and shown in the preview area. See Figure 3-11.

**Figure 3–11**     **Insert Chart dialog box**

selected chart type

Pie chart type

styles for the selected chart type

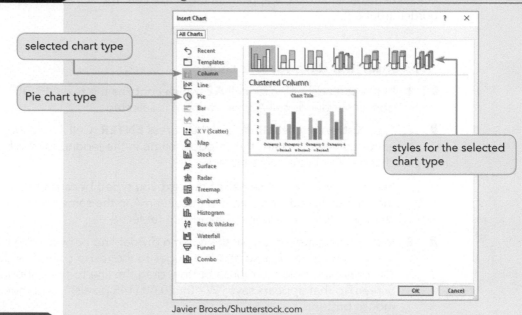

Javier Brosch/Shutterstock.com

**Tip**

After you insert a chart, you can click the Design Ideas button in the Designer group on the Design tab to open the Design Ideas pane with suggestions for the slide layout.

**3.** In the list of chart types, click **Pie**. The row of chart styles changes to pie chart styles. The Pie style is selected.

**4.** Click **OK**. A sample chart is inserted on Slide 2, and a small spreadsheet (sometimes called a datasheet) opens above the chart. In the spreadsheet, colored borders around the cells indicate which cells are included in the chart. At the bottom of the chart, the **legend** identifies how data is represented using colors or patterns. See Figure 3–12.

**Figure 3–12**     **Spreadsheet and chart with sample data**

spreadsheet with sample data

chart contextual tabs

chart created from sample data

legend

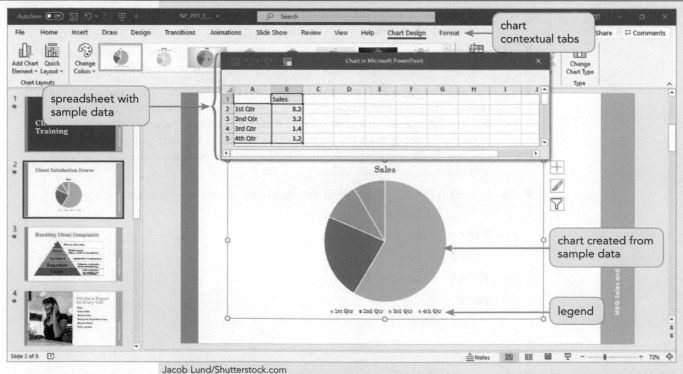

Jacob Lund/Shutterstock.com

To create the chart for Kavita's presentation, you need to edit the sample data in the spreadsheet. When you work with a spreadsheet, the cell that is selected is the **active cell**. When you enter data, it appears in the active cell. The active cell has a green border around it.

### To enter the data for the chart:

1. In the spreadsheet, click cell **A2**, which contains the text "1ˢᵗ Qtr". A green border surrounds cell A2, indicating it is selected.

2. Type **Extremely satisfied**, and then press **ENTER**. Cell A3 becomes the active cell. In the chart, the category name in the legend for the blue pie slice changes to "Extremely satisfied".

   In cell A2, you cannot see all of the text you typed because the text is longer than the cell width. You can widen column A in the same manner that you change column widths in a PowerPoint table.

3. Move the pointer on top of the column divider line between the column A and column B headers so that it changes to the resize column width pointer ✛, press and hold the mouse button, drag the line to the right until the ScreenTip that appears says "Width: 20.00 (145 pixels)", and then release the mouse button.

4. Enter the following in cells **A3** through **A5**, pressing **ENTER** after each entry:

   **Very satisfied**

   **Somewhat satisfied**

   **Somewhat dissatisfied**

**Tip**

To add or remove a row or column from the chart, drag the small sizing handle at the bottom-right of the last column and last row of data in the spreadsheet.

5. In cell A6, type **Not at all satisfied**, and then press **ENTER**. The active cell is cell A7. In the chart, a new category name is added to the legend. Because there is no data for this new category in cell B6, a corresponding slice was not added to the pie chart. Although the shading and colored borders in the spreadsheet did not change, a small sizing handle appears in the corner of cell B6 in the spreadsheet. This indicates that the cells in this row will be included in the chart.

6. Scroll the spreadsheet up, click in cell **B1** to make it the active cell, type **Number**, and then press **ENTER**. The active cell is now cell B2.

7. In cell B2, type **1321**, and then press **ENTER**. The slice in the pie chart that represents the percentage showing the number of clients who are extremely satisfied increases to essentially fill the chart. This is because the value 1321 is so much larger than the sample data values in the rest of the rows in column B. As you continue to enter the data, the slices in the pie chart will adjust as you add each value.

8. In cells B3 through B6, enter the following values, and then compare your screen to Figure 3–13:

   **3527**

   **13290**

   **7544**

   **2637**

| Figure 3–13 | Spreadsheet and chart after entering data |

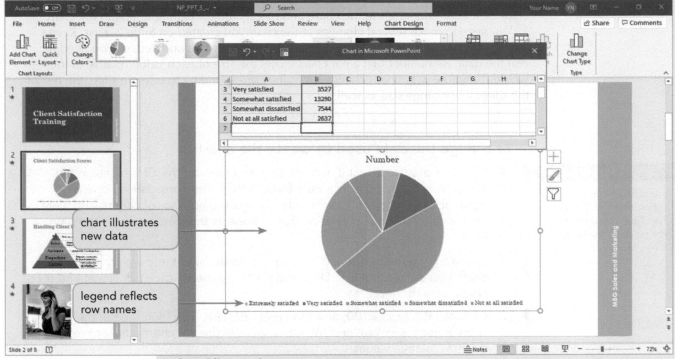

Jacob Lund/Shutterstock.com

Notice that the shading and colored borders in the spreadsheet now includes cells A6 and B6.

9. In the spreadsheet, click the **Close** button ✕. The spreadsheet closes.

10. Save the changes to the presentation.

# Proskills

### Decision Making: Selecting the Correct Chart Type

To use charts effectively, you need to consider what you want to illustrate with your data. Column charts use vertical columns and bar charts use horizontal bars to represent values. These types of charts are useful for comparing the values of items over a period of time or a range of dates or costs. Line charts and area charts use a line to connect points that represent values. They are effective for showing changes over time, and they are particularly useful for illustrating trends. Line and area charts are a better choice than column or bar charts when you need to display large amounts of information and exact quantities that don't require emphasis. Pie charts are used to show percentages or proportions of the parts that make up a whole. Treemap and sunburst charts also show the proportion of parts to a whole. These two chart types also show hierarchical data when the data is grouped into subcategories.

You can change a chart type after you create it. To do this, click the Change Chart Type button in the Type group on the Chart Design tab. The same dialog box appears as when you first create a chart.

## Modifying a Chart

Once a chart is on a slide, you can modify it by changing or formatting its various elements. For example, you can edit the data; apply a style; add, remove, or reposition chart elements; add labels to the chart; and modify the formatting of text in the chart.

You need to make several changes to the chart you created on Slide 2. First, Kavita informs you that one of the values she provided needs to be updated, so you need to edit the data. Remember that a pie chart shows the size of each value relative to the whole. Therefore, when you change the value corresponding to one pie slice, the rest of the slices will change size as well.

**Tip**

To switch to another type of chart, click the Change Chart Type button in the Type group on the Chart Design tab.

### To change the data used to create the chart:

1. Click the chart to select it, if necessary, and then on the Chart Design tab, in the Data group, click the **Edit Data** button. The spreadsheet opens again above the chart. You need to change the number of clients who were "Extremely satisfied". The slice that represents this percentage is the blue slice.

   **Trouble?** If a menu opened instead of a spreadsheet appearing above the chart, you clicked the Edit Data arrow. On the menu, click Edit Data, and then continue with Step 2.

2. Click cell **B2**, type **2100**, and then press **ENTER**. The blue slice in the pie chart increases in size, and the other slices in the pie chart adjust to reflect the new relative values.

3. On the spreadsheet, click the **Close** button ☒. The spreadsheet closes.

Next, Kavita wants you to make several formatting changes to the chart. She would like you to apply a different style to the chart and change its colors. There are several ways to do this. You can use the Quick Layout command, or you can change the style and apply a different palette of colors.

### To change the layout, style, and colors of the chart:

1. On the Chart Design tab, in the Chart Layouts group, click the **Quick Layout** button. A gallery of chart layouts specific to pie charts opens. Each layout includes different chart elements, such as the chart title and legend.

2. Point to several of the layouts to see which elements are added to the chart, and then click **Layout 1**. The category name and percentage of each slice are added as labels on the slices, and the legend is removed. With this layout, there is no need for the legend.

3. To the right of the chart, click the **Chart Styles** button ✎. A gallery opens with the Style tab selected at the top.

4. Point to several of the styles to see the effect on the chart. In addition to changing the colors used, some of the styles include layouts and add or remove chart elements, similar to the Quick Layouts.

5. Click **Style 3**. This style adds the legend and a background that varies from very light gray to a darker gray. The labels that list the category names and percentages of each slice are still included. The labels overlap, but you will fix that in the next set of steps. See Figure 3-14.

Figure 3–14

**Figure 3–14** | **Chart after changing the layout and applying a style**

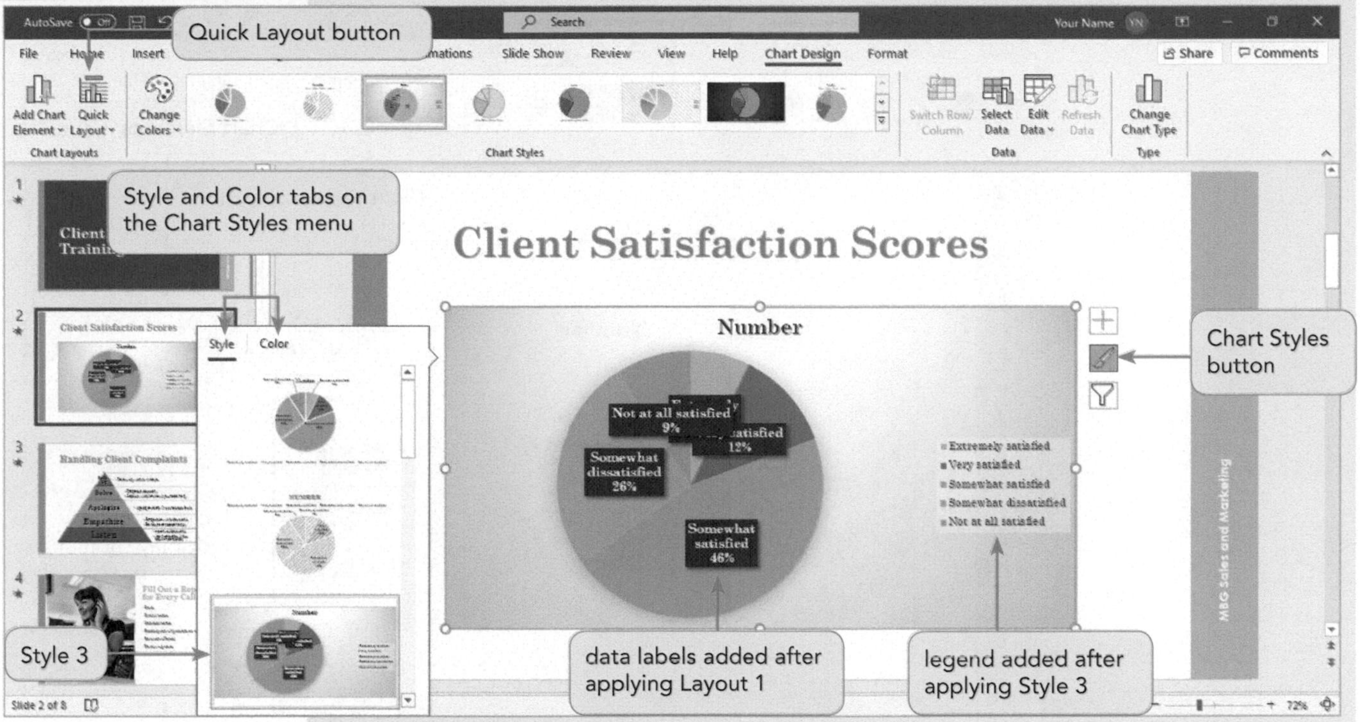

Jacob Lund/Shutterstock.com

**6.** On the Chart Styles menu, click the **Color** tab at the top. A menu containing color palettes appears.

**7.** In the list, click **Colorful Palette 2**. The colors in the chart change to the colors specified in the palette you selected.

There is no need for a title on the chart because the slide title describes the chart. Because the pie slices are labeled with the category names and the percentage values, there is also no need for the legend. You will remove the title and the legend. Then you will reposition the labels on the chart.

**Tip**

Double-click a chart element to open a pane that contains additional commands for modifying that element.

### To remove, reposition, and format chart elements:

**1.** To the right of the chart, click the **Chart Elements** button ⊞. The Chart Styles menu closes, and the Chart Elements menu opens to the right of the chart. The Chart Title, Data Labels, and Legend check boxes are all selected, which means these elements are shown on the chart.

**2.** On the Chart Elements menu, move the pointer on top of **Chart Title** so that an arrow ▶ appears, and then click the **arrow** ▶. The Chart Title submenu opens. See Figure 3–15. The submenu contains two locations where you can place the chart title. The Above Chart option is selected. The submenu also contains the More Options command. If you click More Options, the Format Chart Title pane opens. That pane contains commands you can use to format the chart title.

**Figure 3–15** **Chart Title submenu on the Chart Elements menu**

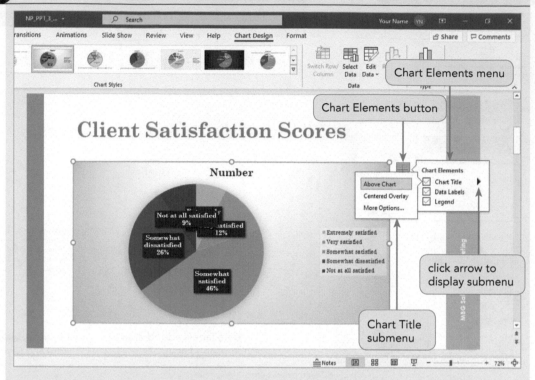

3. On the Chart Elements menu, click the **Chart Title** check box. The check box is deselected, the submenu closes, and the chart title is removed from the chart.

4. On the Chart Elements menu, move the pointer on top of **Legend**, and then click the **arrow** ▶ that appears. The Legend submenu opens listing four locations where you can position the legend.

5. Click the **Legend** check box to deselect it. The legend is removed from the chart.

6. On the Chart Elements menu, move the pointer on top of **Data Labels**, and then click the **arrow** ▶ to open the Data Labels submenu. This time, you will select a command on the submenu.

7. On the submenu, click **Outside End**. The data labels are moved so that they are positioned next to each pie slice.

8. Click the **Chart Elements** button ⊞ to close the menu.

9. Click one of the data labels to select all of them, and then click the **Home** tab.

10. In the Font group, click the **Font** button, and then click **Century Gothic**.

11. In the Font group, click the **Font Size** button, and then click **11**.

12. Click the **Somewhat satisfied 46%** data label. The label you clicked is selected and the rest of the data labels are deselected.

13. Drag the **Somewhat satisfied 46%** data label so it is positioned in the center of the large, light-green slice.

   **Trouble?** If the label moves back to its original position, click the data label to select it, wait for several seconds, and then drag it again.

14. Drag the **Somewhat dissatisfied 26%** data label so it overlaps the dark blue slice.

▶ **15.** Drag the **Very satisfied 12%** data label so its corner overlaps the light olive-green slice.

▶ **16.** Drag the **Not at all satisfied 9%** data label so its corner overlaps the dark olive-green slice.

▶ **17.** Drag the **Extremely satisfied 7%** data label so its corner overlaps the light blue slice and is approximately aligned with the "Not at all satisfied 9%" label. Compare your screen to Figure 3–16 and make any necessary adjustments so that your screen matches the figure.

**Figure 3–16** ▶ **Chart with modified data labels and the title and legend removed**

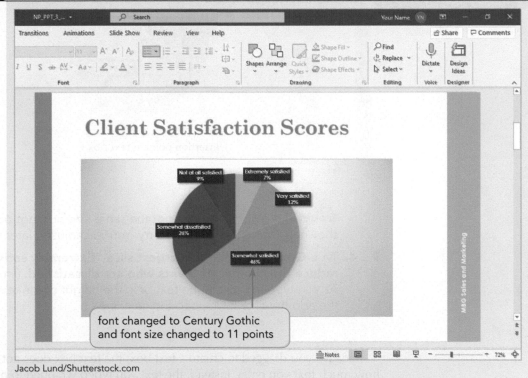

Jacob Lund/Shutterstock.com

▶ **18.** Save the changes to the presentation.

# Inserting and Formatting Text Boxes

Sometimes you need to add text to a slide in a location other than in one of the text placeholders included in the slide layout. Two ways you can do this are to draw a shape and then add text to it, or add a special type of shape called a text box.

Ordinary shapes are filled with the Accent 1 color by default, but text box shapes have no fill when you create them. Therefore, when you place a shape over another object, it obscures the object behind it, while a text box shows the object through the background. With an ordinary shape, the text is center-aligned by default, but the text in a text box shape is left-aligned.

Regardless of the differences, after you create a text box, you can format the text box in all of the same ways you can format a shape, including adding a fill, adjusting the internal margins, and rotating and repositioning it.

Kavita wants you to add text on Slide 2 that describes the goal for her team for the next quarter. You will add a text box to accomplish this.

### To add a text box on Slide 2:

▶ 1. With Slide 2 ("Client Satisfaction Scores") displayed, click the **Insert** tab on the ribbon, and then in the Illustrations group, click the **Shapes** button.

▶ 2. In the Basic Shapes section, click the **Text Box** shape ▣, and then move the pointer to the slide. The pointer changes to the draw text box pointer ↓.

▶ 3. Position the draw text box pointer ↓ below the left edge of the chart, and then click and drag to draw a text box as wide as the chart and about one-half-inch high. See Figure 3–17. The insertion point is in the text box.

| Figure 3–17 | Text box inserted on Slide 2 |
| --- | --- |

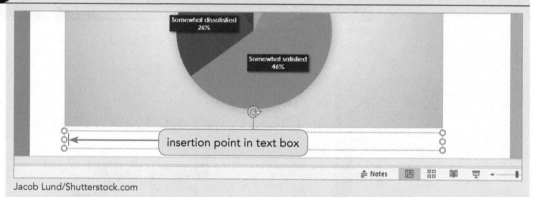

Jacob Lund/Shutterstock.com

**Trouble?** If your text box is not the same size or is not positioned exactly as shown in Figure 3–17, don't worry. You will adjust it later.

▶ 4. Type **Goal is to make the largest slice "Extremely satisfied" and greatly reduce the number of clients who are dissatisfied.** (including the period). As you type the text in the text box, the height of the text box changes, and the additional text wraps to the next line.

Because you dragged to create a text box, the text box does not get wider no matter how much text you enter. Instead, the text you typed wrapped to new lines in the text box, and the height of the text box resized to accommodate the text you typed. If you had simply clicked to place the text box, the text box would have expanded horizontally as wide as necessary to accommodate the text you typed, even if it needed to flow off the slide. This differs from text boxes created from title and content placeholders and shapes with text in them. As you have seen, text boxes created from placeholders have the AutoFit feature applied to reduce the font size of the text to fit if you add more text than can fit in the placeholder. When you add text to a shape, if you add more text than can fit horizontally in that shape, the text wraps to the next line and then extends outside of the top and bottom of the shape if necessary.

Kavita thinks the text below the chart would look better if it were all on one line and italicized. You will change the text wrapping option so that the text does not wrap to the next line.

### To modify and reposition the text box:

▶ 1. Right-click the text box, and then on the shortcut menu, click **Format Shape**. The Format Shape pane opens to the right of the displayed slide. The pane contains two tabs at the top—Shape Options and Text Options—and buttons to display related commands on each tab. The Shape Options tab is selected. This tab contains categories of commands for formatting the shape, such as changing the fill or line. See Figure 3–18.

**Figure 3–18** Format Shape pane and text box with wrapped text

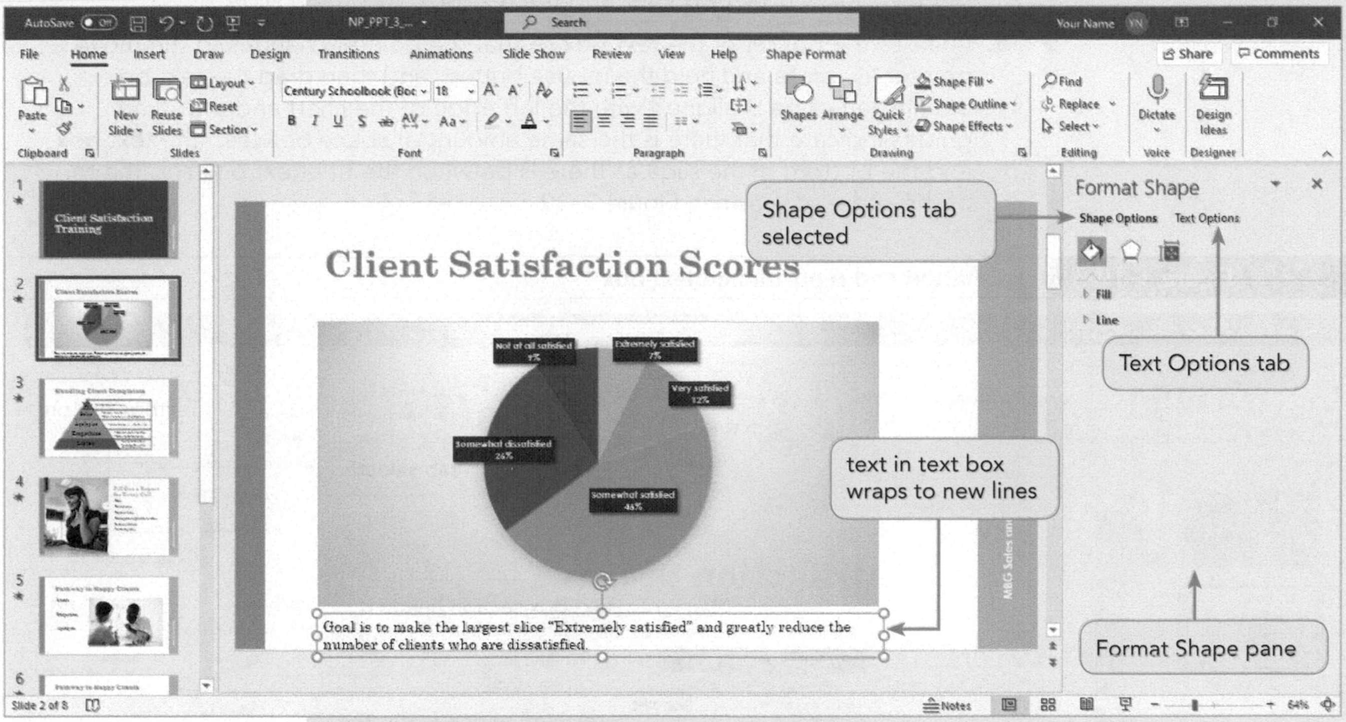


Jacob Lund/Shutterstock.com: fizkes/Shutterstock.com

**Tip**

Clicking any of the Dialog Box Launchers on the Shape Format tab also opens the Format Shape pane.

2. In the Format Shape pane, click **Text Options** to display the Text Options tab. This tab contains commands for formatting the text in the text box.
3. Click the **Textbox** button. The Format Shape pane changes to show the Text Box section, containing options for formatting text in a text box. At the top of the pane, the Resize shape to fit text option button is selected. That is why the height of the text box increased when the text wrapped to a new line. Text and content placeholders have the Shrink text on overflow option button selected by default. And shapes other than text boxes have the Do not Autofit option button selected.

   First you want to change the wrap option so the text does not wrap in the text box.
4. Click the **Wrap text in shape** check box to deselect it. The text in the text box appears all on one line and overlaps the right edge of the slide. Next, you want to decrease the space between the first word in the text box and the left border of the box. In other words, you want to change the left margin in the text box.

   **Trouble?** If the Wrap text in shape check box is not selected, you clicked instead of dragging to create the text box in Step 3 in the previous set of steps. In this case, do not click the check box; leave it unselected.
5. Click the **Left margin** down arrow. The value in the box changes to 0", and the text shifts left in the text box.
6. On the slide, click the text box border to select all of the text in the text box, and then, in the Font group on the Home tab, click the **Italic** button *I*. The text in the text box is italicized.

7. In the Font group, click the **Decrease Font Size** button $\boxed{\text{A}^{*}}$ twice. The text in the text box is now 14 points, and the text box fits on the slide.

8. Point to the border of the text box so that the pointer changes to the move pointer $\overset{\text{⊹}}{\text{↖}}$, press and hold the mouse button, and then drag the text box until its left edge is aligned with the left edge of the chart and the smart guides indicate that there is the same amount of space between the text box and the bottom of the slide as there is between the title text box and the top of the slide, as shown in Figure 3–19.

**Figure 3–19** **Formatted and repositioned text box**

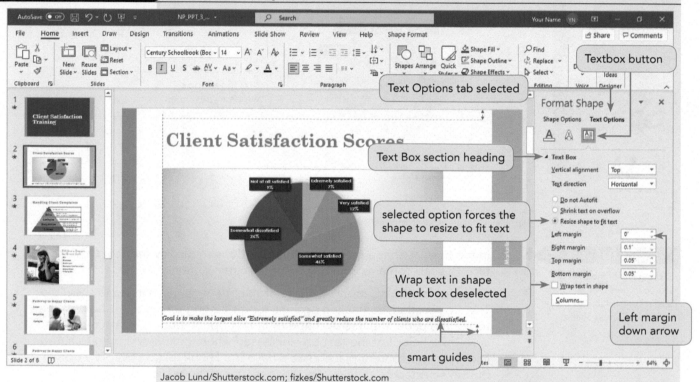

Jacob Lund/Shutterstock.com; fizkes/Shutterstock.com

9. Release the mouse button.

10. In the Format Shape pane, click the **Close** button $\boxed{\times}$, and then save the changes to the presentation.

# Applying WordArt Styles to Text

**WordArt** is formatted, decorative text in a text box. WordArt text has a fill color, which is the same as the font color, and an outline color. To create WordArt, you can insert a new text box by using the WordArt button in the Text group on the Insert tab or format an existing one by applying one of the built-in WordArt styles or using the Text Fill, Text Outline, and Text Effects buttons in the WordArt Styles group on the Format tab.

Kavita would like you to apply a WordArt style to the title of Slide 8.

**To apply a WordArt style to the title of Slide 8 and modify it:**

1. Display Slide 8 ("100% Satisfaction"), click the title **100% Satisfaction**, and then click the title text box border. The entire text box is selected.

2. Click the **Shape Format** tab, and then in the WordArt Styles group, click the **More** button to open the WordArt gallery. See Figure 3–20.

Figure 3–20    WordArt gallery

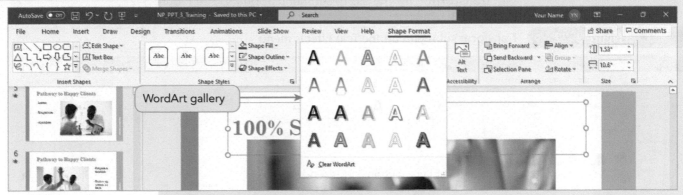

fizkes/Shutterstock.com

**Tip**

To create a new text box containing text formatted with a WordArt style, make sure nothing on the slide is selected, click the WordArt button in the WordArt Styles group on the Insert tab, and then click a style.

3. Click the **Pattern Fill: Brown, Dark Upward Diagonal Stripe; Hard Shadow** style (the last style in the last row). The title text is formatted with the style you selected in the WordArt gallery. This WordArt style doesn't really match the slide theme, so you will change it.

4. In the WordArt Styles group, click the **More** button, and then click the **Gradient Fill: Green, Accent color 5; Reflection** style (the second style in the second row). The style of the text changes to the style you chose. You want to change the color used in the gradient fill from green to blue.

5. In the WordArt Styles group, click the **Text Fill arrow**. The Theme Colors palette appears.

6. Click the **Ice Blue, Accent 1, Darker 50%** color. If you wanted to change the color of the outline of each letter, you would use the Text Outline button.

7. Click the **Home** tab, and then in the Paragraph group, click the **Center** button. See Figure 3–21.

Figure 3–21    WordArt on Slide 8

fizkes/Shutterstock.com

The shape of text in a text box can be transformed into waves, circles, and other shapes. To do this, you use the options located on the Transform submenu, which is accessed from the Text Effects menu on the Shape Format tab.

Kavita wants you to change the shape of the WordArt on Slide 8.

**To change the shape of the WordArt by applying a transform effect:**

▶ **1.** With the WordArt on Slide 8 selected, click the **Shape Format** tab.

▶ **2.** In the WordArt styles group, click the **Text Effects** button, and then point to **Transform**. The Transform submenu appears. See Figure 3–22.

**Figure 3–22**   Transform submenu on the Text Effects menu

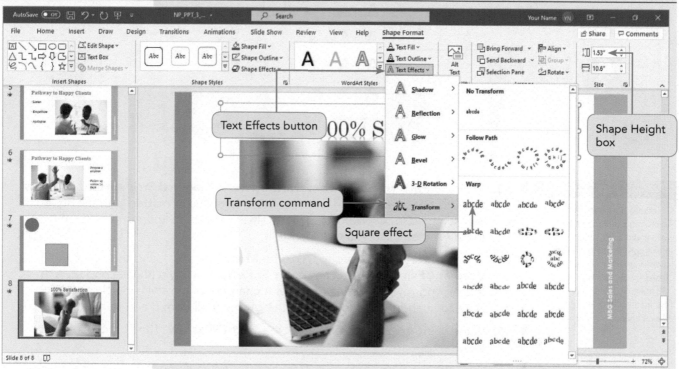

fizkes/Shutterstock.com

▶ **3.** In the first row under Warp, click the **Square** effect. The effect is applied to the text in the text box. The WordArt text box is too large for the space.

▶ **4.** In the Size group, click in the **Shape Height** box, type **0.7**, and then press **ENTER**. Compare your screen to Figure 3–23.

**Figure 3–23**     **Final WordArt**

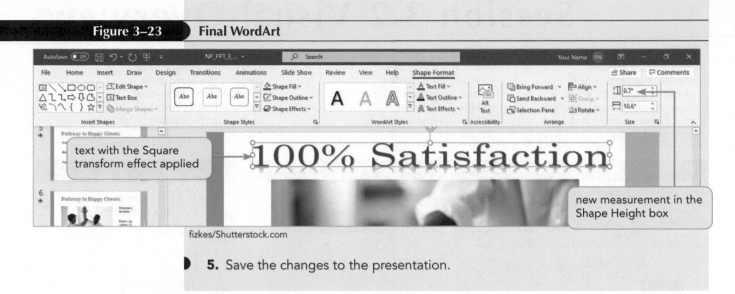

fizkes/Shutterstock.com

**5.** Save the changes to the presentation.

## Proskills

### Decision Making: Selecting Appropriate Font Colors

When you select font colors, make sure your text is easy to read during your slide show. Font colors that work well are dark colors on a light background or light colors on a dark background. Avoid red text on a blue background or blue text on a green background (and vice versa) unless the shades of those colors strongly contrast with each other. These combinations might look fine on your computer monitor, but they are almost totally illegible to an audience viewing your presentation on a screen in a darkened room. Also avoid using red/green or blue/yellow combinations, which many people with color blindness find illegible.

In this session, you created and modified a SmartArt graphic, and then you animated it and changed the effect options for the animation. You also converted a SmartArt graphic to shapes, ungrouped the shapes, and then grouped them in a different organization. You added an audio clip and WordArt to a slide. You learned how to create and modify a chart on a slide, and how to insert and format a text box. In the next session, you will continue modifying the presentation by creating a custom shape, formatting pictures and shapes, and making the presentation accessible.

## Review

### Session 3.1 Quick Check

1. How do you change the animation applied to a SmartArt graphic so that each shape animates one at a time?

2. What happens when you click the Play in Background button in the Audio Styles group on the Playback tab?

3. What happens when you group objects?

4. What is the start setting for an audio clip when you place it on a slide: In Click Sequence, Automatically, or When Clicked On?

5. What is a spreadsheet?

6. How do you identify a specific cell in a spreadsheet?

7. What is WordArt?

# Session 3.2 Visual Overview:

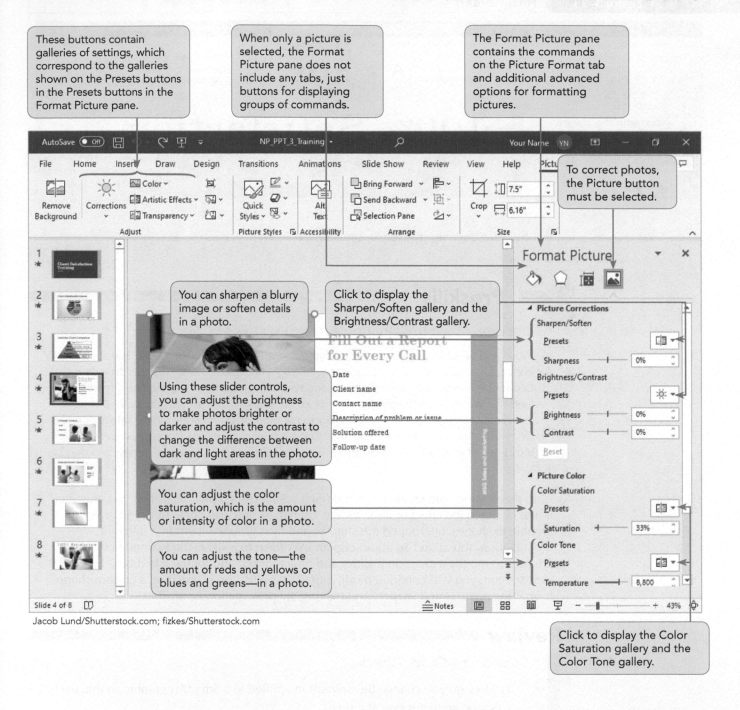

These buttons contain galleries of settings, which correspond to the galleries shown on the Presets buttons in the Presets buttons in the Format Picture pane.

When only a picture is selected, the Format Picture pane does not include any tabs, just buttons for displaying groups of commands.

The Format Picture pane contains the commands on the Picture Format tab and additional advanced options for formatting pictures.

To correct photos, the Picture button must be selected.

You can sharpen a blurry image or soften details in a photo.

Click to display the Sharpen/Soften gallery and the Brightness/Contrast gallery.

Using these slider controls, you can adjust the brightness to make photos brighter or darker and adjust the contrast to change the difference between dark and light areas in the photo.

You can adjust the color saturation, which is the amount or intensity of color in a photo.

You can adjust the tone—the amount of reds and yellows or blues and greens—in a photo.

Click to display the Color Saturation gallery and the Color Tone gallery.

Jacob Lund/Shutterstock.com; fizkes/Shutterstock.com

# Formatting Shapes and Pictures

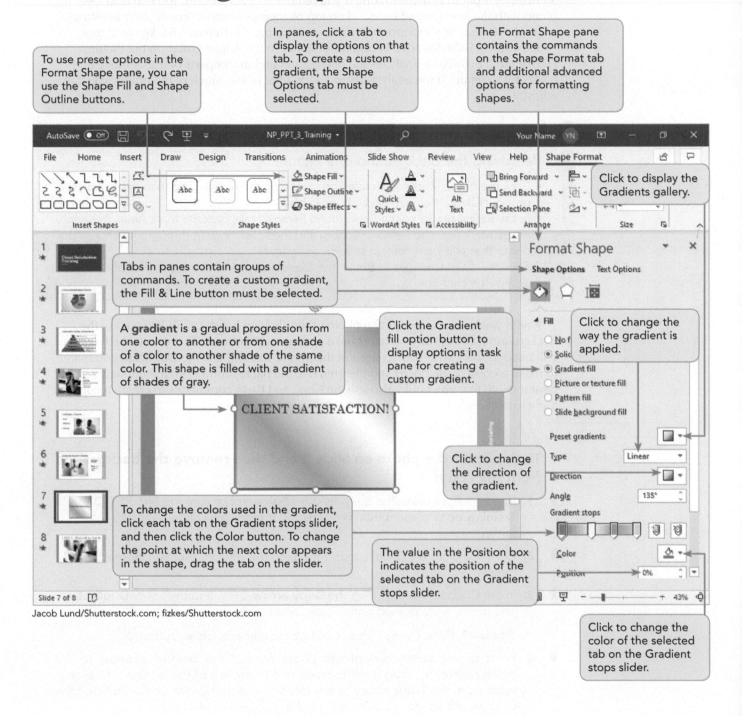

To use preset options in the Format Shape pane, you can use the Shape Fill and Shape Outline buttons.

In panes, click a tab to display the options on that tab. To create a custom gradient, the Shape Options tab must be selected.

The Format Shape pane contains the commands on the Shape Format tab and additional advanced options for formatting shapes.

Click to display the Gradients gallery.

Tabs in panes contain groups of commands. To create a custom gradient, the Fill & Line button must be selected.

A **gradient** is a gradual progression from one color to another or from one shade of a color to another shade of the same color. This shape is filled with a gradient of shades of gray.

Click the Gradient fill option button to display options in task pane for creating a custom gradient.

Click to change the way the gradient is applied.

Click to change the direction of the gradient.

To change the colors used in the gradient, click each tab on the Gradient stops slider, and then click the Color button. To change the point at which the next color appears in the shape, drag the tab on the slider.

The value in the Position box indicates the position of the selected tab on the Gradient stops slider.

Click to change the color of the selected tab on the Gradient stops slider.

Jacob Lund/Shutterstock.com; fizkes/Shutterstock.com

# Removing the Background from Pictures

Sometimes a photo is more striking if you remove its background. You can also layer a photo with the background removed on top of another photo to create an interesting effect. To remove the background of a photo, you use the Remove Background tool. When you click the Remove Background button in the Adjust group on the Picture Format tab, PowerPoint analyzes the photograph and marks parts of it to remove and parts of it to retain. If the analysis removes too little or too much of the photo, you can adjust it.

## Reference

### Removing the Background of a Picture

- Click the photo, click the Picture Format tab on the ribbon, and then in the Adjust group, click the Remove Background button.
- In the Refine group on the Background Removal tab, click the Mark Areas to Keep or the Mark Areas to Remove button, and then click or drag through the area of the photo that you want marked to keep or remove.
- Click the Keep Changes button in the Close group or click a blank area of the slide to accept the changes.

Kavita wants you to modify the photo of the shaking hands on Slide 8 so that the background is blurry, but the handshake is sharp and in focus. To create this effect, you will need to work with two versions of the photo. You will use the Duplicate command to make a copy of the photo and then remove the background from the duplicate photo. (Note that you could also use the Copy and Paste commands to create a copy of a photo on a slide.)

**To duplicate the photo on Slide 8 and then remove the background from the copy:**

1. If you took a break after the previous session, make sure the **NP_PPT_3_Training.pptx** presentation is open, and then display Slide 8 ("100% Satisfaction").

2. Click the picture to select it, and then, on the ribbon, click the **Home** tab if necessary.

3. In the Clipboard group, click the **Copy arrow** 🗎 ˅, and then click **Duplicate**. The photo is duplicated on the slide, and the duplicate is selected.

   **Trouble?** If the Design Ideas pane opens, click its Close button ☒.

4. Point to the selected duplicate photo so that the pointer changes to the move pointer ⊹, drag it left to position it to the left of the original photo so it appears in the blank space to the left of the slide border, and then scroll the window left so that you can see all of the duplicate photo.

5. With the duplicate photo selected, click the **Picture Format** tab on the ribbon.

6. In the Adjust group, click the **Remove Background** button. The areas of the photograph marked for removal are colored purple. A new tab, the Background Removal tab, appears on the ribbon and is the active tab. See Figure 3-24. You need to adjust the area of the photograph that is retained by using the Mark Areas to Keep and Mark Areas to Remove buttons in the Refine group on the Background Removal tab.

**Figure 3–24**    **Picture after clicking the Remove Background button**

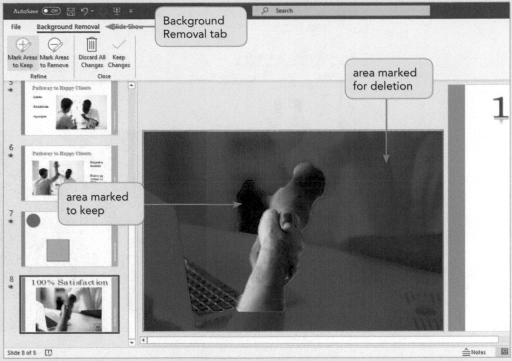

fizkes/Shutterstock.com

7. In the Refine group, click the **Mark Areas to Keep** button if necessary. The pointer changes to the pencil pointer.

8. Drag the pencil pointer on the areas of the arm belonging to the top hand that are colored purple. A green line appears as you drag the pencil. After a moment, the green line disappears and the area you dragged the pointer along changes so it is no longer colored purple. The purple coloring might be removed from some of the other areas of the picture as well.

9. Drag the pencil pointer along the parts of the arm belonging to the bottom hand that are colored purple, and then drag over any other parts of the two arms and hands that are colored purple.

10. In the Refine group, click the **Mark Areas to Remove** button. The pointer is still the pencil pointer.

11. Drag the pencil pointer on the areas of the photo that are not colored purple but are part of the background. A red line appears as you drag the pencil pointer, and then the area you dragged over changes to purple to indicate it will be removed. Compare your modified picture to Figure 3–25. Your picture might not match Figure 3–25 exactly, but as long as most of the handshake is marked to keep and most of the background behind the handshake is colored purple, it's fine.

**Figure 3–25**     **Picture after marking areas to keep and remove**

fizkes/Shutterstock.com

**12.** On the Background Removal tab, in the Close group, click the **Keep Changes** button. The changes you made are applied to the photograph, and the Background Removal tab is removed from the ribbon. Only the two hands and arms are visible now. See Figure 3–26.

**Figure 3–26**     **Duplicate picture with the background removed**

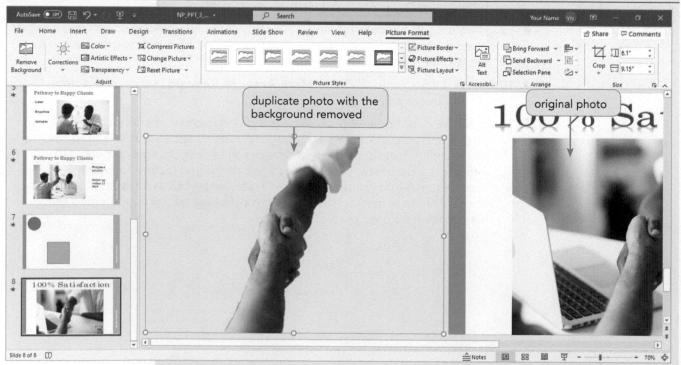

fizkes/Shutterstock.com

**Trouble?** If you want to make more adjustments to the photo, click the Remove Background button again, make the changes you want, and then repeat Step 12.

In the next section, you will complete the effect by modifying the original picture and then moving the picture with the background removed on top of the original picture.

# Editing Pictures

If photos you want to use in a presentation are too dark or require other fine-tuning, you can use PowerPoint's photo-correction tools to correct the photos. These photo-correction tools appear on the ribbon and in the Format Picture pane. Refer to the Session 3.2 Visual Overview for more information about correcting photos and the Format Picture pane.

One way you can edit pictures is to apply an artistic effect to make them look like they are paintings, black-and-white line drawings, under glass, and so on. On Slide 8 (the last slide), you will place the photo with the background removed on top of the original photo. Before you do this, you will apply an artistic effect to the original photo so that when the handshake is placed on top, it will stand out.

**To apply an artistic effect to the original photo on Slide 8:**

1. On Slide 8 (the last slide), scroll right if needed so that you can see all of the original photo with the visible background, and then click the original photo.

2. Click the **Picture Format** tab if necessary, and then in the Adjust group, click the **Artistic Effects** button. See Figure 3–27.

**Figure 3–27**    Artistic Effects menu

fizkes/Shutterstock.com

3. Click the **Glass** effect in the third row. The Glass effect is applied to the photo.

Next, you need to sharpen the photo on Slide 8 that has the background removed so that it is in sharper focus and soften the original photo. Then when you place the photo with the background removed on top of the original photo, there will be more contrast between the two photos.

### To sharpen and soften the photos on Slide 8:

1. On Slide 8 ("100% Satisfaction"), make sure the original photo with the background is still selected, and on the ribbon, the Picture Format tab is the active tab.

2. In the Adjust group, click the **Corrections** button. The options for sharpening and softening photos appear at the top of the menu.

3. Under Sharpen/Soften, click the **Soften: 50%** option. The edges of the objects in the picture are blurred and less distinct.

4. Scroll left, and then click the photo that you removed the background from.

5. In the Adjust group, click the **Corrections** button, and then under Sharpen/Soften, click the **Sharpen: 50%** option. The edges of the objects in the picture are sharper and clearer. Now you will place this photo with the background removed on top of the original photo with the Glass artistic effect and the soften effect applied.

6. Drag the photo with the background removed to the right and position it directly on top of the original photo with the artistic effect applied. Use the smart guides to ensure that it is positioned directly on top of the original photo, not centered horizontally on the slide. See Figure 3–28.

**Figure 3–28**   **Final graphic on Slide 8**

fizkes/Shutterstock.com

Another correction you can make to photos is to change the brightness and contrast. Kavita thinks there is not enough contrast between the dark and light areas in the photos on Slides 5 and 6. You will correct this aspect of the photos.

**To change the contrast in the photo on Slides 5 and 6:**

1. Display Slide 5 (the first "Pathway to Happy Clients" slide), and then click the photo to select it.

2. On the ribbon, click the **Picture Format** tab, and then in the Adjust group, click the **Corrections** button. The options for adjusting the brightness and the contrast of the photo are below the Sharpen/Soften options.

3. In the Brightness/Contrast section, click the **Brightness 0% (Normal) Contrast -20%** style (the third style in the second row). The contrast of the image changes. Because you chose a style with a Brightness percentage of 0%, the brightness of the photo is unchanged.

    You want to decrease the contrast just a little more. However, the gallery provides options that change the contrast in increments of 20 percent, which is more of an adjustment than you are looking for. For selecting a more precise contrast setting, you need to open the Format Picture pane.

4. Click the **Corrections** button again, and then click **Picture Corrections Options**. The Format Picture pane opens with the Picture button selected 🖼 and the Picture Corrections section expanded.

5. Drag the **Contrast** slider to the left until the box next to the slider indicates -30%. The contrast decreases slightly. See Figure 3–29.

**Tip**

Click the Transparency button in the Adjust group on the Picture Format tab to make the picture transparent.

**Figure 3–29**    **Contrast changed to -30%**

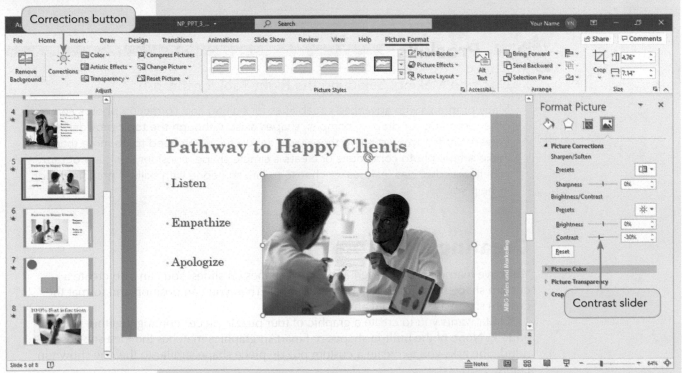

fizkes/Shutterstock.com; Jacob Lund/Shutterstock.com

**Trouble?** If you can't position the slider exactly, click the up or down arrow in the box containing the percentage as needed, or select the current percentage and then type -30.

▶ **6.** Display Slide 6 (the second "Pathway to Happy Clients" slide), and then decrease the contrast of the picture on Slide 6 by **-30%** as well.

▶ **7.** Close the Format Picture pane.

Next, Kavita wants you to adjust the photo on Slide 4. She wants you to make the colors in the photo more realistic by reducing the saturation and the tone.

### To change the saturation and tone of the photo on Slide 4:

▶ **1.** Display Slide 4 ("Fill Out a Report for Every Call"), click the photo to select it, and then click the **Picture Format** tab, if necessary.

▶ **2.** In the Adjust group, click the **Color** button. A menu opens with options for adjusting the saturation and tone of the photo's color.

▶ **3.** Under Color Saturation, click the **Saturation: 33%** option. The colors in the photo are now less intense.

▶ **4.** Click the **Color** button again.

▶ **5.** Under Color Tone, click the **Temperature: 8800K** option. More reds and yellows are added to the photo. The picture now looks like it was taken in an area with natural light.

▶ **6.** Save the changes to the presentation.

**Tip**

To recolor a photo so it is all one color, click the Color button in the Adjust group on the Picture Format tab, and then click a Recolor option.

### Proskills

Decision Making: Selecting the Right Tool for the Job

Many programs with advanced capabilities for editing and correcting photos and other programs for drawing complex shapes exist. Although the tools provided in PowerPoint for accomplishing these tasks are useful, if you need to do more than make simple photo corrections or create a simple shape, consider using a program with more advanced features, or choose to hire someone with skills in graphic design to help you.

## Creating a Custom Shape

You have learned how to insert and format shapes on slides. You can also create a custom shape by merging two or more shapes. Then you can position and format the custom shape as you would any other shape.

Kavita wants you to create a graphic of four puzzle pieces coming together on Slide 7. None of the built-in shapes or SmartArt graphics matches the idea she has in mind. She asks you to create a custom puzzle piece shape similar to the one shown in Figure 3–30.

Figure 3–30    Kavita's sketch of the shape for Slide 7

To create the custom shape for Kavita, you will merge shapes. Kavita already placed the shapes you need to use on Slide 7. To create the puzzle piece, you will first duplicate the circle shape.

**To arrange the shapes on Slide 7 so that you can create a custom shape:**

1. Display Slide 7 (the second to last slide), and then click the circle to select it.

2. On the Home tab, in the Clipboard group, click the **Copy arrow** 📋▾, and then click **Duplicate**.

3. Drag the duplicated circle on top of the top border of the square so that the smart guides show that the center of the circle is aligned with the top of the square and the middle of the circle is aligned with the middle of the square.

4. Drag the other circle on top of the right border of the square so that the smart guides show that the center of the circle is aligned with the center of the square and the middle of the circle is aligned with the right edge of the square.

See Figure 3–31.

Make sure you position the circle as instructed in Step 4 or the final puzzle pieces will not fit together.

| Figure 3–31 | Shapes arranged to form the new shape |

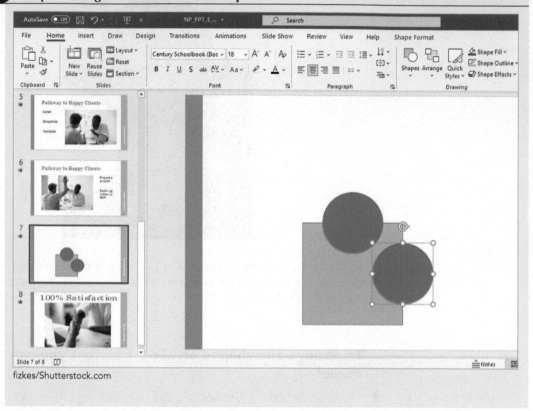

fizkes/Shutterstock.com

To create a custom shape, you use the commands on the Merge Shapes menu in the Insert Shapes group on the Shape Format tab. Each command has a different effect on selected shapes:

- **Union**—Merges selected shapes without removing any portions
- **Combine**—Merges selected shapes and removes the sections of the shapes that overlap
- **Fragment**—Separates overlapping portions of shapes into separate shapes
- **Intersect**—Merges selected shapes and removes everything except the sections that overlap
- **Subtract**—Removes the second shape selected, including any part of the first shape that is overlapped by the second shape

When you merge shapes, you place one shape on top of or touching another, and then you select the shapes. When you use the Union, Combine, Fragment, or Intersect command, the shape you select first determines the format of the merged shape. For example, if you select a red shape first and a blue shape second, and then you unite, combine, fragment, or intersect them, the merged shape will be red. When you use the Subtract command, the shape you select second is the shape that is removed.

To create the puzzle piece, you will use the Union command to combine the square and one of the circles. Then you will use the Subtract command to create the indented part of the puzzle piece.

## To merge the shapes:

1. Click the square shape, and then click the **Shape Format** tab. In the Insert Shapes group, the Merge Shapes button is gray and unavailable. At least two shapes need to be selected to use the commands on the Merge Shapes menu.

2. Press and hold **SHIFT**, click the circle shape at the top of the square, and then release **SHIFT**. The square and the top circle shape are now selected. In the Insert Shapes group, the Merge Shapes button is now available. Because you selected the square first, when you use the Union command, the merged shape will be filled with the fill color of the square.

3. In the Insert Shapes group, click the **Merge Shapes** button, and then click **Union**. The two shapes are merged into a new shape formatted the same blue color as the square shape. The merged shape is selected.

4. Press and hold **SHIFT**, click the circle shape on the right side of the square, and then release **SHIFT**. Because you selected the merged, blue shape first, the circle shape will be subtracted from the blue shape when you use the Subtract command.

5. In the Insert Shapes group, click the **Merge Shapes** button, and then click **Subtract**. The entire orange circle is removed and the part that had overlapped the blue merged shape was removed from the blue shape. See Figure 3–32.

**Figure 3–32**    **Merged shape**

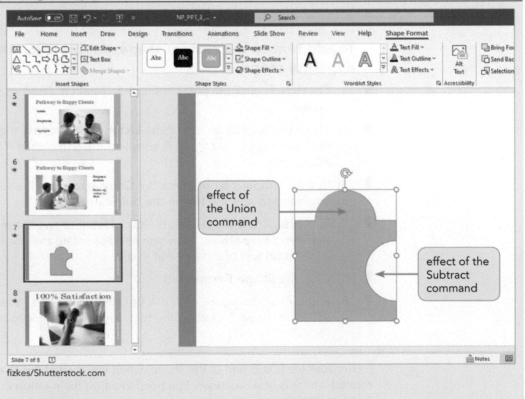

fizkes/Shutterstock.com

Now that the puzzle piece is created, Kavita wants you to save it as a picture so that she can reuse it in the future. You'll do that now.

**To save the custom shape as a picture:**

1. Right-click the puzzle piece shape. A shortcut menu opens.

**Tip**

To convert a drawing to a picture, first copy the drawing. Next, click the Paste arrow, and then click the Picture option on the Paste Options menu.

2. On the shortcut menu, click **Save as Picture**. The Save as Picture dialog box opens. It is very similar to the Save As dialog box you use when you save a presentation with a new name. In the Save as type box, PNG Portable Network Graphics Format is selected. This is one of the file types that pictures are saved as. The temporary file name is selected in the File name box.

3. Type **NP_PPT_3_Puzzle**, navigate to the location where you are saving your files, and then click **Save**. The dialog box closes, and the puzzle shape is saved as a picture in a file.

# Rotating Shapes with Text

You already know that when you rotate a shape that contains text, the text rotates with the shape. There are times when you need to adjust the rotation of the text so that it appears right-side up even after the shape is rotated.

Kavita wants you to add text to the puzzle shape, duplicate the shape so that there are four puzzle piece shapes, and then arrange them so it looks like you put the puzzle together. When you are finished with this slide, there will be four puzzle pieces and each piece will have different text on it.

First, you will add text to the first shape, duplicate the shape, and then rotate it so it is in the correct position to "attach" the original puzzle piece.

**To add text to the custom shape, duplicate it, and rotate the duplicate shape:**

1. On Slide 7, click the custom shape to select it if necessary, and then type **Listen**.

2. Move the pointer on top of the **Listen** shape so that the pointer changes to the move pointer ⊹, click to select the entire shape, and then click the **Home** tab.

3. In the Clipboard group, click the **Copy arrow** 🗐 ▾ , and then click **Duplicate**. You need to edit the text in the duplicated shape.

4. In the duplicate shape, double-click **Listen** to select the entire word, and then type **Empathize**. Now you need to rotate the duplicated shape so that it will fit on top of the original shape.

5. Click the **Shape Format** tab.

6. In the Arrange group, click the **Rotate** button, and then click **Rotate Right 90°**. The shape, including the text, rotates to the right by 90 degrees.

Because the text is part of the shape, when you rotated the shape, the text also rotated, and it is now sideways. You need to adjust the rotation of the text so that the text is right-side-up.

## To adjust the rotation of the text in the rotated shape:

1. On the Shape Format tab, in the Arrange group, click the **Rotate** button, and then click **More Rotation Options**. The Format Shape pane opens with the Shape Options tab selected, the Size & Properties button selected, and the Size section expanded. In the Rotation box, 90° appears. See Figure 3–33. This is because the shape was already rotated once.

**Figure 3–33**    Empathize shape rotated right 90 degrees

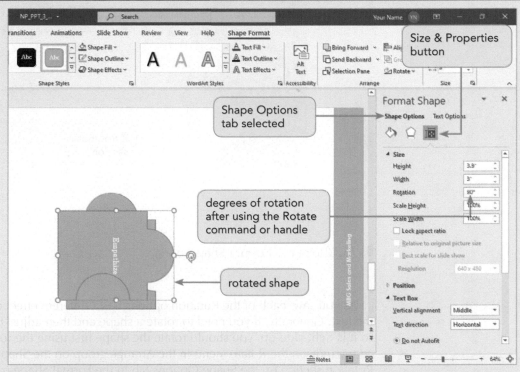

2. In the Format Shape pane, click the **Text Options** tab, click the **Text Effects button**, and then click **3-D Rotation** to expand that section, if necessary.

3. To the right of Z Rotation, click the **Counter-clockwise** button. The text in the Empathize shape rotates five degrees in a counter-clockwise direction. In the Format Shape pane, the number in the Z Rotation box changes to 5°. You need to rotate the text by 90 degrees.

4. In the Z Rotation box, click after 5°, press **BACKSPACE** twice, and then type **90**. The text rotates 90 degrees in a counter-clockwise direction and is now right-side up.

5. Drag the **Empathize** shape above the "Listen" shape, and then place it so that the two puzzle pieces fit together, using the smart guides to ensure that the shapes are exactly aligned with one another. See Figure 3–34.

Figure 3–34 **Empathize shape positioned to fit in the puzzle**

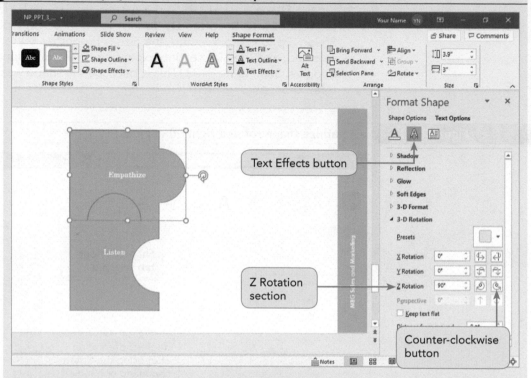

6. Close the Format Shape pane.

As you saw, each of the Rotation options has a different effect on the shape and the text. Generally, if you need to rotate a shape and then adjust the text in the shape so it is right-side-up, you should rotate the shape first using the rotate handle ⟳ , the commands on the Rotate menu in the Arrange group on the Shape Format tab, or the Rotation section on the Shape Options tab in the Format Shape pane when the Size & Properties button 🔳 is selected. Then, you can rotate the text using the Z Rotation command on the Text Options tab in the Format Shape pane when the Text Effects 🅰 button is selected.

Although this method works, editing and formatting the text in the shapes is going to get more difficult because when you are editing, the text flips back to its original rotation. Instead, you can create text boxes to contain the text for each shape. You will remove the text from the two puzzle pieces on the slide and add text boxes instead. Then, you will create the other two missing puzzle pieces.

**To delete the text in the shapes and add text boxes:**

1. Click **Empathize**. The text rotates to its original position.

2. Double-click **Empathize** to select the entire word, and then press **DELETE**.

3. Double-click **Listen**, and then press **DELETE**. Now you will add text boxes to label the two puzzle pieces.

4. Click the **Insert** tab.

5. In the **Text** group, click the **Text Box** button, and then click a blank area of the slide. A text box is inserted.

6. Type **Listen**. As you type, the width of the text box expands to accommodate the text you type. This is because the Wrap Text option is not selected when you click (instead of drag) to insert a text box.

7. Drag the **Listen** text box on top of the bottom puzzle piece so it is approximately centered in the piece.

8. Insert another text box without wrapping the text, type **Empathize**, and then drag the **Empathize** text box onto the top puzzle piece so it is approximately centered in the shape. Now you need to create the final two puzzle pieces.

9. Duplicate the **Empathize** puzzle piece, rotate the duplicate shape, rotate it to the right by 90 degrees, and then position the duplicate shape to the right of the Empathize shape.

10. Duplicate the **Listen** shape, rotate the duplicate shape to the left by 90 degrees, and then position the duplicate shape to the right of the Listen shape.

11. Create a text box that does not wrap, type **Apologize**, and then position the **Apologize** text box so it is approximately centered on the shape to the right of the Empathize shape.

12. Create one more text box that does not wrap, type **Solve**, and then position the **Solve** text box so it is approximately centered on the shape to the right of the Listen shape.

Next you need to adjust the formatting of the text in the puzzle pieces. You will change the color and font size of the text.

**To format and reposition the text boxes:**

1. Click **Empathize**, press and hold **SHIFT**, click each of the other three text boxes, and then release **SHIFT**. The four text boxes are selected.

2. Click the **Home** tab if necessary, and then in the Font group, click the **Increase Font Size** button four times. The text in all of the shapes changes to 32 points.

3. In the Font group, click the **Font Color arrow**, and then click the **White, Background 1** color. All of the text changes to white. Now you need to reposition the shapes.

4. Click a blank area of the slide to deselect all of the text boxes, and then position the **Empathize** text box so that its right edge aligns with the straight edge on the right side of the shape and so its middle aligns with the middle of the shape.

5. Drag the **Apologize** text box so it aligns horizontally with the Empathize text box and just fits between the sides of the piece.

6. Position the **Listen** text box so its left edge aligns with the left edge of the Empathize text box and its middle aligns with the middle of the shape.

7. Position the **Solve** text box so it horizontally aligns with the Listen text box and its left edge aligns with the left edge of the Apologize text box. Compare your screen to Figure 3–35.

**Figure 3–35**    **Final puzzle pieces**

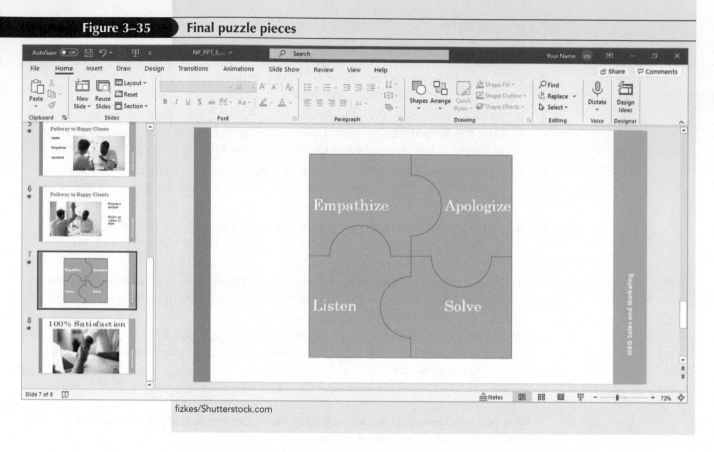

fizkes/Shutterstock.com

Now that the puzzle pieces are created, you need to use the Morph transition so that it looks like the pieces appear on the screen during the slide show and fit together. The first thing you need to do is group each shape and its text box. Then you need to copy the pieces and place the copies on Slide 6.

**To copy the puzzle pieces, place them around Slide 6, and apply the Morph transition:**

1. Click **Listen**, press and hold **SHIFT**, click the **Listen** shape, and then release **SHIFT**.

2. On the Home tab, in the Drawing group, click the **Arrange** button, and then click **Group**. The Listen text box and the shape it is on are grouped into one object.

3. Group each of the remaining text boxes and their shapes so that there are four grouped objects.

4. Select the four puzzle pieces, and then on the Home tab, in the Clipboard group, click the **Copy** button. The four shapes are copied to the Clipboard.

5. Display Slide 6 (the second "Pathway to Happy Clients" slide), and then in the Clipboard group, click the **Paste** button. The four shapes are pasted on top of the Slide 6 content.

6. On the status bar, click the **Zoom Out** button as many times as needed to change the zoom percentage to 40%.

**7.** Click a blank area of the slide to deselect the shapes, and then drag each of the puzzle pieces off the slide and position them so they are off the slide near each corner of the slide. See Figure 3–36.

**Figure 3–36** | **Copies of the puzzle pieces placed next to Slide 6**

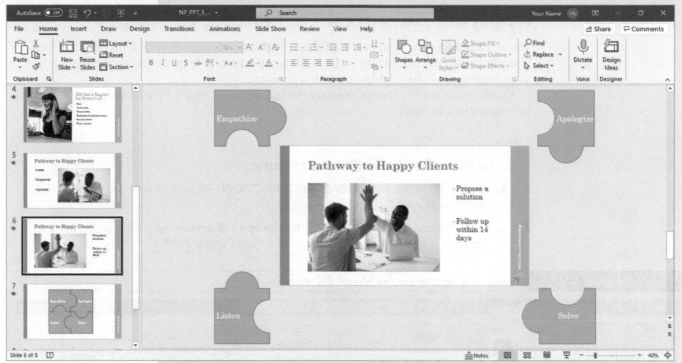

Jacob Lund/Shutterstock.com; fizkes/Shutterstock.com

**8.** On the status bar, click the **Fit slide to current window** button 🔷, display Slide 7, and then apply the **Morph** transition to Slide 7. Now the puzzle pieces will move onto the screen when you display Slide 7 during the slide show.

Finally, Kavita wants the puzzle pieces to appear to change to a solid square that contains the text "Client Satisfaction!" You will create the shape for that next.

### To draw a square on top of the puzzle pieces:

**1.** With Slide 7 (the slide containing the four puzzle pieces) displayed, click the **Insert** tab, in the Illustrations group, click the **Shapes** button, click the **Rectangle** shape, and then click anywhere on Slide 7. A one-inch square is added to the slide and the Shape Format tab is selected.

**2.** In the Size group, click in the **Shape Height** box, type **6**, click in the **Shape Width** box, type **6**, and then press **ENTER**. The shape you added is now six inches square.

**3.** Drag the shape you added directly on top of the four puzzle pieces, using the smart guides to align it.

4. Type **CLIENT SATISFACTION!** in the square, change the font size of this text to **32** points, and then change the color of the text to **Gray, Accent 6, Darker 50%**.

5. Save the changes to the presentation.

# Applying Advanced Formatting to Shapes

You already know that you can fill a shape with a solid color or with a picture. You can also fill a shape with a texture—a pattern that gives a tactile quality to the shape, such as crumpled paper or marble—or with a gradient.

Kavita wants you to change the way the square looks. You'll try changing the fill of the square to a texture.

**To change the shape fill to a texture:**

1. On Slide 7, click the **CLIENT SATISFACTION!** square to select it, and then click the **Shape Format** tab if necessary.

2. In the Shape Styles group, click the **Shape Fill arrow**, and then point to **Texture**. The Texture submenu opens. See Figure 3–37.

**Figure 3–37** Texture submenu on the Shape Fill menu

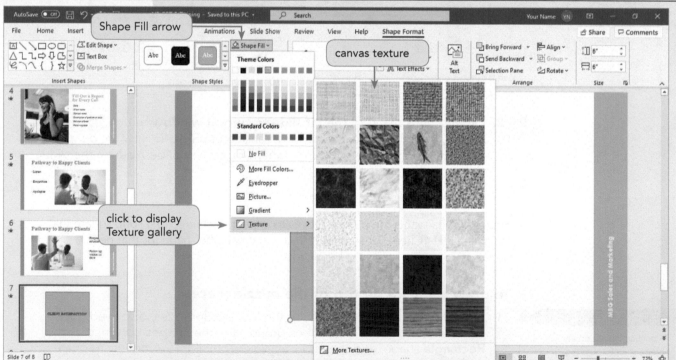

Jacob Lund/Shutterstock.com; fizkes/Shutterstock.com

3. Click the **Canvas** texture (the second texture in the first row). The custom shape is filled with a texture resembling canvas.

The texture did not achieve the effect Kavita wanted for the shape. She asks you to simulate the look of metal or silver. To create this effect, you will use a gradient. You can apply gradients on the Shape Fill menu that use shades of the Accent 1 color in the theme color palette. You can also create a custom gradient using the options in the Format Shape pane. To create a custom gradient, you select a gradient stop, which is a position in the shape at which point the color changes. Then you can change the color and the position in the shape where the color will change. You can also change the direction of the gradient in the shape. If you need to add or remove gradient stops, you can click the Add gradient stop button or the Remove gradient stop button in the Format Shape pane. Refer to the Session 3.2 Visual Overview for more information about using the Format Shape pane to create a custom gradient.

## Reference

### Creating a Custom Gradient in a Shape

- Select the shape.
- Click the Shape Format tab.
- In the Shape Styles group, click the Shape Fill arrow, point to Gradient, and then click More Gradients to open the Format Shape pane with the Fill & Line button selected and the Fill section expanded.
- In the Format Shape pane, click the Gradient fill option button.
- To change the position of a gradient stop, click a tab on the Gradient stops slider, and then drag it to the desired position on the slider or change the value in the Position box.
- To change the color of a gradient stop, select the tab on the Gradient stops slider, click the Color button, and then select a color.
- To add a new gradient stop, click the Add gradient stop button; to remove a gradient stop, click it, and then click the Remove gradient stop button.
- Click the Type arrow, and then click the type of gradient you want to use.
- Click the Direction button, and then click the direction of the gradient.

You will change the fill of the square to a custom gradient. You could remove the texture by clicking No Fill on the Shape Fill menu, but there is no need because you will replace the texture fill with the gradient.

### To create a custom gradient fill for the square:

1. On the Shape Format tab, in the Shape Styles group, click the **Shape Fill arrow**, and then point to **Gradient**. The gradients on the submenu that appears use shades of the Ice Blue, Accent 1 color.

2. In the Dark Variations section, click the **From Center** gradient. The shape fill is changed to a gradient of blues. To create a custom gradient, you need to open the Format Shape pane.

3. In the Shape Styles group, click the **Shape Fill arrow**, point to **Gradient**, and then click **More Gradients**. The Format Shape pane opens with the Fill & Line button ⬧ selected on the Shape Options tab and with the Fill section expanded. In the Fill section, the Gradient fill option button is selected because the shape is currently filled with a gradient. Under Gradient stops, the first tab on the slider is selected, and its value in the Position box is 0%. You will change the position and color of the second tab on the slider.

4. On the Gradient stops slider, click the **Stop 1 of 3** tab (the first tab), and then click the **Color** button. The color palette opens.

5. Click the **Gray, Accent 6** color.

6. On the Gradient stops slider, drag the **Stop 2 of 3** tab to the left until the value in the Position box is 40%.

   **Trouble?** If you can't position the slider exactly, click the Stop 2 of 3 tab, type 40 in the Position box, and then press ENTER.

7. With the Stop 2 of 3 tab selected, click the **Color** button, and then click the **White, Background 1, Darker 5%** color.

8. Click the **Stop 3 of 3** tab, click the **Color** button, and then click the **Gray, Accent 6, Lighter 60%** color.

**Tip**

To remove a tab from the slider, click it, and then click the Remove gradient stop button.

9. To the right of the slider, click the **Add gradient stop** button 🗘. A new tab stop is added to the slider in the third position and is selected.

10. Change the color of the **Stop 3 of 4** tab to **White, Background 1, Darker 35%**. Next you will change the gradient type. Above the Gradient stops slider, in the Type box, Radial is selected. This means that the shading varies from the center out in a circle towards the edges. You will change the type to Linear so that the gradient will change linearly—that is, top to bottom, side to side, or diagonally.

11. Click the **Type** arrow, and then click **Linear**. Next you will change the direction of the gradient.

12. Click the **Direction** button. A gallery of gradient options opens.

13. Click the **Linear Diagonal – Top Right to Bottom Left** direction. The shading in the shape changes so it varies diagonally from the top-right corner to the bottom-left corner. Finally, Kavita wants this shape to look slightly three-dimensional, so you will apply a bevel effect. You could use the Shape Effects button on the Shape Format tab, but you will use a command in the Format Shape pane instead.

14. In the Format Shape pane, click the **Effects** button ⬠, and then click **3-D Format**, if necessary, to expand that section.

15. Click the **Top bevel** button, and then click the **Angle** bevel (first bevel in the second row in the Bevel section). The bevel effect is applied. Compare your screen to Figure 3–38.

**Figure 3–38**    Shape with modified gradient fill and bevel

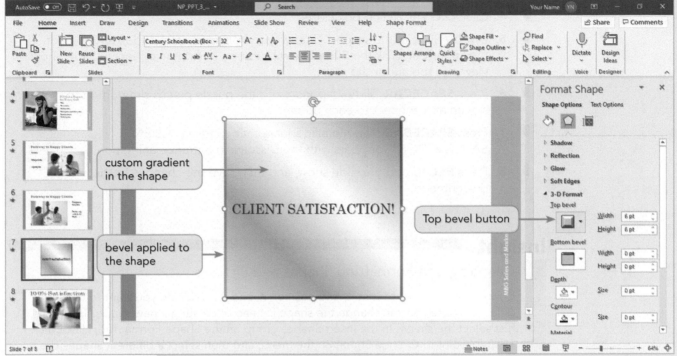

Jacob Lund/Shutterstock.com; fizkes/Shutterstock.com

**16.** Close the Format Shape pane.

Now you will apply an entrance animation to the shape with the gradient fill on Slide 7. Then you will examine Slides 6 and 7 in Slide Show view.

### To animate the shape filled with a gradient:

**1.** Click the Animations tab, and then in the Animation group, click the **More** button.

**2.** At the bottom of the gallery, click **More Entrance Effects**. The Change Entrance Effects dialog box opens. See Figure 3–39.

**Figure 3–39**    Change Entrance Effect dialog box

▶  **3.** In the Basic section, click **Dissolve In**. The animation previews on the slide.

▶  **4.** Click **OK**. The dialog box closes.

▶  **5.** Display Slide 6 (the second "Pathway to Happy Clients" slide), and then on the status bar, click the **Slide Show** button ⬚. Slide 6 appears in Slide Show view and the audio clip plays.

▶  **6.** Press **SPACEBAR**. Slide 7 appears and the puzzle pieces slide onto the screen and connect to each other.

▶  **7.** Press **SPACEBAR**. The metallic square that contains "CLIENT SATISFACTION!" appears with the Dissolve In entrance animation.

▶  **8.** Press **ESC** to end the slide show, and then save the changes to the presentation.

## Insight

### Changing and Formatting Shapes and Pictures

If you insert a shape, format it, and position it, and then decide you want to use a different shape you can change the shape instead of creating a new shape. To do this, first select the shape. In the Insert Shapes group on the Shape Format tab, click Edit Shapes, point to Change Shape on the menu, and then select a different shape. The new shape will replace the existing shape, but the formatting you applied and the shape's position will be the same. Likewise, you can change a picture that you have resized and repositioned. To change a picture, right-click it, point to Change Picture on the shortcut menu, and then click a command on the submenu to replace the picture with one stored in a file on your computer or network, a picture you find online, or an object stored on the Clipboard. You can also change a picture to an icon (also called a scalable vector graphic).

# Making Presentations Accessible

People with physical impairments or disabilities use assistive technology to help them when using computers. For example, people who cannot use their arms or hands can use foot, head, or eye movements to control the pointer. One of the most common assistive technologies is the screen reader. The screen reader identifies objects on the screen and produces an audio of the text in the objects or alt text describing the objects for those with visual impairments.

Graphics and tables cause problems for users of screen readers unless they have alt text. When a screen reader encounters an object that has alt text, it announces that an object is on the slide, and then it reads the alt text. You already know how to add alt text to pictures. Other types of graphics, such as shapes, SmartArt graphics, and charts need alt text as well. You can add alt text to shapes or a SmartArt graphic by clicking the Alt Text button in the Accessibility group on the Format tab for shapes or SmartArt.

After she gives her presentation orally to her team, Kavita plans to post the PowerPoint file on the company server so that others can read it. She asks you to add missing alt text and fix, or at least identify, other issues that might cause accessibility issues. You will use the Accessibility Checker to do this.

## Checking for Accessibility Issues

The Accessibility Checker identifies possible problems on slides that might prevent a presentation from being completely accessible. The Accessibility Checker classifies potential problems into three categories—errors, warnings, and tips. Content flagged as an error is content that people with disabilities cannot access at all or only with great difficulty. Content flagged with a warning is content that is difficult for many people with disabilities to access. Content flagged with a tip isn't necessarily impossible for people with disabilities to access, but the content could possibly be reorganized in a way that would make it easier to access.

You will use the Accessibility Checker to see what adjustments you should consider to make the presentation accessible.

### To use the Accessibility Checker:

1. Display Slide 1 (the title slide), click the **Review** tab, and then in the Accessibility group, click the **Check Accessibility** button. The Accessibility pane opens. See Figure 3–40. At the top of the pane is the list of Inspection Results. At the bottom is the Additional Information section where details about the issues in the Inspection Results list will appear.

**Figure 3–40**  |  **Accessibility pane listing potential issues**

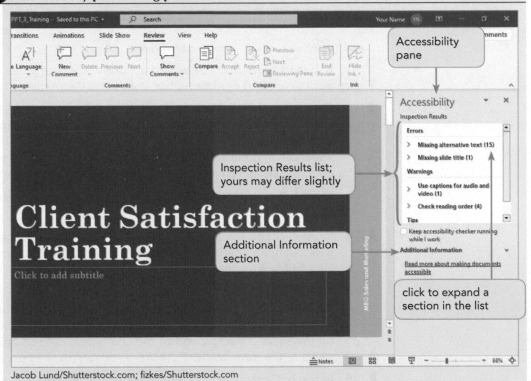

Jacob Lund/Shutterstock.com; fizkes/Shutterstock.com

The Errors section is the first section listed, and the first type of error is "Missing alternative text".

2. In the Errors section, click **Missing alternative text** to expand the issue, click **Content Placeholder 6**, and then click the **arrow**. Slide 2 ("Client Satisfaction Scores") appears, and in the Accessibility pane, a menu listing Recommended Actions and Other Suggestions opens. At the bottom of the pane, the Additional Information section changes to describe the selected problem. See Figure 3–41. Note that the numbers after the word "Group" might be different on your screen.

**Figure 3-41**    **Menu listing recommended actions for missing alt text**

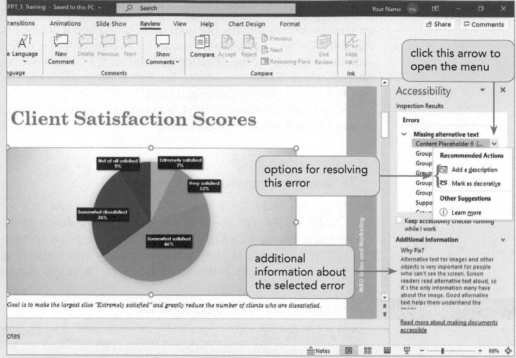

Jacob Lund/Shutterstock.com; fizkes/Shutterstock.com

In this case, the recommended actions are to add a description (which is adding alt text) or marking the graphic as decorative.

3. On the menu, click **Mark as decorative**. The chart is marked as decorative—that is, an object that does not need alt text—and Content Placeholder 6 is removed from the list in the Accessibility pane. However, because the chart conveys important information, Kavita wants you to add alt text to the chart. You could undo the last action, or you can just open the Alt Text pane for the chart.

**Trouble?** If the Notes pane opens, click the Notes button on the status bar to close it.

4. Right-click the shaded background of the chart area, and then on the shortcut menu, click **Edit Alt Text**. The Alt Text pane opens. Because you clicked Mark as decorative on the menu in the Accessibility pane, the Mark as decorative check box is selected.

**Trouble?** If the Edit Alt Text command is not on the shortcut menu, click anywhere on the slide, and then repeat Step 4 making sure you right-click on the shaded background of the chart area, but not on any of the pie chart slices or the data labels.

5. In the Alt Text pane, click the **Mark as decorative** check box to deselect it, click in the white box, and then type **Pie chart showing that almost half of MBG's clients are only somewhat satisfied, 26% are somewhat dissatisfied, and only 7% are extremely satisfied.** (including the period). It is difficult to create alt text that adequately describes charts. The description you typed isn't perfect, but it conveys Kavita's biggest concerns, and will be more meaningful than a recitation of the chart data.

In the Accessibility pane, the next five items listed as missing alt text are all on Slide 3.

6. Close the Alt Text pane, and then, in the Accessibility pane, click **Group X (Slide 3)** (where "X" is the number after the word "Group"). Slide 3 ("Handling Client Complaints") is displayed. The Follow Up grouped object on the slide is selected. Each of the five grouped objects on the slide are graphics that need alt text. Kavita decides that she will keep Slide 3 as is for her presentation to her team, but before she posts the presentation on the company server, she will recreate the SmartArt graphic and add alt text to it by clicking the Alt Text button in the Accessibility group on the Format tab.

The next item in the "Missing alternative text" section is the audio file on Slide 6.

7. In the Accessibility pane, click **Support_PPT_3_Comment**, click the **arrow** ☑ that appears, and then click **Add a description**. Slide 6 is displayed, the speaker icon is selected, and the Alt Text pane opens.

8. In the Alt Text pane, click in the white box, type **Audio object for audio that will play during the slide show.**, and then close the Alt Text pane. This alt text describes the object on the slide. The next four items listed as missing alt text are on Slide 6, and the last four items listed as missing alt text are on Slide 7.

9. In the Accessibility pane, click the first object on Slide 6. Slide 6 appears.

10. Click to the left of the scroll box in the horizontal scroll bar. The slide scrolls right and the Listen grouped shape and text box is selected. The four grouped shapes on Slide 6 can be marked as decorative.

11. In the Accessibility pane, click the **arrow** ☑ next to the first object on Slide 6, click **Mark as Decorative**, and then mark the other three items on Slide 6 as decorative also. The next four items on Slide 7 are the grouped puzzle piece shapes on that slide. Kavita will add alt text for these shapes before she posts the file. The next issue listed is in the Errors section. It identifies a missing slide title on Slide 7.

12. In the Accessibility pane, scroll down, click **Missing slide** title to expand that issue, and then click **Slide 7**. Slide 7 is displayed in Outline view. Like the graphic on Slide 3, Kavita will leave this slide as is (without a title) for her presentation, but she will modify it by adding a slide title before she posts the presentation on the company server.

**Tip**

To add closed captions to a video object, click the Insert Captions button in the Caption Options group on the Playback tab for video or audio, locate the WebVTT file containing the captions, select it, and then click Insert.

13. In the Accessibility pane, scroll the list of Inspection Results down until the Warnings section is at the top. At the top of the Warnings list, click the first warning about audio and video using closed captions to display the audio clip on Slide 6 again. Kavita will create captions for the audio clip using another app, and then she will add them to the audio object.

14. Scroll the list of Inspection Results to the Tips section, click **Duplicate slide title**, scroll down again, and then click **Pathway to Happy Clients**. Slide 6 appears. This Tip tells you that this slide title is the same as another slide title in the presentation. The title of Slide 5 is also "Pathway to Happy Clients". Kavita wants you to change the titles of Slides 5 and 6.

15. On Slide 6, change the title text to **Become Happy Clients**.

16. Switch to Normal view, display Slide 5, delete the title text, and then type **Unhappy Clients...** in the title text placeholder. The Tip section disappears from the list of Inspection Results in the Accessibility pane.

You skipped the "Check reading order" list in the Warning section in the Accessibility pane. You will examine this issue next.

## Checking the Order Objects Will Be Read by a Screen Reader

When a person uses a screen reader to access a presentation, the screen reader selects and describes the elements on the slides in the order they were added. In PowerPoint, most screen readers first explain that a slide is displayed. After the user signals to the screen reader that the user is ready for the next piece of information (for example, by pressing the Tab key), the reader identifies the first object on the slide. For most slides, this is the title text box. The second object is usually the content placeholder on the slide.

To check the order in which a screen reader will describe objects on a slide, you can press TAB or open the Reading Order. You'll start by opening the Reading Order pane using the Accessibility Checker. You can also use the Selection pane by clicking the Select button in the Editing group on the Home tab, and then clicking Selection Pane, or by clicking the Selection Pane button in the Arrange group on the Shape or Picture Format tab.

If an object is listed in the wrong order in the Reading Order pane—for example, if the content placeholder was identified first and the title second—you could change this in the Reading Order pane. To do this, click the object you want to move, and then at the top of the pane, click the Move Up or Move Down buttons at the top of the Selection pane to move the selected object up or down in the list.

### To identify the order of objects on slides:

▶ **1.** In the Accessibility pane, click **Check reading order** to display a list of errors in that section, click **Slide 5**, and then click the arrow ✔ that appears. The only option on the menu to address the problem is "Verify object order."

▶ **2.** On the menu, click **Verify object order**. The Reading Order pane opens. See Figure 3–42. In the Reading Order pane, the first object added to the slide appears at the top of the list, and the last object added appears at the bottom of the list. (The blue bar on the right side of the slide and the gray bar on the left side of the slide aren't listed in the Reading Order pane because they are part of the slide background.)

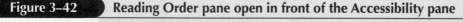

**Figure 3–42**    Reading Order pane open in front of the Accessibility pane

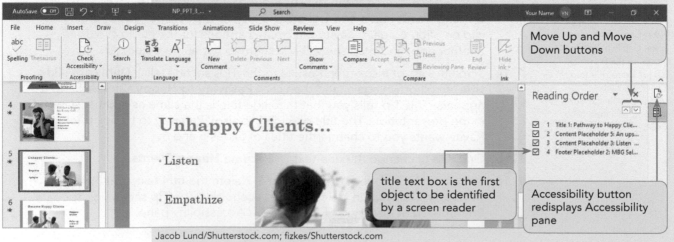

Jacob Lund/Shutterstock.com; fizkes/Shutterstock.com

3. Click a blank area of the slide, and then press **TAB**. On the slide, the title text box is selected. In the Reading Order pane, Title 1 is selected at the top of the list.

4. Press **TAB** three more times. On the slide, the content placeholder with the picture is selected, then the content placeholder with the bulleted list, and finally, the footer on the right. In the Reading Order pane, the items in the list are selected when they are selected on the slide. The reading order of objects on Slide 5 is correct. Slide 7 is the next slide listed in the "Check reading order" section of the Accessibility pane.

5. Display Slide 7 (the untitled slide with the "Client Satisfaction" shape). In the Reading Order pane, **Footer Placeholder 1** is listed first, but it was listed last on Slide 5. It would be best if the footer placeholder was consistently placed in the same position on each slide, so Kavita wants you to make it the last object selected. Click Footer Placeholder 1, and then at the top of the pane, click the **Move Down** button ☑ five times. The Footer Placeholder 1 object moves down the list in the Reading Order pane, and the footer will now be read last on the slide.

6. Display Slide 8 ("100% Satisfaction"), the next slide listed in the "Check reading order" section of the Accessibility pane. The order of objects on Slide 8 is correct, except Footer Placeholder 2 is in the middle of the list in the Reading Order pane. Click **Footer Placeholder 2**, and then at the top of the pane, click the **Move Down** button ☑. The Footer Placeholder 2 object moves to the end of the list. Although Slides 2, 3, 4, and 6 may not be listed in the Check reading order section of the Accessibility pane, you should check the reading order on these slides as well.

7. Display Slide 2 ("Client Satisfaction Scores"). Move Footer Placeholder 3 to the bottom of the list in the Reading Order pane.

8. Display Slide 3 ("Handling Client Complaints"), examine the order of the objects in the Reading Order pane, display Slide 4 ("Fill Out a Report for Every Call"), and then examine the order of the objects in the Reading Order pane. On both slides, the footer placeholder appears at the bottom of the list in the Reading Order pane.

9. Display Slide 6 ("Become Happy Clients"). Footer Placeholder 2 appears in the middle of the list in the Reading Order pane.

10. In the Reading Order pane, click **Footer Placeholder 2**, and then at the top of the pane, click the **Move Down** button ☑ to move it below the Support_PPT_3_Comment audio object. You don't need to move it below the grouped objects because they are marked as decorative.

11. To the right of the Reading Order pane, click the **Accessibility** button 🗔 to redisplay the Accessibility pane if necessary. Close the Accessibility pane, and then, if the Notes pane is open below the slide, click the Notes button on the status bar to close it.

You have addressed all of the issues listed in the Accessibility pane. There is one issue that was not flagged by the Accessibility Checker. On Slide 8, you duplicated the picture before you removed the background from the duplicate. This means the alt text was copied. You should edit the alt text so that one of the images is marked as decorative.

### To rename objects in the Reading Order pane and mark an object as decorative:

▶ 1. Display Slide 8 ("100% Satisfaction"), then in the Reading Order pane, click **Picture 3**, and then click **Picture 4**. On the slide, a selection box appears around the pictures, but you can't tell which picture is Picture 3 and which one is Picture 4.

▶ 2. On the slide, click the picture, and then drag it to the left about one inch. The picture you dragged is the version of the picture with the background removed. In the Reading Order pane, Picture 4 is selected. To avoid confusion in the future, you will rename these objects in the Selection pane.

▶ 3. In the Reading Order pane, click **Picture 4**. Because it was already selected, it changes to a text box displaying a description of the picture.

▶ 4. Press **DELETE** as many times as needed to delete all of the text, type **Picture with background removed**, and then press **ENTER**.

▶ 5. In the Reading Order pane, click **Picture 3**, click it again to display a text box with a description of the picture, delete all of the text, type **Picture with artistic effect**, and then press **ENTER**.

▶ 6. On the slide, drag the picture with the background removed back on top of the other picture. Now that you know which picture is which, you will mark the picture with the artistic effect applied as decorative.

▶ 7. In the Reading Order pane, click **Picture 3: Picture with artistic effect**, click the **Picture Format** tab, and then in the Accessibility group, click the **Alt Text** button. The Alt Text pane opens.

▶ 8. In the Alt Text pane, click the **Mark as decorative** check box to select it.

▶ 9. Close the Alt Text pane, and then close the Reading Order pane.

▶ 10. **sam**⬆ Display Slide 1 (the title slide), add your name as the subtitle, and then save and close the presentation.

You have created and saved a custom shape and used advanced formatting techniques for shapes and photos in the presentation. You also checked the presentation for accessibility and corrected the issues that Kavita wanted you to correct.

## Review

### Session 3.2 Quick Check

1. What happens when you use the Remove Background command?

2. What are artistic effects?

3. What happens when you merge shapes?

4. When you create a custom gradient, how do you change the colors used?

5. What feature can you use to check a file for accessibility issues?

6. What is the Reading Order pane?

# Practice

## Review Assignments

**Data Files needed for the Review Assignments: NP_PPT_3-2.pptx, Support_PPT_3_Compliment.mp3, Support_PPT_3_FollowUp.jpg, Support_PPT_3_Form.jpg, Support_PPT_3_Respect.jpg**

Three months after Kavita Goyal, a client operations manager for MBG Sales and Marketing, created a new training program for her customer service team, the percentage of clients who are extremely or very satisfied has increased and the percentage of clients who are only somewhat satisfied or who are somewhat dissatisfied has decreased. Kavita is very pleased with her team, although they still have room for improvement. She wants to congratulate them, but also point out some areas where there is still room for improvement. She asks you to help her create a presentation she can use when she meets with her team. Complete the following:

1. Open the presentation **NP_PPT_3-2.pptx**, located in the PowerPoint3 > Review folder included with your Data Files, add your name as the Slide 1 subtitle, and then save it as **NP_PPT_3_FollowUp** to the location where you are storing your files.

2. On Slide 2 ("Improved Client Satisfaction Scores"), add a pie chart. Change the width of column A so that the ScreenTip indicates that column A is 145 pixels wide. In cells A2 through A6, type **Extremely satisfied**, **Very satisfied**, **Somewhat satisfied**, **Somewhat dissatisfied**, and **Not at all satisfied**. In cell B1, type **Number**. In cells B2 through B6, type **5700**, **7668**, **5047**, **3419**, and **2250**.

3. Apply Layout 6 to the chart.

4. Apply Style 6 to the chart.

5. Change the number of clients who are Not at all satisfied to **1650**.

6. Remove the title and the legend from the chart, and then change the position of the data labels to the Data Callout option. Change the font size of the data labels to 16 points, and then format them as bold.

7. On Slide 2, add a text box approximately 2 inches wide and one-half inch high. Type **"Extremely satisfied" increased from 7% to 24% and "Very satisfied" increased from 12% to 33%.** (including the period). Change the format of the text box so the text doesn't wrap and so that the left margin is zero. Format the text in the text box with italics and change the font size to 16 points.

8. Align the left edge of the text box with the left edge of the chart, and align it vertically so that there is the same amount of space between the text box and the bottom of the chart as there is between the top of the chart and the bottom of the title text box.

9. On Slide 3, duplicate the square shape. Change the size of the duplicate square so it is 3 inches high and wide, and then move the duplicate shape to the side of the original shape. Insert an oval shape, and then resize it so it is 1.5 inches high and wide. Position the circle on the top edge of the three-inch square so that its center is aligned with the center of the square and so that its middle is aligned with the top edge of the square.

10. Duplicate the circle. Position the duplicate circle on the right edge of the three-inch square so that its middle is aligned with the middle of the square and its left edge is aligned with the right edge of the circle on the top edge of the square.

11. Create two more identical circles and position them on the bottom and left edges of the three-inch square so they are aligned with the circles on the opposite edge. Make sure the right edge of the circle on the left edge of the three-inch square is aligned with the left edges of the circles on the top and bottom edges of the three-inch square.

12. Use the Union command to merge the two side circles with the three-inch square, and then use the Subtract command to remove the top and bottom circles from the square. Make sure to select the square first each time so that the color of the final shape is the same color as the square. The final shape is shown in Figure 3–43.

**Figure 3–43**    **Custom shape on Slide 3**

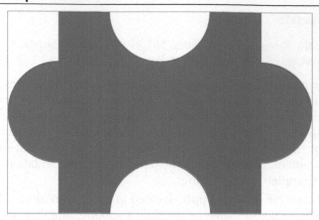

13. On Slide 3, duplicate the merged shape you created, and then place the duplicate on top of the original square in the center of the slide. Make sure it is aligned so that its middle and center are aligned with the middle and the center of the original square. Use the Subtract command to remove the duplicate puzzle piece from the original square.

14. Select the original puzzle piece you created, and then type **YOU!**. Change the font size of this text to 44 points and format it as bold. Move the YOU! puzzle piece above and a little to the left of the slide (zoom out if necessary), and then rotate it to the left about 160 degrees so that 200° appears in the Rotation box in the Size section on the Shape Options tab in the Format Shape pane.

15. Duplicate Slide 3. On the new Slide 4, move the YOU! shape onto the slide, rotate it so the text is right-side up, and then position it on top of the square in the empty space. Apply the Morph transition to Slide 4 and change the speed of this transition to 1.5 seconds.

16. On Slide 4, insert a rectangle shape that is 5 inches high and wide. Position it directly on top of the square with the filled-in puzzle piece. Fill the shape with the From Center gradient in the Dark Variations section on the Shape Fill menu.

17. Customize the gradient in the square by changing the color of the Stop 1 of 3 tab to Gold, Accent 4, Darker 50%. Position the Step 2 of 3 tab at 33% and change its color to Gold, Accent 4, Lighter 40%. Change the color of the Stop 3 of 3 tab to Gold, Accent 4, Lighter 80%. Add a new tab stop at the 66% position and change its color to Gold, Accent 4. Change the Type to Linear, and then change the Direction to Linear Diagonal–Bottom Right to Top Left.

18. Type **Problem Solved!** in the square with the gradient. Change the font size to 40 points and format the text as bold. Apply the Zoom entrance animation to the square with the gradient. (*Hint*: Make sure you apply the animation to the square and not to the text.)

19. On Slide 4, add the audio clip **Support_PPT_3_Compliment.mp3**, located in the PowerPoint3 > Review folder. Hide the icon during the slide show. Position the icon centered below the square so its top edge is aligned with the bottom edge of the vertical Footer text box in the blue bar. Change the order of animations on Slide 4 so that the audio clip plays first.

20. On Slide 5 ("Room for Improvement"), create a SmartArt graphic using the Picture Accent Process layout, which is a Process type graphic. From left to right, replace the first-level placeholder text in the shapes with **Follow up**, **Call sheets**, and **Solve**.

21. Add a new first-level shape as the rightmost shape in the SmartArt graphic, and then replace the placeholder text in it with **Respect**. Move the Respect shape up so it is the second shape in the graphic.

22. Delete the entire Solve shape from the SmartArt graphic.

23. In the Follow Up shape, add **Follow up within two weeks!** as second-level text, and then delete the other second-level item. In the Respect shape, add **Listen respectfully to the client.** as second-level text. In the Call sheets shape, add **Fill out call sheets completely.** as second-level text, and then delete the other second-level item.

24. In the SmartArt graphic, above the Follow Up shape, insert the picture **Support_PPT_3_FollowUp.jpg**, and then increase the brightness of the picture by 10% and increase its contrast by 40%. Above the Respect shape, insert the picture **Support_PPT_3_Respect.jpg**, sharpen it by 50%, and then change its tone by changing the temperature to 5900K. (*Hint*: If you use the Format Picture pane instead of the command on the ribbon to change the temperature, you cannot type the letter "K" in the Temperature box.) Above the Call sheets shape, insert the picture **Support_PPT_3_Form.jpg**, and then decrease its saturation to 66%.

25. Animate the SmartArt graphic with the Wipe entrance animation. Change the effect options to One by One and From Top.

26. Change the style of the SmartArt graphic to the Intense Effect style, and then change the color to the Colored Fill – Accent 2 colors.

27. Convert the SmartArt graphic to shapes. Ungroup the shapes, and then delete the two arrows. Group each picture and its corresponding shape containing text. Apply the Wipe animation to each grouped shape with the From Top effect. Make sure the grouped shapes animate in order from left to right, and that the start setting of each animation is On Click.

28. On Slide 6, format the title as WordArt using the Fill: Green, Accent color 5; Outline: White, Background color 1; Hard Shadow: Green, Accent color 5 style.

29. Change the Text fill color of the WordArt text to Orange, Accent 2, Darker 25%, and then change the font size of the text to 66 points. Apply the Chevron: Down transform effect to the text box.

30. Move the title text box that contains the WordArt down so its bottom is aligned with the bottom of the vertical footer text box in the blue box on the right. Resize the picture on the slide so it is 5 inches high (maintaining the aspect ratio), and then position the picture so it is horizontally centered on the slide and so that its top edge is aligned with the top of the slide.

31. On Slide 6, remove the background of the picture (keep all the people and the monitor on the right). It doesn't need to be perfect. Next, apply the Photocopy artistic effect to the picture.

32. Run the Accessibility Checker.

33. On Slide 2 ("Improved Client Satisfaction Scores"), add the following as alt text for the chart: **Pie chart showing that 24% of MBG's clients are extremely satisfied, 33% are very satisfied, 21% are somewhat satisfied, 15% are somewhat dissatisfied, and only 7% are not at all satisfied.** (including the period).

34. On Slide 4, resolve the duplicate slide title by first changing the title to **YOU!**. Because this title does not need to be seen during the slide show, select the title text box, and then change the text color to White, Background 1.

35. On every slide, the Footer Placeholder object should be the last object selected. Move it to the bottom of the list in the Reading Order pane on each slide if necessary. On Slide 4, select the Rectangle 2 shape and edit the Rectangle 2 shape name in the Reading Order pane to **Problem Solved shape**. (Do not include the period).

36. If necessary, close the Notes pane. View the presentation as a slide show, and then save and close it.

# Apply

## Case Problem 1

**Data Files needed for this Case Problem: NP_PPT_3-3.pptx, Support_PPT_Recovery.mp3**

**Springfield Hospital** Jake Cohen is the director of the physical therapy clinic at Springfield Hospital in Springfield, Georgia. The clinic has a good reputation because their patients have faster recovery times than average. The staff at the clinic has also consistently received positive reviews from their patients. The board of directors asked Jake to talk about the clinic's success at their next meeting. Jake prepared a PowerPoint presentation and asked you to finish it for him. Complete the following steps:

1. Open the presentation **NP_PPT_3-3.pptx**, located in the PowerPoint3 > Case1 folder included with your Data Files, add your name as the subtitle, and then save the presentation as **NP_PPT_3_Therapy** to the location where you are storing your files.

2. On Slide 2 ("Our Clinic"), add a text box, and type **\*American Board of Physical Therapy Specialties** in the text box. Turn off the Wrap text option, change the right margin to 0, and then right-align the text in the text box by clicking the Align Right button in the Paragraph group on the Home tab. Position the text box so that its right edge is aligned with the right edge of the bulleted list text box and its top edge is aligned with the bottom edge of the bulleted list text box.

3. On Slide 3 ("Recovery Time Examples in Weeks"), add a clustered bar chart in the content placeholder. In the spreadsheet, change the width of column A so that the ScreenTip indicates it is 157 pixels wide, and then enter the data shown in Figure 3–44 to create the chart.

**Figure 3–44     Data for Slide 4**

|  | Industry Average | Clinic at Springfield Hospital |
|---|---|---|
| Rotator cuff injuries | 35 | 26 |
| Meniscus tear | 8 | 5 |
| Achilles tendon rupture | 24 | 18 |

4. Drag the small blue box in the lower-right corner of cell D5 up and to the left so that the blue border surrounds cells B2 through C4 and the data in column D and in row 5 is removed from the chart. Close the spreadsheet.

5. Change the style of the chart to Style 7, and then change the colors of the chart to the Colorful Palette 2 palette.

6. Reposition the legend so it is at the top of the chart.

7. Add data labels to the outside end of the bars.

8. Change the font size of the data labels to 16 points and make them bold. Make sure you format the data labels for both the green bars and the red bars.

9. Change the font size of the text in the legend to 14 points, and then change the font size of the labels on the vertical axis to 14 points.

10. Remove the chart title.

11. On Slide 3, insert the audio clip **Support_PPT_3_Recovery.mp3**, located in the PowerPoint3 > Case1 folder. Hide the speaker icon during a slide show and set it to start automatically. Position the speaker icon so it is centered below the slide title and so its bottom edge is aligned with the bottom of the chart.

12. On Slide 4 ("We Love Our Patients"), increase the brightness of the photo by 5% and the contrast by 20%. Sharpen the photo by 25%,

13. On Slide 5 ("Questions?"), change the color saturation of the photo to 66%, and then change its tone to a temperature of 5300K. (*Hint*: If you use the Format Picture pane instead of the command on the ribbon to change the temperature, you cannot type the letter "K" in the Temperature box.)

14. Check the accessibility of the presentation. Add **Audio object for audio that will play during the slide show.** as alt text for the audio icon. Then add **Chart showing that recovery times for certain injuries is faster at our clinic than the industry average.** as alt text for the chart.
15. Check the reading order on all of the slides. Make sure the Title object on each slide is selected first. On Slide 5, move the Text Placeholder so it is selected second.
16. Save and close the presentation.

# Challenge

## Case Problem 2

**Data Files needed for this Case Problem: NP_PPT_3-4.pptx**

**Keystone State Elder Services** Kelly Lewis is the associate director of the Executive Office of Elder Affairs (EOEA) in Massachusetts. The EOEA contracts with home care agencies across the state to provide services for elderly and disabled people so that they can continue to live at home rather than in a nursing home. Kelly was asked to prepare a presentation to explain how people obtain services. She started creating a PowerPoint presentation and asked you to help complete it by correcting photos and adding SmartArt. She also created a design similar to a logo that she wants you to place on the first and last slides. Complete the following steps:

1. Open the file named **NP_PPT_3-4.pptx**, located in the PowerPoint3 > Case2 folder included with your Data Files, add your name as the subtitle on Slide 1, and then save it as **NP_PPT_3_Elder** to the location where you are storing your files.
2. On Slide 2, duplicate the square shape three times. These are the four squares behind the center square in Figure 3–45. Arrange them as shown in Figure 3–45 so that there is about one-quarter inch of space between each square. Merge the four squares using the Union command.

Figure 3–45    Kelly's design

3. Apply the From Center Gradient style in the Dark Variations set of gradient styles to the merged square. Customize this gradient by changing the Stop 2 of 3 tab to the Bright Green, Accent 4, Darker 25% color, and changing its position to 60%. Then change the gradient Type to Rectangular and the direction to From Center.
4. Create a text box, and then type **EOEA** in it.
5. Turn off the Wrap text option in the text box, if necessary.
✦ **Explore** 6. Turn on the Do not Autofit option in the Format Shape pane.
7. Change the size of the text box to 1.5" square.
8. Change the font to Copperplate Gothic Bold, and change the font size to 32 points.

9. Use the Center button in the Paragraph group on the Home tab to center the text in the box horizontally, and then use the Align Text button in the Paragraph group to center the text vertically in the middle of the text box.

10. Fill the text box shape with the White, Background 1 color.

11. Position the text box so it is centered over the custom shape, using the smart guides to assist you.

12. Group the custom shape and the text box.

13. Save the final grouped shape as a picture named **NP_PPT_3_EOEA** to the location where you are storing your files.

14. Delete Slide 2, and then insert the picture **NP_PPT_3_EOEA.png** on Slide 1 (the title slide). Position it to the left of the title so that its bottom edge is aligned with the top of the subtitle text box and so that there is approximately the same amount of space between the picture and the slide title and the picture and the left side of the slide.

15. On Slide 2 ("Services Provided by Home Care Agencies"), decrease the brightness of the picture by -10% and increase the contrast by 20%. Change the color tone to a temperature of 7200K. (*Hint:* If you use the Format Picture pane instead of the command on the ribbon to change the temperature, you cannot type the letter "K" in the Temperature box.)

16. On Slide 3 ("What Is Case Management?"), sharpen the picture by 25%, and change the color saturation to 66%.

17. On Slide 4 ("How Does a New Client Get Services?"), insert a SmartArt graphic using the Horizontal Bullet List layout (in the List category). Type the following as first-level items in the graphic, adding first-level shapes if needed:

**Schedule Services**

**Set Up Appointment with Case Manager**

**Answer Intake Questions**

**Call Elder Line**

18. Add **Talk to Intake Specialist** as a second-level bullet below the Call Elder Line shape. Add **Answer questions about health history and income** as a second-level bullet below the Answer Intake Questions shape. Add **Be prepared to talk about what the client needs** as a second-level bullet below the Set Up Appointment with Case Manager shape.

19. Delete the Schedule Services shape. Remove the unused placeholder text and second-level bullets in the rest of the shapes.

⊕ **Explore** 20. Reverse the order of the boxes in the graphic so that the Call Elder Line shape is the leftmost shape and the Set Up Appointment with Case Manager shape is the rightmost shape. (*Hint:* Use a command in the Create Graphic group on the SmartArt Design tab.)

21. Change the style of the SmartArt graphic to the Cartoon style. Change the color to Colorful – Accent Colors.

22. On Slide 5 ("Questions?"), insert the **NP_PPT_3_EOEA.png** file you created in the content placeholder on the left.

23. Check the accessibility of the presentation file. Add **SmartArt graphic listing the three steps to take to receive services.** as alt text for the SmartArt graphic. Mark the pictures you inserted on Slides 1 and 5 as decorative. On Slide 3 ("What Is Case Management?"), change the selection order of the objects so that the title is selected first, the bulleted list is selected second, and the picture last.

24. Save and close the presentation.

**Module 4**

## OBJECTIVES

**Session 4.1**
- Use guides to place objects
- Add more than one animation to an object
- Set animation triggers
- Change the slide background
- Create and edit links and action buttons
- Create slide zooms
- Hide slides during a slide show

**Session 4.2**
- Create a self-running presentation
- Rehearse slide timings
- Record slide timings and narration
- Set up a presentation for kiosk browsing
- Inspect a presentation for private information
- Save a presentation in other formats

# Advanced Animations and Distributing Presentations

## Creating an Advanced Presentation for Agricultural Development

## Case | Pennsylvania Department of Agriculture

Jack Chu works in the Agricultural Commodity Marketing Division in the Pennsylvania Department of Agriculture. Over the past few years, small family-owned farms have contacted his office requesting suggestions and assistance in expanding and extending their cash flow into the fall and early winter seasons. In response, Jack will begin presenting on this topic at agricultural fairs and trade shows across the state. He wants your help in finishing the presentation he has created.

In this module, you will enhance Jack's presentation by adding multiple animations to objects and setting triggers for animations. You'll also add a picture as the slide background, create links, and create a self-running presentation that includes narration. Finally, you'll save the presentation in other formats for distribution.

## Starting Data Files

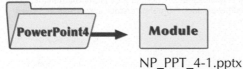

NP_PPT_4-1.pptx
NP_PPT_4-2.pptx
Support_PPT_4_Light.png
Support_PPT_4_Tractor.png

**Review**

NP_PPT_4-3.pptx
NP_PPT_4-4.pptx
Support_PPT_4_Corn.png

**Case1**

NP_PPT_4-5.pptx
Support_PPT_4_Waves.jpg

**Case2**

NP_PPT_4-6.pptx
Support_PPT_4_Bacteria.png
Support_PPT_4_Isopropanol.3mf

# Session 4.1 Visual Overview:

When multiple animations are applied to an object, select one of the animation sequence icons to display its associated animation in the Animation gallery.

To add a second animation to an object, click the Add Animation button in the Advanced Animation group on the Animations tab.

If the second animation applied to an object is set to With Previous or After Previous, the animation sequence icons are stacked on top of one another.

The motion path is indicated by a dashed line. To modify it, click it, and then drag the green circle that indicates the beginning of the path or the red circle indicating the ending of the path.

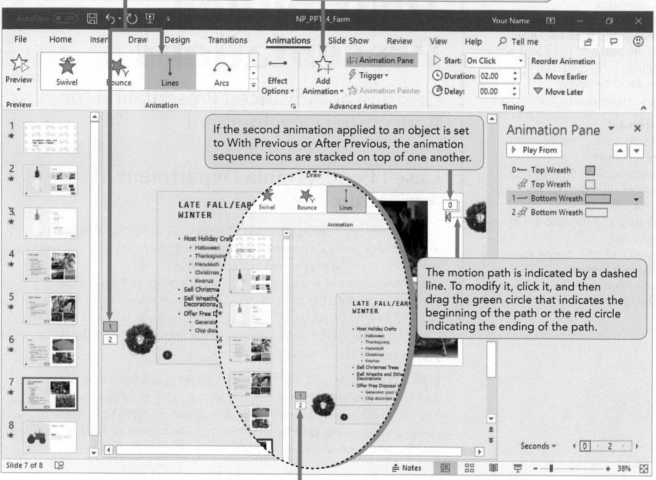

When you add a second animation to an object, a second animation sequence icon appears next to the object.

iStock.com/mediaphotos; iStock.com/FlamingPumpkin; ND700/ Shutterstock.com; Arina P Habich/Shutterstock.com; Love Silhouette/ Shutterstock.com; fokke baarssen/Shutterstock.com; iStock.com/ AzmanJaka; Vicki L. Miller/Shutterstock.com; gvictoria/Shutterstock.com; iStock.com/BanksPhotos; Jack Frog/Shutterstock.com; Heather Stokes/ Shutterstock.com

# Understanding Advanced Animations

When an animation has a trigger, the number in the animation sequence icon is replaced with a lightning bolt. This is because the animation is no longer part of a sequence; it will occur only when the trigger is clicked.

The list of objects on the "On Click of" submenu corresponds to the objects on the slide. You can also see this list of objects in the Selection pane.

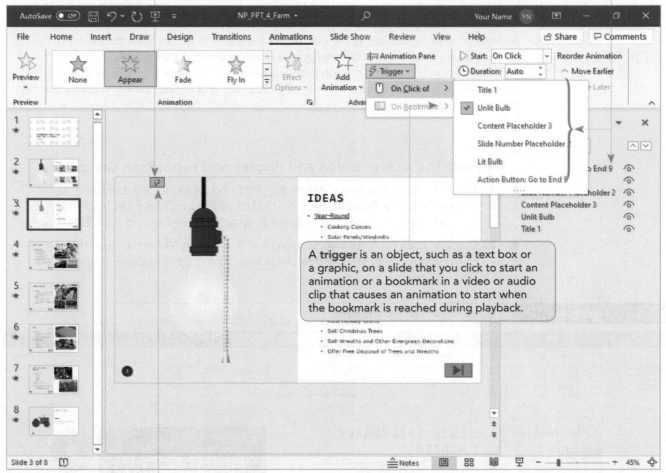

A **trigger** is an object, such as a text box or a graphic, on a slide that you click to start an animation or a bookmark in a video or audio clip that causes an animation to start when the bookmark is reached during playback.

The Play/Pause animation automatically applied to a video when a video is added to a slide is triggered by clicking the video object itself. That is why the animation sequence icon for the Play/Pause animation contains a lightning bolt.

Heather Stokes/Shutterstock.com; Arina P Habich/Shutterstock.com; Love Silhouette/Shutterstock.com; fokke baarssen/Shutterstock.com; iStock.com/AzmanJaka; Vicki L. Miller/Shutterstock.com; gvictoria/Shutterstock.com; iStock.com/BanksPhotos; Jack Frog/Shutterstock.com; iStock.com/mediaphotos; iStock.com/FlamingPumpkin; ND700/Shutterstock.com

# Using Guides

You are already familiar with three tools that help you align objects as you drag them. Smart guides are the dashed red lines that appear when you drag objects on a slide. Gridlines are evenly spaced horizontal and vertical lines that you can display on slides. You also have used the horizontal and vertical rulers. In addition to these tools, you can use **guides**, which are dashed vertical and horizontal lines you display and position on the slide, to help you precisely position objects. When you first display guides, one vertical guide and one horizontal guide appear in the center and the middle of the slide. To reposition the guides, you drag them to a new location on the slide. As you drag, a ScreenTip appears, indicating the distance of the guide in inches from the center of the slide. You can also create additional guides or remove individual guides.

Jack wants you to apply motion path animations to some of the objects in his presentation. To help you position the objects at the end of their paths, you will display and adjust the guides.

### To open the presentation and display and reposition the guides:

▶ 1. **sam** ⬇ Open the presentation **NP_PPT_4-1.pptx**, located in the **PowerPoint4 > Module** folder included with your Data Files, and then save it as **NP_PPT_4_Farm** to the location where you are saving your files.

▶ 2. Display Slide 6 ("Late Fall/Early Winter"), click the **View** tab, and then in the Show group, click the **Guides** check box. The guides appear on the slide. See Figure 4–1.

**Figure 4–1**   **Guides displayed on the slide**

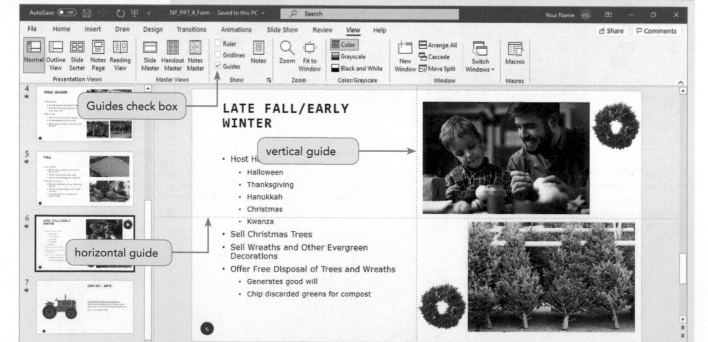

iStock.com/mediaphotos; iStock.com/FlamingPumpkin; ND700/Shutterstock.com; iStock.com/AzmanJaka; Vicki L. Miller/ Shutterstock.com; gvictoria/Shutterstock.com; iStock.com/BanksPhotos; Jack Frog/Shutterstock.com; Heather Stokes/ Shutterstock.com

3. In a blank area of the slide, position the pointer on top of the horizontal guide so that the pointer changes to the move horizontal guide pointer ÷, and then press and hold the mouse button. The pointer disappears, and a ScreenTip appears in its place displaying 0.00. This indicates that the horizontal guide is in the middle of the slide.

   **Trouble?** If the pointer doesn't change, you are pointing to the bulleted list text box or a photo. Repeat Step 3, this time positioning the pointer on top of the guide in a blank area of the slide so that the pointer changes to the move horizontal guide pointer.

4. Drag the guide up until the ScreenTip displays 2.71, and then release the mouse button. The horizontal guide now intersects the middle of the wreath at the top of the slide. Next, you will create a second horizontal guide.

5. Position the pointer on top of the horizontal guide so that the pointer changes to the move horizontal guide pointer ÷, press and hold **CTRL**, press and hold the mouse button, and then start dragging the guide down. A second horizontal guide is created and moves down with the mouse pointer.

6. Continue dragging down past the middle of the slide until the ScreenTip displays 2.67, release the mouse button, and then release **CTRL**. The horizontal guide you created is aligned with the middle of the wreath at the bottom of the slide.

7. Position the pointer on top of the vertical guide so that the pointer changes to the move vertical guide pointer +‖+, press and hold **CTRL**, drag the vertical guide to the right until the ScreenTip displays 0.75, and then release **CTRL** and the mouse button. The copy of the vertical guide is aligned with the center of the wreath at the bottom of the slide.

8. Drag another copy of the vertical guide to the right until the ScreenTip displays 5.92. The second copy of the vertical guide is aligned with the center of the wreath at the top of the slide. You don't need the original vertical guide that is positioned in the center of the slide.

9. Right-click the vertical guide that is positioned in the center of the slide on a part of the guide that is not inside the title text box. A shortcut menu that includes the Delete command appears. See Figure 4–2.

**Figure 4–2** **Shortcut menu for deleting a guide**

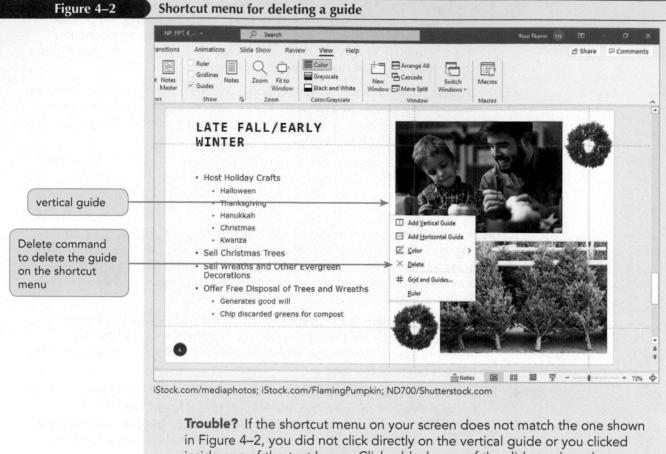

vertical guide

Delete command to delete the guide on the shortcut menu

iStock.com/mediaphotos; iStock.com/FlamingPumpkin; ND700/Shutterstock.com

**Trouble?** If the shortcut menu on your screen does not match the one shown in Figure 4–2, you did not click directly on the vertical guide or you clicked inside one of the text boxes. Click a blank area of the slide to close the menu, and then repeat Step 9.

▶ 10. On the shortcut menu, click **Delete**. The vertical guide in the center of the slide is deleted.

# Adding More Than One Animation to an Object

You can apply more than one animation to an object. For example, you can apply an entrance animation to an object by having it fly into a slide, and then once the object is on the slide, you can animate it a second time to further emphasize a bullet point on the slide or to show a relationship between the object and another object on the slide.

On Slide 6 in the presentation, Jack wants you to add animations to the photos of wreaths to add interest. He wants the wreaths to roll onto the slide.

**To add a motion path animation to the top wreath on Slide 6:**

▶ 1. Click the wreath at the top of the slide, and then on the ribbon, click the **Animations** tab.

▶ 2. In the Animation group, click the **More** button ▾, scroll down to locate the Motion Paths section, and then click the **Lines** animation. The animation previews, and the wreath moves down the slide. After the preview, the motion path appears below the wreath, and a faint image of the wreath appears at the end of the path. At the beginning of the path, the green circle indicates the path's starting point, and at the end of the path, the red circle indicates the path's ending point. See Figure 4–3.

| Figure 4–3 | Wreath with Lines motion path animation applied |

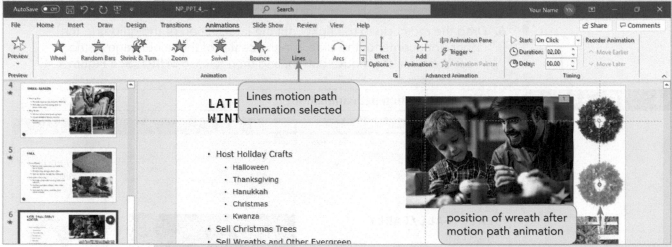

iStock.com/mediaphotos; iStock.com/FlamingPumpkin; ND700/Shutterstock.com; iStock.com/AzmanJaka; Vicki L. Miller/Shutterstock.com; gvictoria/Shutterstock.com; iStock.com/BanksPhotos; Jack Frog/Shutterstock.com

To have the wreath roll onto the slide, you will position the wreath to the right of the slide, and then change the direction of the Lines animation so that the wreath moves to the left instead of down. Then you will adjust the ending point of the motion path so that the wreath ends up in the upper-right corner of the slide when the animation is finished.

### To move the top wreath off the slide and modify the motion path animation:

1. Click the wreath at the top of the slide. The faint image of the wreath at the end of the motion path disappears, and the end points of the motion path change from circles to arrows.

2. Press and hold **SHIFT**, drag the wreath to the right until it is completely off the slide, and then release **SHIFT**. Pressing SHIFT while you drag an object forces the object to move in a straight line. The center of the wreath is still aligned with the horizontal guide.

3. In the Animation group, click the **Effect Options** button, and then click **Left**. The motion path changes to a horizontal line, and the wreath moves to the left as the animation previews. You need to reposition the end point of the motion path so that the wreath ends up to the right of the picture of the man and boy after the animation is finished. First you need to select the motion path. To do this, you click the motion path or the starting or ending point. Because the motion path is aligned with the horizontal guide, you will click the red ending point.

4. Click the red ending arrow. The arrows on the ends of the motion path change to circles, and a faint copy of the image appears at the end of the motion path. Now you can drag the start and end points to new locations.

5. Position the pointer on top of the red circle so that it changes to the double-headed diagonal pointer ⤢, press and hold **SHIFT**, and then press and hold the mouse button. The pointer changes to the thin cross pointer ╋.

6. Drag the red circle to the right until the intersection of the guides in the upper-right corner of the slide is in the center of the faint image of the wreath, release the mouse button, and then release **SHIFT**. See Figure 4–4.

**Figure 4–4** | Modified Lines motion path animation

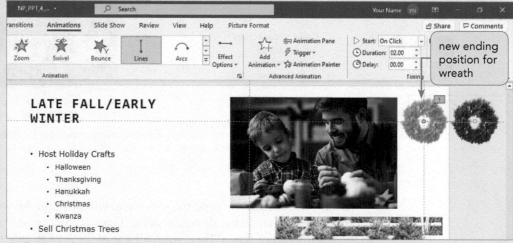

iStock.com/mediaphotos; iStock.com/FlamingPumpkin; ND700/Shutterstock.com

**Trouble?** If the path is slanted, you released SHIFT before you released the mouse button when you were dragging the wreath or the end point of the motion path. Click the Undo button ↺ on the Quick Access Toolbar, and then repeat Steps 4 through 6, this time making sure you release the mouse button before you release SHIFT.

Jack wants the wreath to look like it is rolling onto the slide. To create this effect, you need to add a second animation to the wreath. To add a second animation to an object, you must use the Add Animation button in the Advanced Animation group on the Animations tab. If you try to add a second animation to an object by clicking an animation in the gallery in the Animation group, you will simply replace the animation already applied to the object.

### To add a second animation to the top wreath on Slide 6:

1. Click the wreath positioned to the right of the slide to select it, and then click the **Animations** tab, if necessary.

2. In the Advanced Animation group, click the **Add Animation** button.

   The same gallery of animations that is in the Animation group appears.

Make sure you do not click another animation in the Animation group.

3. In the Emphasis section of the gallery, click the **Spin** animation. Nothing happens for a moment, and then the animations preview very quickly. Next to the top wreath, a second animation sequence icon appears and is selected. In the Animation group, the Spin animation is selected, which means that the 2 animation sequence icon corresponds to the Spin animation. To see both animations, you need to preview them.

4. In the Preview group, click the **Preview** button. The wreath moves left onto the slide, stops to the right of the picture of the man and boy, and then spins once in a clockwise direction.

To make the wreath look like it is rolling onto the slide, you need to change the start setting of the Spin animation to With Previous so that it happens at the same time as the Lines animation. Because two animations are applied to the object, you need to make sure that the correct animation sequence icon and the correct animation in the Animation group on the Animations tab are selected before you make any changes.

**To modify the start setting of the Spin animation applied to the wreath:**

1. Click the top wreath. In the Animation gallery, Multiple is selected. This indicates that more than one animation is applied to the selected object.

2. Next to the top wreath, click the **2** animation sequence icon to select it. In the Animation gallery, Spin is selected. This is the animation that corresponds to the selected animation sequence icon.

3. In the Timing group, click the **Start** arrow, and then click **With Previous**. The two animation sequence icons are now stacked on top of the other and they are both selected.

4. In the Preview group, click the **Preview** button. Because the Lines motion path and the Spin animation happen at the same time, the wreath appears to roll as it moves onto the slide. However, it rolls in the wrong direction. Because the wreath starts from the right side of the slide, it should roll onto the slide in a counter-clockwise direction.

5. With the Spin animation selected in the Animation group, click the **Effect Options** button, click **Counterclockwise**, and then in the Preview group, click the **Preview** button. The wreath rolls onto the slide in a counterclockwise direction.

Next, you need to apply the same animations to the wreath that is positioned at the bottom of the slide. You can follow the same steps you took when you applied the animations to the first wreath, or you can copy the animations and then modify them. You will copy the animations.

**To copy and modify the animations:**

1. Click the top wreath, and then in the Advanced Animation group, click the **Animation Painter** button.

2.  Click the wreath at the bottom of the slide. The animations are copied and preview. Now you need to move the bottom wreath to the left of the slide, and then adjust its motion path.

3.  Drag the bottom wreath off the slide to the left in a straight line, keeping its center aligned with the horizontal guide at the bottom of the slide. Now you need to change the direction and the end position of the motion path so that the wreath stops in the correct position on the slide.

4.  Scroll left if necessary, and then click one of the end points on the motion path applied to the wreath at the bottom of the slide to select the motion path.

5.  In the Animation group, click the **Effect Options** button, and then click **Right**. The end point of the motion path moves so it is below the bulleted list.

6.  Select the motion path again, press and hold **SHIFT**, drag the red circle that indicates the end of the motion path to the right until the intersection of the guides to the left of the picture of the trees is in the center of the faint image of the wreath, release the mouse button, and then release **SHIFT**.

7.  In the Preview group, click the **Preview** button. The wreath at the top of the slide rolls onto the slide, then the wreath at the bottom of the slide rolls onto the slide. The wreath at the bottom rolls in the wrong direction, but you will fix this in the next section. You are finished using the guides, so you can hide them.

8.  Click the **View** tab, and then in the Show group, click the **Guides** check box. The guides no longer appear on the screen.

9.  Click a blank area of the slide, and then save the changes to the presentation.

## Using the Animation Pane

On Slide 6, the bottom wreath rolled onto the slide in a counterclockwise direction. Since it rolls from the left, it should roll in a clockwise direction. But when more than one animation is applied to an object and the Start setting of one of the animations is set to With Previous or After Previous, you can't select only one of the animation sequence icons because they are stacked on top of one another. To select one animation when the animation sequence icons are stacked, you need to open the Animation pane.

**To examine the animations on Slide 6 in the Animation pane:**

1.  To the left of the slide, click the bottom wreath, click the Animations tab, and then in the Advanced Animation group, click the **Animation Pane** button. The Animation pane opens and Multiple is selected in the Animation group on the Animations tab. In the Advanced Animation group, the Animation Pane button is selected. See Figure 4–5.

| Figure 4–5 | Animation pane listing the animations on Slide 6 |

iStock.com/mediaphotos; iStock.com/FlamingPumpkin; ND700/Shutterstock.com; Arina P Habich/Shutterstock.com; Love Silhouette/Shutterstock.com; fokke baarssen/Shutterstock.com; iStock.com/AzmanJaka; Vicki L. Miller/Shutterstock.com; gvictoria/Shutterstock.com; iStock.com/BanksPhotos; Jack Frog/Shutterstock.com; Heather Stokes/Shutterstock.com

**Trouble?** If Lines is selected in the Animation group, click a blank area of the slide, and then click the bottom wreath.

2. In the Animation pane, move the pointer on top of the first animation in the list, **Top Wreath**. A ScreenTip appears, identifying the start setting (On Click), the type of animation (Motion Paths), the direction of the animation (Left), and the full name of the object (Top Wreath). This is the Lines animation applied to the wreath that ends up in the upper-right corner of the slide. The horizontal line to the left of the object name indicates that this is a motion path animation. The number 1 to the left of the object name is the same number that appears in the animation sequence icon for this animation.

3. In the Animation pane, move the pointer on top of the second animation in the list, the second **Top Wreath**. This is the Spin animation applied to the wreath that ends up in the upper-right corner of the slide. There is no number to the left of this animation because this animation occurs automatically (With Previous), not when the slide show is advanced (On Click). The yellow star to the left of the object name indicates that this is an emphasis animation. (Entrance animations are indicated with a green star, and exit animations are indicated with a red star.)

**Tip**

The entrance animation Appear and the exit animation Disappear have no length, so an arrow appears in the Animation Pane instead of a rectangle and the ScreenTip displays only a start time.

4. To the right of the Top Wreath Line animation (the first Top Wreath animation), move the pointer on top of the blue rectangle so that the pointer changes to the horizontal two-headed arrow pointer ↔. The rectangle indicates the length of the animation. The ScreenTip identifies the start time as 0s (zero seconds), which means it starts immediately after the slide show is advanced. The animation takes two seconds to complete so the ending time in the ScreenTip is 2s.

▶ **5.** To the right of the Top Wreath Spin animation (the second Top Wreath animation), move the pointer on top of the yellow rectangle so that the pointer changes to the horizontal two-headed arrow pointer ↔. The yellow rectangle is directly below the blue rectangle, and the ScreenTip identifies the start time and end time as the same as the start and end times associated with the blue rectangle above it (0s and 2s).

▶ **6.** In the Animation pane, click the **Top Wreath Spin** animation. In the Animation group on the Animations tab, the Spin animation is selected instead of Multiple.

▶ **7.** On the Animations tab, in the Timing group, click the **Delay** up arrow once to set a delay of 0.25 seconds. In the Animation pane, the yellow rectangle next to the Top Wreath Spin animation moves to the right.

▶ **8.** In the Animation pane, move the pointer on top of the yellow rectangle to the right of the Top Wreath Spin animation. The ScreenTip now identifies the start time as 0.25s.

▶ **9.** In the Timing group, click the **Delay** down arrow once to change the Delay back to 0.00 seconds.

Now you can change the direction of the Spin animation for the bottom wreath to clockwise. You also might have noticed that when the bottom wreath rolled onto the slide, it seemed to slide part of the way instead of roll completely across the slide. And when the top wreath rolled onto the slide, it continued rolling after it was in position in the upper-right corner of the slide. To make the rolling effects appear more realistic, you will change the number of revolutions each wreath makes.

**To select the Spin animations in the Animation pane and modify them:**

▶ **1.** In the Animation pane, click the **Bottom Wreath Spin** animation. First, you will change the direction of the animation.

▶ **2.** On the Animations tab, in the Animation group, click the **Effect Options** button, and then click **Clockwise**.

▶ **3.** Click the **Effect Options** button again. In the Amount section, Full Spin is selected. Because this wreath needs to travel all the way across the slide, two spins would look better.

▶ **4.** On the Effect Options menu, click **Two Spins**. As the animation previews (which you can't see because the wreath is not on the slide), only the Bottom Wreath Spin animation is shown in the Animation Pane, and a vertical line moves across the pane. You need to preview both animations applied to the bottom wreath.

▶ **5.** Press and hold **SHIFT**, in the Animation pane click the **Bottom Wreath Lines** animation, and then release **SHIFT**. The two Bottom Wreath animations are selected. The button at the top of the Animation Pane changes to the Play Selected button.

▶ **6.** Click the **Play Selected** button. The two selected animations preview, with the bottom wreath rolling onto the slide while spinning twice. Now you need to adjust the number of spins for the top wreath.

▶ **7.** In the Animation Pane, click the **Top Wreath Spin** animation (the second animation in the list). On the Animations tab, in the Animation group, the Spin animation is selected.

8. In the Animation group, click the **Effect Options** button. In the Amount section, Full Spin is selected. Because this wreath needs to travel only a short distance, a half spin might look better.

9. On the Effect Options menu, click **Half Spin**. The menu closes, and the Spin animation applied to the top wreath previews. Again, you can't see this because the wreath is spinning to the right of the slide.

10. In the Animation Pane, click the **Top Wreath Lines** animation, and then at the top of the pane, click the **Play From** button. The four animations preview by starting with the selected animation and playing each animation in the pane.

When the bottom wreath animates, it continues to roll after it is in position. To fix this problem, you will slightly speed up the Spin animation applied to it by shortening its duration. The top wreath seems to roll more slowly than the first wreath. To fix that issue, you will speed up both animations applied to the top wreath.

### To modify the duration of the animations applied to the wreaths:

1. Make sure the Top Wreath Lines animation is selected in the Animation pane, press and hold **SHIFT**, click the **Top Wreath Spin** animation, and then release **SHIFT**.

2. On the Animations tab, in the Timing group, change the value in the Duration box to **0.75**.

3. In the Animation pane, click the **Bottom Wreath Spin** animation.

4. Change the duration of the Bottom Wreath Spin animation to **1.75** seconds.

5. On the status bar, click the **Slide Show** button 🖵, and then press **SPACEBAR**. The top wreath rolls onto the slide faster than before.

6. Press **SPACEBAR** again. The second wreath rolls on and no longer has an extra spin at the end.

7. Press **ESC** to end the slide show and return to Normal view.

Jack wants the wreaths to roll onto the slide automatically after the slide transitions onto the screen during a slide show. In order for this to happen, the start timing of both Lines animations need to be set to After Previous.

### To change the start timing of the Lines animations:

1. In the Animation Pane, click the **Top Wreath Lines** animation. An arrow ▼ appears to the right of the blue rectangle.

2. Click the **arrow** ▼ to the right of the blue rectangle. A menu appears. The first three commands are the same commands that appear when you click the Start arrow in the Timing group on the Animations tab. See Figure 4–6.

**Figure 4-6**   Menu in the Animation pane for the selected Top Wreath Lines animation

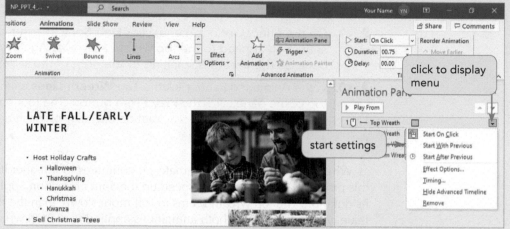

iStock.com/mediaphotos; ND700/Shutterstock.com

> **3.** Click **Start After Previous**. Now the first wreath will roll onto the slide after the slide transitions. Notice that the number 1 that had been next to the animation changes to zero.

> **4.** Click the **Bottom Wreath Lines** animation, click the arrow ⏷ that appears, and then click **Start After Previous**. The blue and yellow rectangles next to the Bottom Wreath animations shift right to indicate that they won't start until after the previous animations finish. See Figure 4-7.

**Figure 4-7**   Modified timeline in the Animation pane

iStock.com/mediaphotos; ND700/Shutterstock.com

> **5.** Point to the blue rectangle to the right of the Bottom Wreath Lines animation. The ScreenTip indicates that the animation will start 0.75 seconds after the slide show is advanced and will end 2.75 seconds after the slide show was advanced. Now preview the animations in Slide Show view.

> **6.** On the status bar, click the **Slide Show** button 🖵. Slide 6 appears in Slide Show view, the top wreath rolls onto the slide, and then the bottom wreath rolls on.

> **7.** Press **ESC** to end the slide show.

On each of the four slides that contain the ideas for generating income, Jack wants the bulleted lists to appear with an entrance animation and for the pictures to appear with the bulleted item they are illustrating. You'll start with Slide 4.

**To animate the bulleted list and pictures on Slide 4:**

1. Display Slide 4 ("Three-Season"), click the bulleted list, press and hold **SHIFT**, click the picture of the boy feeding the goat, click the picture of the red tractor, click the picture of the horses pulling a wagon, and then release **SHIFT**. The four objects you clicked are selected.

2. On the Animations tab, in the Animation group, click the **Fade** entrance animation. The Fade animation is applied to all four objects. In the Animation pane, the bulleted list appears first. The bulleted list animation is collapsed so you can see only the name of the entire object.

3. In the Animation pane, move the pointer on top of the first item in the list. The ScreenTip identifies this item as Content Placeholder 2: Petting Zoo. This is the name of the bulleted list object.

4. In the Animation pane, click the **Click to expand contents** button ⟰ . The list expands and instead of "Content Placeholder 2," the first item is the same as the first item in the bulleted list, the second item is the next item in the bulleted list, and so on. See Figure 4–8.

**Figure 4–8**     Expanded bulleted list in the Animation pane

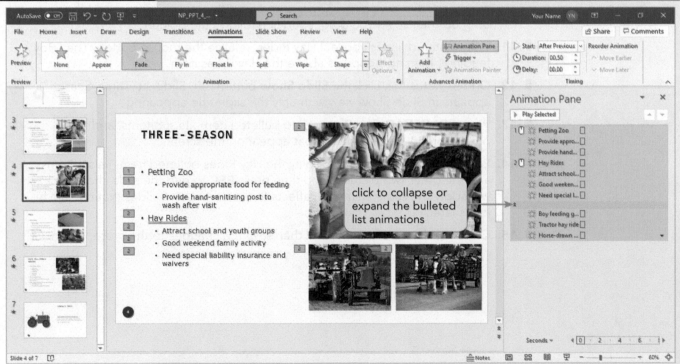

Jack wants the Petting Zoo bulleted item and its subitems to appear first, and he wants the picture of the little boy feeding the goat to appear at the same time. Then he wants the Hay Rides bulleted item and its subitems to appear along with the other two pictures.

5. Move the pointer on top of each bulleted list item in the Animation pane to see how it starts. The Petting Zoo and Hay Rides items are set to start On Click. These two items are first-level bulleted items in the list. All of the other items (the subitems in the bulleted list and the pictures) are set to start With Previous.

6. In the Animation pane, near the bottom of the list, move the pointer on top of **Boy feeding**. The ScreenTip for the "Boy feeding" item shows that the full name of this item is "Boy feeding goat." This picture needs to move up in the list so that it animates at the same time as the Petting Zoo item.

7. On the slide, click the **2** animation sequence icon next to the picture of the boy feeding a goat. In the Animation pane, "Boy feeding," which is just below the "Need special" subbullet near the bottom of the list, is selected.

8. On the Animations tab, in the Timing group, click the **Move Earlier** button. In the Animation pane, the "Boy feeding" item moves up one spot and is now above the "Need special" item. On the slide however, it looks as if nothing has changed—the animation sequence icon next to the picture is still 2. The Animation pane gives you a more complete picture.

9. At the top of the Animation pane, click the up arrow ⌃. The "Boy feeding" item moves up one more position.

10. Move the pointer on top of **Boy feeding** so that the pointer changes to the two-headed arrow pointer ↕, press and hold the mouse button, and then drag up the list. As you drag, a red line follows the pointer.

11. When the red line is above 2 Hay Rides, release the mouse button. The "Boy feeding" item now appears above the Hay Rides item.

12. On the status bar, click the **Slide Show** button 🖵. Slide 4 ("Three-Season") appears in Slide Show view with only the slide title appearing.

13. Press **SPACEBAR**. The Petting Zoo bulleted item, its subitems, and the picture of the boy feeding a goat appear on the screen.

14. Press **SPACEBAR** again to display the Hay Rides bulleted item, its subitems, and the other two pictures, and then press **ESC** to end the slide show. Jack will apply the same animation effects to the other three slides that contain his ideas later.

15. Close the Animation pane, and then save the changes to the presentation.

**Proskills**

### Problem Solving: Solving Animation Problems

Sometimes animations do not work as you expect, especially if you combine triggers, multiple animations, and the Morph transition. This is why you should periodically preview your animations in Slide Show view as you create them. First, make sure that the effect you are trying to create actually enhances your message and does not distract from it. Before fixing the animation, duplicate the slide so that you can return to the original version if you want. On the copy of the slide, open the Animation pane and examine the animations. Make sure objects animate in the correct order and that each animation has the correct start setting. In the Animation pane, click an animation, click the arrow that appears, and then click Effect Options to open a dialog box that offers more options for modifying the selected animation. With a little detective work, you should be able to solve most of your problems. Sometimes, you might decide that you have too many animations occurring on one slide. The solution in that case might be to create two slides instead of just one, and then use a transition to help you create the effect you want.

# Setting Animation Triggers

Jack created an overview slide listing his suggestions for increasing the cash flow for farms in the fall and early winter months. He included a graphic of an unlit light bulb on the slide, and he wants to be able to click it during his presentation to cause a lit light bulb image to appear so it looks like he turned the light on. To do this, you will make the unlit bulb a trigger for that entrance animation. Refer to the Session 4.1 Visual Overview for more information about triggers.

**To set a trigger for an animation on Slide 2:**

1. Display Slide 2 ("Ideas"), and then, on the ribbon, click the **Home** tab. Slide 2 contains a title, a light bulb graphic, and a bulleted list. The white light bulb is a little hard to see because the background on the left side of the slide is very light blue.

2. In the Editing group, click the **Select** button, and then click **Selection Pane**. The Selection pane opens.

3. On the slide, click the light bulb. In the Selection pane, Content Placeholder 5 is selected.

4. In the Selection pane, click **Content Placeholder 5**, drag across **Content Placeholder 5** to select the text, type **Unlit Bulb**, and then press **ENTER**.

5. Insert the picture **Support_PPT_4_Light.png**, located in the PowerPoint 4 > Module folder. Another light bulb graphic is added to the slide, but this one looks like the light bulb is turned on. In the Selection pane, Picture 6 is added to the top of the list.

6. In the Selection pane, rename Picture 6 so it is **Lit Bulb**.

7. On the slide, drag the lit version of the light bulb graphic directly on top of the unlit version, using the smart guides to make sure the two graphics are perfectly aligned.

▶ 8. Click the **Animations** tab, and then in the Animation group, click the **Appear** entrance animation. The Appear animation is applied to the lit bulb. Now you need to make the unlit bulb the trigger for this animation.

▶ 9. In the Advanced Animation group, click the **Trigger** button, and then point to **On Click of**. The same list of objects that appears in the Selection pane appears on the submenu, but in reverse order.

▶ 10. Click **Unlit Bulb**. The animation sequence icon next to the light changes to a lightning bolt. This means the animation applied to the lit bulb will not occur until the trigger happens—in this case, until the unlit bulb is clicked during a slide show.

Next, you will test the trigger. You'll view Slide 2 in Slide Show view and click the unlit bulb to make sure the lit bulb appears.

**To test the animation trigger in Slide Show view:**

▶ 1. On the status bar, click the **Slide Show** button 🖵. Slide 2 appears in Slide Show view displaying the slide title, the bulleted list, and the unlit version of the light bulb graphic.

**Tip**

To remove a trigger, select the animated object, click the Trigger button, and then click the checked object on the menu.

▶ 2. Click the unlit bulb. The light bulb appears to turn on as the lit version of the light bulb graphic appears on top of the unlit version.

**Trouble?** If Slide 3 ("Year-Round") appears instead of the lit bulb appearing on Slide 2, you clicked the slide area instead of clicking the light bulb. Press the Backspace key to redisplay Slide 2, and then click the unlit bulb graphic.

▶ 3. Press **ESC** to end the presentation.

▶ 4. In the Selection pane, click the **Close** button ✖, and then save the changes to the presentation.

## Insight

### Using Bookmarks as Triggers and Using the Seek Animation

When you add bookmarks to video and audio objects, you can click the bookmarks to jump to that point in the clip or set the bookmark to trigger an animation. For example, if you want to skip the first part of a clip, but you don't want to trim the clip, you can click the bookmark to start playback at a point in the middle of the clip. Another example is if you add a video with a bookmark and a text box containing the title of the video to a slide, you could set the bookmark to be a trigger for an entrance animation applied to the text box containing the title. To add a bookmark, first identify the pointer where you want to insert the bookmark by clicking the video or audio toolbar, or by playing the clip and then clicking the Pause button when it reaches the point where you want the bookmark inserted. Then, on the Playback tab for the object, in the Bookmarks group, click the Add Bookmark button. The Remove Bookmark button is in the same group if you no longer need the bookmark.

When a video or audio object has a bookmark, the Seek animation in the Media section is available on the Animations tab. You can use this if you want to play the beginning and end of a clip but skip the middle. To use the Seek animation, insert bookmarks at the beginning and end of the section you want to skip. Select the bookmark at the end of the section you want to clip, and then apply the Seek animation to it. Then set the bookmark at the beginning of the section that you want to clip as a trigger for the Seek animation.

# Changing the Slide Background

The background of a slide can be as important as the foreground when you are creating a presentation with a strong visual impact. To change the background, you use the Format Background pane. When you change the background, you are essentially changing the fill of the background. The commands are the same as the commands you use when you change the fill of a shape. For example, you can change the color, add a gradient or a pattern, or fill it with a texture or a picture.

## Reference

### Modify the Slide Background

- On the Design tab, in the Variants group, click the More button, point to Background styles, and then click a style to apply that background to all of the slides in the presentation.

*or*

- On the Design tab, in the Customize group, click the Format Background button to open the Format Background pane with the Fill button selected and the Fill section expanded.
- Click one of the fill option buttons to select the type of fill you want to use.
- Use the option buttons, menus, and sliders that appear to customize the selected fill option.
- To apply the background to all the slides in the presentation, click Apply to All.

The entire background of Slide 1 is light blue. The layout applied to the rest of the slides includes a white box below the text or pictures in the content placeholder on the right side of the slide. On those slides, the light blue background shows only on the left side of the slide.

On Slide 2, the light blue background makes it difficult to see the unlit light bulb. Jack wants you to change the color of the slide background so that this is not a problem. Then he wants you to apply that background to all of the slides to give the presentation a consistent look.

### To change the fill of the slide background:

1. With Slide 2 ("Ideas") displayed, click the **Design** tab.

2. In the Variants group, click the **More** button ⩒, and then on the menu, point to **Background Styles**. A gallery of color choices appears. See Figure 4–9.

**Figure 4-9** Background Styles gallery

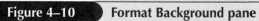

Arina P Habich/Shutterstock.com; Love Silhouette/Shutterstock.com; fokke baarssen/Shutterstock.com; iStock.com/
AzmanJaka; Vicki L. Miller/Shutterstock.com; gvictoria/Shutterstock.com

3. On the menu, click **Style 2** (the second style in the first row). The light blue
   background on the slides changes to the style you selected. Slide 2 is one of
   the slides that has a layout with a white rectangle on the right, so only the left
   side of this slide changed color. Jack thinks this color is a little dark.

4. On the Design tab, in the Customize group, click the **Format Background**
   button. The Format Background pane opens. See Figure 4-10. This pane
   has only one button—the Fill button—and one section of commands—the
   Fill section. It contains the same commands as the Fill section in the Format
   Shape pane. The Solid fill option button is selected, indicating that the
   current background has a solid fill.

**Figure 4-10** Format Background pane

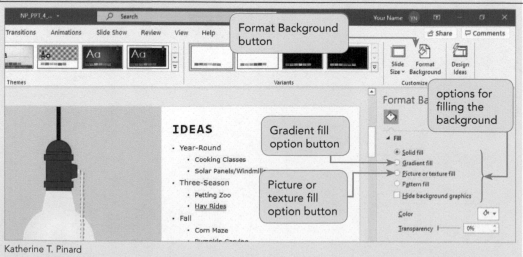

Katherine T. Pinard

5. In the pane, click the **Gradient fill** option button. The background of Slide 2 changes to a gradient fill with the color varying from green to a light yellow orange. Jack wants the background to be a solid green color, but a little lighter than the color that was applied when you changed the background style.

6. In the pane, click the **Solid fill** option button, click the **Color** button, and then click the **Light Green, Background 2, Lighter 40%** color. The background of Slide 2 changes to the green color you selected.

7. At the bottom of the Format Background pane, click **Apply to All**. The light green background is applied to all of the slides in the presentation.

Jack wants the title slide to have a different background than the rest of the slides. You can fill the slide background with a picture, or you can tile the picture, which means to make the picture appear as repeating images across the slide. When you set an image to tile across the background, you can make the tiles smaller so that more tiles appear on the background.

You can also change the offset of a picture in the slide background. This means you can move the picture horizontally or vertically in the background.

You'll add a picture of a tractor as the slide background of Slide 1, and then you will tile it.

### To tile a picture in the background of Slide 1:

1. Display **Slide 1** (the title slide), and then in the Format Background pane, click the **Picture or texture fill** option button. The default texture is applied to the current slide background and the Format Background pane changes to include commands for inserting pictures. Below the Transparency slider, the Tile picture as texture check box is selected. Textures are made up of a picture that is sized much smaller than the slide and then repeated across and up and down the slide.

2. Click the **Tile picture as texture** check box. The check box is deselected, and the texture picture changes to fill the slide. The original picture that was tiled to create the texture background is very small, so when you deselect the Tile picture as texture option, the small image enlarges to fill the screen and is now blurry.

3. In the Picture source section of the pane, click the **Insert** button. The Insert Pictures dialog box opens. Click **From a File**. The Insert Picture dialog box opens.

4. Navigate to the **PowerPoint 4 > Module** folder, click **Support_PPT_4_ Tractor.png**, and then click **Insert**. A picture of a tractor fills the slide background of Slide 1. See Figure 4–11.

**Figure 4–11**   **Picture in background of Slide 1**

Heather Stokes/Shutterstock.com; Arina P Habich/Shutterstock.com; Love Silhouette/Shutterstock.com; fokke baarssen/
Shutterstock.com; iStock.com/AzmanJaka; Vicki L. Miller/Shutterstock.com; gvictoria/Shutterstock.com; iStock.com/
BanksPhotos; Jack Frog/Shutterstock.com; iStock.com/mediaphotos

5. In the pane, click the **Tile picture as texture** check box to select it. The picture changes to a series of tiles on the slide in three rows. You want four rows of tiles to appear, so you will change the scale.

6. To the right of **Scale Y** box, click the down arrow on the box until there are four rows of tractors on the slide and the box contains the value **80%**. Each tile was resized smaller vertically to fit the extra row of tractors on the slide. The aspect ratio was not maintained, but for this picture, that is fine. (If you needed to maintain the aspect ratio, you would change the Scale X value to the same percentage as the Scale Y value.) Now you will move the pictures sideways by changing the horizontal offset.

7. Click in the **Offset X** box, delete the value in it, type **85**, and then press **ENTER**. The tiles on the slide shift sideways so that the front half of a tractor appears on the left and the back half appears on the right.

8. Scroll to the bottom of the Format Background pane, click the **Mirror type** arrow, and then click **Horizontal**. Every other image is flipped horizontally to create mirror images. See Figure 4–12.

**Figure 4-12**    **Picture tiled in background of Slide 1 with a mirror effect**

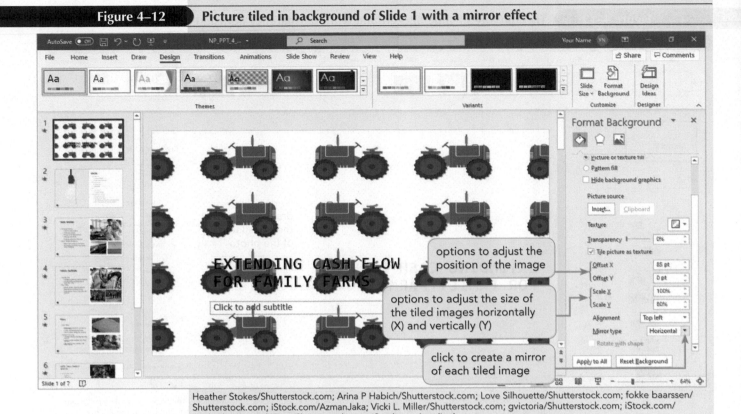

Heather Stokes/Shutterstock.com; Arina P Habich/Shutterstock.com; Love Silhouette/Shutterstock.com; fokke baarssen/
Shutterstock.com; iStock.com/AzmanJaka; Vicki L. Miller/Shutterstock.com; gvictoria/Shutterstock.com; iStock.com/
BanksPhotos; Jack Frog/Shutterstock.com; iStock.com/mediaphotos

The text on the slide is hard to see on the picture background. You could adjust
the brightness and the contrast of the photo, or you could make the photo more
transparent. You'll adjust the transparency of the photo now.

### To change the transparency of the background picture:

1. In the Format Background pane, drag the **Transparency** slider to the right
until the value in the Transparency box is 85%. Compare your screen to
Figure 4-13.

| Figure 4–13 | Tiled picture in slide background with transparency adjusted |

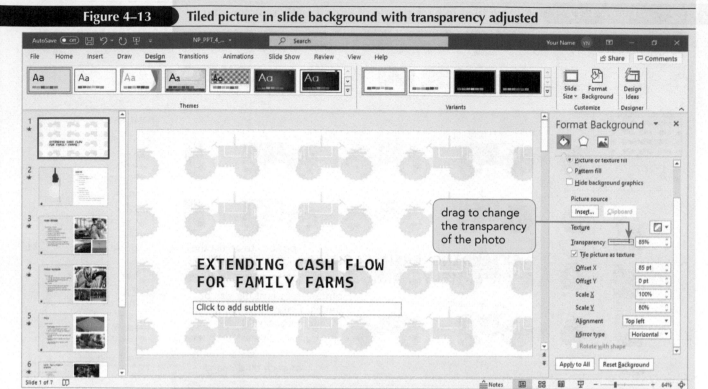

Heather Stokes/Shutterstock.com; Arina P Habich/Shutterstock.com; Love Silhouette/Shutterstock.com; fokke baarssen/
Shutterstock.com; iStock.com/AzmanJaka; Vicki L. Miller/Shutterstock.com; gvictoria/Shutterstock.com; iStock.com/
BanksPhotos; Jack Frog/Shutterstock.com; iStock.com/mediaphotos

**Trouble?** If you can't position the slider so that 85% appears in the Transparency box, click the up or down arrows in the Transparency box as needed to change the value.

The slide appears somewhat gray. This is because the Office theme is set to Colorful. When the slide is displayed during a slide show, the space between the images will be white.

2. On the status bar, click the **Slide Show** button. Slide 1 appears in Slide Show view, and the space between the images is white, not gray. The text is easy to read in Slide Show view.

3. Press **ESC** to end the slide show, and then close the Format Background pane.

4. Save the changes to the presentation.

## Insight

### Hiding Background Graphics

Some themes include graphics as part of the slide background. If you need to print slides with graphics in the background in black and white or grayscale, you might want to remove those graphics before printing the slides because the graphics could make the text difficult to read. To hide graphics in the background, select the Hide background graphics check box in the Format Background pane. Note that selecting this option will not hide anything you use as a fill for the background, such as the picture you added as the background in this module.

# Creating and Editing Links

If you've visited webpages on the Internet, you have clicked links (sometimes called "hyperlinks") to "jump to"—or display—other webpages or files. In PowerPoint, a link on a slide accomplishes the same thing. You can convert any text or object on a slide to a link to another slide in the same presentation, to a different file, or to a webpage. A link can be customized to do several other actions as well.

To create a link from text or a shape, you use the Link button or the Action button in the Links group on the Insert tab. You can use either button to create most types of links; however, the Action Settings dialog box allows you to also run a macro (which is a predefined set of instructions). In addition, when you use the Action button, you can create a link that responds when you simply point to it rather than click it, plays a sound when you click it or point to it, and highlights the link in some way when you click it or point to it.

## Creating and Editing Text Links

As you know, when you type a webpage or an email address, it is automatically converted to a link. If you want, you can change the text that appears on the slide. For example, if you type a webpage address and it is converted to a link, you can change the text of the link to the name of the webpage.

You can also convert any text on a slide to a link. Text links are usually underlined and a different color than the rest of the text on a slide. After you click a text link during a slide show, the link changes to another color to indicate that it has been clicked, or followed.

Slide 7 contains Jack's email address formatted as a link. You can edit this link so that the text displayed on the slide is Jack's name instead of his email address.

**To change the text displayed for a link:**

▶ 1. Display Slide 7 ("Contact Info"), and then move the pointer on top of the email address. The ScreenTip that appears shows the "mailto" instruction followed by Jack's email address. (The "mailto" instruction causes your email app to start and create a new email message addressed to the email address when you click the link.)

▶ 2. Click anywhere in the email address link on the slide, click the **Insert** tab, and then in the Links group, click the **Link** button. The Edit Hyperlink dialog box opens. In the Link to list on the left, the E-mail Address option is selected. The email address, preceded by the "mailto" instruction, appears in the E-mail address box. In addition, the email address that appears on the slide is in the Text to display box at the top of the dialog box. See Figure 4–14.

**Figure 4–14**     Edit Hyperlink dialog box for a link to an email address

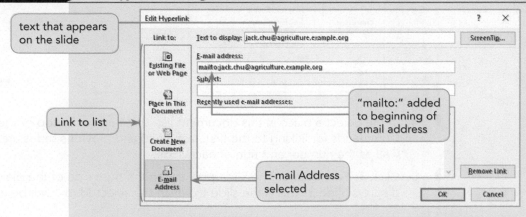

> **3.** Click in the **Text to display** box, delete all the text, and then type **Jack Chu**.

> **4.** Click **OK**. The dialog box closes, and the email address on Slide 7 changes to the text you typed in the Edit Hyperlink dialog box, Jack Chu.

> **5.** Move the pointer on top of **Jack Chu**. The ScreenTip that appears still shows Jack's email address.

Slide 2 in Jack's presentation is an overview slide. Each first-level bulleted item on this slide names another slide in the presentation. Jack wants you to convert each first-level bulleted item to a link that links to the related slide. One way to create links is to use the Insert Hyperlink dialog box.

### To create a link using the Insert Hyperlink dialog box:

> **1.** Display Slide 2 ("Ideas"), and then in the first bulleted item, drag across the text **Year-Round**. The text is selected.

> **2.** Click the **Insert** tab, if necessary, and then in the Links group, click the **Link** button. The Insert Hyperlink dialog box opens. In the Link to list on the left, the E-mail Address option is selected. You need to identify the file or location to which you want to link. In this case, you're going to link to a slide in the current presentation. If you wanted to link to another file on your computer or network, you would click the Existing File or Web Page button. If you wanted to create a new PowerPoint file when you clicked the link, you would click the Create New Document button.

> **3.** In the Link to list on the left, click **Place in This Document**. The dialog box changes to show the Select a place in this document box, listing all the slides in the presentation. See Figure 4–15.

**Figure 4–15** **Insert Hyperlink dialog box with list of slides in this presentation**

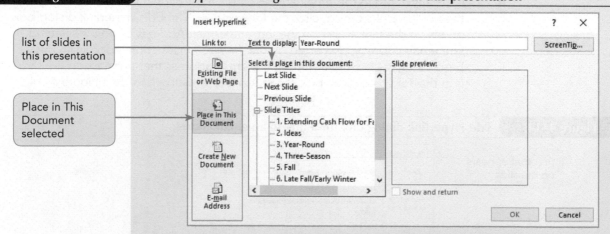

> **4.** In the Select a place in this document list, scroll up to the top of the list. Commands for linking to the first, last, next, and previous slides are listed, as well as the number and title of each slide.

> **5.** Click **3. Year-Round**. The Slide preview on the right side of the dialog box displays Slide 3. This is the slide to which the selected text will be linked.

6. Click **OK**, and then click a blank area of the slide to deselect the text. The text of the first bullet is now a link and is formatted as light-blue and underlined.

You can also create a link using the Action Settings dialog box. You'll create the link to the Three-Season slide using the Action button on the Insert tab.

### To create a link using the Action Settings dialog box:

1. Drag across the text **Three-Season** to select it.

2. On the Insert tab, in the Links group, click the **Action** button. The Action Settings dialog box opens with the Mouse Click tab selected. See Figure 4–16.

**Figure 4–16**   Action Settings dialog box

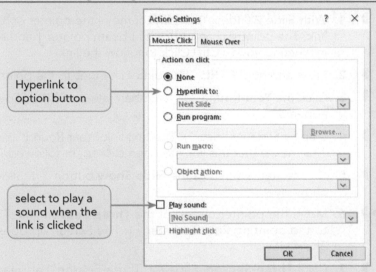

3. In the Action on click section, click the **Hyperlink to** option button. The Hyperlink to box becomes available, and lists the default option, Next Slide.

4. Click the **Hyperlink to** arrow. The commands on the list allow you to create links to the same things you can link to using the Insert Hyperlink dialog box. You want to link to a specific slide in the current presentation.

5. Click **Slide**. The Hyperlink to Slide dialog box opens listing all the slides in the presentation. See Figure 4–17.

**Tip**

Click the Mouse Over tab to create a link that you only need to point to in order to display the linked slide or file.

**Figure 4–17**   Hyperlink to Slide dialog box

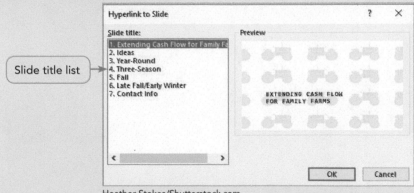

Heather Stokes/Shutterstock.com

6. Click **4. Three-Season**, and then click **OK**. The Hyperlink to Slide dialog box closes and "Three-Season" appears in the Hyperlink to box.

7. Click **OK**. The dialog box closes, and the second bulleted item is formatted as a link.

8. Change the next two first-level bulleted items to links to Slides 5 and 6 respectively, using either the Link or the Action button.

Now you need to test the text links you created. You can press and hold CTRL while you click a text link in Normal view, or you can switch to Slide Show view and then just click the text link.

## To test the links:

1. With Slide 2 ("Ideas") displayed, move the pointer on top of the Year-Round link. The pointer changes to the I-beam pointer $\text{I}$ and a ScreenTip appears instructing you to Ctrl+Click to follow the link.

2. Press and hold **CTRL**. The pointer changes to the pointing finger pointer ☝.

3. Click the **Year-Round** link, and then release **CTRL**. Slide 3 ("Year-Round") appears.

4. Display Slide 2 ("Ideas"). The text link "Year-Round" is now grayish-green. This means that this link has been clicked, or followed.

5. On the status bar, click the **Slide Show** button ☐. Slide 2 appears in Slide Show view.

6. Move the pointer on top of the **Three-Season** link. The pointer changes to the pointing finger pointer ☝. The ScreenTip does not appear in Slide Show view.

7. Click **Three-Season**. Slide 4 ("Three-Season") appears in Slide Show view using the Push transition. (The bulleted list and the pictures do not appear on the slide because you applied entrance animations whose start setting is On Click.)

8. Right-click anywhere on the slide, and then on the shortcut menu, click **Last Viewed**. Slide 2 ("Ideas") appears in Slide Show view also using the Push transition. The first two bulleted items are now grayish-green, indicating that the links have been followed. See Figure 4–18.

**Tip**

To show a ScreenTip in Slide Show view, click the ScreenTip button in the Insert Hyperlink dialog box, and then type the ScreenTip in the box.

Figure 4–18   **Followed and unfollowed links on Slide 2 in Slide Show view**

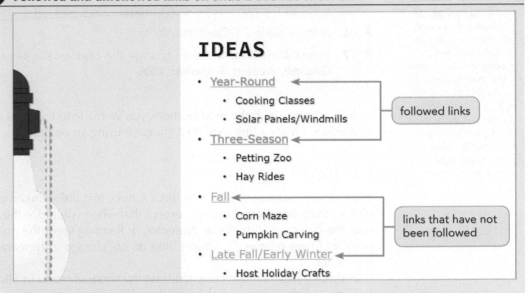

**9.** Click each of the other two links to verify that they link to the correct slides, using the Last Viewed command on the shortcut menu to return to Slide 2 each time.

**10.** Press **ESC** to end the slide show. Slide 2 appears in Normal view. The links are now all grayish-green. They changed color because they have been clicked—followed—during a slide show. They will reset to the light-blue color when you close and reopen the presentation.

**Trouble?** If Slide 2 is not displayed, you did not return to Slide 2 in the Slide Show after clicking the last link. Display Slide 2.

## Changing the Color of Text Links

You can change the color of text links in the same manner you change the color of any text. If you do this, however, the color of followed links will be the same color you choose for the color of unfollowed links.

Jack thinks that both the light-blue color of unfollowed links and the grayish-green color of followed links are hard to see. You'll change the color of the links.

**To change the color of text links:**

**1.** On Slide 2 ("Ideas"), select the text **Year-Round**, press and hold **CTRL**, select **Three-Season**, **Fall**, and **Late Fall/Early Winter**, and then release **CTRL**. All of the text links are selected.

**2.** Click the **Home** tab, and then in the Font group, click the **Font color arrow** A ˅. The palette of colors applied to this presentation appears.

**3.** On the menu, click the **Orange, Accent 3, Darker 25%**, and then click a blank area of the slide. The four text links are now the orange color you selected.

**4.** Click a blank area of the slide, press and hold **CTRL**, and then click the **Year-Round** link. Slide 3 ("Year-Round") appears.

**Tip**

To change the color of a followed link as well, you need to customize the color palette by clicking the More button in the Variants group on the Design tab, clicking Colors, clicking Customize Colors, clicking the Hyperlink and the Followed Hyperlink buttons, and then selecting new colors.

▶ **5.** Display Slide 2 ("Ideas"). On Slide 2, the Year-Round link is still the same color as the other links, even though you clicked it.

▶ **6.** Display Slide 7 ("Contact Info").

▶ **7.** Select **Jack Chu**, and then change the color of the selected link text to **Orange, Accent 3, Darker 25%**.

Jack is happy with the modifications you've made to the presentation so far. Next he asks you to create a link to Slide 2 ("Ideas") using an object.

## Creating Object Links

You can also convert objects into links. Unlike text links, linked objects are not visually distinct from non-linked objects, except that when you move the mouse pointer over the object in Slide Show, Presenter, or Reading view, the pointer changes to the pointing finger pointer 🖑. Object links do not change in appearance after they have been clicked.

Although Jack can use commands on the shortcut menu in Slide Show view to return to Slide 2 after clicking a link to another slide, it would be easier for him to navigate during the slide show if you added a link to Slide 2 on each slide. You'll do this now by adding a shape that you format as a link on Slides 3 through 6.

**To create a shape and format it as a link:**

▶ **1.** Display **Slide 3** ("Year-Round"), and then click the **Insert** tab.

▶ **2.** In the Illustrations group, click the **Shapes** button, and then in the Rectangles group, click the **Rectangle: Rounded Corners** shape.

▶ **3.** Click below the bulleted list to insert the shape, resize it so it is one-half inch high and 1.2 inches wide, and then using the smart guides that appear, position it so that the shape's right edge aligns with the right edge of the bulleted list text box and its bottom edge aligns with the bottom edge of the slide number.

▶ **4.** With the shape selected, type **IDEAS**, and then format the text as bold.

▶ **5.** Click the outside of the shape to select the entire shape, then, on the ribbon, click the **Shape Format** tab if necessary.

▶ **6.** In the Shape Styles group, click the **More** button 🔽, and then in the Presets section, click the **Transparent, Colored Outline – Orange, Accent 3** style. See Figure 4–19.

**Figure 4–19**   **IDEAS shape on Slide 3**

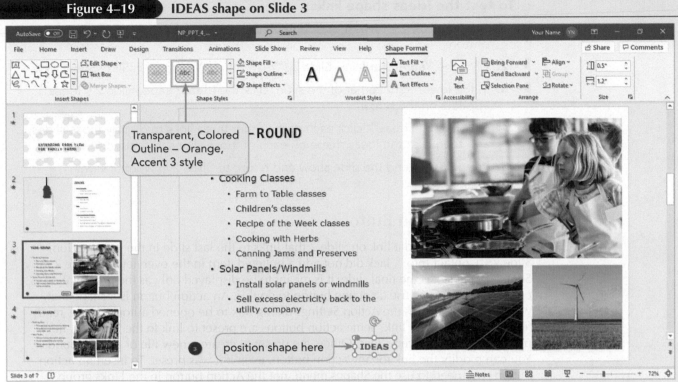

7. On the ribbon, click the **Insert** tab.

8. With the shape selected, in the Links group, click the **Link** button. The Insert Hyperlink dialog box opens. Because Slide 2 is the previous slide, you could select the Previous Slide location instead of clicking the slide number. However, you will be copying this link to other slides, so you will link specifically to Slide 2.

9. With Place in This Document selected in the Link to list, click **2. Ideas** in the Select a place in this document list, and then click **OK**. The shape does not look any different now that it is a link. You want the same link to appear on Slides 4, 5, and 6. You can insert a shape on each slide and format it as a link, or you can copy the shape on Slide 3 and paste it on each slide.

10. With the **IDEAS** shape selected, click the **Home** tab, and then in the Clipboard group, click the **Copy** button.

11. Display **Slide 4** ("Three-Season"), and then in the Clipboard group, click the **Paste** button. A copy of the IDEAS link appears in the lower-right corner of the slide—the same position it was in on Slide 3.

12. Paste the IDEAS link onto Slide 5 ("Fall") and Slide 6 ("Late Fall/Early Winter").

You need to test the Ideas links. As with text links, you can test object links in Normal or Slide Show view.

**To test the Ideas shape links:**

▶ 1. Display Slide 2 ("Ideas"), and then on the status bar, click the **Slide Show** button 🖵.

▶ 2. Click the **Year-Round** link. Slide 3 ("Year-Round") appears in Slide Show view.

▶ 3. In the lower-right corner of the slide, click the **Ideas** shape. Slide 2 ("Ideas") appears on the screen.

▶ 4. On Slide 2 ("Ideas"), click each of the other three links to display those slides, and then click the Ideas shape on each of those slides to return to Slide 2.

▶ 5. Press **ESC** to end the slide show and return to Slide 2 in Normal view.

## Inserting Action Buttons

Jack wants you to add a link on Slide 2 that links to the last slide in the presentation, Slide 7 ("Contact Info"). Jack did not add a bulleted item in the overview on Slide 2 for Slide 7 because, as the final slide, it is meant to be displayed only as the presentation is concluding. You will use an action button to do this. An action button is a shape that, when inserted, causes the Action Settings dialog box to be opened automatically, ready for you to specify the link. Some action buttons are preset to link to the first, last, next, previous, or last viewed slides. Others are preset to create a new file or play a sound. You can modify the link for any action button, even if it was preset. To insert an action button, you need to use the Shapes menu, not the Action button in the Links group.

**To insert an action button on Slide 2:**

▶ 1. With Slide 2 ("Ideas") displayed, on the ribbon, click the **Insert** tab.

▶ 2. In the Illustrations group, click the **Shapes** button, scroll to the bottom of the gallery, and then in the Action Buttons section, click the **Action Button: Go to End** shape.

▶ 3. Click near the bottom-right corner of the slide. The action button is inserted, and the Action Settings dialog box opens. The Hyperlink to option button is selected, and Last Slide appears in the Hyperlink to box.

▶ 4. Click **OK**. On the Shape Format tab, in the Shape Styles group, the Colored Fill – Gold, Accent 1 style is selected.

▶ 5. Resize the action button so it is one-half inch high and one inch wide, position it in the lower-right corner of the slide so its right edge aligns with the right edge of the bulleted list text box and its bottom edge aligns with the bottom of the slide number, and then click a blank area of the slide to deselect the button. Compare your screen to Figure 4–20.

**Figure 4–20**    Action button on Slide 2

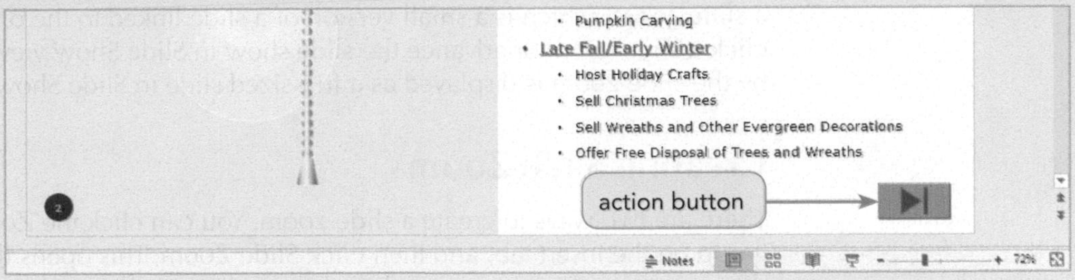

Katherine T. Pinard

Now you need to test the new link. Unlike the other links you have created, you can test action buttons only in Slide Show view.

**To test the action button:**

1. On Slide 2 ("Ideas"), move the pointer on top of the action button. The pointer changes to the move pointer ⁺↖, not the I-beam pointer Ⅰ or the pointing finger pointer 🖑. This means that you cannot click it to follow the link.

2. On the status bar, click the **Slide Show** button 🖵. Slide 2 ("Ideas") appears in Slide Show view.

3. Move the pointer on top of the action button. The pointer changes to the pointing finger pointer 🖑.

4. Click the action button. Slide 7 ("Contact Info") appears.

5. Press **ESC** to end the slide show. Slide 7 appears in Normal view.

6. Save the changes to the presentation.

# Insight

### Linking to Another File

You can create a link to another file so that when you click the link during a slide show, the other file opens. The other file can be any file type; it doesn't need to be a PowerPoint file. To create a link to another file, open the Insert Hyperlink dialog box, click Existing File or Web Page in the Link to list, and then click the Browse for File button. To change the link destination of an action button to another file, open the Action Settings dialog box, click the Hyperlink to option button, click the Hyperlink to arrow, and then click Other PowerPoint Presentation or Other File. For either type of link, a dialog box opens in which you can navigate to the location of the file.

When you create a link to another file, the linked file is not included within the PowerPoint file; only the original path and filename to the files on the computer where you created the links are stored in the presentation. Therefore, if you need to show the presentation on another computer, you must copy linked files as well as the PowerPoint presentation file to the other computer, and then you need to edit the path to the linked file so that PowerPoint can find the file in its new location. To update the path for a link or action button, right-click it, and then click Edit Link on the shortcut menu to open the Edit Hyperlink or the Action Settings dialog box.

# Creating Slide Zooms

Instead of creating text or shape links to other slides in a presentation, you can create a **slide zoom**, which is a small version of a slide linked to the original slide. When you click a slide zoom or advance the slide show in Slide Show view, the slide represented by the slide zoom is displayed as a full-sized slide in Slide Show view.

## Creating Slide Zooms

There are two ways to create a slide zoom. You can click the Zoom button in the Links group on the Insert tab, and then click Slide Zoom. This opens the Insert Slide Zoom dialog box in which you can select the check boxes below the slides you want to insert. Or you can drag a slide thumbnail from the pane that contains the thumbnails onto a slide in Normal view.

When you select a slide zoom, the Zoom contextual tab appears on the ribbon. This tab contains many of the same commands as the Picture Format tab. For example, you can resize a slide zoom or apply a style, border, or effect to it. In addition, you can use the Zoom Background command to remove the background of the slide zoom so that you see the background of the slide that the slide zoom is on.

# Reference

### Inserting Slide Zooms

- Display the slide you want to insert the slide zooms on, and then click the Insert tab.
- In the Links group, click the Zoom button, and then click Slide Zoom.
- In the Insert Slide Zoom dialog box, click the check boxes below the slides you want to create a slide zoom for, and then click Insert.

*or*

- Display the slide you want to insert the slide zooms on, and then in Normal view, drag a thumbnail from the pane on the left onto the slide.

Jack wants you to create another version of the "Ideas" slide that contains slide zooms of the same four slides that the bulleted items on Slide 2 link to.

**To create slide zooms:**

1. Duplicate Slide 2 ("Ideas"). A copy of Slide 2 is inserted as a new Slide 3 and is the current slide. Jack wants you to keep Slide 3 as it is and add the slide zooms to Slide 2.

2. Display Slide 2, click anywhere on the bulleted list, click the text box outline, and then press **DELETE**. The text is deleted, and the content placeholder text and icons appear.

3. Click the border of the content placeholder, press **DELETE**, and then click the **Insert** tab. Now you will insert the slide zooms.

4. In the Links group, click the **Zoom** button, and then click **Slide Zoom**. The Insert Slide Zoom dialog box appears. See Figure 4–21.

**Figure 4–21**  Insert Slide Zoom dialog box

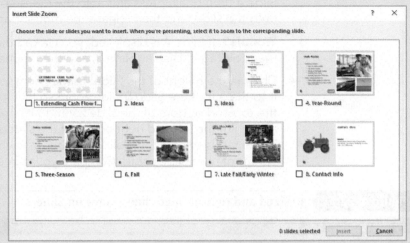

Heather Stokes/Shutterstock.com; Arina P Habich/Shutterstock.com; Love Silhouette/Shutterstock.com; fokke baarssen/ Shutterstock.com; iStock.com/AzmanJaka; Vicki L. Miller/Shutterstock.com; gvictoria/Shutterstock.com; iStock.com/ BanksPhotos; Jack Frog/Shutterstock.com; iStock.com/mediaphotos; iStock.com/FlamingPumpkin; ND700/Shutterstock.com/ Katherine T. Pinard

5. In the dialog box, click the **5. Three-Season** check box, the **6. Fall** check box, and the **7. Late Fall/Early Winter** check box. The three check boxes you clicked are selected.

6. Click **Insert**. The dialog box closes, and three slides you selected appear in the center of Slide 2 as slide zooms. On the ribbon, the Zoom contextual tab appears.

7. Click the **Zoom** tab. The Size group shows that the height of each selected slide zoom is 1.88 inches, and the width is 3.33 inches.

8. In the Size group, click in the **Height** box, type **1.7**, and then press **ENTER**. The height changes to the measurement you typed. The width also changed. This is because the aspect ratio is locked for slide zooms.

9. Click a blank area of the slide to deselect the slide zooms, and then display the gridlines and the ruler.

10. Drag the slide zoom on the top of the stack down and to the right so that its top edge aligns with the gridline at the negative 1-inch mark on the vertical ruler and its right edge aligns with the right edge of the title text box and the action button.

   **Trouble?** If you have trouble aligning the top of the slide zoom with the gridline, press and hold ALT while you are positioning the slide zoom.

11. Drag the next slide zoom on the stack down and position it to the left of the first slide zoom that you positioned so that its top edge aligns with the negative 1-inch mark on the vertical ruler and so that its right edge is one gridline dot away from the slide zoom you already positioned.

12. Drag the third slide zoom to the right so its left and right edges align with the left and right edges of the slide zoom on the bottom-right and so its top edge aligns with the gridline at the 2-inch mark on the vertical ruler. You still need to add a slide zoom of Slide 4. You will insert the last slide zoom by dragging the thumbnail of Slide 4 onto Slide 2.

**Tip**

To unlock or lock the aspect ratio of objects, click the Dialog Box launcher in the Size group on the object's contextual Format tab, and then in the Format pane that opens, click the Lock aspect ratio check box.

**13.** In the pane containing the slide thumbnails, move the pointer on top of the Slide 4 thumbnail, press and hold the mouse button, drag the thumbnail onto the slide, and then release the mouse button.

**Trouble?** If Slide 4 is displayed, you clicked the Slide 4 thumbnail before you tried to drag it. Display Slide 2, and then repeat Step 13.

**14.** Change the height of the Slide 4 slide zoom to **1.7** inches, and then position it to the left of the Slide 5 slide zoom so that its top and bottom align with the top and bottom of the slide zoom to its right and its left and right edges align with the left and right edges of the slide zoom below it. When the Zoom tab is selected, the slide number of each slide is in the lower-right corner of each slide zoom. Compare your screen to Figure 4–22.

**Figure 4–22** **Resized and repositioned slide zooms on Slide 2**

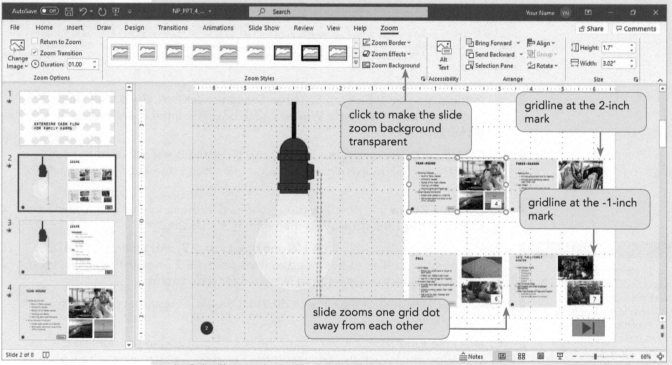

Heather Stokes/Shutterstock.com; Arina P Habich/Shutterstock.com; Love Silhouette/Shutterstock.com; fokke baarssen/ Shutterstock.com; iStock.com/AzmanJaka; Vicki L. Miller/Shutterstock.com; gvictoria/Shutterstock.com; iStock.com/ BanksPhotos; Jack Frog/Shutterstock.com; iStock.com/mediaphotos; iStock.com/FlamingPumpkin; ND700/Shutterstock.com/ Katherine T. Pinard

**15.** Hide the gridlines and the ruler.

Now you will test the slide zoom links. Slide zooms are similar to action buttons in that you cannot test them in Normal view. You need to switch to Slide Show view.

### To test the slide zooms:

**1.** On Slide 2 (the "Ideas" slide with the slide zooms), move the pointer on top of one of the slide zooms. The pointer changes to the move pointer ✛. This is because you cannot test the link in Normal view.

2. On the Quick Access Toolbar, click the **Start from Beginning** button 🖳. Slide 1 (the title slide) appears in Slide Show view with the Push transition.

3. Click anywhere on the slide to display Slide 2 (the "Ideas" slide with the zoom slides), and then move the pointer on top of the **Year-Round** slide zoom (the first slide zoom in the first row). The pointer changes to the pointing finger pointer 👆.

4. Click the **Year-Round** zoom slide. The slide zoom you clicked zooms larger and fills the screen.

5. Press **SPACEBAR**. The view slides out, sideways, and then back in so that the Slide 5 ("Three-Season") slide zoom fills the screen. As Slide 5 slides onto the screen, the bulleted list and images fade away because they have entrance animations applied.

6. Click twice anywhere on the slide except on the IDEAS link to display the slide content, and then click one more time to move to the next slide. The view shifts down and to the left so that the Slide 6 ("Fall") slide zoom fills the screen.

7. Press **SPACEBAR** to slide the view sideways so that Slide 7 ("Late Fall/Early Winter") slide zoom fills the screen. This is the last slide zoom.

8. Press **SPACEBAR**. Slide 8 ("Contact Info") appears with the Push transition.

9. Press **BACKSPACE**. Slide 7 ("Late Fall/Early Winter") appears on the screen with the Push transition. This is the actual Slide 7, not the linked slide zoom on Slide 3.

10. Press **SPACEBAR** to display Slide 8, press **SPACEBAR** again to display the black slide that signals the end of the slide show, and then press **SPACEBAR** one more time to display Slide 8 in Normal view.

## Modifying Slide Zooms

As you saw, the default transition for slide zooms is for the slide zoom to slide into view based on where it is located on the slide that contains the slide zooms. This is what happened when you tested the slide zooms you inserted on Slide 3. You can change this so that clicking a slide zoom will display the slide using whatever transition is applied to that slide instead of the slide zoom transition.

Another setting you can change is what happens when you advance the slide show when a slide zoom is displayed. The default is for the next slide to appear when you advance the slide show. You can change this so that after you click the slide zoom to display it, the next click or pressing SPACEBAR causes the slide that contains the slide zoom to reappear.

Finally, you can change the speed with which the next slide zoom or slide appears by changing the duration of the zoom. You will change some of the settings applied to the slide zooms on Slide 2.

### To modify the slide zooms on Slide 2:

1. Display Slide 2 (the "Ideas" slide with the slide zooms) if necessary, click the **Slide 4** ("Year-Round") slide zoom, and then click the **Zoom** tab. See Figure 4–23.

**Figure 4–23** Zoom Options group on the Zoom contextual tab

click to have the selected slide zoom return to this slide instead of moving to the next slide zoom or slide

click to change the image used for the slide zoom

when Zoom Transition is selected, use this to change the speed of the zoom effect

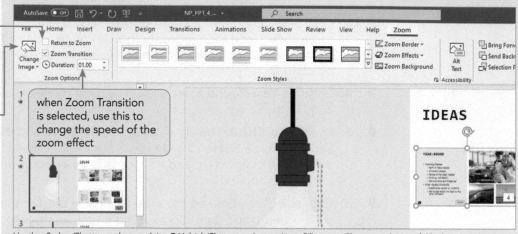

Heather Stokes/Shutterstock.com; Arina P Habich/Shutterstock.com; Love Silhouette/Shutterstock.com; fokke baarssen/Shutterstock.com; iStock.com/AzmanJaka; Vicki L. Miller/Shutterstock.com; gvictoria/Shutterstock.com; iStock.com/BanksPhotos; Jack Frog/Shutterstock.com; iStock.com/mediaphotos; iStock.com/FlamingPumpkin; ND700/Shutterstock.com/Katherine T. Pinard

**Tip**

To change the image used for a zoom slide, in the Zoom Options group, click the Change Image button to open the Insert Pictures window. The image you select replaces the image shown as the zoom slide, but when you zoom into that slide, you will see the slide contents.

2. In the Zoom Options group, click the **Zoom Transition** check box to deselect it.

3. Click the **Slide 5** ("Three-Season") slide zoom, and then in the Zoom Options group, click the **Duration** box down arrow to change the value to **0.75** seconds.

4. Click the **Slide 6** ("Fall") slide zoom, and then in the Zoom Options group, click the **Return to Zoom** check box to select it. An arrow appears next to the slide number on the slide zoom to indicate that advancing the slide show after displaying this slide zoom will cause Slide 2 to reappear.

5. On the status bar, click the **Slide Show** button 🖵. Slide 2 appears in Slide Show view.

6. Click the **Slide 4** ("Year-Round") slide zoom. Because you deselected the Zoom Transition check box for this slide zoom, Slide 4 ("Year-Round") appears on the screen with the Push transition.

7. Press **SPACEBAR**. Because the Zoom Transition check box is still selected for the Slide 5 ("Three-Season") slide zoom, this slide appears using the zoom transition. It appears a little faster than it did in the last set of steps because you changed the time from one second to three-quarters of a second.

8. Press **SPACEBAR** three times to display Slide 6 ("Fall") with the zoom transition, and then press **SPACEBAR** again. Slide 2 (the "Ideas" slide with the slide zooms on it) appears. This is because you selected the Return to Zoom check box for the Slide 6 ("Fall") slide zoom.

9. Press **ESC** to end the slide show. Now that you've seen how the different zoom options affect the slide show, you will adjust them so that they are the same.

10. Click the **Slide 4** ("Year-Round") slide zoom, click the **Zoom** tab, click the **Zoom Transition** check box in the Zoom Options group to select it, and then change the duration to **0.75** seconds.

**11.** Click the **Slide 6** ("Fall") slide zoom, click the **Return to Zoom** check box to deselect it, and then change the duration to **0.75** seconds. You will apply the same settings to the Slide 7 slide zoom, except you will also select the Return to Zoom check box. This is because the Slide 7 slide zoom is the last slide zoom and Jack wants to provide the opportunity to display any of the four idea slides again.

**12.** Click the **Slide 7** ("Late Fall/Early Winter") slide zoom, change the duration to **0.75** seconds, and then click the **Return to Zoom** check box to select it.

**13.** Start the slide show from Slide 2 (the "Ideas" slide with the slide zooms), click the **Slide 4** ("Year-Round") slide zoom, press the **SPACEBAR** five times to display Slide 7 ("Late Fall/Early Winter"), wait for the wreaths to roll onto the slide, and then press **SPACEBAR** again. Slide 2 appears again.

**14.** On Slide 2, click the action button in the lower-right corner of the slide. Slide 8 ("Contact Info") appears.

**15.** Press **ESC**, and then save the changes to the presentation.

## Hiding a Slide

There are now two slides titled "Ideas" in the presentation and both contain a way to jump to the same slides. Jack wants to keep both slides in the presentation, but for now, he wants to use the Ideas slide that contains the zoom slides. He asks you to hide the other "Ideas" slide. When you hide a slide, you can still see it and edit it in Normal view, but it will not appear in Slide Show view.

**To hide Slide 3:**

**1.** Display Slide 3 (the "Ideas" slide with the text links).

**2.** Click the **Slide Show** tab, and then in the Set Up group, click the **Hide Slide** button. The Hide Slide button is selected. In the pane containing the slide thumbnails, a slash appears through the slide number for Slide 3 and that thumbnail appears somewhat faded. See Figure 4–24.

**Tip**

You can also right-click a slide thumbnail, and then click Hide Slide on the shortcut menu.

**Figure 4–24** **Slide 3 hidden**

Hide Slide button

Slide 3 marked as hidden

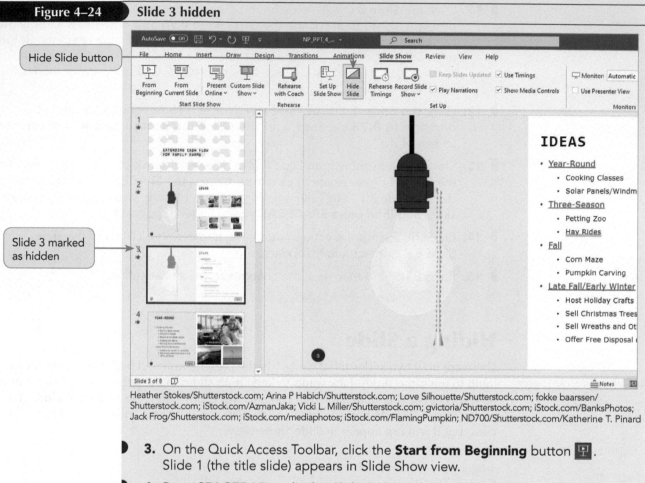

Heather Stokes/Shutterstock.com; Arina P Habich/Shutterstock.com; Love Silhouette/Shutterstock.com; fokke baarssen/Shutterstock.com; iStock.com/AzmanJaka; Vicki L. Miller/Shutterstock.com; gvictoria/Shutterstock.com; iStock.com/BanksPhotos; Jack Frog/Shutterstock.com; iStock.com/mediaphotos; iStock.com/FlamingPumpkin; ND700/Shutterstock.com/Katherine T. Pinard

3. On the Quick Access Toolbar, click the **Start from Beginning** button. Slide 1 (the title slide) appears in Slide Show view.

4. Press **SPACEBAR** to display Slide 2 (the "Ideas" slide with the zoom slides), and then press **SPACEBAR** again. Slide 4 ("Year-Round") appears. Slide 3, the hidden slide, was skipped.

5. Press **ESC** to end the slide show.

6. **sam ↑** On Slide 1 (the title slide), add your name as the subtitle, save the changes to the presentation, and then close it.

Jack is happy with the modifications you've made to the presentation so far. You modified motion path animations. You applied two animations to objects and selected and modified one of them using the Animation pane. You set a trigger for an animation. You also changed the fill of slide backgrounds and filled the title slide background with a tiled picture that you made somewhat transparent. You converted text and a shape to links and added an action button. You changed the color of text links so that they can be more easily distinguished on the slides. Finally, you created slide zooms to link to slides.

In the next session, you will create a self-running presentation by setting slide timings. You will then record a narration to accompany the self-running presentation. You also will save the presentation in other formats so it can be more easily distributed.

# Review

## Session 4.1 Quick Check

1. What happens if you try to add a second animation by using the Animation gallery instead of the Add Animation button?
2. What is a trigger?
3. When you change the background of a slide, can you apply that change to all of the slides in a presentation?
4. What items on a slide can be a link?
5. What is an action button?
6. What is a slide zoom?

# Session 4.2 Visual Overview:

To set automatic timings manually, select the After check box. During a slide show, the slides will advance automatically after the time displayed in the After box.

When the On Mouse Click check box is selected, the slide show can be advanced by clicking the slide, even if there are saved slide timings. If the On Mouse Click check box is deselected, the slide show cannot be advanced by clicking a slide, although users can still use the keyboard or click links to display other slides.

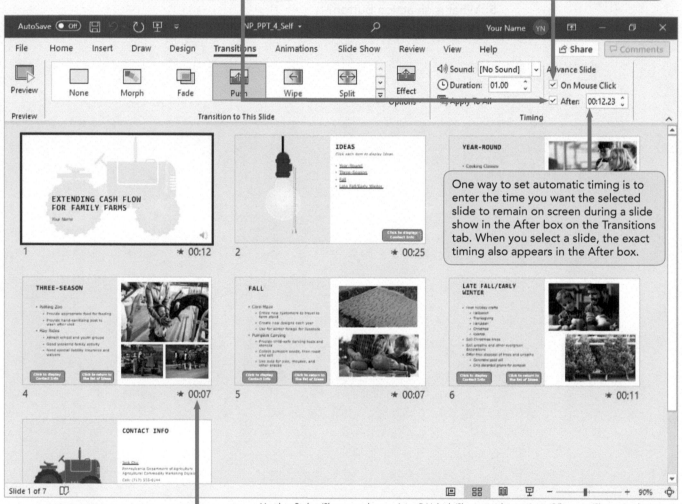

One way to set automatic timing is to enter the time you want the selected slide to remain on screen during a slide show in the After box on the Transitions tab. When you select a slide, the exact timing also appears in the After box.

Automatic timings indicate how many seconds a slide will stay on the screen before transitioning to the next slide during a slide show.

# Automatic Slide Timings

Click the Record button to start recording the slide show. Click the Stop button to stop recording. Click the Replay button to watch the recording of the slide. After you start recording, the Record button changes to the Pause button. You can click the Pause button to pause the recording without stopping it.

If the slide includes speaker notes, you can click the NOTES button to display the notes on the screen. The notes will not be part of the slide show recording.

Click the Clear button to delete the recording from the current slide or from all the slides.

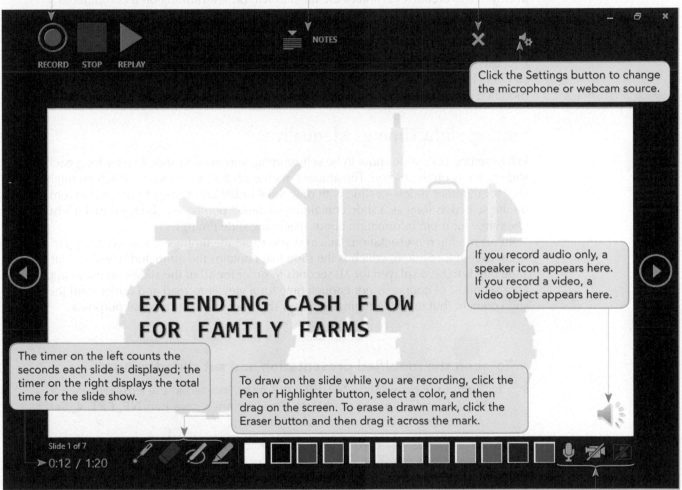

Click the Settings button to change the microphone or webcam source.

If you record audio only, a speaker icon appears here. If you record a video, a video object appears here.

The timer on the left counts the seconds each slide is displayed; the timer on the right displays the total time for the slide show.

To draw on the slide while you are recording, click the Pen or Highlighter button, select a color, and then drag on the screen. To erase a drawn mark, click the Eraser button and then drag it across the mark.

Keep the Microphone button selected to record audio. Keep the Camera button selected to record video. Keep the Camera Preview button selected to see a preview of your webcam recording on the screen while you are recording.

EXTENDING CASH FLOW FOR FAMILY FARMS

Heather Stokes/Shutterstock.com

# Creating Self-Running Presentations

A self-running presentation advances without a presenter or viewer doing anything. Self-running presentations include settings that specify the amount of time each slide is displayed as well as the time at which animations occur. Some self-running presentations include audio that takes the place of the presenter's oral explanations or gives the viewer instructions for watching the slide show. To give the user more control over the viewing experience, you can include links on the slides or allow the user to advance the slide show manually using the mouse or keyboard.

Jack intends to use his PowerPoint file when he gives oral presentations, but he also wants to create a version of the file that will be self-running on a computer at agricultural fairs and trade shows for people who are unable to attend his presentation. Jack made several modifications to the presentation including removing the slide zooms, modifying the links, and removing the trigger from the lit light bulb. This is because in a self-running presentation, trigger animations do not occur automatically, so the lit bulb would never appear unless the viewer knew to click the unlit bulb. This modified presentation can now be set up as a self-running presentation.

## Setting Slide Timings Manually

When setting up a slide show to be self-running, you need to specify how long each slide remains on the screen. The amount of time each slide stays on the screen might vary for different slides—a slide with only three bullet points might not need to remain on the screen as long as a slide containing six bullet points. See the Session 4.2 Visual Overview for more information about specifying slide timings.

In his modified presentation, Jack asks you to set the timings to four seconds per slide, except for Slide 6, which is the slide that contains the animated wreaths. That slide needs to be displayed for 10 seconds in order for all of the slide content to appear. Four seconds, of course, is not enough time for a viewer to read and understand the slide content, but the slide timings are kept short here for instructional purposes.

### To open the modified presentation and set slide timings:

1. Open the presentation **NP_PPT_4-2.pptx**, located in the **PowerPoint4 > Module** included with your Data Files, and then save it as **NP_PPT_4_Self** to the location where you are saving your files.

2. Display Slide 2 ("Ideas"), click the lit bulb graphic, and then click the **Animations** tab. The animation sequence icon does not contain a lightning bolt because Jack removed the trigger. In the timing group, After Previous appears in the Start box, and the delay is set for one-quarter second.

3. Display Slide 3 ("Year-Round"). Jack modified the four slides that contain the ideas so that the first bulleted item animates automatically along with the picture that goes along with that item, and then after a second or two, the next item and its associated picture animates.

4. Display Slide 7 ("Contact Info"), and then click each item in the unnumbered list. You can see that in the Animation group, the Fade entrance animation is selected and the start setting is On Click for each of the three items.

5. On the status bar, click the **Slide Sorter** button 🔡 to switch to Slide Sorter view. Slide 7 is selected.

6. Press and hold **SHIFT**, scroll up if necessary, click the **Slide 1** (the title slide) thumbnail, and then release **SHIFT**. All of the slides are selected.

7. On the ribbon, click the **Transitions** tab. In the Timing group, the On Mouse Click check box is selected in the Advance Slide section. This means that the viewer can take an action to advance the slide show.

8. In the Timing group, click the **After** check box. The check box is selected, and 00:00 appears below each slide thumbnail. See Figure 4–25.

| Figure 4–25 | Transitions tab with the After box selected |
|---|---|

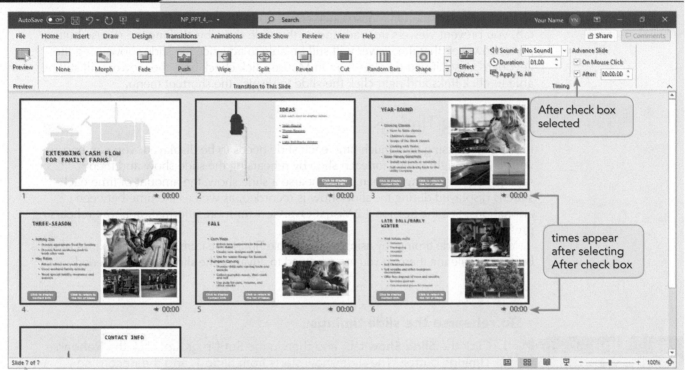

After check box selected

times appear after selecting After check box

Heather Stokes/Shutterstock.com; Arina P Habich/Shutterstock.com; Love Silhouette/Shutterstock.com; fokke baarssen/Shutterstock.com; iStock.com/AzmanJaka; Vicki L. Miller/Shutterstock.com; gvictoria/Shutterstock.com; iStock.com/BanksPhotos; Jack Frog/Shutterstock.com; iStock.com/mediaphotos; iStock.com/FlamingPumpkin; ND700/Shutterstock.com/Katherine T. Pinard

**Tip**

If you want to remove slide timings, select all the slides in Slide Sorter view, click the Transitions tab, and then click the After check box in the Timing group to deselect it.

9. In the Timing group, click the **After up** arrow four times to change the time to four seconds per slide. Under each slide thumbnail, the time changes to 00:04.00. Because Slide 6 contains more information and more animations than the other slides, that slide needs to be displayed longer.

10. Click the **Slide 6** ("Late Fall/Early Winter") thumbnail, and then in the Timing group, click the **After up** arrow six times to change the time for Slide 6 to 10 seconds.

11. On the Quick Access Toolbar, click the **Start From Beginning** button 🖳. Watch as Slide 1 appears, then after four seconds, Slide 2 ("Ideas") appears. After a brief pause, the lit bulb appears, and then after four seconds, Slide 3 ("Year Round") appears.

12. Immediately after Slide 3 appears, click the mouse button twice to display the bulleted list and the pictures, and then click it again to display Slide 4 ("Three-Season"). You are able to advance the slide show by clicking the mouse button because you left the On Mouse Click check box on the Transitions tab selected.

▶ **13.** Watch as the slide show advances through the rest of the slides. When Slide 7 appears, watch as the unnumbered list appears automatically, even though the animation is set to start On Click. This is because the automatic slide timing overrides the animation's On Click start setting.

▶ **14.** When the black slide that indicates the end of the slide show appears, press **SPACEBAR**. The presentation appears in Slide Sorter view.

If you deselect the On Mouse Click check box in the Timing group on the Transitions tab, you prevent viewers from advancing the slide show by clicking the mouse button. Note, however, that the viewer will still be able to advance the slide show using the keyboard. Also, if you deselect the On Mouse Click check box, the viewer will still be able to click links and right-click the slide to display the shortcut menu.

## Rehearsing Timings

Instead of guessing how much time each slide needs to be displayed, you can ensure you have the right timing for each slide by rehearsing the slide show and then saving the slide timings. When you rehearse a slide show, the amount of time each slide is displayed during the slide show is recorded, as well as the time between animations. See the Session 4.2 Visual Overview for more information about rehearsing presentations.

You'll set slide timings by using the Rehearse Timings feature. Read the next set of steps before completing them so you are prepared to advance the slide show as needed.

**To rehearse the slide timings:**

**Tip**

Click the Pause Recording button on the Recording toolbar to pause the timer; click the Repeat button to restart the timer for the current slide.

▶ **1.** Click the **Slide Show** tab, and then in the Set Up group, click the **Rehearse Timings** button. The slide show starts from Slide 1, and the Recording toolbar appears on the screen in the upper-left corner. The toolbar includes a timer on the left that indicates the number of seconds the slide is displayed and a timer on the right that tracks the total time for the slide show.

▶ **2.** Leave Slide 1 on the screen for about five seconds, and then advance the slide show. Slide 2 ("Ideas") appears with the bulleted list and the unlit light bulb, then the lit bulb appears.

▶ **3.** Leave Slide 2 on the screen for about five seconds, and then advance to Slide 3 ("Year-Round").

▶ **4.** On Slides 3 ("Year-Round") through 5 ("Fall"), wait for the bulleted lists and pictures to appear, and then wait for about three more seconds on each slide so that the timer indicates 6 seconds.

▶ **5.** On Slide 6 ("Late Fall/Early Winter"), wait for the bulleted lists and pictures to appear, and then wait for about two to three more seconds so that the timer indicates 10 seconds.

▶ **6.** On Slide 7 ("Contact Info"), wait two seconds, advance the slide three times to display the three items in the unnumbered list, and then advance the slide show once more when the timer indicates 10 seconds. A dialog box opens asking if you want to save the timings.

▶ **7.** Click **Yes**. The presentation appears in Slide Sorter view. The rehearsed time appears below each slide thumbnail. You can also see the timing assigned to the slides on the Transitions tab.

**8.** Click the **Transitions** tab, and then click the **Slide 1** thumbnail. In the Timing group, the recorded timing to the hundredth of a second for the selected slide appears in the After box. The rehearsed timing replaced the four-second slide timing you set previously.

After you rehearse a slide show, you should run it to evaluate the timings. If a slide stays on the screen for too much or too little time, stop the slide show, and then change that slide's time in the After box in the Timing group on the Transitions tab.

### To play the slide show using the rehearsed slide timings:

**1.** On the Quick Access Toolbar, click the **Start From Beginning** button. The slide show starts and Slide 1 appears on the screen. The slide show advances to Slide 2 ("Ideas") automatically after the saved rehearsal timing for Slide 1 elapses. When Slide 7 ("Contact Info") appears, the animation occurs automatically after the two seconds you waited before you advanced the slide show.

**2.** When the final black slide appears, advance the slide show to end it.

Jack wants you to see what happens if the viewer tries to interact with the slide show and clicks one of the shapes that links to the last slide.

### To interact with the self-running presentation:

**1.** Click the **Slide 2** thumbnail, and then on the status bar, click the **Slide Show** button. Slide 2 ("Ideas") appears in Slide Show view.

**2.** Move the mouse to display the pointer, and then in the lower-right corner, click the **Click to display Contact Info** shape. Slide 7 ("Contact Info") appears.

**3.** Press **BACKSPACE** as many times as needed to display Slide 5 ("Fall"), and then wait. After about six seconds, the slide show advances automatically to Slide 6 ("Late Fall/Early Winter").

**4.** Right-click a blank area of the slide, and then on the shortcut menu, click **See All Slides**. The slides appear as thumbnails, similar to Slide Sorter view.

**5.** Click the **Slide 3** thumbnail. Slide 3 ("Year-Round") appears in Slide Show view. After about six seconds, the slide show advances.

**6.** Press **S**. The slide show stops advancing automatically.

**7.** Press **S** again. The slide show resumes advancing automatically.

**8.** Press **ESC** to end the slide show and display the presentation in Slide Sorter view.

**Tip**

You can also right-click a blank area of the screen, and then click Pause to stop the automatic slide advancement or click Resume to resume the automatic advancement.

## Recording a Slide Show

When you use the Rehearse Timings command, only the amount of time a slide is displayed during the slide show and the time when animations occur are saved. In addition to just recording timings, you can record a slide show by recording video of yourself or just narration to give viewers more information about your presentation's content.

To record video or narration to play while a slide is displayed, you use the Record Slide Show command. When you record video, the recorded video for each slide is inserted on the slide as a video object. If you record narration only, the recorded audio is inserted on each slide as an audio object. Refer to the Session 4.2 Visual Overview for more information about recording video or narration.

When you record video or narration for a slide, you should not read the text on the slide—the viewers can read that for themselves. You should provide additional information about the slides or instructions for the viewers as they watch the self-running presentation. For example, you can tell viewers that they can click action buttons to manually advance the presentation.

When you record a slide show, you can also draw on the slides. The default color is red, but you can change this. Or you can use the highlighter tool to draw a thick, transparent line across items on the slide.

## Reference ▮▬▬▬▬▬▬▬▬▬▬▬▬▬▬▬▬▬▬▬▬

### Recording Narration

- Click the Slide Show tab, and then in the Set Up group, click the Record Slide Show button.
- In the recording window, click the Microphone, Camera Off/Camera On, and Camera Preview buttons to select or deselect these options.
- Click the Pen or Highlighter button to select that tool, and then click the color you want to use to draw on the slides.
- At the top of the window, click the RECORD button, and then after the three-second countdown, speak into the microphone to record the narration for the current slide.
- After the desired amount of time, advance the slide show, record the narration for the next slide, and then continue, as desired, to other slides.
- End the slide show after recording the last narration; or continue displaying all the slides in the presentation for the appropriate amount of time, even if you do not add narration to each slide, and then end the slide show as you normally would.
- Click the Close button in the upper-right corner to close the recording window.

Jack wants viewers to have some guidance in navigating through the presentation. You will record narration for Slides 1 and 2 and record new timings for these two slides.

▶ 1. Make sure your computer is equipped with a microphone.

   **Trouble?** If your computer doesn't have a microphone, connect one, or check with your instructor or technical support person. If you can't connect a microphone, read the following steps but do not complete them. If your computer has a webcam, it probably includes a microphone.

▶ 2. Click the Slide 3 thumbnail to select it, if necessary, and then on the ribbon, click the **Slide Show** tab.

**Tip**

You can also right-click a tab on the ribbon, click Customize the Ribbon, and then in the Customize the Ribbon list in the PowerPoint Options dialog box, click the Recording check box. Click OK, and then on the new Recording tab on the ribbon, in the Record group, click the Record Slide Show button.

3. In the Set Up group, click the **Record Slide Show** button. The recording window appears with Slide 3 displayed. If your computer has a microphone and a camera, and if they are turned on, and the camera preview is turned on. The camera preview is the small square at the bottom right of the slide. It shows you how you look as your camera is recording you. In these steps, the camera will be turned off.

4. At the bottom right of the screen, click the **Turn Camera Off** button. Both the camera and the camera preview are turned off.

   **Trouble?** If the camera button is the Turn Camera On button, do not click it or you will turn the camera back on.

5. At the top of the screen click the **Settings** button, and then point to the microphone name listed below the label "Microphone." If the selected microphone is not the one you are using, click the microphone you are using. If there is only one microphone listed, it is probably the built-in microphone.

6. Below the slide, in the Inking section, click the **Pen** button. The Pen button is selected. In the row of color squares, the red color is selected. (It is the only color square without a white outline.)

The information below the bottom left of a slide tells you which slide is displayed and how many slides are in the presentation. It also tells you the timing set for the current slide and how long the entire presentation takes to view in Slide Show view if the slide timings are used.

Now that the recording options are set up, you can start recording. To do this, you click the Record button at the top of the window. You want to start recording from Slide 1.

1. To the left of the slide, click the **Return to the previous slide** button twice. Slide 1 appears.

2. At the top of the screen, click the **RECORD** button. The RECORD button changes to the PAUSE button, and after a three-second countdown, Slide 1 reappears on the screen with the Push transition. The timer below the slide that had indicated the rehearsed timing for Slide 1 starts over at zero.

3. Speak the following into the microphone: **"This presentation describes several ideas for increasing cash flow at your farm. The presentation will advance automatically from one slide to the next."**

4. Wait for a moment, click the **Advance to the next slide button** to the right of the slide to advance to Slide 2, wait for the light to "turn on," and then say into the microphone, **"To go to a specific slide, click its name in this list. Or right-click a blank area of a slide, click See All Slides, and then click the slide you want to view. To pause or resume the slide show, press S on the keyboard. You can also click the buttons at the bottom of the slides."**

5. Wait five seconds, and then at the top of the window, click the **STOP** button. The timer below the slide stops, and the Pause button changed back to the Record button. A speaker icon appears in the bottom-right corner of Slide 2.

**Tip**

Another way to remove a recording on a slide is to delete the speaker icon in Normal view.

6. To the left of the slide, click the **Return to the previous slide** button ◀ to display Slide 1. A speaker icon appears on this slide as well.

   **Trouble?** If you made a mistake and want to re-record, click the Clear button at the top of the window, and then click the command to clear the recording on either the current slide or on all the slides. Next, display the slide that you want to record again, click the Record button, and then click the Stop button when you are finished.

7. In the upper-right corner of the window, click the **Close** button ✕. The recording window closes, and the presentation appears in Slide Sorter view.

8. Double-click the **Slide 1** thumbnail to display it in Normal view, and then click the speaker icon in the lower-right corner. This is the narration you recorded on Slide 1.

9. On the ribbon, click the **Playback** tab. In the Audio Options group, note that the start timing is set to Automatically (not In Click Sequence), and the Hide During Show check box is selected.

10. On the Quick Access Toolbar, click the **Start From Beginning** button 🖳. The slide show starts, the recording that you made for Slide 1 plays, and then the slide show advances to Slide 2 a few seconds after the recording ends. Five seconds after the recording on Slide 2 finishes playing, the slide show advances automatically to display Slide 3. The rest of the slides will continue to appear using the timings you set when you rehearsed the presentation.

11. Press **ESC** to end the slide show, and then save your changes.

## Insight

### Creating a Screen Recording and Inserting Screenshots

In addition to creating a recording of a slide show, you can record your actions on a screen or take a screenshot and insert it on a slide. The commands for both of these actions are on both the Insert tab and the Recording tab.

To create a recording of your actions on the screen, first open the window in which you want to record your actions. Then in the window containing your PowerPoint presentation, click the Screen Recording button in the Media group on the Insert tab. The PowerPoint window you are working in minimizes, the Screen Recording toolbar appears, the pointer changes to the thin cross pointer, and the entire screen is dimmed. Drag the pointer from one corner to the other of the window in which you want to record your actions. The Record button on the toolbar turns red, indicating that you can click it to begin recording. Click the Record button, do the actions you want to record, speaking to record audio if you want. When you are finished, click the Stop button. The screen recording is added to the current slide in the PowerPoint presentation as a video object.

To add a screenshot of a window to a presentation, make sure the window is open. Then click the Screenshot button in the Images group on the Insert tab. This opens a menu. Click one of the windows shown in the menu to insert a screenshot of that window, or click Screen Clipping to drag on the part of the screen that you want to insert as an image on a slide.

## Applying Kiosk Browsing

Jack wants you to set the presentation so that after the last slide appears, it will restart. He also doesn't want the viewer to be able to do anything other than click the links and press ESC to end the slide show. To do this, you'll set up the slide show to be browsed at a kiosk. If you apply kiosk browsing, every slide must have a link or timing assigned to it. Otherwise, after Slide 1 appears, the viewer will be unable to advance the slide show.

**To set up the presentation for browsing at a kiosk:**

1. Click the **Slide Show** tab, and then in the Set Up group, click the **Set Up Slide Show** button. The Set Up Show dialog box opens. See Figure 4–26.

**Figure 4–26    Set Up Show dialog box**

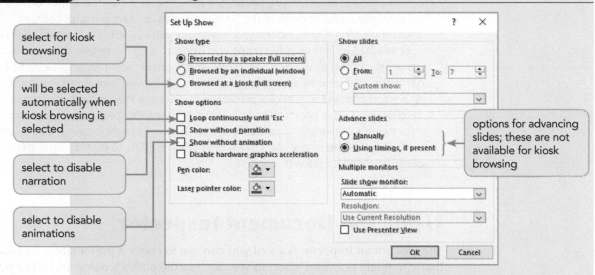

The Advance slides section in the Set Up Show dialog box is similar to the options in the Timing group on the Transitions tab. However, the options in this dialog box take precedence. For example, if the After check box is selected on the Transitions tab, but you select the Manually option button in this dialog box, the slide show will not advance automatically.

2. In the Show type section, click the **Browsed at a kiosk (full screen)** option button. In the Show options section, the Loop continuously until 'Esc' check box becomes selected. That option has also changed to light gray, indicating that you cannot deselect it. The options under Advance slides also cannot be changed now.

3. Click **OK**. The dialog box closes, and the presentation is set up for kiosk browsing.

4. Display Slide 2 ("Ideas"), and then on the status bar, click the **Slide Show** button 🖵. Slide 2 appears in Slide Show view.

5. Click the **Click to display Contact Info** shape. Slide 7 ("Contact Info") appears.

6. Press **SPACEBAR**. The slide show does not advance. Instead, Slide 7 remains on the screen until the saved timing for Slide 7 elapses, and then the slide show automatically starts over with Slide 1.

### Tip

To change the resolution of the slide show, click the Slide show monitor arrow, click the monitor on which the slide show will run, click the Resolution arrow, and then click the resolution you want to use.

▶ **7.** After Slide 1 (the title slide) appears on the screen, press **ESC** to end the slide show.

▶ **8.** Save the changes to the presentation.

 **Proskills**

### Written Communication: Preparing a PowerPoint Presentation for People to View on Their Own

You have learned that when you prepare a PowerPoint presentation to use while you are presenting a topic in front of an audience, the PowerPoint file should only contain content that enhances your oral presentation to keep the audience focused on you. However, when you prepare a PowerPoint presentation for others to view on their own, you need to make sure the slides contain enough content so that anyone viewing it will understand it without you standing in front of them to clarify your message. This usually means you need to add more text than you would if you were presenting orally, use complete sentences rather than one-word bullets, or add narration to explain visuals. Keep in mind that PowerPoint is not just an alternative to a word processor. Unlike a printed document, a PowerPoint presentation can help present your information in a visual manner. People understand and remember information presented graphically better than information presented as text. Take advantage of the many tools available in PowerPoint to display or enhance the content of the slides with graphics.

## Using the Document Inspector

The Document Inspector is a tool you can use to check a presentation for hidden data that you might not want others to see, such as the author's name and other personal information, objects that are in the presentation but are hidden or placed in the area next to a slide instead of on the slide, and speaker notes.

Jack wants to be able to send the presentation to small farmers who call into his office looking for information on expanding their selling season and offerings. Before doing so, he wants to ensure there is no hidden data he wouldn't want to distribute. You will check the presentation for hidden data.

### To check the presentation using the Document Inspector:

▶ **1.** With Slide 1 (the title slide) displayed, on the status bar, click the **Notes** button. There is a note on this slide that Jack added before he gave you the presentation to work with. Jack created this note to remind him to create a self-running presentation. The audience doesn't need to see this note. When you use the Document Inspector, you will remove notes.

▶ **2.** On the ribbon, click the **File** tab, and then click **Info**. The Info screen in Backstage view appears. On the right, file properties are listed, including the number of slides in the presentation and the author name. On the left, next to the Check for Issues button, a bulleted list informs you that the presentation contains document properties that you might want to delete, off-slide objects, presentation notes, and content that people with disabilities are unable to read. See Figure 4–27.

**Figure 4–27** Info screen in Backstage view

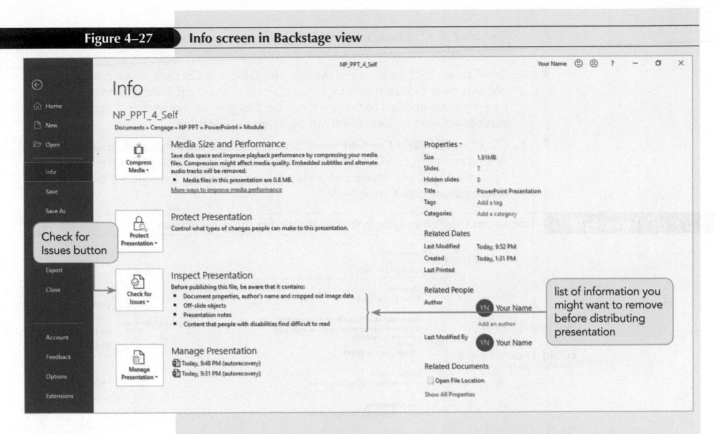

3. Click the **Check for Issues** button, and then click **Inspect Document**. The Document Inspector dialog box opens. All of the visible check boxes are selected. Each section is a category of issues that will be examined. See Figure 4–28.

**Figure 4–28** Document Inspector dialog box

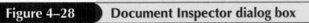

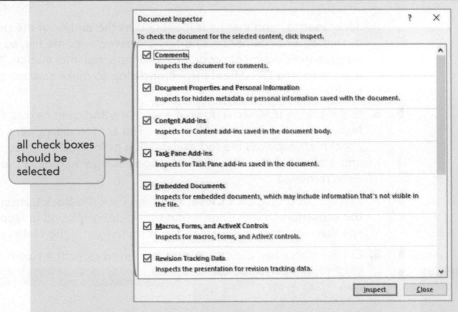

**Trouble?** If a dialog box opens telling you that you need to save the presentation first, click Yes to save the presentation.

4. Scroll down to the bottom of the list. The Off-Slide Content check box is not selected. Notice that it says that objects that are off-slide and have an animation applied to them will not be flagged, so the wreath that is positioned next to Slide 8 will not be listed as a problem.

5. Click the **Off-Slide Content** check box to select it, and then click **Inspect**. After a moment, the Document Inspector dialog box displays the results. Potential problems have a red exclamation point and a Remove All button next to them. See Figure 4–29.

**Figure 4–29** **Document Inspector dialog box after inspecting the presentation**

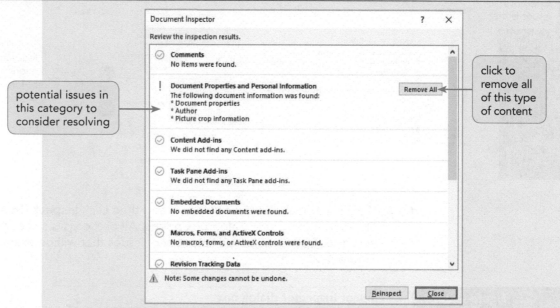

Jack doesn't mind that he is identified as the author of the presentation or that other document properties are saved with the file, so you will not remove the document properties and personal information. You should, however, scroll the Document Inspector dialog to make sure no other potential problems are identified.

6. In the dialog box, scroll down if necessary, and then next to Presentation Notes, click the **Remove All** button. The button disappears, a green checkmark replaces the red exclamation point next to Presentation Notes, and a message appears in that section telling you that all presentation notes were removed.

7. In the dialog box, click **Close**, and then click the **Back** button ⬅ to return to the presentation with Slide 1 (the title slide) displayed in Normal view. The speaker note that Jack had added is no longer in the Notes pane.

8. On the status bar, click the **Notes** button to close the Notes pane.

9. On **Slide 1** (the title slide), add your name as the subtitle, and then save the changes to the presentation.

Save the changes now because next you will be saving the presentation in a different format.

# Saving a Presentation in Other Formats

PowerPoint lets you save presentations in several formats that allow others to view the presentation without allowing them to make any changes to it. Figure 4–30 lists several of the file formats you can save a PowerPoint presentation as.

| Figure 4–30 | File formats that PowerPoint presentations can be saved as |
| --- | --- |

| File Format | Description |
| --- | --- |
| MPEG-4 Video<br>Windows Media Video | A video created from the slides in the presentation. |
| PNG Portable Network Graphics<br>JPEG File Interchange Format | One or all of the slides saved as individual graphic files in the PNG or JPG graphic format. |
| PowerPoint Picture Presentation | Each slide is saved as a graphic object (as if you took a photo of each slide) and then each graphic object is placed on a slide in a new PowerPoint presentation. |
| PDF | Portable Document File format, a file format shows a document as it looks in the app that created it and that can be opened on any make or model of computer, as long as a free PDF reader program is installed, such as the Reader app included with Windows 10. |
| XPS | XML Paper Specification, a file format that lists the content of a document and describes how it should look and that can be opened on any make or model of computer |
| PowerPoint Show | A PowerPoint format that automatically opens in Slide Show view if you double-click the file in a File Explorer window. |
| PowerPoint 97-2003 | A PowerPoint format that can be opened in earlier versions of PowerPoint, specifically, PowerPoint 97, PowerPoint 2000, PowerPoint 2002, and PowerPoint 2003. |
| Outline/RTF | The text of the presentation saved in a Word document. |

Jack wants to be able to post the presentation to his department's website and email the presentation to small farmers when they contact him for information about expanding their season or services. To ensure that the presentation can be opened and viewed by anyone, regardless of the type of computer they have and the programs they have access to, he asked you to save it in several formats.

To save the file in different formats, you can use the Export screen in Backstage view or the Save As dialog box. You'll save the presentation in several different formats now.

**Tip**

In addition to using the Export screen, you can click Save As in Backstage view, and then click Browse to open the Save As dialog box. Click the Save as type arrow, and then click the file type you want to save the presentation as.

## Saving a Presentation as a Video

You can create a video of your presentation that can be viewed the same way you view any digital video, in an app such as the Movies & TV app included with Windows 10. You can save a presentation as a video in either the MPEG-4 or Windows Media Video file format. When you do this using the command on the Export screen in Backstage view, you can choose the resolution of the video, whether to use recorded narrations and timings, or, if you choose not to use saved timings, how long each slide will appear on the screen. After you have created the video, you can play it in any video player.

Jack wants you to save the presentation as a video. When he posts it, he will include instructions to let viewers know that despite the narration on Slide 2, because it is a video and not a PowerPoint file, they will not be able to click the links to control the progression of the slides.

### To save the presentation as a video:

▶ **1.** On the ribbon, click the **File** tab, and then in the navigation bar, click **Export** to display the Export screen in Backstage view.

▶ **2.** In the Export list on the left, click **Create a Video**. Options for saving the presentation as a video appear on the right. See Figure 4–31. The options shown are the default options and are how the video would be created if you used the Save As dialog box to save the presentation as video.

**Figure 4–31**    Export screen in Backstage view when creating a video

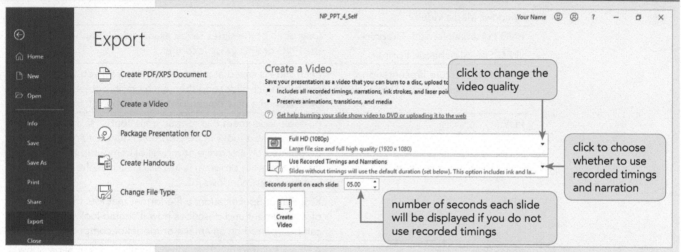

First, you need to select the quality of the video you want to create. Jack wants people to be able to play this presentation on smartphones, tablets, or other mobile devices, so you will create a video with the smallest possible file size.

▶ **3.** Click the **Full HD (1080p)** button. The menu that opens lists four options for selecting the quality of the video. The highest quality—and therefore the largest file size—is Ultra HD (4K), and the lowest quality is Standard (480p).

▶ **4.** Click **Standard (480p)**.

▶ **5.** Click the **Use Recorded Timings and Narrations** button. The menu that opens allows you to choose to use or not use the recorded narrations and timings. You can also preview the timings or record new timings. If you choose to not use the recorded narrations and timings, you could adjust the number of seconds for each slide to be displayed in the Seconds to spend on each slide box.

▶ **6.** Click **Use Recorded Timings and Narrations**.

▶ **7.** Click the **Create Video** button. Backstage view closes and the Save As dialog box opens with MPEG-4 Video selected in the Save as type box and the filename of the presentation in the File name box. If you wanted, you could change the file type by clicking the Save as type arrow and then clicking Windows Media Video. The folder where you are storing your files should be the current folder.

8. Change the name in the File name box to **NP_PPT_4_Video**, and then click **Save**. The dialog box closes, and in the status bar, a progress bar labeled Creating video NP_PPT_4_Video.mp4 appears. After a moment, the progress bar disappears, which means the video has been created.

Now that you've created the video, you can watch it.

**To watch the video:**

1. Open a File Explorer folder window, and then navigate to the folder where you are storing your files. The NP_PPT_4_Video file is included in the file list.

   Double-click the **NP_PPT_4_Video** file. Your video player starts and the video you created starts playing. The narrations and timings you recorded are retained. After the last slide appears, the video ends.

2. Close the video player.

3. On the Windows taskbar, click the **PowerPoint** button [P]. The PowerPoint window appears with the NP_PPT_4_Self presentation displayed.

## Saving Slides as Pictures and a Presentation as a Picture Presentation

If you want to distribute your presentation to others so they can see it but prevent them from modifying it or copying complex animations, backgrounds, or other features, you can save individual slides as graphic files. You can choose the type of graphic file you want to save the slides as. The most common choices are PNG or JPEG. You can also save slides in the TIF, BMP, and other graphic file formats.

When you save slides as graphic files, you can choose to save only the current slide or all of the slides in the presentation. If you save only the current slide, the file is saved in the folder you choose. If you save all of the slides in the presentation as graphic files, a new folder is automatically created with the same name as the presentation file name. Each slide is saved as a graphic file in this new folder. The file name of each file is SlideX where "X" is the slide number in the presentation.

Jack asks you to save the title slide as a graphic file in the PNG format.

**To save a slide as a picture:**

1. Display Slide 1 (the title slide) if necessary.

2. On the ribbon, click the **File** tab, and then in the navigation bar, click **Export**.

3. On the Export screen, click **Change File Type**. The right side of the screen changes to list various file type options that you can save the presentation as. See Figure 4–32. You will save Slide 1 as a PNG file.

**Figure 4–32**   **Export screen in Backstage view with Change File Type selected**

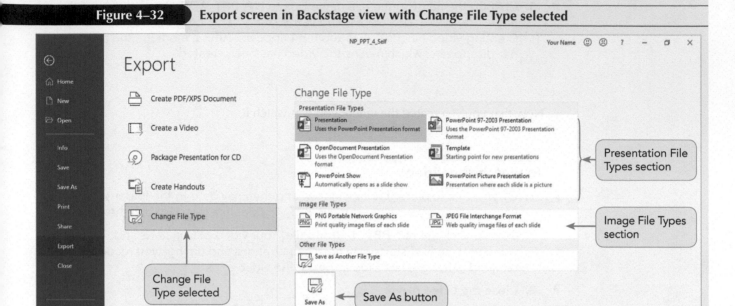

**Tip**

If you want to choose a different file format, click the Save as type arrow, and then click the file format you want to use.

4. In the Image File Types section in the right pane, click **PNG Portable Network Graphics**, and then click the **Save As** button. The Save As dialog box opens with PNG Portable Network Graphics Format in the Save as type box. The name in the File name box is the same as the presentation filename, and the current folder is the folder in which you are storing your files.

5. Change the filename to **NP_PPT_4_PNG**, and then click **Save**. The Save As dialog box closes and another dialog box opens asking which slides you want to export. You can choose to export all of the slides or just the current slide.

6. In the dialog box, click **Just This One**. The dialog box closes and Slide 1 is saved as a PNG file.

7. On the Windows taskbar, click the **File Explorer** button ⬜. The NP_PPT_4_ PNG file is included in the file list.

8. Double-click the **NP_PPT_4_PNG** file. The Photos app opens and Slide 1 of the presentation appears as a picture.

   **Trouble?** If a dialog box opens asking how you want to open this file, click the app you want to use, and then click OK.

9. Close the Photos app window, and then on the Windows taskbar, click the **PowerPoint** button ⬛. The PowerPoint window appears with the NP_PPT_4_Self presentation displayed.

You can also save the entire presentation as a picture presentation. When you save a presentation as a picture presentation, each slide is saved as an image file in the JPEG format, and then that image is placed on a slide in a new presentation so that it fills the entire slide. If there are timings assigned to the slides, the timings will be preserved. Jack asks you to save the presentation as a picture presentation.

## To save the presentation as a picture presentation:

1. On the ribbon, click the **File** tab, and then in the navigation bar, click **Export**.

2. On the Export screen, click **Change File Type**, and then in the Presentation File Types section in the right pane, click **PowerPoint Picture Presentation**.

3. Click the **Save As** button. The Save As dialog box opens with PowerPoint Picture Presentation in the Save as type box. The name in the File name box is the same as the presentation filename, and the current folder is the folder in which you are storing your files.

4. Change the filename to **NP_PPT_4_PicturePres**, and then click **Save**. The Save As dialog box closes and, after a moment, another dialog box opens telling you that a copy of the presentation has been saved.

5. Click **OK**. You can open the picture presentation in the same way you normally open a presentation.

6. On the ribbon, click the **File** tab, and then in the navigation bar, click **Open**. The Open screen appears in Backstage view.

7. Navigate to the folder where you are storing your files, if necessary, click **NP_PPT_4_PicturePres**, and then click **Open**. The presentation opens in Normal view, displaying Slide 1 (the title slide).

8. Click anywhere on the slide. Sizing handles appear around the edges of the slide in the Slide pane and the Picture Format tab appears on the ribbon. This is because all of the objects in the original slide were converted to a single JPEG file and this picture is sized to fill the entire slide. See Figure 4–33.

**Figure 4–33**   Image of Slide 1 selected in the picture presentation

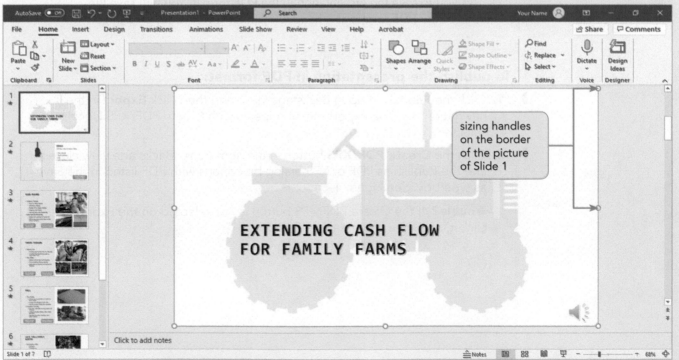

Heather Stokes/Shutterstock.com; Arina P Habich/Shutterstock.com; Love Silhouette/Shutterstock.com; fokke baarssen/Shutterstock.com; iStock.com/AzmanJaka; Vicki L. Miller/Shutterstock.com; gvictoria/Shutterstock.com; iStock.com/BanksPhotos; Jack Frog/Shutterstock.com; iStock.com/mediaphotos

> **9.** Display **Slide 3** ("Year-Round") in the Slide pane, and then click the "Click to display Contact Info" shape. The shape is not selected. Instead, the entire image of Slide 3 is selected.

> **10.** On the status bar, click the **Slide Show button** 🖥. Slide 3 appears in Slide Show view.

> **11.** Click the "Click to display Contact Info" shape. Nothing happens. The links do not function because each slide is just a picture of the original slide.

> **12.** Wait several more seconds. After about eight seconds, Slide 4 ("Three-Season") appears.

> **13.** Press **ESC** to end the slide show, and then click the Transitions tab. The After check box in the Timing group is selected, and the timing you set is in the After box.

> **14.** Close the **NP_PPT_4_PicturePres** file. The original NP_PPT_4_Self presentation appears again.

## Save a Presentation as a PDF

The PDF file format is a format that can be opened on any make or model of computer, as long as a free PDF reader program is installed. It is a good format to choose if you don't know whether the people to whom you distribute the presentation have PowerPoint available. In addition, recipients cannot edit the presentation when it is saved as a PDF. When you save a presentation as a PDF, you can choose the number of slides to include on each page, similar to choosing the number of slides per handout when you print handouts.

Jack asks you to save the presentation in the PDF format. You will save the presentation in the PDF format as a handout with all seven slides on a page.

### To publish the presentation in PDF format:

> **1.** Click the **File** tab to open Backstage view, and then click **Export** in the navigation bar. The Export screen appears with Create PDF/XPS Document selected.

> **2.** Click the **Create PDF/XPS** button in the right pane. Backstage view closes, and the Publish as PDF or XPS dialog box opens with PDF listed in the Save as type box. See Figure 4–34.

> **Trouble?** If the Create PDF/XPS button is not selected on the Export screen, click it, and then continue with Step 2.

**Figure 4–34** Publish as PDF or XPS dialog box

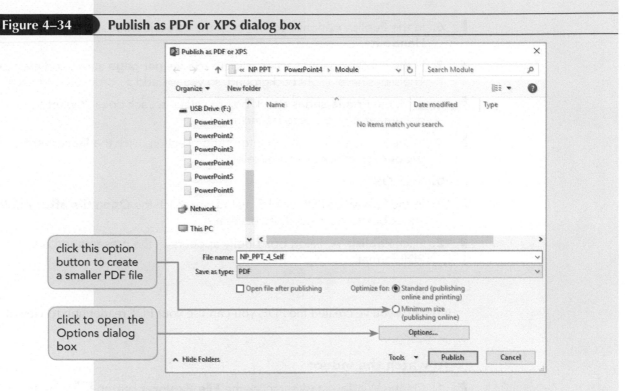

click this option button to create a smaller PDF file

click to open the Options dialog box

**Trouble?** If XPS appears in the Save as type box instead of PDF, click the Save as type arrow, and then click PDF.

3. Navigate to the location where you are storing your files, if necessary, and then change the filename to **NP_PPT_4_PDF**. You want to create a small file size suitable for attaching to an email message.

4. Click the **Minimum size (publishing online)** option button. Now you need to set the option to save it as a handout.

5. Click the **Options** button. The Options dialog box opens. See Figure 4–35.

**Figure 4–35** Options dialog box for saving a presentation as a PDF

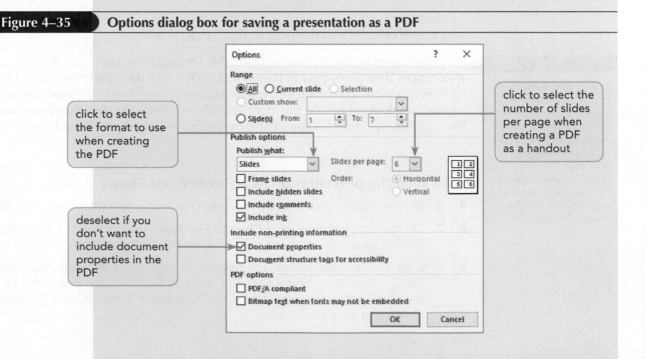

click to select the format to use when creating the PDF

click to select the number of slides per page when creating a PDF as a handout

deselect if you don't want to include document properties in the PDF

6. In the Publish options section, click the **Publish what** arrow, and then click **Handouts**.
7. In the Publish options section, click the **Slides per page** arrow, and then click **9**. The slides have a light background, so you will add a border around each slide.
8. Click the **Frame slides** check box to select it. Jack doesn't want the document properties to be included.
9. In the Include non-printing information section, click the **Document properties** check box to deselect it.
10. Click **OK**.
11. In the Publish as PDF or XPS dialog box, click the **Open file after publishing** check box to deselect it, if necessary.
12. Click **Publish**. A dialog box briefly appears as the presentation is saved in PDF format.

Now that you've created the PDF, you can use your PDF reader app to view it.

**To watch the video:**

1. On the Windows taskbar, click the **File Explorer** button. The NP_PPT_4_PDF file is included in the file list.
2. Double-click the **NP_PPT_4_PDF** file. The PDF reader app on your computer starts and the PDF file you created opens. Each slide in the presentation appears as an image on the page. There is a border around each image.
3. Close the PDF reader app.
4. On the Windows taskbar, click the **PowerPoint** button. The PowerPoint window appears with the NP_PPT_4_Self presentation displayed.

## Save a Presentation as a PowerPoint Show

**Tip**

To save a presentation to a CD, DVD, or folder along with any linked files and embedded fonts, use the Package Presentation for CD command on the Export screen in Backstage view. People can view the presentation even if they don't have PowerPoint installed.

Jack wants to make the presentation available for people to watch as if they are watching in Slide Show view in PowerPoint even if they don't have PowerPoint installed on their computer. When you save a presentation in the PowerPoint Show format, anyone can double-click the file in a File Explorer window to view the presentation in Slide Show view. Jack asks you to save the file in the PowerPoint Show format.

**To save the presentation as a PowerPoint Show:**

1. On the ribbon, click the **File** tab, and then in the navigation bar, click **Export**.
2. On the Export screen, click **Change File Type**, and then in the Presentation File Types section in the right pane, click **PowerPoint Show**.
3. Click the **Save As** button. The Save As dialog box opens with PowerPoint Show in the Save as type box. The name in the File name box is the same as the presentation filename, and the current folder is the folder in which you are storing your files.

4. Change the filename to **NP_PPT_4_Show**, and then click **Save**. The Save As dialog box closes and the file is saved as a PowerPoint show. The PowerPoint show presentation file you just created is the currently open presentation.

5. Close the NP_PPT_4_Show presentation file.

## Insight

### Checking a Presentation for Compatibility with Earlier Versions of PowerPoint

If you want to save a presentation in a format compatible with earlier versions of PowerPoint, you should first use the Compatibility Checker to identify features in the presentation that are incompatible with earlier versions of PowerPoint so that you can decide whether to modify the presentation. To do this, click the File tab, click Info, and then on the Info screen in Backstage view, click the Check for Issues button, and then click Check Compatibility. When you save a presentation in the PowerPoint 97-2003 format, the compatibility checker runs automatically.

In this session, you set slide timings manually, rehearsed slide timings, recorded a slide show, and set up the show to be viewed at a kiosk. You also inspected the file for hidden information and saved the file in other formats. Jack has the presentation in all the formats he needs.

## Review

### Session 4.2 Quick Check

1. How do you manually change the amount of time a slide stays on the screen during Slide Show view in a self-running presentation?
2. Do links work in a self-running presentation?
3. How do you prevent viewers from advancing the slide show by clicking the mouse during a self-running presentation?
4. When you record a slide show, can you save audio or video along with the presentation?
5. What does the Document Inspector reveal?
6. What are the two types of file formats you can save a presentation as when you save it as a video?
7. What file format should you save a presentation in if you want to make sure that almost anyone with a computer can view the contents of the slides?
8. What file format should you save a presentation in if you want to allow anyone to double-click the file to view it in Slide Show view even if they don't have PowerPoint installed?

# Practice

## Review Assignments

**Data Files needed for the Review Assignments: NP_PPT_4-3.pptx, NP_PPT_4-4.pptx, Support_PPT_4_Corn.png**

Some owners of small farms have asked Jack Chu for suggestions on how to create a corn maze. Specifically, farmers have asked about how to design and build the maze, how to monitor customers in the maze, how to advertise the attraction, and how to set ticket prices. Jack created a presentation that he plans to use when he describes building a corn maze, and he wants your help to finish it. Complete the following steps:

1. Open the file **NP_PPT_4-3.pptx**, located in the PowerPoint4 > Review folder included with your Data Files, add your name as the subtitle, and then save the presentation as **NP_PPT_4_Maze** to the location where you are saving your files.

2. Add a gradient fill to the background of Slide 1. Change the color of the Stop 4 of 4 tab to Brown, Accent 4, Lighter 40%. Change the color of the Stop 3 of 4 tab to Brown, Accent 4, Lighter 60% and change its position to 90%. Change the color of the Stop 2 of 4 tab to Brown, Accent 4, Lighter 80% and change its position to 85%. Change the color of the Stop 1 of 4 tab to White, Background 1 and change its position to 75%. Change the Type to Linear and change the Direction to Linear Down.

3. Apply the gradient background to all of the slides in the presentation.

4. On Slide 1 (the title slide), add the photo **Support_PPT_4_Corn.png**, located in the PowerPoint4 > Review folder included with your Data Files as the background fill. Tile the picture as texture, and then change the horizontal offset (Offset X) to 120 pt. Change the transparency of the photo background on Slide 1 to 50%.

5. On Slide 2, display the guides. Reposition the vertical guide at 2.17 inches to the right of center. Reposition the horizontal guide at 0.17 inches above the middle.

6. On Slide 2, move the maze off of the slide to the left, keeping its center aligned with the horizontal guide. (Remember to press and hold SHIFT to move an object in a straight line. Zoom out if necessary.) Apply the Lines motion path animation with the Right effect to the maze. Adjust the ending of the Lines motion path so that the center of the maze ends on the intersection of the guides and so that the maze will travel in a straight line.

7. Add the Spin emphasis animation to the maze. Change the start setting of the Spin animation to With Previous, and then change its duration to 1.75 seconds.

8. Change the start setting of the Lines animation to After Previous.

9. On Slide 2 ("Plan"), format each of the unnumbered list items to links to the corresponding slides.

10. Change the color of the links on Slide 2 ("Plan") to Light Yellow, Background 2, Darker 75%.

11. On Slide 9 ("Questions?"), change the text displayed for the link to **Jack Chu**, and then change the color of the link to the same color as the text links on Slide 2 (Light Yellow, Background 2, Darker 75%).

12. Insert a new Slide 3 using the Title Only layout. Type **Plan** as the slide title. Add Slides 4 through 8 as slide zooms on the new Slide 3. Resize the slide zooms so they are 1.5 inches high.

13. Reposition the vertical guide so it is 4.33 inches to the right of center. Make a copy of the vertical guide and reposition the copy 4.33 inches to the left of center. Make another copy of the vertical guide, and then position it so it is centered on the slide at 0.00 inches. Reposition the horizontal guide so it is in the middle of the slide at 0.00 inches. Make a copy of the horizontal guide and reposition the copy at 1.75 inches below the middle.

14. Position the slide zooms as follows:

    a. Position the "Pricing" slide zoom so the right edge aligns with the vertical guide on the right side of the slide and the bottom edge aligns with the horizontal guide at 1.75 inches below the middle.

    b. Position the "Liability" slide zoom so the center aligns with the guide at the center of the slide and the top and bottom edges align with the top and bottom edges of the "Pricing" slide zoom.

    c.   Position the "Marketing" slide zoom so the left edge aligns with the vertical guide positioned 4.33 inches to the left of center and the top and bottom edges align with the top and bottom edges of the "Liability" and "Pricing" slide zooms.

    d.   Position the "Operation" slide zoom so the bottom edge aligns with the horizontal guide in the middle of the slide (at 0.00 inches) and so the center approximately aligns with the center of the space between the "Liability" and "Pricing" slide zooms.

    e.   Position the "Design and Build" slide zoom so the top and bottom edges align with the top and bottom edges of the "Operation" slide zoom and so the center approximately aligns with the center of the space between the "Marketing" and "Liability" slide zooms.

15. Change the duration of the zoom transitions applied to each of the slide zooms to 1.25 seconds. Change the setting of the "Pricing" slide zoom so that after the slide is displayed, Slide 3 (the "Plan" slide with the slide zooms) reappears.

16. On Slide 4 ("Design and Build"), insert the Arrow: Left shape, and then type **Plan** in the shape. Change the font size to 20 points. Resize the shape so it is 0.5 inches high and 0.9 inches wide. Apply the Intense Effect – Orange, Accent 1 shape style in the Theme Styles section, and then position the shape in the lower-left corner of the slide so that the top of the shape aligns with the bottom of the bulleted list and so its center aligns with the guide 4.33 inches to the left of center.

17. Format the Plan shape as a link to Slide 3 (the "Plan" slide with the slide zooms).

18. Copy the Plan shape on Slide 4 ("Design and Build") to Slide 5 ("Operation"), Slide 6 ("Marketing"), Slide 7 ("Liability"), and Slide 8 ("Pricing").

19. On Slide 3 ("Plan"), insert the Blank action button, and then set it to link to Slide 9 ("Tips"). Enter **TIPS** in the action button, and then format the action button with the Semitransparent – Black, Dark 1, No Outline shape style in the Presets section. Resize the action button so it is one-half inch high and 0.7 inches wide. Position the action button in the upper-right corner of the slide so that the bottom aligns with the bottom of the title text and the center aligns with the right edge of the Slide 8 ("Pricing") slide zoom and the vertical guide at 4.33 inches right of center. Hide the guides.

20. On Slide 6 ("Marketing"), modify the animation of the bulleted list so that the first item ("Put up road signs") animates after the previous action. Then change the start settings of the other three first-level bulleted items so that they animate after the previous action with a delay of one second. Keep the start setting of the animations of the second-level items below "Conventional ads" as With Previous and add a delay of one second if necessary so that their animations start at the same time as the animation applied to the "Conventional ads" bulleted item.

21. On Slide 6, change the start setting of the animation applied to the picture of the corn maze sign to With Previous, and then change the order of the animations so that the animation of the corn maze sign occurs at the same time as the animation of the first-level item "Put up road signs." Preview the animations on Slide 6.

22. Hide Slide 2 (the "Plan" slide with the text links) during a slide show.

23. Save the presentation and close it.

24. Open the presentation **NP_PPT_4-4.pptx**, add your name as the subtitle, and then save it as **NP_PPT_4-MazeSelf** to the location where you are saving your files.

25. Rehearse the timings, displaying the content of Slide 1 for four seconds, and displaying the content of each of the rest of the slides for about one second after the last bulleted item appears, except Slide 2. Display Slide 2 long enough to watch the maze morph onto the screen and the path animate through the maze, and then wait five seconds.

26. Change the timing of Slide 9 ("Questions?") to eight seconds.

27. Record the slide show starting on Slide 2 ("Plan"). After the path through the maze animates, say, **"To skip to the last slide, which contains tips for running the corn maze attraction, click the button in the lower-right corner."** Wait five seconds, and then stop the recording.

28. Set up the show to be browsed at a kiosk.

29. Run the Document Inspector and then remove anything found, except do not remove document properties and personal information.

30. Save the changes to the presentation. Make sure you do this before you continue with the rest of the steps.

31. Save the presentation as an MPEG-4 video at the Standard (480p) size and using the recorded timings and narration. Name the video file **NP_PPT_4_MazeVideo** and save it in the location where you are saving your files.

32. Save Slide 1 of the presentation as a PNG file named **NP_PPT_4_MazeSlide1** to the location where you are saving your files.

33. Save the entire presentation as a picture presentation named **NP_PPT_4_MazePic** to the location where you are saving your files.

34. Save the presentation file as a PDF named **NP_PPT_4_MazePDF** in the location where you are saving your files. Use the Minimum size option, do not include the document properties, and create a handout with nine slides per page with each slide framed.

35. Save the presentation in the PowerPoint Show format with the name **NP_PPT_4_MazeShow**.

36. Close the file.

# Apply

## Case Problem 1

**Data Files needed for this Case Problem: NP_PPT_4-5.pptx, Support_PPT_4_Waves.jpg**

**Shoreside Realty**: Julia Moreno owns Shoreside Realty, a real estate company in Scarborough, Maine, that specializes in selling and renting homes in local beach communities. As part of her marketing, she attends local events, such as the farmer's market, weekly summer concerts, and Chamber of Commerce events, and shows photos of houses near beaches for sale or rent. She created a presentation with slides containing the addresses and brief descriptions of several newly listed properties. She asks you to finish the presentation by adding formatting to the title slide background, and by adding animations to high-light the fact that two of the properties can fit a large number of people. Then she wants you to make the presentation self-running and save it as other file types. Complete the following steps:

1. Open the file **NP_PPT_4-5.pptx**, located in the PowerPoint 4 > Case1 folder included with your Data Files, add your name as the subtitle on the title slide, and then save it as **NP_PPT_4_Realty** in the location where you are saving your files.

2. Apply the Style 6 Background style to all of the slides in the presentation.

3. On Slide 1 (the title slide), fill the background with the picture **Support_PPT_4_Waves.jpg**, located in the PowerPoint 4 > Case1 folder.

4. On Slide 2 ("Available Properties"), change each address to a link to the corresponding slide. Change the color of the links to Ice Blue, Background 2, Darker 75%.

5. On Slide 3 ("18 Oceanside Road"), insert the Rectangle: Rounded Corners shape and resize it so it is 0.7 inches high and 2.5 inches wide. Type **Click here to find out how to contact us!** in the shape, and then apply the Gradient Fill – Brown, Accent 6, No Outline shape style in the Presets section. Position the shape so it is centered below the text boxes in the darker area on the left side of the slide and so the top edge aligns with the bottom edge of the picture of the cottage.

6. On Slide 3, format the shape you drew as a link to Slide 8 ("Schedule an Appointment Today"). Copy this shape link and paste it on Slides 4, 5, 6, and 7.

7. Display Slide 3 ("18 Oceanside Road"), and then display the guides. Drag the horizontal guide up to 2.58 inches above the middle, and then drag the vertical guide to 1.75 inches to the right.

8. On Slide 3, insert a Rectangle shape. Resize it so it is 0.7 inches high and 2.4 inches wide. Fill the shape with the Light Blue color in the Standard Colors section, remove the shape outline, and then insert the text **Sleeps 10!** in the shape. Position the shape so it is centered on top of the intersection of the horizontal and vertical guides. Apply the Wipe entrance animation to the shape, and then change its direction effect to From Left.

9. On Slide 3, insert the Double Wave shape in the Stars and Banners section of the Shapes menu. Resize the shape so it is 0.3 inches high and 2.5 inches wide. Duplicate the shape, and then

position the copy of the shape to the right of the original shape so that the two shapes are aligned horizontally and the ends are touching. Group the two wave shapes.

10. Position the grouped shape above the Sleeps 10! shape so that the top edge of the grouped shape aligns with the top edge of the slide and so it is centered horizontally above the Sleeps 10! shape.

11. Apply the Lines motion path to the grouped shape. Change the direction effect to Right. Move the start point of the motion path in a straight line so it is approximately aligned with the left edge of the Sleeps 10! shape, and then move the end point of the motion path so it is approximately aligned with the right edge of the Sleeps 10! shape.

12. Duplicate the grouped shape. Position the copy of the grouped shape so that it is below the Sleeps 10! shape with the bottom of the grouped shape touching but not overlapping the picture of the cottage, and so it is vertically aligned with the original grouped shape.

13. Change the start setting of the animation applied to the Sleeps 10! shape to After Previous. Make sure the animation applied to the grouped shapes above and below the Sleeps 10! shape occur after the animation applied to the Sleeps 10! shape, and then change the start setting of both animations to With Previous.

14. On Slide 3, select the two grouped shapes and the Sleeps 10! shape, and then copy them. Display Slide 5 ("4 West Beach Road"), and then paste the shapes you copied to this slide. Click a blank area of the slide to deselect the pasted shapes. Click the Sleeps 10! shape, select "10", and then type **14** to change the text to "Sleeps 14!"

15. On Slide 5 ("4 West Beach Road"), select both grouped shapes and fill them with the Ice Blue, Background 2 color (this is the same color as the background fill color). Remove the outline of the grouped shapes. The shapes are now the same color as the slide background and you cannot see them. Preview the animations on the slide.

16. Display Slide 3, and then fill both grouped shapes with the Ice Blue, Background 2 color and remove their outlines.

17. Hide the guides.

18. On Slide 8 ("Schedule an Appointment Today"), edit the link to the website so that the text on the slide is **Click to visit us online!**

19. On Slide 8, change the color of the link text to Ice Blue, Background 2, Darker 75%.

20. Rehearse the timings. Leave Slide 1 (the title slide) and Slide 2 ("Available Properties") displayed for five seconds. Leave Slide 3 ("18 Oceanside Road") through Slide 7 ("31 Island View Road") displayed for four seconds each. Leave the last slide—Slide 8 ("Schedule an Appointment Today") displayed for 10 seconds.

21. Record the presentation starting at Slide 1. After Slide 1 appears, say, **"Shoreside Realty is the answer to your vacation needs."** Wait five seconds, and then stop the recording.

22. Use the Transitions tab to change the timing of Slide 2 ("Available Properties") to 10 seconds.

23. Set up the slide show to be browsed at a kiosk.

24. Run the Document Inspector to remove the note on Slide 2.

25. Save the changes to the presentation.

26. Save the presentation as an MPEG-4 video named **NP_PPT_4_RealtyVideo** using the Standard (480p) option and the recorded timings. Because only two slides have timings assigned, the rest of the slides will be displayed for five seconds each—the time listed in the Seconds spent on each slide box in the Create a Video section of the Export screen in Backstage view.

27. Save the presentation as a picture presentation named **NP_PPT_4_RealtyPic**.

28. Save the presentation as a PDF named **NP_PPT_4_RealtyPDF** in the location where you are saving your files. Use the Minimum size option, do not include the document properties, and create a handout with nine slides per page.

29. Close the presentation.

# Challenge

## Case Problem 2

**Data Files needed for this Case Problem: NP_PPT_4-6.pptx, Support_PPT_4_Bacteria.png, Support_PPT_4_Isopropanol.3mf**

**Northwest Biotech** NMW Medical Manufacturing in Tacoma, Washington, manufactures medical devices. They have recently started helping hospitals reprocess single-use medical devices. They hired Northwest Biotech to advise them so that they can meet FDA guidelines. Ben Yeung is the department head of Vitro Services at Northwest Biotech. Ben has set up a series of meetings at NMW to help them set up their validation process. He created a presentation for his first meeting and he asks you to help him complete it. Complete the following steps:

1. Open the file **NP_PPT_4-6.pptx**, located in the PowerPoint 4 > Case2 folder included with your Data Files, add your name as the subtitle on the title slide, and then save it as **NP_PPT_4_ Reprocess** in the location where you are saving your files.

2. Insert a new Slide 2 with the Blank layout. Add Slides 3 through 11 as slide zooms on the new Slide 2. Resize the slide zooms so they are 1.8 inches high. Arrange them on the side in three rows with the slide zooms for Slides 3 through 5 in the first row, Slides 6 through 8 in the second row, and Slides 9 through 11 in the third row.

3. Change the zoom options for Slides 3, 4, 6, 9, and 10 so that Slide 2 reappears after displaying those slides during a slide show.

⊕ **Explore** 4. On Slide 3 ("Terms"), select "Single-Use Medical Device" and then use the Search button on the Review tab to search for information about this term on the web. Click one of the results to open that webpage in your browser.

⊕ **Explore** 5. Click once in the address bar in the browser to select the entire webpage address, and then press CTRL+C to copy the webpage address. Change the selected text on the slide to a link to the webpage address. Change the text color of the link to Aqua, Accent 1, Darker 50%.

⊕ **Explore** 6. On Slide 5 ("Clean"), insert the Get Information action button. Set it so that if you move the pointer on top of the shape, it will display Slide 3 ("Terms") and so it will play the Click sound when you do this.

7. Resize the action button so it is one-inch square. Position it in the upper-right corner of the slide so the middle aligns with the middle of the title text box and the right edge aligns with the right edge of the picture. Copy the action button and paste it onto Slides 4, 6, 7, 9, and 10.

8. On Slide 8 ("One Bacteria Can Multiply Quickly and Infect Patient"), insert the picture **Support_PPT_4_Bacteria.png**, located in the PowerPoint 4 > Case2 folder. Resize it so it is two inches high, rotate it 180 degrees, and position it above the slide so it aligns with the top and right edge of the slide.

9. Apply the Lines motion path animation to the picture of the bacteria. Drag the ending point of the animation so it is approximately centered on the picture of the medical tubing on the slide.

10. Add the Pulse emphasis animation to the picture of the bacteria. Change the start setting to After Previous, and change the duration to 0.25 seconds.

⊕ **Explore** 11. Change the number of times the picture pulses to three. (*Hint*: Click the arrow for the animation in the Animation pane, and then click Effect Options.)

12. Insert another copy of the picture **Support_PPT_4_Bacteria.png**, and resize it so it is two inches high. Apply the Appear entrance animation to this image. Change its start setting to After Previous and add a delay of 0.50 seconds. Position this image on top of the picture of the tubing near the top-left of the image.

13. Copy the picture of the bacteria that you placed near the top-left of the image, and then paste the copy on the slide. Position the copied image somewhere else on top of the picture of the tubing. Change the delay of the Appear animation to 0.25 seconds. Rotate this image about 45 degrees in either direction.

14. Make a copy of the image that has the Appear animation with a delay of 0.25 seconds. Paste this copy on the slide. Position it on a part of the picture of the tubing that does not already have a picture of the bacteria. Rotate it slightly in any direction.

15. Paste the copied image 10 more times. Arrange the pasted images so they are scattered on top of the picture of the tubing. Rotate the pictures of the bacteria to different orientations.

⊕ **Explore** 16. On Slide 9 ("Isopropanol Alcohol—Common Disinfectant"), insert the 3D model **Support_PPT_4_Isopropanol.3mf**, located in the PowerPoint4 > Case2 folder. Resize the image so it is 3.8 inches high. This is a molecular model of isopropanol alcohol. Use the handle in the middle of the image to rotate and tilt the image in all directions until you can see all of the molecules on the slide at once. Position it so its top edge aligns with the top edge of the bulleted list text box and its left edge aligns with the left edge of the title text box.

17. On Slide 11 ("For More Information"), change the text displayed for Sean's email address to **Sean McLaughlin Email**. Then change the color of the text of both links on Slide 11 to Aqua, Accent 1, Darker 50%.

18. Save the changes to the presentation.

⊕ **Explore** 19. Save all of the slides as PNG files to a folder named **NP_PPT_4_ReprocessAll**.

**Module 5**

## Objectives

**Session 5.1**
- Import a Word outline
- Reset slides
- Reuse slides from another presentation
- Work in Outline view
- Create sections in a presentation
- Create section and summary zooms
- Insert icons
- Use the Effect Options dialog box to modify animations
- Move objects through layers on a slide

**Session 5.2**
- Embed a Word table
- Format a table with advanced options
- Embed an Excel worksheet
- Link an Excel chart
- Format a chart with advanced options
- Break links
- Annotate slides during a slide show
- Create handouts in Microsoft Word

# Integrating PowerPoint with Other Programs

Creating a Presentation for a Rowing Convention

## Case | South Bay College Rowing Team

Tyler Davis has been the head coach of the rowing team at South Bay College in Green Bay, Wisconsin, for the past 10 years. Although some coaches have a hard time attracting and retaining first-time rowers (called novices), Tyler consistently retains 90 percent of his novices. He has been asked to give a presentation describing his approach for coaching novices at an upcoming convention for rowing coaches.

In this module, you will import a Word outline to create slides and insert slides from another presentation. You will also divide a presentation into sections, create and use section and summary zooms, layer objects on a slide, apply advanced animation effects, and embed and link objects created in other programs. Finally, you will annotate slides during a slide show and create handouts in Microsoft Word.

## Starting Data Files

**PowerPoint5** → **Module**

NP_PPT_5-1.pptx
Support_PPT_5_Fitness.xlsx
Support_PPT_5_Olivia.pptx
Support_PPT_5_Outline.docx
Support_PPT_5_Practice.docx

**Review**

NP_PPT_5-2.pptx
Support_PPT_5_Basics.pptx
Support_PPT_5_Erg.xlsx
Support_PPT_5_GPA.xlsx
Support_PPT_5_NovOutline.docx
Support_PPT_5_Races.docx

**Case1**

NP_PPT_5-3.pptx
Support_PPT_5_Budget.xlsx
Support_PPT_5_Hunger.pptx
Support_PPT_5_Plan.docx

**Case2**

NP_PPT_5-4.pptx
Support_PPT_5_Boys.jpg
Support_PPT_5_Data.xlsx
Support_PPT_5_ParentNotes.docx
Support_PPT_5_Slides.pptx

# Session 5.1 Visual Overview:

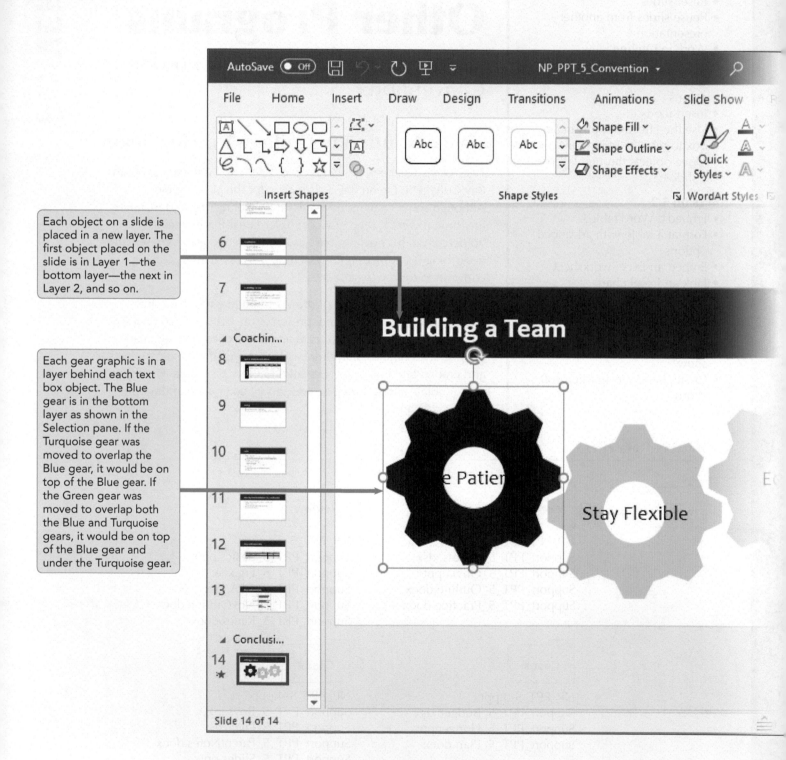

Each object on a slide is placed in a new layer. The first object placed on the slide is in Layer 1—the bottom layer—the next in Layer 2, and so on.

Each gear graphic is in a layer behind each text box object. The Blue gear is in the bottom layer as shown in the Selection pane. If the Turquoise gear was moved to overlap the Blue gear, it would be on top of the Blue gear. If the Green gear was moved to overlap both the Blue and Turquoise gears, it would be on top of the Blue gear and under the Turquoise gear.

# Understanding Layers

Click the Bring Forward button to move an object up in the list in the Selection pane and toward the top layer; to jump an object to the first layer, click the Bring Forward button arrow, and then click Bring to Front.

Click the Send Backward button to move an object down through the layers; to jump an object to the bottom layer, click the Send Backward button arrow, and then click Send to Back.

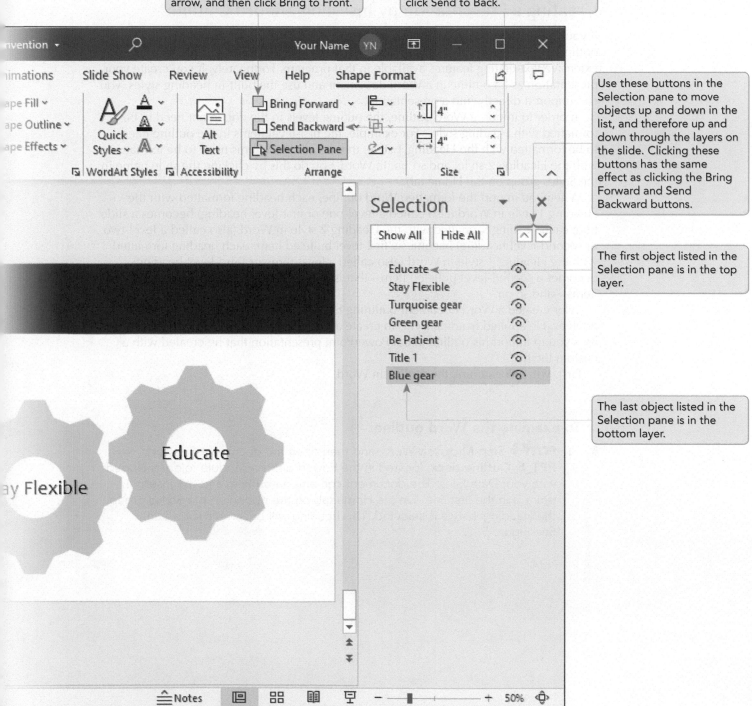

Use these buttons in the Selection pane to move objects up and down in the list, and therefore up and down through the layers on the slide. Clicking these buttons has the same effect as clicking the Bring Forward and Send Backward buttons.

The first object listed in the Selection pane is in the top layer.

The last object listed in the Selection pane is in the bottom layer.

# Creating a Presentation by Importing Content

If content already exists in an outline in a Word document or in another presentation, you can reuse that content in your presentation instead of recreating it. If your content is in a Word document as an outline, when you import the outline, slides and bulleted lists are created. You can also reuse slides from one presentation in another presentation.

## Creating a Presentation by Inserting a Word Outline

If your presentation contains quite a bit of text, it might be easier to create the outline of your presentation in Microsoft Word so that you can take advantage of the extensive text-editing features available in that program. Fortunately, if you create your presentation as an outline in a Word document and use the built-in heading styles, you can import it directly into a presentation.

In order to import a Word outline, the outline levels in the document need to be formatted with Heading styles. For example, the first-level items in the outline need to be formatted with the Heading 1 style, the second-level items need to be formatted with the Heading 2 style, and so on. In Word, you do this by clicking the style name in the Styles group on the Home tab.

When you import the formatted Word outline, each heading formatted with the Heading 1 style in Word (also called a level-one or first-level heading) becomes a slide title; each heading formatted with the Heading 2 style in Word (also called a level-two or second-level heading) becomes a first-level bulleted item; each heading formatted with the Heading 3 style in Word (also called a level-three or third-level heading) becomes a second-level bulleted item—that is, a subitem below the first-level bulleted items—and so on.

Tyler created a Word document outlining his best practices for successfully coaching novices. He applied heading styles to create an outline with text at various levels. He asks you to import his outline into a PowerPoint presentation that he created with a custom theme.

First, you will examine the outline in Word.

### To examine the Word outline:

▶ 1. **sam** ⬇ Start Microsoft Word, and then open the document **Support_PPT_5_Outline.docx**, located in the PowerPoint5 > Module folder included with your Data Files. The document contains an outline, and the insertion point is in the first line. On the Home tab on the ribbon, in the Styles group, the Heading 1 style is selected. This heading will become a slide title. See Figure 5–1.

Figure 5–1    **Outline in Word document**

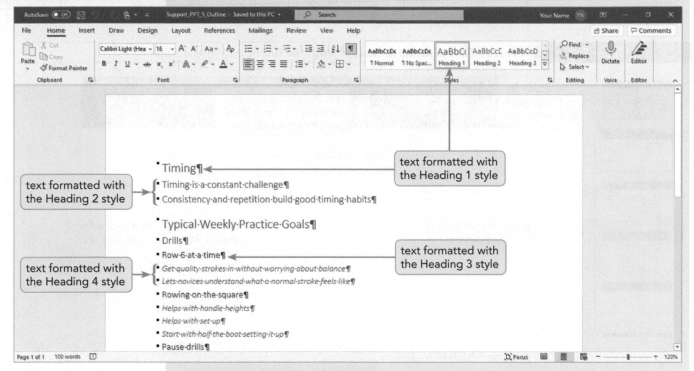

**Trouble?** If you don't see the dots to the left of each line and the paragraph marks at the end of each line, click the Show/Hide button ¶ in the Paragraph group on the Home tab. If the zoom percentage on your screen is not 120%, change it to 120%.

2. Press **DOWN ARROW**. The insertion point moves down one line, and in the Styles group, the Heading 2 style is selected. This heading will become a first-level bullet on a slide.

3. Press **DOWN ARROW** four times. The insertion point is in the line "Row 6 at a time". In the Styles group, the Heading 3 style is selected. This heading will become a second-level bullet on a slide.

4. Close the document.

Now you will import the outline into PowerPoint. You do this using a command on the New Slide menu.

**To import the Word outline into a presentation:**

1. Open the presentation **NP_PPT_5-1.pptx** from the PowerPoint5 > Module folder included with your Data Files, and then save it as **NP_PPT_5_Convention** to the location where you are saving your files. The presentation consists of two slides.

2. On the Home tab, in the Slides group, click the **New Slide arrow**, and then click **Slides from Outline**. The Insert Outline dialog box opens.

3. Navigate to the PowerPoint5 > Module folder, click **Support_PPT_5_Outline.docx**, and then click **Insert**. The Word outline is inserted as new

---

**Tip**

If imported content on a slide creates a bulleted list that is too long, use the Add or Remove Columns button in the Paragraph group on the Home tab to arrange text in multiple columns in a text box.

slides after the current slide, Slide 1, in the PowerPoint presentation. All the Heading 1 text in the outline became new slide titles. Slide 2 ("Timing") is displayed. See Figure 5–2.

| Figure 5–2 | Presentation with slides created from the imported Word outline |

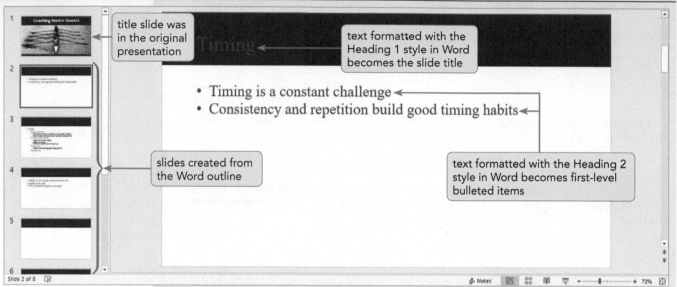

iStock.com/spepple22

> **Trouble?** If Slide 2 is not selected, click the Slide 2 thumbnail in the pane on the left.

▶ **4.** In the Slides group, click the **Layout** button. Notice that a new layout, Title and Text, was created and applied. This layout was created when you imported the outline and it was applied to each slide created by importing the outline.

▶ **5.** Press **ESC** to close the Layout menu.

The text of the slides created by importing the outline retained the fonts and text colors of the outline document rather than picking up those of the presentation theme. You can fix this by resetting the slides. You can reset a slide any time that formatting is changed unexpectedly or isn't applied as you intended, or if placeholders are modified. When you reset slides, you reset every object on the selected slides, so you might need to reapply any formatting that you added.

You'll reset the slides created when you imported the Word outline.

### To reset the imported slides:

▶ **1.** With the Slide 2 thumbnail selected, scroll down to the bottom of the pane containing the slide thumbnails, press and hold **SHIFT**, and then click the **Slide 7** thumbnail. The six slides that were created when you inserted the outline are selected.

▶ **2.** On the Home tab, in the Slides group, click the **Reset** button. The slide fonts now match the presentation theme. See Figure 5–3.

| Figure 5-3 | Slides reset to the presentation theme |

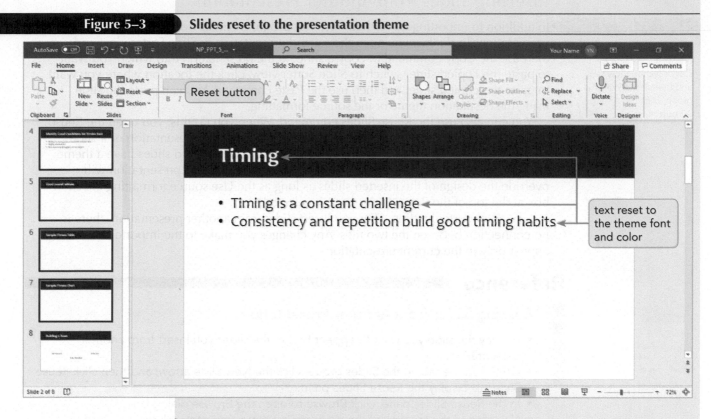

**3.** Save the changes to the presentation.

The imported Word outline is now in the PowerPoint presentation with the custom theme of the NP_PPT_5_Convention presentation applied. Because you imported the outline, the text is now part of the PowerPoint file. Any changes you make to either the PowerPoint or the Word file will not be reflected in the other file.

## Insight

### Changing Slide Size and Orientation

The default for PowerPoint presentations is for slides to be sized for wide screen displays at an aspect ratio of 16 to 9. This is written as 16:9. To change the slide size, click the Slide Size button in the Customize group on the Design tab. To change the slide size to a 4:3 aspect ratio, click Standard (4:3) on the menu. To select other sizes or to create a custom size, click Custom Slide Size to open the Slide Size dialog box, and then select the size from the Slides sized for list.

Slides in a presentation can be in **landscape orientation**, which is wider than tall or **portrait orientation**, which is taller than wide. Handouts can also be formatted in either orientation. To change the orientation of slides or handouts, open the Slide Size dialog box. In the Orientation section of the dialog box, click the Portrait or Landscape option button in the Slides section or the Notes, Handouts, & Outline section.

## Inserting Slides from Another Presentation

In addition to importing a Word outline, you can insert slides from another presentation. To do this, you open the second presentation in Slide Sorter view and then use the Copy command to copy a slide. In the presentation into which you want to paste the copied slide, switch to Slide Sorter view, click the location where you want to paste the copied slide, and then use the Paste command. You can paste the slide using the destination theme or the source formatting.

You can also use the Reuse Slides command. When you do this, you open the Reuse Slides pane, in which you can access the slides from another presentation or a slide library. Then you click the slides you want to insert. If the inserted slides have a theme different from the current presentation, the design of the current presentation will override the design of the inserted slides as long as the Use source formatting check box at the top of the Reuse Slides pane is selected.

Like an imported outline, after you insert slides from another presentation, there is no connection between the two files. Any changes you make to the imported slides appear only in the current presentation.

## Reference

### Reusing Slides from Another Presentation

- Display the slide you want to appear before the slides you insert from another presentation.
- On the Home tab, in the Slides group, click the New Slide arrow, and then click Reuse Slides to display the Reuse Slides pane.
- In the Reuse Slides pane, click Browse to open the Browse dialog box.
- Navigate to the location of the presentation that contains the slides you want to insert, click the file, and then click Choose Content.
- In the Reuse Slides pane, make sure the Use source formatting check box is not selected to have the inserted slides use the theme in the current presentation, or click the Use source formatting check box to retain the theme of the slides you want to import.
- In the Reuse Slides pane, click each slide that you want to insert into the current presentation.

Tyler asked his assistant coach, Olivia Connor, to create slides that describe the best practices to use when coaching novice rowers. You will insert the slides that she created into the NP_PPT_5_Convention presentation.

### To insert slides from another presentation:

1. Display Slide 7 ("Sample Fitness Chart"). You want to insert slides from Olivia's presentation after Slide 7.

2. On the Home tab, in the Slides group, click the **New Slide arrow**, and then click **Reuse Slides**. The Reuse Slides pane opens.

3. In the Reuse Slides pane, click **Browse**. The Browse dialog box opens.

4. Navigate to the PowerPoint5 > Module folder, click **Support_PPT_5_ Olivia.pptx**, and then click **Choose Content**. Thumbnails of the five slides in the Support_PPT_5_Olivia presentation appear in the Reuse Slides pane. The theme applied to this presentation is different from the theme applied to the NP_PPT_5_Convention presentation. At the top of the pane, the Use source formatting check box is unchecked. See Figure 5-4.

Figure 5–4 **Reuse Slides pane with slides from another presentation**

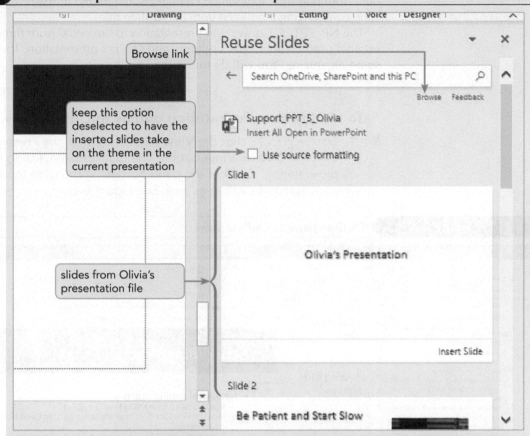

5. In the Reuse Slides pane, click the **Be Patient and Start Slow** thumbnail, which is the second slide. The slide is inserted into the NP_PPT_5_ Convention presentation after the current slide (Slide 7). Because the Use source formatting check box is not checked, the theme used in the NP_ PPT_5_Convention presentation is applied to the slide instead of the theme used in the Support_PPT_5_Olivia presentation.

6. In the Reuse Slides task pane, scroll down if necessary, click the **Educate and Explain** thumbnail, click the **Stay Flexible** thumbnail, and then click the **Scheduling Practice** thumbnail. The slides are added to the NP_PPT_5_ Convention presentation. (You do not need to insert the first slide, which is Olivia's title slide.)

7. Close the Reuse Slides pane.

8. Save the changes to the presentation.

The four slides you inserted from the Support_PPT_5_Olivia presentation are now Slides 8 through 11 in the NP_PPT_5_Convention presentation.

# Working in Outline View

**Outline view** displays the outline of the presentation in the Outline pane, which appears in place of the pane that contains the slide thumbnails. In the Outline pane, presentation text is arranged as in an ordinary outline. Slide titles are the top levels in the outline, and the bulleted lists are indented below the slide titles.

You can use the Outline pane to see the outline of the entire presentation, move text around, and even change the order of slides. For example, you can move a bulleted item from one slide to another, change a subitem into a first-level item, or create a new slide by changing a bulleted item into a slide title.

The NP_PPT_5_Convention presentation has material from three sources: Tyler's original presentation, Tyler's outline, and Olivia's presentation. The presentation needs some organizing. You will do this in the Outline view.

### To modify the presentation outline in Outline view:

1. On the ribbon, click the **View** tab, and then in the Presentation Views group, click the **Outline View** button. The Outline pane, listing the outline of the presentation, replaces the pane containing the slide thumbnails. The Notes pane becomes visible as well. See Figure 5–5.

**Figure 5–5**  **Outline pane in Outline view**

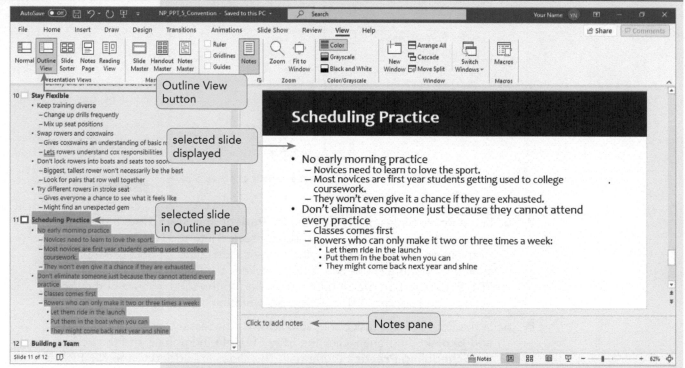

You need to change the first-level bulleted item "Drills" on Slide 3 ("Typical Weekly Practice Goals") so it becomes a slide title. You want the subitems below "Drills" to move with the "Drills" bulleted item so that they become bulleted items on the new Slide 4.

2. Scroll up in the Outline pane, and then on Slide 3 ("Typical Weekly Practice Goals"), move the pointer on top of the bullet next to "Drills" so that the pointer changes to the four-headed arrow pointer ⬥.

3. Click the bullet next to "Drills". The bulleted item "Drills" and all of its subitems are selected in the Outline pane.

4. On the ribbon, click the **Home** tab, and then in the Paragraph group, click the **Decrease List Level** button ⬚. "Drills" becomes the title for a new Slide 4, and all of the bulleted items below it are moved up one level.

Next, you need to change the slide title on Slide 6 ("Good overall athlete") so it becomes a first-level bulleted item on Slide 5 ("Identify Good Candidates for Stroke Seat").

▶ **5.** In the Outline pane, move the pointer on top of the **Slide 6** ("Good overall athlete") slide icon ☐ so that the pointer changes to the four-headed arrow pointer ✥, and then click the **Slide 6** slide icon ☐. Slide 6 is selected in the Outline pane and Slide 6 is displayed.

▶ **6.** Press **TAB**. The selected text is demoted so that the slide title becomes the last first-level bullet on Slide 5. Now you need to move Slide 2 ("Timing") so it appears before Slide 4 ("Drills").

▶ **7.** Move the pointer on top of the **Slide 2** ("Timing") slide icon ☐ so that the pointer changes to the four-headed arrow pointer ✥, press and hold the mouse button, and then drag the pointer down so that the horizontal line indicating the position of the item you are dragging appears above Slide 4, as shown in Figure 5–6.

| Figure 5–6 | Dragging an item in the Outline pane |

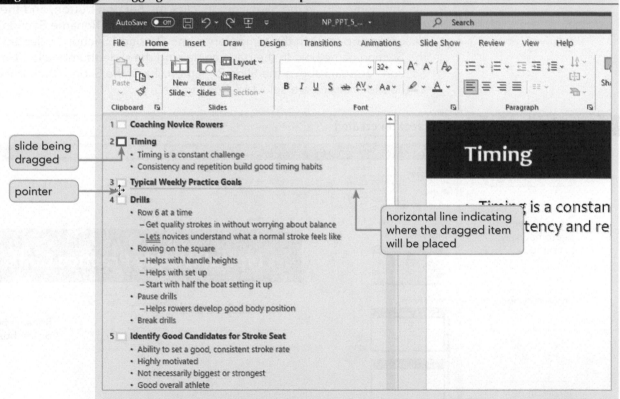

▶ **8.** With the horizontal line positioned above Slide 4, release the mouse button. The "Timing" slide is now Slide 3. You are finished working in Outline view. On the status bar, the Normal button is selected, but you can click it anyway to return to Normal view.

▶ **9.** On the status bar, click the **Normal** button 🗔. The presentation appears in Normal view, but the Notes pane is still visible.

▶ **10.** On the status bar, click the **Notes** button. The Notes pane closes.

▶ **11.** Save the changes to the presentation.

# Organizing a Presentation Using Sections and Zooms

When you work with a long presentation, it can be helpful to divide it into sections. It can also be helpful to your audience if you create a summary slide from which you can link to each section.

## Creating Sections in a Presentation

Tyler wants you to create a section that consists of the slides created from his outline. To do this, you need to first select the slide that will mark the beginning of the section. You can do this in Normal view or in Slide Sorter view.

### To create sections in the presentation:

1. In the pane containing the thumbnails, scroll up, and then click the **Slide 2** thumbnail. Slide 2 ("Typical Weekly Practice Goals") is displayed. This will be the first slide in the section you will create.

2. On the Home tab, in the Slides group, click the **Section** button, and then click **Add Section**. The new section is created, and the Rename Section dialog box opens with the temporary name "Untitled Section" selected in the Section name box. In the pane containing the slide thumbnails, "Untitled Section" appears above the Slide 2 thumbnail and the Slide 2 thumbnail and all the slides after it are selected. See Figure 5–7.

| Figure 5–7 | New section created |
|---|---|

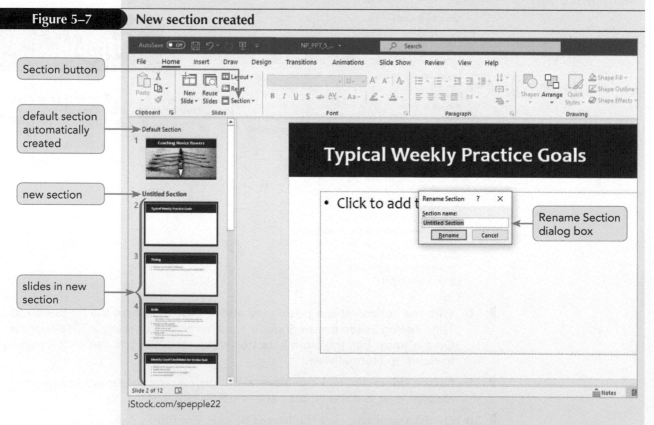

iStock.com/spepple22

3. In the Section name box, type **Coaching Suggestions**, and then click **Rename**. The dialog box closes, and the section is renamed. At the top of the pane containing the thumbnails, the section name "Default Section"

appears. When you create a section in a presentation that does not contain any other sections and you selected a slide other than Slide 1, all the slides before the new section are placed in a section as well. This first section is automatically titled "Default Section". Because you created a section that starts with Slide 2, the Default Section includes only Slide 1. You will rename this section.

▶ **4.** In the pane containing the thumbnails, click **Default Section**. The section name changes to orange, and the thumbnail in the section is selected.

▶ **5.** On the Home tab, in the Slides group, click the **Section** button, and then click **Rename Section**. The Rename Section dialog box opens.

▶ **6.** Type **Introduction**, and then click **Rename**. The section is renamed.

The Coaching Suggestions section that you created should include only the six slides that Tyler created. You need to create another section that includes the last five slides in the presentation.

▶ **7.** Create a new section named **Best Practices** with Slide 8 ("Be Patient and Start Slow") as the first slide in the section.

## Creating Section Zooms and a Summary Zoom

You already learned how to create slide zooms on a slide. You can also add section zooms to a slide. A **section zoom** is a slide zoom linked to the first slide in a section that you click to display that slide followed by the rest of the slides in the section. When you use the Section Zoom command, only the first slide in each section appears in the dialog box for you to select.

Tyler wants you to add a slide containing section zooms to the presentation.

**To create section zooms:**

▶ **1.** Create a new Slide 2 in the Introduction section with the **Title Only** layout, and then add **Sections** as the slide title.

▶ **2.** On the ribbon, click the **Insert** tab, and then in the Links group, click the **Zoom** button. The Zoom menu opens.

▶ **3.** On the menu, click **Section Zoom**. The Insert Section Zoom dialog box opens. Unlike when you created slide zooms, only the three slides that are the first slides in the three sections appear in the dialog box.

▶ **4.** Click the **Section 1: Introduction** and **Section 2: Coaching Suggestions** check boxes, and then click **Insert**. The dialog box closes, and two section zooms are inserted on Slide 2.

▶ **5.** Click a blank area of the slide, click the top section zoom, and then drag it to the right so it is no longer on top of the other section zoom. The exact position doesn't matter.

Tyler tells you that the two sections that should have been added as section zooms are the Coaching Suggestions section and the Best Practices section.

▶ **6.** Click the **Introduction** section zoom ("Coaching Novice Rowers"), and then press **DELETE**.

▶ **7.** In the pane containing the slide thumbnails, scroll down until you can see the Best Practices section name, click the **Best Practices** section name but do not release the mouse button.

**8.** Drag the **Best Practices** section name onto Slide 2 somewhere to the left of the section zoom already on the slide. When you start dragging, the sections in the pane on the left collapse to show just the other two section names. See Figure 5–8.

**Figure 5–8**    Dragging a section name to create a section zoom

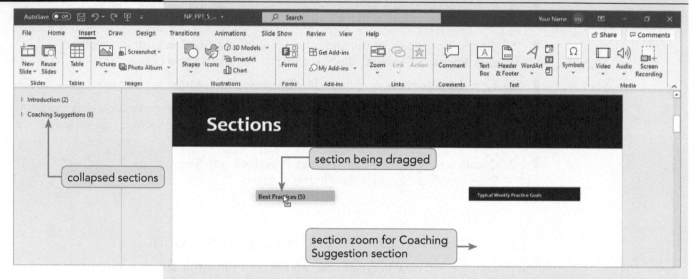

**9.** Release the mouse button. The section zoom for the Best Practices section is added to the slide and is selected.

**10.** Click the **Zoom** tab. See Figure 5–9.

**Figure 5–9**    Slide 2 with two section zooms

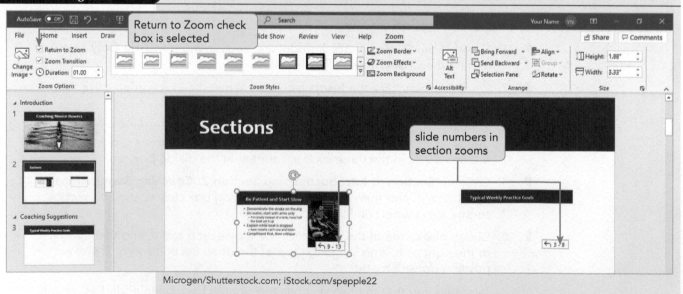

Microgen/Shutterstock.com; iStock.com/spepple22

Section zooms differ from slide zooms in three ways. First, when the Zoom tab is selected, a box on the section zoom lists the range of slide numbers included in that section. Second, the Return to Zoom check box is selected by default in the Zoom Options group on the Zoom tab. Finally, when you click a section zoom during a slide show, that slide appears with the Zoom transition (if you leave the Zoom Transition check box in the Zoom Options group selected), then each slide in the section appears using whatever transition is applied to it. After the last slide in the section appears, the slide that contains the section zooms reappears with the Zoom transition.

### To align and use the section zooms on Slide 2:

1. On Slide 2, click the "Be Patient and Start Slow" section zoom, press and hold **SHIFT**, click the "Typical Weekly Practice Goals" section zoom, and then release **SHIFT**.

2. Click the **Zoom** tab if necessary, and then in the Arrange group, click the **Align** button. The Align menu opens. At the bottom of the menu, Align Selected Objects is selected. This means that commands you use on the Align menu will align the selected objects with each other.

3. Click **Align Middle**. The menu closes, and the selected section zooms are vertically aligned with each other.

4. In the Arrange group, click the **Align** button, click **Align to Slide**, and then click the **Align** button again. The Align menu opens. At the bottom of the menu, Align to Slide is now selected. Now commands you select on the Align menu will align selected objects with the slide.

5. Click **Align Middle**. The two selected objects shift so that their middles are aligned with the middle of the slide.

6. In the Arrange group, click the **Align** button, and then click **Distribute Horizontally**. The two selected section zooms are positioned so there is the same amount of space on either side of them and between them.

7. On the status bar, click the **Slide Show** button 🖵. Slide 2 appears in Slide Show view.

8. Click the **Be Patient and Start Slow** section zoom. That slide appears on the screen with the Zoom transition.

9. Press **SPACEBAR** four times. The next four slides in the Best Practices section—Slides 10, 11, 12, and 13—appear on the screen.

10. Press **SPACEBAR** once more. Slide 2—the slide that contains the section zoom—reappears with the Zoom transition.

11. Press **ESC** to end the slide show.

You can also create a summary zoom. A **summary zoom** is a slide that contains section zooms, usually for all of the sections in the presentation. When you use the summary zoom command, the dialog box that appears contains all of the slides in the presentation. If the presentation contains sections, the first slide in each section is already selected in the dialog box. You can deselect any of these slides or select additional slides. If you select a slide that is not the first slide in a section, a new section is created with the slide you selected as the first slide in that section.

If you deselect a slide that is the first slide in a section, the section is not removed from the presentation when you create the summary zoom, but a section zoom for that section will not be created.

When you create a summary zoom, a new slide containing the section zooms is added before the first section you select. This slide is in a new section named "Summary Section".

## To create a summary zoom:

1. Click the **Insert** tab.
2. In the Links group, click the **Zoom** button, and then click **Summary Zoom**. The Insert summary zoom dialog box opens. The first slide in each of the three sections is selected. See Figure 5–10.

| Figure 5–10 | Insert Summary Zoom dialog box |

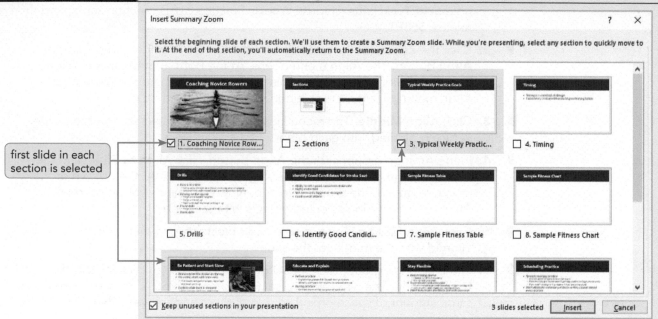

first slide in each section is selected

iStock.com/spepple22; Microgen/Shutterstock.com

Tyler wants Slides 7 and 8—the slides that will contain sample data—to be in their own section, and he wants Slide 13 to be in its own section.

3. Click the **7. Sample Fitness Table** check box, scroll down in the dialog box, and then click the **13. Building a Team** check box. Slides 7 and 13 are now selected as well and each will become the first slide in a new section. The section created that begins with Slide 7 will contain Slides 7 and 8. Slide 9 is the first slide in the next section.

4. Click **Insert**. A new Summary Section is created at the beginning of the presentation with a single summary zoom in it, and the Introduction section is now the second section. There are five section zooms on the summary zoom.

5. In the pane containing the slide thumbnails, scroll down to the bottom. Slide 14 is in a new section titled "Building a Team", which is the same as the slide title of Slide 14.

6. Scroll up until the section name above Slide 8 is visible in the pane that contains the slide thumbnails. Slides 8 and 9 are in a section titled "Sample Fitness Table". This is the slide title of the first slide in that section. See Figure 5–11.

### Tip

If you want to add or remove section slides from the summary zoom, click one of the section zooms, click the Zoom tab, and then in the Zoom Options group, click the Edit Summary button.

**Figure 5–11**    Slides 8 and 9 in the new section

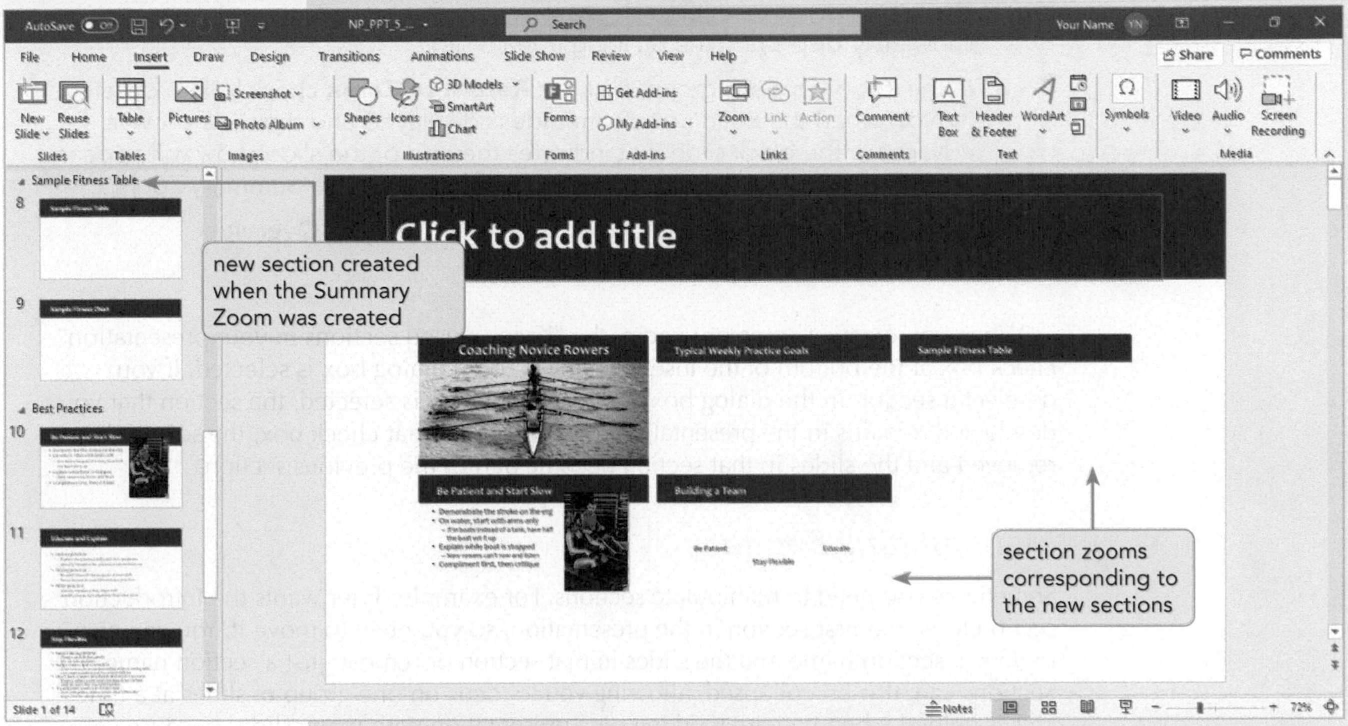

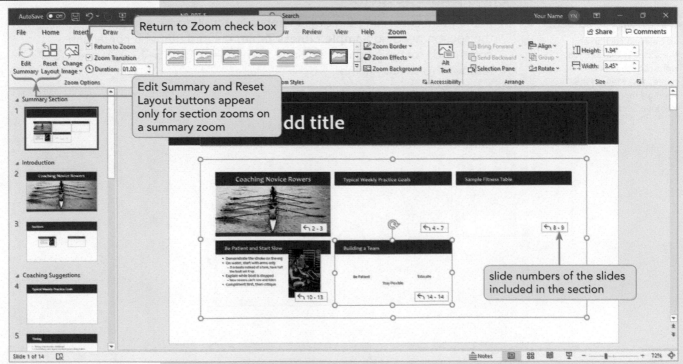

iStock.com/spepple22; Microgen/Shutterstock.com

7. On Slide 1 (the summary zoom), click the **Building a Team** section zoom, and then click the **Zoom** tab. As with the section zooms you created on Slide 3, the slide numbers on each section zoom indicate the slides that are included in the section. In the Zoom Options group, there are two additional buttons that did not appear when you selected a slide zoom or the section zooms that you added to what is now Slide 3 ("Sections"). See Figure 5–12.

**Figure 5–12**    Zoom tab for a section zoom on a summary zoom

iStock.com/spepple22; Microgen/Shutterstock.com

Because the summary zoom contains section zooms, the Return to Zoom check box is selected for each section zoom. Tyler wants to end the slide show after displaying the Building a Team slide.

▸ **8.** In the Zoom Options group, click the **Return to Zoom** check box to deselect it. Now when the Building a Team slide is displayed and the slide show is advanced, the black slide that indicates the end of the slide show will appear instead of returning to Slide 2. You will add a title to the Summary Zoom.

▸ **9.** On Slide 1, click in the title placeholder, and then type **Overview**.

When you create a summary zoom, the "Keep unused sections in your presentation" check box at the bottom of the Insert summary zoom dialog box is selected. If you deselect a section in the dialog box and that check box is selected, the section that you deselected remains in the presentation. If you deselect that check box, the section is removed and the slides in that section become part of the previous section.

## Manipulating Sections

Sometimes you need to manipulate sections. For example, Tyler wants the Introduction section to be the first section in the presentation, so you need to move it. You can also remove a section name and the slides in that section or remove just a section name. Sections can also be collapsed, allowing you to focus on one group of slides at a time. This is helpful when you are working on a presentation with many slides because you can collapse the sections containing slides you are not working on.

In addition to making the Introduction section the first section, Tyler wants the Best Practices section to appear before the Coaching Suggestions section. He also decided that he doesn't want the two slides in the Sample Fitness Table section to be in their own section and he wants you to make them part of the Coaching Suggestions section again. Finally, he wants you to rename the last section. You'll make these changes now.

### To manipulate sections:

**Tip**

To delete a section and the slides in that section, right-click the section name, and then on the shortcut menu, click Remove Section & Slides.

▸ **1.** In the pane containing the slide thumbnails, scroll down, and then right-click the section heading **Sample Fitness Table**. A shortcut menu containing commands for working with sections opens. See Figure 5–13. You need to remove this section name.

**Figure 5–13**    Shortcut menu for a section name

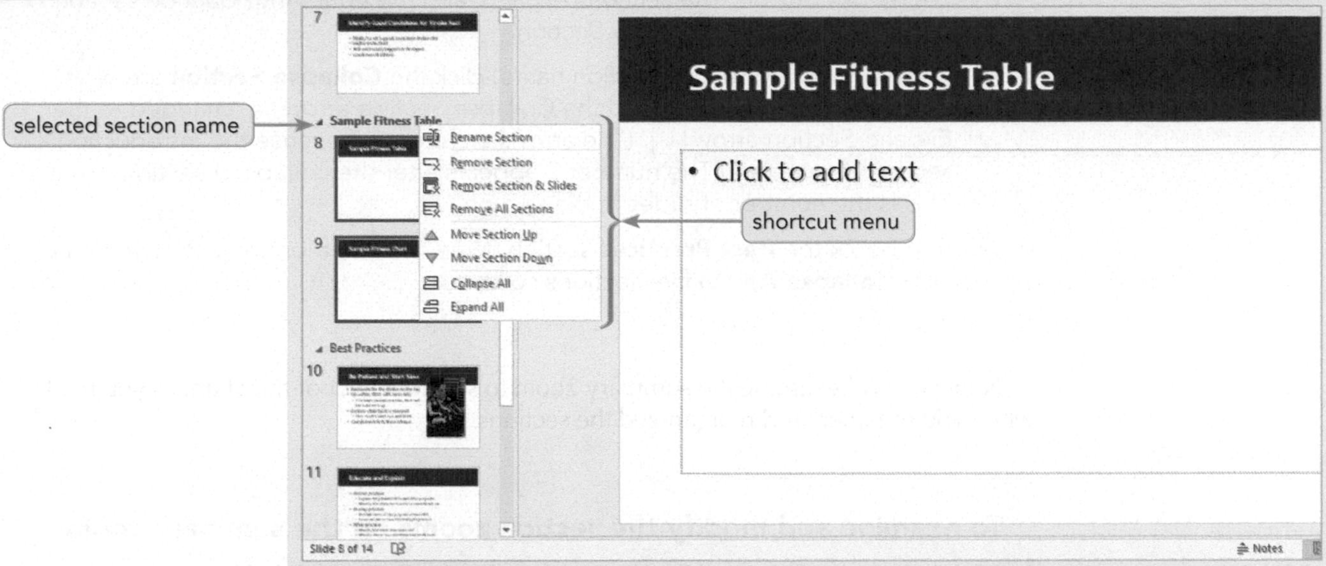

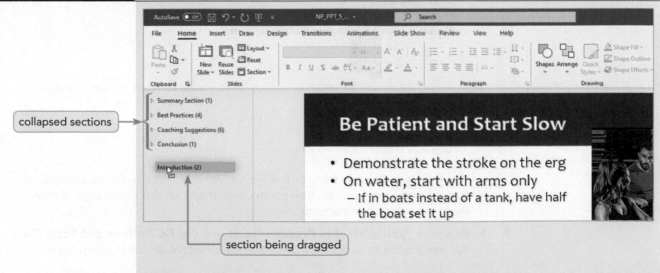

Microgen/Shutterstock.com

2. On the shortcut menu, click **Remove Section**. The selected section name is deleted and Slides 8 and 9 are now part of the Coaching Suggestions section. Next, you will rename the last section.

3. Scroll down, right-click the **Building a Team** section name, click **Rename Section**, type **Conclusion** in the Rename Section dialog box, and then click **Rename**. The section is renamed. You need to reorganize the sections.

4. Scroll up, right-click the **Best Practices** section name, and then on the shortcut menu, click **Move Section Up**. The entire Best Practices section moves up above the Coaching Suggestions section. You can also drag a section to a new position.

5. Scroll up, move the pointer on top of the **Introduction** section name, press and hold the mouse button, and then move the pointer up slightly. When you start dragging the section name, all of the sections collapse and the section you are dragging moves below the other four sections. See Figure 5–14.

**Figure 5–14**    Dragging a section to a new position

Module 5 Integrating PowerPoint with Other Programs | PowerPoint

6. Drag the **Introduction** section above the Summary Section, and then release the mouse button. The sections expand, and the entire Introduction section appears above the Summary Section.

7. Next to the Introduction section name, click the **Collapse Section** arrow ◢. The section is collapsed, and the Collapse Section arrow ◢ changed to the Expand Section arrow ▷. (The arrows are orange because the Introduction section is selected.) The number 2 appears after the collapsed section name. This is the number of slides in the section.

8. Right-click the **Best Practices** section name, and then on the shortcut menu, click **Collapse All**. All five sections collapse.

Now you will examine the summary zoom to see the effect of the changes you made when you renamed and reorganized the sections.

### To examine and modify the section zooms on the summary zoom:

1. Next to the Summary Section name, click the **Expand Section** arrow ▷. The Summary Section expands, and the Slide 3 thumbnail is visible.

2. Click the **Slide 3** thumbnail, click one of the section zooms, and then click the **Zoom** tab. Because you reorganized the sections, the slide numbers on the Coaching Novice Rowers, Typical Weekly Practice Goals, and Be Patient and Start Slow section zooms have changed to reflect the new slide numbers in those sections. Also, because you deleted a section, there is a broken link symbol on one of the section zooms. See Figure 5–15.

| Figure 5–15 | Summary zoom after manipulating the sections |

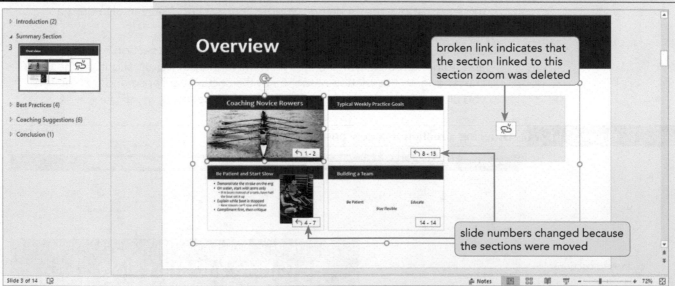

iStock.com/spepple22; Microgen/Shutterstock.com

You will swap the positions of the Typical Weekly Practice Goals and the Be Patient and Start Slow section zooms, and then use the Reset Layout command to align them correctly.

3. Drag the **Typical Weekly Practice Goals** and the **Be Patient and Start Slow** section zooms to swap their positions. Don't worry about aligning them.

4. On the Zoom tab, in the Zoom Options group, click the **Reset Layout** button. The two section zooms you moved jump back to their original position. You need to recreate or edit the summary zoom.

5. In the Zoom Options group, click the **Edit Summary** button. The Edit Summary Zoom dialog box opens. Similar to the Insert Section Zoom dialog box, it contains only the first slide in each section. The only section not selected is the Summary Section. In the dialog box, the sections are listed in the order they appear in the pane containing the thumbnails. Before you update the summary zoom, Tyler wants you to remove the Introduction section from it.

6. Click the **Section 1: Introduction** check box to deselect it, and then click **Update**. The dialog box closes. On the summary zoom, the Introduction section zoom and the section zoom with the missing link are deleted and the three remaining section zooms are now in the correct order. You need to format the section zooms so that they stand out more on the slide. There is a selection box around all three section zooms.

7. Click a blank area inside the selection box around the section zooms.

8. On the Zoom tab, click the **Zoom Border arrow**, and then click the **Indigo, Text 2** color.

9. Drag the **Building a Team** section zoom to the right to center it below the other two section zooms. Now that you have created the summary zoom, you can hide Slide 2 with the section zooms.

10. Expand the Introduction section, click the **Slide 2** thumbnail, click the **Slide Show** tab, and then in the Set Up group, click the **Hide Slide** button.

11. Save the changes to the presentation.

# Proskills

## Problem Solving: Creating a Slide Show with Two Orientations

There may be times that the content of your presentation requires you to use a combination of portrait and landscape slide orientations. For example, suppose you are creating a presentation that contains some photos in portrait orientation and some in landscape orientation. In PowerPoint, you cannot create a single presentation file with slides in both orientations; rather, you need to create two presentations and create links between them. To do this, create one presentation using the default landscape orientation, create a second presentation and change the orientation to portrait, and then add the appropriate photos to each file. The primary file should be the presentation that you want to use at the start of your presentation. Then, decide the order in which you want the photos to appear. When you want to display a slide using the orientation used in the other presentation, insert a link on the slide that will appear prior to displaying the slide with the other orientation. To use the Link command, in the Insert Hyperlink dialog box, click Existing File or Web Page in the Link to list, click the file you want to link to, and then click the Bookmark button to open the Select Place in Document dialog box listing the slides in the presentation you selected. Click the slide you want to link to, and then click OK in the dialog boxes. If you need to, add a link in the second presentation back to the appropriate slide in the first presentation. You should store the two presentations in the same folder so that they will always be together.

# Inserting Icons

In PowerPoint, icons are a type of graphic called a scalable vector graphic (SVG). SVGs are graphics created with drawing programs and do not lose quality when they are resized.

Icons share some characteristics with both pictures and shapes. For example, you can crop icons the same way you crop pictures. You can change the color of icons just as you can change the outline and fill color of shapes. And like both types of graphics, you can apply effects or styles to change the way an icon looks. If you want, you can convert an icon to shapes and then format each shape differently.

In PowerPoint, icons are sorted into categories, such as People, Education, Vehicles, Sports, and so on. To insert icons, click the Insert tab, and then in the Illustrations group, click the Icons button to open the Insert Icons dialog box. Click as many icons as you want to add to the slide, and then click Insert.

When you select an icon on a slide, the Graphics Format tab appears on the ribbon. Because icons share some characteristics with pictures and shapes, you can modify them in many of the same ways. Similar to the Shape Format tab, the Graphics Format tab contains buttons that let you change the fill color and the outline color, weight, and style of an icon. Like the Picture Format tab, the Graphics Format tab contains the Crop button. The Graphics Format tab contains commands to apply a style or effects, such as shadows or bevels, to the icon, and commands to align, group, rotate, and resize icons—all of which are available on both the Shape and Picture Format tabs.

> **Tip**
>
> To insert scalable vector graphics that are stored on your computer or network, use the Pictures button in the Images group on the Insert tab.

## To insert an icon and modify it:

▶ 1. Expand the Conclusion section, display Slide 14 ("Building a Team"), and then click the **Insert** tab.

▶ 2. In the Illustrations group, click the **Icons** button. The Insert Icons window opens. The icons in the window are arranged into categories.

   **Trouble?** If a message appears telling you that you need to be online in order to use icons, click Cancel, connect to the Internet, and then repeat Step 2.

▶ 3. In the category list near the top, use the right arrow, if necessary, and then click **Analytics**. The window displays icons in the Analytics category. See Figure 5–16.

**Figure 5–16**    **Insert Icons dialog box**

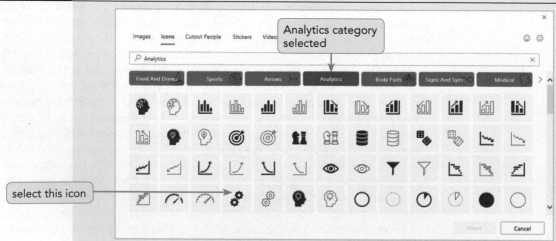

4. In the Analytics category, click the dark gray gears icon, as indicated in Figure 5–16. A box around the selected icon and a check mark in the upper-right corner appear. If you wanted, you could click more than one icon before clicking Insert.

5. Click **Insert**. The Insert Icons window closes and the icon of two gears is inserted on the slide. The icon is selected, and the Graphics Format contextual tab appears on the ribbon and is selected. You will resize the icon larger. Like pictures, icons also have their aspect ratios locked.

6. Resize the icon so it is six inches square, and then position it so that it is centered on the slide below the title. It will be on top of some of the text that is already on the slide.

7. On the Graphics Format tab, in the Graphics Styles group, click the **Graphics Fill arrow**, and then click the **Turquoise, Accent 2** color. Both gears are filled with the turquoise color.

If you want to recolor or manipulate different parts of the icon, you need convert it to shapes or ungroup it. To do this, select the icon, and then in the Change group on the Graphics Format tab, click the Convert to Shape button. Then you can click each shape that makes up the icon and format it any way you want using the tools on the Drawing Tools Format tab.

Tyler wants each gear to be a different color. You will convert the icon to shapes.

### To convert an icon to shapes:

1. On the Graphics Format tab, in the Change group, click the **Convert to Shape** button. Although the icon does not look any different, the Graphics Format tab disappears, and the Shape Format tab appears instead. The selected object is now two grouped shapes instead of a single icon. The Home tab is selected, and there is still a selection box around the two grouped icons.

2. On the Home tab, in the Drawing group, click the **Arrange** button, and then in the Group Objects section of the menu, click **Ungroup**. The selection box around the two icons disappears and each gear has a selection box around it.

3. Change the height of the selected shapes to **4"**. Because the gears are now shapes instead of icons, their aspect ratios are not locked.

4. Change the width of the selected shapes to **4"**.

5. Click a blank area of the slide, click the top gear, and then change its fill color to the **Green, Accent 3** color.

6. Position the turquoise gear so it horizontally aligns with the center of the slide and so its middle vertically aligns with the middle of the "Stay Flexible" text box underneath it.

7. Duplicate the green gear, and then change the color of the duplicate to the **Indigo, Text 2** color.

8. Position the blue and green gears as shown in Figure 5–17. They should be middle-and center-aligned with the text boxes underneath them and their top and bottom edges should align with each other.

**Figure 5–17** **Gears positioned on Slide 13**

**Figure 5–17** **Gears positioned on Slide 13**

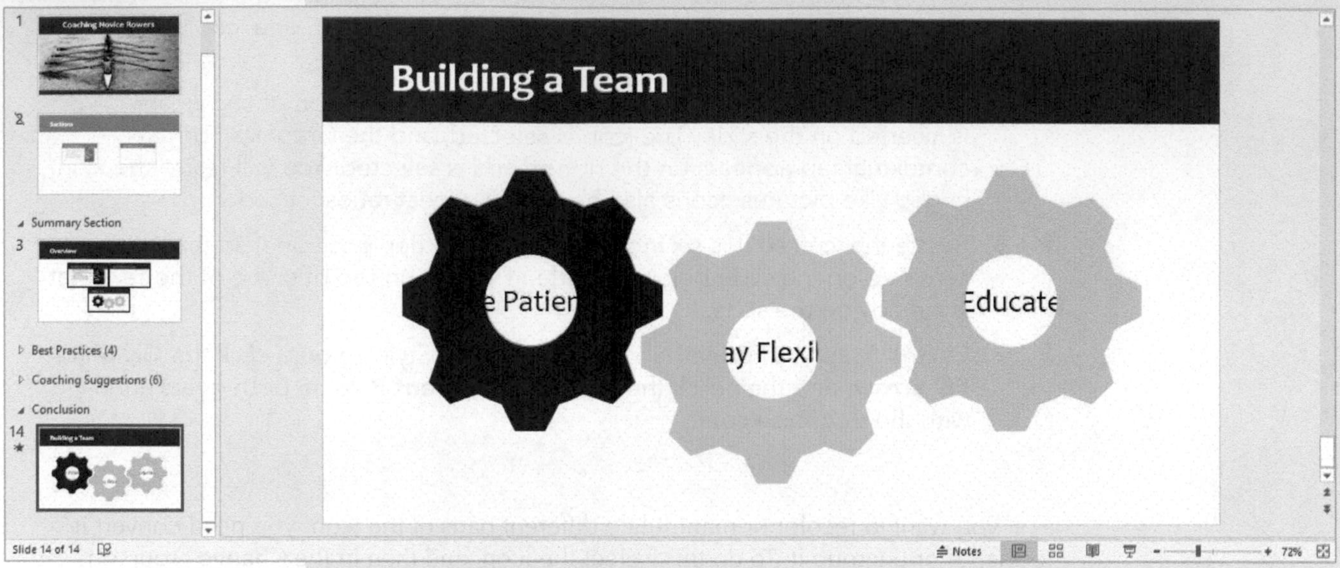

iStock.com/spepple22; Microgen/Shutterstock.com

9. Open the Selection pane, click each Freeform object to figure out which name in the Selection pane corresponds to each shape, and then rename the three shapes as **Blue gear**, **Turquoise gear**, and **Green gear**.

10. Close the Selection pane, and then save the changes to the presentation.

# Using the Effect Options Dialog Box to Modify Animations

Tyler wants you to apply animations to Slide 14 ("Building a Team") so that the gears appear one at a time after the slide transitions, then change to a light color and rotate. Then he wants the text boxes to appear on top of the gears.

You could duplicate the gears, change the color of the duplicate gears to the lighter color, and then add exit animations to the original gears and entrance animations to the duplicate gears. Instead, you will modify the entrance animation that you will apply to the gears so that the gears change color when the slide show is advanced.

To modify an animation this way, you need to use the Effect Options dialog box. The exact title and contents of this dialog box vary depending on the selected animation, but it always contains an Effect tab and a Timing tab. For entrance, exit, and emphasis animations, the title of the dialog box matches the name of the animation. For most motion path animations, the title of the dialog box matches the selected direction effect.

The first thing you need to do to create the effect Tyler wants is to apply the Appear animation to the gears and then modify that animation so that the gears change to a lighter color when the slide show is advanced.

**Tip**

To select all of the objects on a slide, click the Select button on the Home tab in the Editing group, and then click Select All.

**To change the fill color of shapes when the slide show advances:**

1. Click the blue gear, press and hold **SHIFT**, click the turquoise gear, click the green gear, and then release **SHIFT**.

2. Apply the **Appear** entrance animation to the three selected objects. Tyler wants the gears to change to a lighter color when the slide show advances.

3. On the Animations tab, in the Animation group, click the **Dialog Box Launcher** 🖼. The Appear dialog box opens with the Effect tab selected. This is the Effect Options dialog box for the Appear animation. In the After animation box, Don't Dim appears. This means that nothing will happen to the selected objects when the slide show advances.

4. Click the **After animation** arrow. A menu opens listing options that will be applied to the selected objected once the slide show advances. See Figure 5–18.

**Figure 5–18**       **Effect Options dialog box titled "Appear"**

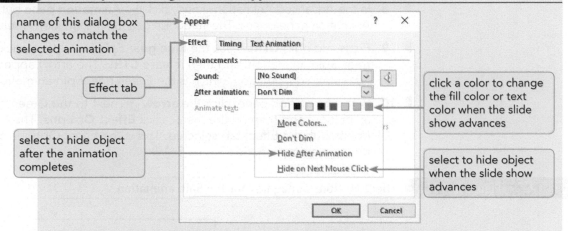

name of this dialog box changes to match the selected animation

Effect tab

select to hide object after the animation completes

click a color to change the fill color or text color when the slide show advances

select to hide object when the slide show advances

If you select either of the Hide options, the selected object will act as if the Disappear exit animation was applied to it when the slide show advances. If you select a color, the fill color of the shape will change to that color when the slide show advances. If the selected object was a text box, the font color would change to the selected color, and if the selected object was a shape with text in it, the fill color of the shape would change.

5. On the menu, click the third color square, which is light blue. The menu closes and the light blue color you selected appears in the After animation box.

6. Click **OK** to close the dialog box.

Now you need to add the Spin animation to the gears. You also need to modify this animation so that the gears keep spinning until the next slide appears.

### To modify an animation so that it does not end until the next slide appears:

1. Select all three gears.

2. On the Animations tab, in the Advanced Animation group, click the **Add Animation** button, and then click the **Spin** emphasis animation. The Spin animation previews and the three gears spin in a clockwise direction. To make it look like the gears are operating together, you need to change the direction of the turquoise gear to counter-clockwise.

3. To the left of the turquoise gear, click the **2** animation sequence icon to select only the Spin animation applied to the turquoise gear. In the Animation group, the Spin animation is selected.

4. In the Animation group, click the **Effect Options** button, click **Counterclockwise**, and then on the status bar, click the **Slide Show** button. Slide 14 appears in Slide Show view.

5. Press the **SPACEBAR**. The three gears appear and are three different colors.

6. Press the **SPACEBAR**. The gears all change to light blue and spin once. Now it looks like the gears are rotating so that each gear is making the gears touching it rotate.

7. Press **ESC** to end the slide show. You need to modify the Spin animations so they continue until the slide is no longer on the screen.

8. In the Advanced Animation group, click the **Animation pane** button. The Animation pane opens. The Turquoise gear Spin animation is selected in the pane.

9. Press and hold **CTRL**, click the **Blue gear Spin** animation, click the **Green gear Spin** animation, and then release **CTRL**. The arrow appears next to the last selected animation, which is the Green gear Spin animation.

10. In the Animation pane, click the **arrow** ⏷ next to the Green gear Spin animation, and then on the menu, click **Effect Options**. The Spin dialog box opens with the Effect tab selected. This is the Effect Options dialog box for the Spin animation. See Figure 5–19.

---

**Figure 5–19**    **Effect Options dialog box for the Spin animation**

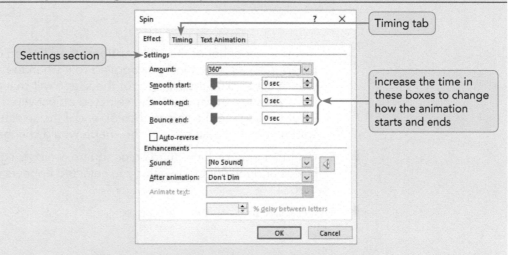

The Effect tab for the Spin animation contains a Settings section which was not in the Appear Effect Options dialog box. For the Spin animation, you can change how the animation starts and ends. If you increase the time in the Smooth start box, the animation will start more slowly and then increase to the appropriate speed. Likewise, if you increase the time in the Smooth end box, as the animation ends, it will slow down over the course of that time. And if you increase the time in the Bounce end box, the object will bounce in the direction of the animation at the end of the animation.

11. Click the **Timing** tab, click the **Repeat** arrow, click **Until End of Slide**. Now the gears will continue to spin until the next slide is displayed. You also want to slow the animation down a little. You can change the Duration on the Animations tab or in this dialog box.

12. Click the **Duration** arrow, click **5 seconds (Very Slow)**, and then click **OK**. The animation previews and the gears spin more slowly.

Tyler wants the text boxes that appear under the gears to appear on top of the gears after they start spinning, and he wants the characters in the text boxes to appear one letter at a time. He also wants a typewriter sound to play as each character appears. You will apply an animation to the text boxes.

**To modify an animation applied to text so that the text appears one character at a time with a sound effect:**

1. On Slide 14 ("Building a Team"), click the text in the center of the blue gear, press and hold **SHIFT**, click the text in the center of the turquoise gear, click the text in the center of the green gear, and then release **SHIFT**. The three text boxes are selected.

2. Apply the **Appear** entrance animation to the text boxes. The three Appear animations are added to the Animation pane and are selected.

3. In the Animation pane, click the **arrow** ▼ next to the Educate Appear animation, and then click **Effect Options**. The Appear Effect Options dialog box opens. Because the selected objects are text boxes, this dialog box now includes the Text Animation tab and an Animate text box on the Effects tab. In the Animate text box, All at once is selected.

4. On the Effect tab, click the **Animate text** arrow. The menu that opens contains two additional choices for the text: By word and By letter.

5. Click **By letter**.

6. Below the Animate text box, change the value in the box to **0.1**. This changes the pause between each letter appearing to 0.1 seconds.

7. At the top of the dialog box, click the **Sound** arrow, scroll down in the menu, click **Typewriter**, and then click **OK**.

8. On the status bar, click the **Slide Show** button 🖵. The slide appears in Slide Show view displaying only the slide title.

9. Press the **SPACEBAR**. The gears appear.

10. Press the **SPACEBAR**. The gears change to light blue and start spinning.

11. Press the **SPACEBAR**. The text in the three text boxes appears, one letter at a time, accompanied by a typewriter sound. You can't read the text because it is behind the gears.

    **Trouble?** Depending on your computer, the Typewriter sound might not play properly. Don't worry about this.

12. Press **ESC**, and then save the changes to the presentation.

# Working with Layers

Every time you add an object to a slide, a new layer is created on the slide to hold that object. As illustrated in the Session 5.1 Visual Overview, you can send objects to the back (bottom) of the layers on a slide, or you can bring an object to the front (top) of the layers. To change an object's layer, you use commands in the Arrange group on the Format tab or on the Arrange menu in the Drawing group on the Home tab for whatever type of object is selected. You can also move objects through layers using the Selection pane.

You do not need to open the Selection pane to move an object through the layers on a slide, but if a slide contains many objects, it can be easier to work with them if you can see the complete list in the Selection pane.

You need to move the text boxes so that they are in layers on top of the gears.

### To move objects through the layers on a slide:

1. On Slide 14 ("Building a Team"), click the blue gear, click the **Shape Format** tab, and then in the Arrange group, click the **Selection Pane** button. The Blue gear object is the first item in the list in the Selection pane because it is in the top layer on the slide. The Title 1 object is the last item in the list, indicating it is in the bottom layer. See Figure 5–20.

**Figure 5–20**    **Selection pane listing objects in layers**

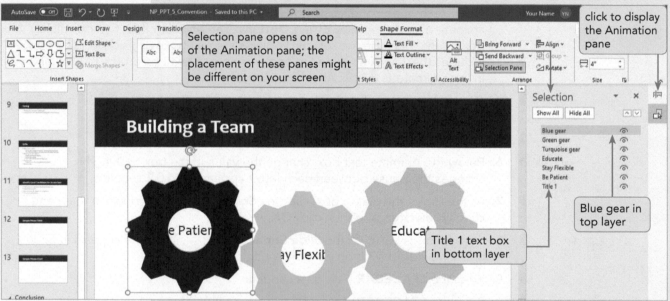

iStock.com/spepple22; Microgen/Shutterstock.com

**Tip**

If you are working with a slide containing multiple objects, you can click the eye icon in the Selection pane to hide an object on a slide to get it out of your way while you work with another object.

2. On the Shape Format tab, in the Arrange group, click the **Send Backward arrow**, and then click **Send to Back**. In the Selection pane, Blue gear moves to the bottom of the list, and on the slide, the blue gear is now behind the "Be Patient" text box.

3. In the Selection pane, click the **Stay Flexible** object, and then in the Arrange group, click the **Bring Forward** button. On the slide, nothing appears to change, but in the Selection pane, the selected Stay Flexible object moved up one place in the list.

4. At the top of the Selection pane, click the **Bring Forward** button twice. In the Selection pane, the selected object moves up two more positions so it is above the Turquoise gear object. On the slide, Stay Flexible text box now appears on top of the turquoise gear.

5. In the Selection pane, click the **Educate** object.

6. In the Arrange group, click the **Bring Forward arrow**, and then click **Bring to Front**. The Educate object moves to the top of the list in the Selection pane. On the slide, the Educate text box is now on top of the green gear.

During the slide show, Tyler wants the three gears to appear at the same time, one-half second after the slide transitions. After a one-second delay, he wants the gears to fade and start spinning and the text boxes to appear one at a time. You'll modify the start settings of the animations.

### To modify the animations so that they start automatically:

1. Click the Animation Pane icon 📹 to the right of the Selection pane to display the Animation pane, click the **Blue gear Appear** animation, click the **arrow** ▾ , and then click **Effect Options**.

2. In the Appear dialog box, click the **Timing** tab.

3. Click the **Start** arrow, and then click **After Previous**.

4. Change the value in the Delay box to **0.5** seconds, and then click **OK**. The start setting of the Turquoise gear and Green gear Appear animations is set to With Previous. In the Animation pane, you can see by the position of the green arrows that they will appear before the Blue gear appears. See Figure 5–21. You need to add the same delay to these animations.

**Figure 5–21**    **Animation pane showing the timing of the animations**

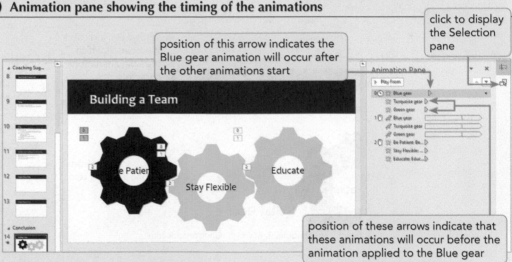

iStock.com/spepple22; Microgen/Shutterstock.com

5. In the Animation pane, select both the **Turquoise gear Appear** and **Green gear Appear** animations, click the **Animations** tab, and then in the Timing group, click the **Delay** up arrow twice. The green arrows now show that the three animations will occur at the same time.

6. Select the **Blue gear Spin** animation, change its Start setting to **After Previous**. The yellow bars for all three Spin animations shift right.

7. With the Blue gear Spin animation selected, change the Delay to **1.00** second. The yellow bar shifts right. This time, instead of adding the same delay to the other two Spin animations, you will reapply the With Previous start setting.

8. Select the **Turquoise gear Spin** animation and the **Green gear Spin** animation.

9. Next to the Green gear Spin animation, click the **arrow** ▾ . There is a check mark next to Start with Previous.

10. On the menu, click **Start with Previous** to reapply this start setting. The two yellow bars shift right so that they are aligned with the yellow bar of the Blue gear Spin animation.

Now you need to modify the Appear animations applied to the text boxes so that the first text box appears at the same time the gears start spinning, followed by the other two text boxes one at a time.

▶ **11.** In the Animation pane, select the three Appear animations applied to the text boxes, and then change their Start setting to **After Previous**. In the Animation pane, the green arrows shift right. The arrow indicating the Appear animation applied to the Be Patient text box is aligned with a vertical line through the three Spin animations. Even though the Appear animations are set to start After Previous, they can't start after the Spin animations end because the Spin animations are set to repeat until the end of the slide. The vertical line indicates the point at which the Spin animations complete one revolution. This shows that the Appear animations will start after the Spin animations complete one revolution. See Figure 5–22.

**Figure 5–22**  **Animation pane showing the Appear animations shifted right**

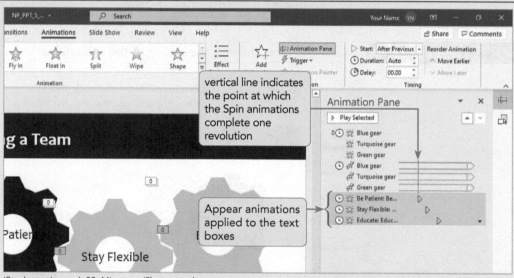

iStock.com/spepple22; Microgen/Shutterstock.com

▶ **12.** Select the **Stay Flexible Appear** animation, set a Delay of **0.50** seconds, and then do the same for the **Educate Appear** animation.

▶ **13.** On the status bar, click the **Slide Show** button 🖵. Slide 14 appears in Slide Show view. After one-half second, the three gears appear. After one second, the gears fade to blue and start spinning. Then there is a delay of six seconds, then the three text boxes appear, one after the other, with one-half second between each one. The reason the first text box appeared after a six-second delay is because the Spin animation was slowed down so that it takes five seconds to complete one full spin. Then you applied a one-second delay to the Appear animation applied to the text box. The six-second delay is too long.

▶ **14.** Press **ESC** to end the slide show. You will modify the Appear animation applied to the Be Patient text box so that it starts one second after the gears start spinning.

**Tip**

To zoom in or out on the animation time line in the Animation pane, click the Seconds button at the bottom of the Animation pane, and then click Zoom In or Zoom Out.

▶ **15.** Change the Start setting of the Be Patient Appear animation to **With Previous**, and change the Delay to **2.00** seconds. Remember that the Spin animations have a delay of one second applied to them. You need to set the delay of the Appear animation to two seconds because you want the text to appear one second after the spin animations start.

▶ **16.** Change the start setting of the Stay Flexible Appear and the Educate Appear animations to **With Previous**. Tyler wants a little more time between the text box animations.

▶ **17.** Change the Delay for the Stay Flexible animation to **3.50** seconds, change the Delay for the Educate Appear animation to **5.00** seconds, and then on the status bar, click the **Slide Show** button 🖵. The animations now appear as Tyler wants.

▶ **18.** Press **ESC** to end the slide show, close the Animation and Selection panes, and then save the changes to the presentation.

You have created a presentation by importing an outline and inserting slides from another presentation. You modified the presentation outline in Outline view, divided the presentation into sections, and created a summary zoom. You moved objects through layers and modified animation effects using the Effect Options dialog box. In the next session, you will insert and modify objects created in Excel and Word and format them. You will also annotate slides during a slide show and create handouts in Microsoft Word.

# Review

## Session 5.1 Quick Check

1. Describe how you use a Word outline to create slides in PowerPoint.

2. Describe how you insert slides from one presentation into another.

3. When you insert slides from one presentation into another, how do you apply the colors and other formatting from the destination presentation to the newly inserted slides?

4. What happens when you select a first-level bulleted item in the Outline pane in Outline view, and then click the Decrease List Level button?

5. Describe the two ways to create sections.

6. How are layers created on a slide?

7. How can you change the color of a shape or text to which an animation is applied when a slide show is advanced?

# Session 5.2 Visual Overview:

### source file (Word table)

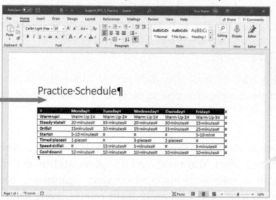

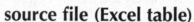

The program used to create an object that you want to copy, embed, or link is called the **source program**; the file that initially contains the object is called the **source file**.

When you paste an object, a copy of an object created in a source program becomes part of the destination file; you can edit the object with the tools available in the destination program. There is no connection between the inserted object and its source file.

### source file (Excel table)

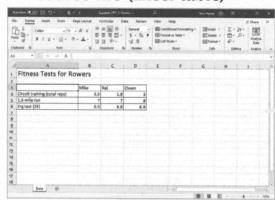

When you **embed** an object, a copy of the object along with a one-way connection to the source program become part of the destination file, and you can edit the object using the source program's commands. Changes made do not appear in the source file.

### source program

You must have access to the source program to edit an embedded object; however, you do not need access to the source file.

### source file (Excel chart)

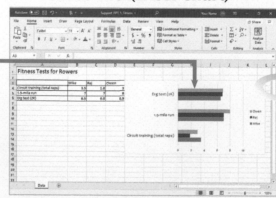

When linking an object, you must have access to the source file if you want to make changes to the source object.

# Importing, Embedding, and Linking

### destination file
### (PowerPoint presentation)

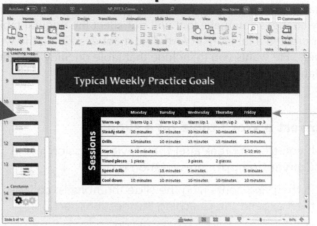

The program used to create the file into which you want to paste, embed, or link an object from a source file is called the **destination program**; the file in which you want to insert the object is called the **destination file**.

### destination file
### (PowerPoint presentation)

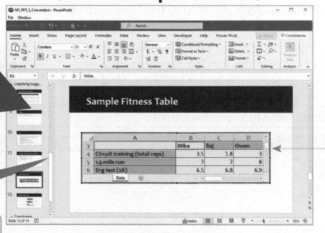

There is no connection between an embedded object and its source file; therefore, changes made to the object in the source file do not appear in the destination file.

When you **link** an object, a connection is created between the source and destination programs so that the object exists in only one place—the source file—but the link displays the object in the destination file as well.

### destination file
### (PowerPoint presentation)

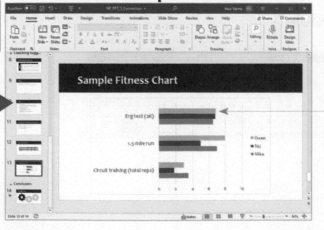

If you edit a linked object in the source file, the link ensures that the changes appear in the destination file.

# Inserting a Word Table

You know how to use PowerPoint commands to create a table on a slide, but what if you've already created a table in a Word document? You don't need to re-create it in PowerPoint. Instead, you can copy the table from the Word document and then paste it on a slide. Similar to importing a Word outline or inserting slides from another presentation, once you paste the table, the table becomes part of the PowerPoint file, and any changes you make to it will not affect the original table in the source file.

Tyler created a table in a Word document describing the weekly practice plan for his rowers. He wants you to include that table on Slide 8 in the NP_PPT_5_Convention presentation.

## To insert a Word table on a slide:

1. If you took a break after the previous session, make sure the **NP_PPT_5_ Convention.pptx** presentation is open.

2. In the pane containing the slide thumbnails, collapse all of the sections, and then expand the Coaching Suggestions section.

3. Display Slide 8 ("Typical Weekly Practice Goals"), and then change the layout to **Title Only**.

4. Start Microsoft Word, and then open the document **Support_PPT_5_ Practice.docx**, located in the PowerPoint5 > Module folder included with your Data Files.

5. Move the pointer on top of the table so that the Table Select Handle ⊞ appears in the top-left corner, and then click the **Table Select handle** ⊞ to select the entire table. See Figure 5–23.

| Figure 5–23 | Selected table in Word document |
|---|---|

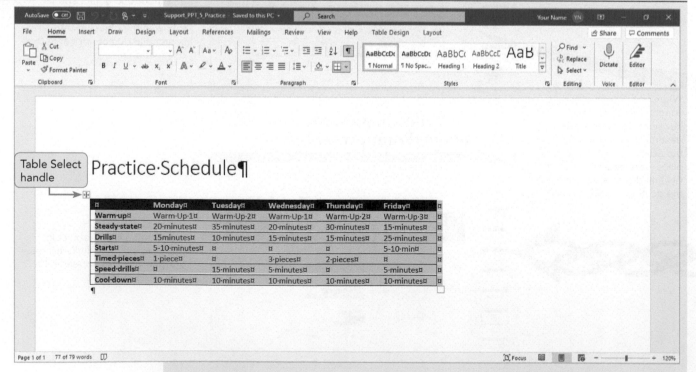

**6.** On the Home tab, in the Clipboard group, click the **Copy** button.

**7.** On the Windows taskbar, click the **NP_PPT_5_Convention – PowerPoint** button 🅿 to switch back to the NP_PPT_5_Convention presentation.

**8.** On the Home tab, in the Clipboard group, click the **Paste arrow**, and then click the **Keep Source Formatting** button 📝. The table is pasted on the slide as a PowerPoint table with the formatting from the source file (the Word file). You need to make the table larger.

**9.** On the ribbon, click the **Layout** tab.

**10.** In the Table Size group, click in the **Height** box, type **4.2**, click in the **Width** box, type **9.5**, and then press **ENTER**.

**11.** Make sure the entire table is still selected, and then on the ribbon, click the **Home** tab.

**12.** In the Font group, click the **Font Size arrow**, and then click **18**. The font size of the text in the table increases to 18 points.

**13.** Point to the table border so that the pointer changes to the move pointer ↖, and then drag the table to position it so its center aligns with the center of the slide and so it is approximately vertically centered in the white area on the slide.

**14.** On the Windows taskbar, click the **Support_PPT_5_Practice – Word** button ⬛, and then close the document and exit Word. You return to the NP_PPT_5_Convention presentation.

## Formatting Cells in Tables

Your previous work with tables focused on formatting and modifying a table's appearance and structure. You can also make formatting changes to individual cells. For example, you can merge cells, rotate text in cells, and change the width of borders.

When you merge cells, you combine two or more cells into one. You can merge cells in the same row, the same column, or the same rectangular block of rows and columns. Merging cells is especially useful when you need to enter large amounts of information into a single cell, or when you want to add a heading that spans more than one column. To merge cells, you use the Merge Cells button, which is located in the Merge group on the Layout tab.

Tyler recommends that practices be divided into seven sessions devoted to specific activities. You will create a new first column and merge the cells in that column to create one larger cell containing the label "Sessions".

**To create a new first column and merge cells:**

**1.** Click in any cell in the first column in the table, and then on the ribbon, click the **Layout** tab.

**2.** In the Rows & Columns group, click the **Insert Left** button. A new first column is added to the table.

**3.** Click in the second cell in the new column to position the insertion point, press and hold the mouse button, and then drag down to select the rest of the cells in the column.

**4.** On the Layout tab, in the Merge group, click the **Merge Cells** button. The seven selected cells are merged into one cell. See Figure 5–24.

Figure 5–24 **Merged cell in imported table**

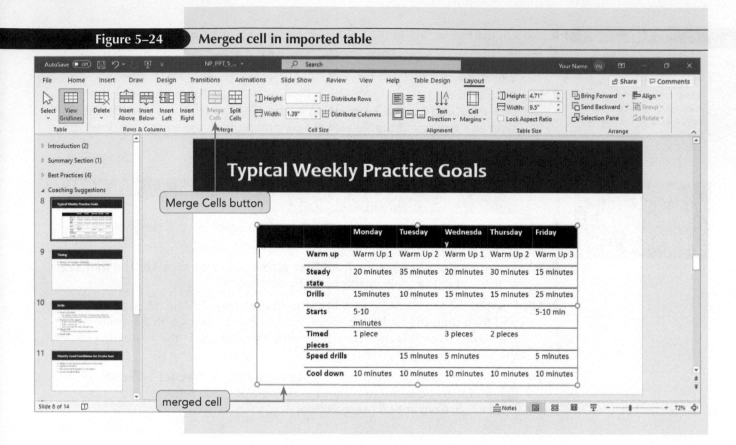

You can rotate text in a cell to read from the top to the bottom or from the bottom to the top. You will enter the label in the merged cell and then rotate it so it is read from bottom to top.

### To enter, rotate, and format text in a cell:

1. Click in the merged cell, if necessary, and then type **Sessions**.

2. On the Layout tab, in the Alignment group, click the **Text Direction** button, and then click **Rotate all text 270°**. The text in the cell rotates so it reads sideways from the bottom up. See Figure 5–25.

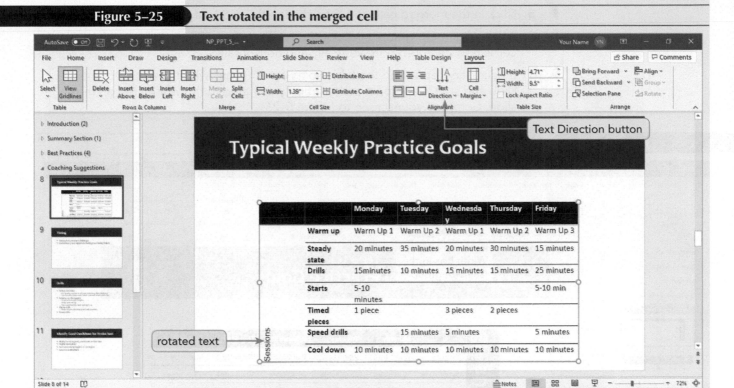

**Figure 5–25** — Text rotated in the merged cell

3. Double-click **Sessions** to select it, click the **Home** tab, and then in the Font group, click the **Bold** button B. The text is small and hard to read.

4. In the Font group, click the **Font Size arrow**, and then click **44**.

5. Click the **Table Design** tab.

6. In the WordArt Styles group, click the **Text Fill arrow** A and then click the **White, Background 1** color.

7. In the Table Styles group, click the **Shading arrow**, and then click the **Black, Text 1** color.

To finish formatting the table, you'll adjust the width of the columns and align the cell contents so that the table elements are properly proportioned. Finally, you will center-align the text in the first column.

**To resize columns and align the text in cells:**

1. Click the **Layout** tab.

2. In the Table group, click the **Select** button, and then click **Select Table**.

3. In the Cell Size group, click in the **Width** box, type **1.56**, and then press **ENTER**. All the columns are resized to 1.56 inches wide.

   **Trouble?** If all of the columns resize so they are extremely narrow, click the Undo button on the Quick Access Toolbar. Then repeat Step 3, this time making sure you click in the Width box that is in the Cell Size group (not the Width box in the Table Size group).

4. In the Alignment group, click the **Center Vertically** button. The content of each cell in the table is centered vertically.

**5.** Click in the merged cell, and then change the width of this column to **1"**.

**6.** In the Alignment group, click the **Center** button ▤. The text in the merged cell is now centered both vertically and horizontally.

**7.** If necessary, reposition the table so its center aligns with the center of the slide and so it is approximately vertically centered in the white area on the slide. Compare your screen to Figure 5–26.

**Figure 5–26** **Formatted and repositioned table**

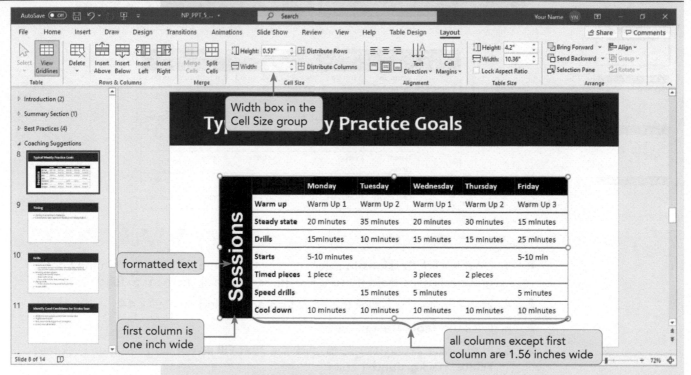

**8.** Save the changes to the presentation.

# Insight

### Inserting Equations

If you need to add a complex mathematical equation to a slide, you can use the Equation button in the Symbols group on the Insert tab. Click the Equation button arrow, and then click one of the common equations on the menu to insert that equation. If the equation you want to enter is not listed in the menu, click the Equation button to insert an equation text box, and then type the equation, using the buttons in the Symbols group on the Equation tab to insert mathematical symbols, such as the square root sign ($\sqrt{\ }$). You can also click buttons in the Structures group on the Equation tab to insert mathematical structures such as fractions ($\frac{3}{4}$ or ¾) or the integral sign that is used in calculus ($\int$). You can also click the Ink Equation button in the Tools group on the Equation tab to open the Math Input Control window. Using a stylus or your finger if you have a touchscreen device or using the pointer, drag to write the equation in the window. When you are finished, click Insert to close the window and insert the equation you drew in the equation text box on the slide.

# Inserting Excel Data and Objects

If you created a table or a chart in Excel, you can insert those Excel objects on slides instead of recreating them in PowerPoint. In addition to pasting an object from the Clipboard, you can embed or link it. Pasting, embedding, and linking all involve inserting an object from a source file into a destination file. The difference is where the objects are stored and which program's commands are used to modify the object. Refer to the Session 5.2 Visual Overview for more information about the differences between pasting, embedding, and linking.

When you embed an object, you insert a link to the source program as well as the object itself, and this increases the file size. If you do not need to access the source program commands from within the destination file, pasting an object is probably a better choice than embedding it.

## Embedding an Excel Worksheet

You can insert a worksheet created in Excel on a slide. When you do, you can choose to paste it as a table or a picture, embed it, or link it. To paste a worksheet as a table or a picture or to embed it, you use one of the buttons on the Paste menu. Note that when you paste Excel data as a picture, you cannot edit the data, but you can format the object using commands on the Picture Format tab. If you want to link the data in the worksheet, you need to click the Paste Special command on the Paste menu and then click the Paste link option button in the Paste Special dialog box that opens.

Tyler regularly has his rowers perform fitness tests. They are timed when they row two kilometers on a rowing machine called an ergometer (or erg, for short) and when they run one and a half miles. The number of times they complete a circuit of exercises is also counted. Tyler tracks this data in an Excel workbook. He uses this data to create charts that he posts so that the rowers are motivated to try to improve their numbers. Tyler asked you to embed sample data from the workbook into Slide 11 of the presentation.

## Reference

### Embedding an Excel Worksheet in a Slide

- Start Excel (the source program), open the file containing the worksheet you want to embed, and then select that worksheet's sheet tab.
- In the Excel worksheet, click and drag to select the cells you want to copy, and then on the Home tab, in the Clipboard group, click the Copy button.
- Switch to the PowerPoint presentation, and then display the slide in which you want to embed the copied cells.
- On the Home tab, in the Clipboard group, click the Paste arrow, and then click the Embed button, or click the Paste arrow, click Paste Special, make sure Microsoft Excel Worksheet Object is selected in the As list, and then click OK.

First, you will open the Excel workbook and then copy the cells containing the sample data to be embedded in Slide 11 of the NP_PPT_5_Convention presentation.

### To embed Excel worksheet data in Slide 11:

1. Display Slide 12 ("Sample Fitness Table"), and then change the layout to **Title Only**.

2. Start Microsoft Excel, open the file **Support_PPT_5_Fitness.xlsx**, located in the PowerPoint5 > Module folder included with your Data Files, and then save the workbook as **NP_PPT_5_Fitness** to the location where you are storing your files. See Figure 5–27.

**Figure 5-27** Data in Excel file

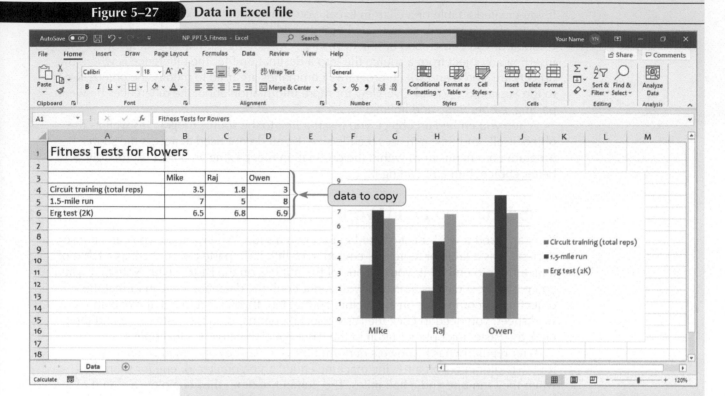

**Trouble?** If the worksheet is not at 120% zoom, use the Zoom slider on the right end of the status bar to change the zoom to 120%.

3. Move the pointer on top of cell **A3**, press and hold the mouse button, drag down to cell **D6**, and then release the mouse button. Cells A3 through D6 are selected.

4. On the Home tab, in the Clipboard group, click the **Copy** button.

5. On the Windows taskbar, click the **NP_PPT_5_Convention – PowerPoint** button [P] to switch back to the NP_PPT_5_Convention presentation with Slide 12 displayed.

6. On the Home tab, in the Clipboard group, click the **Paste arrow**, and then click the **Embed** button [icon]. The worksheet is embedded in the slide with the presentation theme. Instead of the table contextual tabs, the Shape Format tab appears on the ribbon.

7. Resize the worksheet object so it is 2 inches high and 10.27 inches wide. (Change the measurements on the Shape Format tab in the Shape Height box in the Size group if necessary.)

8. Center align the embedded object on the slide and then drag it so it is approximately vertically centered in the white area on the slide.

**Tip**

To create an embedded Excel worksheet from within PowerPoint, click the Insert tab, click the Table button in the Tables group, and then click Excel Spreadsheet.

To modify an embedded worksheet, you double-click the selected worksheet object to display the Excel tabs and commands on the ribbon in the PowerPoint window. You can then change the data or format the table using the Excel commands on the ribbon.

Tyler wants you to fill the cells with color. He also wants the column and row labels to be bold. You'll make these changes now.

### To modify the embedded worksheet:

1. On Slide 12 ("Sample Fitness Table"), double-click the worksheet object. The ribbon changes to display the Excel tabs and commands, although the program title bar indicates you still are working in PowerPoint. Cells A3 through D6 in the worksheet are selected. See Figure 5–28.

**Figure 5–28**    Embedded Excel object with Excel active

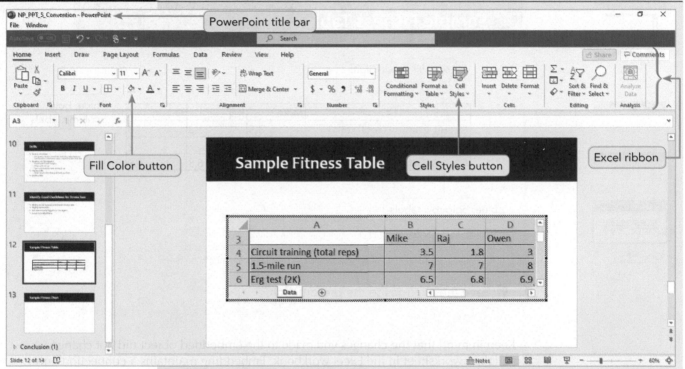

2. On the Home tab, in the Font group, click the **Fill Color button arrow**, and then click the **Blue, Accent 1, Lighter 80%** color. The selected cells are filled with the light blue color.

3. Move the pointer on top of cell **A4**, press and hold the mouse button, drag down to cell **A6**, and then release the mouse button. Cells A4 through A6 are selected.

4. Press and hold **CTRL**, drag to select cells **B3** through **D3**, and then release the mouse button and **CTRL**. Cells A4 through A6 and cells B3 through D3 are selected.

5. In the Styles group, click the **Cell Styles** button, and then click **Heading 4**. The selected cells are formatted with the Heading 4 style, which formats the text as bold and blue.

6. Click a blank area of the slide. The ribbon changes back to the PowerPoint ribbon, and then the Excel window may become the active window.

7. If necessary, on the Windows taskbar, click the **NP_PPT_5_Convention – PowerPoint** button to switch back to the NP_PPT_5_Convention presentation with Slide 12 displayed. The embedded object is still selected.

8. Click a blank area of the slide again to deselect the object. See Figure 5–29.

Figure 5–29 **Formatted data in the embedded Excel workbook**

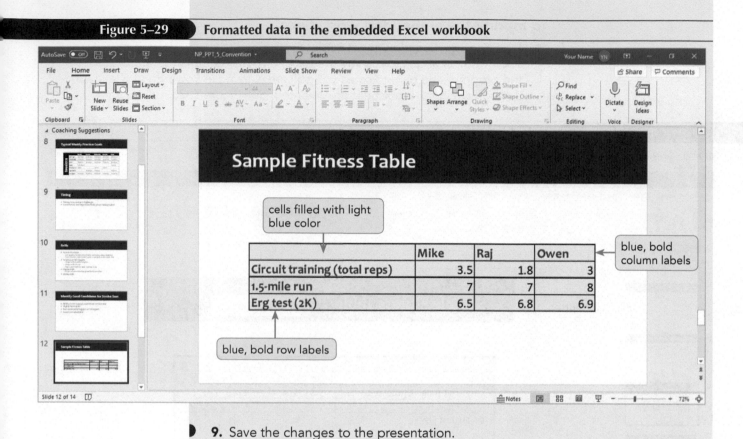

**9.** Save the changes to the presentation.

Keep in mind that the changes you made to the embedded object did not change the original worksheet in the Excel workbook. Embedding maintains a connection only with the program that was used to create the object, not with the original object itself.

## Linking an Excel Chart

If you need to include an Excel chart in your presentation that is based on data that might change, you can link the chart instead of embed it. For example, you might need to include a chart on a slide, but you know that the final data is not available yet or that the chart data will change over time. In this case, you should link the chart so that when the source file is updated, the linked chart in the destination file is updated and reflects the changes made to the source file.

There are two ways to link a chart from an Excel workbook to a presentation. After copying the chart, you can click the Paste arrow in PowerPoint and then click the Use Destination Theme & Link Data button or the Keep Source Formatting & Link Data button. Both of these options link the data of the chart, but not the chart itself. This means that if you change the way the chart looks in the Excel file, that change will not be reflected on the slide. Instead, when you click the chart on the slide, the chart tools contextual tabs appear on the PowerPoint ribbon and you can use the commands on those tabs to modify the chart.

If you want to link both the data and the chart, you need to use the Paste Special dialog box, which you open by clicking the Paste Special command on the Paste button menu. When you link a chart or data using the Paste Special dialog box, you do not have the option to use the style of the destination file, but any changes you make to the chart in the Excel file will be reflected in the PowerPoint file.

# Reference

## Linking Excel Chart Data and Format to a Slide

- Open the Excel file containing the chart to be linked, and then select the sheet tab that contains the chart.
- Point to the chart to display the ScreenTip "Chart Area", click the chart to select it, and then copy it to the Clipboard.
- Switch to the PowerPoint presentation, and display the slide to which you will link the chart.
- On the Home tab, in the Clipboard group, click the Paste arrow, click Paste Special to open the Paste Special dialog box, click the Paste link option button, and then click OK.

In the Excel workbook, Tyler created a column chart to illustrate the sample data. He wants you to link it to Slide 13 in the NP_PPT_5_Convention presentation.

### To insert a chart linked to the Excel worksheet:

1. Display Slide 13 ("Sample Fitness Chart"), and then change the layout to **Title Only**.

2. On the taskbar, click the **NP_PPT_5_Fitness – Excel** button ⊠. The workbook appears with the Data worksheet selected. The column chart was created from the sample data.

3. Move the pointer on top of the chart so that the ScreenTip "Chart Area" appears, and then click to select the chart.

   **Trouble?** If the ScreenTip displays something other than "Chart Area", move the pointer closer to the top or bottom edge of the chart.

4. On the Home tab, in the Clipboard group, click the **Copy** button.

5. On the taskbar, click the **NP_PPT_5_Convention – PowerPoint** button ⊡. The NP_PPT_5_Convention presentation appears with Slide 13 displayed.

6. In the Clipboard group, click the **Paste arrow**, and then click **Paste Special**. The Paste Special dialog box opens. See Figure 5–30.

**Figure 5–30**    **Paste Special dialog box**

click to paste copied chart as a link

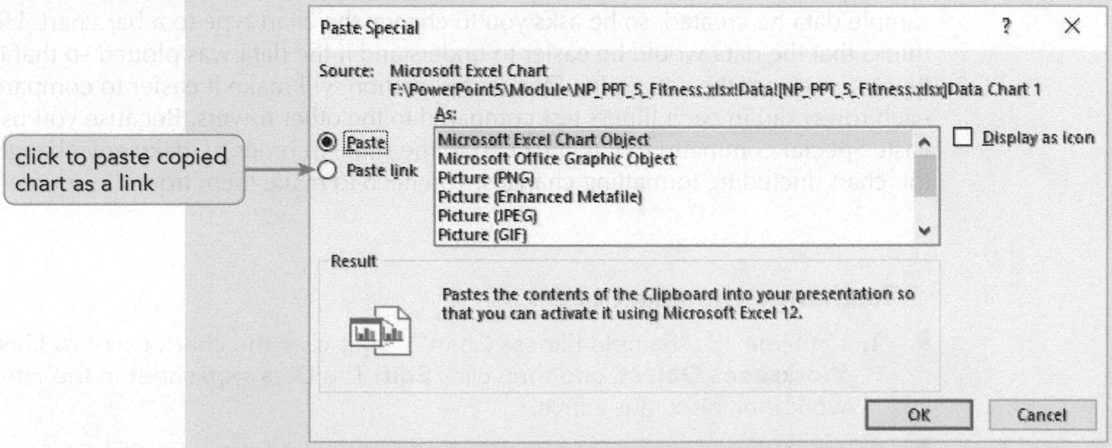

**Tip**

If you want to link worksheet cells, you must use the Paste Special dialog box.

7.  In the dialog box, click the **Paste link** option button. The As list changes to include only one object, a Microsoft Excel Chart Object.

8.  Click **OK**. The chart is linked to Slide 13 using the style of the source file. On the ribbon, the chart contextual tabs do not appear. Instead, the Shape Format tab appears.

9.  On the ribbon, click the **Shape Format** tab, and then resize the chart so it is **5.3** inches high and about **9.84** inches wide, using the Shape Height and Shape Width boxes in the Size group on the Shape Format tab to help you.

10. Position the chart so its center aligns with the center of the slide and so it is approximately vertically centered in the white area on the slide.

Tyler wants to make some changes to the chart. First, he wants to change the sample data for Raj's time for the run so there is a greater difference in this data for the three rowers. He asks you to make the changes in the Excel worksheet and then make sure the changes are reflected in the PowerPoint presentation.

### To modify the linked chart:

1.  On Slide 13 ("Sample Fitness Chart"), double-click the linked chart. The NP_PPT_5_Fitness workbook becomes active.

    **Trouble?** If you store your files on the cloud, the workbook might open in the Excel 365 app in your browser. Your steps may differ slightly.

2.  Click cell **C5**, type **5**, and then press **ENTER**. The column in the chart that shows Raj's time for the run changes to reflect the new data.

3.  Switch to the NP_PPT_5_Convention presentation. The chart on Slide 13 has been updated to reflect the changed data.

    **Trouble?** If the chart on Slide 13 did not update, right-click the chart, and then on the shortcut menu, click Update Link.

The linked chart is a column chart with the rowers' names as the categories and each type of test as a data series. Tyler thinks that a bar chart would better illustrate the sample data he created, so he asks you to change the chart type to a bar chart. He also thinks that the data would be easier to understand if the data was plotted so that the types of tests are the categories. This representation will make it easier to compare how each rower did in each fitness test compared to the other rowers. Because you used the Paste Special command to link the chart to the slide, in order to make any changes to the chart, including formatting changes, you need to make them from the source file.

### To change the chart type:

1.  On Slide 13 ("Sample Fitness Chart"), right-click the chart, point to **Linked Worksheet Object**, and then click **Edit**. The Data worksheet in the Fitness workbook becomes active.

2.  Move the pointer on top of the chart so that the ScreenTip "Chart Area" or "Chart" appears, and then click to select the chart.

3. Click the **Chart Design** or **Chart** tab, and then, in the Type group, click the **Change Chart Type** button. The Change Chart Type dialog box opens.

   **Trouble?** If you are using the Excel 365 app in your browser, click the **Change Chart Type arrow**, and then click **Clustered Bar** on the menu. Skip Step 4. In Step 5, click the **Switch Row/Column** button on the left of the ribbon.

4. In the navigation pane on the left, click **Bar**, and then click **OK**. The dialog box closes, and the chart is now a bar chart. Next you need to change how the rows and columns of source data are plotted on the chart.

**Tip**

You can also click the second option in the Change Chart Type dialog box to insert a chart with the rows and columns switched.

5. On the Chart Design tab, in the Data group, click the **Switch Row/Column** button. The chart changes so that the types of tests are the categories of data and each person's data is a data series. This means the legend identifying each bar color now contains the column labels Owen, Raj, and Mike, and the labels identifying the bars are now the row labels.

6. Save the changes to the Excel workbook, and then close the workbook and exit Excel. You return to the NP_PPT_5_Convention presentation. All the changes you made to the chart are shown in the chart on Slide 13. See Figure 5–31.

| Figure 5–31 | Updated linked chart on Slide 13 |
|---|---|

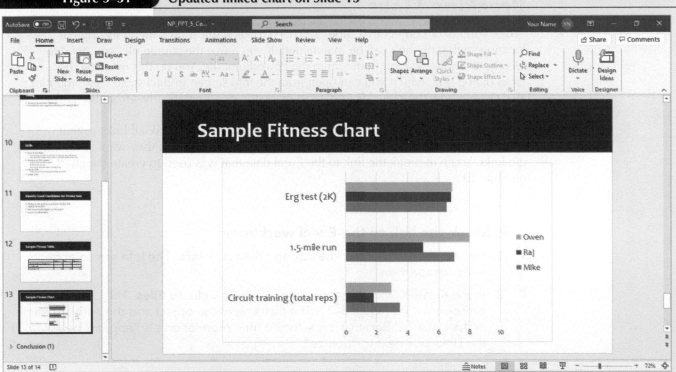

**Trouble?** If the changes were not applied to the chart on the slide, right-click the chart, and then on the shortcut menu, click Update Link.

7. Save the changes to the presentation.

You have now linked and edited an Excel chart in a PowerPoint presentation. Any additional changes made to the workbook will be reflected in the linked chart in the PowerPoint slide.

**Proskills**

Decision Making: Comparing Paste, Embed, and Linking Options

Each method of including objects from another file has advantages and disadvantages. The advantage of pasting or embedding an object instead of linking it is that the source file and the destination file can be stored separately. You can make changes to the object in the destination file, and the source file will be unaffected. The disadvantage of pasting or embedding an object is that you do not have access to the source program from within the destination file to modify the object. Another disadvantage of embedding an object is that the destination file size is somewhat larger than it would be if the object were simply imported as a picture or text or linked.

The advantage of linking an object instead of embedding it is that the object remains identical in the source and destination files, and the destination file size does not increase as much as if the object were embedded. The disadvantage is that the source and destination files must be stored together. When you need to copy information from one program to another, consider which option is the best choice for your needs.

## Breaking Links

When you link an object to a slide, you need to keep the source file in its original location so that the link can be maintained. If you move the source file, you need to identify the new location from within the PowerPoint file. You do this by using the Links dialog box, which you can open from the Info screen in Backstage view. You can also change how the object is updated—manually or automatically—from the Links dialog box.

If you plan to send the presentation to others, you should break all links so that when they open the file, they don't see a message asking them if they want to update the links. You will break the link to the Excel data that was used to create the chart on Slide 13.

**To break the link to the Excel workbook:**

1. On the ribbon, click the **File** tab, and then click **Info**. The Info screen appears in Backstage view.

2. In the Related Documents section, click **Edit Links to Files**. The Links dialog box opens. See Figure 5–32. The filename of the object and the path appear in the Links list. Because it is selected, this information also appears below the Links box next to "Source".

| Figure 5–32 | Links dialog box on the Info screen in Backstage view |

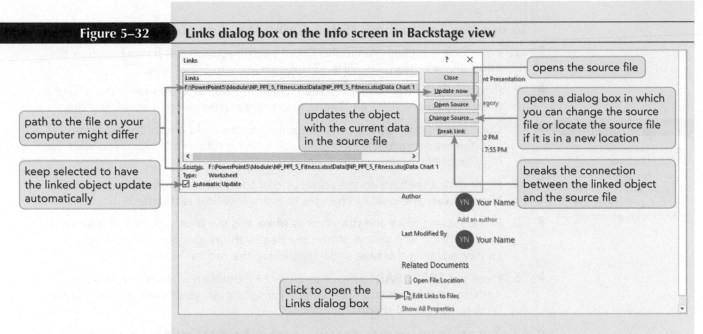

3. In the Links list, make sure the linked object is selected, and then click **Break Link**. The selected item in the list is removed. Now, if you change the data on which the chart is based in the Excel worksheet, the chart on Slide 13 will not reflect that change.

4. In the Links dialog box, click **Close**.

5. At the top of the navigation bar, click the **Back** button ⊙ to close Backstage view. On Slide 13, the chart is selected, and on the ribbon, the Picture Format tab appears. This happened because you broke the link to source file.

6. Save the changes to the presentation.

# Annotating Slides During a Slide Show

During a slide show, you can annotate—add markup to—the slides to emphasize a point. To do this, you change the pointer to a pen, which allows you to draw lines on a slide during a slide show, or to a highlighter, which allows you to highlight something on a slide during a slide show. (As you saw when you recorded a slide show, you can also annotate a slide using the pen or highlighter while you are recording.) For example, you might use the Pen to underline a word or phrase that you want to emphasize or to circle a graphic that you want to point out. You can change the ink color of the Pen or Highlighter you select. You can also select the Eraser tool to remove Pen or Highlighter lines that you draw

After you go through a presentation and mark it, you have the choice of keeping the markings as drawn objects in the presentation or discarding them. If you keep them, you can convert them into text or shapes if you want.

## To use the Pen to mark slides during the slide show:

1. With Slide 13 ("Sample Fitness Chart") displayed, on the status bar, click the **Slide Show** button ⬚. Slide 13 appears in Slide Show view.

2. Right-click anywhere on the screen, point to **Pointer Options** on the shortcut menu, and then click **Pen**. The mouse pointer changes to a small, red dot.

3. Click and drag to draw an arrow pointing to the right end of the bottom blue bar (the bar representing Mike's circuit training total reps). Next, you want to highlight Mike's name in the legend.

4. Right-click anywhere on the screen, point to **Pointer Options**, and then click **Highlighter**. The pointer changes to a small, yellow rectangle.

5. In the legend, click and drag across **Mike** and the blue square in the legend to highlight it with yellow. When the Pen or the Highlighter is active, you cannot advance the slide show by clicking the mouse button.

6. Press the **SPACEBAR** to move to Slide 14 ("Building a Team"). There is nothing on this slide that you want to annotate, so you'll change the pointer back to its normal shape.

7. Right-click anywhere on the slide, point to **Pointer Options**, and then click **Highlighter** to deselect it. The pointer changes to its normal shape. While you are changing the pointer options, the animations stop, and then restart when you are done.

8. Advance the slide show to display the black slide that indicates the end of the slide show, and then advance once more. A dialog box opens asking if you want to keep your ink annotations.

9. Click **Keep**, and then return to Slide 13 ("Sample Fitness Chart"), which displays the annotations you made during the slide show. See Figure 5-33.

**Tip**

To erase an annotation in Slide Show view, right-click anywhere on the slide, point to Pointer Options, click Eraser, and then click the annotation.

**Figure 5-33** **Annotated Slide 13 in Normal view**

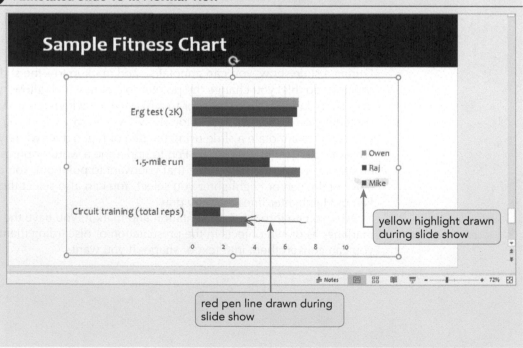

The marks you drew in Slide Show view can be manipulated or deleted just like any object on a slide. Annotations are treated as drawings, like shapes, so when you select an annotation on the slide, the Shape Format tab appears on the ribbon. You can change the color and width of annotations, as well as move them through layers, align and rotate them, and change their overall size. You can also convert annotations to text or shapes.

You will delete the highlight mark on Slide 13.

**To delete an annotation mark on Slide 13:**

1. On Slide 13 ("Sample Fitness Chart"), click the highlight mark in the legend that you drew during the slide show. The highlight mark is selected.

2. Press **DELETE**. The highlight is deleted.

3. In the pane containing the thumbnails, collapse the Conclusion and Coaching Suggestions sections, and then expand the Introduction section.

4. Display Slide 1 (the title slide), and then change the name in the subtitle to your name.

5. Save the changes to the presentation.

## Insight

### Using the Laser Pointer During a Slide Show

You can change the pointer into a red dot that looks like a laser pointer during a slide show so that you can point to objects or text on a slide during your presentation. To do this, right-click a slide during the slide show, point to Pointer Options on the shortcut menu, and then click Laser Pointer. As when you change the pointer to a Pen or Highlighter, you cannot click the mouse button to advance the slide show while the pointer is the Laser Pointer.

# Creating Handouts by Exporting a Presentation to Word

You know how to print a presentation using the Handouts setting on the Print screen in Backstage view so that one or more slides are printed per page. Another way you can create handouts is to export your slides to a new Word document. When you do this, you can choose from the following options:

- **Notes next to slides**—lists the speaker notes next to each slide; the number of slides per page depends on how many lines of speaker notes are on each slide
- **Blank lines next to slides**—adds blank lines next to each slide, three slides per page
- **Notes below slides**—lists the speaker notes below each slide; one slide per page
- **Blank lines below slides**—adds blank lines below each slide, one slide per page
- **Outline only**—lists the outline of the presentation as a bulleted list with first-level bulleted items at the same level as slide titles and second-level bulleted items indented

Tyler wants you to export the presentation to Word to create handouts displaying thumbnails of the slides with lines for notes to the right of each thumbnail.

## To create handouts by exporting the presentation to Word:

1. On the ribbon, click the **File** tab to open Backstage view, and then in the navigation bar, click **Export**. The Export screen appears.

2. Click **Create Handouts**. The screen changes to display a description of creating handouts in Microsoft Word and a button for doing this. See Figure 5–34.

**Figure 5–34** Export screen in Backstage view with Create Handouts selected

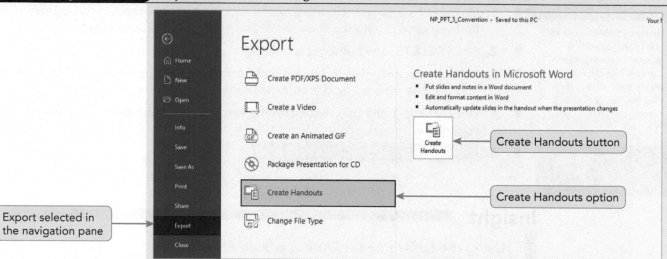

Export selected in the navigation pane

Create Handouts button

Create Handouts option

3. Click the **Create Handouts** button. Backstage view closes, and the Send to Microsoft Word dialog box opens. You can choose from five options for creating handouts, and you can choose to link the slides instead of simply exporting them. If you choose to link the handouts, when you modify the presentation, the change will be reflected in the handouts. See Figure 5–35.

**Figure 5–35** Send to Microsoft Word dialog box

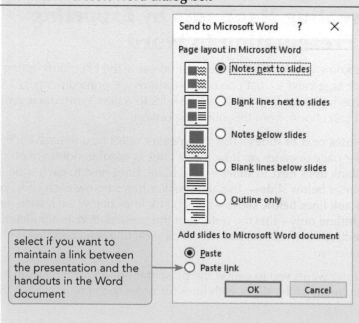

select if you want to maintain a link between the presentation and the handouts in the Word document

▶ **4.** Click the **Outline only** option button, and then click **OK**. The dialog box closes, and a new Microsoft Word document is created. On the taskbar, a Microsoft Word button appears and starts blinking, indicating the document is being created. After the document is created, the button stops blinking. The time it takes for this to happen depends on the speed of your computer—it may take a minute or two.

▶ **5.** On the taskbar, click the **Document1 – Compatibility Mode – Word** program button ![W]. The handouts appear in a Word document with each slide title and first-level items in the bulleted lists in large font size (44 points in this case) and formatted as bold, and the sub-bullets in a smaller font size (18 points in this case).

**Trouble?** If the pointer blinks and changes to a blue circle, the document is still being created. Wait until the pointer is no longer a circle before continuing.

▶ **6.** Click the **File** tab, and then in the navigation bar, click **Save As** ![icon]. The Save As screen in Backstage view appears.

▶ **7.** Click **Browse** to open the Save As dialog box, type **NP_PPT_5_Handouts** in the File name box, navigate to the location where you are storing your files, and then click **Save**. A dialog box appears telling you that the document will be upgraded to the newest file format.

**Trouble?** If the dialog box telling you that the document will be upgraded to the newest file format doesn't appear, skip Step 8.

▶ **8.** Click **OK**. The file is saved.

▶ **9.** Close the NP_PPT_5_Handouts document and exit Word.

▶ **10.** **sam** ↟ Close the NP_PPT_5_Convention presentation.

In this session, you copied a table from a Word document and formatted the table in PowerPoint. You also inserted Excel objects by embedding them and linking them to their source files. Finally, you broke the links, annotated slides during a slide show, and then created handouts by exporting the presentation to a Word document. Tyler is satisfied with the presentation.

# Review

## Session 5.2 Quick Check

**1.** What does it mean to embed an object in a presentation?

**2.** If you modify the source file of a linked object, what happens to the linked object in the PowerPoint slide?

**3.** Why would you link an object instead of embed it?

**4.** If you link an Excel chart to a slide with one of the Paste Link buttons on the Paste menu, is the chart formatting linked as well?

**5.** How is an annotation that you created during a slide treated in Normal view?

**6.** Describe how to create handouts in Word.

# Practice

## Review Assignments

Data Files needed for the Review Assignments: **NP_PPT_5-2.pptx, Support_PPT_5_Basics.pptx, Support_PPT_5_Erg.xlsx, Support_PPT_5_GPA.xlsx, Support_PPT_5_NovOutline.docx, Support_PPT_5_Races.docx**

Tyler decided to create a presentation describing basic rules and procedures to new rowers at South Bay College. He prepared an outline of part of the presentation, and his assistant coach, Olivia, prepared slides describing basic terminology. He asked you to help create the final presentation. Complete the following steps:

1. Open the presentation **NP_PPT_5-2.pptx**, located in the PowerPoint5 > Review folder, add your name as the subtitle on Slide 1, and then save the file as **NP_PPT_5_Orientation** in the location where you are storing your files.

2. After Slide 1, create slides from the outline in the Word file **Support_PPT_5_NovOutline.docx**, located in the PowerPoint5 > Review folder. Reset the six slides you create.

3. After Slide 7 ("Average GPA"), insert Slides 1 through 3 from the **Support_PPT_5_Basics.pptx** presentation, located in the PowerPoint5 > Review folder, so they become Slides 8 through 10 in the NP_PPT_5_Orientation presentation.

4. In Outline view, on Slide 6 ("Average 5K Erg Test Scores in Minutes"), change the "Student Athlete" bulleted item into a new Slide 7 with its subitems as bulleted items on the new Slide 7. Then reorder the presentation by moving Slide 4 ("2021-2022 Race Schedule") so it becomes Slide 8, and moving Slide 12 ("If You Can't Make a Practice") so it becomes Slide 4.

5. Create four sections in the presentation and a summary zoom containing the four sections. One section should include Slide 1 (the title slide) and be named **Title**; another section should include Slide 2 ("Safety") and be named **Safety**; another section should include Slides 3 ("Typical Practice Schedule") through 9 ("2021-2022 Race Schedule") and be named **Routine and Expectations**, and the final section should include Slides 10 ("Terminology") through 12 ("Identifying the Rowers") and be named **Basics**.

6. Reorder the sections in the following order: Summary Section, Title, Basics, Safety, and Routine and Expectations. Add **Overview** as the slide title on the summary zoom, and then edit the summary zoom so that the section zooms appear in the correct order.

7. On Slide 8 ("If You Can't Make a Practice..."), insert two icons: in the Technology And Electronics category, a smartphone icon in the top row, and in the Communication category, the open envelope with the @ symbol on a piece of paper. Resize both icons so they are 3.5 inches high, and then duplicate the smartphone icon.

8. Position one of the smartphone icons above the text "Call" so its center aligns with the center of the "Call" text box. Position the other smartphone icon above the "Text" text box so its center aligns with the center of the slide. Position the envelope icon above the "Email" text box so its center aligns with the center of the "Email" text box.

9. Select all three icons, and then use the Align Middle command so that the middles of the three icons align with each other. With the three icons still selected, position them vertically so there is approximately one-half inch between the tops of the smartphone icons and tops of the green boxes and one-half inch between the bottom of the icons and the text below each icon.

10. Convert the Email icon to shapes. Ungroup the shapes, and then change the fill color of the @sign shape to Red, Accent 6, Darker 50%.

11. In the Selection pane, rename the two smartphone icon objects to **Call smartphone** and **Text smartphone**. Rename the envelope image to **Envelope** and the @ sign to **At sign**.

12. Open the Animation pane. Each green rectangle has the Collapse exit animation applied to it. The Left rectangle will animate when the slide show advances (On Click), and the animations applied to the other two rectangles will start after the previous action with a delay of one second.

13. Apply the Teeter emphasis animation to the Call smartphone object. Use the Teeter Effect Options dialog box to add the Chime sound to the animation. Change the order of this animation so it starts after the Left rectangle exit animation. Change the start setting so it starts after the previous animation.

14. Apply the Appear entrance animation to the Coach text box object (the text box that contains the message to the coach in the center of the smartphone icon on the middle green rectangle). (*Hint*: Use the Selection pane to select the Coach text box object.) Modify the animation using the Appear Effect Options dialog box by doing the following:
    a. Add the Typewriter sound to the animation.
    b. Change the color of the text when the slide show advances to the blue color that is fifth from the left on the menu.
    c. Change the animation of the text so that the letters appear one character at a time with 0.1 second delay between each letter.

15. Change the order of the Appear entrance animation applied to the Coach text box object so that the animation starts after the Middle rectangle exit animation, and then change its start setting to After Previous.

16. Apply the Blink emphasis animation to the At sign object. (*Hint*: Use the More Emphasis Effects command at the bottom of the Animations gallery.) Use the Timing tab in the Blink Effect Options dialog box to make the animation repeat three times and change the duration to 0.5 seconds. Make sure the Blink animation will occur after the Right rectangle exit animation, and then change the start setting to After Previous.

17. In the Selection pane, examine the layers on Slide 8. The green rectangles need to be on top of the icons so that Tyler can click them during the slide show to display the icons. Move the three green rectangles to the three top layers so that they are in layers on top of the icons and text boxes. Change the fill color of the rectangles to Blue, Accent 1, Darker 50%.

18. View Slide 8 in Slide Show view. Advance the slide show once to start the animations. End the slide show after the last animation.

19. Start Excel, open the **Support_PPT_5_GPA.xlsx** file located in the PowerPoint5 > Review folder, and then copy cells A3 through F5. In the NP_PPT_5_Orientation PowerPoint file, display Slide 12 ("Average GPA"), change the layout to Title Only, and then embed the cells you copied. Resize the embedded object so it is 1.5 inches high and 12.28 inches wide, and then position it so it is centered horizontally and vertically on the slide.

20. On Slide 12, fill cells A3 through F5 in the embedded workbook with the Gray, Accent 3, Lighter 80% color. Format cells A4 through A5 and cells B3 through F3 with the Heading 4 cell style, and then change the font size of the text in these cells to 14 points.

21. Open the Excel file **Support_PPT_5_Erg.xlsx**, located in the PowerPoint5 > Review folder, and then save it as **NP_PPT_5_Erg** in the location where you are saving your files. Copy the chart. Switch to the NP_PPT_5_Orientation presentation, display Slide 10 ("Average 5K Erg Test Scores in Minutes"), change the layout to Title Only, and then use the Paste Special command to link the copied chart to Slide 10. Use the Shape Height box in the Size group on the Shape Format tab to resize the linked chart so it is five inches high. Position the chart so its center aligns with the center of the slide and there is about one-quarter of an inch between the chart and the blue title rectangle.

22. Update the data on which the chart is based by typing **7:45** in cell B7 (indicating that the Novice Women's average score in Week 8 is 7:45 minutes), and then pressing ENTER. Change the chart type of the chart in the Excel workbook to Clustered Bar, and then switch the columns and the rows so that the team names are the categories. Save the changes to the NP_PPT_5_Erg workbook, and then close it. Close the Support_PPT_5_GPA workbook (do not save changes if asked) and exit Excel.

23. Break the link between the NP_PPT_5_Orientation presentation and the NP_PPT_5_Erg workbook.

24. On Slide 13 ("2021-2022 Race Schedule"), change the layout to Title Only. Copy the table in the Word file **Support_PPT_5_Races.docx**, located in the PowerPoint5 > Review folder, to Slide 13 using the source formatting. Close the Support_PPT_5_Races document and exit Word.

25. Resize the table so it is four inches high and 10.3 inches wide, and then change the font size of all the text in the table to 18 points.

26. Insert a new first column. In the new first column, merge the second through sixth cells, and then merge the seventh through eleventh cells. In the top merged cell, type **Fall**, and in the bottom merged cell type **Spring**.

27. Change the font size of the text in the merged cells to 36 points, and then rotate the text in the merged cells so it reads from the bottom of the cell up. Center the text in the merged cells both horizontally and vertically.

28. Resize the first column so it is 0.75 inches wide, resize the second column so it is 5.5 inches wide, and then resize the third column so that it is 3.8 inches wide. Position the table so its center aligns with the center of the slide and so there is approximately one inch between the table and the blue title rectangle.

29. Display Slide 6 ("Safety") in Slide Show view, circle the "Report all injuries" bulleted item using the red Pen, and then end the slide show, keeping the annotation.

30. Save the changes to the NP_PPT_5_Orientation presentation.

31. Create handouts in a Word document using the Outline only option. Save the Word document as **NP_PPT_5_NoviceHandouts** in the location where you are storing your files. Close the NP_PPT_5_NovicesHandouts file and exit Word.

32. Close the NP_PPT_5_Orientation presentation.

# Apply

## Case Problem 1

**Data Files needed for this case Problem: NP_PPT_5-3.pptx, Support_PPT_5_Budget.xlsx, Support_PPT_5_Hunger.pptx, Support_PPT_5_Plan.docx**

**Community Kitchen** Grace Kim works for Sullivan and Sanchez Consulting, a consulting firm that helps nonprofit organizations fundraise. Community Kitchen is a new nonprofit organization in Albuquerque, New Mexico, that was founded by local civic and religious groups to provide meals in a comfortable, welcoming atmosphere for people in need. Their goal is to provide family-style dining rather than a soup kitchen buffet line. They hired Sullivan and Sanchez Consulting to help them raise money to get started, and Grace was assigned to the project. Complete the following steps:

1. Open the presentation **NP_PPT_5-3.pptx**, located in the PowerPoint5 > Case1 folder included with your data files, replace the subtitle on Slide 1 with your name, and then save the file as **NP_PPT_5_Community** in the location where you are storing your files.

2. Create additional slides after Slide 4 from the outline contained in Word file **Support_PPT_5_Plan.docx**, located in the PowerPoint5 > Case1 folder. Reset the 11 newly created slides.

3. Demote all the text on Slide 6 ("Create partnerships") so "Create partnerships" becomes a first-level bulleted item on Slide 5 ("Building the Team").

4. Demote all the text on Slide 8 ("Equipment") so "Equipment" becomes a first-level bulleted item on Slide 7 ("Supplies"), and then move the "Equipment" bulleted item and its subitems up so the "Equipment" bulleted item is the second first-level bulleted item in the bulleted list on Slide 7.

5. On Slide 2 ("One Person in Six Is Hungry in New Mexico"), insert the filled icon of a person standing with arms down in the People category. Position the icon so its top aligns with the 2-inch mark on the vertical ruler and its left edge aligns with the left edge of the title text box.

6. Duplicate the icon, and then position the duplicate to the right of the original so that the two icons are horizontally aligned and there is about one-eighth of an inch between the "hands" of the two icons. Keep the icon selected.

7. Duplicate the selected icon. Another duplicate appears to the right of the second icon, positioned at the same distance from the second icon that the second icon is from the first icon. The third icon is selected.

8. Continue duplicating the selected icon nine more times so that there is a total of 12 icons in a row. (*Hint*: Press CTRL+D to execute the Duplicate command.)

9. Change the fill color of the sixth and the twelfth icon to Green, Accent 5.

10. Select all 12 icons. (*Hint*: On the Home tab, in the Editing group, click the Select button, click Select All, press and hold SHIFT, click the title text box border to deselect it, and then release SHIFT.) Apply the Appear entrance animation to the selected icons. Change the start setting to After Previous, and add a delay of 0.50 seconds.

11. Add the Blink emphasis animation to the green icons. (*Hint*: Make sure you use the Add Animation button and then use the More Emphasis Effects command at the bottom of the Animation gallery.) Change the duration of the Blink animations to 0.50 seconds. Modify the Blink animation applied to the green icons so that they repeat three times. Reorder each Blink animation so it occurs after the Appear animation applied to the same icon, and then change the start setting of the Blink animations to After Previous with a 0.25 second delay.

12. Change the delay applied to the seventh icon to 0.25 seconds. View Slide 2 in Slide Show view.

13. Insert Slide 2 and Slide 3 from the file **Support_PPT_5_Hunger.pptx**, located in the PowerPoint > Case1 folder, as Slides 3 and 4 in the NP_PPT_5_Community presentation. Apply the Morph transition to Slide 4.

14. Move Slide 2 so it becomes Slide 15, the last slide in the presentation. Create a new section named **Unused** that includes only Slide 15.

15. Start Excel, open the **Support_PPT_5_Budget.xlsx** workbook, located in the PowerPoint5 > Case1 folder, and then save it as **NP_PPT_5_Budget**.

16. In the NP_PPT_5_Budget workbook, copy the Projected Monthly Expenses column chart. Switch to the NP_PPT_5_Community presentation, display Slide 10 ("Monthly Expenses"), change the layout to Title Only, and then link the copied chart to Slide 10 using the Paste Special dialog box.

17. Edit the chart source file by changing the value in cell B8 to **-3500**, and then change the chart type in the source file to a pie chart.

18. On Slide 10, resize the chart so it is five inches high and 8.37 inches wide, and then center it in the space below the slide title.

19. Break the link between the NP_PPT_5_Community presentation and the NP_PPT_5_Budget workbook.

20. In the NP_PPT_5_Budget workbook, copy cells A17 through B33. Switch to the NP_PPT_5_Community presentation, display Slide 11 ("Annual Estimated Income"), and then change the layout to Title Only. Embed the copied data on Slide 11, resize the Excel object so it is five inches high and 5.31 inches wide, and then position it so it is centered in the blank area on the slide.

21. On Slide 11, double-click the embedded workbook, and then format cells A20 through B27 so that black border lines appear between all the cells. (*Hint*: Click the Borders arrow in the Font group on the Home tab, and then click More Borders. In the Format Cells dialog box, on the Border tab, click in the middle of the large box in the Border section to insert a horizontal line. If you accidentally add a line somewhere else, click it to remove it.) Save the NP_PPT_5_Budget workbook, and then close Excel.

22. In the presentation, create the following sections:
    - **Intro**, which includes Slides 1 through 4
    - **Organization**, which includes Slides 5 through 8
    - **Finances**, which includes Slides 9 through 11
    - **Menu & Operations**, which includes Slides 12 and 13
    - **Advertising**, which includes Slide 14

23. Create a summary zoom that contains section zooms for all of the sections except the Intro section and the Unused section. Leave the summary zoom as Slide 5. Change the layout of the summary zoom to Title Only. Select the four section zooms on the summary zoom, and then add a Red, Accent 1 border to the section zooms.

24. Create handouts in Word using the Outline only option. Save this file as **NP_PPT_5_ CommunityHandouts** in the location where you are saving your files, and then exit Word.

25. Save the changes to the NP_PPT_5_Community file, and then close it.

# Troubleshoot

## Case Problem 2

**Data Files needed for this case Problem: NP_PPT_5-4.pptx, Support_PPT_5_Boys.jpg, Support_PPT_5_Data.xlsx, Support_PPT_5_ParentNotes.docx, Support_PPT_5_Slides.pptx**

**Northgate Counseling Center**  Donna Teton is a licensed social worker at Northgate Counseling Center in Idaho Falls, Idaho. Donna specializes in providing therapy to children. She has been hired by several school districts to talk to teachers, school support staff, and parents about ways they can identify and stop bullying. Complete the following steps:

1. Open the presentation **NP_PPT_5-4.pptx**, located in the PowerPoint5 > Case2 folder included with your data files, add your name in the subtitle on Slide 1, and then save the file as **NP_PPT_5_Bully** to the location where you are saving your files.

2. On Slide 1 (the title slide), select the six photos, and then group them together. (Each photo has a six-point black border.) Duplicate the grouped object, and then place the duplicate to the right of the original grouped object. Align the top and bottom edges of the two grouped objects. Position the left black border of the duplicated object directly on top of the right black border of the original grouped object. Finally, select both grouped objects and group them together.

3. Apply the Lines motion path animation to the grouped object, change its effect to Left, change its duration to 14 seconds, and change its start setting to With Previous. Click the motion path so that the red triangle that indicates the end of the motion path changes to a red circle. While pressing SHIFT to maintain a straight line, drag the red circle to the left until the images you are dragging are no longer blurry because they are directly on top of the original grouped object.

4. Open the Effect Options dialog box for the Lines animation (it will be titled "Left"). Change the Smooth start and end times to 0 seconds, and then have the animation repeat until the end of the slide. View Slide 1 in Slide Show view and watch until you see each image three times. If the transition between the end of the second set of images and the beginning of the third set of images is bumpy, repeat Step 3, and try to get the images exactly aligned on top of one another.

5. On Slide 2 ("What Is Bullying?"), insert the picture **Support_PPT_5_Boys.jpg**, located in the PowerPoint5 > Case2 folder.

6. Apply the Lines motion path animation to the picture of the boys. Drag the end point of the line up in a straight line to shorten the path so it is one and one-eighth inch long.

7. Add the Grow/Shrink emphasis animation to the picture of the boys. In the Grow/Shrink Effect Options dialog box, change the size to 73%. (*Hint*: Type the value in the Custom box on the menu.) Change the duration to 1.25 seconds.

8. Add the Fade exit animation to the picture of the boys.

9. Duplicate the picture of the boys. On the Picture Format tab, apply the Washout effect in the Recolor section of the Color menu. In the Selection pane, rename the picture with the washout effect applied to **Boys washout**. Rename the original picture **Boys**.

10. Resize the Boys washout picture so it is 5.5 inches high. Position it so its center aligns with the center of the slide and the center of the original picture of the boys and so its bottom edge aligns with the bottom edge of the slide. Remove the animations from the Boys washout picture.

11. Reorder the animations so that Lines animation applied to the Boys object occurs first, the Grow/ Shrink animation applied to the Boys object occurs second, the Fade animation applied to the Boys object occurs third, the entrance animation applied to the title text box occurs fourth, and the entrance animation applied to the content placeholder occurs fifth.

12. Change the start setting of the Boys Grow/Shrink emphasis animation to With Previous and set a delay of 0.50 seconds. Set the Boys Fade exit animation to After Previous. Change the start setting of the Title Fade entrance animation to With Previous.

⚙ **Troubleshoot** 13. View Slide 2 in Slide Show view, pressing SPACEBAR to advance the slide show four times. Modify the slide as needed so that you see the Boys picture object at the beginning and the bulleted list on top of the Boys washout picture at the end.

14. Start Excel, and then open the file **Support_PPT_5_Data.xlsx**, located in the PowerPoint5 > Case2 folder, and then save it as **NP_PPT_5_Data**. Copy the column chart. In the PowerPoint file NP_PPT_5_Bully, link the chart to Slide 3 ("Bullying Behaviors Reported by Children 12-18") so that when the chart's format is changed in the Excel file, it will change in the PowerPoint file as well. Resize the chart so it is 5.25 inches high and 9.31 inches wide. Center it in the area below the slide title.

15. In the Excel file NP_PPT_5_Data, click cell C5, type **17**, and the press ENTER. Change the chart type to a clustered bar chart, keeping the types of behaviors as the categories. Save the file and exit Excel.

⚙ **Troubleshoot** 16. Donna sent the presentation to a colleague, and the colleague reported that every time she opens the file, she is asked if she wants to update the links. Modify the file so that this does not happen.

17. Reuse Slides 2 through 6 from the **Support_PPT_5_Slides.pptx** presentation file, located in the PowerPoint5 > Case2 folder by inserting them in order after Slide 3 in the NP_PPT_5_Bully file.

18. Insert slides from the outline **Support_PPT_5_ParentNotes.docx** after Slide 8.

⚙ **Troubleshoot** 19. The new Slides 9 and 10 don't look the same as the other slides. Change them so they match the look of the other slides.

20. Create a summary zoom by selecting Slides 2, 4, and 8 as the first slide in sections. Display the Zoom tab to see that the first section zoom contains Slides 3-4, the second section zoom in the first row contains Slides 5-8, and the section zoom in the bottom row contains Slides 9-11.

21. Rename the Default Section section to **Title**. Rename the What Is Bullying? section to **Introduction**. Rename the Behaviors to Look For section to **For Teachers**. Rename the Warning Signs section to **For Parents**.

22. Move the For Parents section so it comes before the For Teachers section.

⚙ **Troubleshoot** 23. Display Slide 2 (the summary zoom), and then display the Zoom tab. The slides are out of order. Fix this slide so that the first section is the section zoom that contains the picture of the boys, the second section zoom in the first row is the Warning Signs section zoom with Slides 5-7, and the Behaviors to Look For section zoom is in the third row on the left.

24. View Slide 9 ("Addressing Bullying Behaviors with Students") in Slide Show view. Draw a red line under the slide title, and then keep the annotation.

25. Create handouts in Word using the Outline only option. Save the Word document as **NP_PPT_5_BullyHandouts**. Exit Word.

26. Save the changes to the presentation, and then close it.

Module **6**

# Customizing Presentations and the PowerPoint Environment

## Creating a Presentation for a City-Wide Green Challenge

## Objectives

**Session 6.1**
- Compare presentations, and accept or reject changes
- Add, reply to, and delete comments
- Modify the slide master
- Modify the style of lists
- Create and modify slide layouts
- Create custom theme fonts and colors
- Fill text and shapes with a color on the slide
- Save a presentation as a theme

**Session 6.2**
- Create a custom show
- Create and modify custom file properties
- Encrypt a presentation
- Mark a presentation as read-only
- Present a presentation online

## Case | Rockland, Missouri City Government

The city council in Rockland, Missouri, issued a "Green Challenge" to the city department heads to come up with plans to make their departments more environmentally friendly. Each department head needs to present their ideas at the next city council meeting. Veronica Soto, the director of the Parks and Recreation department, created a plan to reduce the amount of trash collected at city parks and nature trails by placing recycling containers and dog waste receptacles next to all trash bins. She asks you to help her as she works on the presentation.

In this module, you will compare presentations and use comments. You will modify the slide master and layouts, and create a custom theme font set and color palette. You will fill shapes with a color from the slide. Then you will save the presentation as a theme. You will also create a custom show and create and modify custom file properties. Finally, you will encrypt a presentation, mark it as read-only, and then learn how to present the presentation online.

## Starting Data Files

**PowerPoint6** →

**Module**

NP_PPT_6-1.pptx
Support_PPT_6_Aiden.pptx
Support_PPT_6_Park.jpg
Support_PPT_6_Receptacle.jpg
Support_PPT_6_Recycle.png
Support_PPT_6_Tree.jpg

**Review**

NP_PPT_6-2.pptx
Support_PPT_6_Dan.pptx
Support_PPT_6_Night.jpg

**Case1**

NP_PPT_6-3.pptx
Support_PPT_6_Background.jpg
Support_PPT_6_Password.jpg
Support_PPT_6_Side.jpg

**Case2**

Support_PPT_6_Bullet.png
Support_PPT_6_Logo1.png
Support_PPT_6_Logo2.jpg

# Session 6.1 Visual Overview:

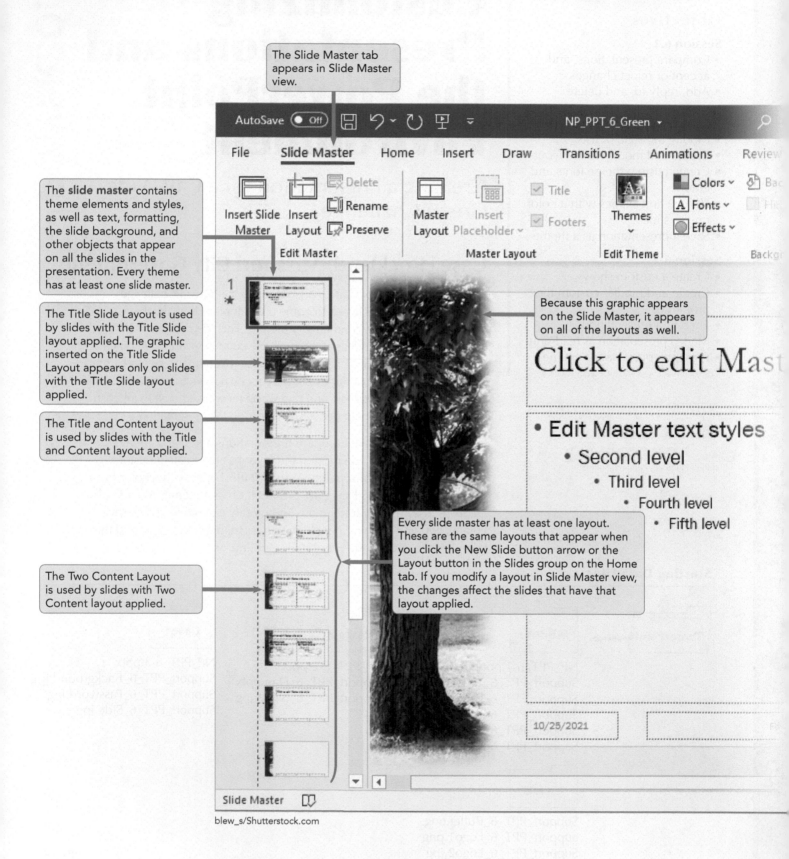

The Slide Master tab appears in Slide Master view.

AutoSave ● Off   💾   ↺ ˅   ↻   📺   ≂    NP_PPT_6_Green ˅    🔎

File    **Slide Master**    Home    Insert    Draw    Transitions    Animations    Review

Insert Slide Master | Insert Layout | Delete | Rename | Preserve | Master Layout | Insert Placeholder ˅ | ☑ Title | ☑ Footers | Themes | Colors ˅ | Fonts ˅ | Effects ˅ | Back...

Edit Master     Master Layout     Edit Theme     Backg...

The **slide master** contains theme elements and styles, as well as text, formatting, the slide background, and other objects that appear on all the slides in the presentation. Every theme has at least one slide master.

The Title Slide Layout is used by slides with the Title Slide layout applied. The graphic inserted on the Title Slide Layout appears only on slides with the Title Slide layout applied.

The Title and Content Layout is used by slides with the Title and Content layout applied.

The Two Content Layout is used by slides with Two Content layout applied.

Because this graphic appears on the Slide Master, it appears on all of the layouts as well.

Click to edit Mast

- Edit Master text styles
  - Second level
    - Third level
      - Fourth level
        - Fifth level

Every slide master has at least one layout. These are the same layouts that appear when you click the New Slide button arrow or the Layout button in the Slides group on the Home tab. If you modify a layout in Slide Master view, the changes affect the slides that have that layout applied.

10/25/2021

Slide Master

blew_s/Shutterstock.com

# Slide Master View

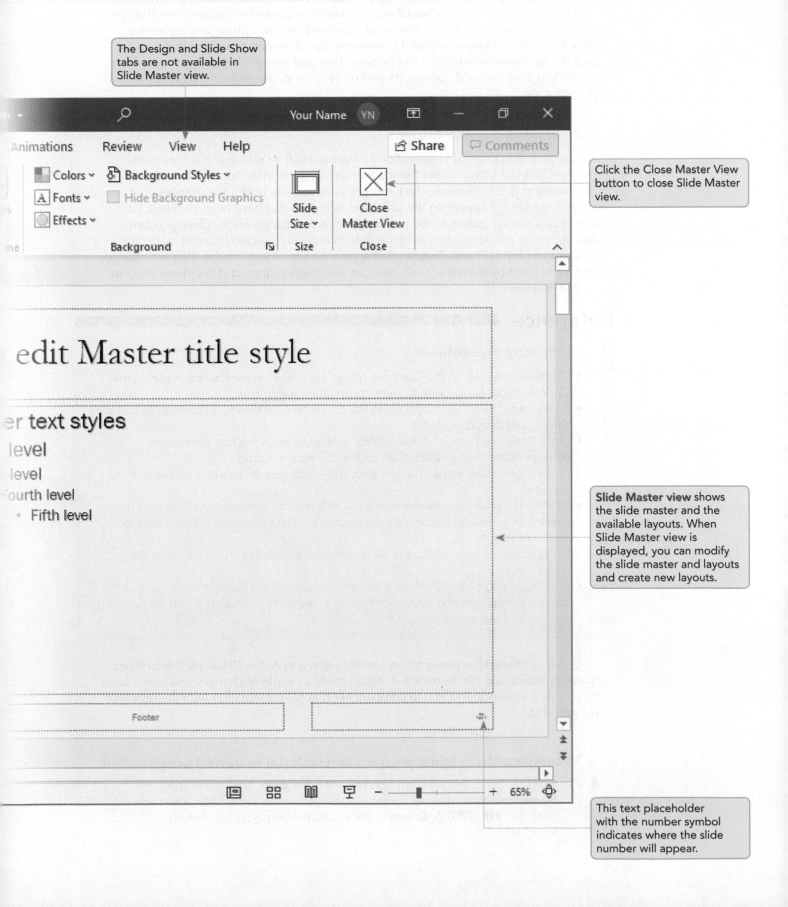

The Design and Slide Show tabs are not available in Slide Master view.

Click the Close Master View button to close Slide Master view.

Slide Master view shows the slide master and the available layouts. When Slide Master view is displayed, you can modify the slide master and layouts and create new layouts.

This text placeholder with the number symbol indicates where the slide number will appear.

# Sharing and Collaborating with Others

It is a good idea to ask others to review your presentations before you finalize and present them. Another set of eyes can spot errors or inconsistencies that you might otherwise miss. When you send a presentation to colleagues for review, they can make changes and add comments. You then can compare the original and the reviewed versions of the presentation and accept the changes or ignore them. You also can add comments and reply to or delete existing comments in a presentation.

## Comparing Presentations

To compare your original presentation to a version that a colleague has reviewed, use the Compare button in the Compare group on the Review tab. While you are comparing two presentations, the Revisions pane appears listing the changes, and change buttons ▨ appear on the slide next to objects that have been changed. You can click a change button to see a description of the change made. Change buttons that appear in the pane containing the slide thumbnails indicate changes made at the presentation level. Change buttons that appear next to objects on the slide are changes that affect that object on that slide. You can view each change and decide whether to accept it or reject it.

# Reference ▉▉▉▉▉▉▉▉▉▉▉▉▉▉▉▉▉

### Comparing Presentations

- On the Review tab, in the Compare group, click the Compare button to open the Choose File to Merge with Current Presentation dialog box.
- Navigate to the location containing the presentation with which you want to compare, click it, and then click Merge.
- In the Revisions pane, click each listed revision to open the box next to the corresponding change button; or, click each change button.
- In the box describing a change, click the check box to select it to see the change.
- To keep the change, keep the check box selected; to reject the change, click the check box to deselect it; or, click the Accept or Reject button in the Compare group on the Review tab.
- In the Compare group, click the Next button to display the next change in the presentation.
- After reviewing all the changes in the presentation, in the Compare group, click the End Review button, and then in the dialog box that opens asking if you are sure you want to end the review, click Yes.

Veronica created her presentation and then sent it to Aiden Callahan, the facilities manager, and asked him to review it. Aiden made a couple of changes and sent it back to Veronica. Veronica asks you to compare her original presentation with the reviewed presentation.

**To compare the original presentation with the reviewed presentation:**

▶ **1.** **sam** ⬇ Open the presentation **NP_PPT_6-1.pptx**, located in the **PowerPoint6 > Module** folder included with your Data Files, and then save it as **NP_PPT_6_Green** in the location where you are storing your files.

**2.** On the ribbon, click the **Review** tab, and then in the Compare group, click the **Compare** button. The Choose File to Merge with Current Presentation dialog box opens.

**3.** Navigate to the **PowerPoint6 > Module** folder if necessary, click **Support_PPT_6_Aiden.pptx**, and then click **Merge**. The Revisions pane opens with the DETAILS tab selected. Slide 4 ("Recycling Program") is displayed. See Figure 6–1.

**Figure 6–1**    **Slide 4 after using the Compare command**

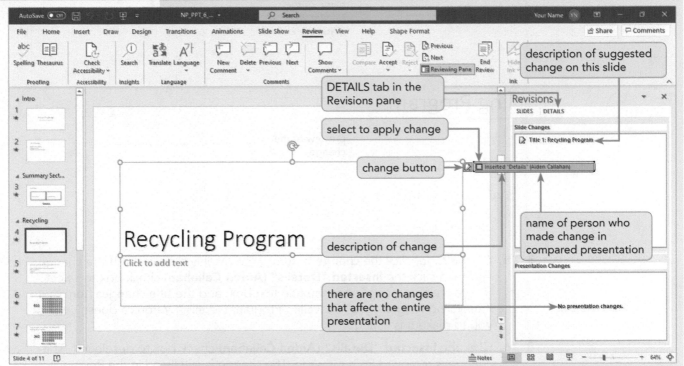

Changes that affect only the current slide are listed in the Slide Changes box at the top of the Revisions pane. Changes that affect the entire presentation would be listed in the Presentation Changes box at the bottom of the Revisions pane. The change button to the right of the title text box is selected and a description of the change is displayed. In this case, the description indicates that Aiden Callahan added the word "Details" to the text box.

**4.** At the top of the Revisions pane, click **SLIDES**. The SLIDES tab appears. There is one change listed on this slide. See Figure 6–2.

**Figure 6–2** SLIDES tab in the Revisions pane listing a change on Slide 4

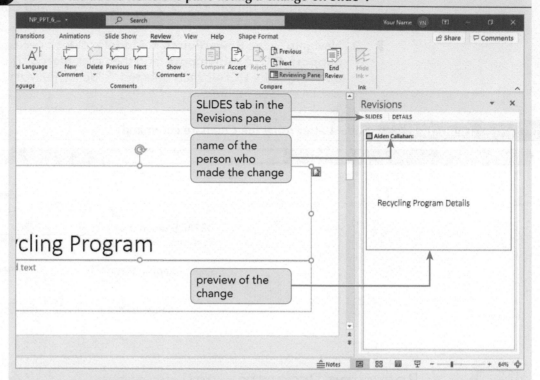

5. On the slide, click the **change** button ![icon] to display details about the change, and then click the **Inserted "Details" (Aiden Callahan)** check box to select it. The change is applied to the title text box, and the title changes from "Recycling Program" to "Recycling Program Details." Veronica doesn't want you to make this change.

6. Click the **Inserted "Details" (Aiden Callahan)** check box to deselect it. The change is removed from the slide. The change is still listed in the Revisions pane because it is something that is different between the two presentations.

**Tip**

You can also click the Accept and Reject buttons in the Compare group on the Review tab to accept or reject a selected change.

7. On the Review tab, in the Compare group, click the **Next** button. Slide 5 ("Reduce Amount of Trash Collected at Parks") appears with a change button and a description of the changes next to the content placeholder. The description says that "40" was inserted and "60" was deleted. On the slide, the last bulleted item ends with "60%." This is the original text. In the Revisions pane, on the SLIDES tab, the last bulleted item ends with "40%." This is Aiden's suggested change. He is correct—the expected percentage reduction of non-recyclable trash is 40%, not 60%. Veronica tells you to accept this change.

**Trouble?** If the Comments pane and a dialog box open, you clicked the Next button in the Comments group instead of in the Compare group. Click Cancel in the dialog box, close the Comments pane, and then repeat Step 7.

**Trouble?** If the description of the changes does not appear next to the change button on the slide, click the change button ![icon].

8. On the slide, click the **All changes to Content Placeholder 2** check box to select it. Check marks appear in all three check boxes, on the change button, and in the Aiden Callahan check box in the Revisions pane. On the slide, the last bulleted item now ends with "40%."

9. On the Review tab, in the Compare group, click the **Next** button. A dialog box opens, telling you that was the last change in the presentation and asking if you want to continue reviewing from the beginning. Because Slide 1 was displayed when you clicked the Compare command, you don't need to continue from the beginning.

10. Click **Cancel**. You are finished reviewing the merged changes. You need to end the review in order to accept the changes you selected, reject the changes you did not select, and remove the change buttons.

11. In the Compare group, click the **End Review** button. A dialog box opens, asking if you are sure you want to end the review and warning that any unapplied changes will be discarded.

12. Click **Yes**. The dialog box and the Revisions pane close, and the change button on Slide 5 disappears. On Slide 5, the last bulleted item now ends with "40%." This is the change you accepted.

13. Display Slide 4 ("Recycling Program"). The word "Details" is not included in the slide title. That was the change you rejected.

The changes made to the presentation were recorded with Aiden's Microsoft username that he is signed into Office with. (The username is shown in the upper-right corner of the PowerPoint window.) If you are not signed into a Microsoft account when you use Office, when you save a file, the name in the User name box on the General tab in the PowerPoint Options dialog box is applied. You can change the username in the PowerPoint Options dialog box by clicking the File tab and then clicking Options in the navigation bar of Backstage view.

## Working with Comments

When a colleague reviews a presentation, they can add comments to ask a question or make a suggestion. You can also add comments to direct others' attention to something on a slide or reply to a comment that someone else has placed on a slide.

**Tip**

If you save your presentation to OneDrive, you can click the Share button on the right end of the ribbon and invite others to edit it. They can then edit it at the same time you are editing.

If you are signed in to Office with a Microsoft account, when you insert a comment in a presentation, the comment is labeled with your Microsoft account username (in the upper-right corner of the PowerPoint window). If you are not signed in to Office with a Microsoft account, comments are labeled with the name in the User name box on the General tab in the PowerPoint Options dialog box. Signing in with your own name makes it obvious to the reviewer who made what changes. This is helpful when comparing revisions from multiple reviewers at once.

You will insert a comment labeled with your username.

### To insert a comment on Slide 5:

1. Display Slide 5 ("Reduce Amount of Trash Collected at Parks"), and then on the Review tab, in the Comments group, click the **New Comment** button. The Comments pane appears with a box labeled with your username, and on the Review tab, in the Comments group, the Show Comments button is selected. A comment balloon appears in the top-left corner of the slide. See Figure 6–3.

| Figure 6–3 | New comment added to Slide 5 |
|---|---|

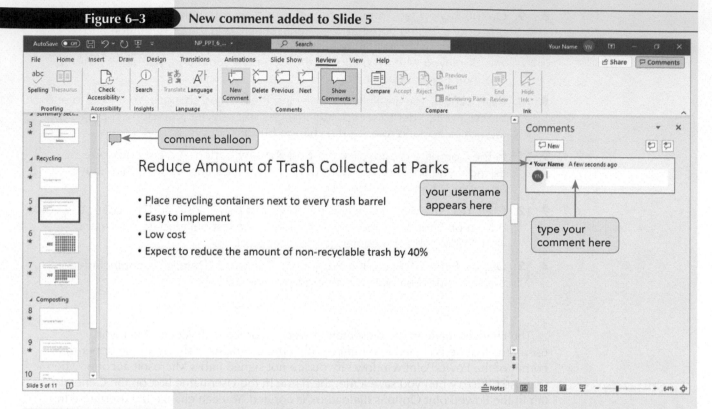

2. In the box in the Comments pane, type **In the third bullet, maybe add details about the cost per container.** (including the period).

3. On Slide 5, drag the comment balloon down to position it to the left of the "Low cost" item in the bulleted list.

If you need to change the username, click the File tab, click Options, and then in the User name box in the PowerPoint Options dialog box, type your name. To use this username instead of the username associated with your Microsoft Office account, click the "Always use these values regardless of sign in to Office." check box.

Veronica added a comment on Slide 2 ("The Challenge"). Instead of making the change the comment suggests, you will reply to her comment.

### To reply to a comment:

1. On the Review tab, in the Comments group, click the **Next** button. A dialog box opens asking if you want to continue from the beginning of the presentation.

2. Click **Continue**. Slide 2 ("The Challenge") appears, and the comment that Veronica inserted appears in the Comments pane. A Reply box appears below the comment in the Comments pane.

3. Click in the **Reply** box, and then type **I agree.** (including the period).

4. Press **ENTER**. The reply is labeled with your username. On the slide, a second comment balloon appears on top of the first balloon. See Figure 6–4.

**Figure 6–4**    **Reply to the comment on Slide 2**

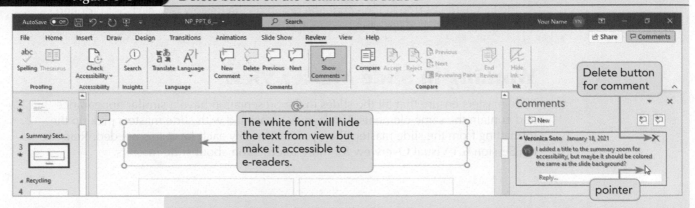

You need to check if there are any additional comments in the presentation. You can decide what to do based upon a comment, and then you can delete the comment when you are finished, if appropriate.

**To review and delete a comment:**

1. In the Comments pane, click the **Next** button. Veronica's comment on Slide 2 is selected.

2. In the Comments pane, click the **Next** button to select your reply, and then click the **Next** button again. Slide 3 (the summary zoom slide titled "Overview") appears, and another comment from Veronica appears in the Comments pane.

3. Read the comment in the Comments pane. Veronica added a title to the slide to keep the content accessible, but she thinks it shouldn't appear during a slide show. To hide the title, she asks if the slide title text should be the same color as the slide background.

4. On the slide, change the text color of **Overview** to **White, Background 1**, and then click the **Review** tab if necessary. Now that you've made the change, you can delete Veronica's comment.

5. In the Comments pane, move the pointer on top of Veronica Soto's comment. A border appears around the comment, and a Delete button appears. See Figure 6–5.

**Tip**

To hide an object on a slide, in the Selection pane, click the eye icon to the right of the object name. Doing this also makes that object invisible to screen readers.

**Figure 6–5**    **Delete button on the comment on Slide 3**

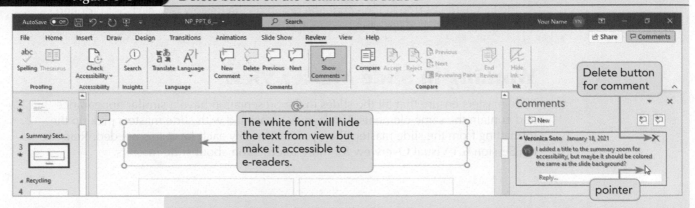

▶ 6. In the Comments pane, click the **Delete** button ☒. The comment is deleted. The Comments pane now displays a message telling you that there are comments on other slides in this presentation.

▶ 7. In the Comments pane, click the **Next** button ⟳. Slide 5 ("Reduce Amount of Trash Collected at Parks") appears. This is the slide to which you added a comment earlier.

▶ 8. In the Comments pane, click the **Next** button ⟳. The dialog box asking if you want to continue from the beginning of the presentation appears again. You have seen all of the comments in the presentation.

▶ 9. Click **Cancel**, and then on the Review tab, in the Comments group, click the **Show Comments** button. The Comments pane closes, and the Show Comments button is no longer selected.

▶ 10. Save the changes to the presentation.

## Proskills

### Teamwork: Preparing Presentations for an International Audience

If you work for a company that conducts business internationally, you should evaluate your presentations to make sure they contain information that is appropriate for and clear to an international audience. For example, when a date is written using numbers in the United States, the first number is the month and the second number is the day of the month. In most of the rest of the world, the order is reversed—the first number is the day of the month and the second number is the month. For example, August 12, 2021 would be written as 8/12/2021 in the United States, and as 12/8/2021 in most of the rest of the world. Someone who lives in a country that uses the day first format could incorrectly interpret the United States format of 8/12/2021 as December 8, 2021. To avoid confusion, you should use a date format that includes the month name, such as August 12, 2021 if the presentation is intended for mostly audiences in the United States or 12 August 2021 if the presentation is intended for international audiences.

If you need to translate words in your presentation, you can use the Translate button in the Language group on the Review tab. Keep in mind that translations generated by PowerPoint are not always perfect. After you translate all or part of a presentation, you should have an expert in the language review the translation and make any necessary corrections.

If your presentation includes foreign words, the spell checker will flag those words as spelled incorrectly. This is because the proofing language for the presentation is set to English. To change the proofing language for a word, select the word, click the Language button in the Language group on the Review tab, click Set Proofing Language, and then click the language of the selected word.

## Working in Slide Master View

Slide masters ensure that all the slides in the presentation have a similar appearance and contain the same elements. The layouts associated with slide masters pick up the formatting from the slide master. Then you can modify each layout as needed. Refer to the Session 6.1 Visual Overview for more information about slide masters.

You can modify a slide master and layouts in many ways. For example, you can change the size and style of text in the placeholders, add or delete graphics, change the slide background, and change the style of lists.

Changes you make to the slide master affect all of the slides in the presentation. For example, if you modify the font, font size, or font style of the title text or content placeholder on the slide master, or if you add an image or an animation to the slide master, it will appear on all the slides in the presentation. Changes you make to a layout in Slide Master view appear only on slides with that layout applied.

## Modifying the Slide Master

Veronica wants you to make several changes to the appearance of the slides in the presentation. Because she wants the changes to be applied to all of the slides in the presentation, you will modify the slide master. First, you will switch to Slide Master view and examine the slide master and its layouts. All presentations contain at least one slide master and one layout. Most themes include multiple layouts.

### To switch to Slide Master view:

1. On the ribbon, click the **View** tab, and then in the Master Views group, click the **Slide Master** button. The view changes to Slide Master view. A new tab, the Slide Master tab, appears on the ribbon to the left of the Home tab. In place of the slide thumbnails in the pane on the left, the master layout thumbnails appear.

2. In the pane on the left, move the pointer on top of the selected layout thumbnail. The ScreenTip identifies this layout as the Title and Content Layout and indicates that it is used by Slides 2-3, 5, and 9-11. In addition to placeholders for the title and content, there are placeholders for the slide number, date, and footer.

3. Scroll to the top of the pane on the left, and then move the pointer on top of the top thumbnail, which is larger than the other thumbnails. This is the slide master, and it is named for the theme applied to the presentation—in this case, it is the Office Theme Slide Master because the theme applied to the presentation is the Office theme. The ScreenTip also indicates that it is used by slides 1-11, which are all the slides in the presentation.

4. Click the **Office Theme Slide Master** thumbnail. The slide contains the same elements as the Title and Content layout.

To begin creating the custom theme for Veronica, you will change the background color. She wants you to use a light shade of blue because the recycling bins she will put in the parks will be blue.

### To change the fill color of the background of the slide master:

1. On the Slide Master tab, in the Background group, click the **Background Styles** button. The gallery of background styles opens. This is the same gallery that appears when you click this button on the Design tab in Normal view.

2. At the bottom of the gallery, click **Format Background**. The Format Background pane opens. The Solid fill option button is selected.

3. Click the **Color** button, and then click the **Blue, Accent 1, Lighter 80%** color. The blue color fills the background of the slide master and the background of all of the layouts as well. You didn't need to click Apply to All at the bottom of the Format Background pane because changes you make to the slide master appear on all of the layouts.

4. Close the Format Background pane.

Veronica wants a picture of a tree to appear along the left edge of the slides in the presentation. First, you need to adjust the placeholders on the slide master to make room for the picture.

## To modify the size and position of the placeholders on the slide master:

1. On the slide master, change the width of the title text placeholder to **10"**, and then drag the title placeholder so its right edge aligns with the right edge of the content and slide number placeholders.

2. Change the width of the content placeholder to **10"**, and then drag it so its right edge aligns with the right edge of the title and slide number placeholders.

3. Change the width of the date placeholder to **1.5"**, and then drag it to the right so its left edge aligns with the left edge of the title and content placeholders.

4. Click the **Title and Content Layout** thumbnail. The changes you made to the slide master appear on this layout.

5. Click the **Title Slide Layout** thumbnail. The changes you made to the date placeholder appear on this layout, but the title and subtitle text placeholders did not change.

Now you will add Veronica's picture of a tree to the left side of the slide master. Then you will modify it by applying a soft edge effect so the edge blends into the background.

## To add and format a picture to the slide master:

1. Display the Office Theme Slide Master.

2. On the ribbon, click the **Insert** tab, in the Images group, click the **Pictures** button, and then click **This Device**.

3. Navigate to the **PowerPoint6 > Module** folder, click the **Support_PPT_6_Tree.jpg** file, and then click **Insert**. The picture is inserted on the slide master. In the pane containing the thumbnails, you can see that the picture also appears on all of the layout thumbnails.

4. On the Picture Format tab, in the Arrange group, click the **Align Objects** button, and then click **Align Left**. The picture is now aligned with the top, bottom, and left edges of the slide master. Veronica wants the right edge softened so it looks like it fades into the slide.

5. On the Picture Format tab, in the Picture Styles group, click the **Picture Effects** button, point to **Soft Edges**, and then in the Soft Edge Variations section, click the **25 Point** style. A 25-point soft edge effect is applied to the picture. But now you can see blue around the top, left, and bottom edges of the picture.

6. Change the height of the picture to **8.3"**. The height and width of the picture increased so that you can no longer see blue below the picture. You need to move the picture to the left and up off the slide a little so that you cannot see any blue on those edges. To do this, you will adjust the picture position to exactly match the figures in this text.

7. Right-click the picture, and then on the shortcut menu, click **Format Picture**. The Format Picture pane opens.

8. In the Format Picture pane, click the **Size & Properties** button 📷, and then click **Position** to expand that section. The current horizontal and vertical position of the picture is zero inches from the top left corner. This means that the top of the selected object is aligned with the top of the slide and the left edge of the selected object is aligned with the left edge of the slide. See Figure 6–6.

| Figure 6–6 | Position section in the Format Picture pane for the selected picture |
|---|---|

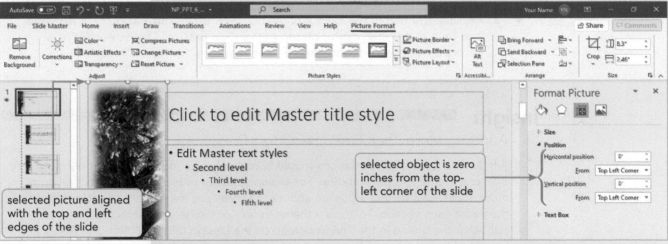

blew_s/Shutterstock.com

9. Click the **Horizontal position** down arrow five times. The value in the Horizontal position box changes to -0.5" and the picture shifts one-half inch to the left of the edge of the slide. The value is negative because the left part of the object is off the slide by one-half inch.

10. Click the **Vertical position** down arrow four times. The value in the Vertical position box changes to -0.4" and the picture shifts down. Now the edges of the picture hang off the edges of the slide and the blue background is no longer visible above, to the left, and below the picture.

When you make changes to the slide master, you should check the layouts you want to use to make sure the changes you made were applied.

11. Click the **Title and Content Layout** thumbnail, and then click the picture of the tree on the slide. The picture is not selected. This is because the picture was not placed on this layout. You placed it on the slide master.

▶ **12.** In the pane containing the thumbnails, click the **Two Content Layout** thumbnail (the fourth small thumbnail). The picture appears on this layout, and the title text and date placeholders match the size and position of those placeholders on the slide master. The sizes of the two content placeholders need to be adjusted so they align with the title text and date placeholders. Veronica will modify this layout later if she needs to use it.

▶ **13.** Click the **Title Only Layout** thumbnail (the sixth small thumbnail). This layout looks fine.

▶ **14.** Close the Format Background pane.

Now that you have made changes to the slide master, you should rename it because it is no longer the Office Theme slide master.

### To rename the slide master:

▶ **1.** In the pane containing the thumbnails, click the slide master.

▶ **2.** Click the Slide Master tab, and then in the Edit Master group, click the **Rename** button. The Rename Layout dialog box opens. The current name "Office Theme" is in the Layout name box.

▶ **3.** Replace the text in the Layout name box with **Rockland Parks**, click **Rename**, and then move the pointer on top of the slide master. The ScreenTip now shows the name Rockland Parks Slide Master.

## Insight

### Applying More Than One Theme to a Presentation

Although in general presentations should have a cohesive look, you can apply more than one theme to a presentation. For example, if your presentation is about different music styles, and several slides are about each style, you might want to use a different theme for each section. To apply a theme to only one slide or to selected slides, right-click the theme in the Themes group on the Design tab, and then click Apply to Selected Slides.

When multiple themes are applied to a presentation, each theme has a slide master and its associated layouts. You can see the additional themes in the pane containing the thumbnails in Slide Master view. The layouts for additional themes appear on the New Slide and Layout menus in Normal view.

Sometimes, if more than one slide master is applied to a presentation and no slides in the presentation use a layout connected to that slide master, the slide master is automatically deleted. To prevent that from happening, click the Preserve button in the Edit Master group on the Slide Master tab to select it.

## Modifying the Style of Lists

Good presentation design dictates that list styles should be consistent across all slides in a presentation. You can modify the style of lists in many ways. For example, you can change the bullet symbol, size, and color or change the font used for numbers in a numbered list. If you modify the style of lists in a presentation, you should make these formatting changes to the slide master, ensuring that the changes appear on all layouts.

## Reference

### Modifying the Bullet Symbol

- To modify the bullet symbol for all the list levels, select the content text box. To modify the bullet symbol for only one list level, click in the placeholder text for that level.
- On the Home tab, in the Paragraph group, click the Bullets button arrow, and then click Bullets and Numbering to open the Bulleted tab in the Bullets and Numbering dialog box.
- To change the bullet symbol, click Customize to open the Symbol dialog box, click the new symbol, and then click OK; or, click Picture to open the Insert Pictures window, click the location of the picture you want to use as a bullet symbol, click the file, and then click OK.
- To change the size of the bullet symbol relative to the size of the text, adjust the percentage in the Size box.
- To change the color of the bullet symbol, click the Color button, and then click a color.
- Click OK.

Veronica would like you to change the color of the bullet symbols used in her presentation to a darker shade of the blue color used for the background of the slides. She also wants you to increase the size of the bullet symbols. You'll make this change on the slide master.

### To modify the bullet character on the slide master:

**Tip**

To modify the bullet character of one level of bulleted items, place the insertion point in that level, and then click the Bullets arrow.

1. Display the Rockland Parks Slide Master if necessary, and then on the slide, click the border of the content placeholder. Now the change you make to the bullet symbol will affect all bullet levels.

2. Click the **Home** tab, and then in the Paragraph group, click the **Bullets arrow** ☰ ▾. The Bullets gallery opens. See Figure 6–7. You can select one of the styles in the gallery or open a dialog box where you can customize your bullets.

**Figure 6–7**     **Bullets gallery**

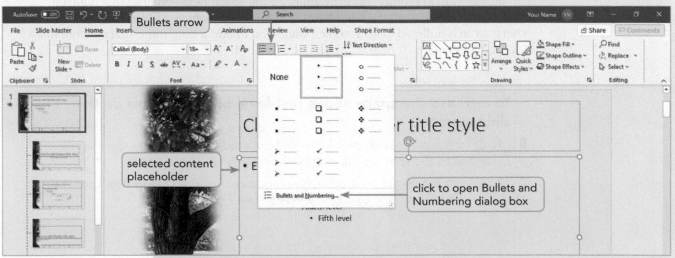

blew_s/Shutterstock.com

> 3. Click **Bullets and Numbering**. The Bullets and Numbering dialog box opens with the Bulleted tab selected. See Figure 6–8.

| Figure 6–8 | Bulleted tab in the Bullets and Numbering dialog box |

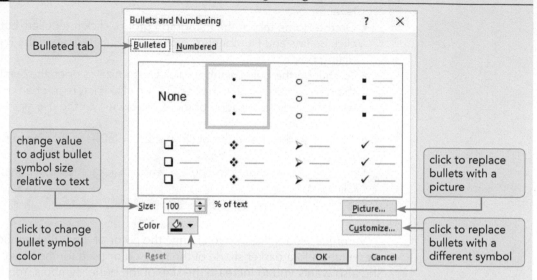

> 4. Click the **Color** button, and then click the **Blue, Accent 1, Darker 25%** color.

> 5. Select the value in the Size box, type **110**, and then click **OK**. The bullet symbols in the content placeholder change to the blue color you selected and are 10% bigger than they were.

You can customize the style of numbers in numbered lists in the same manner. To do that, you click the Numbering arrow in the Paragraph group on the Home tab. Then click one of the styles in the gallery, or click Bullets and Numbering to open the Bullets and Numbering dialog box with the Number tab selected. You can change the color and size of the numbers, and you can change the starting number if you want the list to start with a number other than 1.

Another way to modify lists is by adjusting the space between lines in a bulleted item, the space between bulleted items, and the space between bullets and the first character in a bulleted item. Veronica wants you to add a little more space before first-level bulleted items.

**To increase the space above first-level bulleted items on the slide master:**

> 1. On the slide master, click in the first bulleted item. Now the change you make to the spacing will affect only first-level bulleted items.

> 2. On the Home tab, in the Paragraph group, click the **Dialog Box Launcher** 🔲. The Paragraph dialog box opens. See Figure 6–9.

**Figure 6–9**  Paragraph dialog box

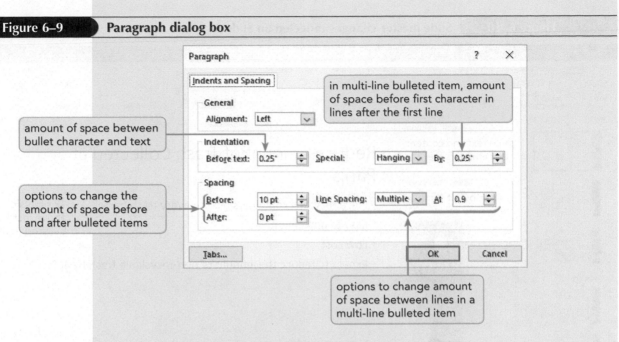

amount of space between bullet character and text

options to change the amount of space before and after bulleted items

in multi-line bulleted item, amount of space before first character in lines after the first line

options to change amount of space between lines in a multi-line bulleted item

> **3.** In the Spacing section, click the **Before** up arrow. The value in the Before box changes to 12 pt, which means now there will be 12 points of space above each first-level bulleted item instead of 10 points. If you change the Line Spacing value, you would change the space between each line in a first-level bulleted item that contained more than one line.

> **4.** Click **OK** to close the dialog box. On the slide master, the change is not apparent. You will see the change in Normal view.

Now you will examine the slides in Normal view to see the effect of the changes you made to the slide master.

### To examine the changes made to the slide master in Normal view:

> **1.** On the ribbon, click the **Slide Master** tab, and then in the Close group, click the **Close Master View** button, and then click the Slide 5 thumbnail if necessary. The Presentation appears in Normal view with Slide 5 ("Reduce Amount of Trash Collected at Parks") displayed. The slide background is light blue; the title text and content text boxes are not as wide as they were; the picture of the tree appears on the left side of the slide; the bullets are dark blue and a little larger than they were; and the space between the bulleted items increased by two points. These changes correspond to the changes you made to the slide master. See Figure 6–10.

**Figure 6–10**    Slide master changes reflected on Slide 5

blew_s/Shutterstock.com

2. Click the picture of the tree on the slide. Nothing happens. You cannot select or modify the picture because it is on the slide master.

3. Click the title, and then change the width of the title text box to **5"**. This time, the change happens. For placeholders, the format of the placeholders is specified on the slide and layout masters, but you can override this with direct formatting on the slide.

4. On the Quick Access Toolbar, click the **Undo** button ⟲. The Comment balloon that you had positioned next to the "Low cost" bulleted item needs to be moved because the bulleted items moved.

5. Drag the Comment balloon to the right and position it next to the "Low cost" bulleted item, and then close the Comments pane.

6. Display Slide 3 (the summary zoom titled "Overview"). Because of the changes to the slide master, you need to modify the placement of the section zooms.

7. Click one of the section zooms, and then drag the grouped object to the right so that the right edge of the grouped object aligns with the right edge of the slide. Visually, there is approximately the same amount of space between the section zoom on the right and the right edge of the slide as there is between the section zoom on the left and the picture of the tree. (The image of the slides on the section zooms contains text that runs into the tree. You will fix this in the next set of steps.)

8. Click **Questions**, and then drag that text box to the right until a vertical smart guide indicates that the text box is centered below the space between the two section zooms.

## Insight

### Using the Font Dialog Box

Additional options for formatting text that are not included in the Font group on the Home tab are in the Font dialog box. To open this dialog box, click the Dialog Box Launcher in the Font group on the Home tab. The Font tab in the dialog box lets you change the underline style and color. You can also format text in the following ways:

- with a double strikethrough
- as superscript and subscript
- as all caps
- as small caps (where all the letters in a word are uppercase but when a letter is typed as a capital letter, that letter is somewhat larger than the rest of the letters)
- with equal character heights so that all the characters are the same height, even if they are a combination of upper and lowercase letters

On the Character Spacing tab, you can change the spacing between pairs of characters (called kerning). The default is for characters to be spaced normally, but when there is too much or too little space between characters with the normal spacing applied, the spacing will be adjusted to fix this problem, as long as the text is at least as large as the point size specified.

## Creating Slide Layouts

If the theme you are using does not contain a layout that suits your needs, you can create a new layout. You do this in Slide Master view. After you create a new layout, it will be listed on the New Slide and Layout menus in the Slides group on the Home tab.

In Veronica's presentation, Slide 4 is the first slide in the Recycling section and Slide 8 is the first slide in the Composting section. Veronica applied the Section Header layout to these slides, but she wants to add a photo to each one. She wants you to create a custom section header layout. The custom layout will have a placeholder on the left side of the slide that can be used to add a picture to the slide.

**To create a custom layout:**

1. Switch to Slide Master view, and then in the Slides pane, click the **Section Header Layout** thumbnail (the third small thumbnail).

2. On the Slide Master tab, in the Edit Master group, click the **Insert Layout** button. A new layout is inserted below the Section Header Layout. The new layout contains the picture of the tree that is on the slide master. The new layout also includes placeholders for the slide title and the slide number, date, and footer. See Figure 6–11.

**Figure 6–11**     New layout added in Slide Master view

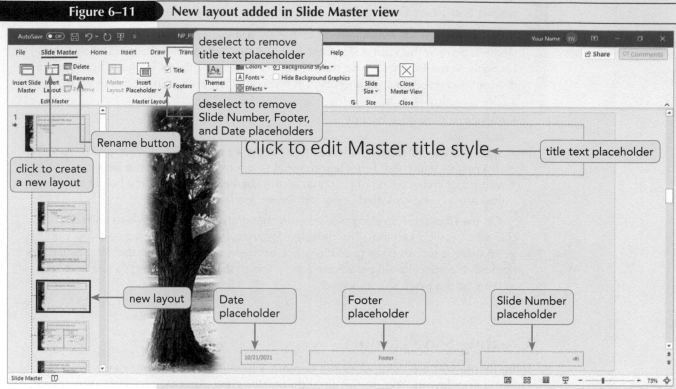

blew_s/Shutterstock.com

3. Change the width of the title text placeholder to **6.1"**, and then position it so its middle is vertically aligned with the middle of the slide and its right edge is approximately one-quarter of an inch from the right edge of the slide.

4. Click the Slide Master tab if necessary, and then in the Master Layout group, click the **Insert Placeholder arrow**. A gallery of placeholders opens. See Figure 6–12.

**Figure 6–12**     Placeholder gallery

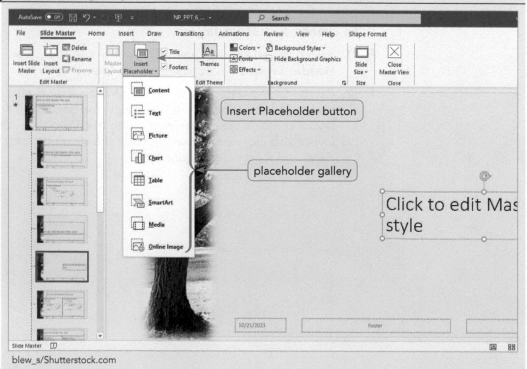

blew_s/Shutterstock.com

5. Click **Picture**. The pointer changes to the thin cross pointer ╋.

6. On the slide, click and drag to create a placeholder, and then resize it so that it is **7.5"** high and **6.5"** wide. The picture placeholder contains only one button—the Pictures button 🖻.

7. On the Shape Format tab, in the Arrange group, click the **Align** button, and then click **Align Top**. The top and bottom edges of the placeholder align with the top and bottom of the slide.

8. In the Arrange group, click the **Align** button, and then click **Align Left**. The left edge of the placeholder aligns with the left edge of the slide. (Remember that the picture of the tree overlaps the top, left, and bottom edges of the slide.)

   If you insert a picture that fills the placeholder, the tree will be covered. However, if you insert a picture with a transparent background, such as a logo, the tree will be visible. To fix this, you will hide the background graphics on this layout master.

9. Click the **Slide Master** tab, and then in the Background group, click the **Hide Background Graphics** check box. The check box is selected, and the picture of the tree is removed from this layout master. The blue fill in the background is not removed.

10. Reposition the title text placeholder so that there is the same amount of space between the left edge of the title text placeholder and the center of the slide as there is between the right edge of the picture placeholder and the center of the slide. See Figure 6–13.

**Figure 6–13    Completed custom layout**

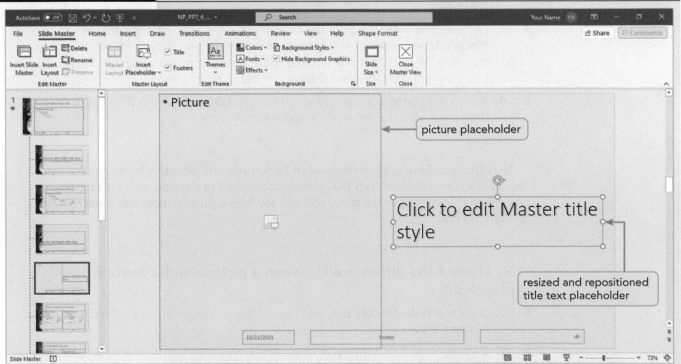

blew_s/Shutterstock.com

Now you need to rename the layout.

▶ **11.** Move the pointer on top of the new layout thumbnail that you created. The ScreenTip shows the name "Custom Layout Layout."

▶ **12.** On the Slide Master tab, in the Edit Master group, click the **Rename** button. The Rename Layout dialog box opens. The current name "Custom Layout" is in the Layout name box.

▶ **13.** Replace the text in the Layout name box with **Picture Section Header**, click **Rename**, and then move the pointer on top of the new layout. The ScreenTip now shows the name Picture Section Header Layout.

As you know, you can also insert a picture using a content placeholder. When you insert a picture using a *picture* placeholder, the picture fills the placeholder even if some of the picture needs to be cropped in order to make this happen. When you insert a picture using a *content* placeholder, the placeholder resizes to exactly fit the picture. To see the difference, you will create another custom section header layout, this time with a content placeholder. To do this, you will duplicate the Picture Section Header layout to create the new layout.

### To duplicate and modify a layout:

▶ **1.** Right-click the **Picture Section Header Layout** thumbnail, and then on the shortcut menu, click **Duplicate Layout**.

▶ **2.** Rename the new layout as **Content Section Header**.

▶ **3.** Click the border of the picture placeholder to select it, and then press **DELETE**.

▶ **4.** On the Slide Master tab, in the Master Layout group, click the **Insert Placeholder arrow**, click **Content**, and then drag to draw a placeholder on the slide. The content placeholder looks like the content placeholder you have seen on the Title and Content layout in Normal view.

▶ **5.** Resize the content placeholder so that it is **7.5"** high and **6.5"** wide, and then align with the top and left sides of the slide.

Now that you have created the custom layout, you will decide which layout you want to use—the one with the picture placeholder or the one with the content placeholder. To make this decision, you will see how a picture looks using each layout in Normal view.

### To explore the difference between a picture and a content placeholder:

▶ **1.** Click the **Slide Master** tab, and then in the Close group, click the **Close Master View** button.

▶ **2.** Display Slide 8 ("Composting Program"), and then on the Home tab, in the Slides group, click the **Layout** button. The Section Header layout is selected, indicating that it is applied to the slide. The two new layouts you created appear on the next line in the gallery.

**3.** In the gallery, click the **Picture Section Header** layout, then close any open task panes, if necessary. The layout is applied to Slide 8.

**4.** Duplicate Slide 8, and then apply the Content Section Header layout to the new Slide 9.

**5.** On Slide 9, click the **Pictures** button 🖾 in the content placeholder, and then insert the picture **Support_PPT_6_Receptacle.jpg**, located in the PowerPoint6 > Module folder. The entire picture is visible and is as high as the content placeholder. The width of the content placeholder was reduced to five inches to just fit the picture. The picture *fits* inside the placeholder.

**6.** Display Slide 8, click the **Pictures** button 🖾 in the picture placeholder, and then insert the picture **Support_PPT_6_ Receptacle.jpg**, located in the PowerPoint6 > Module folder. The picture completely fills the inside of the picture placeholder, but because the aspect ratio is locked, the top and bottom of the image are cut off so that the picture can be wide enough to fill the placeholder horizontally. The picture *fills* the placeholder.

**7.** On the status bar, click the **Zoom Out** button ➖ as many times as needed to change the zoom percentage to 50%.

**8.** With the picture on Slide 8 selected, click the **Picture Format** tab, and then in the Size group, click the **Crop** button. Crop marks appear around the picture, and you can see the top and bottom parts of the picture that were cropped off. See Figure 6-14.

**Figure 6-14**    Crop marks around a picture set to fill the placeholder

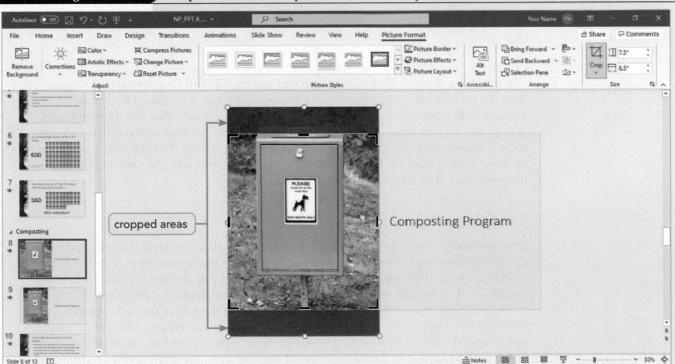

Rob kemp/Shutterstock.com; blew_s/Shutterstock.com

**9.** In the Size group, click the **Crop arrow**, and then click **Fit**. The entire picture now fits inside the placeholder, similar to the way it appears on Slide 9. However, the placeholder is still the same size.

▶ **10.** In the Size group, click the **Crop arrow**, and then click **Fill**. The picture fills the entire placeholder as it did when you inserted it, and the top and bottom of the image is again cut off. When the picture fills the placeholder, you can adjust the position of the picture in the placeholder.

▶ **11.** Within the crop marks, drag the picture down so that you can see the top of the receptacle, and then click a blank area of the slide.

▶ **12.** On the status bar, click the **Fit slide to current window** button 🔲, display Slide 9, click the picture to select it, and then display crop marks. The crop marks appear around the outer edges of the picture. None of the picture was cropped off to make the picture fit, and the placeholder was resized.

▶ **13.** Click the **Crop arrow**, and then click **Fill**. Nothing happens to the image. This is because the placeholder was resized to fit the picture exactly when you inserted it, so the picture already fills the placeholder.

▶ **14.** Click the **Crop** button to remove the crop marks, and then align the left edge of the picture with the left edge of the slide. Veronica wants you to use the layout with the content placeholder for the two section headers because she wants to be sure the entire picture will be displayed.

▶ **15.** Delete Slide 8, apply the Content Section Header layout to Slide 4 ("Recycling Program"), and then insert the picture **Support_PPT_6_ Recycle.png**, located in the PowerPoint6 > Module folder in the content placeholder on Slide 4. Now you need to delete the Picture Section Header layout.

▶ **16.** Switch to Slide Master view, click the **Picture Section Header Layout** thumbnail, and then in the Edit Master group, click the **Delete** button. The Picture Section Header layout is deleted.

If you fill a shape with a picture, you can use the Fill and Fit commands to adjust how the picture appears in the shape. When you first use the Shape Fill command to fill a shape with a picture, depending on the shape, the picture either fills the shape and is cropped, or it fills the shape but is distorted because the fill command overrode the locked aspect ratio. You can override the settings by clicking the Crop arrow and then clicking either Fill or Fit. Likewise, if you crop a picture to a shape, you can modify it by using the Fill or Fit command on the Crop menu.

## Modifying a Slide Layout

Changes you make to the slide master are applied to all of the layouts associated with the slide master and, consequently, to all the slides in the presentation. You can also modify individual layouts in Slide Master view. When you do this, only the individual layout—and, therefore, only slides that have that layout applied—are affected.

Veronica wants the title slide to look different than the rest of the slides in the presentation. The picture of the tree that you placed on the left side of the slide master was cropped from a larger picture of one of the city parks. Veronica wants the picture of the park to appear as the background of the title slide. You will modify the Title Slide layout.

### To modify an individual layout:

1. Display the Title Slide layout. You will fill the background of this layout with the picture of a park.

2. In the Background group, click the **Dialog Box Launcher** to open the Format Background pane, and then click the **Picture or texture fill** option button. A texture is applied to the background of the Title Slide Layout. Notice that the picture of the tree on the left is on top of the texture. Even though you cannot select the picture of the tree on this slide because it is on the slide master, it is still in a layer on top of the slide background.

3. In the Format Background pane, click the **Hide background graphics** check box to select it. The tree is removed from the layout.

4. In the Format Background pane, click the **Insert** button, click **From a File**, click **Support_PPT_6_Park.jpg** located in the PowerPoint6 > Module folder, and then click **Insert**. The picture of the slide fills the background. Now you need to reposition and format the text placeholders so that they are readable.

5. Close the Format Background pane, and then resize the title text placeholder so it is **1.5"** high and **13.33"** wide.

6. Align the top of the title text placeholder with the top of the slide and align the left edge with the left edge of the slide.

7. Click the **Home** tab, and then change the color of the title text to the **White, Background 1** color and format it as bold. Next you will change the vertical alignment of the text in the title text placeholder.

8. In the Paragraph group, click the **Align Text** button. On the menu, Bottom is selected, and the text in the title text placeholder is vertically aligned at the bottom of the text box.

9. On the menu, click **Top**. The text in the text placeholder is now top-aligned.

10. Resize the subtitle text placeholder so it is **1"** high and **5"** wide, change the font size of the text in the subtitle text placeholder to **20** points, and then format the text as bold.

11. On the Home tab, in the Paragraph group, click the **Align Right** button. The horizontal alignment of the text changes to it is right-aligned in the text placeholder.

12. Align the right edge of the subtitle text placeholder with the right edge of the slide.

13. Right-click the subtitle text placeholder border, and then click **Format Shape**. The Format Shape pane opens.

    **Trouble?** If Format Shape is not on the shortcut menu, you didn't right-click directly on the border of the subtitle placeholder. Repeat Step 13, this time making sure that you right-click directly on the border of the subtitle placeholder.

14. In the Format Shape pane, click the **Shape Options** tab if necessary, click the **Size & Properties** button, click **Position** if necessary to expand that section, and then change the value in the Vertical position box to **5.12"**. The placeholder text in the subtitle text placeholder is on top of the part of the grass that is very light. See Figure 6–15.

Figure 6–15          **Final Title Slide layout**

blew_s/Shutterstock.com

▶ **15.** Close the Format Shape pane, and then save the changes to the presentation.

# Changing Theme Fonts and Colors

Recall that theme fonts are two coordinating fonts or font styles, one for the titles (or headings) and one for text in content placeholders and other text elements on a slide. You know that you can change the theme fonts and theme colors in Normal view. You can also change them in Slide Master view. If you don't like any of the built-in theme font sets, you can create a set of custom theme fonts. Likewise, you can create a custom theme palette.

**To change the theme fonts:**

▶ **1.** Click the **Slide Master** tab, and then in the Background group, click the **Fonts** button. The gallery of theme fonts opens.

▶ **2.** Scroll to the bottom of the list, and then click **Garamond-TrebuchetMs**. The font of the slide titles changes to Garamond, and the font of the lists changes to TrebuchetMs. Veronica likes the Garamond font for Headings, but she wants you to change the Body font to Franklin Gothic Book.

▶ **3.** In the Background group, click the **Fonts** button and then click **Customize Fonts**. The Create New Theme Fonts dialog box opens. See Figure 6–16.

| Figure 6–16 | Create New Theme Fonts dialog box |
| --- | --- |

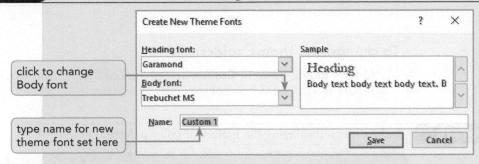

click to change Body font

type name for new theme font set here

4. Click the **Body font** arrow, scroll up the alphabetical list, and then click **Franklin Gothic Book**.

5. Click in the **Name** box, delete the text in the box, type **Parks Dept Fonts**, and then click **Save**.

6. In the Background group, click the **Fonts** button. The new custom font set appears above the list of built-in font sets. See Figure 6–17.

| Figure 6–17 | Custom theme font set in the Fonts gallery |
| --- | --- |

custom theme font set

blew_s/Shutterstock.com

7. In the Close group, click the **Close Master View** button, and then in Normal view, click the **Design** tab.

8. In the Variants group, click the **More** button ⏷, and then point to **Fonts**. The custom font set you created appears at the top of this Fonts gallery as well.

Veronica used the default Office theme and color palette when she created her presentation. She asks you to apply a different color palette that has more green colors in it.

## To change the theme colors:

1. On the menu, point to **Colors**. The gallery of theme colors opens. See Figure 6–18. The Office color palette is selected.

Figure 6–18
**Colors menu displaying the gallery of color palettes**

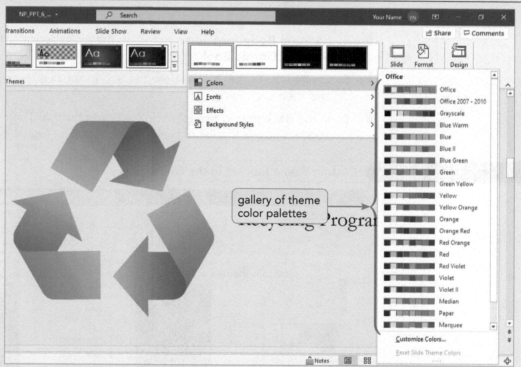

Kostenyukova Nataliya/Shutterstock.com; blew_s/Shutterstock.com; Rob kemp/Shutterstock.com

**Trouble?** If the menu in the Variants group is not still open, click the More button in the Variants group, and then do Step 1.

2. Click the **Green** palette. The Green palette is applied to the presentation. The background color of all of the slides changed to light green. Veronica likes the green background better than the blue one you applied earlier.

3. Display Slide 3 (the Summary Zoom titled "Overview"). The text link at the bottom of this slide is a darker green than the slide background, but is a little difficult to see. Veronica wants you to change the color of unfollowed links, but she wants followed links to be a different color. To accomplish this, you need to create a custom color palette.

4. In the Variants group, click the **More** button, point to **Colors**, and then click **Customize Colors**. The Create New Theme Colors dialog box opens listing the 12 colors included in the current color palette. At the bottom of the list, you can see that the Hyperlink color is green, and the Followed Hyperlink color is brown. See Figure 6–19.

**Figure 6–19**     **Create New Theme Colors dialog box**

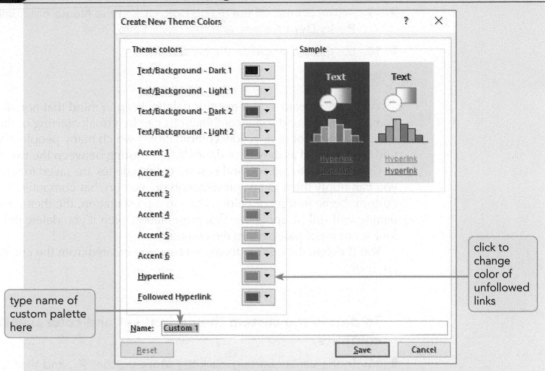

type name of
custom palette
here

click to
change
color of
unfollowed
links

5. Click the **Hyperlink** button. The current color palette appears with the theme color in the second to last column selected. You can select one of the colors in the palette or choose another color.

6. On the menu, click **More Colors**. The Colors dialog box opens with the Custom tab selected.

7. Click the **Standard** tab, and then click the red color as shown in Figure 6–20.

**Figure 6–20**     **Standard tab in the Colors dialog box**

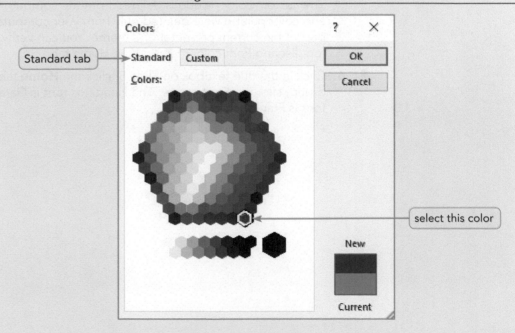

Standard tab

select this color

▶ **8.** Click **OK**. The Hyperlink color in the list is now the red color you selected.

▶ **9.** At the bottom of the dialog box, click in the **Name** box, delete the text, type **Parks Dept Colors**, and then click **Save**.

▶ **10.** Save the changes to the presentation.

When you create a custom color palette, keep in mind that not all colors are complementary, and some combinations can be visually jarring or illegible. Also avoid using red/green or blue/yellow combinations, which many people who are color-blind find hard to read as they have difficulty contrasting between the two colors.

Custom theme font sets and custom color palettes are saved to your computer, and you can apply them to any presentation opened on that computer. After you apply a custom theme font set or color palette to a presentation, the theme fonts or the color palette will still be applied to that presentation even if you delete the custom theme font set or color palette from the computer.

You'll delete the custom theme font set you created from the computer you are using.

**To delete the custom theme font set and color palette from the computer:**

▶ **1.** In the Variants group, click the **More** button ⬇, and then point to **Fonts**. The custom theme font set you created appears at the top of the menu.

▶ **2.** Right-click **Parks Dept Fonts** on the menu, and then on the shortcut menu, click **Delete**. A dialog box opens, asking if you want to delete these theme fonts.

▶ **3.** Click **Yes**.

▶ **4.** In the Variants group, click the **More** button ⬇, and then point to **Colors**. The custom theme font set you created appears at the top of the menu.

▶ **5.** Right-click **Parks Dept Colors** on the menu, click **Delete**, and then click **Yes**. The custom color palette is deleted from the computer. The custom font set and color palette were deleted only from your computer. They are both still part of the current presentation's theme. You can verify this by looking at the font list and Font color menu on the Home tab.

▶ **6.** Click in the title text box on Slide 3, click the **Home** tab, and then in the Font group, click the **Font arrow**. The Headings font is Garamond and the Body font is Franklin Gothic Book.

**Proskills**

### Problem Solving: Should You Create Your Own Theme?

PowerPoint comes with professionally designed themes, theme colors, and theme fonts. You can also create a presentation based on a template stored on Office.com. If you decide you need to create a custom theme, you can start "from scratch" and assign every theme color and create your own combination of fonts. But unless you are a graphic designer, consider starting with a theme or theme colors that most closely match the colors you want to use, and then selectively customize some of the colors, fonts, or styles. By creating a theme this way, you can take advantage of the professional designs available in PowerPoint and on Office.com to create your own custom look.

## Filling Text and Shapes with a Color Used on the Slide

To fill a shape with a color used on a slide, you click Eyedropper on the Shape Fill menu, and then click an area of the slide. The shape is then filled with the exact color that you clicked.

When you point to a color using the Eyedropper tool, a ScreenTip appears listing a general name for the color, such as Light Green, Gold, or Black, and the color's RGB values. RGB stands for Red, Green, and Blue. Every color is made up of some combination of these three colors on a scale of 0 through 255. For example, pure red has a Red value of 255 and Green and Blue values of 0, but a shade of orange has a Red value of 229, a Green value of 128, and a Blue value of 27.

Earlier, you changed the color of the title text on Slide 3 (the Summary Zoom titled "Overview") so that it would not be visible on the slide. You changed the text to white because the slide background was white. You need to change the color again now that the slide backgrounds are filled with green. The summary zoom has the Title and Content layout applied. Because many of the slides in the presentation have that layout applied, you will change the title text color on Slide 3, not on the Title and Content layout in Slide Master view.

### To use the Eyedropper to select a fill color:

1. On Slide 3 (the Summary Zoom titled "Overview"), click **Overview**, and then click the border of the title text box. The entire text box is selected.

> **Tip**
>
> If you select the Eyedropper tool and then decide you don't want to use it, press ESC.

2. Click the **Home** tab if necessary, in the Font group, click the **Font Color** button A ⋅ , and then click **Eyedropper**. The pointer changes to the eyedropper pointer 🖊 .

3. Move the pointer on top of a green area of the slide. A box containing the color you are pointing to appears above the pointer, and a ScreenTip appears identifying the color as RGB(219,239,212) Light Green. See Figure 6–21.

| Figure 6–21 | Eyedropper showing the ScreenTip identifying a color on a slide |

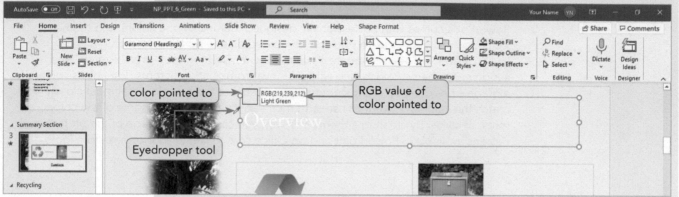

Kostenyukova Nataliya/Shutterstock.com; Rob kemp/Shutterstock.com; blew_s/Shutterstock.com

> **4.** Click the light green slide background. The text in the selected text box changes to the same color and is no longer visible.

On the title slide, the title text is hard to see on top of the picture. To fix this, you will try adjusting the transparency of the picture in the background. You will make this change in Slide Master view.

### To change the transparency of a picture:

> **1.** Display Slide 1 (the title slide). The title "Green Challenge" is somewhat hard to read.

> **2.** Switch to Slide Master view to display the Title Slide layout, and then in the Background group, click the **Dialog Box Launcher** 🔲. The Format Background pane opens.

> **3.** In the Format Background pane, drag the **Transparency** slider to the right until the percentage in the Transparency box is 65%. The title is a little easier to read, but the picture looks washed out. Veronica doesn't like this effect.

> **4.** In the Transparency box, select **65%**, type **0**, and then press **ENTER**. The picture is again opaque—not transparent at all.

Making the picture transparent helped make the title text a little clearer, but it muted the colors in the picture too much. Instead, you will fill the title text box with a gradient of a color in the photo.

### To use the Eyedropper to fill a text box with a gradient color:

> **1.** Click the title text placeholder, and then click the **Shape Format** tab. Because a shape (the title text placeholder) is selected, the pane changes to the Format Shape pane. The Shape Options tab and the Fill & Line button 🖍 are selected, and the Fill section is expanded. The No fill option button is selected.

> **2.** On the Shape Format tab, in the Shape Styles group, click the **Shape Fill arrow**, and then click **Eyedropper**.

3. Move the pointer below the letters "a" and "s" in "Master." The rectangle that shows the color should be labeled Dark Green, and the ScreenTip should identify the color as something close to RGB(153,172,41). It's fine if your RGB values do not match this exactly.

4. When the pointer is positioned, click. The fill of the title text box changes to the color you clicked. In the Format Shape pane, the Solid fill option button is now selected, and the Color button has a green stripe.

Although you can now see the title text, it looks a little odd to have the green rectangle on top of the picture. To fix this, you will make the fill semi-transparent to see if that looks better. First, you will change the fill color so that it matches the color shown in the figures exactly.

### To change the fill transparency of the title text box:

1. In the Format Shape pane, click the **Color** button. Below the Standard Colors row, a Recent Colors row appears. The green color you selected in the previous set of steps appears in the Recent Colors row. See Figure 6–22.

**Figure 6–22** | **Color palette showing recently selected colors**

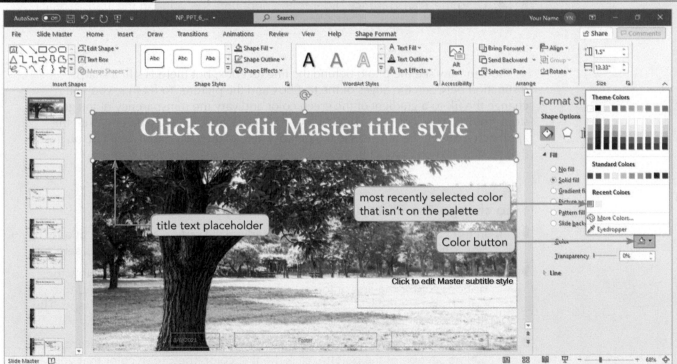

blew_s/Shutterstock.com

**Trouble?** If there is more than one color below the Recent Colors label, the most recently selected color—the green color you selected in the previous set of steps—is the first color in the row.

2. Click **More Colors**. The Colors dialog box opens with the Custom tab selected. See Figure 6–23.

**Figure 6–23      Custom tab in the Colors dialog box**

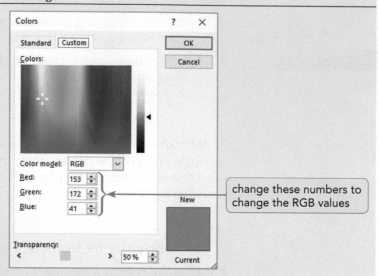

change these numbers to change the RGB values

3. If necessary, change the value in the Red box to **153**, change the value in the Green box to **172**, change the value in the Blue box to **41**, and then click **OK**. Now you need to make the text box semi-transparent.

4. Drag the **Transparency** slider to the right until the value in the Transparency box is 50%.

You can now see the photo behind the title text box, but there is still a sharp distinction between the edges of the text box and the picture. To fix this, you will change the fill to a gradient of the green color and vary the transparency of the gradient stops from 100%—not transparent at all—to 0%—completely transparent. With this approach, you will be able to see the photo and read the text, and it won't be obvious that the title text box has a fill.

**To change the fill to a gradient of transparencies:**

1. In the Format Shape pane, click the **Gradient fill** option button. The title text box is filled with a gradient of a green color. In the Type box, Linear is selected.

2. Click the **Direction** button, and then click the **Linear Down** style. Now the options set for the first gradient stop will affect the top of shape, and the options set for the last gradient stop will affect the bottom of the shape. The first gradient stop on the slider is selected.

3. In the Format Shape pane, click the **Color** button, and then in the Recent Colors section of the palette, click the first color (the green color that you used to fill the title text placeholder shape).

4. Click the **Stop 2 of 4** tab, change its color to the same color as the Stop 1 of 4 tab, and then change its position to **50%**. You need to change the transparency of this gradient stop to 50%.

5. Scroll to the bottom of the Format Shape pane, and then drag the **Transparency** slider to the right until the Transparency box contains 50%.

6. Click the **Stop 4 of 4** tab, change its color to the same color as the Stop 1 of 4 and Stop 2 of 4 tabs, and then change the transparency to 100%.

7. Click the **Stop 3 of 4** tab, and then click the **Remove gradient stop** button 🔯.
   With the title text vertically aligned at the top of the text box, the text is
   clearer on the green background that is not transparent. See Figure 6–24.

| Figure 6–24 | Final gradient for the title text placeholder on the Title Slide layout |
|---|---|

blew_s/Shutterstock.com

The middle stop on the gradient slider is not necessary to create this effect.
However, if you keep it, you can change its position from 50% to either
extend or reduce the part of the text box that is not at all transparent.

8. Close the Format Shape pane, and then switch to Normal view.

9. **sam** ⬆ Save the changes to the presentation.

> Make sure you save
> the changes to the
> presentation because you
> will be saving the file in
> another format in the next
> set of steps.

# Insight

## Creating a Photo Album

PowerPoint includes a built-in Photo Album command, which allows you to create a photo
album with one, two, or four pictures per slide, and optionally, with titles and captions.
The advantage of this feature is that you can insert a large number of photographs all at
once into a presentation without needing to insert each picture individually. To create this
type of photo album, you click the Insert tab, and then, in the Images group, click the
Photo Album button to open the Photo Album dialog box. To add a photo, click the File/
Disk button, select the photo or photos you want to add from the Insert New Pictures
dialog box, and then click the Insert button. To modify a photo, click the check box next
to it in the Pictures in album list, and then click one of the Rotate buttons to rotate the
picture 90 degrees, and click one of the Brightness or Contrast buttons to make the
image brighter or darker or to increase or decrease the contrast. To add text boxes below
each photo for captions, click the Captions below ALL pictures check box.

To change the layout of the slides, click the Picture layout arrow, and then click a
layout. Note that when you do this, you are not actually changing the layout of the
slides. All of the options on the Picture layout menu that do not include a title place
the slides on the Blank layout from the Office theme; all of the options that include
a title place the slides on the Title Only layout from the Office theme. When you are
finished setting up the photo album, click Create to create the photo album.

# Saving a Presentation as a Custom Theme

Now that you have created a custom theme for Veronica, she asks you to save the theme so that she can apply it to other presentations. When you save a presentation as a theme, the changes are saved to the Document Themes folder. The Document Themes folder is created on the hard drive when Office is installed and is where the built-in themes are installed. If you save to this folder, the custom theme will appear in the Themes gallery on the Design tab. You can also save a theme to another folder, but then you will need to apply it in the same way you apply a theme that is used by another presentation.

When you save a presentation as a theme, it needs only one slide. The first thing you will do is delete all the slides except the title slide.

## To save a presentation as a theme:

1. Delete Slides 2 through 11. The section names are still listed.

2. Right-click any section name, and then on the shortcut menu click **Remove All Sections**.

3. Click the **File** tab, and then in the navigation pane, click **Save As** or **Save a Copy**. The Save As or Save a Copy screen in Backstage view appears.

4. Click **Browse** to open the Save As dialog box. At the top of the dialog box, the path to the folder and the name of the folder containing the NP_PPT_6_ Green presentation appears. At the bottom of the dialog box, the name of the open file appears in the File name box. Below that, the file type appears in the Save as type box. The current file type is PowerPoint Presentation.

5. Click the **Save as type** box. A list of file types appears.

6. In the list, click **Office Theme**. At the top of the dialog box, the path changes to show the path to the folder Document Themes. See Figure 6–25.

**Figure 6–25**    Save As dialog box showing the Document Themes folder

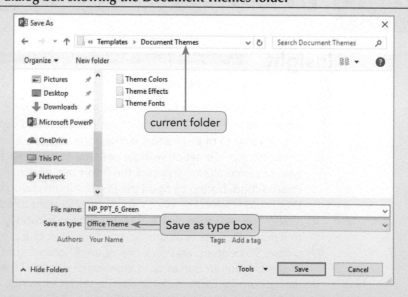

7. In the File name box, change the file name to **NP_PPT_6_ParksTheme**, and then click **Save**. The dialog box closes, and the theme is saved. You could also click the More button ⬆ in the Themes group on the Design tab, and then click Save Current Theme to save the presentation as a theme.

8. Click the **Design** tab, and then in the Themes group, click the **More** button ⬆. The custom theme appears in a new Custom section in the Themes gallery. See Figure 6–26.

| Figure 6–26 | Custom theme in the Themes gallery |

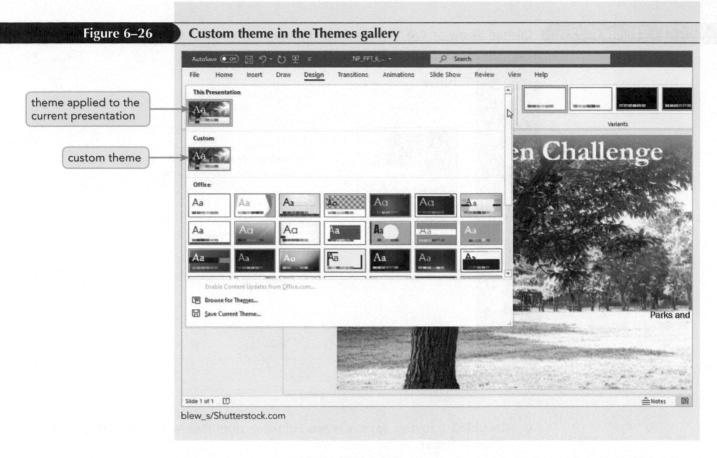

theme applied to the current presentation

custom theme

blew_s/Shutterstock.com

Recall that a template is a PowerPoint file that has a theme applied and also contains text, graphics, and placeholders that help a user create a final presentation. You can also save a presentation as a template if you want to preserve some of the content. To save a presentation as template, select PowerPoint Template in the list of file types on the Save As screen in Backstage view or in the Save as type box in the Save As dialog box. When you do this, the folder path you are saving to changes to the path to the Custom Office Templates folder.

Once you have saved a custom theme, there are several ways you can apply it to a presentation. If you saved it to the Document Themes folder, the theme will appear on the Design tab in the Themes group, and you can click the custom theme to apply it to the current presentation. Or when you are creating a new presentation, you can click Custom on the New screen in Backstage view, click the Document Themes folder, and then click the custom theme. You can also apply a custom theme to the current presentation using the same method you use to apply a theme from any presentation by clicking the More button ⤓ in the Themes group on the Design tab, and then clicking Browse for Themes.

### To create a new presentation using a custom theme:

▶ 1. Click the **File** tab, and then in the navigation pane, click **New**. The New screen appears in Backstage view. The Office tab is selected. This tab contains all of the built-in themes. If you click one, a new presentation will be created with that theme applied. You can also click one of the Suggested searches links or type in the "Search for online templates and themes" to find templates that have a theme applied as well as placeholder content.

▶ 2. Click **Custom**. The New screen changes to show themes and templates stored in the Document Themes folder on your computer. See Figure 6–27.

**Figure 6–27**    **Custom theme on the New screen in Backstage view**

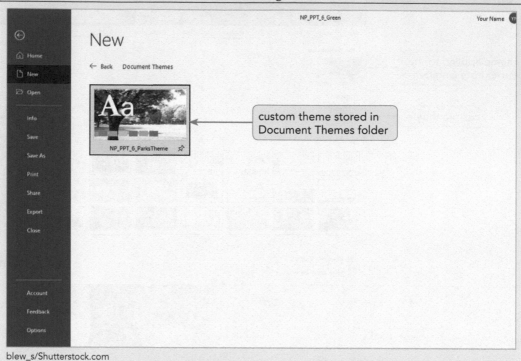

blew_s/Shutterstock.com

> **Trouble?** If folders appear instead of the custom theme, click the Document Themes folder.

▶ **3.** Click **NP_PPT_6_ParksTheme**. A window opens showing the Title layout of the selected theme. See Figure 6–28.

**Figure 6–28**    **Window that appears when a theme is selected on the New screen**

blew_s/Shutterstock.com

▶ **4.** Click the **Create** button. The window and Backstage view close and a new presentation is created with the custom theme you created applied.

▶ **5.** Add a new Slide 2 with the Title and Content layout.

▶ **6.** Add your name as the title on the title slide, save the new presentation as **NP_PPT_6_ThemeTest** to the location where you are saving your files, and then close it. The NP_PPT_6_Green presentation is the active presentation again. It contains only the title slide. You saved the completed presentation before you saved the file as a theme, so you will close this version without saving changes, and then reopen the version you saved.

▶ **7.** Click the **File** tab, and then click **Close**. A dialog box opens asking if you want to save the changes to the presentation.

**Tip**

If you have AutoSave enabled, click the Undo button on the Quick Access Toolbar as necessary to undo the deletion of Slides 2-11 and skip steps 7-9.

▶  **8.** Click **Don't Save**. The dialog box and the presentation close.

▶  **9.** Open the file **NP_PPT_6_Green** from the location where you are storing your files.

If you open a template from the New screen in Backstage view, a new presentation will be created based on that template. If you open a template from the Open screen in Backstage view, the template itself will open.

You'll delete the custom theme you created from the computer you are using.

### To delete the custom theme from the computer:

▶  **1.** Click the **Design** tab. In the Themes group, the custom theme applied to the current presentation appears. The second theme is the custom theme you saved.

▶  **2.** Move the pointer on top of the first theme. The ScreenTip that appears says "Rockland Parks: used by all slides."

▶  **3.** Move the pointer on top of the second theme. The ScreenTip that appears says "NP_PPT_6_ParksTheme."

▶  **4.** In the Themes group, right-click the second theme with the ScreenTip "NP_PPT_6_ParksTheme." A shortcut menu opens.

▶  **5.** On the shortcut menu, click **Delete**. A dialog box opens, asking if you want to delete this theme.

▶  **6.** Click **Yes**. The custom theme is deleted from the computer.

In this session, you compared presentations and worked with comments. You also modified the slide master by changing the formatting and adding pictures on the slide master and on individual layouts, by changing the bullet style, by modifying a layout, and by creating a custom layout. You also created a custom theme font set and theme color palette. You used the Eyedropper tool to fill text and a shape with a color used on the slide, and you modified a title text box by making part of it transparent. Finally, you saved the custom theme. In the next session, you will create a custom show, modify and create advanced file properties, encrypt the presentation, and mark it as final.

## Review

### Session 6.1 Quick Check

1.  What types of changes are listed when you compare presentations: changes to individual slides, changes to the entire presentation, or both?

2.  What happens to the layouts when you modify the slide master?

3.  What happens to Title and Content layout when you modify the Title Slide layout?

4.  Describe how to create a new layout.

5.  Describe how to add a placeholder to a layout.

6.  If you delete a custom theme font set from your computer, does the presentation revert back to its original theme font set?

7.  When describing a color, what do the letters R, G, and B stand for?

8.  How do you get a custom theme to appear in the Themes gallery on the Design tab?

# Session 6.2 Visual Overview:

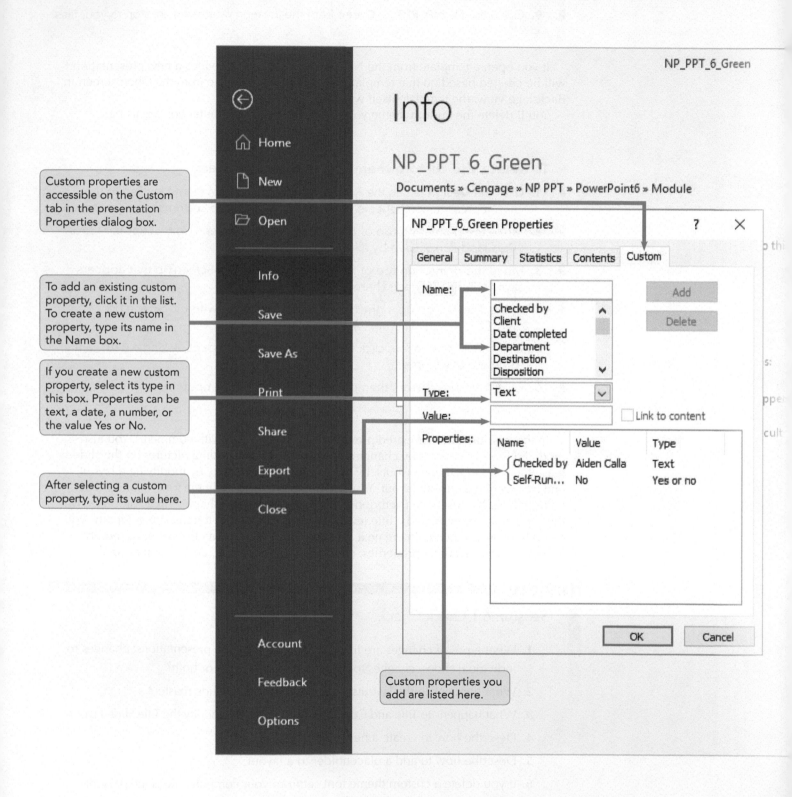

Custom properties are accessible on the Custom tab in the presentation Properties dialog box.

To add an existing custom property, click it in the list. To create a new custom property, type its name in the Name box.

If you create a new custom property, select its type in this box. Properties can be text, a date, a number, or the value Yes or No.

After selecting a custom property, type its value here.

Custom properties you add are listed here.

NP_PPT_6_Green

Info

NP_PPT_6_Green

Documents » Cengage » NP PPT » PowerPoint6 » Module

Home
New
Open
Info
Save
Save As
Print
Share
Export
Close
Account
Feedback
Options

**NP_PPT_6_Green Properties**          ?   ✕

General | Summary | Statistics | Contents | Custom

Name:
Checked by
Client
Date completed
Department
Destination
Disposition

Add
Delete

Type:   Text

Value:                     ☐ Link to content

Properties:

| Name | Value | Type |
|------|-------|------|
| Checked by | Aiden Calla | Text |
| Self-Run... | No | Yes or no |

OK     Cancel

# Advanced File Properties

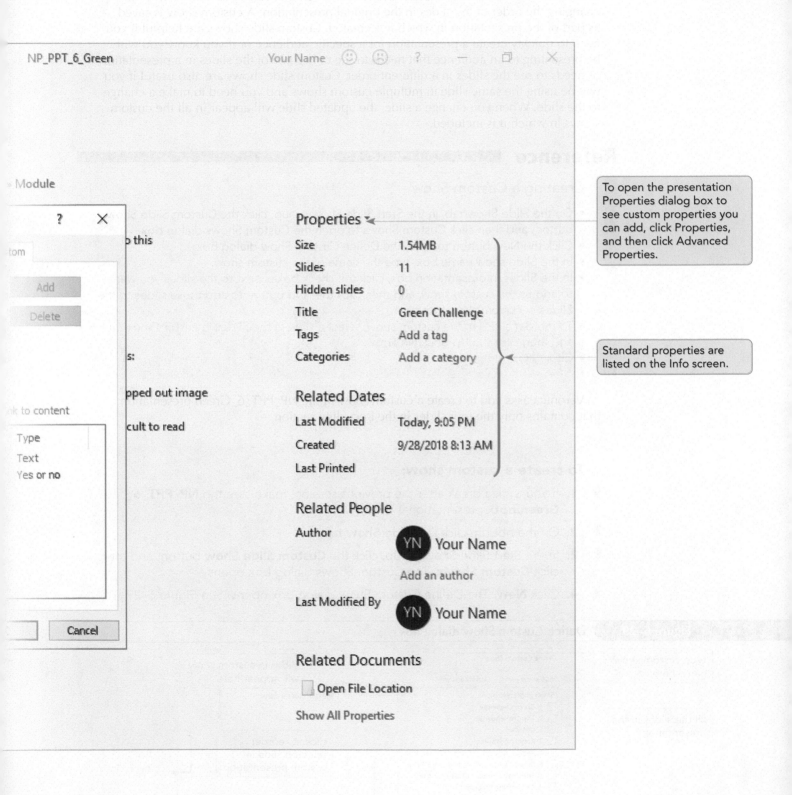

NP_PPT_6_Green    Your Name

Module

? ×

tom

Add

Delete

s:

pped out image

nk to content    cult to read

Type
Text
Yes or no

Cancel

**Properties**

| Size | 1.54MB |
| Slides | 11 |
| Hidden slides | 0 |
| Title | Green Challenge |
| Tags | Add a tag |
| Categories | Add a category |

**Related Dates**

| Last Modified | Today, 9:05 PM |
| Created | 9/28/2018 8:13 AM |
| Last Printed | |

**Related People**

Author    YN  Your Name
Add an author

Last Modified By    YN  Your Name

**Related Documents**

Open File Location

Show All Properties

> To open the presentation Properties dialog box to see custom properties you can add, click Properties, and then click Advanced Properties.

> Standard properties are listed on the Info screen.

# Creating a Custom Show

A **custom show** is a subset of slides in a presentation that can be reordered without changing the order of the slides in the original presentation. A custom show is saved as part of the presentation in which it is created. Custom slide shows are helpful if you need to quickly create a presentation for a specific audience or if you know you will be presenting to an audience that needs to see only some of the slides in a presentation or needs to see the slides in a different order. Custom slide shows are also useful if you will be using the same slide in multiple custom shows and you need to make a change to the slide. When you change a slide, the updated slide will appear in all the custom shows in which it is included.

## Reference

### Creating a Custom Show

- On the Slide Show tab, in the Start Slide Show group, click the Custom Slide Show button, and then click Custom Shows to open the Custom Shows dialog box.
- Click the New button to open the Define Custom Show dialog box.
- In the Slide show name box, type the name of the custom show.
- In the Slides in presentation box, click the check boxes next to the slides you want to add to the custom show, and then click the Add button to add those slides to the Slides in custom show box.
- To reorder slides in the custom show, select a slide in the Slides in custom show box, and then click the Up or Down arrow.
- Click OK, and then click Close.

Veronica asks you to create a custom show in the NP_PPT_6_Green presentation that contains only the four slides in the Recycling section.

### To create a custom show:

1. If you took a break after the previous session, make sure the **NP_PPT_6_ Green.pptx** presentation is open.

2. On the ribbon, click the **Slide Show** tab.

3. In the Start Slide Show group, click the **Custom Slide Show** button, and then click **Custom Shows**. The Custom Shows dialog box opens.

4. Click **New**. The Define Custom Show dialog box opens. See Figure 6-29.

**Figure 6-29** **Define Custom Show dialog box**

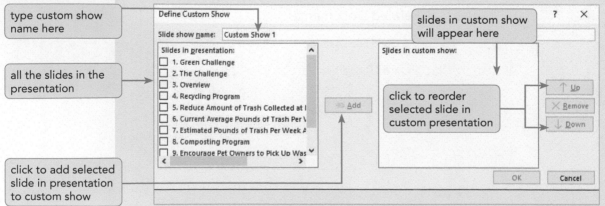

5. In the Slide show name box, delete the text, and then type **Recycling**. Next, you'll select the slides that you want to use in the custom show.

6. In the Slides in presentation box on the left, click the check boxes next to **4. Recycling Program**, **5. Reduce Amount of Trash Collected at Parks**, **6. Current Average Pounds of Trash Per Week**, and **7. Estimated Pounds of Trash Per Week After Adding Recycling Bins**.

7. Click **Add**. The selected slides on the left are added to the Slides in custom show box on the right and are renumbered 1-4 in the box on the right.

8. Click **OK**. The custom show you created is added to the list in the Custom Shows dialog box.

9. Click **Close** in the dialog box.

To run the custom show, you can click the Show button in the Custom Shows dialog box, or you can run it from Normal, Slide Show, or Presenter view.

### To run a custom show:

1. On the Slide Show tab, in the Start Slide Show group, click the **Custom Slide Show** button. The menu now includes the custom show you created. See Figure 6–30.

**Figure 6–30**    **Custom Slide Show menu listing a custom show**

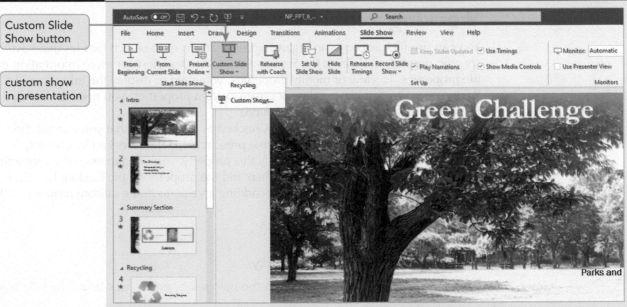

Custom Slide Show button

custom show in presentation

blew_s/Shutterstock.com; Kostenyukova Nataliya/Shutterstock.com; Rob kemp/Shutterstock.com

**Tip**

You can format text or an object on a slide as a link to a custom show. In the Insert a Hyperlink dialog box, click Place in This Document in the Link to list, and then click the custom show name.

2. Click **Recycling**. The first slide in the custom show, "Recycling Program", appears in Slide Show view.

3. Advance the slide show four times to display the remaining slides in the custom presentation and the black slide that indicates the end of a slide show, and then advance it once more to return to Normal view.

4. Save the changes to the presentation.

## Insight

### Working with 3D Models

You can insert 3D models on a slide. To do this, click the 3D Models arrow in the Illustrations group on the Insert tab. To insert a 3D model stored on your computer or network, click From a File. To insert a 3D model from an online library called Remix 3D, click Stock 3D Models. Remix 3D contains 3D models uploaded by members of the Remix community.

The 3D Model tab appears on the ribbon when a 3D model is selected. Like any other object on a slide, you can resize a 3D model by dragging a sizing handle or by changing the measurements in the Height and Width boxes in the Size group. In addition, you can click a view in the 3D Model Views group to rotate the model as indicated or you can drag the 3D control in the middle of the image to rotate the object in three dimensions. You can also click the Pan & Zoom button in the Size group to add a magnifying glass icon to the right of the model. If you drag the magnifying glass icon up or down, the model increases or decreases in size inside the object border.

You also have access to additional animations when a 3D model is selected. You can apply the 3D Arrive animation, which is an entrance animation for 3D models. You can also apply the 3D Turntable, Swing, and Jump & Turn animations, which are emphasis animations for 3D models. And you can apply the 3D Leave animation, an exit animation for 3D models. The Effect Options menus for all of the 3D animations contain options to change the direction and the rotation axis of the animation. Some of the animations allow you to change the intensity of the animations and some allow you to change amount of the animation.

# Working with File Properties

You can use file properties to organize presentations or to search for files that have specific properties. Refer to the Session 6.2 Visual Overview for more information on file properties. To view or modify properties, you need to display the Info screen in Backstage view. To view, modify, or create custom properties, you need to display the Properties dialog box for the presentation.

Veronica wants you to modify the Checked by property so that you can list the names of people who have reviewed the presentation. The Checked by property is not listed on the Info screen. To modify this property, you need to open the Properties dialog box for the presentation, and then add the property on the Custom tab. Even after you modify a custom property by adding a value to it, the custom property will still not appear on the Info screen.

### To add a custom file property:

1. Click the **File** tab, and then in the navigation pane, click **Info**. The Info screen in Backstage view appears.

2. At the top of the list of document properties, click the **Properties** button, and then click **Advanced Properties**. The NP_PPT_6_Green Properties dialog box opens.

3. Click the **Custom** tab. This tab lists additional properties you can add. See Figure 6–31.

**Figure 6-31**     Custom tab in the NP_PPT_6_Green Properties dialog box

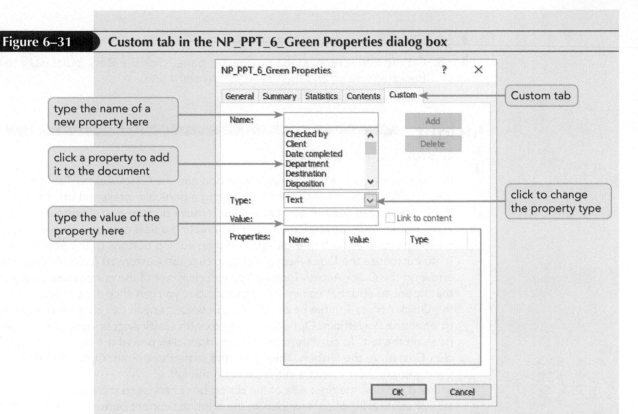

**4.** In the Name list, click **Checked by**. "Checked by" appears in the Name box above the list.

**5.** Click in the **Value** box, type **Aiden Callahan**, and then click **Add**. "Checked by" and the value you gave it appear in the Properties list below the Value box.

Properties are one of four types: Text, Date, Number, or Yes or no. All of the properties you have worked with so far are Text properties and contain text as their value. A property with the Date type can contain only a date as its value, and a Number type property can contain only a number. Yes or no type properties have the value Yes or No.

Veronica will use the NP_PPT_6_Green presentation when she speaks in front of the city council. The council wants the department heads to post self-running versions of their presentations on the city's website as well. Veronica plans to create another version of her presentation for the website that contains a little more explanatory text. She will also review the presentation for accessibility. To help her keep track of her presentations, she wants you to create a new custom Yes or no property named Self-Running. The current version of her presentation will have No as the Self-Running property. The version that she will post on the city's website will have Yes as the Self-Running property.

**To create a new custom file property:**

**1.** In the NP_PPT_6_Green Properties dialog box, click in the **Name** box, and then type **Self-Running**.

**2.** Click the **Type** arrow, and then click **Yes or no**. The Value box changes to show Yes and No option buttons.

**3.** Click the **No** option button, and then click **Add**. "Self-Running" and the value you gave it appear below "Checked by" in the Properties list.

▶ 4. Click **OK**. The dialog box closes.

▶ 5. On the Info screen, in the navigation pane, click the **Back** button ⊙ to close Backstage view, and then save the presentation.

## Insight

### Customizing PowerPoint

In PowerPoint, you can customize the ribbon and the Quick Access Toolbar to suit your working style or your needs for creating a particular presentation. To customize the Quick Access Toolbar, you can add or remove buttons and change its location in the window. You customize the ribbon by creating a new group on an existing tab or creating a new tab with new groups and then adding buttons to the new groups.

To customize the Quick Access Toolbar, click the Customize Quick Access Toolbar arrow on the Quick Access Toolbar. You can click one of the commands on the menu that opens to add that command to the toolbar, you can click the command to move the Quick Access Toolbar below the ribbon below, or you can click More Commands to open the PowerPoint Options dialog box with Quick Access Toolbar selected in the pane on the left. To customize the ribbon, right-click one of the ribbon tabs, and then click Customize the Ribbon. This opens the same PowerPoint Options dialog box with Customize Ribbon selected in the pane on the left.

In both cases, the right side of the dialog box changes to show two lists. On the left is an alphabetical list of commands. On the right, the current buttons on the Quick Access Toolbar or the current tabs and groups on the ribbon are listed. The list of commands on the left are Popular Commands; to see all the commands in PowerPoint, click the Choose commands from arrow, and then click All Commands. To add a command to the Quick Access Toolbar or to the selected group on the ribbon, click the command in the list on the left, and then click Add. To add a command to the ribbon, you must create a new group first. Select the tab on which you want to create the new group (or click the New Tab button to create a new tab), and then click the New Group button.

## Encrypting a Presentation

To **encrypt** a file is to modify it to make the information unreadable to anyone who does not have the password. When you encrypt a PowerPoint file, you assign a password to the file. The only way to open the file is by entering the password. When you create passwords, keep in mind that they are case sensitive; this means that "PASSWORD" is different from "password." Also, you must remember your password. This might seem obvious, but if you forget the password you assign to a file, you won't be able to open it.

## Reference

### Encrypting a Presentation

- On the ribbon, click the File tab, and then click Info to open the Info screen in Backstage view.
- Click the Protect Presentation button, and then click Encrypt with Password.
- In the Encrypt Document dialog box, type a password in the Password box, and then click the OK button to open the Confirm Password dialog box.
- Retype the password in the Reenter password box.
- Click OK.

Veronica wants you to encrypt the NP_PPT_6_Green file so that it can be opened only by people with whom she has shared the password.

### To encrypt the presentation with a password:

1. On the ribbon, click the **File** tab, and then click **Info** to open the Info screen in Backstage view.

2. Click the **Protect Presentation** button. A menu opens listing options for protecting the presentation. See Figure 6–32.

**Figure 6–32**   Protect Presentation menu on the Info screen

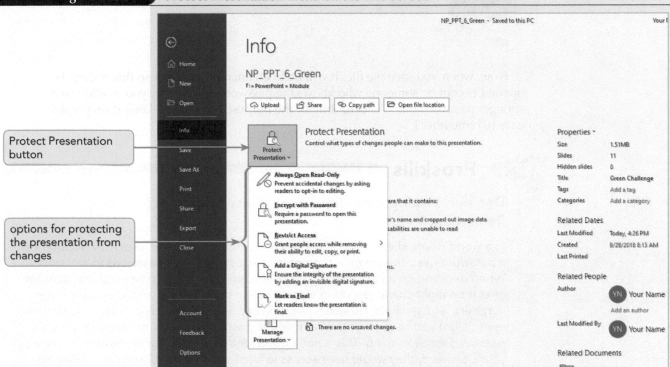

Protect Presentation button

options for protecting the presentation from changes

**Tip**

To remove the password, delete the password in the Encrypt Document dialog box, and then click the OK button.

3. Click **Encrypt with Password**. The Encrypt Document dialog box opens. Here you'll type a password.

4. Type **Green**. The characters you type appear as black dots to prevent anyone from reading the password over your shoulder.

5. Click **OK**. The dialog box changes to the Confirm Password dialog box.

6. Type **Green** again to verify the password, and then click **OK**. The Protect Presentation section heading and the Protect Presentation button are yellow to indicate that a protection has been set, and the message in the Protect Presentation section explains that a password is required to open the presentation. See Figure 6–33.

Figure 6–33    Info screen after encrypting a file

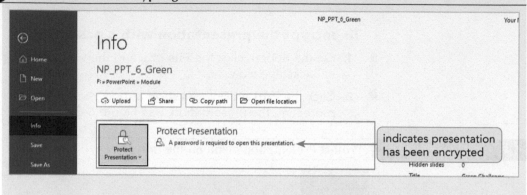

Now, when you save the file, it will be in an encrypted format so that it can't be opened except by someone who knows the password. (Normally, you would use a stronger password than "Green," but for the purpose here, you'll keep it simple and easy to remember.)

 **Proskills**

Decision Making: Creating Strong Passwords You Can Easily Remember

In a world where sharing digital information electronically is an everyday occurrence, a password used to encrypt a presentation is just one more password to remember. When deciding on a password, you should consider a strong password that consists of at least eight characters using a combination of uppercase and lowercase letters, numbers, and symbols. However, this type of password can be difficult to remember, especially if you have to remember multiple passwords. Some people use the same password for everything. This is not a good idea because if someone ever discovered your password, they would have access to all of the data or information protected by that password. Instead, you should come up with a plan for creating passwords. For example, you could choose a short word that you can easily remember for one part of the password. The second part of the password could be the name of the file, website, or account, but instead of typing it directly, type it backwards, or use the characters in the row above or below the characters that would spell out the name. Or you could split the name of the website and put your short word in the middle of the name. Other possibilities are to combine your standard short word and the website or account name, but replace certain letters with symbols—for example, replace every letter "E" with "#," or memorize a short phrase from a poem or story and use it with some of the substitutions described above. Establishing a process for creating a password means that you will be able to create strong passwords for all of your accounts that you can easily remember.

# Making a Presentation Read-Only

You can make a presentation **read-only**, which means that others can read but cannot modify the presentation. There are two ways to make a presentation read-only. You can mark the presentation as final or you can set the presentation to always open as read-only. The next time you open a presentation marked as final, it will be read-only. If you turn off the read-only status, make changes, and then save and close the file, it will no longer be marked as final. If a presentation is set to always open as read-only and you turn off the read-only status to make changes, the next time you open that presentation, it will still be marked as read-only.

When Veronica posts her revised presentation on the city's website, she wants to make it read-only. She asks you to experiment with the two ways to do this and decide which method would be a better choice for this purpose.

### To mark the presentation as final and as read-only:

1. On the Info screen in Backstage view, click the **Protect Presentation** button, and then click **Mark as Final**. A dialog box opens stating that the presentation will be marked as final and then saved.

2. Click **OK**. The dialog box and Backstage view close, and another dialog box opens telling you that the document has been marked as final.

   **Trouble?** If the dialog box stating that the document has been marked as final does not appear, a previous user clicked the Don't show this message again check box in that dialog box. Skip Step 3.

3. Click **OK**. The ribbon is collapsed, a yellow MARKED AS FINAL bar appears below the collapsed ribbon, the Marked as Final icon appears in the status bar, and "Read-Only" appears in the title bar. See Figure 6–34.

---

**Figure 6–34**    **Presentation after marking a file as final**

blew_s/Shutterstock.com; Kostenyukova Nataliya/Shutterstock.com; Rob kemp/Shutterstock.com

▶ 4. Close the NP_PPT_6_Green file, and then reopen it. The Password dialog box appears.

▶ 5. In the Password box, type **Green**, and then click **OK**. The presentation opens, and the yellow MARKED AS FINAL bar appears.

▶ 6. In the MARKED AS FINAL bar, click **Edit Anyway**. The bar disappears and the ribbon is displayed.

▶ 7. Save the presentation, close it, and then reopen it, typing **Green** in the Password box when asked. The yellow MARKED AS FINAL bar does not appear.

▶ 8. Click the **File** tab, click **Info**, click the **Protect Presentation** button, and then click **Always Open Read-Only**. Additional text added below the Protect Presentation button name tells you that the presentation has been set to read-only.

▶ 9. In the navigation pane, click **Save**.

▶ 10. Close, and then reopen the presentation. The yellow bar appears again. This time, it is labeled READ-ONLY.

▶ 11. In the READ-ONLY bar, click **Edit Anyway**, display Slide 1 (the title slide), click **Parks and Recreation Department** in the subtitle text box, move the insertion point to the end of the line, press **ENTER**, and then type your name.

▶ 12. Save the presentation, close it, and then reopen it. The yellow READ-ONLY bar appears. If you want to remove the Always Open as Read-Only status, you need to click Edit Anyway in the READ-ONLY bar first.

▶ 13. Close the presentation file.

Now if you want to modify the presentation, you must remove the editing restriction by clicking the Edit Anyway button in the yellow MARKED AS FINAL bar.

# Insight

## Adding a Digital Signature and Restricting Access

A **digital signature** is an electronic attachment not visible in the file that verifies the authenticity of the author or the version of the file by comparing the digital signature to a digital certificate. A **digital certificate** is a code attached to a file that verifies the identity of the creator of the file. When you digitally sign a document, the file is marked as read-only. If anyone removes the read-only status so that you can make changes to the document, the signature is marked as invalid because it is no longer the same document the signatory signed. You can obtain a digital certificate from a certification authority.

To add a digital signature to a file, click the Protect Presentation button on the Info screen in Backstage view, and then click Add a Digital Signature. If the Get a Digital ID dialog box opens indicating that you don't have a digital ID and asking if you would like to get one from a Microsoft Partner, that means no digital certificate is stored on the computer you are using. If you click Yes, your browser starts and a webpage opens, listing certificate authorities from whom you can purchase a digital certificate.

If you or your company has access to a Rights Management Server or you are using Office 365 with RMS Online, you can restrict access to a presentation so that others can read it but not make any changes to it or copy or print it. To do this, click the Protect Presentation button, and then use the Restrict Access command.

# Presenting Online

You can run a slide show over the Internet so that anyone with a browser and the URL (the address for a webpage on the Internet) for the presentation can watch it while you present. When you present online, you send the presentation to a special Microsoft server that is made available for this purpose. (If you have access to a SharePoint server, you can send the presentation to that server instead.) A unique web address is created, and you can send this web address to anyone you choose. Then, while you run your presentation on your computer in Slide Show view, your remote audience members can view it on their computers in a web browser at the same time. Note that viewers will not be able to hear you unless you also set up a conference call.

In order to present online, you need a Microsoft account (or access to a SharePoint server), and you need to be connected to the Internet. If you don't have a Microsoft account, you can get one by clicking the Sign in link in the upper-right corner of the PowerPoint window or on the Microsoft webpage at microsoft.com. Once you have a Microsoft account, you can connect to the Microsoft server from within your PowerPoint presentation to create the unique web address for your presentation and start presenting online.

To present a slide show online, click the Slide Show tab, and then in the Start Slide Show group, click the Present Online button to open the Present Online dialog box, as shown in Figure 6–35.

**Figure 6–35**   Present Online dialog box

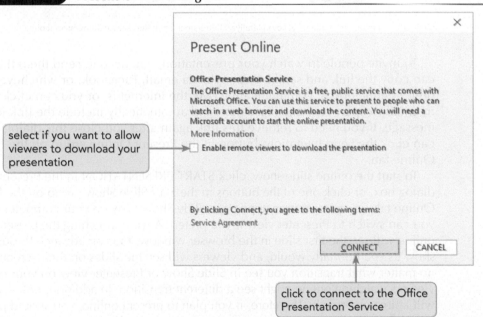

select if you want to allow viewers to download your presentation

click to connect to the Office Presentation Service

Click CONNECT. If you are signed into your Microsoft account in Office, the dialog box changes to display the link to your presentation on the Microsoft server and a new tab—the Present Online tab—appears on the ribbon, as shown in Figure 6–36. If you are not signed in to your Microsoft account, you will need to sign in before the link is created. (To present online, the file cannot be marked as file or set to always save as read-only, and it cannot have a password.)

**Figure 6–36**    **Present Online dialog box after web address is created**

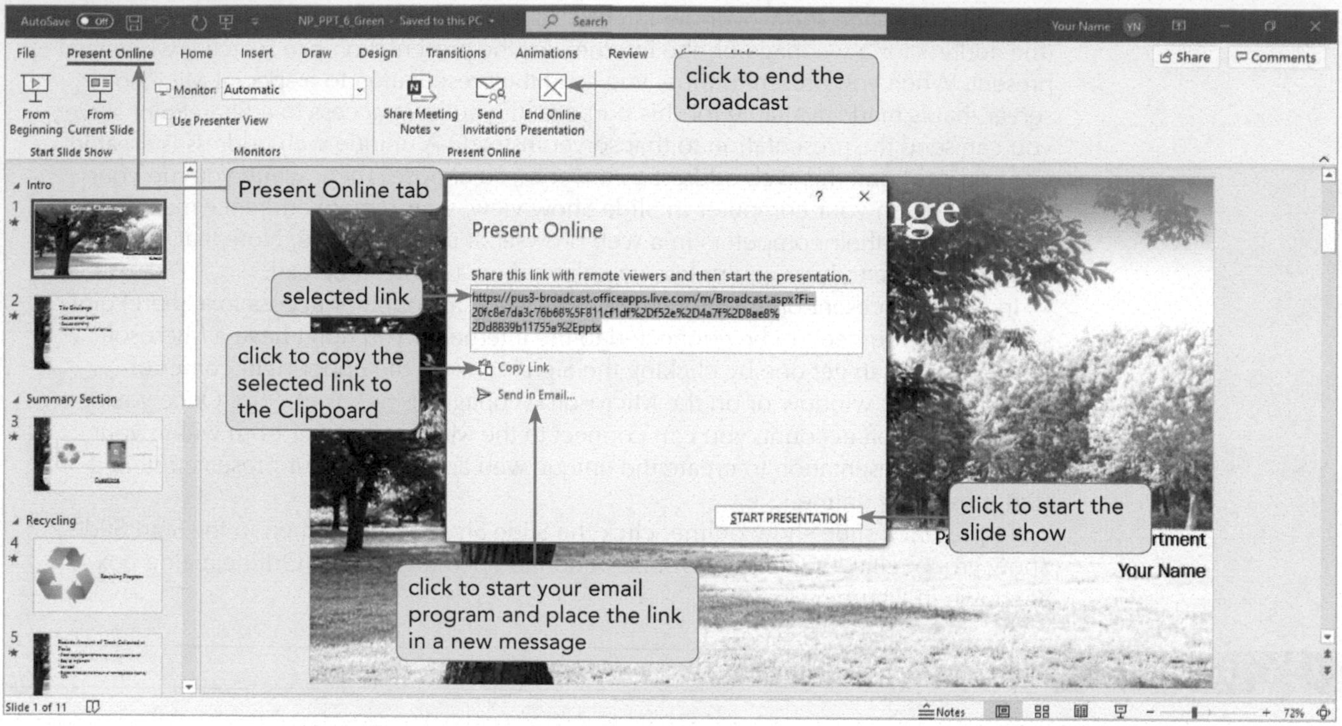

blew_s/Shutterstock.com; Kostenyukova Nataliya/Shutterstock.com; Rob kemp/Shutterstock.com

To invite people to watch your presentation, you need to send them the link. You can copy the link and send it to people via email, Facebook, or whichever your preferred method of communicating over the Internet is, or you can click Send in Email to open your email program and automatically include the link in the message. If you need to retrieve this link again after you close this dialog box, you can click the Send Invitations button in the Present Online group on the Present Online tab.

To start the online slide show, click START PRESENTATION in the Present Online dialog box, or click one of the buttons in the Start Slide Show group on the Present Online tab. The presentation appears in Slide Show view on your computer (although you can switch to Presenter view if you prefer). Anyone watching the presentation online will see the first slide in the browser window. You can advance through the slide show as you normally would, and viewers will see the slides on their screens. Note that no matter what transition you see in Slide Show or Presenter view on your computer, viewers watching online might see a different transition. In addition, not all animations will animate correctly. Therefore, if you plan to present online, you should preview the presentation in your own browser first and make sure the transitions and animations are acceptable.

To end the online slide show and disconnect from the Microsoft server, click the End Online Presentation button in the Present Online group on the Present Online tab. In the dialog box that opens warning you that everyone watching the online presentation will be disconnected, click the End Online Presentation button.

If you needed to sign into your Microsoft account in order to present online, you are now signed into that account in Office. To sign out, click your username in the upper-right corner of the PowerPoint window, and then click Account settings to open the Account screen in Backstage view. Below your username, click Sign out.

You have finished working on Veronica's presentation. She has the versions she needs to effectively share and collaborate with her staff to create consistent presentations to meet multiple purposes.

# Review

## Session 6.2 Quick Check

1. What is a custom show?
2. Can you modify custom properties on the Info screen in Backstage view?
3. What are the four types of properties?
4. What is an encrypted presentation?
5. What are the two ways to make a presentation read-only?
6. What happens when you present online?

# Practice

## Review Assignments

**Data Files needed for the Review Assignments: NP_PPT_6-2.pptx, Support_PPT_6_Dan.pptx, Support_PPT_6_Night.jpg**

Veronica Soto, the head of the Parks and Recreation department in Rockland, Missouri, researched another idea for meeting the Green Challenge issued by the city council. Currently, lights on walkways and in ball fields in city parks are on seven days a week from dusk until 11:00 p.m. She will present a plan to light certain fields only when a group has been issued a permit, but she wants to discuss the idea of leaving some fields lit for pick-up games. She gave a copy of her presentation to Dan Yost, the head of the department of public works. He reviewed it and returned it to her. She asks you to help her evaluate Dan's comments and complete her presentation. Complete the following steps:

1. Open the file **NP_PPT_6-2.pptx**, located in the PowerPoint6 > Review folder included with your Data Files. On Slide 1, add your name as the subtitle, and then save the file as **NP_PPT_6_Lights** in the location where you are saving your files.

2. Compare the NP_PPT_6_Lights presentation with the file **Support_PPT_6_Dan.pptx**, located in the PowerPoint6 > Review folder. Do not accept the change that says that Dan deleted your name on Slide 1 (the title slide), accept the change on Slide 2 ("Who Uses the Ball Fields?"), and then end the review.

3. On Slide 2 ("Who Uses the Ball Fields?"), read and then delete Dan's comment.

4. On Slide 7 ("Concerns"), read the comment from Dan, and then type the following as a reply: **That's a good idea. I'll look into the feasibility of that.** (including the period).

5. On Slide 4 ("New Lighting Plan"), insert the following as a new comment: **Maybe extend the time to 11:00 p.m. on weekend nights?**. Reposition the comment balloon to the left of the second bulleted item.

6. Apply the Parallax theme, and then choose the third variant. Change the theme fonts to the Consolas-Verdana theme font set, and then customize that theme font set so that Heading text uses the Arial font. Save the custom theme font set with the default name.

7. Delete the custom theme font set from the computer.

8. Modify the slide master by doing the following:
   a. Change the width of the title text placeholder to 10", and then align its right edge with the right edge of the content placeholder.
   b. Change the width of the content placeholder to 10", and then align its right edge with the right edge of the title text placeholder.
   c. Change the width of the footer placeholder by to 7.98", and then align its left edge with the left edge of the content placeholder.
   d. In the content placeholder, change the font size of the first-level items to 28 points, and change the font size of the second-level items to 24 points. Change the vertical alignment of the content placeholder to Top.
   e. Change the color of the bullet characters to Green, Accent 2, Darker 25%, and change their size to 150% of the text.
   f. Change the space before every bulleted item to 12 points.
   g. Ungroup the graphic on the left side of the slide master. Change the fill of the top green shape to Green, Accent 2, and then change the fill of the bottom green shape to Green, Accent 2, Darker 25%.

9. Duplicate the Title Slide Layout. Rename the new layout to **Title Slide Alternate**.

10. Delete the graphic on the Title Slide Alternate layout. Deselect the Footers check box in the Master Layout group on the Slide Master tab.

11. In the new layout, change the height of the title text placeholder to 1.8", change its width to 13.33", align its center to the center of the slide, and align its top to the top of the slide. Change the vertical alignment of the text in the title text placeholder to Top.

12. Change the width of the subtitle text placeholder to 7". Align its right edge with the right edge of the slide. Position it horizontally 6.33" from the top-left corner and vertically 4.88" from the top-left corner.

13. Fill the background of the Title Slide Alternate layout with the picture in **Support_PPT_6_ Night.jpg**, located in the PowerPoint6 > Review folder.

14. Fill the title text placeholder shape with a gradient with three gradient stops, all three formatted with the color with the RGB value of 5,21,36. Position the first stop at 0% and format it so it is completely opaque (0% transparent). Position the second stop at 50% and format it so it is 50% transparent. Position the third stop at 100% and format it so it is 100% transparent.

15. Change the color of the text in the title text placeholder and the subtitle text placeholder to White, Background 1. Format the text in the title text placeholder as bold.

16. Rename the slide master to **Alt Parks Theme**.

17. In Normal view, change the layout of Slide 1 (the title slide) to the Title Slide Alternate layout. Then reset Slide 5.

18. Create a custom show named **New Plan** that contains Slide 4 ("New Lighting Plan"), Slide 5 ("Projected Reduction in Kilowatt Hours"), and Slide 6 ("Projected Reduction in Kilowatt Hours").

19. Add the custom property Editor with your name as the value of that property. Create a new custom property named **Draft** of the type Yes or no, and select Yes.

20. Save the changes to the presentation.

21. Make sure you saved the changes to the presentation, delete Slides 2 through 7, and then save the presentation as a theme named **NP_PPT_6_ParksTheme2** in the location where you are saving your files. (Make sure you change the folder to the folder where you are saving your files. Do not save the theme to the Document Themes folder.)

22. Undo the slide deletions from the NP_PPT_6_Lights presentation, and then save it.

23. Encrypt the presentation with the password **Lights**, and then mark the presentation as final.

# Apply

## Case Problem 1

**Data Files needed for this Case Problem: NP_PPT_6-3.pptx, Support_PPT_6_Background.jpg, Support_PPT_6_Password.jpg, Support_PPT_6_Side.jpg**

**Pascal Cybersecurity**    Michael Petrakis was hired as an intern at Pascal Security in Minneapolis, Minnesota. When Pascal Security is hired by a new client, Michael's supervisor, Anjali Krishnamurthy, visits that client and presents an overview of the services that Pascal Cybersecurity will be providing. Anjali asked Michael to create a PowerPoint presentation to be used as a starting point for this talk. She also asked Michael to create a theme that others can use. Michael created a presentation with four sections: an Introduction section, a section about the importance of using strong passwords, a section about the new network policies that will be introduced, and a section about new policies for employees' mobile devices. Anjali will add the content to the last two sections when she reviews the presentation. Complete the following:

1. Open the file **NP_PPT_6-3.pptx**, located in the PowerPoint > Case1 folder included with your Data Files, add your name as the subtitle, and then save the file as **NP_PPT_6_Cyber** in the location where you are saving your files.

2. Change the color palette to Blue Warm.

3. Change the theme font set to a custom set that uses Gill Sans Nova for Headings and Garamond for Body text. Delete the custom font set from your computer.

4. On the slide master, change the width of the title text placeholder to 10.8", and then left-align it with the content placeholder, if necessary.

5. Change the width of the content placeholder to 10.8", and then left-align it with the title text placeholder, if necessary.

6. Change the width of the slide number placeholder to 2.3", and then right-align it with the content placeholder if necessary.

7. Change the color of the bullet characters in the bulleted list to Blue-Gray, Accent 1, Darker 50%, and change the size of the bullet characters to 110% of text.

8. Increase the space before first-level bulleted items to 12 points.

9. On the Title Slide layout, remove the date, slide number, and footer placeholders by using the appropriate command in the Master Layout group on the Slide Master tab.

10. On the Title Slide layout, change the width of both the title text placeholder and the subtitle text placeholder to 13.33". Change the height of the title text placeholder to 2", and change the height of the subtitle text placeholder to 0.6". Top- and left-align the title text placeholder with the top and left edges of the slide. Bottom- and left-align the subtitle text placeholder with the bottom and left edges of the slide.

11. Change the vertical alignment of the text in the title text placeholder so it is middle-aligned. Horizontally align the text in the subtitle text placeholder so it is right-aligned, and vertically align it so it is bottom-aligned.

12. Format the text in both placeholders as bold, and change the text color to White, Background 1.

13. On the slide master, insert the picture in **Support_PPT_6_Side.jpg**, located in the PowerPoint6 > Case1 folder. Resize it so it is 8" high and 1.52" wide, and then apply a 10-point soft edge to the picture. Position it so that it is horizontally 12.22" from the top-left corner of the slide and vertically -0.25" inches from the top-left corner of the slide.

14. On the Title Slide layout, hide the background graphics, and then fill the background of the Title Slide layout with the picture **Support_PPT_6_Background.jpg**, located in the PowerPoint6 > Case1 folder.

15. On the Title Slide layout, fill the title text placeholder with the dark blue color above the "le" in "style." Change the fill color to the color with an RGB value of 12,28,44, if necessary.

16. Change the fill of the title text placeholder to a gradient fill with five stops of type Linear and direction Linear Down. Set the positions of the five gradient stops to 0%, 20%, 50%, 80%, and 100%. Change the color of each stop to the recent blue color (with the RGB value of 12,28,44). Change the transparency of the stops at 0% and 100% to 100% transparency. Change the transparency of the stops at 20% and 80% to 50% transparency.

17. Insert a new layout named **Content Section Header** after the Section Header layout. Resize the title text placeholder so it is 1.45" high and 4.6" wide. Position it so that it is vertically centered in the middle of the slide and horizontally its position is 6.02" from the top-left corner of the slide.

18. Insert a content placeholder that is 5" high and 5.5" wide. Left-align it with the left edge of the slide. Vertically, align it with the middle of the slide.

19. Modify the Two Content layout by changing the width of the two content placeholders to 5.3". Align the content placeholder on the left so its left edge aligns with the left edge of the title text placeholder. Align the content placeholder on the right so its right edge aligns with the right edge of the title text placeholder.

20. Rename the slide master to **Cyber Theme**.

21. In Normal view, reset Slide 5, if necessary. Change the layout of Slide 4 to the Content Section Header layout, and then insert the picture **Support_PPT_6_Password.jpg**, located in the PowerPoint6 > Case1 folder, in the content placeholder.

22. Create a custom property named **Draft** of the type Yes or no. Set its value to Yes.

23. Encrypt the presentation with the password **Cyber**, and then set the presentation to always be read-only.

# Create

## Case Problem 2

**Data Files needed for this Case Problem: Support_PPT_6_Bullet.png, Support_PPT_6_Logo1.png, Support_PPT_6_Logo2.jpg**

**Smith Harris Accounting**   Victoria Hofbauer is an associate staff auditor at Smith Harris Accounting in Phoenix, Arizona. Her manager asked her to create a simple custom theme that the department will use for presentations. Refer to Figure 6–37 as you complete the following steps:

**Figure 6-37**    Slide master and Title Slide layout for the custom theme

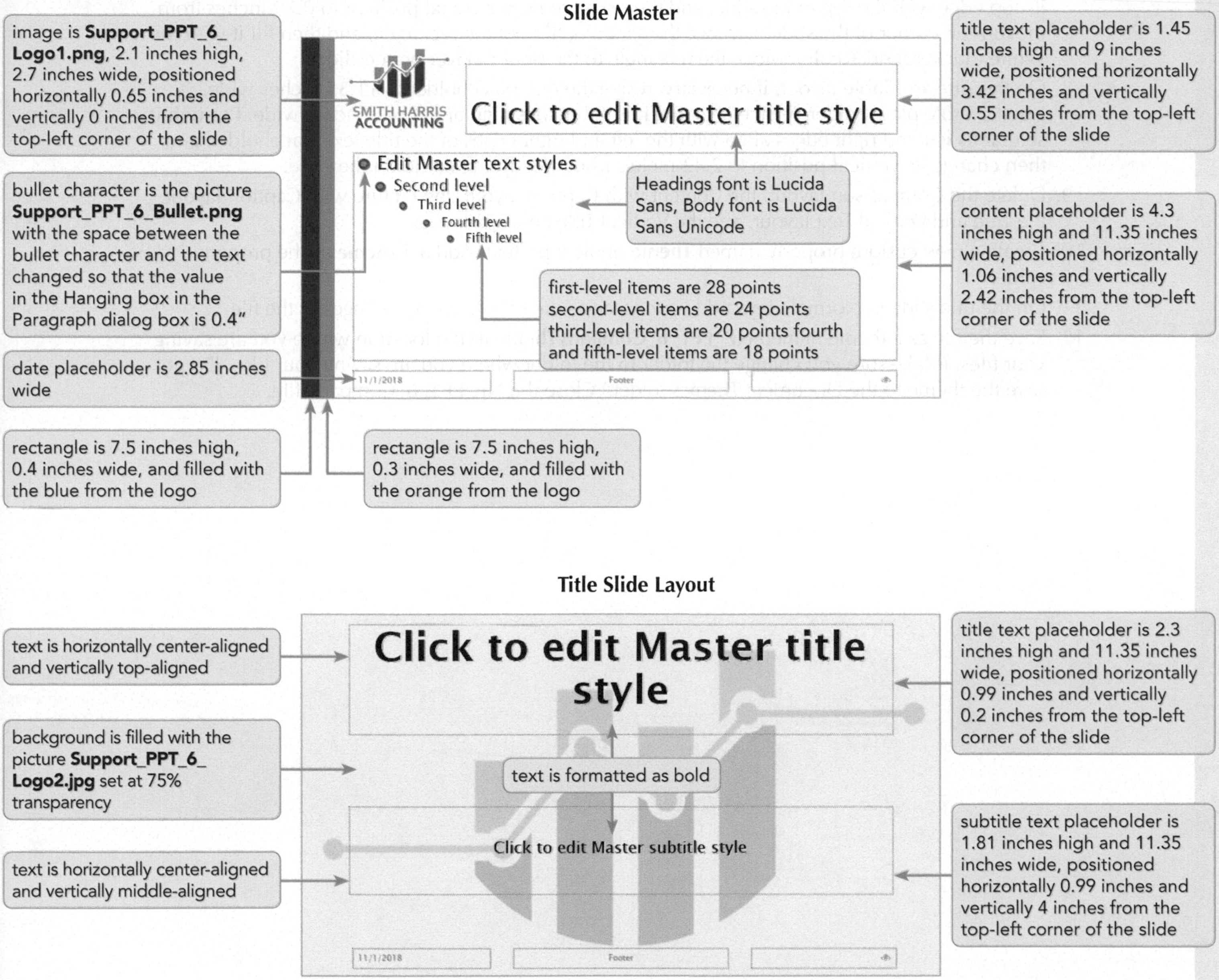

**Slide Master**

image is **Support_PPT_6_Logo1.png**, 2.1 inches high, 2.7 inches wide, positioned horizontally 0.65 inches and vertically 0 inches from the top-left corner of the slide

bullet character is the picture **Support_PPT_6_Bullet.png** with the space between the bullet character and the text changed so that the value in the Hanging box in the Paragraph dialog box is 0.4"

date placeholder is 2.85 inches wide

rectangle is 7.5 inches high, 0.4 inches wide, and filled with the blue from the logo

rectangle is 7.5 inches high, 0.3 inches wide, and filled with the orange from the logo

title text placeholder is 1.45 inches high and 9 inches wide, positioned horizontally 3.42 inches and vertically 0.55 inches from the top-left corner of the slide

content placeholder is 4.3 inches high and 11.35 inches wide, positioned horizontally 1.06 inches and vertically 2.42 inches from the top-left corner of the slide

Headings font is Lucida Sans, Body font is Lucida Sans Unicode

first-level items are 28 points second-level items are 24 points third-level items are 20 points fourth and fifth-level items are 18 points

**Click to edit Master title style**

● Edit Master text styles
  ● Second level
    ● Third level
      ● Fourth level
        ● Fifth level

SMITH HARRIS ACCOUNTING

11/1/2018    Footer

**Title Slide Layout**

text is horizontally center-aligned and vertically top-aligned

background is filled with the picture **Support_PPT_6_Logo2.jpg** set at 75% transparency

text is horizontally center-aligned and vertically middle-aligned

title text placeholder is 2.3 inches high and 11.35 inches wide, positioned horizontally 0.99 inches and vertically 0.2 inches from the top-left corner of the slide

subtitle text placeholder is 1.81 inches high and 11.35 inches wide, positioned horizontally 0.99 inches and vertically 4 inches from the top-left corner of the slide

**Click to edit Master title style**

text is formatted as bold

Click to edit Master subtitle style

11/1/2018    Footer

onep99/Shutterstock.com

1. Create a new, blank presentation, and then save the file as **NP_PPT_6_Company** in the location where you are saving your files.
2. Create the slide master and Title Slide layout as described in Figure 6-37. Rename the slide master to **Smith Harris**.
3. Delete the custom font set from your computer.
4. On the Two Content layout, resize the two content placeholders so that they are 4.3 inches high and 5.5 inches wide. Position the content placeholder on the left so that its left edge aligns with the left edge of the date placeholder, and position the content placeholder on the right so that its right edge aligns with the right edge of the title text placeholder. Change the vertical position of both content placeholders so they are 2.42 inches from the top-left corner of the slide.
5. On the Blank layout, hide the background graphics. Copy the blue and orange bar from the slide master, and then paste them on the Blank layout.

6. After the Title and Content layout, insert a new layout. Rename it to **Title and Table**.

7. On the new Title and Table layout, insert a rectangle two inches high and 2.4 inches wide. Align its top edge with the top of the slide, and then change its horizontal position to 0.75 inches from the top-left corner of the slide. Remove the shape outline of the rectangle, and then fill it with the White, Background 1 color. Move the rectangle to the bottom layer on the slide.

8. On the Title and Table layout, if necessary, resize the title placeholder to 11.35 inches wide. Insert a Table placeholder. Resize it so that it is 4.3 inches high and 11.35 inches wide. Position it so that its left and right edges align with the left and right edges of the title text placeholder, and then change its vertical position to 2.42 inches from the top-left corner of the slide.

9. Delete the Comparison layout, the Content with Caption layout, the Picture with Caption layout, the Title and Vertical Text layout, and the Vertical Title and Text layout.

10. Create a new custom property named **Theme** of the type Text. Add **SH Theme** as the property value.

11. On the title slide in Normal view, add your name as the title. Save the changes to the file.

12. Save the file as a theme named **NP_PPT_6_CompanyTheme** to the location where you are saving your files. (Make sure you change the folder to the folder where you are saving your files. Do not save the theme to the Document Themes folder.) Close the NP_PPT_6_Company file.

# INDEX